# PROTECT & AVENGE
## The 49th Fighter Group
## in World War II

# PROTECT & AVENGE

# THE 49TH FIGHTER GROUP IN WORLD WAR II
## S.W. FERGUSON & WILLIAM K. PASCALIS

Schiffer Military/Aviation History
Atglen, PA

**Dust jacket and color profile artwork by Steve Ferguson, Colorado Springs, CO.**

**THE EIGHTBALLS OF ORO BAY**
The May 14, 1943 mission depicted here is described in detail in Chapter 11.

*PAGE 1*
*9 FS Flt Ldr Lt. Ralph Blachly, the only Flying Knight to reach the bombers over Oro Bay on May 14th.*

*PAGE 2-3*
*Terrors of Tacloban, early November, 1944: Above lt.-rt. Krankowitz, Kirkland, Curl, Swift, Helterline, Curton, Fisher, Curley, Boyd, Campbell, Norton, Nelson and Mathre. Below lt.-rt. Morrissey, Walker, DeHaven, Drier, Smerchek, Estes, Jordan, Bong, Johnson, Lewelling, McElroy, Wood, Williams, Forgey, Smith, and Gupton. Of the pilots seen here, only Lt. Forgey would be lost in action after the New Year.*

*PAGE 8*
*7 FS pilot Jim Mathis next to A/C #18 "BILLIE JEAN" after the 49ers settled in Japan.*

Book Design by Robert Biondi

Copyright © 1996 by S.W. Ferguson & William K. Pascalis.
Library of Congress Catalog Number: 94-68964

Printed in China
ISBN: 0-88740-750-1

We are interested in hearing from authors with book ideas on related topics.

Published by Schiffer Publishing Ltd.
77 Lower Valley Road
Atglen, PA 19310
Please write for a free catalog.
This book may be purchased from the publisher.
Please include $2.95 postage.
Try your bookstore first.

# PREFACES

## First Preface

From model airplanes to mechanic, from the P-35 to Boeing 747, I've spent over half my lifetime working and maintaining airplanes. I didn't particularly want to fly, but was more curious to know how and why these machines could fly.

I was a "Flying Knight" crewman and eventually a crewchief in the Southwest Pacific Theater of World War II. What follows is a small part of my life in the 49ers. We turned our peacetime 49th Pursuit Group of 1941 into a first class fighting machine and became the first group to go overseas together. We were the only group to engage the enemy over Darwin, and became the first unit of World War II to win a Presidential Unit Citation for our part in the defense of the Northern Territory. After a year of combat, we were the first group to shoot down one-hundred enemy aircraft.

For some twenty years after the war, we always heard parts of the story such as "the Fighters of Humpty Doo," or the tales of the individuals in the Screamin' Demons, the Blacksheep and the Flying Knights. There were so many stories about the legend of pilot Dick Bong that most of the veterans were overshadowed and the whole story was never told. If all the stories were written, there would be volumes to fill a library. This is the first time in half a century that this story has ever been told this way.

Of all my memories, there are so many friends now lost that it is hard to choose the most important to me. They all seemed to play their part in our magnificent story. And so I quote from General MacArthur's radiogram of November 3, 1944, from the Philippines, "They are unsurpassed in the air." This echoes my sentiments of having served with the best.

William K. Pascalis
Author and 49th FG Historian

## Second Preface

Excerpt from an interview with Gen. Hutchinson held in Niagara Falls, New York, 1984.

I have related so many anecdotes of the 49ers, it is difficult to choose my favorite. I suppose the one that sticks out in my mind is not a combat story, but a brief story about Squeeze Wurtsmith and his days at Dobodura.

Our 5th Fighter Command headquarters shack was on a knoll overlooking the airfield and V.I.P.s were usually taken there when they toured the area. Squeeze was the consummate command officer, always proper and extremely accommodating to the officers or news journalists who came to our camp. Eventually, the quests would ask to tour the flight lines and that's when the fun began.

There was always a vehicle available at HQ, usually Squeeze's personal jeep, and unlike other command types, the general loved to drive. Unbeknown to his guests, Squeeze loved to drive fast. After everyone climbed on board his jeep, he would tromp down on the accelerator and turn the thing straight down the hill. Their eyes popped out and they grabbed hold of one another as the general tore down the slope, flashing his famous grin.

That's the way I like to remember General Wurtsmith. He was the finest man I ever knew and was superior as a commander. If I had to choose a hero, and we had so many good men, I would have to select the general, or probably, the man of lowest rank, the private. I suppose that was the way with the 49ers. We had the best, where ever you looked. Men came forward to lead when it was necessary and they were superior, too.

We didn't really follow any rules. We made up our own rules as we went along and no one seemed to care at the time. At least, neither Squeeze, nor Enis (Whitehead), not even Kenney said anything. We had a job to do, and as long as it got done, no one asked about our business. We took great pride in being operators. We had to win and everyone did his part.

My group? I never felt that it was my group. Everyone knew what they had to do. They were superior.

Major General Donald R. Hutchinson
Commander, 49th Fighter Group
November 1942 to July 1943

Chief of Staff,
FEAF November 1944 to August 1945

# CONTENTS

# INTRODUCTION

Colonel Jerry Cox, commander of the 49th Tactical Fighter Wing in 1983, was in attendance at a formal "Dining-In" with the host Blacksheep at Holloman AFB in the New Mexico desert. We sat together at the guests' table, he being the senior flight officer present and myself being a pretentious artist and historian thinking I knew enough to carry on a bull session with a group of modern day fighter pilots.

It turned out to be quite a humiliating evening. The pilots, regardless of rank or their phenomenal capacity for the libation of the day, obviously were educated far beyond my meager liberal arts experience and were just as conversant in art, music, politics and philosophy as they were in aerodynamics and combat maneuvering. The enlisted men and women introduced to me were equally as glib. At first impressed and finally overwhelmed, this reticent artist returned quietly to his chair as the party accelerated beyond my means. It was best to remain an observer of the flying community rather than ply my wits as an intruder.

It was then that Col. Cox very pointedly asked if I was going to write the history of the unit. When I offered that a great deal had already been written about the 49th Group, the colonel graciously pressed the issue a bit further.

"No", the colonel continued, "I mean a real book about where all this began. We have a new program called the Warrier Program which requires all unit commanders to become aware of their unit history. The 49ers have an association of World War II veterans and I believe they have a historian who already has an outline of the 49ers history."

So it was, forty years after the first Blacksheep commander had an idea and put it into operations, another Blacksheep "operator" had set the wheels in motion. Once again Group Historian Bill Pascalis and I began the process of putting this history into print. We originally thought the book would be resolved within a year, but eight years later, it finally took on a form of its own.

I have always been fascinated by flight. I understand the reasoning of biologists who profess our origins began in the sea, and those who sail or swim certainly have an affinity with our aquatic past. If the archaeologists are correct, our later ancestors on terra firma were very likely somewhere quite low in the food chain, and anyone who moves quickly over the land, either fleet of foot or in control a formula one race car is parenthetically carrying on the survivalist instinct to escape in haste.

Flight seems to be the exception. We have no reason to be up there, accept for some obscure laws of physics which the Wright brothers adapted to their own curiosity, to hence, introduce Americans to the strange realm above the earth where only daredevils would go. They left terra firma and for a brief moment, left the rest of us behind.

When my time on earth came to pass, as with most in my post-World War II generation, it seemed the aerial daredevils were all legendary. It was many years later that my father and his brothers boasted they had once been daredevils and had lived in the air during the war in the forties. As difficult as it was to believe that my grey kith and kin were those very legends of my youthful imagination, further pursuit of the truth in my formal education put me in contact with many living legends. The men, and women too, seemed to generally share a common demeanor. It is my studied opinion that these very common folks accomplished an incredible feat in their youth that probably is unparalleled in any other generation in our country's history.

This book retells a very small portion of the human experience in the generation preceding mine. Within the ruthless intrigues and embroiled politics of the world gone mad for the second time in the same century, a team of young flyers and crewmen rose up from the common folk and fought their war to save the life of freedom that was uniquely American. Some were volunteer reservists before the war and others were citizens who suffered personal loss in the Great depression and found refuge in the military, simply to survive. They were neither politically astute, philosophically clever, nor prophetically aware. The Army Air Corps would call them the Forty-Ninth Pursuit Group and their country would send them off to war. Too young to be worldly and often to ignorant to be afraid, their adventure was greater than any fantasy and as distant as any heroic odyssey.

Their air group would remain in combat for three and a half years. They would live in the most hostile terrains ever negotiated by troops in war. They sustained against heat, monsoons, disease, the enemy and the lonely isolation in the most dense jungles on earth. The crews kept their aircraft in service through sheer creative genius and the pilots fought in every major engagement in the Southwest Pacific theater. And far too many of the young men would not come home.

You're going to relive this story; you're in the "Forty Niners" now. This is the First Team. Strap on your fighter plane and hang on for dear life.

S.W. Ferguson

# 1

# SELFRIDGE AIR FIELD

The formation of the 49th Pursuit Group (Interceptors) was by decree of the U.S. Army Air Corps staff and Congressional advisors following strategic conferences held in Washington, D.C. during the Battle of Britain. The U.S. Army observers in England provided glaring reports of new Luftwaffe and RAF standards in contrast to the undermanned and poorly equipped Army and Navy units in the States. The 350 men in the 94th Pursuit Squadron at Selfridge Field, Michigan, were selected as a nucleus for the necessary new squadrons in the Army Air Corps to remedy the disparity. On November 20, 1940, Major Glen Davasher was authorized by the War Department to take command of the 49th Pursuit Group and its three newly designated squadrons; the 7th, 8th, and 9th. Two officers were posted to each squadron. An adjutant and personnel officer were assigned to assist Davasher and as of January 16, 1941, the 49th PG was officially activated with 130 non-commissioned men and 9 pilots appointed to their ranks.

The 31st Pursuit Group was activated in parallel with the 49th, and duties would often overlap within these separate units. Several different types of fighter aircraft were in service at Selfridge and limited maintenance was performed by all crews on attached assignments. The greatest test of man and machine was the severe Michigan winter. Unfortunately for Davasher, he collapsed with influenza in February, 1941 and relinquished command to Major John Egan. Illness did not recognize rank and PFC William Riley died in the hospital of infectious pneumonia on the 17th, the first Group fatality.

The swelling ranks of the Selfridge units soon made maintenance assignments for all impossible. New planes would soon ar-

rive in April, but not for Major Egan's Group. The 49th would instead get a new CO and assignment to a new base.

## HEADING SOUTH WITH McCOY

In May, 1941, the 49th's increased roster of 19 officers and 280 enlisted men was appointed to the command of Major George "Snuffy" McCoy. Now that the unit would begin receiving aircraft, they would require an experienced flying officer to lead them and McCoy was the senior pilot in line for such an assignment at Selfridge. His first assignment however, would not be in airplanes, but trucks. On May 16, his convoy of 75 vehicles set off for the Group's new base at Morrison Field, West Palm Beach, Florida. The 1100 mile trip took four uneventful days, and the spring weather in Florida was a welcome relief to the harshness of the previous Michigan winter.

Morrison Field, commanded by LtC. John Monohan, was a large new air base on the west side of West Palm Beach. Several barrack buildings and flight support facilities were still under construction. Sidewalks were not complete, lawns were not seeded and parking lots were only graveled. The 51st Base Materiels Group had also arrived and soon, LtC. Monohan and Major McCoy would incorporate all personnel to finish the construction. Many a young airplane mechanic would sow grass seed, plant trees and pour concrete for walkways at Morrison Field in the summer of 1941.

Anticipating the arrival of new aircraft also required improving the Group administration. Flying officers were chosen to fill the Squadron command positions. Headquarters Squadron, as an administrative unit, was given to amiable Capt. Don Hutchinson. Lieutenant Allen Bennett took the 7th Pursuit, Lt. Robert Van Auken took the 8th Pursuit and Capt. Victor Pixey took the 9th Pursuit. These four men had been on flying status at Selfridge. Irving Amidon was assigned as 1st Sgt. to assist Hutchinson administratively. Line chiefs were designated as the experienced M/Sgts. Earl McCullum, Hal Hays, Paul Marlin and Charles Jauga. Each new Squadron CO would in turn appoint subordinate officers for mess hall, operations, communications and supply duties. Van Auken also commanded the radiomen of the 49th Interceptor Controllers.

With a properly designated staff, and the air base near completion, the 49th Pursuit Group was placed under the auspices of the 3rd Air Force headquartered at Drew Field, Florida, by direct order of USAAC Commanding Gen. Hap Arnold, effective June 20, 1941. Now that Morrison was an official active duty training base, the aircraft began to arrive.

*HQ and flight control center at Morrison Field.*

*Stearman PT-17 assigned to Morrisson Field*

## FLYING IN AMERICA

The flying schedule at Morrison Field was rather simple. Each squadron received a PT-17 Stearman two seat biplane, a PT-13 Ryan Basic Trainer two seat monoplane and three P-35 Seversky Advanced Trainer fighter aircraft. A P-40C Curtiss Warhawk was assigned to each Squadron also as an advanced trainer fighter. All cadet pilots were required to log hours through certain proficiency ratings on the fabric covered Stearman, then the all-metal Ryan, and finally to fighter pilot status on the P-35. Crew chiefs were also required to log "back seat" time on either the PT-17 or the PT-13. Pilots immediately began filing flight plans and the citizens of West Palm Beach soon saw Army planes buzzing the beaches and country roads of southern Florida. The 49ers were making themselves right at home.

Enlisted personnel continued on work details at Morrison Field, but also increased their technical skills at 3rd Air Force schools in communications and aircraft maintenance throughout the southeastern United States. In August and early September, a break in the training schedule came with severe rain that flooded the field, causing water damage on some first floors in the barracks area. But little else affected the 49ers. The country was still deep in the Depression and a young private would divide his pay between a weekend pass and the family back home. As the nation braced for a possible involvement in the European War, the young troops of Morrison Field seemed more concerned with the long hours of their daily routines.

Flight training continued in the sweltering summer heat. The weather added to the frustrations that began to surface with the Seversky P-35. Maj. McCoy grew increasingly annoyed with the overweight, underpowered, radial-engined planes. The 1050 hp rated

*Troop trucks for work details at Morrison.*

*Flooded barracks at Morrison in September, 1941.*

Pratt & Whitney engines never delivered the power. The propellers were constantly out of balance, causing excessive engine wear and heavy oil leaks. Young mechanics spent their maintenance training mopping up oil from taxi ways, hangar floors and cowling panels. A private once reported that the Florida humidity would never get through the oil coating on the P-35 to cause any corrosion. "It's a self-maintaining plane", he surmised.

More concerns arose. McCoy's squadron commanders and senior flying officers were ordered to attend Army war maneuvers in September near Alexandria, Louisiana. The men would have to attend as observer pilots and fly restricted duty, because so few were checked out on the Severskys.

The worst happened on September 20th. Second Lt. Caryle Loverud was killed when his P-35 engine seized and crashed near Jackson, Georgia, on a cross country flight during the maneuvers. The commanders were deeply saddened, and they returned to Morrison to ground the remaining Severskys. All aircraft received complete overhauls by months end. Even after these preventive measures, the ungainly machines were not considered airworthy by either the crews or the pilots.

In November, Capt. Pixey was asked to send a contingent from the Group to march in the Armistice Day parade in Stuart, Florida. Ironically, the contingent was unknown to the citizenry and the men returned to West Palm Beach rather disappointed. By the end of November, they were an unknown, under trained, poorly equipped pursuit group. Morale was beginning to wane. Rain on the 30th truly dampened their spirits.

## PEARL HARBOR AND A NEW COMMANDER

The lack of progress in McCoy's training plan had now reached the attention of 3rd AF command. McCoy was notified that his replacement would arrive in the last week of November, 1941. The news of world tensions was all the more unsettling as the British and Germans spread their war across Africa and Russia. Some newspapers even spoke of the veiled dangers within the Japanese and American negotiations over vested interests in the Pacific. America's entrance into the war became more imminent. Surely, the Squadron leaders hoped, the new commander would bring the Group new energy and purpose.

On the morning of December 7th, most of the enlisted men had begun to return from weekend passes. Bunks soon were occu-

*2Lts. Manning (#90) and Porter on patrol, December, 1941. Aircraft cowlings already display the red designator of the 9th squadron.*

pied by drowsy crewmen who recalled their weekend events with friends. A few card games began indoors while more hardy souls went outside and started a sandlot baseball game.

Off base at the residence of Lt. Van Auken, new friend Lt. Bob Morrissey of the 51st Base Materiels unit, and their families were having a birthday party. Familiar radio music crackled in the background of the festivities. Mrs. Morrissey called attention to the abrupt end of the melody and everyone presently heard an announcer flatly read the United Press wire bulletin, "Honolulu, Hawaii time . . . two, possibly three waves of attacking planes . . . navy ships lost . . . all military personnel report to their stations . . ."

Neither lieutenant spoke. They finished their whiskeys and Van Auken called Morrison Field. Lt. Allen Bennett was Officer of the Day at that hour while LtC. Monohan and Major McCoy were both on extended weekend leave. Bennett curtly declared the base was closed and all personnel leaves were canceled. He hung up on Van Auken.

Men on the base were stunned as the word spread of the attack in Hawaii. Card games stopped and radios were tuned for more details from the news wires. Men who were en route to the Field found it hard to get taxis or make long distance calls to their families in other cities. On that quiet Sunday morning, the events far out in the Pacific Ocean had thrown all of America into disarray.

Mrs. Morrissey and Mrs. Van Auken saw their husbands drive off toward the Field. They would not spend much time with them after that evening.

## OPERATIONAL TRAINING AND DEPLOYMENT

The next two weeks at Morrison Field saw a transformation of the entire 3rd AF and the 49th Pursuit Group. The first change was the formal transfer of command to Major Wurtsmith on December 12, 1941. Immediately, the Squadron leaders recognized the new CO's ability.

Paul Wurtsmith was a fighter pilot of substantial experience, even if gained in peace time. After enlisting in 1928, he qualified for Cadet Pilot training and was commissioned in 1932. Though not physically large, his air of confidence was overwhelming. Never coarse, he was exact in his speech and had an amiable manner. Most important was his skill as a flyer.

The Major excelled in airmanship and formation flying, particularly in fighters. He had achieved a reputation as a outstanding tactician while on staff at Selfridge Field in the late 30's. He knew the Squadron Commanders personally and his transition to the 49ers was quite smooth.

Capt. Hutchinson was not only an old comrade, but was similar in personality to the Major and they were complementary in their style of command. The two men immediately streamlined the administration of the Group, enabling their pilots and crews to take on the greater requirements of an air force at war.

Wurtsmith ordered an increase of flying hours and school attendance for his Group. Flying and maintenance of the Stearman and Ryan trainers nearly doubled in December. The P-35 Seversky's

*9 PS patrolling the inner coastal canal off West Palm Beach. Trailing P-35 is one of the few to be camouflaged per USAAC directives of late 1941.*

*7 PS P-35 with squadron insignia-blue cowling just off the coast.*

*Group CO Paul Wurtsmith (Australian era photo)*

were pressed into coastal submarine patrols along Florida's Atlantic coast. Crews were justifiably tired at the end of each duty day.

Only one tragic setback marred the events of the month. Lt. Van Auken had filed a flight plan for the longest cross-country trip to date. Three P-40's would make the trip which ran from Morrisson Field to Macon, Georgia, then north to Dayton, Ohio. From there, they would fly west to St. Louis, Missouri and then return through Macon. Sadly, during the flight out of Dayton on the 20th, heavy weather separated the planes and Lt. Howard Cory died when his Curtiss fighter struck a fog covered hill as he approached St, Louis.

It was the last long distance flight in the United States. On Christmas, orders arrived from Army Air Corps HQ for mobilization and deployment of the 49th Pursuit Group. Priority was given to the construction of crates for tools, office equipment and the distribution of new uniforms. Two troop trains arrived in West Palm Beach on the 28th and work details included loading gear on the trains, as well as providing military security accompanied by civilian police.

## NEW SQUADRON COMMANDERS AND TRAVEL ORDERS

Favoritism soon affected changes within the Group. New arrival Lt. Morrissey was also an accomplished pilot and an old acquaintance of the new commander. By month's end, he replaced Bennett

*9 PS P-40C similar to the type lost with Lt. Cory at St. Louis on December 18th.*

as CO of the 7th Squadron. Bennett had become an excess command rated officer, and was therefore grudgingly transferred out of the Group. He stayed on attached duty until the Group left Morrison Field.

Lt. Jim Selman relieved Capt. Pixey in the 9th and the Captain joined HQ as deputy to Hutchinson. Lt. George Powell took command of the 49th Interceptor Squadron that allowed Van Auken to focus command of his 8th Sqn pilots.

Other units at Morrison were absorbed into Wurtsmith's command. Two ordinance companies, a signal company, an air base ground personnel company and quarter master company joined the ranks preparing for the move.

Men began to wonder which front they would be sent to, but rumor of going to England, or Africa, was quickly put down. Wurtsmith had orders by the end of the month to send an advance team to San Francisco, California. Second Lts. Owen Fish and John Livingstone headed a contingent of six section chief sergeants and left by commercial flight to make ready for the Group's embarkation by ship from the West Coast port. At Morrison Field, each man was given travel orders and base restrictions, but still no one was certain of their final destination.

The waiting and speculation ended on January 4, 1942. Trucks carried the pilots, crews, and support personnel to the rail station in the early morning hours. The HQ Squadron and 7 PS on the first train left that afternoon, and the 8th and 9th squadrons followed in the second train in evening twilight. The troop trains went north through the flat countryside of Florida and into Georgia. They reached Atlanta late that night and switched to the west-bound line.

## CALIFORNIA AND THE VOYAGE DOWN UNDER

The train trip across the southern United States took four days, with one brief stop in El Paso, Texas, to take on additional troops. Arriving in California on January 8, the 49ers were more than happy to leave the crowded cars and cramped seats, even if to walk in the sprawling San Francisco railyards. They marched in loose formation quite some distance across the yards to the huge glass and steel building, officially the County Livestock Pavilion, but referred to by those who entered as "the Cow Palace." It was far from being royal.

The Cow Palace was filled with the din of thousands of troops. Men were crowded everywhere inside the big dusty arena on cots laid end to end, and many others stretched out on the bleachers above the dirt floor. Hot during the day and cold at night, the men milled about looking like so many bewildered cattle. Uncertain of how long the 49ers would be there, the section chiefs instructed their men to keep the outfit together and not to stray from the pavilion.

It was total chaos for the 49ers after their relatively quiet departure from Morrison Field. It was, however, prime hunting ground for Wurtsmith and Hutchinson who were looking for more men and pilots to fill the ranks of their Group. The U.S. Army had advised the 49ers commanders that transport pilots, sergeant pilots, bomber pilots and even navigators who were pilot qualified would be available at San Francisco. They also inducted enlisted men on the spot; cooks, clerk typists, electricians and more mechanics. By

*Folding cots cover the arena of dusty "Cow Palace" in San Francisco, early January, 1941.*

January 8th, the 49ers signed on 75 new pilots and 587 more enlisted personnel from the troops in transit at the Cow Palace.

Some were able to take leave on the 9th, and those lucky few wandered into the strange atmosphere of the famous harbor town. Following the attack at Pearl Harbor, all of the West Coast was in a state of panic, and this city had transformed into an odd blend of tourist town and armed camp. Gift shops and restaurants carried on business behind sandbags and barbed wire barricades. Auto traffic was restricted everywhere and most people travelled by trolley or on foot. Curfew and off-limits were posted everywhere and strictly enforced by well armed Military Police. The city was blacked out at night. Shop keepers made windfall profits as civilian and soldier alike horded cigarettes, candy, liquor and packaged food in anticipation of a Japanese invasion of the California coast. A few 49ers found lady companions for their last hours in the States. There was excitement, bravado, mystery, anxiety, hurried phone calls and scribbled post cards. It all came to an abrupt end.

All passes were revoked on January 10th and embarkation orders were issued to the 49ers. On the 12th, the men were trucked to the Matson Ship Line docks in San Francisco Bay to board commercial liners assigned to the U.S. Transport Services. The majority of the Group boarded the USAAT *Mariposa*, while the remainder went over to the *Coolidge*. The USAAT *Monroe* took on men and supplies of other units for their own obscure mission. By mid-afternoon, with the light cruiser U.S.S. *Phoenix* as escort, the four-ship convoy sailed beneath the Golden Gate Bridge and out into the broad Pacific. The 49th Pursuit Group was the first fighter group

formed in the States to be sent overseas as a unit and they were off to confront the ominous and mysterious Japanese Empire.

## ABOARD THE MARIPOSA

All the while leading up to their departure, the men of the 49th tried to keep pace with the news coming from the war fronts. The headlines told of the Europeans fighting in Norway, North Africa and Russia. Halfway around the world, the Japanese forces were advancing on three different fronts around the South China Sea against the British in Malaysia, the Dutch in the Celebes and the American forces in the Philippines. Since the Pearl Harbor catastrophe, few Americans had any facts of the staggering losses that followed in the Pacific. The true nature of the enemy forces were also unknown. General Douglas MacArthur, commander of the embattled forces in the Philippines, had urgently requested reinforcements for his headquarters in Manila on Luzon, but the delivery of new men and supplies had become too dangerous as the Japanese closed in on the Philippines capital.

## CONQUEST BEYOND THE SOUTH CHINA SEAS

To the rest of the world, Japan seemed a medieval enigma struggling to join the scientific industrial age of the 20th Century. But the success of the Imperial forces was not a military feat of mere coincidence or luck. The Japanese were hardened by centuries of feudal civil wars, having stoically accepted personal suffering and sacrifice to their warrior kings and emperors for many generations.

Consequently, the island empire had raised a modern Navy and Army amidst the challenges of its global neighbors in the preceding three decades. By the late 1930s, a military government loyal to the sovereign boy-king Hirohito, had acquired control of the east coast of China and the island of Formosa by armed exploitation. Since the "China Incident" of 1937 and the subsequent occupation of Korea and Manchuria, the military leaders fashioned a plan to eliminate all foreign influence in the Pacific, and particularly the British interests in Indo-China. In 1940, Japan joined the Axis coalition of Germany and Italy in a hardened stance against the British Commonwealth, declaring their Oriental empire to be the "Greater East Asia Co-prosperity Sphere."

As the European war grew on the far side of the world in 1941, the Japanese took advantage of the tactical situation and advanced

*USAT Coolidge in the Pacific bound convoy.*

*USS Phoenix destroyer escort to the January convoy.*

into the South China Sea area with minimal opposition from the English Royal Navy. Primarily intent to isolate the British fleet in the west and the American fleet in the east, they anticipated a twelve month long offensive to engulf all of the Malay Peninsula, the Dutch West Indies, the Philippines and the central Pacific islands, ridding the entire eastern hemisphere of the exploitative foreigners for ever. Few Allied strategists could perceive the audacity of this conquest, particularly by a oriental people considered provincially quaint and ruled by courtly medieval royalty. Japan's three-pronged lunge into the Pacific stunned the western world.

The three simultaneous assaults on December 7 and 8, 1941, were at Pearl Harbor in the eastern Pacific, the Marshal, Gilbert, Marianas and Caroline Islands in the central Pacific and the Philippines and Indo-China in the west. The invasion into the South China Sea drew the British warships from the Indian Ocean to protect the small garrisons at Hong Kong and Singapore, but the cruisers H.M.S. *Prince of Wales* and the *Repulse* were summarily sunk by enemy aircraft off the west coast of the Malay Peninsula on December 10th. The British garrison at Hong Kong was therefore trapped and forced to surrender three weeks later. Thailand soon bowed to uncontested occupation. All of the Malay peninsular "arch," and the spiny tail of islands from Sumatra on the west through Java to tiny Timor on the east, were stepping stones to the exposed northwest coast of Australia. Even the British Commonwealth nations of Burma and India, far to the northwest, were vulnerable to invasion.

In the first week of January, 1942, the Japanese Army was able to press south toward the strategic British port of Singapore, Malaya, against meager opposition that had no reinforcements. Eventually, the port city protectors consolidated their defense on Singapore Island on January 31st. Only a few refugees would escape across the Molucca Straits to Sumatra, let alone the 600 mile flight south to Java. The American, British and Dutch losses of pilots, crews, and shipping soared as the left flank of the invaders swung south from Malaya into Borneo and further severed the supply route from Australia, eventually forcing an Allied withdrawal from the Philippines, Borneo, Halmahera Island and the Celebes Islands. By the end of January, the retreat halted in a line extending from Java on the west through the southwestern Celebes port of Kendari, and to remote Ambon Island 400 miles on the east.

As the Allied bases in Indonesia fell, some veteran survivors escaped by ship or plane to Australia's northern port of Darwin. The U.S. Army Chief of Staff Gen. George Marshall, had sent his personal observer, Gen. George Brett, to tour USAAC bases in India, China and Australia immediately after the Pearl Harbor attack. Once Brett arrived in Darwin on December 31, 1941, he was ordered to take command of all U.S. Army refugees. They were renamed the new U.S. Army Forces In Australia (USAFIA) and Brett would determine the redeployment of these veterans to relieve the Dutch and British in the East Indies, and MacArthur in Manila. He would likewise deploy the reinforcements arriving from the States.

## REINFORCEMENT FROM THE U.S.A.

Previously in December, there had been initial discussion between Major Wurtsmith and the USAAC staff in Washington, D.C. that the 49ers might be sent to relieve MacArthur's Far East Air Force (FEAF) defenses on Luzon. But in two desperate months, every-thing in the conflict had changed and time ran out for the Air Corps in the Philippines. Many of the Wurtsmith's old flying mates from the earlier days at Selfridge would be lost fighting against over-whelming odds in defense of Manila. The group leader expressed his anguish to deputy Hutchinson in being so isolated at sea aboard the *Mariposa*, but nothing could be done. They settled in for the long voyage to what they thought would surely be a base in the southern Philippine Islands.

The other 49ers had no idea where they were headed and after a few days at sea, hardships soon preoccupied the novice voyagers. Many experienced severe motion sickness and melancholia. The quarters were crowded, privacy was impossible and both soldier and seaman sacrificed many privileges. Cigarettes became scarce, food was often cold, and many were forced to take cold saltwater showers from a hose on the main deck.

On January 24th, the *Mariposa* had mechanical failure in her steering. After a hard 360 degrees to starboard, she stopped dead and the men anxiously watched the sister ships and Navy escort disappear over the west horizon. A rumor that an enemy submarine had been sighted was quickly put down. Following repairs, she got under way at full speed and to the relief of all on board, caught up with the convoy the next morning.

On the 26th, the 49ers spirits lifted when treated to the traditional celebration for novice seamen who cross the equator for the first time. All joined in the fanfare and blessings of King Neptune. Their spirits dimmed again on the following day when the steering failed a second time. After repairs, the *Mariposa* again rejoined the convoy only to see two British Royal Navy escort destroyers lead the USAAT Monroe off to an unknown port. The remaining three ship convoy steamed on. On the 28th, the ship's captain relayed a radio message to Wurtsmith that their course had been altered and that they would reach the new destination of Melbourne, Australia, by the first week of February.

## MELBOURNE AND THE ALLIED COMMAND

On January 31, 1942, after three weeks at sea, the American convoy bearing the 49th Pursuit Group came within sight of Cape Howes on the southeast coast of Australia. As the convoy hugged the coastline, the men could just make out the rolling foothills and more distant peaks of the blue Australian Alps, locally called the Snowy Mountains. The next day, the first of February, the ships passed Wilsons Promontory where the escort U.S.S. *Phoenix* gave the *Coolidge* and the *Mariposa* over to tugs from Port Phillip Bay. The cruiser then turned and sailed back to the east, never to be seen again.

The tugs guided the two liners north into bustling Melbourne harbor and the capital city of Victoria province. There was a curious similarity to San Francisco, even though much smaller. It was a handsome city with wide boulevards and squares, tall office buildings, shops and churches. Past bridges spanning the inner harbor and beyond the docks, was a community of 7,000 inhabitants. It was a commerce center of shipping, railyards, and streets busy with pedestrians, buses, and carts. Further beyond rose the forested slopes of the Snowy Mountains. No barricades were seen in the avenues, but there were armed guards at the docks and the American section chiefs were informed of restricted zones in the town. The nation had been in a state of war since the British declaration against the Nazis in 1939, but the grand city was void of any sign of hostilities.

Originally a penal colony for the dregs of the British Empire in the 1800s, the resilient Britons had proved their worth by carving out a nation on the southeastern shores of the vast, primitive continent. Beyond the hills outside Melbourne lay nearly 3 million square miles of mainland called the Outback. Only slightly smaller in area than the continental United States, the great southern continent was sparsely populated by a mere two million European citizens. Magnificent vacant prairies, deserts, intermittent coastal forests and the resident aboriginals made her mysterious and foreboding, and only a few hardy ranchers (station masters) or mining prospectors had ventured into the hostile interior.

Australia arose from an upstart, rebel colony to become a strategic Commonwealth member in a mere 170 years of maturity. From the nation's capital of Canberra in the Snowy Mountains, Prime Minister John Curtin and the Parliament administered to the ports at Perth, Port Pirie, and Melbourne along the south coast, and Sydney and Brisbane to the east. They were gateways to trade routes in the Orient and Central Pacific. The British Royal Navy also used these ports, and Australia became highly dependent on England's fleet for protection in perilous times. Canberra intended to establish her own Navy squadrons after the First World War, and improve her ports on the west and north coasts, but found costs too restrictive in the wake of the world economic depression in the 1930s. Only the harbor shanty town of Darwin, at the northern most point of the Northern Territory, was upgraded to service ships with fuel and supplies. By 1939, the British high command had settled for the "Singapore strategy," a plan to focus Royal Navy strength at the southern most port of the South China Sea. Certain that such a location would hold any Oriental expansion in check, Darwin was designated as a principal staging base for flights and voyages to the north.

Now the country was drawn into a second world conflict, and still, Australia had neither a navy, nor an air force. Curtin's administration reluctantly conscripted the nation's young men for the

British war effort in Europe. At that critical juncture in the spread of the Pacific war, Canberra, London and Washington's governments knew the isolation of the great southern continent would sound the death knell of the Royal Navy's authority over the sea lanes to the South China Sea and the South Pacific. The 49ers were but a small consolation group sent to help bolster the withering Allied forces which fought a conqueror who stood at the threshold of the Australia's Northern Territory.

## ASHORE DOWN UNDER

The Mariposa and Coolidge anchored on Sunday, and small craft soon surrounded the ships as the news spread that American troops were on board. The raising of Aussie voices brought great excitement to the Yanks as they made ready for debarkation. They slept on board that night for the last time.

On the morning of February 2nd, the first of the Group stepped down the gangway and boarded busses that carried them to the Flinders Street station. Trains then transported the Americans to several different sites around Melbourne for temporary quarters. When a staff car arrived, Major Wurtsmith immediately set off to report to Commodore F. M. Bladin, Deputy Chief Air Staff of RAAF, at Allied HQ in the city.

The Major left Hutchinson in the care of the ships captains and the military harbor authority. The Deputy Group CO was only then informed that as it was so early in the day and with such a small dock force of "wharfies" available, the Captain should organize Air Corps work details to help unload the heavy cargo from the hold of the troop ships. The few Aussie stevedores that were available simply refused to handle the munitions. Over one hundred 49ers served for the next three days removing ammunition, vehicles and tool crates from both the Mariposa and the Coolidge.

At the initial meeting in Allied HQ, Commodore Bladin proved himself early on to be an efficient administrator. The Commodore was an older man, but very friendly and an able diplomat for the

*8 PS lieutenant pilots at Canberra. Front: Dennis (MIA), Martin, Davis Back: Eisenburg, Gelatka, Java veteran Morehead, Kingsley*

*8 PS pilots. Front: Duke, Jordan, Java vet Johnsen, Werner, Smith Back: Day, Steddom, Harris, Java vet Docksteder, Fish (KIA)*

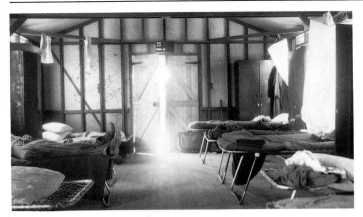

*Camp Darley temporary quarters, Melbourne.*

*USAT Mariposa bearing the main 49ers contingent in Australian coastal waters, February, 1942.*

task of introducing the newly arrived 49er CO to the struggling Allied command. Bladin informed Wurtsmith of his promotion to lieutenant colonel and his Deputy CO Hutchinson to major. All the Pursuit Squadron COs, and 49th Interceptor CO Powell, were promoted to captain. Second Lt. Bill Ladendorf was then given command of the 49th Interceptor Controllers, enabling Capt. Powell to join Hutchinson's HQ staff. From that moment on, the 49er were integrated into the woeful abyss of the remnant Allied fighter command.

In the next few days, it became quite evident to the 49ers enlisted people that very few men 20 to 30 years of age were available to work in all of Australia. The British Empire had again taken all of the country's available men for service in Europe. Only the very young, the old, or an occasional veteran just released from hospital were present. Each day, as the 49er work details met their Australian counterparts, the Yanks were made aware of just how desperate the situation in this great country had become. Australians were very cordial to the "colonial lads" from America, but after brief exchanges with their hosts, one soon learned of the fear that Japanese troops would land on their northern shores at any moment. Many locals expressed contempt for England and the "bloody Churchill business" in Africa. The older veterans and families of the conscripted voiced a resentment for what most considered England's theft of the nation's youth. The Australians were a bitter, war weary people without an army to protect themselves.

## CAMPS IN VICTORIA TERRITORY

The men of the 49ers were now scattered all around the city, both at military encampments and civilian quarters. At Camp Darley west of Melbourne, 600 men left the train to walk two miles across an open field to the very foothills of the Alps. This site was to be their bivouac, but the hosts had not provided any gear. Some spent the first few nights curled up under makeshift windbreaks of truck tarpaulins, or canvasses from the ships. The few barracks assigned were tin shacks and those within who thought themselves lucky, soon suffered in the cold night drafts pouring through the floor planks. Work details tried to secure equipment from nearby Australian units, but little came forth.

One man rose up from the encampment who set a precedent for "Yankee ingenuity" that would eventually make the 49ers infa-

mous. The fellow was S/Sgt Wesley Downer, head of the armament section in the 8th Pursuit Squadron. The small, portly NCO was unassuming in appearance, but would soon become the nemesis of every supply depot in the Australian theater. His commander, Capt. Van Auken, called him the "thief who kept them alive."

After the first few uncomfortable nights, Capt. Van Auken designated a work detail to acquire camp supplies. Tents in a supply dump, some five miles on the other side of Camp Darley, were the objective of the detail and they set off on foot shortly after breakfast. After about a mile of walking in the Australian summer sun, the 8th PS detail was passed by a horse drawn cart, driven by the larcenous S/Sgt. Downer. It was a humorous sight at first, but he didn't stop and the detail cursed as Downer disappeared in a swirl of red dust. When they reached the supply dump, the Sergeant was already returning in the cart stacked high with tent kits.

Upon the return to the 49er's camp, Van Auken called Downer over to explain how he got his equipment. The horse cart was one the sergeant had seen two days earlier and he was purposely vague beyond that point. There had been no guards posted when he arrived at the dump. He simply took the gear. Downer told the captain, "Next time, "I'll get a truck." He did and the most nefarious acquisition network in the Allied forces was placed in operation for the duration.

## ABDACOM; FEBRUARY 1942

The Australians were not distracted by such minor diversions as stolen tents in New South Wales. The ominous task of resupplying the crumbling defenses far to the north-west was a much more serious concern for ABDACOM, the Australia-British-Dutch-American command.

ABDACOM had been formed on January 2nd at Batavia, Java, with British Gen. Sir A.P. Wavell as its head, to align all the member nations toward a coordinated counter offensive to save the besieged port of Singapore. The Allied forces had been in a dismal retreat from the onset of the wide spread attacks, brilliantly executed by the superior forces. The logistics to cover the 5000 mile front now set from Singapore on the west to the Solomon Islands on the east, was far beyond the scope of Allied forces, even when combined. ABDACOM soon proved to be too complicated an answer to resolve the dilemma, and was a political nightmare.

## BRERETON'S ROUTE

As early as the summer of 1941, Gen. MacArthur had foreseen the impending Japanese treachery and wisely sent his new FEAF CO, Gen. Lewis Brereton, from Manila to Australia to designate a southern supply route across the continent that would serve his Philippines forces in the event of an invasion from the north. With the aid of RAAF field officers, the FEAF commander designated a network of northern air strips and supply bases across the sprawling Outback by the end of November that would be known as the "Brereton Route."

The newcomer USAFIA commander, Gen. Brett, had arrived in December to ensure the Brereton Route was a priority operation, but the fields along the Route were merely dirt strips dragged out in the 1930s by bush pilots and flying physicians. The dusty, narrow runways could only support fighters and light bombers. The RAAF simply did not have the engineering units available to upgrade the rustic landing areas. USAAC B-17 Fortress or B-24 Liberator bombers would have to make the 1100 mile flight nonstop between Darwin on the northwest coast and Townsville on the east coast of Queensland Territory. Only the hardpacked runways at Katherine Field 100 miles south of Darwin, Batchelor Field 50 miles south of Darwin, or RAAF Field at Darwin proper, were judged sturdy enough to receive the heavy four-engine planes.

Fighter aircraft and light bombers shipped from the U.S. were initially intended to be assembled on the airfields in the Philippines, but by late December, that was impossible. All shipments of pilots and crews from the States were diverted in January to the eastern ports of Australia, principally to Brisbane and Townsville where air bases and assembly facilities were fully operational. Once the American and Australian mechanics, often with the help of the pilots, made a plane ready it would be sent west. From Brisbane, they would fly 400 miles due west to Charleville. After refueling there, they took off to the northwest, following ranch trails and the telegraph line, for 550 miles to the sheep station community of Cloncurry, Queensland. The ferry flights from Townsville flew directly to Cloncurry, due west 400 miles along the railroad.

Once aircraft were deep in Queensland's western wilderness, the next leg was possibly the most hazardous on the continent. They would fly northwest 500 miles across the barren, red Outback called Barkley Tablelands to the dreary station of Daly Waters, Northern Territory. The lands there were flat, dotted by sparse stands of trees and coursed by broad, shallow winding creeks. Only the low bluffs of a once great mountain range broke the horizon of the Tablelands beyond Daly Waters. Further up the dirt road "track", beyond the stations of Katherine and Adelaide River, lay the grasslands of the Northern Territory.

Beyond the grasslands was the lime green eucalyptus forest, the "bush", which eventually melded with the swampy tidal flats of the north coast. At the jigsaw shoreline of Beagle Gulf, Brereton designated the little harbor shanty town of Darwin as "Base One". Allied airmen and their valiant crews would gather at the remote port town, the last safe harbor in the Southwest Pacific, until they were called to enter into the 2000 miles long void of the Malay arch battle front.

The Brereton Route was nearly 3600 miles long from Brisbane to Java, and if guide aircraft were available (they rarely were), the course was at least passable. It was the best the general could devise in such arduous circumstances. It was the longest supply line ever established to reach a single campaign in the history of warfare, was as delicate as a cobweb and could easily be broken anywhere along the "Malay Barrier" beyond Base One-Darwin.

## ABDACOM IN CRISIS

In mid-January, Gen. Wavell had asked the Australian government at Canberra to clarify if his area of command included Brett's Base One and the Brereton Route, and Prime Minister Curtin said it did. Thereafter, all American aircraft in the north, from Brisbane to Darwin, were placed under order of the British, to serve the direct concerns of the Dutch. At the insistence of Gen. Marshall in Washington D.C., Brereton was named as Deputy to Wavell so that an American staff general officer would still administer the USAAC needs, but Brereton instantly found the political arrangement incompatible with his combat duties. He relinquished the Deputy role to Gen. Brett, who in turn passed his USAFIA command to B.Gen. Julian Barnes as of the end of January.

Wavell was persistent, however, and still wanted Brereton and his invaluable FEAF under the close scrutiny of British Air Chief Marshal Peirse of ABDAIR. The Australians succeeded in convincing Gen. Marshall to direct Brereton to become ABDAIR Deputy. Brereton agreed, and with the ABDACOM staff politically aligned at Batavia's HQ, a battle plan was finally drawn on February 7th for the relief of Singapore. Far down the ABDACOM chain of command in Air Marshal Peirse's ABDAIR, was the new 49th Pursuit Group, led by Maj. Paul Wurtsmith.

The political shuffling sent shock waves all the way to Melbourne. Wurtsmith was bewildered by the endless communiques of staff changes. His 49th Pursuit Group was scheduled for deployment by the end of February, and yet the major was uncertain who would be his field general, or if the desperate ABDACOM would leave the 49ers any planes to fulfill their mission. Commodore Bladin had the keen sense to understand Wurtsmith's frustration and together, the RAAF Deputy and the 49er CO initiated the training plan for the newcomer American pilots camped in New South Wales.

## MISSIONS IN ABDACOM

Previously in late December, the Dutch command in charge of the Allied forces in the Celebes had convinced Brereton that his FEAF B-17 Fortress' great range would better serve over the widening front from the large airstrip at Malang, Java, only 60 miles south of FEAF HQ at Soerbaja. Brereton therefore ordered the last twelve heavy bombers up from Batchelor Field to Malang on the 30th. From this new base on the eastern tip of Java, the Fortresses staged 1400 miles through the Dutch base at Kendari in the Celebes to hit targets in the Philippines. At further Dutch insistence the Americans also flew against Japanese shipping on the Sumatran coast, over 800 miles to the west.

It was brutal logic that on January 21, Gen. Wavell would likewise face the deterioration of the east flank. The Australian garrison at Rabaul, New Britain, 2500 miles east of the Java campaign, came under attack from the Japanese aircraft carrier force that sailed from the new Imperial Navy stronghold at Truk lagoon in the Caroline Islands. Two days later, Japanese Marines entered Simpson Harbor and landed at Rabaul, forcing the garrison troops to escape south into the jungle. The loss of the strategic New Britain port demanded redesignation of planes at the bases of northern Queensland for the defense of eastern New Guinea, but the diversion brought a furious response from the Dutch staff. They questioned if Australia favored defense on the northern continent and abandonment of Java all together. The argument was rhetorical, since the ways and means to cover both the western and eastern flanks did not exist.

On February 15, the "Singapore strategy" and the relief schemes for the trapped Allies in Malaya vanished as the Singapore island defense capitulated to Gen. Yamashita's surrounding Imperial Army. The men of Java's tiny defense force knew the end was near.

*Fuel tanks at the Darwin docks set ablaze in the air raid.*

## THE VETERANS ARE TOO LATE

During January, Brereton had demanded more base defense and he implored the floundering RAAF to expedite the advance of all available P-40 units. Only one squadron of seventeen serviceable P-40s, flown by Philippines veterans renamed the 17th Provisional Pursuit, had made the trip to Java via the "Route" by mid month. Douglas A-24 dive bombers of the 27th Group reached Darwin, but the planes lacked essential equipment for combat. They withdrew to Batchelor Field to be refitted, but only a few would reach Timor Island, 500 miles short of their intended destination of Kendari and Ambon Island which were captured by the end of the month.

However, a few P-40s with veteran replacement pilots of the 20th Squadron and the 3rd Squadron were delivered to the 17th Provisional on Java. By mid-February, the Japanese Army and Navy air units were raiding the length of the Malay arch and the surrounding sea lanes. FEAF losses soared.

## A SEABORNE DIVERSION AT PERTH

The logistical riff between USAFIA and ABDACOM widened as more aircraft and crews became hopelessly mired along the Brereton Route. In mid-February, exasperated Gen. Wavell and A.M. Peirse preempted USAFIA authority and commandeered all fighter aircraft en route. They were to divert to Perth, Western Australia, to be partially disassembled and brought aboard ships for Java.

## USAFIA CO

Barnes grudgingly promised 140 Warhawks in the network, and notified the appropriate bases to divert the pilots and planes immediately. ABDACOM chose the old aircraft tender U.S.S. *Langley*, and the freighter U.S.S. *Seawitch*, to take the fighters to the Java port of Tjilatjap.

*Port Moresby after the February 19th attack. Salvage crews work over a freighter capsized at the dock. The water tower on the horizon at far left marks the location of the Darwin RAAF airfield.*

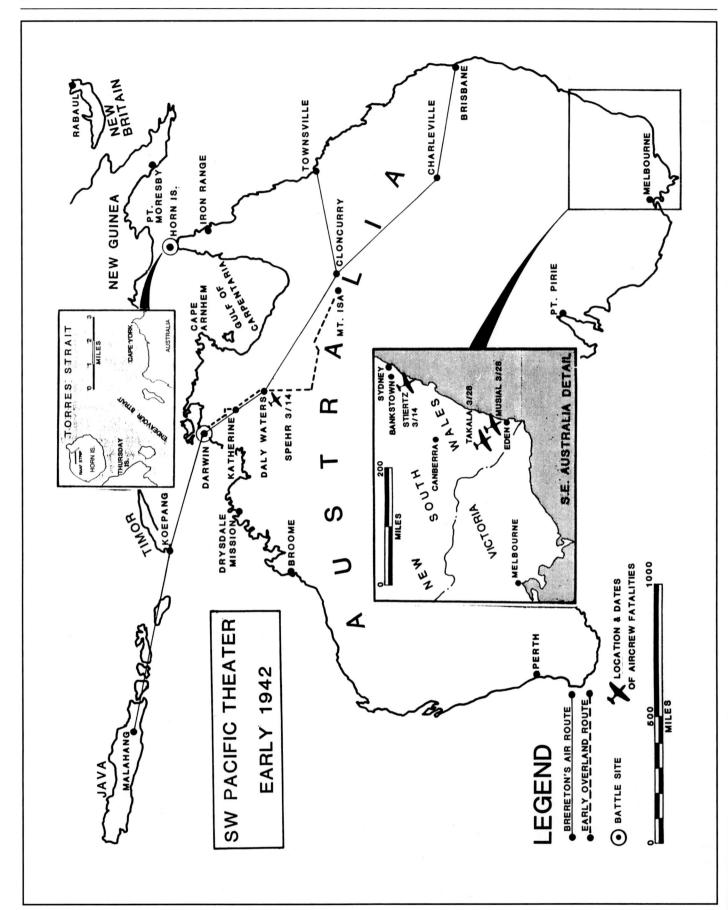

*Burned out remains of a P-40 Warhawk from Pell's ill-fated 33 PS at RAAF Darwin Airfield.*

*USAAC Douglas A-24 dive-bomber at RAAF Batchelor A/F in early March after the Darwin raid, obviously inadequate for the defense of the vulnerable northern Australian coast.*

The new diversion completely disrupted the operations in both ABDAIR and USAFIA. Experienced pilots from the training bases far to the south were pressed into ferry duty. Aircraft intended for the 49ers were diverted for the seaborne venture. Lt. Earl Kingsley, just arrived on the USAAT *Coolidge* at Melbourne, was inducted into a provisional squadron flying to Perth, but was forced down at Port Pirie with engine trouble. He returned to Canberra and was then inducted into Van Auken's 8 PS. In a similar vane, Captain Morrissey made the trip all the way from Sydney to the Perth docks and was instrumental in getting the P-40s on the deck of the Langley. The captain hoped to embark for Java, but Wurtsmith ordered his immediate return to Melbourne. With USAAC pilots scattered the width and breadth of the continent without a well planned order of battle, it was little wonder all of the ventures would fail.

## DARWIN; FEBRUARY 19, 1942

There was yet another diversion within the reinforcement attempt which underscored the total futility of the Java campaign. The 33rd Pursuit Squadron led by Maj. Floyd Pell which was Perth-bound for the Langley venture had just been diverted from Port Pirie, two-thousand miles across the Outback to Base One-Darwin for convoy escort to Timor, and subsequent ferry to Koepang, Java. At Darwin by the 18th, the 33rd was unable to follow the lead B-17 to Timor's fogged-in landing site, and instead, waited for clearer weather the next day.

Indeed, Pell's squadron was on the flight line that fateful morning of the 19th where they fell victim to fifty-four Mitsubishi G4M heavy bombers that had staged from newly captured Ambon and Kendari, plus the carrier based assault force of eighteen dive-bombers with thirty-six Zero-sen fighters in escort. Nine of their ten Warhawks were destroyed and four pilots, including Pell, were killed by strafing enemy fighters. Only Lt. Bob Oestricher and his plane survived. Eleven RAAF planes were also wiped out in the raid.

Darwin's shanty houses near the harbor were flattened by the awesome explosion of an oil tanker, a troop ship carrying ammunition, and a freighter loaded with depth charges that were all simul-

taneously hit in the harbor. Fuel tanks on the docks were set ablaze. Other ships were sunk or damaged, and the RAAF runways were pitted as the enemy made two bombing passes unopposed.

On the morning of the 20th, the few remaining Allied air crews and dock workers abandoned the smoking ruins and headed south along the Track for Batchelor Field, or even further to Adelaide River station. Others scattered into small camps in the gumtree forests south of the strip. Over 240 civilians and military personnel were dead or missing.

Oestricher's P-40E was the last real fighter in all the Northern Territory. Only sixteen worthless 27th BG A-24 dive-bombers were left at Batchelor Field. Brereton's Route was cleanly severed at Base One.

## THE FALL OF JAVA AND THE END OF ABDACOM

Of the 140 Warhawks rushed into the fray in late February, only thirty-nine ever reached Brereton's Java defense force. The twenty-five crated aircraft on board the Seawitch were abandoned on the docks at Tjilatjap while the port was under siege on the 26th. Mere hours later, the *Langley*, with her crew and thirty-two planes with nearly all the pilots, was sent to the bottom of the Java Trench by enemy bombers.

The losses were all the more pathetic as Gen. Wavell had abandoned his ABDACOM headquarters at Batavia and had withdrawn to Australia that very same day. Later that night, the remnant Allied navy under Dutch command was sacrificed in one final, futile engagement against the superior Mobile Fleet. On March 1st, a few minor skirmishes with the surviving Dutch ships marked the end of the fight for Java.

ABDACOM was finished. Just after midnight on the morning of March 2nd, the last men of the allied forces lifted off in a B-24 transport from a strip near the village of Jogjakarta on the southern shore. Seven hours later, they landed at the seaplane haven at Broome, Australia, 900 miles to the southeast. Others had returned to Darwin, a ghost town on the tide flats, still in the path of the great invasion fleet that lurked just beyond the northern horizon.

# 2

# THE ALLIES REGROUP IN AUSTRALIA MARCH 1942

The events in the Australian-Java campaigns of February, 1942, were marked by the disastrous counter measures of the Allied command. Neither American nor Australian intelligence accurately measured the strength or position of the Japanese. Allied units were massacred while replacements languished in the maze of cumbersome ABDACOM.

During those last frenzied hours on Java, USAFIA reserves were scattered 3000 miles to the southeast, refitting planes at assembly bases on the east coast, or on the dusty airfields across the Outback. While those relief flights struggled westward along the Brereton Route, the "Malay Barrier" line of defense toppled until the last of the FEAF units were swept off the island of Java. The February 19th air raid on Base One sent ABDACOM and the Australian people reeling. Only the dregs of a battered, obsolete air force stranded at Batchelor Field in the Northern Territory stood before the impending landings at Darwin in early March. Further to the west, the successful Japanese advance up the Burmese coast and imminent capture of the capitol city of Rangoon threatened the eastern provinces of India. Prime Minister Churchill of England asked the American Chief of Staff, Gen. Marshall, to release Brereton's heavy bomber force from the hopeless Malayan campaign. Marshall acquiesced and the FEAF commander summarily withdrew his bombers to India by the end of February. General Brett was the highest ranking U.S. Army staff officer left in Australia and he resumed command of the USAFIA with General Barnes as his deputy on February 24th. The Allied command withdrew to Melbourne and the Australian Chiefs of Staff argued as to what final stand they could mount on their northern shores against the Japanese landing forces. Neither the Americans nor the Chiefs of Staff could totally agree on a projected invasion place or date. The entire nation braced as the huge enemy juggernaut queued up off Java for the next strike, somewhere on the northern coast.

## RANK AND ORDER UNDER RAAF COMMAND

Wurtsmith and his immediate superior, Deputy Chief of Staff Commodore Bladin, had in the meantime become a most effective team. The 49er CO impressed his superior with his direct "Yankee" manner and eagerness to utilize his Group at the earliest moment. In the debacle of the ABDACOM era, the elderly Bladin had come forward as the most accommodating foreign officer and was instrumental in assuring that facilities for the American group would be a priority in the turbulent command that now retreated to Melbourne. Bladin and Wurtsmith concurred on the tactic of Group strength for Darwin, and not the wasteful sacrifice of individual squadrons by ABDACOM. Estimates by the Allied Chiefs of Staff for an enemy landing on the north coast varied from the last week in March to no later than early April, and indeed, part of the defense logistics called for a fighter unit of group strength. The 49ers were the only fully manned outfit in all the country and 100 P-40s from Brisbane and Townsville had been promised as early as February in anticipation of their arrival. Training facilities, however, were critically sparse. The pivotal task was to put pilots, crews and planes together at a base via the primitive transportation network on the continent. LtC. Wurtsmith was disturbed that in all the vast surroundings, there was no base large enough to accommodate his whole Group. Three training bases were in New South Wales, but they were miles apart from each other, and more than 2000 miles from the front.

The underdeveloped Australian Outback was comparable to the western U.S. in the 1800s. Only sea routes, air travel, and the southeast coastal railroad linked the greater harbor towns. Dirt roads inland in the north were usually washed out in "gudjewg", the monsoonal wet season of January through March. Railroads of different gauges required wheel changes in each province making overland travel lengthy for anyone in peace time, and a tactical night-

*7 PS Warhawk #8 bellied in at Bankstown RAAF Airfield, New Castle, N.S.W. All three squadrons adopted the single or two-digit numbering system early on in the operational training era.*

*8 PS Warhawk #41 with broken left gear on RAAF Fairbrin Airfield, Canberra, N.S.W.*

*8 PS aircraft #52 bellied in on dry river bed near Canbera.*

*Pranged 8 PS ship #61 dragged aside at Fairbrin for parts salvage.*

mare during war. Telegraph was transcontinental to most towns, but breaks due to natural causes could isolate thousands of square miles for weeks before repairs could be made. Most sheep stations relied on short wave radio to communicate with the railhead towns or coastal trade centers. Within this archaic system, the 49er Squadrons were sent off to their operational training bases.

## WARHAWKS IN NEW SOUTH WALES

On February 14, Capt. Selman and his 9 PS were first to take the train north from Camp Darley, through Canberra, and on to Williamstown RAAF Airdrome at Newcastle, N.S.W., 550 miles up the coast. Billeting was provided in the town of Newcastle, just across the bay from the landing field, as well as in the RAAF field barracks.

The next day, Maj. Hutchinson with his HQ staff and Capt. Morrissey with his 7 PS pilots and crews, took the same route, but stopped 75 miles short of Newcastle at the harbor town of Sydney. They joined the RAAF at Bankstown Airdrome just west of the harbor. Hutchinson set up his HQ in the golf course club house just across the road from the landing area. The 7 PS crews bivouacked in the surrounding forests and shared some barracks quarters with the RAAF. In two days, Lt. Ladendorf brought up his Group Interceptors team to Bankstown to begin earnest training in RAAF air control systems.

On February 16, Capt. Van Auken and his 8 PS took the rails into Canberra's valley to reside at Fairbrin RAAF Airdrome, just

east of the capitol. Officers were billeted in the town and the enlisted shared barracks with the RAAF crews.

Engineering section Lts. George Hermanson of the 7th, Dick Illing of the 8th, Fred Hollier of the 9th and Paul Werner of HQ had a special assignment. They took an 80-man team of line crews 900 miles by rail to the assembly base of Amberly Field at Brisbane. Amberly was the source of Curtiss P-40 Warhawks for their squadrons in New South Wales.

## THE FIRST 49ERS TO BASE ONE
## AND A NEW OPERATION OFFICER

The gravity of the 49ers schedule was certainly underscored by the Darwin raid on the 19th. Gen. Brett ordered an advance team of 49ers air crews immediately to Base One-Darwin and Sgt. Fred Quick with 16 men from the 9th Squadron were mobilized. Quick's people were driven from Williamstown Field back to Sydney, and were then flown by RAAF 4-engine flying boat to a one-night layover at Townshend Island, just offshore of Townsville, Q.T., on the 21st. They flew the final leg to Darwin the next day.

The squadron commanders all wondered if the March 1st readiness date was realistic, but the Chiefs of Staff and Gen. Brett were resolute. The 49ers had two weeks to get ready for combat. As incomprehensible as it seemed, USAFIA at that precise moment absconded with the 49ers' most experienced flyers for the Perth-Langley debacle, eliminating key personnel in that critical training period. Wurtsmith was dumbfounded and adamantly asked for any

*Lt. Fielder put #40 down on a coastal sandbar east of Melbourne where 8 Squadron engineers set it upright.*

*Aircraft #40 next floated to the mainland for removal of its wings and portage by lorry back to Fairbrin.*

*Temporary Group Ops officer Major Buzz Wagner.*

senior flight officers from USAFIA that were unattached to fill the void. Luckily for Wurtsmith, USAFIA relinquished veteran Capt. Boyd "Buzz" Wagner to the novice pursuit group. An old acquaintance of Wurtsmith from the prewar days, Wagner was a perfect choice for the 49ers new Operations Executive.

Captain Wagner's exploits in the Philippines campaign were nothing less than of legendary. He was the first official USAAC ace with 5 confirmed kills and numerous probable victories. After his virtual one-man reign of terror against the Japanese over Luzon in December, an eye wound forced him out of combat and MacArthur personally ordered him back to Australia to take charge of reorganizing the replacement fighter units in USAFIA. Hense, Wagner became one of the most influential leaders to effect all of the new fighter units in the Allied build-up.

## 49ER WARHAWKS IN NEW SOUTH WALES

The engineers and crews soon passed new fighters to ferry pilots

for delivery to the three Operational Training sites in New South Wales. Each 49er squadron was allocated twenty-five Curtiss Warhawk P-40E fighters from the first, second and third production blocks and P-40E1CU types from the fourth block. Several of the third and fourth block planes were in earth brown and dark green with pale grey underside camouflage, indicating RAF-contract machines for Europe or China duty. They had been commandeered from RAF distribution after America joined the war effort. The other planes were standard USAAC overall olive drab with grey undersides. All bore star-in-circle insignia and "U.S. ARMY" beneath the wings. The three squadrons drew plane assignments at random from the first and second blocks, while 10 were held out for reserve with the HQ Squadron at Bankstown A/D. Approximately 10 more were allocated at Melbourne's Laverton airstrip in an RAAF reserve pool as a source for spare parts.

The Curtiss P-40E was the most advanced fighter plane available in large numbers to the USAAC in 1942. Essentially the same design as the old C-model ships flown by the 49th Group in the Florida 1941 era, the E-model was distinguished by an increase in firepower to six .50 caliber machine guns, three in each wing and 1600 rounds when fully armed. An increase in the size of the coolant radiator beneath the Allison in-line engine gave a jut-jawed, repugnant look to the otherwise, overall streamlined machine. The "Warhawk", known as the "Kittyhawk" by the RAF veterans on the African front, had proved to be a rugged and dependable combatant, and had again displayed incredible adaptability in the hands of the Yanks over the Philippines and Java. Although a 350 mile radius was far below the range of contemporary Japanese types, the P-40 proved its worth in base defense and excelled in ground attack. The heavy combat losses of the tough fighter-bomber was sorely felt by all the Allied air forces. The training losses in Australia alone would result in the attrition of approximately 140 of the available 330 Warhawks in March, 1942.

## PILOTS AND LEGENDS ARE BORN

Very few 49er pilots had proceeded much beyond their advanced cadet training. Perhaps a dozen had flown the more advanced P-40

*Early 7 PS markings on Lt. George Prentice's P-40E #11, late March, 1942. The white #11 is painted over the original black 3-digit identifier. The small emblem on the rudder is a devil cartoon which would later become the namesake of Prentice's famous 475th FG Satan's Angels.*

in the States, and fewer still had any gunnery flights. To become a Warhawk pilot in Australia was painfully simple. At each base, the squadron CO, or experienced senior pilot, would follow the novice up the wing-walk of a P-40E, and help "the candidate" strap into the cockpit. After the rudimentary identification of flight controls, throttle settings, radio operations and fuel-ignition sequences, the instructor departed for the control tower. From the tower at the edge of the RAAF "pasture", the instructor ordered the 1150 hp Allison engine "fired up." After insuring the prop was in correct pitch and all switches were on, the pilot was told to take his foot off the brake and "gently" advance the throttle.

The adventure, or chaos, then began. At the Bankstown, Fairbrin and Williamstown airdromes, Yankee fighter pilots careened their Warhawks across the fields to the shouts of squadron mates waiting their turns, and the anxious plea of the instructor over the radio to "trim it up, Lieutenant." The first flight was once around the pattern, with gear in the down position, to a final approach "talk-down" and landing back at the drome. Proceeding flights summarily included retracted landing gear and greater distances.

No one was killed in these early flights, but the torque of the Allison engine was treacherous. Ground loops and swerving take-offs were common, but landing took the greater toll. The gear of the P-40 was wide, but not well suited for grass landings by novice pilots. Over 30 wrecks were logged in two weeks time and maintenance crews worked continuously to straighten propellers and landing gears of the pranged Warhawks. Flight surgeons patched up the bruised limbs and cracked heads of young lieutenants from the abrupt stops after botched landings, but very few were sent to hospital.

Some aircraft were carried by lorry or train to Laverton's reserve base for a complete overhaul, and the worst were cannibalized for the vital spare parts.

The advanced pilots were required to upgrade their formation flying skills. LtC. Wurtsmith and Capt. Wagner were advocates of sound flight leader training (both men were accomplished in "the Selfridge tradition"). The Ops man was particularly adamant and told the new pilots that "Many a good wingman in the fight is why I'm in New South Wales today." Good formation in combat was the key to victory. By month's end, the Group could hear the CO on training flights badgering a reluctant lieutenant wingman, "Squeeze it in here, man. Squeeze it in."

Nicknames were traditional for pilots as well as planes in the flying community, and a legend was born in New South Wales; "Squeeze" Wurtsmith was leaving his personal mark on the 49ers. By March, four ship flights of P-40s in tight formation roamed the skies over southeastern Australia.

## ANOTHER STRIKE ON AUSTRALIA

On March 3, 1942, 800 miles south of Darwin, many refugees had just arrived at Broome, Western Australia, by several different flights from Java and Celebes to wait for evacuation to the south and east. Certain that an enemy reconnaissance flight had passed over the day before, the air transport commanders thought to depart in the early morning light, but the wait proved costly. Staging from the Celebes through newly captured Timor, nine pale grey fighters swept in at 0920 and shot down a B-24 transport just as it crossed the

beach on takeoff. Next, they destroyed sixteen flying boats floating in the shallow harbor, and then two B-17s, two RAAF Hudsons, another B-24 and a civilian DC-3 were all torched on the landing field by the strafing Japanese. On departing, one enemy fighter was shot down on the beach by machine gun fire from a Dutch air crewman in meager retribution for the appalling carnage.

A final Dutch DC-3, perhaps the last Allied flight from Java, was shot down off the shoreline during the enemy's return to Timor. As in Darwin just two weeks past, the Broome survivors counted their dead, and abandoned the smoldering ruins by nightfall. They escaped south along the coast road on foot, or by car, for any small town that had portage to Perth, 1300 miles distant. The government in Canberra rocked under the blow of the news; approximately 70 civilians and Allied servicemen were dead or missing on their western shore.

On March 6th, the Dutch formally conceded Java to the Oriental victors. The Allies rushed more reserves to Base One, sure that Darwin would be revisited at any moment.

## VETERANS FROM JAVA FOR THE 49ERS

Melbourne, Sydney and Brisbane were soon host to more veterans from the north. After the Darwin raid and fall of Java, detached Allied airmen roamed the streets of every town, many combat weary beyond hope and looking for a pub that was not off limits. Others were desperate to keep the belief that their comrades in the Philippines, or the Celebes, were still alive. Those faithful few reported to the Allied commands in Brisbane and Melbourne for another assignment up north.

By the first week of March, Wurtsmith was introduced to several veterans of the Philippines and Java FEAF units still looking for a vehicle north. They were hardened men, anxious to exact vengeance on the Japanese and Squeeze Wurtsmith took advantage of their circumstance. The 49ers needed more experienced men like Wagner, the new Operations officer, and the veterans would afford invaluable experience and instruction for the novice pilots.

To Morrissey's 7 PS came Captains Nate Blanton and Bill Hennon and Lt. Lester Johnsen as new flight leaders. Bowing to demands of USAFIA and Com. Bladin from the beginning, Morrissey's "can-do" ability (including the ill-fated *Langley* scheme) caused his absence more often than he or Wurtsmith liked. His capable Deputy, Lt. George Prentice, had seen to the training schedule, but the added authority in the veterans' presence was most welcome.

Van Auken inducted two new Captains, Al Strauss, a quiet, calculating former B-17 pilot, and "the Kentucky gentleman" George Kiser, as flight leaders into the 8 PS. Young firebrand Lieutenants R.C. Dockstader and Jim Morehead added more depth as element leaders.

Selman took on Capt. "Bitchin" Ben Irvin as a senior flight leader in the 9 PS. Lieutenants Joe Kruzel, and the future high scoring ace for the Darwin campaign, Andy Reynolds, filled in the element leader slots.

Major Hutchinson also received help from senior Captains Walter Coss and Jack Dale in HQ at Bankstown. The Group now had experience at every level and as more P-40 time was logged, Wurtsmith felt more confident they would be ready to meet the

*7 PS 2Lt. Lee's rebuilt Charters Towers derelict #15 "BITZAHAWK" meant for Horn Island, but flown instead throughout the Darwin campaign.*

Japanese, somewhere "up North." In the first week of March, his Group was assigned their first mission.

## DEPLOYMENT ACROSS THE FRONT

Commodore Bladin and Wurtsmith had agreed from the onset that the 49ers should be deployed at group strength, but as of late February, that theory was set aside by shear necessity. Japanese aircraft probed as far south as Guadalcanal and San Cristobal in the Solomon Islands on Australia's exposed east flank. The RAAF was sending its next defense effort to Port Moresby on the southeastern coast of New Guinea, fearing the loss of the entire Coral Sea area and its sea routes to America. Senior Australian staff officers prepared a contingency "Brisbane Line" defense to submit to the Parliament as, "the quaking roof might collapse" at any point between Darwin and Cape York. For the first time since the war began, PM John Curtin declared martial law and curfews in the nation.

Despite the flounderings of the Allied command, Squeeze Wurtsmith's team in New South Wales had actually met their operational training objective. Maj. Hutchinson claimed all three squadrons could muster at least a dozen elements each for the northern defense and it was none too soon.

## 7th PURSUIT TO HORN ISLAND

Without warning on March 4th, Maj. Wurtsmith confronted Capt. Morrissey and asked how many pilots in his 7th Squadron were combat ready. The captain readily named eleven men, and Wurtsmith told them to get their flight gear ready immediately. Morrissey and his officers were being sent into combat.

After three days of hectic preparations, Morrissey and his 7th Squadron wingmen finally lifted off at daybreak from Bankstown RAAF Field for the mission which was not to Darwin, but to Queensland Territory in the northeast. Morrissey had no idea of the complexity of the deployment, but it was certain that something big was in the works. His team of novice pilots had been selected to advance to an airfield which had no USAAC mechanics, so line

chief Msgt. Hays provided small tool kits, spark plugs and the most rudimentary instructions on maintenance of the Allison engine. The armament people had likewise instructed the pilots on the loading procedures for the six .50 caliber wing guns. Hopefully there would be RAAF crewmen at the advanced field to offer further assistance if necessary.

Only road maps were available to guide them to their first stop at Brisbane. Once there, maritime maps were used to guide them northward up the coast, but three of the P-40s aborted and had to let down at Charters Towers. Two of the pilots returned south while 2Lt. Don Lee remained there to join the RAAF lads in a complete overhaul his ship. Lee never completed the trip to north Queensland, but he would eventually fly on to Darwin in late March in his Charters Towers scrapheap fighter, aptly named "BITZAHAWK."

The nine remaining P-40s pressed on to stay overnight at Townsville. On the following morning of March 8th, they flew 500 miles north to the small mining town of Iron Range, Q.T., to top off their tanks for the final leg up the coast to the very tip of Cape York. At that point of the flight, new maritime maps were used for the short overwater hop northwest to Thursday Island. Adjacent to Thursday lay smaller Horn Island with an RAAF staging strip only 75 miles from the south coast of the great island of New Guinea.

By late afternoon, the nine weary pilots in their sputtering Warhawks strung out in the landing pattern over the brilliant blue Torres Straits and turned toward the small circular island with its "T" runways on the north shore.

Their 2000 foot dispersal strip ran NW to SE across the end of the longer runway that ran due east-west. Morrissey and his pilots taxied to the south end of the shorter strip and parked there, wingtip to wingtip. RAAF crews helped them bivouac in the shrub covered flatlands not far from their P-40s. When Morrisey signalled Melbourne of their arrival, Wurtsmith soon responded with orders for Morrissey to wait until the further notice. Thusly, the 7th Squadron team sat broiling in the tropical sun on the two-mile wide sand spit in the middle of nowhere.

## MELBOURNE PATROLS

Ironically, rumor once again overwhelmed reliable intelligence, and the purported sighting of a Japanese seaplane tender in the southern Solomon Islands caused an uproar in the Canberra Parliament. Commodore Bladin ordered Capt. Van Auken to take his senior pilots for harbor defense and coastal patrol for the entire southeast territory, effective as of March 5th.

Only the 8 PS CO and three of his pilots had any gunnery experience. The fact was moot, since the eighteen Warhawks sent south were far from combat ready. The planes had not had their guns boresighted and the RAAF lacked a supply of .50 caliber ammunition. Only a few of the P-40s were fitted with oxygen gear for high altitude patrols. The ordinance, armament and engineering sections bartered and pilfered from every unit they confronted in New South Wales to refit their planes, but they would never resolve their base assignment obstacle. Laverton Field, from which their patrols were mounted, was just west of the harbor but command logistics there were preposterous. The RAAF had positioned anti-aircraft gun crews along the approach and around the harbor with instructions for all aircraft in the Melbourne vicinity, including the 8 PS, to operate with gear down for ease of identification. Van Auken's protests of the ridiculous setup went unheeded.

Only once in three weeks was the 8th actually alerted to intercept a purported intruder. Residents on the coast had seen a suspicious aircraft and reported the sighting to authorities. Capt. Van Auken's patrol was vectored eastward for the interception and in the haze above the sea off Wilsons Promontory, the Captain saw the faint image of a twin engine plane. The CO set up for a head on pass against the suspect, only to identify the markings of a wayward RAAF Hudson bomber at the last second. Van Auken pulled the P-40 nose up as the "sand and spinach" camouflaged Lockheed sped past and on toward Port Phillip Bay. Van Auken notified Wurtsmith that their situation in the Melbourne defense was intolerable having, "nearly shot down one of our own", but the 8 PS would stay in Victoria Territory until early April, constrained to their absurd assignment.

## SELMAN AND THE BRERETON ROUTE

While the 7th Pursuit made ready for Queensland and the 8th set up operations back at Melbourne, Capt. James Selman's task was to oversee the move of his entire 9 PS organization 2000 miles across the Australian continent to Base One.

Engineering officer Lt. Hollier was recalled from the Amberly Field assembly group to organize the new team for Darwin's RAAF field. Hollier and a ground crew contingent flew north by RAAF transport from Sydney on March 6th.

On March 8th, the Captain set off from Williamstown RAAF airdrome with twenty-five Warhawks on the infamous Brereton Route. When they reached Brisbane, two P-40s stopped with engine trouble. Lieutenants Bud Howk and John Sauber would reach Darwin several days later after necessary repairs. The remaining twenty-three flyers staged on to Charleville where another pair of the Warhawks had mechanical failure. Twenty-one ships then pressed on to Cloncurry with a B-17 in the lead. At Cloncurry, two heavy landings occurred, one by Lt. Ed Smith which damaged his plane beyond repair. Smith was not seriously injured and joined the crew on the Fortress. Captain Selman was left with nineteen planes for the dangerous crossing to Daly Waters, and his frustration soon deepened.

On the 14th, the Barkley Tablelands was dotted with thunderstorms and four P-40s became separated from the 9 PS formation. The four landed at an isolated sheep station far off the Brereton Route, out of fuel and would have to be recovered later.

The fifteen remaining aircraft landed between rain storms at Daly Waters and took advantage of the break for maintenance at the primitive USAFIA facilities. The little shanty trade station and red dust runway was an oasis in the midst of a rolling, barren prairie. That evening, the Captain radioed Melbourne of the weather-forced layover, and was somewhat unnerved by the terse reiteration from HQ that their arrival at Darwin must be accomplished immediately.

The dreary surroundings and belligerence of HQ did not enhance the meal of mutton-suet 'bullybeef', and strong coffee served beneath a swarm of ravenous black flies. The dismal settings seemed to foretell of the pending tragedy.

## THE FIRST 9 PS DEATH IN AUSTRALIA; MARCH 17, 1942

After three days layover at Daly Waters field, Lt. Al Spehr was up on a test flight before the final leg to Base One on the 17th. He attempted an aerobatic "barrel roll" at low altitude, but his plane stalled out and he died in the fiery crash not far from the strip. Selman was heartbroken and radioed Melbourne of the fatal accident. They buried Spehr in the little prairie outpost cemetery that evening.

With improved weather on the March 18th, yet another P-40 failed to get airborne. The last 13 Warhawks finally reached Darwin at noon. Capt. Selman reported to the RAAF skeleton crew at the rickety control shack not far from the bombed-out RAAF hanger. He received updated orders radioed prior to their arrival, and now understood the urgency of the earlier radio communique at Daly Waters. The 7 PS had already made an intercept at Horn Island four day earlier. The 9th was ordered to start patrols immediately.

On the 19th, the four pilots lost at the sheep station had been rescued by a refueling transport flight and they also landed their P-40s at Darwin RAAF strip. The advance team under Lt. Hollier had done what little they could to make the RAAF strip serviceable, but the Nippon marauders had been all too efficient. After consulting with the RAAF command, the Darwin field was designated as an emergency strip for patrol fighters and the 9 PS withdrew 50 miles south to Batchelor Field.

Other 9th Squadron pilots struggled along the Route in March as well. On the 26th, 2Lt. Sid Woods failed a landing while in transit at Daly Waters. The Warhawk was written off and Woods was injured badly enough to require medical leave for the next month. But by the end of March, there were 21 fighters and 25 pilots in Selman's command and they regularly sortied 4-plane patrols north to orbit the red sand beaches and tide flats of Port Darwin.

The Australians had affected changes at Darwin as well. On the 27th, Major Gen. Edmund Herring, an "old charger" infantry commander recently returned from the North Africa campaign, was posted to Darwin as the new area commander of all ground forces in the Northern Territory. A decisive officer with a "no-nonsense" attitude toward the acquisition of materials for his men in the field, Herring immediately took charge of the Allied troops in the area and set them to the task of airstrip construction. The U.S. Army 147th and 148th Artillery regiments, stranded in Darwin since the February raid, were commandeered to improve the Darwin-Daly Waters highway. In the first week of April, the USAAC 808th Aviation Engineers battalion was assigned to complete the new airstrips already initiated by the RAAF. The runways were cut out of the eucalyptus forests adjacent to the highway and named by the milage distance to Darwin; hence, two of the strips would be "27 Mile" and "34 Mile", both intended for the American 49th Pursuit Group due to arrive in the second week of April. Just two miles south of 34 Mile was a camp site being built for the 49ers' HQ staff.

## THE 9th GROUND ECHELON ON THE 'TRACK'

On March 8th, Selman had instructed his entire 9 PS ground echelon to follow on to Darwin, but the USAFIA strategic materials services were severely depleted. After consulting with Gen. Barnes

*Primitive operations setup for 9 PS at Batchelor Field south of Darwin.*

for transport service, Lt. Arthur Patterson of the 9th Squadron staff was assigned the Herculean task of getting all the unit's equipment to Darwin by rail and truck, as no transport planes were available for such a large group. Patterson and Ssgt. Hickman assembled a team of 35 enlisted men and loaded 15 trucks with crates of camp equipment, tools, plane and auto parts. They drove the trucks on to flatcars at Newcastle rail station and traveled four days by rail to Townsville, and then 70 miles beyond Cloncurry to the western most railhead of Mount Isa.

On the 12th at Mt. Isa, they took the packed trucks from the rail station and headed west with Australian guides across the Barkley Tablelands. A staff car was commandeered in Mt. Isa for the Lieutenant, but it was abandoned in the choking red dust of "the Track" that first day. For 1600 miles, the men endured rain swollen streams, temperatures near 100 degrees, weak coffee and the mysterious "bullybeef" that the Aussies generously provided at the desolate stations throughout the Outback. Water was rationed for man and vehicle alike, as the sun beat down on them for 11 days in their trek along the Brereton Route.

On the 22nd, they drove through dismal Daly Waters and turned northwest to follow the narrow railroad track up to Katherine where their spent the night. The next day, Lt. Patterson's dusty convoy motored through the bright green grass lands and sparse forests, coming to rest at RAAF Darwin Field. After reporting to Capt. Selman, the truck convoy was ordered due south down a dirt road through a forest with plush green undergrowth, finally coming to rest at the Allied refugee encampment called Camp Connelly, five miles east of Darwin town. The camp people were the survivors of the February raid and even some of the Americans of the artillery brigades from the voyage on the Mariposa were there. Just as in all of Australia, many of these Yankee survivors were unattached and served with the RAAF while they waited for American units to arrive.

Upon parking their trucks, the men of the convoy were thrilled with the loud reception from the Allied refugees in the forest. However, the howl of a siren and shouts from the camp had not signalled the arrival of the 9 PS ground echelon trucks, but the approach of enemy planes. Lt. Patterson's men joined in the mad dash for slit trenches as a Japanese bomber force struck the RAAF airstrip at that precise moment. Luckily, the camp was spared.

In the next few days, work details included delivery of bivouac supplies to the 9 PS area personnel and camp construction at 34 Mile Field. There were also scavenger hunts in the harbor ghost

town and the men were warned that unexploded aerial bombs might be anywhere. Only the black and white checker board water tower rose above the trees of the wrecked coastal village. They were stunned by the devastation that marked their new home. The desolation here was more sobering than their solemn passage had been upon "the Track."

## WURTSMITH WAITING IN MELBOURNE; MARCH 1942

It was the lowest point in LtC. Paul Wurtsmith's career. His three squadrons were at the far corners of the immense continent and his only contact was via the troublesome communications network of short wave radio, or hand written messages via USAAC couriers. He had likewise become unabashedly leery of the tenuous stance of his superior, Gen. Brett of USAFIA, in the political circus of the Allied command. Brett's own supply command was an abyss of red tape and a frustration to all Allied commanders who waited weeks for supplies to reach their units. The general was not an effective spokesman and was a scapegoat for much of the muddle in Melbourne.

Wurtsmith's first meeting with Gen. Brett was in a very strained atmosphere and the interview turned sour as the two Americans took an immediate dislike of each other. Wurtsmith found the general unable to explain the long stratagem in the deployment of the 49ers. The partially manned 8th Pursuit Group consisting of two squadrons gathered from the surplus personnel who arrived on the USAAT Mariposa was scheduled for deployment in March for the northeast, purportedly to replace Capt. Morrissey's 7 PS and join the RAAF defense at Port Moresby. But the 8th Group was still awaiting assembly of P-39 Bell Airacobras at Amberly Field, Brisbane. Fearing his 7th Pursuit commander had been squandered in another debacle, the 49er CO pointedly asked if the 7th Squadron team was considered an expendable force. Gen. Brett flared at the allegation and thereafter became pointedly evasive.

Squeeze had nothing to loose at that juncture, and asked to be dismissed to join his men at Darwin, but Brett refused, unwilling to send his remaining Group commander in the south to the front. Com. Bladin counseled the Yankee Colonel for restraint and to await the formation of the 8th Group organization. After the March 8th confrontation, Wurtsmith and Brett shared military bearing and courtesies, but little else. The true concern was the fate of all the Allied troops who waited to meet the conquerors on the mainland. None of the Allies could know that the events about to take place in the third week of March, 1942 would forever change the face of the war in the Southwest Pacific.

## A SPECIAL FLIGHT FROM MINDANAO TO DARWIN

On March 17th, a faded B-17 Fortress had made the long, dangerous escape flight from the southern Philippines Island of Mindanao and landed at RAAF strip, Darwin, in the late afternoon. The RAAF and advance ground crew teams of the 9 PS quickly serviced the bomber-transport with their meager equipment. An old Aussie troop lorry brought up several barrels of aviation fuel and the crews formed a bucket brigade to hand fill the main wing tanks of the big plane. The silent, weary flight crew made a brief preflight check of their

*RAAF advisors Noel Leach (lt.) and Ron Pederrick at 8 PS camp, Fairbrin Airfield*

Fortress, accepted a few simple provisions of food, cigarettes and coffee and then took off into a brilliant red sunset for Brisbane.

The Darwin crews were most anxious to see the Fortress go, because they were already hard pressed to service the newly arrived P-40s of the 9 PS for their routine patrols.

The presence of the big four-engine Fortress surrounded by several Warhawks on the forward RAAF strip would only make a prime target for the Japanese bomber force that could return at any time. Anxious to clear their field, the crews actually paid little attention to the passengers aboard the transport and were shocked to learn several days later that the refugees were none other than Gen. Douglas MacArthur and his staff. The Philippines Commander had been ordered out of his surrounded headquarters on Bataan peninsula, Luzon, as of March 14th by American President Roosevelt, who feared the loss of his most capable field officer would destroy any hope of an Allied counteroffensive against Japan.

Accompanying MacArthur was his Deputy and Philippines air defense commander, Gen. Hal "Pursuit" George, who had replaced Gen. Brereton when the FEAF bombers withdrew to Java in December, 1941. At Brisbane, MacArthur was ordered by Gen. Marshall in Washington, D.C., to take supreme command of all American Army ground and air units in the Southwest Pacific at the earliest date, and "Pursuit" George was assigned the responsibility of reorganizing the entire fighter defense force under American command. Considered by his contemporaries from the prewar Selfridge era as the most astute tactician in fighter aircraft logistics, George had directed a brilliant defensive campaign in the Philippines with a skeleton force that had won him the admiration of both his superior commander and his pilots. General George would soon bring his experience and genius into play for the benefit of all the American flyers, and particularly his old friends, LtC. Paul Wurtsmith and the Philippine-Java veterans of the 49th Pursuit Group.

# 3

## THE FIRST COMBAT

### WAITING AT HORN ISLAND; MARCH 14, 1942

The 7th Squadron had been at Horn Island for a week and had only been authorized to fly in two-ship patrols within sight of the airdrome. Once the P-40s landed, there was little Capt. Morrissey could do to get the planes fully refit. Without crews, his pilots were kept on the ragged edge of exhaustion while both flying and maintaining their own planes. Line crews were absolutely essential to their mission, but Com. Bladin and Gen. Brett had no means to quarter more men at the meager island garrison.

Unknown to Morrissey was the Allied Command's desperate, elaborate plan to strike the Imperial Mobile Fleet recently seen in anchorage at the newly captured Simpson Harbor on northern New Britain. The bold scheme entailed a combined effort of the American Air Corps and the Navy, but weather and unreliable intelligence scuttled the counter-offensive early on. Regardless of the desperate scheme having gone awry, fate would momentarily be played out in a fringe engagement between an advanced Japanese aerial reconnaissance flight and an Allied fighter squadron placed in the Torres Straits as point defense for the northern cape of Queensland Territory. That very squadron was Bob Morrissey's 7 PS at Horn Island.

### THE ENEMY AT THE THRESHOLD

The Japanese had likewise struggled with their own tangle of priorities. The Navy's Adm. Yamamoto adamantly stressed for the completion of the original plan to destroy the American Pacific fleet, but the Army commanded by General Tojo prevailed for the strategy to isolate Australia by moving south to take the Solomon, the New Hebrides, and the Fiji Islands, which would ultimately isolate New Guinea.

To that latter purpose, the fall of Port Moresby became a vital link-pin in the master scheme for the capture of the Southern Area. Port Moresby was targeted by Gen. Tojo as the primary target for the first week in May while Yamamoto's role in the northern Pacific was to enact a tactical feint to further isolate the American fleet.

To press the Port Moresby schedule, on March 8th the Japanese landed at the mining town of Lae at the mouth of the Markham River on New Guinea's northern coast. Just 180 air miles over the Owen Stanley Mountains from Port Moresby, the port and airstrip at Lae provided a major staging area for land and sea assaults against both Moresby and Milne Bay at the far eastern tip of New Guinea. As an added measure, the next strategy was to neutralize Allied air units in northeast Australia.

Immediately, reconnaissance flights by the Japanese increased throughout the eastern Papuan region. On March 14th, eight Mitsubishi G4M heavy bomber with a dozen ZEROs of the 4th Kokutai in escort flew an armed surveillance all the way to the Northern Territory's Cape York to find the landing fields of the American heavy bomber forces. They would be the first combatants to test the 7th Squadron of the 49ers.

### THE FIRST COMBAT; HORN ISLAND, MARCH 14, 1942

In the late morning hours of the 14th, coast watchers on the southern shore of New Guinea in the village of Kerema, just west of Moresby, radioed an urgent coded message to the RAAF Thursday Island area defense commander, LtC. R.J. Hurst. A large formation of silver twin-engined planes and escort fighters estimated above 20,000 feet were headed for the Australian mainland.

The alert was forwarded to the RAAF base on Horn Island and the "scramble call" fortunately reached Morrissey and his pilots all

*The superlative JNAF Mitsubishi A6M2 ZERO-Sen, the type shot down by Morrissey for the Group's first victory.*

*Mitsubishi G4M heavy bomber type that was the 49ers principal target throughout the Australian campaign.*

*7 PS CO Maj. Bob Morrissey (then captain) leader of the Horn Island team.*

On climbing to 10,000 feet through the towering clouds just south of the island, the CO ordered all pilots to charge their guns, but Morrissey found his own gun switch was dead. He gave the Squadron over to Reddington and made an emergency descent to the field where alerted RAAF crews desperately cleared the six .50 caliber weapons and recharged the gun battery. After 30 minutes, the repaired P-40 was fired up again and Morrissey took off to re-join his orbiting squadron south of Horn Island. It was another fifteen minutes before he found them in a trailing formation nearly a mile long. It was then that the RAAF ground controller reported bomb strikes on the west end of their strip. The late start of the Warhawks would cost the destruction of a Hudson bomber, a small fuel dump and strikes in the RAAF bivouac area. It was to get even worse.

Indeed, the Japanese had planned their attack for a heavily defended target, yet when Horn Island was reached, the force was unchallenged by Allied fighters. After the bombers pounded the RAAF camp, several ZEROs dropped down to strafe targets of opportunity.

When Morrissey finally regained the lead of his rambling Warhawks, B Flt Ldr Reddington reported his guns had failed. The skipper ordered him back to base at once and assigned B Flight lead to 2Lt. Johnson, but in the maneuvering to reposition, yet another man went missing. The squadron had lost two men without a shot being fired, none of the P-40s were equipped with drop tanks for prolonged flight and Sanford was far in trail. Morrissey quickly weighed the chances of his six untried fighter pilots against the superior force. Despite the odds, the captain ordered them to close up their ragged formation and to climb at full throttle to the northeast.

The Torres Strait was by then covered by a thick haze and cumulus billowed up to 9000 feet. As the raiders swung about through a wide turn for their escape, the bombers entered into a shallow descent from their 23,000 foot altitude to increase speed. Their gunners watched the smoke from Horn Island fade into the misty southern horizon when a lone in-line engine fighter suddenly appeared off the left flank of their formation. The bomber formation closed ranks at 20,000 feet to fend off the enemy interceptor.

Of course, the fighter was the other missing Yank from B Flight. Second Lt. Hal Martin had reckoned Morrissey would not rejoin the interception in time, and after the RAAF strip was bombed, the lieutenant set off alone for the raiders. He closed the distance to the enemy formation after a 30 minute-long climbing pursuit, and was unseen by the escorts until the very last moment.

At maximum range, novice Martin opened fire on the three planes furthermost to the left, vainly attempting to hit them all. Finally at optimum range, he drew down on the big brown and green bomber to the far left and held the trigger down until his ammo was spent. Sure that the last target was mortally hit, he rolled away to the left as return gun fire clattered against his diving Warhawk. Martin immediately set course for Horn Island.

It was just at that time that Morrissey also caught sight of the eight bombers with what appeared to be a single escort on their left flank, and he was quite unaware the fighter was actually 2Lt. Martin on the attack. At 1300 hours precisely, just as Morrissey's pursuit team drew within firing range, the Yankee Squadron Leader caught sight of six light gray ZEROS closing in on his right. He ordered A Flight to engage.

down from their patrols as of 1130 hours. The captain instructed his pilots carefully and quickly, "Take off together. Stay together. Don't wander from your wingman. Take off to the northwest and make a left climbing turn at full power. Form up on me."

They ran to their Warhawks at the east end of their strip and strapped in. Second Lt. Clarence Sanford was told to join the scramble, even if his P-40 had not been flown since the deployment north. They needed all nine planes up, and auspiciously, all the Allison engines coughed and roared into life. They rolled in single file to take-off position with Morrissey in the lead of A Flight 2Lts. A.T. House, Claude Burtnette and Sanford. The B Flight Leader was 2Lt. Bill Reddington with wingmen C.T. Johnson, Wilson Chapman, Hal Martin and Stephen Andrews. They lifted off the main runway at 1145 hours in 15 second intervals.

*Lt. Wilson "Chip" Chapman, one of three interceptor pilots to claim a ZERO kill over Horn Island.*

## THE FIRST OFFICIAL GROUP KILL

The ZEROs that had remained in high escort had obviously focussed solely on the lone enemy fighter attacking the bombers' left flank, since Morrissey's initial approach was not countered. Slightly higher than the ZEROs, the captain was in a descent at full throttle with wingman House just seconds in trail. Morrissey opened fire at the minimum range of 200 yards on the nearest element of the ZEROs and the trailing wingman erupted in flames. The remaining five Japanese looped and rolled to avoid the Americans who flashed by to strike at the bomber formation. The nimble ZEROs wheeled in behind the P-40s and a swirling dogfight began.

Far above the Torres Straits, the fight raged for nearly 10 minutes from 19,000 feet down to the cloud deck. The Warhawks' advantage of surprise was quickly erased as young 2Lts. Burtnette and Andrews were given a rude aerobatic lesson by the enemy aviators who promptly riddled their P-40s with machine gun fire. Both Americans broke off for Horn Island. In the meantime, the bombers had increased their descent and left the escorts to their task.

In the twisting clash, 2Lt. House swung about and fired at a ZERO which rolled sharply away, trailing smoke. He tightened his turn to follow, but his gun jammed from the added G-forces. Immediately, another ZERO turned to the attack on Morrissey, and despite his malfunctioning guns, House descended against the new threat. Deliberately driving the right wingtip of his sturdy Curtiss fighter into the enemy's cockpit, three feet of wingtip was torn away. House descended out of the battle and saw his victim falling toward the sea in a wild spiral.

Meanwhile, 2Lts. Johnson and Chapman ganged up on a ZERO to bracket it in tracers, and the smoking Mitsubishi wheeled off into the overcast. Both Americans were counter-attacked by another ZERO and Johnson was hit by a slug that ricocheted through his cockpit and struck his right foot. Chapman was hit by a round that exploded on the armor plate of his seat, cutting his left shoulder. The Yanks barrel rolled into "terminal velocity" dives through the clouds. They leveled out far below and turned for Cape York in their holed Warhawks.

The other Yanks likewise dove away as the Mitsubishis followed them to the cloud tops. The scattered 7th squadron elements individually dead-reckoned for the east coast of the Cape, then turned northwest to settle down on dusty Horn Island. The Kokutai escorts regrouped above the clouds and cruised back to Lae with two of their own missing, but they were certain they had shot down all eight interceptors. The phenomenal range of the G4M bombers allowed them to return to Rabaul where all landed safely. Only the ship flown in the left wing element reported hits from the lone enemy fighter at the onset of the air battle.

## THE AFTERMATH AT HORN ISLAND

Down on Horn Island, the ripped wingtip of 2Lt. House's P-40 caused for both a hair raising 100 knot landing and the profound amazement of the crews who met him off the end of the strip. By 1330, all the survivors gathered and recounted their incredible luck in the clumsy scramble to get airborne. Each man acknowledged the phenomenal performance of the ZERO and they were flush with their success over the legendary enemy fighter that had been the scourge of the Philippines.

In the debriefing, everyone tried to sort out the first kill claims for their pursuit group. Morrissey chided Martin for bolting from his wingman position and also praised him for the sheer bravery of his single-handed attack on the bombers. An RAAF-Navy communique later reported a large, burning plane had fallen into the sea northeast of Horn Island which consequently confirmed Martin's claim.

All agreed the CO had burned a ZERO on his first pass. Johnson and Chapman settled on a ZERO being destroyed by Johnson and another ZERO was confirmed as a second victory for "rammer" House. Morrissey radioed five confirmed kills to Melbourne and requested reinforcements as they wrote off House's heavily damaged aircraft and grounded the wounded Chapman and Johnson. An area search was out for 2Lt. Clarence Sanford who was last seen being chased by an enemy fighter.

However, the 7 PS was down to seven operational planes and six flyers, and Melbourne ordered them to withdraw to Iron Range immediately. Their retreat was appropriate, for more enemy reconnaissance flights pressed further down the Cape for several days. Another encounter would surely have finished off the diminished 7 PS team. Ultimately, the Japanese Imperial staff was confident their schedule was well in hand. In the interim, the Mobile Fleet vacated Simpson Harbor and the Allies abandoned the plans for the Rabaul raid. There was no reason for Morrissey's fighters to stay in Queensland and they headed off to Darwin by month's end.

## SANFORD'S DIVERSION

As for 2Lt. Sanford, in RAAF parlance, he had certainly "gone missing." His oil spewing P-40 had not been fit for combat and once he was engaged by the superior ZEROs, he wisely chose retreat. The close call with the enemy had completely broken his confidence and in his attempt to find the Cape York coastline, he became hopelessly disoriented in the haze above the Torres Strait. He passed over Horn Island and haphazardly flew for 400 miles to the west across the Gulf of Carpentaria until his fuel ran out just off Cape Arnhem.

To add to his ordeal, he bailed out safely, but nearly drowned swimming to tiny Bremer Island. Aboriginals found him passed out on the beach late that afternoon and carried the exhausted flyer to the Yirrkala missionary post on the mainland where he convalesced for ten days. Morrissey was notified of the lost man's fate on the 15th by the RAAF, but he would not see his pilot again. Sanford was eventually transported all the way to the Darwin RAAF hospital by motor launch, but he never recovered well enough from the incident to ever fly again. He was transferred out the 7 PS to the south in early April, and ultimately, Clarence Sanford returned Stateside, never to be seen again.

## STIERTZ DEATH IN BANKSTOWN; MARCH 14, 1942

The good news of Sanford's recovery on the 15th was paradoxically offset by the tragic loss of 2Lt. Frank Stiertz on the same day of the battle. The brash Stiertz had advanced to cross country flights at Bankstown RAAF field in February, only to anger the authorities at Melbourne by flying beneath the span of one of the harbor bridges.

Grounded for two weeks, the lieutenant returned to the flight schedule and was practicing touch-and-go landings at the Bankstown strip on March 14th. He had just skipped off the runway for another go around and swerved to miss a road grader, but his right wingtip clipped the tractor and the plane stalled out.

The Warhawk struck the runway hard, then skidded into a newly built hangar and flipped over on its back. It did not burn, but Pvts. Paul Manget, Tom Hooper and S/Sgt. John Bush could only watch helplessly as a work group brought out a block and tackle to lift the crumpled plane. Trapped beneath the crushed canopy, Steirtz was asphyxiated by steaming glycol fumes before he could be extricated.

Once the pilot was dragged free, he was rushed to the field dispensary, but the flight surgeon pronounced Frank Steirtz dead. Morrissey learned of the man's fate shortly after the Horn Island mission and he anguished over the loss of such a promising young flyer.

*Derelict "MAC" cannibalized at Adelaide River Airfield. Many early issue 8 PS aircraft retained a remnant red dot on the altered fuselage insignia while upper wing red centers were painted out entirely.*

## THE 9 PS DARWIN DEFENSE

The Japanese continued to send armed reconnaissance to the northwest coast of Australia to keep the Allies off balance during March as the main thrust was planned against Port Moresby in the east. A fighter sweep went to Broome on March 20th, but only confirmed the little harbor had been abandoned. Attention was turned back to the harbor and airstrip at Darwin.

Ironically, the Chiefs of Staff had rushed several ground units to Darwin to upgrade the defenses in early February. The town's harbor facilities were situated on a small square peninsula with yet a smaller narrow finger of land called East Point. The western shoreline of the main peninsula was called Larrakeyah Beach and new anti-aircraft batteries of 40 mm Bofor guns were posted there, while just to the north at Dripstone Cliffs, an early warning radar unit was set directly on the course between the RAAF airdrome and Timor Island. Actually operational on the day of the infamous raid, the Dripstone Cliffs radar was not running simply due to the unknown nearness of the Imperial Mobile Fleet. Hence, there was not a sense of urgency to operate the unfamiliar device. By the end of March, the radar was operated diligently by the RAAF as an integral part of Darwin's early detection system.

Protected Darwin Harbor spread to the south into a very irregular flood plain with a meandering shore line. Its easterly predominance was the East Point headlands with the town and the docks. The harbor proper was the delta of the Elizabeth River whose mouth jutted into the desert to the southeast and it was called East Arm. Immediately to the west was the abrupt natural land jetty called Middle Point. The inlet on Middle Point's west side was the delta of the Blackmore River, a crocodile infested wilderness of mangrove trees locally known as Middle Arm.

West of the Middle Arm mangroves was the greater square headland of Cox Peninsula whose northeastern horn was called West Point and whose northwestern horn was called Point Charles where the lighthouse stood. The eastern shore of forested Cox Peninsula was Swires Bluff, a ragged stony mass which faced the Darwin docks three miles across the harbor.

The 9 PS pilots used Middle Point as the principle land mark for the flight path to the harbor area. Once a pilot left the runway at

Batchelor and turned north, he could follow the "Track" highway and its parallel railroad to the Elizabeth River crossing, then turn west-northwest up the river bed. He would fly straight out over Middle Point, then cross the harbor at 10,000 feet to pass above the Aussie dock hands and gunners. The 49ers would then climb to a patrol altitude of 20,000 feet or more above Beagle Gulf. They were the last real hope for the refugees of Darwin.

## FIRST BLOOD AT DARWIN; MARCH 22, 1942

In the same March time frame, the 3rd Kokutai of the Japanese Navy had moved its reconnaissance squadron and fighter units to the abandoned Allied air strip at Koepang, Java. On March 22nd, a Mitsubishi Ki-15 reconnaissance plane was sent to probe the defenses of Darwin in advance of a larger strike force of Takao Kokutai G4M bombers.

Just 50 miles due north from Darwin across Beagle Gulf lay Melville and Bathurst Islands, separated by a narrow strait. Smaller Bathurst to the west of the strait was inhabited by European missionaries and an aboriginal community. Incorporated as part of the network of coast watchers for the Northern Territory defense, the islanders notified the mainland of an approaching plane at midday, just as they had done on the first raid. Unlike the snarled communications of February, the sighting was confirmed by the RAAF radar specialists at Dripstone Cliffs and urgently relayed to the 9 PS four-plane patrol just south of Melville Island.

*Looking S-SE over the crossed landing strips of spacious Batchelor Airfield. 7 PS eventually set up permanent camp in the forested area at the SE end of the shorter oiled strip.*

*2Lt. Stephan "Polly" Poleschuk, several days after the first 9 PS victory. "HUYEBO" roughly translated as "not worth much" which was the Russian-American flyer's homage to Group CO Wurtsmith's assessment of the lieutenant's landing skills.*

The 9 PS foursome searched to the west in the swelling clouds above the Gulf. They broke into two hunting flights, and at 1310 hours, wingmen 2Lts. Clyde Harvey and Steven Poleschuk spotted the lone brown and green radial engine plane with red wing roundels, its long canopy glinting in the sun. The enemy pilot saw the climbing interceptors, but his attempt to elude them was futile. Both Yanks made firing passes until the Ki-15 trailed heavy smoke and dropped seaward just west of Bathurst Island. One of its crew parachuted out, but he was never found. The Yanks made an orbit of the area until their fuel was critical and then turned back to Darwin's RAAF strip. They were hailed "well done" and after the P-40s were refueled by bucket brigade crews, they departed south for Batchelor. It had been a perfect interception and a coin toss gave confirmation of the aerial kill to "Polly" Poleschuk. More flights were sent north to patrol until dark, but no other contact was made.

As planned, the Takao Kokutai followed shortly thereafter in a raid farther inland to the landing field at Katherine in an unsuccessful hunt for Allied heavy bombers. Now that fighter defense had returned to Darwin, the Timor invaders would momentarily turn their attentions back to the harbor town and the RAAF airfield there.

## THE GROWING 9TH PURSUIT AT DARWIN

In the last week of March 1942, CO Captain Jim Selman had a growing contingent of 9th Pursuit pilots and crews in two separate teams that served at the advanced RAAF air strip, Darwin, and the larger crew at the RAAF air drome at Batchelor field. After the successful interception of the lone Japanese reconnaissance flight

*Mitsubishi Ki-15 scout aircraft similar to the one accredited to Poleschuk.*

on March 22nd, more pilots and their planes arrived directly from the assembly base at Brisbane's Amberly field or from the 9 PS training team in reserve at Williamstown field. Four plane patrols were sent north from Batchelor in an attempt to have eight ships constantly air borne and four P-40s in standby.

Selman had grown impatient with the abysmal RAAF detection system that did not seem to account for the P-40s' performance. The coast watchers and RAAF radar team could not warn his squadron in sufficient time to allow the slow climbing P-40s a chance to intercept the bomber formations crossing the coast at 20,000 feet or more.

The RAAF was equally perturbed that the Americans had not been immediately effective against the raiding bombers from Timor Island. The Japanese had sent a small raid against Darwin on the March 16th, the day before Selman arrived. On the 19th, and 23rd, they had struck Darwin's ghost town and pitted the runway again. When the Takao Kokutai reached 100 miles inland on the 22nd to Katherine Field in search of the Allied bomber forces, Selman's Squadron only intercepted the reconnaissance plane. Fortunately, overall damages had been minimal.

Since the Allies fighters had not made interceptions of the more recent raids, the Takao Kokutai determined it was safe to send an unescorted sortie to Darwin on the 28th. Selman's new patrol system paid off. When the signal came from Darwin's early warning team, one flight was already up over Beagle Gulf. Second Lt. Mitch Zawisza's four ship flight over the harbor turned to pursue the enemy bombers which had already reached the RAAF strip. The Mitsubishis bombed the dusty red runway, causing minimal dam-

*A later photo of mustached Poleschuk and wingman Clyde Harvey. "Polly" stepped down from combat at the end of his first year's tour, but popular Harvey made the transition to the P-38 era.*

age and then turned back to the west toward Timor. As they passed over the docks in their routine descent from the target, Zawisza's flight hit the raiders at 18,000 feet, just before noon.

## VAUGHT'S VENDETTA; MARCH 28, 1942

The alarm at Adelaide River was answered by Flight Leader 2Lt. Bob Vaught, formerly of the ill fated 33rd PS which had mustered for Java in February. Forced to relinquish his plane to Capt. Pell and wait at Amberly Field, Brisbane, the lieutenant had avoided the infamous Darwin massacre on February 19th. When Selman's 9th Squadron passed through Amberly Field enroute to Darwin in mid March, Vaught signed on and soon followed in his P-40 which he helped Amberly personnel rebuild from RAAF relics. His Warhawk #94 displayed a gaudy, grimacing shark's mouth on the deep radiator tub, adopted from the famous RAF 12 Squadron of North Africa, and the rather demure name "BOB'S ROBIN" on the fuselage beneath the cockpit. An ornery and compassionate character, Vaught swore he would exact vengeance on the Japanese for Capt. Pell's death and he eagerly took his five interceptors north for the vendetta.

In the meantime, Flight Leader Zawisza, his wingman Bill Sells, and the "first-kill" team of Poleschuk and Harvey, overtook the descending raiders and peeled off in a line attack on the right flank of the Vee formation. The 9th pilots strafed the length of the marauders formation, then swung to the right and wheeled back for a second pass. They repeated their attacks a third time.

Following the third pass by Zawisza's flight, Vaught's flight could only chase the straggler G4Ms that were fleeing across the Gulf. Vaught swept down beneath a smoking bomber and pulled his "ROBIN" into a climbing attack on the Mitsubishi's underside where his tracers hit the left side of the G4M's rotund fuselage. It spun down, erupted in flames and slammed into the blue-green sea.

As the bombers reached the relative safety of heavy clouds 100 miles out to sea, Poleschuk made a final pass at the last enemy machine and saw pieces fly off as his tracers struck home. Of the five Americans who had reached the unescorted heavy bombers, all claimed heavy damage inflicted on the enemy flight. The P-40s had been hit by turret gunners aboard the bombers but damage was easily repaired and all the pilots were safe. The jubilant 9 PS returned to Batchelor and after the debriefing, they were credited with aerial kills for Vaught and Sells, and a probable victory for Poleschuk.

## ESCORTED MISSIONS BECAME THE RULE

The initial engagements over Darwin were essentially litmus tests for the opposing intelligence teams. The apparent conclusion of the Imperial staff was that the interceptor force at Darwin confirmed the presence American bombers still operating in the immediate area. Conversely, the persistence of the Imperial raiders sustained the threat of an amphibious landing in the Northwest Territory at any moment. Therefore, the Japanese were committed to find the American bomber bases prior to invasion of Port Moresby, still scheduled for May, and to never fly another unescorted mission to Darwin.

*Lt. Bob Vaught and his 9 PS shark.*

Consequently, the Allies continued to strengthen the defenses of their remote garrison. Wurtsmith's pursuit group was equally resolved to make a stand at their desert outpost. The battle at Darwin in 1942 would result in the classic case of an enemy offensive that never fully discovered the true nature of its objective.

Therefore, on March 31st, the first major engagement between the opposing fighter forces would take place. Regardless of the strategies and logistics, the battle over Darwin was established from that day forth as a vendetta for the Americans.

## 9 PS INTERCEPTION; MARCH 31, 1942

The 9 PS patrol over Beagle Gulf, led by the combat veteran 2Lt. Andy Reynolds, was vectored southwest toward the mainland and met the enemy in a brief, vicious dogfight just after one o'clock. Only Reynolds' experience saved him in the skirmish with the superior force as he shot down one of the ZEROs off the north shore of Cox Peninsula.

Up against the veteran 3rd Kokutai, the rookie 2Lts. Jim Porter and Bob McComsy fared badly. Porter's P-40 rudder was shredded by machine gun fire and he quickly dropped out of the fight for Batchelor. Porter bellied in next to the runway and the ship was dragged off for salvage parts. McComsy's P-40 was hit and in his descent toward East Arm inlet, the Allison engine overheated, seized up and he "hit the silk" just over the tip of Middle Point. McComsy drifted in his chute on to the marshy tide flat not far from where his stricken Warhawk had splashed down. The second flight scrambled from Batchelor had joined the fight too late to sway the odds, and only two other fliers reported bullet holes in their Warhawks.

Fortunately, neither of the two lieutenants who had lost planes in the dogfight were wounded, but McComsy soon fell victim to the cruel elements of tropical Australia. RAAF gunners and dock hands had seen McComsy's smoking P-40 going down three miles off on the south side of the harbor, but the poor flyer might as well have settled down on the moon. The RAAF struggled to reach the stranded American but the terrain of twisted tree roots, underbrush, marshes, and mud flats made an overland rescue nearly impossible. They would try again by boat after high tide in the morning.

In the meantime, fellow 9 PS pilots returned to the Gulf patrols. As they flew north along Middle Point, each pilot swept low over the tip of the marshy peninsula and vainly tried to drop water canteens and provisions to McComsy on his high ground perch above the rising evening tide. Only one can of tomato soup fell within his grasp. He was at the mercy of swarms of flies and mosquitoes, and played a deadly one-sided game of tag with an ocean-going crocodile. Dehydrated by the broiling sun and nearly driven crazy by the relentless insects, he tried to rest in the branches of a small tree just after sunset. Unable to sleep, McComsy was totally exhausted when the RAAF picked him up by motor launch from his personal "piece of hell" just after sunrise. They took the lieutenant to the RAAF hospital on the west side of Darwin, where he recuperated for several days.

## REPLACEMENTS FOR THE 9 PS IN APRIL, 1942

Capt. Selman's only consolation was that all his men were safe and had survived another attempt by the Japanese to knock them out of the Darwin defense. In the first week of April, more Java veterans and replacement pilots from the training reserves back at Williamstown Field in Newcastle began to arrive, but the increase of raids in the Northern Territory taxed the 9 PS beyond their means. The area of their patrols was far too expansive for a single squadron with only 16 fighters serviceable at any given time. LtC. Wurtsmith had to bring up the other two squadrons of his group if the defense was to succeed.

The new "34 Mile" landing strip north of Batchelor Field was nearing completion and Gen. Herring ordered the 9th Pursuit to start moving P-40s there immediately. Some crews had already begun to bivouac around the dispersal area in the forest and were ready to service the first flights on the 30th. Eight planes in two flights went north immediately to help relieve the heavy air traffic on Batchelor, and the 9th team was proud to have the first "all American" air strip in operation.

*2Lt. Bob McComsey, victim of ZEROs on March 31.*

On April 2nd, an enemy reconnaissance flight reported the construction of a suspected air strip 20 miles due south of Darwin along side the Daly Waters-Darwin "Track." Later that day, the new RAAF strip, Sattler field, was struck, but there was no damage done, nor were any Allied airplanes seen there.

## THE LAST SOLO INTERCEPTION OF THE 9 PS; APRIL 4, 1942

The Japanese persisted in their search for the Allied air fields and returned two days later to deliver another heavy blow to Darwin strip. Six bombers with six ZEROS in close escort sortied there shortly after one o'clock. Capt. Selman could answer the alarm from the Dripstone radar station with fourteen Warhawks in service. The scramble was to be the 9th Squadron's bloodiest Darwin interception.

A patrol of four Warhawks of C Flight lead by 2Lt. Grover Gardner from Batchelor Field was already at 25,000 feet just north of the Dripstone Cliffs and they swung to the south to meet the enemy Vee formation of bombers head-on. The standby B Flight of six P-40s lead by Lt. Reynolds at Darwin RAAF strip immediate got air borne and headed north at full throttle to join Gardner's flight in the assault. B Flight lost 2Lt. Jim Watkins who made an emergency landing at the Darwin after his engined seized during the initial ascent. The other five pressed ahead.

Gardner's C Flight attacked at once in a line formation as the raiders approached the Dripstone Cliffs. Gardner led wingman Livingstone, element leader John Sauber and his wingman John Kelting, head-on for the G4M furthermost to the right in the on-coming Vee formation. Smoke and flame belched from the Mitsubishi's left engine as the P-40s flashed down and away, then wheeled hard to their right, falling in for the second attack against the Vee formation's rear quarter.

Gardner's men flew headlong into the 3rd Ku ZEROS that were now descending from their trailing high escort position. "Tail-end" Kelting was cut off by the ZEROS and he rolled downward into a full throttle escape for home. The other C Flight pilots turned in a hard circle with the ZEROS and veteran Sauber fired a stream of tracers through the path of an escort attacker which banked off trailing smoke.

At this precise moment, 2Lt. Reynolds' B Flight arrived to attack head-on through the lead bomber element of the Vee formation, and then roared into the fray of the dogfight. Reynolds fired a wide angle deflection at a ZERO that soon dropped away toward the mainland. The five remaining ZEROS could not keep the P-40s in check and the 3rd Ku pilots wheeled around to assume a better defensive position. The Yanks broke away to pursue the descending bombers.

Gardner and Livingstone had avoided the ZEROS and pressed ahead to continue their attack on the raiders now bombing the Darwin airdrome. Gardner pulled in behind the stricken G4M on the far left and poured a murderous stream of tracers into its fuselage. Livingstone closed in on the next target to the right of Gardner's victim, and quickly, both bombers fell away trailing heavy smoke.

After Sauber and Reynolds had dealt with their ZERO opponents and had become separated from their respective flights, the two men joined up and roared off after the bombers that had turned west in retreat. Both Yanks closed in on three bombers that had dropped to about 11,000 feet over the harbor. As they crossed the shore of Cox Peninsula, Sauber drew within range and expended the last of his ammunition at a straggler, then broke off for home. Reynolds made his last attack until low fuel forced him to withdraw. The Yanks saw their victims still dropping northward toward the Gulf.

Gardner and Livingstone had momentarily been shot at by ZEROs as they began their final assault on the bombers nearer the town. Both men maneuvered away and had descended to a lower altitude to escape over the protective anti-aircraft batteries on Larrakeyah Beach, but as they crossed the shore line, the anxious RAAF gunners mistook the approaching Warhawks for enemy fighters. Two ZEROs had already strafed the RAAF drome. The Aussies sent up a brief, accurate 40 mm barrage that hit both of the Yanks.

Gardner's Warhawk #74 spewed flames from the engine and the pilot did not hesitate. He pulled the canopy back, unhooked his belt and rolled the P-40 over. He fell free of the burning craft that continued to arc down and across the harbor to crash on Cox Peninsula. The Flight Leader dropped in his chute into the bay, just off shore near the batteries that had shot him out of the air only seconds before. An Aussie launch soon plucked the Yank from the bay, mad and wet but not hurt.

Lieutenant Livingstone was not as lucky. He radioed ahead he

*(Lt. to Rt.) 2Lts. John Landers, Jack Donaldson, Flt Ldr Andy Reynolds and John Sauber. Donaldson replaced fallen Livingstone of the original B-Flight team which later became the high scoring Blue Flight.*

*2Lt. Jim Watkins, forced out early on in B-Flight's interception on April 4th. Watkins would remain in combat for more than a year to become one of the most able flight leaders in the 5 AF.*

was wounded and might not reach the field. Crewmen at 34 Mile gathered near the runway and soon caught sight of Livingstone's P-40 staggering to stay air borne above the trees just north of their air field.

## LIVINGSTONE'S DEATH AT 34 MILE FIELD

Wounded Livingstone was fading and his radio messages became slurred. His Warhawk passed over the strip, but he failed to set it down and circled to approach a second time. He fared better on the next approach and the Warhawk flared out at the end of the runway. Dust swirled beneath the tires, and it appeared he would be all right.

"He's too fast", cried out a crewman and everyone froze as the Warhawk began to swerve on the dirt runway in its high speed roll-out. The ship slammed into the trees and the residual fuel in the main fuselage tank ignited. Men sprinted to the aid of the motion-less pilot.

Sergeants Fred Quick, Bill Knickerbocker, Al Petraitis and Bob Oestreich bolted onto the wing of the wreck, but the flames leaped higher and forced them back to safe ground. The cockpit exploded into a raging inferno as the pilot eerily, slowly, sat upright within the flames. No one dared imagine Livingstone was conscious of the horror.

## THE REVIEW OF THE APRIL 4TH BATTLE

As with the previous debriefings, some discrepancies arose in the pilots claims. The intercepting pilots claimed victories over all six G4M bombers and two ZEROs, but very likely, only three bombers were shot down over the target. Most probable was the first line attack by C Flight's Gardner, Livingstone, and Kelting, had all been on the same raider. The second attack by Gardner and Livingstone resulted in the RAAF observation of the two G4M crashes, one near Dripstone Cliffs and the other just off shore from the Larrakeyah AA batteries. In the subsequent attacks by Sauber and Reynolds at the lower altitude over Cox Peninsula, the same bomber elements that had been hit in the first pass by C Flight were probably hit a second time by these two men.

Finally, 2Lt. John Landers in Reynolds' flight had nursed his rough running P-40 to the interception, but only reached the fight in time to catch three straggler bombers over Cox Peninsula. Landers attacked the nearest G4M just inland after Sauber's assault, and it descend into the haze over the Gulf to the north. His second target was already aflame from the earlier attack by C Flight, and "Big John" hit it with a coup de grace that forced it down on the north shore. The RAAF would salvage its wreckage on the beach the next day.

The ZERO pilot shot at by Reynolds in the dogfight was ap-parently mortally wounded. Whether the 3rd Ku man was disori-ented or dead, his Mitsubishi eventually crashed 150 miles south of the harbor near Katherine air field.

The surviving three Takao Ku raiders and five escorts returned to Koepang and reported their losses against five enemy fighters destroyed. They also reported heavy damage to "Darwin West" strip which was actually the abandoned civilian landing field west of their intended military target. The damage was insignificant. Re-

*Memorial stone marker for 2Lt. John Livingstone at field entrance, namesake of Livingstone Airfield.*

gardless of the errors and duplication of the reports on either side, the 9 PS had by far been the victor. One aerial kill each was posted for Gardner, Livingstone, Kelting, and two each for Sauber, Reynolds and Landers. Their interception had killed 25 Japanese airmen in exchange for the death of Livingstone. In honor of the first 9th Pursuit man killed in the Darwin campaign, 34 Mile strip was renamed Livingstone Field for the young man who had been with the 9 PS from the first days at West Palm Beach, Florida.

## MOMENTARY WITHDRAWAL OF THE 3RD KU AND TAKAO KU

Although the 3rd Kokutai had reported numerous kills over Dar-win Harbor, they could not totally negate the Allied fighter force that staged from their hidden air field further inland. A second strike to Darwin after the mid-day dogfight of March 31st and subse-quent search further south to Batchelor did not yield a worthwhile target. A third strike returned at midnight for the first night sortie in

*Looking S-SE across Livingstone Airfield. The darkened runway resulted from sprayed fuel oil which held down the permeating red dust.*

*P-40E cannibalized at Batchelor Field. Early 9 PS aircraft often retained the red circle in the fuselage star insignia while upper wing red centers were painted out entirely.*

the Northwest Territory campaign, but they only struck the harbor ghost town and a vacant air drome.

Despite their losses in the April 4th interception, the Timor wing concluded their operations a success and they stood down to refit their damaged aircraft for the preliminary assaults against Port Moresby.

## UNCOMPROMISING ENEMIES; APRIL, 1942

The Java-based Imperial air force had grossly over estimated its performance against Capt. Selman's 9 PS at Port Darwin, but their reasoning was effected by an Oriental conscience that few foreigners could understand. There was the element of honor, or self worth, that was manifested in the individual Japanese serviceman. The honor was called "bushido", an ancient and elaborate tradition of self sacrifice and moral obligation to their revered ancestral authority. There was great ceremony in the acknowledgment of national heros and religious fervor in the planning of battles. With racial hatred for all foreign devils, the Imperial warriors swore to the fanatical bushido code of the destruction and enslavement of their

*Allison engine maintenance at primitive Livingstone facilities, April, 1942.*

enemies in veneration of their Emperor, their commanders and the Japanese people. Compromise for conditional victory was considered dishonorable, and any display of weakness would justify either corporal punishment, or lastly, purification in "harikari" suicide.

In only four months of the new war, the unvanquished Imperial Fleet had swept over nearly 10 million square miles of the Pacific Ocean and the Orient. On April 9th, again the English Royal Navy was engaged. Two of her aircraft carriers and two cruisers were sunk off the cape of India, just east of Ceylon. Japan thought its army and navy were driven by a divine, spiritual force that made them invincible.

The sea battle off Ceylon was Japan's last unqualified victory of the war. No longer overrunning small garrisons on tropical islands, nor crushing weaker opponents with their superior numbers, the Imperial forces momentarily stumbled at the greater obstacles of overtaking China, Burma, New Guinea and the Pacific islands at the same time. The Imperial Staff was faced with the dilemma of supplying huge occupation armies on too many distant fronts.

## THE HORNET'S RAID - APRIL 18th, 1942

The Imperial commanders also failed to accurately judge the resolve of their cornered opponents. The colonials from Australia and America were equally proud of their own rebellious, combative heritage and they showed great resolve. Admiral Yamamoto, a former diplomatic attache to Washington D.C. and subsequent architect of the Pearl Harbor raid, had advised early on that America was an untested industrial giant and must be isolated from the Pacific campaign at the onset, or it would bring that great industry to bare against Japan. His warnings were proven on April 18th, when sixteen B-25 Mitchell bombers launched off the U.S. Navy carrier *Hornet* and struck five cities on Japan's mainland. The peril of the war now loomed over the Japanese people for the first time. Their original strategy to destroy the American fleet, isolate Australia and occupy the Pacific islands had not accounted for a comparable American bushido. The Imperial command had gone much too far in the venture and could not retain its honor with a negotiated peace. America declared a vendetta over the infamy at Pearl Harbor. Two proud enemies were now committed to a long and bloody war.

The contrast of the rank and order of the two adversaries would turn in the Allies favor. The Australian and Americans were commanded by men who did not await consensus of their superiors. Although rancorous at times, the independent nature of the "Yankees and Aussies" field officers made them adaptive and quick to seize any advantage in a fight. Colonel Paul Wurtsmith and his people would soon prove to be such men.

# *4*

# THE AMERICAN COMMAND IN DARWIN APRIL 1942

As the war raged on in the north during March, 1942, the Allied command in Melbourne was undergoing revolutionary change. Since Gen. MacArthur's arrival on March 17th, he had commandeered the entire continent to his own purpose. On April 20th, he was officially appointed Supreme Allied Commander of all forces west of the Solomons and in the Southwest Pacific theater. MacArthur was determined to initiate a counter offensive on New Guinea by the end of the winter monsoons of June and July, for he accurately deduced that the Japanese would attempt the capture of Port Moresby, possibly in May before the winter monsoon floods. Allied intelligence had also broken the code of the Japanese radio communiques with their front line commands at this time and soon confirmed MacArthur's assessment.

The Supreme Commander counselled with his Brisbane staff for a comprehensive defense of New Guinea's southern port. The Australians continued to urge for both Queensland and North Territory air defense until their ground forces could re-equip and land on New Guinea. MacArthur agreed to bolster the defenses and meanwhile queue up the Allies for an August counter attack. Australian and American troops with a combined RAAF-USAAC air force, would be equipped and trained at sights designated in Queensland Territory where rail and air services had already been established.

Generals R. B. Sutherland, Chief of Staff to the commander, and Robert Richardson, a staff advisor from Washington D.C., both warned the Supreme Allied Commander that there was growing resentment in the American ranks of the cross purposes in RAAF demands. Both generals also recommended replacing the inept USAFIA commander, George Brett, and MacArthur agreed but there was no immediate, logical replacement. Although his Staff Air Commander Gen. George was present, that officer's immediate concern was to coordinate the fighter units in Australia for defense. Meanwhile, Brett was familiar with the status of current logistics in Australia and could continue the management of the USAFIA facilities in Melbourne until a new man could be found.

To insure that the existing American fighter air units would serve MacArthur's needs, Gen. George was authorized to overrule any RAAF order and commandeer any personnel or materials to fit the USAAC defenses at both Port Moresby and Port Darwin. In this regard, Gen. George knew that the two 8th Pursuit Group squadrons designated for the newly constructed air strips on the south coast of New Guinea would be up against the most dangerous Philippines veteran pilots of the Japanese Navy. Only two ranking Group Leaders in New South Wales were capable of commanding a novice fighter squadron in such a predicament. They were LtC.

Wurtsmith, CO of the 49th Pursuit Group and Major Wagner, his Operations executive.

George chose Maj. Wagner to lead the 8th PG squadrons to Port Moresby by the end of April. Wurtsmith readily agreed Wagner was the right man and assured "Pursuit Hal" that the influx of combat veterans in the 49ers had sufficiently fortified their ranks.

The 49er CO also knew from Capt. Selman's reports that the early warning system at Darwin would have to be greatly improved. Capt. Van Auken was wisely chosen as the 49er's new Operations Executive, due to his vast experience in radio communication and knowledge of the RAAF interceptor air control systems. Van Auken was also a tough administrator who had handled the Aussies at Melbourne and was well liked by Bladin's staff. Although the 49er staff changes would not be official until the 21st, Van Auken was promoted to the rank of major and actively planned for the move of the 49th Controllers into the Darwin defense while Veteran Capt. Al Strauss would lead the 8 PS into combat. The pilots and their fighters headed for Darwin on April 8th, and Van Auken followed shortly after.

## THE FIRST 8 PS LOSSES IN AUSTRALIA; MARCH 28, 1942

It was a very difficult transition period for all the 8 PS personnel. The unit had to overcome the sad loss of two pilots in a fatal crash on a cross country flight on March 28th. Second Lts. John Musial

*8 PS pilots at Canbera. The two men standing to the right are 2Lts. John Musial (in cap) and Neal Takala were both killed in crashes on March 28th near Eden, N.S.W.*

*Wreckage of Takala's aircraft.*

and Neal Takala had become separated from their training flight in the storm clouds over the Snowy Mountains and blindly flew their planes into a hillside near the town of Eden, just north of Cape Howes. Van Auken, though far off with the his flying mates at Adelaide River, took the responsibility of writing to the families of the dead flyers.

As for Captain Strauss, he had already displayed his serious demeanor to his more novice 8 PS pilots only a few days after their arrival at Adelaide River. Second Lt. Bill Day had struck a eucalyptus tree off the end of the main runway on April 18th. Strauss sternly ordered the shaken pilot to walk the 4000 foot length and 400 foot width of the strip as a pointed lesson of the lieutenant's narrow escape. It was apparent the quiet nature of the new CO was not to be taken for granted.

During the same time frame, Capt. Morrissey and the 7 PS organization mobilized from New South Wales. They arrived at Batchelor to take over the facilities there as Selman's 9th Squadron continued to move north to Livingstone Field. By the 14th, the 49er squadron scroungers were ranging up and down the Track, taking possession of every conceivable item to make their desolate, tropical hell an easier place in which to live.

## WURTSMITH AND HERRING

The Australians had their hands full with the upstart American Pursuit Group that seemed to lack every vestige of military bearing and organization. General Herring and Commodore Bladin were besieged by every unit in the region to curtail the larcenous 49ers from stealing the RAAF blind.

Although they did directly command Wurtsmith's band, the General and Commodore conceded that the Americans were in-

deed "operators" who did not take direction well. The Aussie commanders sent communiques to Wurtsmith, but the messages were summarily ignored.

The 49er organization was truly independent of the RAAF. Squeeze Wurtsmith knew most of his pilots and enlisted by first names, and the RAAF was appalled that Americans did not salute their officers, nor could 49er officers be recognized as they rarely wore rank insignia or issue uniforms. The question of clothing was left strictly to the person in the stifling tropical sun of the Outback. Only twelve degrees below the equator, 100 degree temperatures were common and crews on work details stripped down to cut-off trousers and shoes. Crews set up their primitive airplane engineering stations in the shade of the forest dispersal areas beneath camouflage netting, but the black flies and mosquitoes even made the shade unbearable.

Everyone was dirty. The wind carried the red sand into every tent shack, vehicle radiator, tool box and mess kit. The most valuable commodities on base were water and mosquito nets. Each section at Livingstone, Batchelor and Adelaide Field jury rigged a hanging water barrel for showers, and central laundries were constructed by the Engineers. All were required to take their daily tablets of atabrine and quinine to ward off infections from the swarms of biting, flying insects.

They stole everything. The civilian administrator for Darwin was forced to issue "salvage vouchers" to Wurtsmith's men to circumvent the total sacking of Darwin's private homes but it was to little avail. The 9 PS acquired a barber chair for Livingstone Field and the 8 PS stole the organ from the Anglican chapel. Furniture, fixtures and telephones were ferreted out of the abandoned offices and homes of the harbor town. Any vehicle left with keys in the ignition was soon commandeered and later found out of gas at a 49ers air field.

In the pandemonium and to the chagrin of the RAAF, the Yanks fit a well organized, independent Pursuit Group operation.

## NEW OPERATIONS UNDER VAN AUKEN

Operations Executive Van Auken was determined that the 49ers would not suffer the frustrations that the 8 PS had faced during Melbourne's harbor defense in March. The Major initiated a comprehensive overhaul of all aircraft, designed a patrol grid to maximize the dispersal of their patrols and created a mobile interceptor control team to ensure that the Group would always have a warning system, even if they were forced to retreat.

All three squadrons were assigned to bases that were surrounded by vast wilderness. Each ordinance section chief was instructed to

*Warhawks in transit at Cloncurry, Q.T., April, 1942.*

*Tanker at Adelaide River A/F serving 8 PS Warhawks.*

*8 PS ground personnel Pvts. Edholm, Gerot and Downard at an Outback sheep station on the Track to Darwin.*

find a area near their strip and lay out a gun range 300 yards long, construct gun crew trenches and build a target buttress. Each armament chief in his respective squadron was to schedule the extraction of every .50 caliber weapon for a gun plumbing inspection of all P-40s in the 49er inventory. After refitting the overhauled ordinance, each plane was to have the guns bore sighted for convergence on targets at 300 yards. The targets were 10 foot square cloth panels suspended by ropes from posts cut from the surrounding forest. A hill side at each of the three operational bases provided an ideal backstop, but the 8th armament crew actually constructed a mammoth earthworks shored up by cut trees for their gun buttress at 27 Mile Strip.

Most of the P-40s required heavy maintenance as few had been overhauled since their assembly in Australia. As the poorly equipped crews in the forest dispersal areas had no powered hoists or steel

*A mobile twin-.50 AA rig built by the 8 PS armament section. The armor plate is an inverted P-40 backrest and the 30 mm plexiglass on top is salvaged from a Navy vessel at the harbor.*

framework stands, crude platforms of empty fuel drums and wooden planks were assembled where ever a plane broke down. A normal engine change for the 1200 pound Allison engine required a crew chief, two mechanic assistants and six hours of labor. Curtiss provided tools to service the Warhawk and its power plant, but most were of poor quality and wore out from daily use. Mechanics improvised hand tools and found the most reliable screwdriver for the Zeus fasteners (flush headed screws) was a crucible-steel "T" handled implement made in Japan and acquired through a blackmarket trader at Townsville. Even aviation gas was transferred by handpumps from 55 gallon drums that were transported in jeep drawn trailers or flatbed trucks.

Van Auken also incorporated a broad adaptation of the RAF system used to defend London during the German Luftwaffe raids of 1940. A grid system of ten square-mile flight sectors was designed for the air spaces above the landing strips along the Track, the harbor area, and Beagle Gulf. The RAAF HQ interceptor team on Larrakeyah Beach posted the current courses of P-40 patrol flights, now color coded (instead of by letter) for greater clarity, on a big table map surrounded by radio operators, who directed the proper P-40 interceptors into the corresponding sectors. The individual squadrons would in turn hold two 4-plane "color" units in stand-by alert with takeoff intervals of 5 minutes, and 10 minutes respectively, to avoid snarling the air lanes above the Track.

Another early warning innovation was the creation of the mobile interceptor truck units. Major Van Auken, 49th Controller Sqn CO Lechleitner and radio specialist, Lt. Joseph Fields, devised a plan to modify two 2 and 1/2 ton flatbed trucks with a controller team each of radioman, plotter, communications officer and pilot (on rotation from the flight schedule). The intention was to provide a mobile air and ground controller team that could operate from any location with these independent battery powered radio systems, should the Japanese land and overrun Darwin.

Much to the consternation of Selman's 9 PS pilots with their 14 confirmed kills, their prime hunting ground over Beagle Gulf was reassigned to the flights of the 8 PS. After the forceful demands of Capt. Strauss that his "Java clan" veterans should have first chance against the return of the raiders, Van Auken had consented to put them directly on the path where the enemy normally approached. The 9 PS was set for coastal defense over Darwin proper and the 7 PS was set above Cox Peninsula along the normal escape route where the Java raiders retreated.

Herring, Bladin and Wurtsmith were rightfully impressed. By the third week in April, Van Auken had modernized the defense of the Darwin-Adelaide River area like none before. After the intensive maintenance and overhaul of the Warhawks, the 49ers could answer an alert with as many as 40 to 50 aircraft within a highly coordinated network. The fighters from Livingstone, Batchelor and Adelaide River could now more effectively cover all of the approaches, coastal targets and escape routes of the Japanese.

The news of the April 18th raid on Japan by LtC. Jimmy Doolittle and his B-25 Mitchell outfit aboard the carrier *Hornet* was also an immense boost to the morale of the 49ers who were stranded at this most remote Yankee outpost. With their own past successes at Darwin and the "all American" Air Corps-Navy "whack at the Japs" on their own homefront, LtC. Wurtsmith and his staff were certain they could turn their own dire situation around. As the 49ers reached a new level of confidence, the cruel nature of the

*(Lt. to rt.) Group CO Wurtsmith, Group Ops Exec Jim Porter, Asst. 7 PS Ldr George Prentice and Deputy Group CO Don Hutchinson at their new 49ers HQ known as 27 Mile Camp.*

Outback again underscored how truly isolated their bases were in the war.

## THE LOSS OF THE INTERCEPTORS TEAM; APRIL 21, 1942

The men and equipment of the 49th Interceptors Control Squadron had temporarily detached from the Group and left the HQ training center in Sydney in mid March for additional classified training with the RAAF at Brisbane. The Controllers completed their advanced training in teletype, radio, and wireless by mid-April and Wurtsmith ordered them to rejoin their unit at Darwin. The Controllers were to refit at Batchelor Field by month's end, and eventually set their permanent base at "Jungle Jump" about 5 miles north of the 8th Pursuit's new 27 Mile Strip. Tragically, 10 of them would never see their unit again.

On the 21st, one of three scheduled RAAF transport flights that was expected to arrive before sunset could not find Batchelor strip beneath the low clouds of a broad weather front. The ground crews at Batchelor heard a twin engine Lockheed pass overhead above the darkening overcast that covered the Track from Darwin to Katherine Field. The plane, with twelve Allies aboard, droned off to the south and was never heard from again.

The burned out Lockheed wreckage was found two months later by Constable Joe Doyle and his aboriginal trackers near Burrundie station, 60 miles southeast of Adelaide River. The two bodies of the RAAF crew were turned over to the proper authorities, and on June 28th, the ten bodies of Controllers Cpls Bill Bedford, Tony Gattamelata and PFCs Robert George, Nick Hinch, Ray Love, John Faris, Walt Feret, Dick Schmidt, Buford Wilard and Wyatt Wiley were interred at Adelaide River's American cemetery. Lieutenant Lechleitner and Major Van Auken never fully recovered from the emotionally devastating loss of the men they had known since the West Palm Beach era.

## WHERE ARE THE JAPANESE? APRIL, 1942

In the three weeks following their apparent March victory over the Darwin defenders, the Japanese air forces in the Celebes had swung

*Early May, 1942, publicity flight of Philippines-Java aces to Darwin RAAF.*

*Allied refugees who sailed from Mindanao, P.I. and reached Pt. Darwin in mid-April when the 7th and 8th Squadron echelons arrived. All were too travel weary to remain with the 49ers and were evacuated to the safety of Australia's east coast.*

to the east in support of their army that was overrunning northern New Guinea. By the end of April, the Imperial troops had captured new bases at Babo, Hollandia, Wewak, Finschhafen and Lae that established a critical supply route from the Philippines to support the Port Moresby operation. Once the route was secured, the Takao wing returned to Java and resumed their armed reconnaissance of the Northern Territory. New bases south of Darwin had been detected and 24 G4M bombers with 13 ZERO escorts sortied from Koepang on April 25th, to remove the Allied threat once more. It would be an appropriate display of contempt by the proud, victorious Takao Ku, for on that day, the Australians celebrated the past glories of their veterans who fought in World War I. Confident of their veterans who would strike with the largest Takao formation since the great February raid, the Imperial air crews launched the air armada in the fair weather of mid morning.

The thirteen 3rd Kokutai escorts failed to keep close contact with the Takao Ku bombers in the huge cumulus clouds east of Timor. By the time the strike group reached Darwin, the ZEROs were spread widely about the three-chevron bomber formation. The dispersal of the 3rd Ku would soon prove disastrous as the ensuing 49er interception would be the bloodiest of all the Darwin confrontations.

### ANZAC DAY, APRIL 25, 1942

General Herring and his staff had reasoned that after such a lengthy absence, the Japanese might well choose to return on the national holiday of the World War I Armistice and "crook the celebrations." Wurtsmith was advised to raise his three squadrons to full alert status for the last week of April, particularly on April 25th, Anzac Day.

Although the early warning system could not circumvent the Japanese from reaching their Darwin objective that afternoon, a swarm of 49ers were able to pursue the raiders out to sea with murderous results. Of fifty fighters that took off in answer to the alarm

that Saturday afternoon, eight pilots in the first combat engagement for the 8 PS would tear the heart out of the raider formation.

The fiery veteran Yellow Flight Leader, 2Lt. Jim Morehead, scrambled his flight of wingman "Big Ed" Miller, element leader Dick Dennis and wingman Montie Eisenberg from Adelaide River at 1330 hours and set off to the north in a climbing pursuit of the raider who had already struck Darwin's RAAF field. Blue Flt Lr Lt. Mitchell "Eck" Sims followed at the five minute interval with wingman 2Lts. Clyde "Smiley" Barnett, element leader Don Morse and wingman Harvey Martin.

En route to the interception, Eisenberg dropped out with engine trouble as the others pushed on. After a 30 minute chase beyond the harbor, Morehead could just see the escaping raiders above the cumulus clouds about 1000 feet higher than his Warhawk flight. Aware of his rookies in line formation behind him, he calmly called out, "Enemy bombers at 3 o'clock high...with fighters. Be careful."

Morehead's Yellow Flight continued upward and crossed behind the bombers to place themselves "up sun" at 18,000 feet on the right flank of the triple chevron Vee formation. Now able to make good his vendetta, he rocked his wings to signal the attack and performed a complete barrel roll to, "show the goddamn Japs I mean business." The rookies of Yellow Flight "with dry mouths and sweat on their throttles", followed Morehead into hell itself. Only seconds later, Lt. Sims' Blue Flight would also descended upon the enemy formation.

Yellow Flt Ldr Morehead and wingman Miller plunged into the midst of the chevron formation in a line assault on the right hand elements in the second Vee. Element leader Dennis was just to their left and followed a similar path through the hail of tracers that flashed from the bomber gun turrets. Morehead was considered "kind of dangerous" in his own ranks, but none of the pilots had ever seen such daring as displayed by their Flight Leader. Morehead recklessly closed in on his quarry and his marksmanship was exact. Element Dennis was just as deadly on the left flank.

Miller stayed in near proximity to the Yellow Leader as they streaked toward the lead elements of the Takao Ku. Morehead and Miller broke off to the right while Dennis wheeled left. Yellow Flight's divided elements looked back from their respective flank positions as three flaming bombers descended from the enemy ranks. Morehead looked all about for ZEROs, and seeing none, rolled his Warhawk back toward the bombers. Miller hung on in tight wing position for a second pass.

Element Ldr. Dennis was momentarily averted in his second pass by the ZEROs, and first dropped away for safety, then pressed back toward the bombers. He was aided this time by the strike of Sims' Blue quartet.

Sims' Blue Flight had run head on into the 3rd Ku escorts before they could reach the ever descending bombers. Sims could see the chevron formation was breaking up and one bomber was trailing heavy white smoke on the right hand side of the formation after Yellow Flight's first pass. Blue Flight's Barnett had kept his eye on two ZEROs that had slipped behind his own element and turned toward them to cut off the threat to Blue Flight Leader Sims.

A whirling dogfight broke out at that instant as two more ZEROs threatened the four Warhawks of Blue Flight. Blue element leader Morse fired across the path of a twisting ZERO and it fell out of the fight in flames. Barnett also fired a broad deflection shot that enveloped a ZERO in tracers.

*Aircraft #51 flown by Jim Morehead, #36 flown by Bill Hennon, Vaught's shark flown by Andy Reynolds and #57 flown by George Kiser to Darwin for the press corps. Morehead detested the name "L'ACE" painted on #51 for the publicity affair and had it painted out by month's end. Ironically, the publicity shots included background views of Darwin's shattered hanger.*

Wingmen began to separate on either side and soon dove away to safety as the fight broke off. Sims and Barnett both wheeled around to pursue the bombers. After a brief descent, they caught up with the last Vee remnant of five raiders in loose formation, just southwest of Bathurst Island.

At that precise moment, Morehead, Miller, Sims, Barnett and Martin all closed in on the fleeing stragglers that broke out in singular escapes. The Americans chased them out to sea and butchered three of the Nippon bombers until their ammunition was expended. Two of the G4Ms trailed great ruby flames and the third slowly dropped into the clouds, leaving a wake of black smoke and burning debris. The 8 PS pilots were now equally separated and the ZEROs made one last intervention. The Yanks broke off at full throttle and turned south to navigate as best they could for Adelaide River.

The other 49ers were not quite finished with the escorts and as the 3rd Ku tried to reform far out over the Gulf, they were jumped by one of the flights of 7 PS Warhawks that had scrambled from

Batchelor Field. Only Flt. Ldr. Hennon in #36 prevailed in the chase and tagged onto a ZERO which still carried its centerline droptank.

The Warhawk ace rapidly closed unseen to within 200 yards dead astern. His accurate stream of .50 caliber tracers detonated the enemy's ship into a ball of fire, and #36 was spattered by the smoldering debris. The 7 PS wingmen confirmed Hennon's sixth kill as they watched the flaming wreckage tumbled into the sea.

For nearly an hour, the skirmishes in the clouds had extended the fight over 100 miles out to sea. The scattered combatants withdrew to their respective bases as twilight settled over the Gulf.

## LOSSES IN THE ANZAC DAY BATTLE

The 49ers were scattered all over the Darwin region. The 8 PS men flew for Adelaide River, but fuel forced them to several alternative landings. Second Lt. Harvey Martin of Blue Flight could not find Adelaide beneath the extensive cloud cover after his pursuit of the

*7 FS Java veteran ace Lt. Bill Hennon who scored April 25th.*

bomber victim and flew 70 miles beyond Adelaide to Pine Creek station. Sims' plane had taken a 7mm round through its oil tank and he set the over-heated Warhawk down on the south beach of Bathurst Island. He was rescued by an RAAF plane the following day, and after minor repairs, he flew his Warhawk home to Adelaide.

Second Lt. "Big Ed" Miller had indeed become separated in his dash for Cox Peninsula and was so disoriented, he flew southwest 250 miles. He barely reached Drysdale Mission near Kalumburu, Western Australia, and put down with empty tanks in a tipped-up landing on the short dirt runway. A truly gentle giant, hefty Big Ed later tolerated his squadron mates' good hearted jibes of having gone "absent without leave."

Flight Leader Morehead likewise suffered from a jolting embarrassment at Adelaide River. Upon his arrival over the field, he performed three victory rolls at low altitude, flared out over the runway in a perfect landing and abruptly stood his Warhawk #44 on its spinner hub in front of Capt. Strauss. A 7 mm machine gun round from an enemy gunner had struck the leading edge of his

right wing and destroyed the landing gear mechanism. The P-40 would be uprighted and repaired, but Morehead's ego had truly been roughed up.

All of the 8 PS men and aircraft were accounted for and the combat damage to the Warhawks had been slight. Strauss congratulated Morehead with three confirmed bombers, Dennis and Miller with two each and Sims, Barnett and Martin with single kills. The 8th's 2Lt. Morse and the 7th's Capt. Hennon, also had their ZERO claims confirmed for a mission total of twelve enemy aircraft shot down. The first combat for the 8 PS was celebrated with lemonade and sandwiches at Adelaide River air strip as the debriefing turned into a social gathering for the pilots and crews.

## MORE DUPLICATIONS

The Americans, just as in the previous encounters, had attacked several of the bombers in multiple passes, and again duplicated their claims. In sorting out the confirmations, Barnett was hesitant to claim the ZERO he had fired at in the early engagement, and was surprised that HQ accredited his victory over a bomber that he himself had reported was already in flames when he attacked.

The ultimate fact was that the 3rd Ku had failed to protect the vulnerable bomber crews. Four heavy bombers had fallen near the target while many more of the survivors would return critically wounded. Not only was the overall scope of their strategic mission in jeopardy, it was now a matter of honor. After two days of rest and repairs, the Timor wing retaliated against the devils at Darwin.

## APRIL 27th REPRISAL

LtC. Wurtsmith's 49ers were alerted to reconnaissance flights on the 26th, but no raids followed them. Squeeze encouraged his squadron commanders to be prepared for a reprisal raid, but the Japanese returned to exact a tragic vengeance on the very next day.

The alert came to Wurtsmith's squadrons shortly after the noon hour, and again, some 50 Warhawks from all three squadrons were able to get airborne and half of them made contact. This time, however, an equal number of enemy escorts stayed together in their approach through the heavy cumulus cloud cover and met the 49ers head-on directly over the little harbor town. The 8 PS made first contact with the enemy again, but the outcome would be costly and

*Jim Morehead's pranged P-40 after the April 25th fight.*

*Close-up of the 7 mm round entry point in Morehead's right wing which destroyed his landing gear mechanism. Luckily, the round did not detonate and rebuilt #44 was issued to 2Lt. Eisenburg.*

CHAPTER 4: THE AMERICAN COMMAND IN DARWIN; APRIL 1942

*2Lt. Clyde "Smilely" Barnett points to the 7 mm round entry point in the leading edge of #51's horizontal stabilizer. The round traveled the full cord of the stabilizer and exited at the hinge line without causing any permanent damage.*

*Senior Lt. George Kiser in the cockpit of his Warhawk just days after the fight of April 25th. The shiny red lacquer victory circles display the resultant sixth and seventh career kills.*

the final debriefing at Adelaide River would end in a rather pointed controversy.

## THE DEATHS OF FISH AND STRAUSS

Squadron Leader Al Strauss led two P-40s at the head of the four flights that scrambled from Adelaide River Field. Strauss' Green Flight, with wingmen 2Lts. Earl Kingsley and Pierre Alford, approached the great swarm of escort fighters just beyond the tip of Middle Point, and though outnumbered at the outset by seven to one, they flew straight into the enemy formation with their guns blazing.

Strauss attempted to fight through to the bombers but was drawn into a turning fight with the aggressive escorts. As the Green Flight trio became separated in the dogfight, Strauss was hammered by the enemy and his P-40 suddenly snapped straight up through the swirling fighters.

The stricken Warhawk stalled out above the fight, rolled over and plunged straight down into Darwin Harbor. Kingsley turned hard into a ZERO and lost sight of the falling Squadron Leader, then managed to hit yet another Mitsubishi with a steady stream of tracers. More ZEROs regained the advantage and Alford followed Kingley down and away for the safety of Adelaide where they reported the loss of Capt. Strauss.

The other flights scrambled in the alert also entered into this same fray and a great maze of tracers and planes filled the sky. White Flight Leader 2Lt. C.C. Johnson lost wingman 2Lt. Owen Fish in the first pass made by the ZEROs and the lieutenant's burning P-40 dropped toward the harbor, duplicating the fate of his fallen squadron leader.

Blue Flt Ldr Capt. George Kiser caught the bombers just before they crossed the shore west of the Darwin proper. Kiser was equally as skilled at gunnery as his veteran cohort, Jim Morehead. The Captain, however, preferred to remove his two outboard guns and reduce the ammunition for the remaining four weapons in order to better challenge the nimble ZERO one-on-one. All in the

Pursuit Group agreed that the "Kentucky Gentleman" in his lightened Warhawk was the most capable and dangerous combat pilot in Australia. After he and wingman Barnett swept through the enemy formation, two flaming G4Ms and a ZERO littered the harbor as proof of the Captain's skill. His element wingman, 2Lt. Harvey Martin, did not fare as well. Martin lost his flight leader in the clouds above Cox Peninsula and was shot down by an enemy fighter. He crashed on the shore just south of the light house on Cape Charles. He would spend the night in a tree overlooking the Timor Sea.

Lt. Sims' Yellow Flight also lost out early in the fight as both 2Lts. Chet Namola and Dick Werner were cut off in their attacks on the bombers by the escorts. The lieutenants were both slightly wounded but both safely returned to Adelaide. Namola's left hand was creased by shattered plexiglass from his holed canopy. Werner's Warhawk was hit by an armor piercing round that entered the fuselage from the left side and shattered on his seat's armor plate. The squadron Flt Surgeon, Capt. Grable, after removing the shrapnel

*Kiser's cartoon lion on the fuselage of his aircraft #57. The beast holds down a ZERO while about to devour its aviator sitting in the upheld paw.*

*Combat novice 2Lt. Barnett readily put his prewar training to proper use. A 3 AF champion aerial gunner in the cadet competitions in Florida, the lieutenant marksman scored again on April 27th.*

splinters from Werner's right shoulder and bandaging Namola's cut hand, pronounce both of the lieutenants fit to return to duty.

The 9 PS had also made limited contact with the 3rd Ku over the harbor, and 2Lts. Mitchel Zawisza and wingman Dick Taylor claimed a ZERO victory and another likely destroyed. Zawisza was credited with the kill and Selman was most thankful that all his flights had returned to Livingstone with minimal damage. After nearly 20 minutes of scattered engagements, all the Warhawks had been forced to dive away from the aggressive ZERO escorts. The Takao bombers retreated to the west into the heavy clouds without further pursuit.

## THE 49ERS RECOVER AFTER THE APRIL 27th RAID

Capt. Morrissey of the 7 PS at Batchelor would learn that one his pilots, 2Lt. Steven Andrews, was shot down but resting safely at Cape Charles' light house. As an element leader in Capt. Hennon's Yellow Flight, Andrews had attacked the bombers head-on over Cox Peninsula and was then met by the cursed ZEROS. One he claimed as a victory before an enemy wingman riddled his Warhawk and forced him to jump from the smoking fighter very near Cape Charles Point. Andrews had settled down into the surf after parachuting from about 12,000 feet. He drifted for some time until he chose to cross over the reef to the open ground within the heavy coastal forest. Being shoeless to make for easy swimming, his bare feet were torn by the sharp coral. Luckily, an RAAF patrol led by Lt. Molyneux which was seeking the 8th Squadron's Lt. Martin, found the bare footed Andrews and delivered him to the light house where he spent the night.

On the following day, tracker John Murry delivered the missing 8th Squadron pilot to the Light House as well. Both Martin and Andrews were taken to Darwin by motor launch. All the 49ers were accounted for, accept in the odd circumstances surrounding the recovery made at Swires Bluff.

## THE BODY OFF SWIRES BLUFF

As for the two dead officers from the 8th Squadron, a bewildering controversy arose from the wreckage found in the harbor that marked the crashes of Strauss and Fish. A floating oxygen bottle was retrieved from Fanny Bay, just offshore of the RAAF AA battery and was tentatively identified by serial number as coming from the plane lost with Strauss whose body was purportedly never found. Directly across the harbor on rugged Swires Bluff, RAAF and USAAC authorities recovered the body originally identified as Owen Fish which was carried to the RAAF hospital. When the body was released for burial, it was interred under the name of the senior officer, Capt. Allison Strauss.

The theory that the body of Owen Fish was spuriously buried in tribute to a fallen Squadron Leader so as to instill a greater sense of resolve in the 49ers, and particularly in the battered 8 PS, appears to be rather contrived at best. Few of the cadre knew the captain well at all, and the allegiance would certainly have been just as strong for the popular young cadre lieutenant. Whether a poorly contrived ruse, or a simple case of muddled records in a besieged command, it is a matter likely never to be resolved.

Regardless of the mystery, the new air strip nearing completion 27 miles down the Track from Darwin was officially dedicated as Strauss Field. It was a fitting tribute to the quiet stranger who had lead the 8 PS cadre into their first successful encounter with

*Veteran Capt. Allison Strauss who was killed over Darwin Harbor, April 27th.*

*Capt. Eck Sims, the oldest fighter pilot in the 49ers who assumed command of his 8 PS unit after Strauss death.*

the Japanese. Major Van Auken remained in his role as Group Operations Executive and Eck Sims was recommended to take command of the 8th Pursuit.

## TO THE EAST FRONT FOR THE TAKAO KU

As for their enemy, the vendetta against the Allies at Darwin had retrieved the honor of the bloodied Takao and 3rd Kokutais. In high spirit, they would meet the deadline for joining the May campaign against Port Moresby. Their most recent combat losses only hardened their resolve.

## THE DEATH OF GENERAL GEORGE; APRIL 29, 1942

With the loss of a squadron leader in combat and still no source of reliable intelligence as to the enemy's next move, it seemed unlikely that Paul Wurtsmith's command dilemma could get much worse. But as fate would have it, before the Group could readjust to the terrible setback of the 27th, the entire Allied command in the Southwest Pacific would suffer the setback that took place at Batchelor Field, just two days later.

Gen. MacArthur had sent his air force coordinator, Gen. Hal George, on an inspection tour of the base facilities throughout the Northern Territory, for both the publicity and for strategic planning in the struggling defense. "Pursuit Hal" and a small press corps toured the north by Lockheed C-40 transport and were due to reach the new Livingstone Field airstrip in the late afternoon of April 29th. The general had personally intended to congratulate the highly successful veterans from the Philippines, particularly his old friends now in the 49th Group, but the transport pilot, Lt. Joe Moore, could not find the well camouflaged Livingstone Field. The Lockheed returned to Batchelor and landed in the evening twilight. Just as the Lockheed taxied to a stop at the end of the runway, two Warhawks rolled into takeoff position. Lieutenant Jack Dale and 2Lt. Bob Hazard were practicing "dual takeoff" procedures and revved up their engines.

The George party had just stepped down from the C-40 and were visiting with the group of men that had brought vehicles to the strip to convey the general back to the 49th Group HQ. Everyone turned to watch the P-40s that began to creep forward. As Dale started off first and Hazard followed only seconds later for a tandem lift off, the right tire blew out on Hazard's machine and it violently swerved to the right across the runway. There was no chance to escape.

Hazard's Warhawk smashed into the terrified travelers and killed war corespondent Mel Jacoby and jeep driver Lt. Bob Jaspers instantly. The general was struck in the chest and head by flying debris and thrown several feet from the tangled aircraft. A young second lieutenant standing near was knocked unconscious, but was not seriously hurt.

An ambulance carried the unconscious general to the Batchelor Field dispensary, but the RAAF surgeons had to transfer the mor-

*Looking northward up the Track at Strauss Field. The large pipe behind the sign is the fresh water viaduct from Manton reservoir which supplied Port Darwin.*

*Harrowing landing for 9 PS 2Lt. John Roth in his brand-new P-40 at Batchelor Field. The retainer hinge atop the rudder broke during flight and Roth skillfully brought the "bent bird" down for an easy repair.*

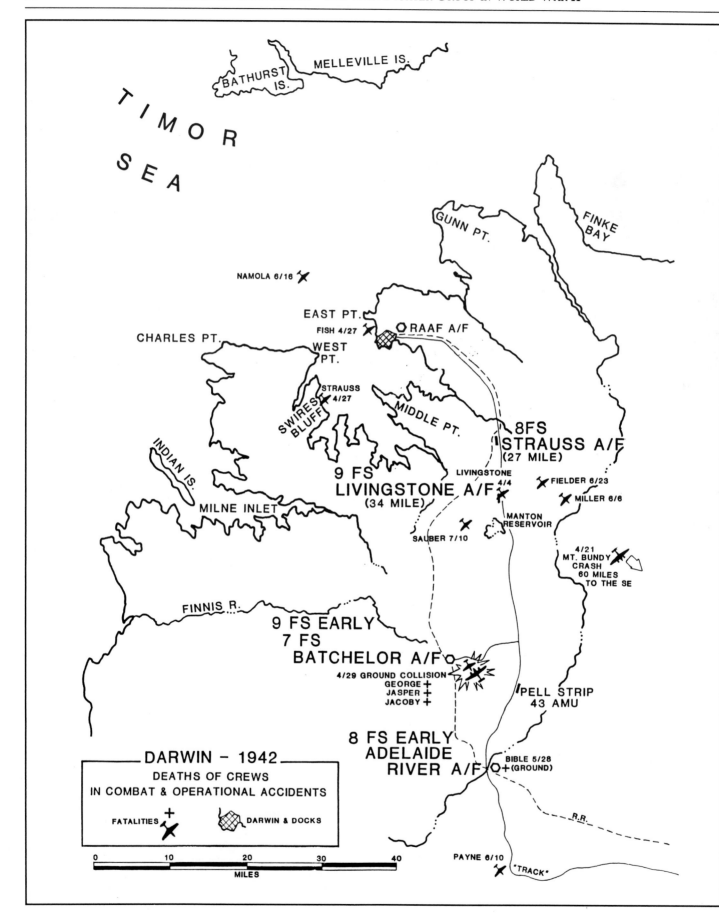

TIMOR

SEA

BATHURST IS.          MELLEVILLE IS.

GUNN PT.                          FINKE
                                  BAY

NAMOLA 6/16 ✈

                    EAST PT.
                            ○ RAAF A/F
CHARLES PT.    FISH 4/27 ✈
               WEST
               PT.

                    STRAUSS
               ✈   4/27
          SWIRES
          BLUFF              MIDDLE PT.
                                          8FS
                                          STRAUSS A/F
                                          (27 MILE)
INDIAN IS.
                              LIVINGSTONE
                    9 FS          ✈ 4/4    ✈ FIELDER 6/23
          MILNE INLET  LIVINGSTONE A/F              ✈ MILLER 6/6
                    (34 MILE)
                                          MANTON
                              ✈          RESERVOIR
                         SAUBER 7/10                    4/21
                                                       MT. BUNDY
                                                       CRASH
                                                       60 MILES
                                                       TO THE SE
          FINNIS R.

               9 FS EARLY
               7 FS
               BATCHELOR A/F ○    ✸
          4/29 GROUND COLLISION ✈
               GEORGE +
               JASPER +                    PELL STRIP
               JACOBY +                    43 AMU

               8 FS EARLY
               ADELAIDE              BIBLE 5/28
               RIVER A/F ○ +(GROUND)
                                              R.R.

DARWIN - 1942
DEATHS OF CREWS
IN COMBAT & OPERATIONAL ACCIDENTS

FATALITIES  ✈           ▨ DARWIN & DOCKS

                              PAYNE 6/10
0        10       20       30       40    ✈   "TRACK"
          MILES

*When Morehead wasn't hitting enemy aircraft in combat, he was hitting home runs in baseball. Squadron mates Werner, Martin and catcher Teahan watch as the ball sails into the outfield of the dispersal area.*

*Werner watches as Ben Duke gives Barnett a haircut at Strauss Field. Hair was kept short, not to meet regulations, but to help keep cool in the stifling tropical heat.*

tally wounded officer south to more modern facilities at Coomalie Creek Field Hospital. At Coomalie, American surgeon Lawrence Braslow tended to the traumatic wounds, but George died the next morning. General MacArthur in Brisbane openly wept at the news that his most valuable field general and dear friend was gone. At the funeral back in the States, George's widow asked never to know the poor young fighter pilot's name who had caused the fateful mishap. Bob Hazard was not injured in the collision, but would never fully recover from the tragedy. Severely despondent, he was

eventually relieved from combat duty. It would be months before he flew again.

The Allied command was stunned. Surely "Pursuit Hal" had been the man that General MacArthur would have chosen to replace General Brett. Who in the Air Corps in Australia could be George's equal?

There was no one, and the Allied intelligence staff confirmed that the Japanese would send a combined force against Port Moresby in the first week of May.

# 5

# METAMORPHOSIS IN MAY 1942

A relative period of calm settled over Darwin as the Japanese forces moved against the eastern front in the New Guinea-Australian campaign in early May, 1942. The majority of the Imperial Navy air units on Java had been temporarily reassigned to the support of their forces who would attempt to occupy Port Moresby. A much smaller force of Mitsubishi heavy bombers remained at Koepang and sent night raids against the Allied air bases along the Track, but neither Livingstone, Strauss nor Batchelor Fields were ever hit during this interim. The 49ers would not meet any opposition in their air patrols above Darwin for nearly six weeks.

From May 5th through the 8th, a U.S. Navy fleet commanded by Adm. Fletcher and based in the southern Solomon Islands, successfully foiled the Japanese in their attempt to land troops on the south coast of New Guinea in the great Battle of the Coral Sea. The battle ultimately resulted in a tactical draw between the combatants, but it completely realigned the direction of the war in the Pacific.

The Doolittle air raid on the Japanese homeland in the previous month and the successful thwarting of the Port Moresby invasion had effectively caused the Japanese Imperial staff to postpone their original May strategy for the assaults into the Central Pacific and simultaneous strike in the south against the New Hebrides and Samoan Islands. As the Imperial staff reassessed the objectives for their invasion fleets across the broad expanse of the Pacific, the Allies in Australia were given time to refit for the counter offensive in New Guinea.

## REALIGNING THE U.S. COMMAND IN AUSTRALIA; MAY, 1942

The American command in Australia was at a critical impasse. A personal rift had arisen between Gen. Douglas MacArthur and his Air Corps commander, Gen. George Brett, which would affect the entire Allied organization. Brett presided over an incredibly elaborate maze which encompassed two regions of authority with separate commanders; the western area under Gen. A.L. Sneed and eastern area under Gen. M.F. Martin. These American staff officers duplicated the RAAF commands and Allied command initiatives were continuously snarled in the process. Another new command for the logistics of the USAAC in Australia was also created, but the reorganized air force was too ungainly. Bomber units of the combined Allied air force continued to sortie against enemy targets on either flank of the Australian front. The USAAC 19 BG had effectively supported the Coral Sea navy operations from Iron Range, but supplies and replacements for the majority of the Allied squadrons were woefully mired in Brett's administrative labyrinth. MacArthur grew impatient with Brett, who continuously promised planes and air crews for the pending spring offensive, yet no personnel or planes were forthcoming. Brett fell far from the favor of the Supreme Commander and was ostracized by Chief of Staff Sutherland at Brisbane HQ.

The exploits of LtC. Paul Wurtsmith's Pursuit Group at the remote outpost of Port Darwin were the brightest spots in the USAAC record. MacArthur called Wurtsmith to Brisbane on May

*The 49ers HQ construction by aboriginals at 27 Mile Camp.*

*Wurtsmith's completed command center atop the hill at 27 Mile.*

*C-47 Dakota transport at Daly Waters, bringing up new supplies in mid-May, 1942.*

*Constant flying in the desert realm required constant changing of spark plugs and fuel filters in the Allisons.*

8th, congratulated Squeeze on the 49er's thirty-nine confirmed victories against the Japanese and personally promoted the Group Leader to the rank of full colonel. The Supreme Commander also informed Wurtsmith that his unit must hold Darwin until an RAAF replacement could release the 49ers for the forthcoming New Guinea counter-offensive in August.

Colonel Wurtsmith returned to Darwin the following day and conveyed the rank of lieutenant colonel to Deputy CO Hutchinson and the personal praise from General MacArthur to the men at Strauss, Livingstone and Batchelor Fields. The 49ers continued to upgrade their airfield system, but in the aftermath of the Coral Sea engagement, the principal Allied endeavor was to concentrate on MacArthur's counter-offensive in the east. The 49ers languished in what seemed to be the most isolated outpost in the South Pacific theater. In the enemy's absence, the pilots and crews waited for news of the fighting in the other fronts, while their dreary routine of coastal patrol flights and desert camp life was interrupted by random mishaps and coveted leaves to the southern cities.

## A FEW DIVERSIONS IN MAY, 1942

The life of the servicemen in the Northern Territory was quite diversified, considering the great distances between their tropical-

*Lts. Illing, Morehead, Werner and Philippines veteran Flt Ldr Randall Keator acquired shotguns and rifles from the 8 FS ordinance, then killed a pair of wild hogs and nearly a hundred ducks. The fresh meat was distributed to all the Yankee units.*

desert wilderness and more civilized places. The Americans in particular had created their own "tent town" versions of a typical country borough at various sites along the Track. The Group Chaplain had begun mimeographing a newspaper. There was a "hanging bedsheet and projector" movie theater at Batchelor Field, a shallow swimming hole in Adelaide River, the newly constructed Manton reservoir south of Livingstone Field, and squadron "stores" that sold any number of items at the respective airfields.

The men of the American air force ventured into the bush that surrounded their field bivouacs to wonder at the ten foot high, concrete-like termite mounds that towered above the forest floor. Some men caught the odd marsupial creatures and exotic birds for pets, but learned the mouse-like gray bandicoots, or even the smallest kangaroos, were nearly impossible to keep in bivouac with human tent mates. The local aboriginals warned the newcomers to be especially cautious of the numerous poisonous snakes in the area.

The Yanks considered the aboriginals to be a very simple people and although very mysterious, the "Aussie Abos" were truly friendly. Many of the men traded for native souvenirs and learned the curious sing-song pidgin English that flavored much of the local dialect. The Yanks also swapped cigarettes for fresh fruit and wild yams to improve their dismal army mess, but few 49ers could tolerate the flesh of the lizards, snakes, fish and flying foxbats that their native hosts considered the delicacies of the "yegge" winter season. Some of the 49ers learned of the shotguns supplied to their armament sections and requisitioned the weapons for bird hunting to enhance their meals. Visitors to Strauss Field were often surprised by a full course roast duck banquet, made possible by the marksmanship of Jim Morehead.

The European-Yankee community was forced to tolerate many of the strange customs of the local aboriginals, but none more peculiar than the annual ritual burning of the surrounding forest in preparation for the new growing season of the coming spring. There was a constant smokey haze over the region and the sun rose and set in prolonged equatorial twilights of brilliant vermillion. The Australians called this place the "land of dreamtime" and the Yanks indeed thought the lime green bush and red desert skies made their new home both mysterious and beautiful.

Life there was not always so mysterious to the newcomer Yanks. The contesting Aussies proved their genuine comradery with their common love of sports. American baseball diamonds were scraped in the sand at every unit location and the Aussie sportsmen even

*The RAAF provided liaison travel and air searches at Darwin Field in this Supermarine Walrus amphibian.*

*The 49ers North American O-47 "The Pregnant Foose", was maintained for liaison flights at Batchelor Field.*

joined in on the Yank basketball tournaments at the beckon of a friendly challenge. The "blokes" returned the favor with an invitational swim meet at Berry Springs, just west of Strauss Field, where the Yanks were trounced by the Aussies who used the famous "Australian crawl" stroke.

The diversions were critical to the sanity of everyone since the more pressing military duties were such drudgery. Although more vehicles were acquired to help lighten the tasks of the poorly equipped crews, labor gangs still provided human muscle for much of the construction throughout the Darwin area. Supreme Commander MacArthur received a highly critical official report of Australian Commander Herring's unauthorized use of American enlisted personnel on labor details. The Aussie versus Yank command continued to struggle without a common resolve.

General MacArthur wisely laid the controversies aside and chose to make use of the positive news of the successful defense of Darwin. Civilian journalists were sent to Batchelor Field in a conscious effort to inform the American public of the critical nature of the Yankee presence in Australia. The heroic exploits of Wurtsmith's 49ers were the truest success stories in the war for the remnant American Army. Soon, the American papers and military Stars and Stripes featured articles of the Yanks "down under" at the exotic bases of Humpty Doo and Rumjungle. The articles were obviously censored for military reasons but families in the U.S.A. could thrill to the exploits of "Big Stoop" Landers, Andrews' breathtaking escape from the sharks, "Baldy Blanton Battlin' Bastards", "Chip

Chapman's Chargin' Chumps", "Parson Posten's Piss Poor Pilots", and "Johny Johnsen's Jap Jumpers." Soon the photographs and articles extolled the victories of aces Kiser, Morehead, Hennon and Reynolds who flew in the defense of their Australian Allies. It was pretty heady stuff and the 49ers basked in the publicity.

## THE FLYING KNIGHTS OF LIVINGSTONE FIELD; MAY, 1942

More veteran pilots and new P-40E aircraft arrived every day at each of the 49er squadrons. Even the Lockheed copilot, 2Lt. Jack Donalson, who had accompanied Gen. George on that fateful flight, stayed to join his old Philippines campaign mates at Livingstone Field. By the end of the month, Captain Selman had enough pilots and planes available at Livingstone to provide a rotation of four flights for standing patrols over Darwin.

In this interim, someone on the 49ers command staff had likened the first team of 9th Pursuit men, who had come to Darwin in March, to the freelance knights of ancient history who served in hopeless causes, but always prevailed. The simile caught Captain Selman's fancy. By mid-May, a road sign at Livingstone appeared, followed by jacket patches, showing a winged knight's helmet on a blue shield and a broad red band running diagonally from the upper right to lower left behind the helmet. An Australian officer jokingly asked if the banded heraldry of the shield might possibly be mis-

*8 FS acquired this deHavilland Tiger Moth two-seater for search and rescue, or crew flights.*

*Barnett attends the bore-sighting of his new aircraft #55 replete with sky-blue forward half of spinner and the name "SMILELY" painted in yellow on the radiator tub.*

taken as the sign of the bastard. Selman drily replied that as regarded his ornery gang, it probably did not matter. The shield of the Flying Knights was forever fixed in history.

## THE EIGHTBALLS OF STRAUSS FIELD

The 8th Pursuit, under command of the Captain Eck Sims, completed their move into the dispersal area of Strauss Field by mid-May and took more men into their flight schedule. Sims was a curious contrast in command to the studious, business-like Van Auken and the silent resolve of veteran Strauss. Eck Sims was a cadre pilot from the Morrison Field era who simply lived to fly. He was loved by his whole squadron and looked upon with disdain by the more proper RAAF types. The 8th Pursuit Commander rarely wore his captain's insignia, drank with his crew chiefs and owned only one regulation uniform that was never pressed. At a May staff meeting, an RAAF contemporary criticized the rough appearance of the "rejects" and "trouble makers" that operated at Strauss Field. Sims wryly quipped that his reject "eightball" outfit with their 17 confirmed victories could out fight anybody and that was the final measure of his men. It was an appropriate retort. They were indeed the "Eightballs" of the 8th Pursuit, and though never official, the name was used proudly by the men at Strauss Field.

## THE SCREAMIN' DEMONS OF BATCHELOR FIELD

The past two months had been somewhat disruptive for Capt. Bob Morrissey and the new facilities at Batchelor Field. The Captain spent an inordinate amount of time at the field HQ in countless staff meetings with Com. Bladin, Wurtsmith, Hutchinson and Van Auken. The squadron level administration once again fell upon his

Deputy, George Prentice, while the operations were coordinated by the combat veteran ace, Bill Hennon. A confrontation arose between the two subordinates for clarification of either man's authority and Morrissey sided with the hotheaded veteran, much to Prentice's disdain. Although Prentice had been with the Group since its inception, he asked for a transfer to another unit at the earliest opportunity. Neither Morrissey nor Prentice would yield in their respective stands on the matter and both were thereafter antagonistic. Col. Wurtsmith, however, readily decided that Prentice's transfer was necessary to settle the rift.

As for the veteran Hennon, Morrissey could not rebuke such an able combat leader. On the rudder of Hennon's Warhawk was a painting of the mythological Java jungle demon called the "bunyap." Legend claimed if a man should encounter this dangerous evil creature and survive to tell the tale, he would inherit the creature's great powers. It was indeed so with "Bunyap" Hennon who displayed a supernatural fierceness in combat over Darwin. His bravery endowed the more eager 7th Pursuit pilots and they adopted the "Screamin' Demons" name in a befitting tribute to their veteran Operations Executive and his bunyap legacy from Java.

## ROUTINE PATROLS AND NO ENEMY IN MAY

The 49er pilots fared well in the routine missions and training flights during May. Only one aircraft was lost out of two flying incidents and both were attributed to the same pilot. On May 5th, "bomber killer" 2Lt. Harvey of the 9 PS was returning after the last sortie of the day. In the twilight, the pilot misjudged the Track for the runway and set his old reliable Warhawk, #92, down on the narrow highway just north of Livingstone Field. The plane's right tire caught on the shoulder of the road which pitched the fighter off to the side. Old #92 rushed toward the trees, and suddenly lurched to a crunch-

*M/Sgt. Paul "Pop" Marlin in his jeep and T/Sgt Art Lightcap – 8 FS welders.*

*8 FS Flt Surgeon Irv Grable and one of the many parakeets kept in the Strauss camp.*

*2Lt. Watkins' new ship in Livingstone bore-sight stand.*

ing halt in a cloud of dust against the big water pipeline which paralleled the Track. When the rescue group from Livingstone drove up to the crash site, they found the lieutenant calmly sitting in the cockpit filling out his accident report. The ship required only minor repair and #92 was turned over to crew chief Akin, who had it back in the air three days later. Unfortunately for Harvey and #92, they were never destined to land together at Livingstone in the month of May.

On the 8th, while returning from patrol over East Arm inlet, #92 ran out of gas and Harvey was forced to bring the sputtering Warhawk in for a belly landing on adjacent Middle Point. The P-40 plowed into the turf approximately ten miles from the Track, but it was much too rugged a terrain to be recovered. Harvey's Warhawk was written off and the "bomber killer" pilot was issued a new "sand and spinach" camouflaged mount from the P-40 replacement pool at Batchelor Field. The lieutenant numbered the new ship "92" and had a gaudy shark mouth painted on the radiator tub for good luck.

### THE NEW FIGHTER AIR FORCE; MAY 26, 1942

A Curtiss Aircraft Company inspection team, accompanied by Army inspectors, toured the 49ers' operations during May, and although they questioned the unorthodox engineering and maintenance of the Warhawks, their reports to the Brisbane command HQ greatly favored the Group Leader of the 49th Pursuit.

*9 FS CO Selman's command ship in the gun stand.*

Meanwhile, Squeeze Wurtsmith restlessly awaited intelligence communiques on the position of the Japanese who only occasionally struck in small night raids nearer to Darwin. There was only word of an official United States Army decree, effective on the 26th, that all pursuit group and squadron units were to be named with the new designator, "fighter group and fighter squadrons" of the United States Army Air Force. Back pay for the troops was also brought up to date and some promotions in ranks for the enlisted men were authorized. Still, the Japanese did not strike in the daylight.

### THE FATAL ACCIDENT OF PFC DAVID BIBLE; MAY 28, 1942

The routine work around a combat aircraft was just as dangerous on the ground as when a ship was aloft. At the Adelaide River gun range, armament chief Ssgt. Downer and a work detail were boresighting an 8th Squadron P-40. Downer climbed into the cockpit to make a final inspection of the gun switch wiring and turned off the electrical power to the instrument panel as a routine safety precaution. As he set about his work after switching off the power, the sergeant was startled by the report of the right outboard .50 caliber weapon. A live ammo round had failed to eject from the weapon's breech during preparations. The crewmen cried out and Downer quickly crawled from the cockpit and hurried to the front of the ship to join the small group of men hovering over the still body of PFC David Bible. One of the mechanics had inadvertently caused a short while refitting the breech mechanism beneath the right wing and the overlooked round discharged with Bible standing only a few feet from the muzzle of the gun. The bullet struck him behind the right ear and nearly decapitated the young private, killing him instantly. Van Auken and Sims were stunned at the news of yet another man dead in their squadron in such a senseless accident, but no one blamed the distraught section chief, Wes Downer. David Bible was buried at the Adelaide Field American cemetery the next day and they mourned for the boyish young man who had died so far from his Florida family. The month of June came and two more fatalities mysteriously occurred in the Group.

### THE DEATHS OF MILLER AND PAYNE

On June 6th, the 8th Squadron's Big John Miller, the peaceful giant and combat veteran, took his P-40 on a high altitude flight for the purpose of testing new oxygen gear. It was presumed the lieutenant's gear had failed which caused him to blackout from oxygen starvation, but little evidence was recovered from the crater where the plunging P-40 had exploded on impact ten miles east of Livingstone Field. Miller's body was torn apart in the crash.

Four days later, the 7th Squadron lost Lt. Bill Payne under similar circumstances in a fatal crash 20 miles due south of Adelaide River. The remains of Miller and Payne were buried in the Adelaide River American cemetery. A full inspection of all high altitude gear in the Warhawks was ordered for the group, but operations were not interrupted.

The Group also reported flying accidents that were not fatal. On June 5th, Lt. Sells of the 9th Squadron lost a P-40 on the

*P-40 in the Strauss Field bore-sight stand.*

Charleville-Cloncurry leg of the Brereton Route when the engine overheated and he was forced to land near the tiny station of Longreach. The fighter was abandoned there and Sells reached Batchelor by RAAF transport a few days later.

On June 6th, Lt. C.C. Johnson of the 8th Squadron brought in a P-40 for a heavy landing at Adelaide River Field. The wrecked fighter was carried off by truck to the 43rd Air Maintenance Unit depot at Pell strip, just a few miles up the Track from the crash site. The ship was repaired and returned to the squadron within a few days. Johnson was uninjured and returned to the flight schedule immediately.

On June 11th, another 7th Squadron man narrowly escaped tragedy on a cross country training flight 20 miles southeast of Adelaide River. Lt. Don Dittler had tried to nurse the overheating Allison engine of his P-40 back to the north, but the motor burst into flame over the mining town of Brocks Creek and Dittler safely parachuted out.

## A CRITICAL VICTORY AT MIDWAY ISLAND; JUNE 3-7, 1942

Col. Wurtsmith was duly worried that some of the older Warhawks were now falling victim to the rigors of the harsh environment and constant flying. Two pilots and an enlisted man had died in opera-

tional accidents that could have been avoided and the squadron leaders agreed that lethargy was as dangerous an enemy as the Japanese. Under the circumstances, their "outpost in hell" was holding up amazingly well. News of fighting in other parts of the Pacific would provide a terrific uplift for the 49ers.

By mid-month, the long awaited intelligence information began to pour into the 49ers HQ. Japan had now suffered a second major setback in a sea battle during the first week in June, far out in the northern Pacific near the tiny American navy base of Midway Island. Word spread quickly throughout the services and civilian newspapers of the Imperial Fleet's losses of four aircraft carriers with over 300 planes, plus a heavy cruiser and 5000 Imperial troops and sailors. It was an unqualified victory for Adm. Fletcher, the same man who had led the American fleet in the Coral Sea encounter.

The Japanese commanders of the Imperial Staff had erroneously assumed that the concentrated Allied defenses in Australia and the Solomon Islands had left a void further east in the central and northern Pacific. In a bold gamble during May, 1942, the Imperial forces were divided into two fleets that executed a daring dual attack on the American navy.

First, a decoy attack was launched in the western Aleutian Islands of Alaska, and second, the main assault was launched to capture Midway Island as a staging base for missions against the American fleet in Hawaii. The American intelligence people again decoded the intercepted radio communiques from the Japanese command and circumvented the objective. Fortunately, Adm. Fletcher's carrier force from Pearl Harbor reached the main enemy invasion fleet and completely terminated the threat to the central Pacific stronghold at Hawaii. In the wake of the great battle near Midway Island, the focus of the remainder of the Pacific war shifted to the southwest. Although the Japanese did successfully land troops on the islands west of Alaska, those Imperial forces were eventually withdrawn after a year of isolation, too far from the more decisive campaigns in the Southwest Pacific.

## THE JUNE, 1942 DARWIN CAMPAIGN

The Japanese had hoped to eliminate the vast resources of American industries with the capture of the central Pacific sea routes and

*Louisiana native Keator and his "Cajun" aircraft #68. The cartoon pelican fighter-bomber includes a frog bombardier on the nose of the bomb and a dangling crayfish tail gunner to fire the shotguns under wing. The port-side name translates into the veteran's own description of how fast he left the Philippines – like a "spotted-ass-ape."*

*Lt, Jack Donaldson's first #83 "MAUREE." Several 9 FS aircraft displayed their numeral designator on the lower surface of the radiator tub.*

a quick victory in the Solomon Islands. But the venture had gone totally awry following the stiff opposition in the Coral Sea and the lethal blow at Midway. The Imperial Staff refocussed their efforts in early June against the remaining Allied air units in the Southwest Pacific, fearing that American General Douglas MacArthur would use that air force in support of an invasion campaign in New Guinea,

*After his close call in April, 2Lt. Werner had heavy angled plates added to his cockpit rear armor plate.*

or the Solomon Islands. An intense maximum effort was launched out of the great stronghold of Rabaul to defeat the Allied flyers who staged from their bases in Australia and the southern islands of the New Hebrides. The island of Guadalcanal in the east, Port Moresby in the center and Darwin in the west were targeted for immediate neutralization.

**THE FIRST RAID; JUNE 13th**

The Allied intelligence staff in Australia advised of probable reprisal raids in the northwest area following the rout at Midway. Japanese reconnaissance flights had been reported throughout the May doldrums, and the flights increased in the second week of June.

Although tiny Port Darwin and its small air defense force was comparatively isolated as an effective participant in the Port Moresby/Guadalcanal campaign, the Japanese could not accurately determine the exact strength of the units there. From June 13th through the 16th, the Takao and 3rd Kokutais returned to Java and launched daily raids against the Darwin area. The Takao wing altered their strategy in that the chevron Vee formations would attack at altitudes well above 20,000 feet with heavy fighter escort to avoid the intercepting Warhawks that had ravaged their crews in April. At mid-day on June 13th, after six weeks of relative calm, the radar

*Crewchief Sgt. Marmaduke (lt.), crewman Pvt. Carney and pilot 2Lt. Alford next to their aircraft #50 which was shot down on June 13th.*

*Eisenburg's "DOLLEYE" before the June 13th fight.*

*DOLLEYE's demise at Strauss Field.*

*DOLLEYE herself beneath the pilot's crushed cockpit. Eisenburg miraculously survived with minor injuries.*

station at Dripstone Cliffs picked up an image of a very high formation which approached from the northwest near Melville Island. Thirty-six 49ers answered the alarm.

The Group Operations Executive Major Bob Van Auken, in borrowed HQ Squadron Warhawk #5, and newcomer 2Lt. Ben Brown in Van Auken's #4, were airborne at 5,000 feet above the harbor in a training exercise with the RAAF coastal anti-aircraft batteries. The Yankee duo first circled back to the north to confirm a coast watcher's sighting of unidentified planes over the islands, but as Van Auken received the report from Dripstone, he gave Brown the order to ascend at full throttle westward toward the approaching enemy. High overhead, the Takao Ku formation of 27 heavy bombers beneath an awesome fighter cover of 45 ZEROs had just turned into their bomb run on the docks and RAAF strip.

The standing Eightball patrol of eight P-40s led by 2Lt. Earl Kingsley reached the raiders as they paraded over their Darwin runway target. The Warhawks were immediately hammered by the 3rd Ku who knocked 2Lt. Pierre Alford out of the Eightball formation in the first pass. Alford bailed out at 3000 feet over Gunn Point and as he descended in his parachute, two grey fighters dropped to his level and sent a burst of tracers unnervingly close to the dangling Eightball pilot. The lieutenant desperately pumped his chute straps and had begun to swing crazily from side to side to foil the Japanese gunners' aim when Flt Ldr Kingsley roared in behind the attackers and shot down the would-be assassin. The other ZERO broke away and Alford landed safely on the beach of Shoal Bay where an RAAF pilot in a deHavilland Tiger Moth picked him up the next day.

The remaining 8th Squadron men were hopelessly outnumbered and were swarmed by the aggressive enemy escorts. All the Eightballs dropped out of the foiled intercept as three of them had received heavy damage. Back at Strauss Field, Lt. Dick Dennis barely managed to set his riddled P-40 down, and luckily avoided injury. Second Lt. Monty Eisenberg reached the runway in his shot up Warhawk #44 which ground looped and crunched inverted in the middle of the strip. He was able to crawl from beneath the twisted wreckage, but was badly shaken up with cuts and bruises. He would not return to the flight schedule for several days. Hapless Lt. C.C. Johnson had been wounded by a ZERO's 20 mm round that exploded in the cockpit and he bellied his #60 in beside the main strip. The squadron had been clobbered by the 3rd Ku, with only one kill awarded to Kingsley. Later, the men grew increasingly worried when they learned their old boss, Bob Van Auken, was missing.

## THE ODYSSEY OF MAJOR VAN AUKEN

Group Exec Van Auken and his rookie wingman, Lt. Brown, had climbed for nearly 20 minutes during the initial stage of the fight, when Brown dropped out of the chase with engine trouble. Even though the Major had flown #4 the previous day and doubted the malfunction claimed by the lieutenant, Van dismissed the timid rookie and continued on alone in #5 following the marauders far out to sea. Van Auken caught the Takao formation as the G4Ms routinely descended over the Gulf near Bathurst Island and closed in on the left flank of the last Vee element. He was at 16,000 feet when the escorts made their first pass at his lone Warhawk. Van slipped past two ZEROS and closed in on the trailing bomber to deliver a long burst of .50 caliber fire. He broke away to the right, leveled out on the far side of the elements just above Bathurst Island's shoreline and was about to swing into a second pass when 20mm explosions upon both wings forced him to dive for safety. At 10,000 feet, the Major's Warhawk was hit a second time and he peeled off again within a hail of tracers. Old #5 was a goner. The engine burst into flame as the Major dived toward the sea. Van attempted to roll the ship over at 800 feet of altitude to let himself drop free of the cockpit, but another exploding round abruptly forced the Warhawk down and momentarily trapped the Major in the seat. He stuck his arms into the slipstream of the blazing Warhawk and was pulled by the wind into the open air. He grabbed the ripcord of his chute pack with a seared right hand and instantly drifted beneath the white nylon of his chute for a short fall into the shallow surf just offshore.

The ZEROS were not finished, and just as they had fired upon Pierre Alford only minutes before, the 3rd Ku pilots tried to murder the Major as he hung in his parachute. The tracers whizzed by until Van Auken splashed down, and he laid motionless in the water, pretending to be dead. Only then did the growling grey hunters overhead break off for Timor.

The Major thought he had come down on Bathurst, but had actually descended to the shore of Melville Island. After walking the shoreline for several hours, the badly burned flyer was found by aboriginals and taken to their village where their tribal doctor treated "goodfella" Van Auken's severely scorched legs with a vegetable paste. The pungent medication soothed the blistered flesh and enabled the "goodfella" to sleep through the night. The islanders carefully transported the weakened Major by large canoe to the mainland on the following day and the authorities immediately placed him in the little Darwin RAAF dispensary known as Kahlin Hospital.

## THE SECOND RAID; JUNE 14th

The 49ers barely had time to dwell on the losses of the previous day. At one o'clock on the following afternoon, the alarm sounded the next raid. For this engagement, the Kokutais switched tactics.

The 3rd Ku sent 27 ZEROs via the approach flown nearer Bathurst Island while 9 G4M Takao raiders took a more direct westerly route over Cox Peninsula to their targets of the harbor and docks. It foiled an effective interception by the twenty-eight Warhawks that scrambled in the alert. The scrambled flights from the 49er's three southern strips could not find a bomber formation but instead ran into the 3rd Ku escorts over Middle Arm Inlet. The 8th completely missed the sweep of the enemy fighters as the 7th and 9th Squadrons bore the weight of the fight.

Capt. Nate "Baldy" Blanton, the grinning cantankerous Java veteran who had come to the Screamin' Demons during the May buildup, led his flight from their standing patrol at 20,000 feet over Cox Peninsula in a shallow dive down into the fighter opposition. Blanton quickly bested a pair of ZEROS but the other Demons could not corner the wily 3rd Ku veterans so easily. Rookie Lt. Keith Brown was caught by a pair of Ku wingmen and his Warhawk exploded in flames from their concentrated cannon fire. Brown barely escaped from the plunging fighter and bailed out just south of Darwin RAAF strip. Burned and weak, he landed in a tree and broke his left leg on impact. The ground crews at RAAF field, and the 49er Controllers, had watched the whole affair and quickly rescued the stranded flyer who was now in the path of the brushfire that had started from the crash of his burning plane.

Of the twelve 9th Squadron men who scrambled from Livingstone Field, only the lethal Blue Flight team could find the enemy. Blue Flt. Ldr. Andy Reynolds lifted off with Sauber, Landers, and Donalson to reach the battle at the same moment as the 7 FS

*Big John Lander's eagle on his aircraft #81 "SKEETER."*

*Lander's machine gun toting "SKEETER" of 9 FS's deadly Blue Flight.*

*Lt. Gil Portmore gives his crewchief a taxi ride just days after his successful engagement on June 15th.*

departed. Three grey fighters immediately fell from the swirling dogfight before the guns of Andrews' quartet. After nearly 30 minutes of continuous engagements, the opponents withdrew from the area and the Americans brought home their holed Warhawks for fast repair. Only Brown's 7 FS Warhawk was lost in exchange for single kills awarded to Flt Ldr Blanton, and to Donalson, Landers and Reynolds of the 9th Squadron.

## THE THIRD RAID; JUNE 15th

The raiders repeated the same tactics with 21 fighters preceding 27 high flying bombers on the next day. Of the 28 Warhawks that went aloft, the 8th Squadron was again unable to break through the escorts and could not hit the bombers in the initial contact over Beagle Gulf. The 9th and 7th Squadrons again were heavily engaged.

The 9 FS was routinely up above Darwin proper with 2Lts. George "Red" Manning leading the flight of wingmen Tom Fowler, Clay Peterson and "crocodile bait" Bob McComsey who had only recently returned to flight status. Red Manning was a short, sandy-haired German-American who loved to argue and set up a personal confrontation with an element of the 3rd Ku directly above the docks. After wingman Fowler joined in the fray, and McComsey with wingman Peterson followed, three ZEROS reeled out of the fight.

The enemy bombers had reached the docks by this time, dropped their ordinance and set fire to some of the nearby buildings. Even the convalescing Van Auken and his attending physician were forced to seek refuge beneath the Major's hospital bed as bombs struck near the Kahlin dispensary. As the raiders turned west and began to accelerate in a descent over Cox Peninsula, they were met by the 7th Squadron.

The Screamin' Demons were in two flights at 24,000 feet to ensure they would intercept the bomber formation which had been missed at their higher altitudes in the two previous raids. With Blue Flight led by ace Ops Exec Hennon, and Red Flight led by Squadron Deputy CO Capt. Prentice, they dived to the left rear quarter attack on the G4M raiders, but only Hennon and wingman 2Lt. C.T. Johnson closed to within firing range before the ZEROS intervened. Johnson lost power momentarily and a ZERO quickly cut him off from his flight. The 3rd Ku aviator riddled the sputtering

Warhawk, and Johnson tried to escape in the stricken fighter, but the Allison engine caught fire. He bailed out at nearly 18,000 feet over hazy Cox Peninsula.

In the meantime, Red Flt Ldr Prentice and wingman 2Lt. Claude Burtnette had engaged two escorts and both men opened fire, sending the ZEROS spinning down toward the Gulf. Second Lt. Gil Portmore in the second Red element also fired a broad deflection volley at a third ZERO which plunged downward, but the Demons were quickly overwhelmed. Red Flight was engaged by an enemy quartet and in the ensuing maneuvers, the Demon team split up. After shaking a ZERO off his tail, Burtnette of Blue Flight set off alone after the escaping bombers beyond Cox Peninsula, but was attacked again off the west shore by a 3rd Ku escort whose 20mm cannon fire blew off the ammo bay panel from the top of his right wing. He bailed out into the sea just west of Indian Island and floated in his Mae West vest while Capt. Hennon circled over his downed wingman until the ZEROS left the area. Burtnette reached Quail Island over two hours later and was spotted by a pair of RAAF Wirraway patrol planes who radioed his location to the Navy. The Australian lugger Kuru picked him up early the following morning from the north beach of Quail Island.

## THE FOURTH RAID; JUNE 16TH

On the last June raid, 27 bombers were escorted by an equal number of ZEROS using the same successful high altitude formations. The Eightballs of Strauss Field seemed to have been marked by fate as three more of their pilots fell victim to the 3rd Kokutai. Although the Eightballs had soared to 26,000 feet over Bathurst Island, they were woefully outmaneuvered by the superior Mitsubishi fighters which dropped from a greater altitude and scattered their flight.

## THE LOSS OF LT. NAMOLA

Second Lt. Chester Namola was hit hard by an escort fighter in the enemy's first pass and his Warhawk was last seen spiraling down toward the harbor. After several days of extensive searching, no trace of him was ever found.

*Crewmen attend to Lt. Chester Namola just days before the pilot's loss on June 16th.*

## MARTIN ON MELVILLE ISLAND

Second Lt. Harvey Martin was not as fortunate against the enemy on this clear Monday afternoon as he had been in his first interception in April. The veteran was cut out of the fight in the first pass at 22,000 feet and Martin was forced to escape in a terminal velocity dive that burned out the Allison engine. He made a perfect flaps-down belly landing in the surf on the south shore of Melville Island. The remaining 8th Squadron also dived away as the 3rd Ku swept south toward the port town.

Even though the RAAF had designated the southern shores of Bathurst and Melville as suitable emergency landing sites, the mud flats were rugged and when covered by tide were not at all safe. Martin's Warhawk sank immediately and he struggled ashore in the rising tide, only to become disoriented in the dense jungle. He spent that night in a tree wrapped in his parachute to ward off the mosquitos and fired his pistol as a signal but only heard its echo deep in the darkness of the coastal swamps. The lieutenant returned to the beach at low tide in the morning, and luckily, he found his wrecked P-40. Martin only ventured inland to find fresh water that day and remained with his downed plane until the following morning when a Royal Navy launch reached his crash site and took him back to Darwin.

## HARRIS DOWN AT FOG BAY

The 8 FS flight led by Capt. Kiser which scrambled from Strauss Field had included #4 man, 2Lt. Bruce Harris, who was forced to dive away in the first contact with the 3rd Ku escorts. Determined to make use of his sound aircraft and remaining fuel, Harris set off in a climbing pursuit almost due west over Cox Peninsula and caught up with the Takao formation nearly 75 miles beyond the west shore. The pursuing Eightball pilot had reached a height 2,000 feet above the enemy formation when he crossed over their line of flight. Harris banked over in a diving attack on the trailing right flank of the last Vee in the triple chevron formation and closed in, firing on the "tail-end-charlie" until his guns jammed. Harris broke off for the

*2Lt. Bruce Harris prior to the June 13th mission.*

long flight home, but his fuel gauge indicated the P-40 would not reach Strauss Field. The landing gear collapsed as he tried to set down on the west coast of Cox Peninsula and he was forced to withdraw from the ship as the residual fuel in the fuselage tank ignited. After waiting near his burned-out Warhawk for the rest of the day, he soon realized he was further south than where he had originally thought he had crossed the shoreline. Harris cut a large piece out of his chute for a mosquito net, left a note on the wreckage for rescuers and set off north along the mud flats. The next day, Harris found the mouth of the Finis River but the broad outlet was full of crocodiles. The stranded pilot reasoned it was better to conserve his energy and stay near the sandy ocean shore. On the second day, Harris was spotted by one of the reliable Wirraway scout planes which soon returned to drop him rations and provisions, including a .45 caliber pistol to deal with the crocs. On the morning of the third day, June 19th, Flt. Lt. Pye of the RANAF landed a deHavilland Tiger Moth in the deep grass area inland of the sandy beach and picked up Harris, fit and uninjured, for an uneventful return flight to Darwin RAAF Field.

*9 FS Lt. Tommy Fowler scored a kill on June 15th.*

*Alford's replacement aircraft #52 "BLUEBEARD II."*

*"BLUEBEARD II" carried a cartoon silkworm on the starboard side to signify the pilot's induction into the parachutists' "caterpillar club."*

In the 9th Squadron, Java veteran Lt. Joe Kruzel led Yellow Flight into a distracting engagement with the ZEROs that permitted the lethal quartet of Reynolds, Sauber, Landers and Donalson to reach the bomber formations. Yellow Flight element 2Lt. Tom Fowler mortally hit his target in the exchange.

Indeed, Lt. Reynolds had brought his Blue Flight up from Livingstone Field at the alarm and after a thirty minute ascending pursuit, they caught the Takao Ku in their escape descent over Cox Peninsula. Just as Kruzel's P-40s broke off for Livingstone, Reynold's Blue team approached from a height of nearly a mile above the raider formation which was at 21,000 feet. Reynolds brought his flight down in a line attack against the last Vee of nine G4Ms above Pt. Charles and immediately set fire to the two rearmost ships before the ZEROs intervened. As the four Yanks fought for position, Landers lost the flight and dropped out for home. Donalson and Sauber kept their wing element intact and successfully countered the ZEROs by twisting through a hard diving turn. Both men fired and two enemy wingmen spiralled down toward the sea.

A turret gunner aboard one of the G4M bombers had hit Reynolds' borrowed plane, and the flight leader wisely rolled out of the contest for home. Oil and radiator coolant soon streamed down the cowling and fouled the windshield, which forced Reynolds to shut down the engine for a dead-stick landing in a clearing on central Cox Peninsula. Luckily, the plane slid to a halt in good shape, not far from the road to the Pt. Charles light house. The lieutenant radioed his location when the combatants had all departed and an RAAF lorry was able to reach him late that afternoon. The P-40 was also recovered by a lorry and returned to the 43rd Air Maintenance Unit the next day.

Only Lt. Bob McComsey from Yellow Flight had been hit in the scrap with the ZEROs and he bellied in on the artillery range west of the Track, twenty miles south of Livingstone Field while trying to reach Adelaide River Field and the 43rd AMU strip. All of the Flying Knights were safe.

So ended the June campaign over Darwin. For the next few days, additional patrols were flown in the schedule but no enemy aircraft were seen. The 49th Fighter Group quickly recovered their downed flyers and refit their damaged Warhawks while the Japanese mysteriously ceased their most successful series of raids.

## REVIEW OF THE JUNE ENGAGEMENTS

Oddly enough, the reported losses on either side did not reflect the true outcome of the fierce encounters. At such great altitudes, with the brevity of the engagements and the escape descents through the great cloud formations, most of the victory confirmations were based on conjecture. The pilots of both air forces assumed that the damage to each other was more severe than had actually been inflicted.

The 49er pilots all expressed frustration with their attempted interceptions at the extreme limit of the Warhawk's altitude capability. The Ops Execs, particularly Capt. Hennon of the 7FS, admonished the inexperienced pilots who chose to attempt individual combat with the ZERO at high altitude. All the veterans advised any pilot to use the "hit-and-run" tactic whenever possible.

*7 FS flight line at Batchelor Field. aircraft #10 with dual yellow stripes of CO Morrissey. aircraft on right is #34 (formerly #11) assigned to Lt. Steere. In the background is Portmore's #16 "ELMER."*

*C.C. Allen (left) and A.C.C. Bracewell just hours before pilot Fielder's death.*

*8 FS Crewchief Sgt. Mel Allen (rt.), with fated Lt. Art Fielder and their aircraft SISSY.*

In contrast to the thirteen ZERO kills awarded to the Group, the 3rd Kokutai records only confirm 2 planes lost on the 13th and another damaged on the 15th. Only the interception on the 15th caused any serious damage to nine of the Takao bombers, but none were lost over the Darwin target, despite the 49ers' claims of two bombers shot down on the 16th.

The Japanese exaggerated their claims over the Warhawks which had safely dived out of the numerous engagements above the harbor and peninsula. Presuming the P-40s were mortally hit, the 3rd Ku boasted forty-three destroyed, when indeed, only nine P-40s were lost in the four days of combat.

For the remainder of the month, the Group returned to the doldrums of their routine patrols and base duties in the tropical heat. The Wet season was little respite and only increased the humidity. A week after their last combat, Capt. Sims not only listed Lt. Namola as missing in action for the 8th Squadron, but was forced to preside over yet another fatal training accident investigation.

### THE DEATH OF LT. ARTHUR FIELDER; JUNE 23, 1942

While stunting in his P-40 #48 named SISSY, Lt. Art Fielder momentarily lost control of his ship when it went into a flat spin and sank toward the desert. Ground observers were certain that Fielder had regained control, for the Warhawk appeared to have pulled out, but it was far too low and struck the trees just a few miles east of Livingstone Field. Fielder's body was recovered from the burned wreckage and was interned at Adelaide River American cemetery. Sims joined crewmen Sgt. Herman Bracewell and PFC Mark Allen to drink a toast to the fallen pilot. The three men agreed that Darwin was the worst place on earth. Their squadron had lost eight men to date and it seemed they were truly the "hard luck" outfit.

Bracewell and Allen were back on the line at Strauss Field the next day and were reassigned to a new plane and pilot.

### VISITORS FROM BRISBANE

In the last week of the June, Generals Brett and Deputy Chief of Staff Richardson led a large contingent on tour of the Darwin defenses. A great ceremony was held by the 49ers at Livingstone Field during the week of the American's July 4th Independence Day and many citations, promotions and congratulations added to the esprit de corps. To Wurtsmith's surprise, Gen. Brett declared this was his farewell tour and a new man would soon be in Australia to take over the USAAF command.

The American air force in Australia would soon be charged to General George Kenney who would forever change the entire organization, and in particular, set a complete transformation of the fighter commands in the theater and affect Wurtsmith's career. Gen. Richardson confirmed that the 49ers must start making plans to gear up for the move east by the end of the month as the Australians planned to bring up a RAAF Warhawk squadron to take over the Darwin defense, tentatively by mid-August.

In the meantime, the training in the fighter squadrons was stepped up appreciably after the assessment of the combat losses in June. New pilots continued to muster into the squadrons and the veterans began a series of rigorous training flights to simulate combat as realistically as possible. One such sortie would prove disastrous for one of the Group's most accomplished combat veterans.

### SAUBER-PREDDY COLLISION; JULY 10, 1942

Shy 2Lt. John Sauber, the tenacious wingman of the 9th Squadron's Blue Flight, was leading a four-plane training flight of 2Lts. George Preddy, Clay Tice and Deems Taylor in the late afternoon over Manton Reservoir. Sauber separated the flight into two elements and instructed wingman Preddy to simulate an attack while Sauber would demonstrate the proper escape maneuver. The Warhawks split up and Preddy went to a greater altitude, but in his descent against the flight leader, the rookie misjudged their separation and the Warhawks collided. Sauber most certainly died on impact and his ship #87 broke up as it fell toward the ground. Preddy was badly injured, but miraculously was able to escape from his plunging #85, TARHEEL, and pull the ripcord of his chute. The two stricken P-40s fell west of the reservoir and crashed only 800 yards apart in the rugged forest terrain.

Tice, meanwhile, flew over descending Preddy and directed the rescue team to him within the dense forest west of the reservoir. Unconscious Preddy was found hanging in his chute harness from a eucalyptus tree and was quickly carried back to Kahlin Hospital. He had a broken right leg, right arm, and cracked ribs, but was conscious enough on the following day to recognize his squadron mates. Major Van Auken was still recuperating there and became Preddy's guardian angel during his convalescence.

After Flt Ldr Reynolds was notified of the accident back at Livingstone Field, on the following morning he gathered Landers, Donalson and Sauber's crew chief, Sgt. Harley Yates, and set off by truck to the west through the bush to find the crash sites. The

*2Lt. George Preddy and his "dragon flight" aircraft #85 "TARHEEL."*

*Another view of "TARHEEL", lost on July 10th collision with Sauber.*

four men reached the crumpled Warhawk #87 and took Sauber's body from the wreckage. The loss of the accomplished Sauber weighed especially heavy on Reynolds, Donalson and Landers. They had lost their dear friend who had proven himself in battle on more than one occasion. Sgt. Yates eventually took charge of Lt. Tice's ship #85, ELSIE, and Tice joined Reynolds' flight at Livingstone as the Flying Knights and Blue Flight soldiered on.

## THE CURIOUS ADVENTURE OF LT. VAUGHT; JULY 16, 1942

Only six days later, another combat veteran went missing from the 9th Squadron, and under the strangest circumstances. Lt. Bob Vaught had just gotten airborne in BOB'S ROBIN for a routine patrol when he realized he was not alone in the cockpit. Beneath the rudder pedals on the floor of the ROBIN lay a three foot snake that was obviously agitated by the presence of the human. After the two occupants shared a brief dance in the crowded cockpit, the snake latched onto Vaught's leg. The pilot grabbed the reptile's head, extracted its fangs from his calf muscle and threw the rascal out the open canopy. Uncertain of the potency of the venom that immediately began to tingle in his lower limb, Vaught hurriedly set his

Warhawk down near a sheep station and set off on foot for help from one of the locals. The terrain was more heavily forested than Vaught had first assumed and he eventually became lost. His leg swelled from the snake venom and he fashioned a crutch from a heavy branch to aid in his trek back to his plane.

It was not Vaught's day to negotiate with Mother Nature. He found BOB'S ROBIN surrounded by several wild water buffalo and one was scratching its rump on the rudder. Vaught cautiously climbed up into the cockpit, charged his guns and fired a burst that scared the beasts away. The day ended as Vaught crawled from the cockpit, totally exhausted. He curled up beneath the wing where he fitfully slept the night.

In the mean time, Lt. Jack Donalson returned from patrol in his #83 MAUREE, refueled and went off again in search of Vaught. Darkness soon curtailed the hunt for the missing man and Donalson returned to land at Livingstone in the twilight, but misjudged the highway for the runway. MAUREE first hit a tree in the descent, then she struck the roadway hard, broke off the left landing gear and came to rest in a cloud of dust. An ensuing engine fire destroyed MAUREE and the shaken pilot set off on foot for Livingstone Field.

The next morning, Vaught decided he would have to gamble on a takeoff from his remote landing site as his snake bitten leg had

*Lt. Sauber killed in July 10th collision.*

*Reynold's aircraft #86 "STARDUST."*

*Whimsical C.C. Al Petraitis (lt.) and Pvt. Lloyd Olsen with their aircraft #94 "BOB'S ROBIN." Flying skull is on both sides of the fuselage.*

*"Snake-bite" Bob Vaught.*

not stopped throbbing. With his makeshift crutch, he was able to manipulate the pedals of the ROBIN well enough to trim it out for takeoff. He made a tenuous return flight and once down at Livingstone Field, he was promptly sent off to Kahlin Hospital for a week's rest to allow the swelling in his bitten leg to subside. Thankfully, the entire incident had been a great humorous relief in the troubled Knights.

## VAN AUKEN, PREDDY AND VAUGHT

Of the three 49ers pilots who had taken up residence in the little dispensary, only Vaught would return to flight duty. Neither Van Auken, nor Preddy, would be able to recover from their injuries well enough to return to their respective squadrons. They were later transferred to the American medical dispensary at Coomalie and eventually sent back to the United States by year's end.

The political rift in the 7th Squadron with temperamental Capt. Prentice was partially resolved with Van Auken's departure. Col. Wurtsmith and Capt. Morrissey concurred that Prentice was a logical choice for Operations Executive and Prentice accepted the Group post effective on July 25th.

*9 FS officers – late July, 1942. Kneeling lt. to rt.; McComsey, Auvil, Taylor, Tice, Landers, Angel, Irvin, and Smith Standing lt. to rt.; CO Selman, Ball, Fowler, Oestreicher, Porter, Howk, Donaldson, Petersen, Kruezel, Sells (KIA), Reynolds, Harvey, Manning, Peaselee, Vaught*

## THE "ABO ATTACK" AT BATCHELOR FIELD

Mother Nature turned on the Allied camp at Batchelor Field, just as dangerously as she had turned on "snake bite" Vaught. Oddly enough, the infamous "abo attack" occurred on the same morning that Vaught went missing, and caused more damage to a 49ers' camp than any Japanese air raid. While the 9th Squadron lieutenant wrestled with the errant reptile and buffaloes further north, the lads of the 7th Squadron at Batchelor Field found themselves in the path of a great prairie fire. It had been set by the Aboriginals as part of the annual rite of the "wurrgeng" growing season. Fire fighters at Batchelor were ill equipped to control the wind driven brush fire and it swept into the armament supply dump, scattering the airfield personnel. The .303 and .50 caliber ammunition fired off and several men were pelted by the explosion's debris, including the crews in the breakfast chow line who were knocked flat by the blast, but no one was hurt too seriously. Thankfully, nature had run her course against the 49ers, and none too soon. A week passed and the Japanese returned.

## ANOTHER JAPANESE TACTICAL VARIATION; JULY 1942

The Takao Ku was back on the night of the 25th. Unlike the earlier night attacks, the sorties of late July ranged farther down the Track and were of substantial concern to the Yanks. Though never a direct threat to the 49ers at Strauss, Livingstone or Batchelor Fields, the crews none the less were constantly shuffling off to air raid shelters in the dead of night and the stress began to show on their faces. The RAAF attempted some abortive night interceptions with Wirraways fighter-bombers thinking their rear gunners might get a shot at the night intruders, but the RAAF failed to ever reach the altitude of the Mitsubishi formations. From the 25th through the 29th, the Takao Ku sent two sorties per night along the Track against the helpless Darwin defender.

Just after midnight on the fifth night, rambunctious 8th Squadron veteran Jim Morehead declared he had been rudely awakened for the last time. The men at Strauss Field peered from their bomb shelters to see the flaming exhausts of Morehead's Warhawk streaking down the runway. Morehead kept his canopy drawn back to afford better night vision and possibly let him hear the drone of the

*Quiet times in August at the 8 FS officers day-room.*

*Peaceful duty at the Strauss Field communications center during the August lag.*

G4M bomber formations above the Track in the moonless sky. But after circling up and down the highway, it became apparent that the one-man hunt would have to be aborted. The glowing exhausts of the Allison engine blinded his forward vision and made the search impossible.

The lieutenant turned southward and tried to find Strauss Field, but it was invisible in the dark desert. He radioed ground control to have a truck shine its lights down the Strauss runway, but clearance was denied as the air raid alert was still in effect. Growing more angry by the minute, the frustrated flyer cursed and set off south for Batchelor Field which was equipped with emergency flood lights on the main runway, but once above the RAAF strip, he was informed the alert was in effect there, too. The RAAF controller directed him to orbit until the all-clear was sounded. Morehead grudgingly trimmed out his P-40 for the duration of its fuel.

The lieutenant was cleared for landing at Batchelor just at sunrise. He quickly refueled and immediately took off for Strauss Field. CO Sims was waiting for him there, summarily congratulated Lt.

Morehead for his initiative and grounded him for a week. The lieutenant had endangered himself and his ship on the absurd, unauthorized night flight. The disciplinary action was most inopportune for the exuberant ace, for at noon that day, the Japanese returned and Morehead was consigned to watched from the flight line as the Eightballs scrambled for the pursuit to Darwin.

## THE SOLO DAYLIGHT JULY RAID; JULY 30, 1942

On July 30th, the Takao Ku sent their bombers with the dreaded escorts against the Darwin airfield and docks once again in daylight. The 49ers rallied 46 Warhawks in the scramble of which 36 made contact with the invaders over the harbor in the cloudless sky. All three squadrons of the 49ers were able to reach the bomber formation of nine Vees of three G4Ms each, while avoiding a prolonged dogfight over the target. Although the Eightballs would not claim any kills, they suffered no losses while firing upon both fighters and bombers as they passed over the harbor town. Again, the Screamin' Demons and Flying Knights would post victory claims from their pursuits west of the harbor town.

For the 7th Squadron, Lt. Ray Melikian led wingmen 2Lts. Gene Drake, Don Lee, and John Fisher of "X" Flight. Capt. Blanton led 2Lts. John Yancey, Gil Portmore and Oliver Vodrey of White Flight. A third make shift flight of 2Lt. John Posten and Ed Steere was joined by Sqn Ldr Morrissey, and was designated "Sterling White."

*7 FS C.C. Ackerman sitting on "PEGGY" (named OBEE on the left. side) above pilot Lt. Gene Drake. The other two are unknown. Drake proved his leadership on the July 30th and August 23rd interceptions, then opted for advanced training with Republic Aviation by year's end, only to vanish on a training flight over the Atlantic coast on February 11, 1943.*

*9 FS Reynolds scored his last victory on July 30th in his trusty aircraft #86 "STARDUST."*

Melikian "X" Flight was at 25,000 feet and Blanton's White Flight elements were at 27,000 when they entered into their diving head-on attacks in single file against the lead bomber Vee. The aggressive 3rd Ku did cut them off in mid-descent, and as White Flight dispersed, only 2Lt. Portmore in his #16 ELMER could handedly counter-attack an escort successfully from head-on. In the exchange, the lieutenant's right leg was grazed by a 7 mm round that ricocheted through ELMER's cockpit. Trailing Wingman Yancey was also hit when he was momentarily caught in a crossfire that riddled the aft of his ship. Blanton and Vodrey were forced to dive away at 400 mph without having fired a shot.

The 7th Squadron's part only lasted ninety seconds, but it resulted in the 49ers only loss of the day. At the onset, the "X" Flight team was barely above the bombers whose trailing elements were stacked in a downward slant to the left. Tail-end, 2Lt. Drake, had fallen behind his three wingmen, but he still chose to attack the second Vee to his right at his lower altitude. Machine gun fire from the bombers filled the sky as "X" Flight closed in from head-on, and in their return fire, Flt Ldr Melikian was certain he mortally hit his target. There would be no chance for a second pass as nine gray fighters quickly swung behind Melikian, Lee and Fisher who dove beneath the bombers that doggedly held formation as they dropped their ordnance on the docks below.

In that same instant, straggler Drake in his #27 OBEE, shoved the throttle to the limit and pressed on in his lower-level assault. As the G4M before him filled the gun sight ring, he held the trigger down on the control stick. The bomber lurched down-ward and Drake rocketed past with the ZEROs now curling toward him in hot pursuit. Recklessly, Drake swept upward in a chandelle and fired at the third Takao element Vee flight, but his aim was bad and he pulled away within a hail of tracers. OBEE shuddered as two ZEROs with guns ablaze closed the gap. Fumes filled the cockpit as the engine streamed oil and glycol down the cowling, fouling the windshield. At 12,000 feet, the fumes nearly overwhelmed the pilot and he took to his parachute. Drake landed in the shallow surf off the tip of West Point on Cox Peninsula. He waded ashore as bombs exploded in the town across the harbor and wisely stayed put until a navy motor launch picked him up later that afternoon.

Lt. Posten's "Sterling White" was the most successful Demon flight in the encounter despite having been engaged by the ZEROs from the start. The White Flight trio attacked the superior force just

*9 FS Donaldson became an ace on July 30th.*

*Lt. Johnson's aircraft had been renamed "MAYBELLE" by the time he scored his August 23rd victory. Note the new belly shackles.*

as the escorts regrouped over the bomber echelons off Cox Peninsula. Their plung from 25,000 feet out of the sun placed Posten and Steere in perfect firing position against the escorts on the left flank of the Takao formation. The escorts' turn into the descending Warhawks was too late as both Posten and Steere first fatally hit their targets from head-on, then Posten damaged yet another. Trailing Capt. Morrissey could not get his sights on the swift opponents and wisely chose retreat. With the advantage of surprise spent, Posten and Steere quickly followed the Squadron Leader in a full throttle escape for Batchelor Field.

The lethal 9th Squadron Blue Flight led by ace Reynolds had meanwhile set upon the right flank of the escorts at about the same time that the 7th Squadron's Sterling White team struck the left flank. Blue Flt Ldr Reynolds, Donalson, Landers, and Clay Tice each declared victory over an enemy fighter in a perfect hit-and-run sweep before the Japanese elements could counter-attack.

Blue Flight's diversion with the ZEROs simultaneously allowed the Flying Knights' Yellow Flight to strike the bombers. Yellow Flt Ldr Clyde Harvey closed in for a head-on pass that left a smoking bomber dropped toward the peninsula. After a brief maneuver through the swirling escorts where the flight leader heavily damaged his second target, the Knights all safely dropped away for Livingstone Field.

## A NEW ACE AT DARWIN

The experience of the 7th Squadron's rescued flyer had pointedly underscored the hit-and-run tactic preached by the veterans. Drake's foiled attempt at a second climbing pass in the vicinity of the ZEROs was in stark contrast to the pilots who prevailed in a single firing pass. Luckily for Drake, his confirmed kill offered a bit of a reprieve. With squadron mate Melikian's bomber kill, plus 9th Squadron Lt. Harvey's kill over Cox Peninsula, the exchange of one Warhawk for three enemy bombers seemed justified.

The burning aircraft that was seen falling into the harbor may well been either one of the two ZEROs awarded respectively to Screamin' Demons Posten, or one of the four confirmed for the Flying Knights. For Java veteran Jack Donalson, it was his fifth and last career kill, making him the newest ace in the Southwest Pacific theater. Big John Landers aggressiveness was cited again with an oak leaf cluster for his Silver Star.

Just as before, the great altitude where the engagements had taken place made accurate debriefings most difficult on either side. Despite the enemy's exaggerations in their victory claims, the ultimate effect was their continued failure to find the Allied fighter bases who interceptors continued to exact a heavy toll of Kokutai bomber crews. Wurtsmith's 49ers kept a substantial enemy air force occupied on the Australian western flank, denying the Imperial Empire vital air power to support its offensive in the east.

The Takao Ku reverted to their night operations once more, but they still failed to hit the 49ers bases. An early morning sortie on the 27th would send an errant Mitsubishi bomber roaring through the tree tops at Strauss Field, but it growled off to the south, it's crewmen never knowing how close they had been to their objective.

## GENERAL KENNEY AND A NEW AIR FORCE

The 49ers had held off the greater daylight raids of June and July, much to the satisfaction of Gen. MacArthur. In the first week of August, Col. Wurtsmith was again called to Brisbane by the command staff to confer on what the Colonel assumed would be details of the new assignment for his fighter group in New Guinea. For the 49ers, the move to Pt. Moresby would begin by mid August, but Squeeze Wurtsmith would only be with them in part. His command skills would take him into the higher ranks of a new American air force.

General Brett was correct in his disclosure to Wurtsmith in early July of the USAAFIA commander's impending replacement. The new man, Major General George Kenney, had arrived in Brisbane on July 29th, and as of the first week in August, was about to revolutionize the air war in Southwest Pacific. The pop-eyed Irish-American from Massachusetts was short haired, short in stature and short on ceremony. He did not care for administrative rhetoric and was appalled by the staff lackeys that crowded the Brisbane offices of MacArthur's command center. From the moment of their first conference, the new air commander promised MacArthur that he would effect changes for an all-American command. Kenney set off at once to assess his new domain.

After a whirlwind tour of bases in northern Queensland, Kenney informed the Supreme Allied Commander in Brisbane that the current air operations were untenable and summarily fired the entire command air staff, keeping only the most able men for a new organization. On August 9th, American Chief of Staff Gen. Marshall radioed from Washington D.C. the authority for Kenney to designate the new command as the 5th Air Force and for him to take charge all Allied air units in the Southwest Pacific, effective immediately. Kenney kept his headquarters in Brisbane, chose B.Gen. Enis Whitehead as his Deputy to command at the advanced base of Pt. Moresby, then chose B.Gen. Ken Walker as 5th Bomber Commander to serve at Townsville and selected Major Victor Bertrandais as his logistics expert to head the new Services Command at Townsville.

General Kenney needed a 5 AF Fighter Commander and met with Squeeze Wurtsmith after MacArthur's personal recommendation of the 49er leader. Kenney was readily impressed with Wurtsmith's ornery demeanor, and even perceived the cocky, somewhat larcenous trait that had lent to the Colonel's success in Darwin. The general promised him the staff Fighter Command with the arrival of new aircraft for his 49ers in late September. Wurtsmith's most pressing responsibility was the realignment of his group staff and he returned to Darwin, one last time, to organize the transfer of their operations to Port Moresby.

## THE ASSAULT ON PORT MORESBY; AUGUST 1942

The Japanese had continued their quest of capturing eastern New Guinea and put a large army ashore at the small village of Buna on the north side of the island as of July 21st. The Australian army under command of Gen. Sir Thomas Blamey, had already countered with forces of the 7th Division in brigade strength south of the Japanese at Milne Bay and two brigades at Port Moresby. One of the Moresby brigades attacked up the south slope of the towering Owen Stanley range along a narrow foot path called the Kokoda Trail. It was the only route through the dense jungle which linked Port Moresby to Buna on the north shore. The other brigade pushed up the coast toward the main enemy force at Buna and by the end of August, the Aussies were heavily engaged in fierce ground fighting against more than 11,000 Japanese troops on the Kokoda Trail and along the north shore of New Guinea.

The Allied air contingent of RAAF P-40s, and USAAF P-39s under command of LtC. Buzz Wagner at Pt. Moresby, were principally stationed for base defense, but the Japanese Navy's infamous Lae Wing had pressed the Allied pilots to their limits. The Allied fighter losses were not being readily replaced as only four interceptions had been flown for all of July and the 41st Squadron had already been forced to withdraw back to Townsville for rest. More air support was critical to sustain the 7th Division assault along the Kokoda Trail.

In the meantime, the U.S. Navy was moving against the Japanese in the Solomon Islands at strategic Guadalcanal. The U.S. Marines landed there on August 7th, the same day that Kenney officially took command of all Allied air forces in the Southwest Pacific. Only the sixteen B-17s of the 19 BG from Townsville could strike at Rabaul in minimal strategic support of the Americans in the Solomons.

## THE 49ERS COMMAND CHANGES HANDS; AUGUST, 1942

Some pilots and crews from the 49ers had already left Australia as replacements for the war weary 35 FG at Port Moresby buildup. Effective August 19th, Capt. Prentice was designated as the relief commander for the war-weary 39th Squadron. Wurtsmith wished him good luck with the besieged command and assured the Captain he would do everything possible to help once the new 5th Fighter Command moved to New Guinea. Thereafter, Capt. John Randolph took up the Group Operations job at Darwin as more staff changes occurred at the squadron level.

The command of the 49ers had essentially been given over to Maj. Don Hutchinson since Wurtsmith's first meeting with Gen. MacArthur in April. As Wurtsmith was occupied with a myriad of communiques from Brisbane, it was certain he would be called away at any time. Hutchinson had actually taken an overseer position while running Headquarters, Group Operations and assisting the 49er Interceptor Controllers after the loss of Ops Exec Van Auken.

After direction from the USAAF command in Washington, the 49ers formally disbanded their Headquarters Squadron on August 22nd. Major Hutchinson ask Capt. Morrissey to join the group staff as Deputy Group CO and help reassemble the 49ers' organization. Morrissey passed his Screamin' Demons command over to Capt. Hennon, while the released HQ personnel, their planes and their

*8 FS Lt. C.C. Johnson in May when his aircraft #60 was first named NIP'S NIGHTMARE.*

*April crash survivor Eisenburg flew the last interception on August 23rd in his "DOLLEYE" 2nd for the last combat mission of his career.*

equipment, were absorbed by other squadrons. The cadre members of the HQ Squadron were disappointed to see that the oldest unit of the Group, formed way back in the Selfridge era, was now to be dispersed. There was little time to reminisce for the Japanese had kept up their nightly raids over Darwin and in mid-month, they demonstrated another tactical shift.

## THE LAST DARWIN ALERT; AUGUST 23, 1942

It was ironic that the only injury to a 49er on August 23rd occurred before the interception. Lt. Larry Hansen of the 7th Squadron had been forced to bail out of his P-40 just after he had taken off from Batchelor Field for a routine morning patrol. The engine seized at 2800 feet of altitude and Hansen could not see through the oil that smeared the windscreen. He was scraped and bruised from his descent into the bush, but safely returned to Batchelor Field before the raid began.

The final interception of the 49ers was against a totally new tactic flown by the Takao bombers. The enemy reconnaissance flights had detected the location of the RAAF landing strip named Hughes Field that lay just on the east side of the Track, half way between Strauss and Livingstone Fields. An enemy formation of nine Vees of three G4Ms each, plus an equal number of ZEROs in high cover, would pass southwest of the harbor and head straight for the homes of the Flying Knights and Eightballs. The 49ers would inflict the heaviest losses on the 3rd Ku in the ensuing battle.

During the August lull in the daylight raids, the RAAF had increased the number of radio communications teams along the north shore of Cox Peninsula and their vigilance immediately paid off. The radar scanned the approach of the bombers well out to sea and provided ample warning to the Americans who met the Takao Ku 25 miles off the west coast. The 8th Squadron was first to make contact, and this time, it was with resounding success.

Capt. Kiser led 2Lts. Marlin Smith and Don Morse in a head-on run against the lead Vee of the long line of three-ship chevrons that approached Cox Peninsula at 25,000 feet. Three G4M bombers took heavy hits as the P-40s poured tracers into their ranks. Kiser's flight broke away before the escorts could descend from their high cover position. In perfect timing, the 7th Squadron fell upon the raiders while the Eight Balls plunged away.

Screamin' Demon Lt. Melikian brought his flight of 2Lts. Lee, Drake and Chapman down in the next head-on attack from nearly a thousand feet above the elongated bomber formation which was still over the Timor Sea. The Yanks raced past the lead element and chandelled up to engage the descending ZEROs who had already failed to catch the previous lightning-quick interception. Second Lt. Lee separated from his element momentarily in the ensuing dogfight, but the other three Demons held their formation and each man clobbered an enemy fighter. Melikian, Drake and Chapman immediately rolled out of the fight and safely dropped away as the next blow fell on the raiders.

The next Yankee trio was another 8th Squadron flight led by Lt. C.C. Johnson who hit the bombers just as the greater formation crossed the western shore. Johnson engaged a threatening ZERO as wingmen Rufus "Bo" Jordan and Bill Day closed in on the burning bomber on the right flank of the lead Vee. Both the G4M and ZERO were seen to drop from the enemy formation as the Eightball trio dived for safety.

Meanwhile, 7 FS Lt. Lee had regained altitude. Though separated from Capt. Melikian's flight, the lieutenant reasoned he was homeward bound on the same path as the enemy and chose to uphold the chase inland. Luckily, clouds over the peninsula obscured his approach to the scattered 3rd Ku escorts and he was able to flame a lone ZERO from dead astern.

Soon, squadron mates Lts. John Posten and Olie Vodrey hove into view as the bombers turned north over the Track and commenced their bomb runs. Lee, Posten and Vodrey joined forces and

*The cartoon characters of Axis dictators Tojo of Japan, Hitler of Germany and Mussolini of Italy on Johnson's MAYBELLE.*

*2Lt. Clay Tice scored his first victory on July 30th in his aircraft #72 named "ELSIE," as all his planes would be named.*

*Deems Taylor and his "dragon flight" aircraft #88.*

harassed the escorts all the way to Middle Arm inlet before they were forced to break off due to spent fuel and ammunition.

A third trio flight of Screamin' Demons had scrambled from Batchelor to 22,000 feet and caught the bombers as they accelerated in a shallow descent back to the northwest above the harbor. Java veteran Flt Ldr Lt. Les Johnsen, with wingmen 2Lts. Ed Steere and Fred O'Riley, pressed into the trailing Vee elements of the escaping Takao Ku where O'Riley struck one of the rotund raiders from dead astern while Johnsen and Steere fired on four others. They sustained their attacks due to a flight of 8th Squadron Warhawks which engaged the escorts directly overhead.

The dogfighting Eightballs were led by the redoubtable veteran Jim Morehead. With wingmen Kingsley and Eisenberg, they twisted through the looping ZEROs and sent three enemy fighters trailing smoke down toward the Gulf. Then the Strauss Field trio chased the others all the way to the shores of Bathurst Island before the fight subsided.

Only the 7th Squadron's Lt. O'Riley of Johnsen's flight would be forced down in the fight. He turned back from his pursuit over the Gulf, but became momentarily disoriented searching for the harbor in the growing cloud formations over the sea. He ran out of fuel just as he crossed the shore 40 miles north-east of Darwin and safely set the sputtering Warhawk down on the beach of Finke Bay. He radioed his position to the RAAF who recovered the downed P-40 by lorry the next day.

The Takao raiders had only marginal success against the Yankee air fields. Strauss Field's runway was pitted by a single bomb which caused Lt. Day a momentary distraction while dead-stick landing his P-40 with dry fuel tanks. Livingstone Field had been reached by the bombers, but only one string of ordinance fell near the runway and northern dispersal area. One explosion cratered the parking area just ten feet from Andy Reynolds' STAR DUST and showered the Warhawk with dirt. Crewchief Sgt. Elwood Barden surveyed his ship for damage and joked with the ace, informing him STARDUST could be easily repaired "with a broom." Unfortunately for the Flying Knights, none of their pilots were cleared for takeoff in the raid and they missed the last scoring opportunity in Australia.

## NO MORE BATTLES IN DREAM-TIME

The August 23rd interception had been an outstanding conclusion for the 49ers Darwin mission, considering only sixteen pilots made contact out of the thirty-six planes that went aloft at the sounding of the alarm. Just as in the previous engagements, the attacks on the bombers at the great altitudes within the clouds surely caused for

*Killer Morehead scored his seventh confirmed victory in an unnamed aircraft believed to be #51.*

*Java veteran Capt. Ben Irvin inherited the 9 FS in September, 1942, only to resign within a month's time. His "Pegasus" a.k.a. the "REBEL" would go to the front with the Flying Knights.*

*Morehead left the 49ers in late October in the New Guinea mobilization. He flew in the ETO, but never scored again.*

*8 FS Pvt. Naughton looks on as crewchief Sgt. Waln cleans the goggles for Flt Ldr Don "Porky" Morse.*

more duplications of kill claims as the 49ers crisscrossed the enemy bomber formation. Of the eight kills awarded, one each was allotted to the 7th Squadron's Drake, Vodrey and O'Riley. In the 8th Squadron, pilots Morse, Smith and Jordan also were awarded single bomber kills, while Kiser, the top ace of the Eightballs, was awarded two more.

There were just as likely duplications in claims against the widely scattered escorts as they passed over Cox Peninsula to the Track, then retreated to the north over the harbor to distant Melville Island. Of the eight ZERO kills confirmed, one each went to the 7th Squadron's Chapman, Drake, Lee and Flt Ldr Melikian, while single ZERO kills went to the 8th Squadron's Johnson, Kingsley, and ace Jim Morehead was awarded the last two victories of his combat career.

A precise accounting of the exchanges in the remote campaign for the Northwest Territory will likely never be achieved. Incomplete USAAF mission records and certain curiosities in the translation of the Japanese archives leave far too many voids for a faithful correlation. Certainly, far more Japanese casualties were suffered in the campaign than those of the Allies. As for the 49ers, what mattered most was that nine of their pilots and eleven enlisted men had paid the ultimate price in their desert stand.

For a final brief interim, the 49ers settled in for the relative calm in their wilderness dream-time world. Although Americans at home would wonder more of the exploits of the sailors and Marines who fought in the pivotal battles in the Central Pacific and Solomon Islands, or of their men who set off for the European theater, the Australians would forever remember Colonel Paul Wurtsmith and his 49th Fighter Group, the unvanquished defenders of Darwin.

# 6

# THE END OF THE 49ERS' DEFENSIVE MISSION

The Allied Command had continuously brought additional ground and air units for the defense of Darwin from the onset of the war. However, after the transfer of Gen. Brereton's bomber command to India in February, 1942, only General Herring's RAAF Hudson squadrons in the Northern Territory had remained as the last Allied offensive weapon to strike back at the Japanese forces on Ambonia, Timor and Java in the grim Australian winter campaign of 1942. Few Aussie units were available to sway the direction of the battle on the western flank of the Allies' Southwest Pacific defense, and those few RAAF crews served with great distinction. On several occasions, the 49ers had provided safe in-bound escort over Beagle Gulf to the brave, battle weary RAAF Hudson bomber crews of No. 2 and No. 13 Squadron who returned from sorties flown to the far reaches of the Timor Sea area.

By mid-year, the RAAF had recovered some of their veterans from the fighting in North Africa, and as promised to the Darwin defenders, the veteran Aussies soon arrived to take up duties in their northern homeland. On August 19th, Sqn Ldr Dick Cresswell and his 77 Squadron arrived at Batchelor Field as the first RAAF "Kittyhawk" unit to relieve the 49ers. Though not assigned to interceptions or patrols until the first week of September, 49er Operations Exec Capt. Randolph began to alter the 49er schedule accordingly. Capt. Hennon and his 7th Squadron were advised to pre-

*Java veteran Flt Ldr Joe Kruzel in his aircraft #80 "BICKY" with wingmen Landers in new aircraft #81, Deems Taylor in #88, and Reynolds in #86.*

pare for deployment to the east immediately, while Cresswell's people slowly took over the Screamin' Demon facilities at Batchelor.

The RAAF relief pilots effected great changes for all the Americans and particularly for the Philippines-Java veterans of the USAAF. As more patrol duties were assumed by the Aussies, the veteran Yanks were eventually released for Stateside duty in the last week of August. Some of the Yankee pilots showed signs of stress after nearly seven months of continuous flight duty.

It was now the "gurrung" season when the coastal prairies were swept by hot dry winds and the swallows soared on the rising thermals high above the parched bush of the Northern Territory. Flt Ldr Nate Blanton dripped a torrent of sweat in the hot fumes inside the cockpit of his P-40 #13, PHILIPPINES OR BUST, which reverberated in idle on the taxi way to the main Batchelor strip. The propeller ticked over slowly while he waited for takeoff clearance to lead the next routine patrol over the Gulf. Only minutes before, Capt. Hennon had informed the 7th Squadron veteran that his name had appeared on the home transfer list. Now strapped into his Warhawk and prepared to go on yet another mission, the weight of CO's remark struck Blanton consciously for the first time. He was

hot, on the brink of total exhaustion and actually had not comprehended the good news of his orders for home. Blanton hurriedly radioed the Batchelor Field controller to signal his standby pilot, then unhooked his seat straps, locked the brakes and walked away from the P-40 with the engine still running. By mid-September, Blanton and many of the other veterans had caught flights from Darwin for Brisbane, and eventually, took berths on the first troopships bound for America.

For the 49ers who remained, the unit would undergo yet another transformation in the great confusion of the move to Port Moresby. MacArthur's counteroffensive was already being fought on the southern slopes of the Owen Stanley Mountains of eastern New Guinea. LtC. Hutchinson's fighter group would again be scattered across the Outback in their mobilization to eastern front.

## THE FIRST 49ERS FOR NEW GUINEA; SEPTEMBER, 1942

On September 5th, 5th Air Force Fighter Commander designate Paul Wurtsmith took his S-2 intelligence man, Capt. Moore, Flight Surgeon Capt. George Greaser, chief radio specialist Sgt. Ed Frink and clerk Cpl. Tom Lyle to Port Moresby in order to set up his command center in the tiny harbor village. The Colonel and his small staff reported to B.Gen. Whitehead at 5 AF advanced head-

*Below: Strauss Field dispersal area on stand-by for the New Guinea mobilization as of early September. First aircraft to the right is Bo Jordan's #62 "SARAH 2nd."*

*Flying Knights in the September publicity formation over Livingstone Field.*

quarters and began to plan for the distribution of the American squadrons that would soon move into the newly constructed bases in the Moresby area. Six airfields had been hacked out of the mountainous jungle terrain that surrounded the tiny peninsula where the port town and harbor lay. Dirt roads twisted through the ravines and gulches to the strips, and just as in Darwin, the mileage to each gave them their names. Down the coast, just south of the harbor was Kila Drome (3 Mile), named after the nearby native village. Inland up the steep winding track past Ward Drome (4 Mile) and Jackson Drome (7 Mile), were Berry Drome (12 Mile) and Durand Drome (14 Mile) which lay north of the great Waigani swamps. Three miles beyond lay Schwimmer Drome (17 Mile). All the proper names honored Allied heroes of the earlier Port Moresby defense.

## THE 7th SQUADRON LEAVES FOR MORESBY; SEPTEMBER 1942

Capt. Bill Hennon was to bring the first air echelon of the 7th Fighter Squadron into the New Guinea offensive at 14 Mile Strip, but the Demons' aircraft had to be refitted in Australia before they were flown into combat. On September 7th, all Screamin' Demon pilots with their P-40s, and forty crewmen on board RAAF transports, flew east for Townsville Airfield. Some ground echelon followed by truck and rail.

All 8th Squadron pilots were to deliver their planes to Townsville as well, but until space could be made available at one of the Port Moresby fields, the most sound Eightball aircraft would be turned over to the 7th Squadron. Capt. Eck Sims took the first Eightball air echelon to Townsville on September 24th as Sqn Ldr "Bluey" Truscott brought up his RAAF 76 Squadron Kittyhawks to take over at Strauss Field. Meanwhile, the remaining enlisted men at Batchelor and Strauss Fields had already crated their camp equipment for portage aboard the Java battle survivor U.S.A.T. *Seawitch* at Port Darwin.

On September 8th, the 49th Fighter Controllers had already broken camp at Jungle Jump and essentially had become an independent unit. After detached service in eastern Australia, the Controllers would eventually reach Milne Bay, and later Oro Bay in January, 1943.

The 9th FS was designated for the task of staying in Darwin as a quasi-operational training squadron and host to the newly arrived RAAF 77 Squadron pilots who would fly as attached elements on the routine patrols. The Flying Knights were shocked at Capt. Selman's announcement of his promotion and temporary reassignment to Brisbane headquarters on the 20th. Capt. "Bitchin'" Ben Irvin would lead the Knights to Port Moresby, but in the interim, the squadron would languish in Australia for many weeks before they could return to combat. The Flying Knights were about to be cast into a very difficult transition period that would effectively remove them from the strategic operations flown by the 7th and 8th squadrons in the growing New Guinea offensive.

*Flt Ldr Jordan with the 8 FS September 4th flight roster and typical scramble intervals for Green Flight at 5 minutes and Yellow flight at 15 minutes.*

## HUTCHINSON'S FIRST TACTICAL FIGHTER SQUADRON

At the maintenance center at Townsville airdrome, Allied aircrews hurriedly refit the Warhawks that were judged combat worthy for the 700 mile ferry flight to Port Moresby. A few of the Warhawks had been refit at Batchelor Field, but the 75 gallon long-range belly tanks were a priority item only available for the demanding logistics in New Guinea. At Townsville, there was equipment available to rig all of the 49ers aircraft. Once the fuselage plumbing and belly shackles were installed, the P-40s were capable of carrying either a belly tanks or a 500-pound bomb and pilots were given rudimentary instructions in glide and dive-bombing techniques.

On September 11th, the first 7th Squadron pilots ventured north for New Guinea. Leaving Townsville, they staged to Cairns and then to Iron Range. If available, transports or bombers would lead them over the sea to Port Moresby. More often, fighter pilots had to dead-reckon for the Papuan coast alone. Of all the P-40 flights along this route, only one 49er was destined to fail the September crossing.

*8 FS Flt Ldr Robb, one of many able Darwin cadre pilots who never fired at an enemy aircraft.*

*Farewell figure-8 formation of Strauss Field P-40s at the September citations ceremony.*

*RAAF 77 Sqn joined the Darwin defense with new issue P-40M aircraft, an export version of the short-fuselage K-model which would reach the 7 FS at Pt. Moresby in October.*

*Gen. Blamey's farewell address at Batchelor Field.*

## THE DEATH OF LT. HAZARD; SEPTEMBER 11, 1942

Three months had passed since Lt. Bob Hazard's takeoff accident which had resulted in the death of General George. Hazard's combat career was over due to his broken spirit, but the urgent need for ferry pilots forced him back into the air and the flight surgeons deemed the sullen lieutenant fit for limited flight duty. On the 11th, Hazard was in the flight that had left Cairns, but he soon reported engine trouble and turned back. Hazard made radio contact with the Cairns flight controller, but his Warhawk never reached the RAAF strip. A search of the coastline of Princess Charlotte Bay found no trace of the unlucky aviator. The tragic life of Bob Hazard had come to an end, and with great remorse, LtC. Hutchinson notified the missing pilot's family of their loss.

On September 14th, newly promoted Major Morrissey and Screamin' Demons CO Hennon led twelve P-40s to 14 Mile Field. Five days later, the 7th Squadron was hitting targets in the hills just a few miles east of their new home.

Meanwhile to the west, the old stager Warhawks of the 8th and 9th Squadrons continued to roll up more flight hours, but time took a toll of several ships en route to Townsville. On the 24th, Lt. Earl Kingsley sadly abandoned #42 EDIE, the ship that was named for his girl in the States and had vindicated him against three enemy planes over Darwin. EDIE blew a tire on takeoff at Daly Waters, dug in a wingtip and split open her belly tank which splashed gasoline up through the cockpit floor. The fuel doused Kingsley cleaned himself up, returned to Strauss Field and nursed another oil spewing Warhawk into Townsville. Kingsley complained to the Eightball CO of his suspect mount, but Capt. Sims coaxed him into flying the rough running machine up to 14 Mile. The lieutenant landed in New Guinea without incident.

The flying echelon at Livingstone Field soldiered on in the daily patrols with 77 Squadron. On September 8th, Lt. Clyde Harvey bellied in his shark-mouthed #92 on the runway for the loss of his third ship and the dubious distinction of setting the crash record for the Yankee pilots of Darwin. The bent P-40 was commandeered by

*9 FS Lt. Harvey's shark aircraft #92 was adopted by 77 Sqn following its safe belly-landing on September 8th.*

*9 FS Lt. Vaught's old stager #94 "BOB'S ROBIN" was scrapped out for parts at Townsville, Q.T.*

the able Aussies who eventually put it back in service, still displaying its lucky shark smile. Old #92 was the 9th Squadron's last emergency landing at Livingstone.

Capt. Irvin's pilots soon became restless in the September doldrums and were afforded a brief diversion when "Bitchin' Ben" ordered all the 9th Squadron ships up on September 14th for an aerial publicity photo of the famous Flying Knights. An RAAF Oxford twin-engine transport took a film crew up to scan the line abreast formation of Yankee pilots and even a few 8th Squadron ships sneaked up for the publicity shot.

An evening raid on the 26th by a small enemy formation caused some concern when bombs fell near Livingstone, but there was no damage. The Japanese had again taken to raiding the RAAF strips nearer Darwin and there were no daylight raids. The Flying Knights relinquished more of their patrol schedule to the RAAF and on the 28th, Darwin's defense was officially returned to the Australian command. The proud Knights were now temporarily attached to the RAAF, but Capt. Ben Irvin approached his grumbling veterans with a new plan that had been passed down by the 5 AF staff.

## THE POLITICS OF KENNEY'S NEW AIR FORCE

In the third week of September, LtC. Hutchinson was informed by General Kenney that new aircraft were designated for the 49th Fighter Group, but that his squadrons would not all receive replacement Warhawks in New Guinea. Colonel Wurtsmith was likewise informed that the new order of battle for the 5th Fighter Command would include a substantial number of new generation fighter airplanes due for delivery to Townsville airdrome in October. Kenney had successfully won the favor of the Chiefs of Staff in Washington

to supply his Southwest Pacific theater fighter groups with the revolutionary Lockheed P-38 Lightning, a twin-engined, heavily armed fighter of phenomenal range and 400 knot speed. Each Group commander was to select one of his squadrons to reassemble at Townsville and take intense training in the new Lockheed ships at the earliest possible date. Colonel Wurtsmith and Major Hutchinson

*9 FS Lt. Bill Levitan and his shark aircraft #73 "THE LITTLE VIRGIN."*

*9 FS Lt. Larry Smith's aircraft #91 at Livingstone was the only "shark" to reach the New Guinea front and was left in the P-40 pool at 4 Mile Field at Pt. Moresby. Smith continued in the P-38 era.*

*7 FS new bivouac at 14 Mile Field.*

agreed that Capt. Ben Irvin and the high scoring veterans of the 9th Squadron already in Australia would be the logical choice for the P-38 program in the high scoring 49th Group.

However, the new directive caught the Flying Knights at a most difficult crossroad in their manpower logistics. Several of their most senior flight leaders were ready to return to America and no one begrudged any veteran who had completed his tour and opted for the next voyage home. The more aggressive pilots of similar rank willing to carry on the fight found it was difficult to be chosen as the "right man for the right command." The situation had arisen that not all of the senior flyers were eligible for the P-38 pilot program at Townsville. There were very few Warhawk assignments in the sister squadrons and virtually no chance for promotions in rank.

To further add to Capt. Irvin's problem, when the orders came on October 8th for his air and ground echelons to move up, those crews not assigned to the Lockheed school at Townsville were directed to take their gear to Port Darwin and board the Dutch transport SS Van Heutz. The logistical rift infuriated "Bitchin' Ben" and when his name appeared on the list for home on the 15th, he resigned in protest. Capt. Irvin joined Ops Exec Randolph, and veteran pilots Ben Brown, Jack Donalson and Andy Reynolds on the next troop ship at Brisbane bound for the States. Now that Major Selman had gone to 5 AF staff, the disheveled 9th Squadron was passed to the next senior captain, Jesse Peaslee, who honorably administered to the closing of the operations at Livingstone Field

and at the same time inherited the critical staffing problems at Townsville.

## DARWIN; A PLACE OF HONOR

The three airfields south of the harbor had been a Yankee community for nearly seven months and the sacrifices of the Americans there were forever honored by the Australians who permanently adopted the names of Livingstone and Strauss for those respective landing areas. America also venerated the 49ers with the first Presidential Distinguished Unit Citation to be awarded to an American combat unit in the Southwest Pacific. As cited in the document, the 49th Fighter Group had established an exemplary record "made possible by the determined courage, the uniform high morale and the technical ability of the group as a whole." The unit could boast 76 confirmed aerial victories and only four pilots lost in combat. They were indeed the pride of the service and Colonel Paul Wurtsmith considered them his first team of 5th Fighter Command. Regardless of the current dispersal of their squadron personnel and the 9th Squadron's administration deadlock, Wurtsmith assured Gen. Kenney that LtC. Don Hutchinson was an able, admired commander who would bring the honored unit back into full operations at Port Moresby in October.

*Fighter Control at Port Moresby.*

*Crews at the open air showers of 3 Mile camp.*

## THE VOYAGE OF THE *SEAWITCH* AND *VAN HEUTZ*

While the first pilots and air echelons were in transit through Queensland to the steaming jungle airdrome in New Guinea, the ground echelons of the 7th and 8th Squadrons were forced to endure the miserable conditions on board the troop carrier *Seawitch* off the north coast of Australia. The *Seawitch* bore the majority of the two squadrons' enlisted ground personnel who huddled together on the crowded deck as they embarked from Port Darwin on September 24th. They sailed 800 miles in five days through the Arafura Sea, but the crowded harbor at Port Moresby would not receive the *Seawitch*. She anchored off Thursday Island at the tip of Cape York, and after being confined aboard the stinking little freighter for two nights, the men went ashore to share the enlisted mess with their Australian island hosts, including the island's entire stock of beer. Much to the garrison commander's relief, the beer guzzling Yanks were ordered to cross over the Coral Sea to Moresby on October 9th, and the 7th Squadron organization immediately began their bivouac at 14 Mile Field. The 8th Squadron personnel began to set up camp at 3 Mile Field in preparation for CO Eck Sims to bring up the air echelon contingent by the end of the month.

As the *Seawitch* passengers disembarked in Moresby on the 30th, the SS *Van Heutz* set off from Darwin harbor, just as crowded as the *Seawitch* had been. The "Hoots" carried Lt. Carl Zeeuw in charge of the last of 49ers to leave Darwin, including the 9th Squadron ground echelon, their camp gear, forty-four men of the 445th Ordnance Company and a barge in tow that carried a huge cache of ammunition.

The men aboard suffered in the stifling tropical heat for over two weeks along the same route as the *Seawitch*, but not all on board would find relief at Port Moresby. The 445th Ordnance Company and four trucks were unloaded at the Moresby docks, only to have the unit disbanded and the majority of its personnel reassigned to other units in the Moresby area. And the Flying Knights voyage was not yet over. The 5 AF staff ordered the 9 FS contingent on the next day to continue aboard the "Hoots", with ammo barge in tow, back up the coast thirty miles to the newest Allied base near the village of Rorona.

In the meantime, the 9th air echelon at Darwin, by truck and by RAAF air transport, followed their pilots with the last P-40s to

*Below: New 5 AF 3 Mile airdrome overlooking the 3 AG A-20 dispersal area. The 8 FS bivouac was in the foothills out of view to the right.*

*An unidentified 7 FS pilot kneels before Flt Ldr Chapman's old Darwin stager #25 "PATRICIA ANN" at 14 Mile. Just above the exhaust stubs is the stencilled sobriquet "CHIP CHAPMAN'S CHARGIN CHUMPS."*

Townsville. The Warhawks were added to the pool of planes to be refit and held in reserve for 5th Fighter Command.

As of October 15th, the 49ers operations consisted of the 7th Squadron flying missions from 14 Mile in New Guinea, the 8th Squadron flying shuttle service from Townsville, and the 9th Squadron pilots and crews awaiting new P-38s at Townsville while their ground echelon set up camp at Rorona.

Group Commander Don "Fighter Hutch" Hutchinson finally arrived in Port Moresby with his group staff on the 15th and reported to his old group commander, Paul Wurtsmith, who introduced him to his field general, Enis Whitehead. After the formalities, the burly 5 AF Deputy Commander asked the weary, diminutive 49er commander if he needed anything special after his arrival in New Guinea. Hutch smiled at Squeeze Wurtsmith, turned back to Whitehead and responded, "General, just keep my boys out of the brig and we'll beat these damn Japs."

*Lt. to rt.: 9 FS Capt. Taylor, Lt. Poleschuk, Capt. Petersen, Lt. Landers and engineering chief Lt. Hollier wait at Townsville in late September, 1942.*

*Collapsed left gear of 8 FS old stager #51 at 3 Mile.*

Whitehead flashed his famous broad grin and knew he had the right man in the right place. "Well, Hutch, that's all I needed to hear."

## THE NEW GUINEA OFFENSIVE; 1942

Lieutenant Colonel Don Hutchinson said good-bye to his 5 AF commanders, and with a three-man infantry escort, he and his Deputy Major Powell, and new Operations Executive Major Bill Redding, set off in a pair of jeeps up the ascending mountain track. Hutch was anxious to find his 7th Squadron pilots and crews who had been in combat since mid-September. He was also duly concerned about establishing a central command post for his scattered fighter group, but in this primitive setting, their reorganizing would not come about for several weeks.

The jeeps sped along as fast as possible through the heavily forested foothills, following signs and the directions of Australian military police. They passed the construction site of 5 Mile Strip where crews were cutting away the forest and grading a narrow, mile-long runway.

They pressed on for nearly 30 minutes, waiting for numerous Army Engineer road gangs, squeezing beneath rocky overhangs

and the negotiation of some very narrow wooden bridges. They passed an immense swamp and the Durand Field ammo dump, then drove through the forested dispersal area before entering the clearing that displayed 14 Mile Strip, the home of the Screamin' Demons.

Hutchinson found the operations tent and 7 FS CO Bill Hennon. It was a wonderful reunion after their scrambled Australia mobilization. Following a glass of "G.I. lemonade" laced with Aussie bootleg gin, the Java veteran brought Hutchinson up to date of the past month of combat flights over the Owen Stanley Mountains.

## BLOODSHED ON THE KOKODA TRAIL

As of their prior arrival on September 19th, Hennon's Screamin' Demons had flown a grueling schedule of fighter-bomber support missions to the Australians. There had been vicious fighting along the Kokoda Trail since the first land force engagement that had begun in July.

The Maroubra Force, a combined group of Australian and Papuan native infantry, was assembled under the New Guinea area command of Australian Gen. Rowell. The Marouba Force had advanced from Port Moresby on foot over 60 miles up the roller coaster

*Left: Prop specialist Sgt. Charlie Bell whose wizardry kept flight-weary P-40E's airworthy at 3 Mile field. Right: 9 FS line chief M/Sgt. Fred Beech who simultaneously oversaw the operations at Rorona, Townsville and 4 Mile fields.*

*14 Mile shower al fresco of the 7 FS.*

mountain track, the "golden staircase" of bamboo steps wide enough for one trooper at a time, to occupy Kokoda village at the crest of the pass. The Japanese attack lead by Colonel Yokoyama on July 7th dislodged the Allied force out of Kokoda village. The village again was taken by the Marouba Force on August 8th with a reinforcement battalion of the 7th Division lead by Gen. Allen. But Yokoyama retook Kokoda a second time with the massive reinforcements from Gen. Horii's South Sea force that arrived via Rabaul on August 26th. In a bloody rear action Allied retreat southward over the Trail, Yokoyama's 12,000 man army fought to Imita Ridge by mid-September, only 30 miles east of Port Moresby. MacArthur was furious with the failure of the rearguard action and approached PM Curtin and Supreme Australian Commander Blamey with the demand that Gen. Rowell be replaced. A great political rift grew within the Allied command, but the American general prevailed and Gen. Herring of the North Territory was called in to replace Rowell. The defenders at Imita Ridge held.

At this point in the campaign, the 7 FS joined the battle, flying bombing and strafing sorties only minutes from their jungle airstrip in support of the regrouping Allied army. In a second counterattack by Allen's 7th Division reinforced with American troops, the Aussies finally repulsed the threat at Imita Ridge on September 26th. Another counteroffensive further east by two other 7th Div. battalions at Milne Bay forced the enemy's complete withdrawal from the southern slopes of the range by month's end. The com-

bined American, Australian and Papuan armies immediately chased the retreating Japanese to a second fierce confrontation on the north slope of the Owen Stanley Mountains. The fighting was restricted to small arms and hand-to-hand combat on the bamboo steps of the Kokoda Trail. Col. Yokoyama withdrew along the mountain track to the north slope village of Wairopi on the Kumusi River.

At Wairopi, Col. Yokoyama set up a staunch rear guard defense that covered the Trail fifteen miles back up the mountain to Eora Creek. At its 7000 foot elevation, the Japanese line held the Allied force at bay in the narrow canyon while Gen. Horii attempted to further fortify his major force at Buna on the coast.

General Allen was given the task of reaching Wairopi in early October while Gen. MacArthur rallied a second flanking attack on Kapa Kapa Trail south of the Kokoda track and a third attack south of Buna at Pongani Mission. The three Allied forces would converge on the northern shore at Buna, hopefully by the first week of November.

Without heavy artillery, the Aussie forces on the Kokoda Trail faltered at Eora Creek and stalled MacArthur's offensive. After Herring and Blamey consulted with Gen. Whitehead of the 5 AF, the Deputy Commander agreed to make the P-40s of Capt. Bill Hennon's 7th Squadron into Herring's personal mobile artillery. In the ensuing October assault, the Screamin' Demons sent eight ship flights, three times a day, to glide bomb down the slopes of the mountains against targets between Eora Creek and the Kumusi River.

*Refit P-40E with an plain white star on its fuselage on the 8 FS alert line at 3 Mile.*

*Refit 7 FS aircraft "IRENE" on the alert line at 14 Mile.*

*3 AG A-20s roll out past 8 FS Warhawks at 3 Mile.*

The Warhawk pilots had developed a murderous efficiency with their new tactics and soon were dropping 500 pounders over the heads of Aussie infantry patrols who directed the American fighter-bombers against the Japanese fortified positions. MacArthur also pressed the Demon Warhawks to cover his Pongani forces, divebombing gun emplacements and flying high escort for 5th BC medium bombers that struck the Buna forces.

Hennon's men flew multiple sorties every day and he expressed his anxiety for the great combat burden that was being borne on the oldest wings in the 5th Fighter Command inventory. His squadron crew chiefs worked around the clock to ensure his pilots would keep up the rigorous flight schedule, but the old model E fighters could not last much longer. The flak put up by the Japanese was light but accurate, and many of the P-40s returned with holes in them. Hennon also considered his squadron lucky that the Japanese had not offered any aerial opposition.

Hutchinson passed on Gen. Kenney's promise that the 7th Squadron held priority for receipt of new Warhawks due at any moment. As for Hennon, it would no longer be his problem, as Hutchinson informed the Java veteran ace that his tour had come to an end. As of October 20th, he was ordered to relinquish command of the 7th Squadron and return to the States on the next available flight. Hennon at first protested, but he was not vehement. Anxious

*New P-40K delivered to 14 Mile and assigned to senior Lt. A.T. House. aircraft became #13 "POOPEY II."*

to return home after a year at war, the weary fighter pilot ace left 14 mile before the end of the month.

As for the leadership of the 7th Squadron, there was no one immediately available of command rank who could take Hennon's place at 14 Mile Field. Major Morrissey was in the Port Moresby hospital being treated for malaria and Hutchinson was reluctant to give up the capable staff leadership of either Majors Powell or Reddington. A new man yet unassigned, senior Capt. Bill Martin, came forward from Fighter Command and was immediately effective in taking over the 7th Squadron. The Demon pilots and crews carried on their duties without the slightest sign of concern for such politics.

Finally on October 28th, the Eora Creek line was broken and the 7th Division brought its full weight down the Trail against Kokoda village. Gen. Horii was drowned at Wairopi while trying to raft his men down the Kumusi River to the coast, but the main body of his troops succeeded in their withdrawal from the Trail for their final bloody defense of Buna.

*9 FS flight line at Rorona Field with well traveled aircraft #84, s.n.42-5170, flown by Fowler, then Blachly and finally 33 PS survivor Oestreicher. The next aircraft carries a black panther on its rudder that signifies a plane flown by a former 17 PS veteran, but the man is not identified. Both #84 and "the panther" would be handed over to the Screamin' Demons where the latter was last seen at 14 Mile strip in mid-October, then numbered #14 and named "SPARE PARTS." The panther was retained.*

## NEW PLANES IN NEW GUINEA; OCTOBER, 1942

General George Kenney made good his word when the new aircraft he had promised were delivered by the 49ers ferry pilots from Townsville. On the 24th, eight new P-40K-5 model Warhawks turned into the landing pattern over 14 Mile and wheeled to a halt on the dispersal area near the 7 FS operations shack. The P-40K was essentially an upgraded version of the earlier model P40-E and differed most in a supercharged Allison powerplant that gave higher power at lower altitude. Physically, the outline of the ship differed by the addition of a fillet added to the leading edge of the tailfin and a slightly broader rudder to accommodate the increased torque of the extra horsepower. Just as with their first P-40s, these new ships were from British contract production blocks and some were camouflaged in sand-and-olive drab amongst the standard USAAF olive drab and gray.

Although the new K ships would not meet the demands of the 49er pilots for a better high altitude interceptor, the lifting power for their tactical role was greatly improved. The Ks were immediately commandeered by the senior pilots and pressed into the flight schedule. For the missions against the toughest ground targets, the squadron's armament chief, M/Sgt. Ed Currie, found the K was fully capable of hefting a 1000 pounder off the runway and his section successfully rigged three 300 pounders, one under each wing and the third on the belly rack. The engineers advised that operational limits of maximums loads be made up of a single 500 pound bomb, or only a pair of 300 pounders and a belly tank, but regardless of those restrictions, the Demons' tactical punch per plane was nearly doubled.

The Demons' operations and facilities at 14 Mile Strip became much more crowded when another unit moved in across the runway. Major George Prentice was back, but this time as commander of the 39 FS, and he brought in twelve new Lockheed P-38s which were assigned to the north end of the field. Ground control became a real headache for tower operators who now directed Warhawks taking off from the south against the Lightnings departing from the north.

More pilots reported at 14 Mile in late October and many had numerous hours of flight time in the P-40s from training in the U.S. during the first months of the war. A small contingent arrived from Hawaii and some had even been airborne the day of the Pearl Harbor raid. The pilots were sarcastically dubbed the "Pineapple Boys" and there arose some spirited jibes between the Darwin veterans

*14 Mile Field "pilots hut" alert shack near the runway.*

and the newcomers, but these replacement pilots soon mixed in with the daily operations of the group and demonstrated their high proficiency in the mission formations.

As the squadron rosters grew, the commands changed as well. Horn Island veteran Capt. Wil Chapman was now the 7 FS Ops Exec and found the new senior lieutenant, Frank Nichols, to be a sharp character and appointed him as his assistant. There were also some former 9th Squadron men who were now posted to 14 Mile roster, in particular the ornery redhead, Capt. George Manning, who had opted out of the strained politics which had arisen in the 9 FS at Townsville. Capt. Manning would eventually usurp the Operations slot from Lt. Nichols when Chapman transferred home in early November.

## NEW PLANES AND BAD POLITICS IN TOWNSVILLE; OCTOBER, 1942

Kenney's P-38s had also arrived in Northern Australia for the Flying Knights, but the resultant hassle that erupted in the 9th Squadron sent shock waves all the way to Squeeze Wurtsmith's Fighter Command headquarters. Sixteen new Lockheed fighters arrived under the guise of the 17th Fighter Squadron (Provisional), much to the consternation of the last 17 PS Java veterans at Townsville

*8 FS refit P-40E with a 500 pounder about to sortie into the Papuan hills.*

*9 FS Warhawks moved into 4 Mile Field. The front aircraft is Tice's "ELSIE." The next aircraft #83 last flown by Capt. Taylor (after McComsey first flew it as #71).*

*Jacketed 9 FS Capts. Petersen and Taylor meet newcomer Lightning pilot Carl Planck at Townsville.*

*Lt. Bill Day and #43 "JERRY" (the first) at 3 Mile.*

awaiting their next combat assignment. Furthermore, the P-38 Lightnings were replete with permanent pilots and those aviators were attached to the 9 FS, swelling the Knights flight roster to nearly 60 pilots. The net result left the majority of Capt. Jesse Peaselee's flyers without aircraft, and he immediately appealed to Wurtsmith to find combat assignments for his senior officers in any available slot in 5 FC. For the month of October, 9th Squadron men languished in Townsville, not knowing if they would go back into combat, nor in what type of aircraft they would fly.

As for the Lightnings, after initial inspection at the Townsville maintenance center, the 9 FS ships were judged not to be combat ready. They would have to go through a complete workup, including the installation of rubber self-sealing tanks in the leading edges of the wings. There were also additional refinements to be made with the radio equipment and the gun camera systems in the tips of the fuselage nose were found to be susceptible to corrosion.

Five of the big fighters were flown to Rorona by month's end to make room at crowded Townsville airdrome. The rubber tanks and modifications were effected by the Rorona line crews, but each plane requiring four men and a minimum of three days labor. Ninth CO Peaselee was stunned to learn that the highly touted P-38s would not be ready for another six weeks. There were more defections by the impatient Flying Knights to the other units in New Guinea. For those qualified Lightning pilots, their combat career would begin in temporary duty assignment to Major Prentiss' 39 FS whose P-38s were already combat modified.

## THE AIR RAIDS AGAINST LAE; NOVEMBER, 1942

The ferocity of the 5 AF offensive in support of MacArthur and Blamey's combined land assaults was devastating to the enemy forces pinned down at Buna. On November 1st, Allen's advanced battalion took Kokoda village while the Japanese command at Rabaul was desperately trying to reinforce their embattled armies at Buna and further east at Guadalcanal. The Imperial Navy air groups at Rabaul's Lakunai airdrome were hopelessly committed to air support in both campaigns. The famous ZERO Tainan Kokutai that had recorded so many kills in the Philippines, the Celebes and the Port Moresby offensive, were now operating under worsening conditions. The once victorious Kokutai now suffered irreplaceable losses on the long range escort missions against either Port Moresby, or the Solomon Islands, while many of their ground crews in New Britain and New Guinea fell ill with malaria, scurvy or dengue fever. Taking advantage of the minimal interventions of the enemy air force, Gen. Whitehead sent strikes against the Lae airfield complex in an attempt to establish Allied air supremacy over the New Guinea front in the beginning of November.

## THE EIGHTBALLS ENTER THE FRAY

Due to the intensified air offensive, Capt. Eck Sims was ordered to bring his squadron up to the front by the end of October. Hutchinson was initially hesitant to permit Sims an extended tour, owing to the 8th Squadron CO being the oldest flying officer by several years in the 49ers ranks. But Sims was a consummate squadron commander and his leadership in New Guinea was sorely needed. The captain agreed to take his unit to Port Moresby, and to cease flying combat.

The old E model Warhawks of the 8th Squadron were overhauled once more, and since the arrival of new K ships for the 7 FS, the Demons' old planes were transferred over to the 8 FS who took up residence at 3 Mile Strip. Since the 3rd Attack Group also operated from the strip and had need of the dispersal area for their larger

*39 FS aircraft of Flt Ldr Capt. King at 14 Mile Field in early October.*

twin-engine A-20 Havocs, the refitted Warhawks were dispersed along the inland side of the runway that ran parallel to the coastline. The 8 FS bivouac was inland to the south, overlooking the sea and the runway which was surrounded by rolling hills and dense brush. The Darwin veteran flight leaders began patrolling above the Moresby area on the 25th.

The Eightballs flew their first escort mission on October 29th as high cover for the Demons and the medium bomber strikes that initiated Gen. Whitehead's offensive against the three airstrips which surrounded Lae village. Two days later, eight Eightballs flew cover above fourteen 3rd AG A-20s and met the first aerial opposition against the 49th Fighter Group in New Guinea. The P-40 pilots soon learned that the diminished Japanese Navy Air Force was still a lethal adversary.

## FIRST AIR COMBAT AT LAE; NOVEMBER 1, 1942

Darwin veteran Lt. Dick Dennis, senior Flight Leader for the escort mission on November 1st, led eight Warhawks in the their takeoff from 3 Mile in the morning twilight, before the sun rose above the mountains. Dennis and fellow flight leader Lt. Bruce Harris, formed up their quartets with the A-20 Havocs over the harbor and the twenty-two ship strike force set a northerly course for the 200 mile hour long overland flight to Lae. The clouds in the morning humidity had already built up to 18,000 feet and the shadows on the mountains were a deep emerald green. They broke out over the Huon

Gulf just south of Salamaua and looked north toward their objective.

The glistening landmark river delta of the Markham Valley appeared on the hazy northern horizon. The A-20s, modified with forward firing machine guns for low-level assault, dropped down to make their wild strafing runs over the main runway of Lae Airdrome, which ran north to south on the east bank of the river delta. Mission leader Dennis spread his Warhawks apart to provide the largest possible coverage. Dennis, still keeping Harris' men in sight, took the Eightballs inland in a wide sweep over the area until the last Havoc signalled its withdrawal from the airfield target. The Eightball flights momentarily separated in the billowing cumulus and Dennis called his Warhawks to regroup for their return to Moresby.

## FIRST LOSS IN NEW GUINEA; LT. GLENN WOHFFORD

By 0745 hours, Flt Ldr Dennis, with wingman Bill Day, element leader Ross Baker and rookie Glenn Wohfford, had egressed south only ten miles from the target and were still separated from Harris' flight in the towering cumulus when Dennis' quartet was "bounced" from the rear by eight Lae-based ZEROs. The four Eightballs dropped their belly tanks and rolled into the enemy, then dove to gain enough speed for a climbing counter-attack. As Dennis and Day swept upward, trailing Baker and Wohfford were forced to continue down and away by the wheeling ZEROs. Baker looked

*7 FS McHale and "GERRY" about to go on patrol.*

*8 FS Warhawk lifts off from 3 Mile past a burning A-20.*

back to see Wohfford's smoking P-40 plunging toward the jungle with two enemy fighters close behind.

At the odds of four-to-one, the Eightball Flight Leader and his wingman turned hard several times into the ZEROS until Dennis was able to hit a victim which snap rolled and fell away in an inverted spin. Then Day hammered a Mitsubishi from head-on which fell in flames, but the odds against them were still too high. Separated and low on fuel, the American stragglers broke off the fight and dropped away for Port Moresby. Seven Warhawks landed at 3 Mile strip where Day inspected three 7mm bullet holes in the rear fuselage of his #43, JERRY. Since there was no internal damage, water-proof tape was secured over JERRY's bullet holes so that Day could sortie again that afternoon. The Eightballs found neither the ZEROS, nor any trace of fallen Glenn Wohfford.

## BRAVE SERGEANTS OF 3 MILE; THE EVENING OF NOVEMBER 1ST

Although several ensuing flights continued to search for Wohfford throughout the day, CO Eck Sims was forced to post the downed pilot as missing in action that evening. Wohfford was the squadron's first man to fall in this great island wilderness, but the hardened Eightball veterans could not anguish long for the newcomer. At 6:00 o'clock, word came down to the 3 Mile flight line that a B-25, badly damaged in combat over Lae, was coming in for an emergency landing with bomber pilot and co-pilot both wounded and the sergeant crew chief at the controls. The surrogate pilot bravely risked the landing, but lost control of the crippled bomber in the stiff cross winds on the runway.

Eightball Sgt. Harley Wisehart was inspecting one of the Warhawks at the strip when the bomber crashed. Wisehart valiantly rushed to the broken bomber and helped pull survivors from the flaming wreckage. After the debris was hauled aside, the Eightball sergeant wearily returned to his duties, for maintenance on the old E Warhawks had become an ongoing nightmare. The next escort missions to Lae were posted for the very next morning.

## THE FIRST P-38 ESCORTS OF THE 5 AF; NOVEMBER 2, 1942

On the 2nd, more strikes were sent against enemy supply ships at Buna and the airdrome at Lae. However, the mission was of marginal success, as eight Lightnings of the 39 FS and eleven Screamin' Demon P-40s in escort of nine RAAF Beaufighters, searched for a purported convoy, but no enemy ships were found. The Allied force instead returned to strafe the Buna garrison.

That afternoon, ten B-26 Marauders escorted by sixteen Eightballs, were intercepted by ten Tainan ZEROS south of Lae and in the brief skirmish, shots were exchanged but no 49ers claimed any hits on the nimble grey fighters. Upon return to 3 Mile, the old stager Warhawk flown by Lt. Bryant Wesley had its engine seize up in the landing pattern and the lieutenant put the sputtering Warhawk down in the shallows of Bootless Bay, just south of the strip. Wesley swam ashore as the P-40 sank out of sight, and was picked up minutes later in a jeep driven by Sqn CO Sims who was directed to the location by attentive wingman Bill Day. The CO broke out a bottle

*Newcomer Lt. Bob McHale and his aircraft #12 "GERRY."*

of whiskey and the three pilots toasted the successful recovery of the drenched man, then drove back up the coast road for home.

## LT. BROWNNELL DIES AT KOKODA STRIP; NOVEMBER 8, 1942

As the Warhawk missions continued to range over the north coast, the flak that rose up from Buna soon proved as deadly as the fighters from Lae. On the 8th, newcomer Lt. Nelson Brownnell of the 8th Squadron had his P-40E heavily damaged by the AA at Buna and could not rise above the mountains to return to 3 Mile Field. At Kokoda village, the Aussies had cut a 3000 foot runway out of the forested hillside for smaller liaison craft. Brownnell tried to reach the strip, but his engine gave out east of Kokoda and the Warhawk crashed. Natives pulled the dead airman from the wreckage and turned the body over to the Australians. Brownnell was interred at Port Moresby a week later.

The next day, rookie 2Lt. Bob Howard failed to get enough power out of #61, the Warhawk he had borrowed from veteran Bill Day for the morning mission. Only minutes from 3 Mile, #61 seized up and Howard attempted an emergency belly landing on the tiny supply flight strip on the southern slope near the village of Myola. The fighter slid off the wet runway and slammed into the undergrowth. He emerged from the wreck with minor abrasions and was soon found by an Aussie patrol who escorted him back down the Trail to the Port Moresby dispensary. Howard was on flight duty at 3 Mile two days later when he expressed his regrets to Day for the loss of the new plane. The men became fast friends as Day held no hard feelings, and besides, the veteran had already been issued another ship. He aptly named it #43, JERRY 2nd.

While the 7th and 8th fought on, on November 16th, the 9th Squadron moved the last of their old Warhawks to Rorona and also increased the count of Lightnings there to ten. The 17th Provisional was officially disbanded and those flight officers were permanently assigned to the 9th Squadron roster, even though they would fly in the 39 FS mission schedule. Meanwhile, the crews of line chief M/Sgt. Bob Oestreich worked around the clock on the Lockheeds and Curtiss fighters while senior Warhawk pilots began to temporarily stage south to the newly completed 4 Mile Field to top off their tanks and begin escort missions in Major Reddington's group operations.

On the 17th, Hutchinson had all three of his Warhawk squadrons in the air in New Guinea for the first time. The 9th Squadron flew its first mission in New Guinea escorting C-47 transports to a new advanced strip just north of Pongani without incident. However, when the Flying Knights returned to the south coast, Lts. Floyd Finberg and Bill Hanning flew past the Pt. Moresby complex in the heavy overcast and both P-40s were lost after the two men bellied in 60 miles down the coast at Point Hood. The pilots were unhurt and Finberg spent the night in a coastal native village before returning to Moresby by RAN launch the next day. Hanning was separated in the heavy forest from his wingman and after reaching an inland Australian outpost, he returned to Rorona five days later.

On the 17th, the 7th and 8th Squadrons also flew escort once more over Lae. On the early morning flight, only Flt Ldr Ray Melikian in his new P-40K gained advantage against one of the eight ZEROs that rose up in the interception. The quarry escaped into the heavy cloud cover south of Lae airfield, and all sixteen Demon Warhawks returned safely to 14 Mile Field.

## LOSSES RISE IN THE 8 FS; NOVEMBER 18, 1943

The next day, the 8th Squadron's mid-day mission was uneventful, but their late afternoon scramble for an interception over Buna nearly ended in disaster. Eight Warhawks lifted off from muddy 3 Mile, and slipped beneath heavy overcast to reach the north coast, but the enemy planes had long departed. On their return flight, two more P-40Es were lost to mechanical failure. Lt. Bernard Makowski was forced to attempt a landing at tiny Kokoda strip after his Allison engine had burned out in his return ascent over the mountains. Unlike deceased Brownnell who had failed a similar emergency landing there only ten days before, Makowski's P-40 reached the narrow dirt runway. Sadly for "Mak", the rains that day had made it impossible for the hefty Warhawk to stop on the short muddy strip and the fighter slid off the end of the strip, crashing into the trees. Australian commandos pulled the injured pilot from the twisted wreckage.

Several minutes later on the south side of the peaks, Lt. Bill McConnell's overheating engine seized in his descent for 3 Mile's coastal strip. He tried to set down at 4 Mile Field which was still under construction, but the smoking Warhawk dropped onto the rugged terrain north of the runway. Badly injured, McConnell was quickly rescued and taken to the Port Moresby hospital. Capt. Sims wrote off two more old stagers, but more importantly, he had lost two valuable men for several weeks due to their crash injuries. The Eightball CO pressed Group Ops Exec Reddington for more replacement Warhawks and the Major was forced to commandeer ships from the beleaguered 9th Squadron. The Flying Knight's new CO hardly needed the added pressure.

## WRETCHED RORONA AND CPL. BRADLEY'S SUICIDE

Ninth Squadron CO Jesse Peaselee and his Rorona team had come up against another hardship in New Guinea, equally as dangerous as the enemy on the north side of the Owen Stanley range. Rorona

*Newcomer 8 FS 2Lts. Blakely, Bellow, Drier and Key at the 3 Mile camp.*

airdrome took its named from the gorgeous waterfall and is plunging river which eventually spread out into an immense swamp on the coastal plain that was now flooded by the November monsoons. The resultant hatch of malarial infected mosquitoes which rose from the swamp swarmed the Flying Knights. Flight Surgeon Jacque Ahronheim declared the base unfit for service as a multitude of line personnel reported to his dispensary with high fevers and blinding headaches.

Unfortunately, there would be no immediate respite for the bug besieged men of Rorona. Peaselee and Ahronheim scrounged the entire theater for more netting, quinine, attabrine and sulfa while waiting for the availability of the new bivouac down south at 4 Mile Field. After six weeks, the horrendous conditions finally took its toll of despondent Cpl. Alvin Bradley. His tent mates found him in his quarters on December 11th, dead of a self inflicted gun shot to the head. Peaselee was visibly shaken and he again pleaded for a speedy evacuation from the hell at 30 Mile airdrome.

## BUNA AND LAE; NOVEMBER, 1942

The Imperial Fleet supreme commander, Adm. Yamamoto, attempted a daring dual campaign to defeat the Allied armies in both the Solomon Islands and New Guinea in mid-November, but neither Allied force would collapse. The impending disaster at Buna would be due in part to the JNAF loss of air superiority in the eastern New Guinea theater.

The Australian 7th Division on the central Kokoda Trail had pushed to within 35 miles of the coast, while MacArthur's southern force pushed in closer from Pongani. By November 15th, the Australian brigades with 7 FS and 8 FS close air support, crossed the Kumusi River. Next, the brigades ran headlong into the fortifications of the last line of the Japanese defenses 15 miles from the coast and for two weeks, the Aussies battered the enemy all the way back to the coastal village of Gona, just north of Buna. An all out last ditch stand by the Imperial army stopped the Allied advance there. The month long assaults against Buna had cost the Aussie battalion over 1400 dead and wounded, but their sacrifice underscored their determination that this campaign was to be the death knell of Japan's conquest for New Guinea and the Southwest Pacific.

# 7

# DARING COMMANDERS
## OF 5 AF

**D**ue south of Buna, roughly half way to Pongani and ten miles inland, lay the newly captured village of Dobodura on the north bank of the rocky stream called the Samboga River. North of Dobodura laid an immense flatland covered with five foot high kunai grass. The broad plain had long been coveted by the 5 AF planners as their next strategic landing area and would soon become the most important advanced base in the New Guinea campaign. Once the area was secured by the advancing American infantry, C-47 transports began to land near both Pongani and Dobodura with supplies for MacArthur's army.

Until more of the superior Lockheed P-38s were available, the 5 AF missions would be flown by the Moresby based P-40s whose operations were hampered by the 13,000 foot spine of the Owen Stanley Range and subsequent descent to distant Lae. The P-40s had to be based much closer to Lae to be more effective tactically, as well as open the Port Moresby air strips for bomber aircraft. The plain adjacent to Dobodura was the answer to the logistics dilemma.

From his Fighter Command HQ at newly completed 17 Mile Field, Squeeze Wurtsmith summoned 49er CO Hutchinson in the early morning hours of November 21st. Squeeze told him to bring a sidearm and overnight gear, so Hutch left the Group administration to Deputy Powell, not knowing when he might return. Later that morning, Squeeze, Hutch and a jeep were loaded on a C-47 to be delivered after an hour's flight to the kunai stubbled landing strip at Dobodura. The colonels, their gear and jeep were unloaded,

*Late December, 1942, at Dobodura Airfield looking N-NE down the main runway which became known as Horanda Strip. The opening in the forest to the right is the entry point to the Flying Knights dispersal area. The dispersal for the Screamin' Demons and Eightballs P-40s is far to the left off the photo, but the rough emergency landing strip adjacent to the steel-matted Kalamazoo strip is plainly seen.*

*8 FS aircraft #51 pranged again at 3 Mile. A bent prop meant a complete engine replacement and three days of labor for a three-man flight crew.*

*Lutton revs up the Allison in the pre-flight check. Lutton flew #46 and named her "LADY JANE," but the old girl gave out in an aborted lift-off in late December and was scrapped out at 3 Mile. Four month's later, Lutton transferred to the new Lightning group, became a successful flight leader and scored five aerial victories in his P-38.*

and after being assured the way was clear of enemy patrols, the two men drove north across the broad grassy plain.

Hutchinson drove and Wurtsmith sat atop the windshield to ensure the way through the deep kunai was void of ravines. They drove northeast to southwest, and when the odometer ticked off a mile travelled, they stuck long stakes topped with white flags in the kunai field to mark the distance. Next they drove northwest to mark the next mile in the same manner. The designated landing zone, looking like an inverted "T", proved to span nearly a square mile of virtually flat savannah.

Back at Dobodura village that afternoon, Col. Wurtsmith instructed the Corps of Engineers to immediately begin preparation of the landing field marked by the stakes. In only a few days, heavy trucks and scrapers cut and dragged two rudimentary landing strips. The main 5500 foot runway lay northeast to southwest, and the other 4500 foot perpendicular strip lay southeast to northwest. By the end of December, the engineers began to set perforated steel matting upon the shorter strip and a bamboo control tower was erected at the north-east corner of the runway intersection. The 78th Squadron signal corps quickly established air traffic control for the increased transport landings and the many types of Allied aircraft that staged there in the continuing offensive against Lae.

Changes also quickly took place within the 49er's leadership by late December. LtC. Don Hutchinson's unique ability to orga-

nize and administrate the myriad functions of a headquarters was an asset that Wurtsmith was unable to do without. Wurtsmith acquired approval from Gen. Whitehead to take Hutchinson as 5FC Chief of Staff. Major Bob Morrissey had recovered from his malaria bout and replaced Group Adjutant Powell who had transferred home to the States before Christmas. Morrissey logically inherited command of the group and then directed the 49ers' HQ in its move to the larger building at 17 Mile to operate in closer proximity to Wurtsmith's 5 FC center.

Until Dobodura's strip was completed, all 5th AF fighter sorties would stage to Wurtsmith's command center at 17 Mile Field on the preceding day of a given mission. Likewise, the 7 FS at 14 Mile, the 8 FS at 3 Mile, and the 9 FS temporarily at 4 Mile, would each keep two flights of aircraft on alert for Port Moresby's defense.

## DEATH OF LT. DITTLER; NOVEMBER 22, 1942

The Screamin' Demons had been incredibly lucky with such a high mission count and no airborne challenges. Their good fortune ended on November 22nd when the Lae Wing mustered the largest fighter force to engage the American units since the November build-up. Poor weather held down both air forces until mid-afternoon when a

*8 FS newcomer Lt. Lowell Lutton "saddling-up" in C.C. Bill Bean's old stager at 3 Mile.*

*Aircraft #40 bellied in at Dobodura after a routine patrol in late December. The attrition rate of the old aircraft was critical for 8 FS CO Sims sincearrival of new Warhawks was still six months away for the Eightballs.*

*Senior Lt. Sid Woods and his aircraft #74 "ARIZONA" before the 9 FS left for New Guinea.*

*Woods and his crewmen with their aircraft before the New Guinea mobilization.*

flight of eighteen ZEROs, likely from the 252 Kokutai struck the Allied troops and their new airfield on the kunai plains above Pongani. They would be met by fifteen Warhawks of the 7th Squadron, and twelve Airacobras of the 41st Squadron.

Seventh Sqn Ldr Bill Martin had once again brought up his Warhawks to provide egress cover for a bomber strike force in retreat from Lae. At 1710 hours, Martin's squadron passed over the north point of Cape Ward Hunt at 15,000 feet and the elements spread out in their search for the returning A-20s and Beaufighters in the dense cumulus clouds.

Suddenly, eight of the 252nd Ku who had stayed together above the heavy clouds, swept down and hit Lt. Paul Slocum's flight. In seconds, ZEROs, Warhawks and Airacobras fought for advantage within the billowing cumulus. Both of the opposing flights separated as the wingmen struggled to keep their elements intact, but losses soon occurred for the enemy and the Screamin' Demons alike.

Flight Ldr Slocum was already short a man when Lt. Hood failed to take off at 14 Mile. The leader tried to hold his trio intact, but the ferocity of the 252nd Ku attack soon forced the Americans apart. Element Lts. Baker and Quivilan lost contact and withdrew from the match.

Immediately, Lt. Frank Nichols' flight of four P-40s swept into the fray, soon followed by the circling attack of Capt. Martin's quartet on the rear of the Kokutai formation. A brief, ferocious dogfight exploded north of Buna in a roar of mind dimming maneuvers and gunfire.

The duo of Flt Ldr Don Dittler and wingman Lt. Ken Johns was cut off from the other elements, and as Johns safely evaded the ZEROs, he last saw his leader under attack by two other enemy planes.

Immediately, the Demons retaliated by claiming three destroyed. Capt. Martin and element leader Lt. Carl Aubrey succeeded in outflanking two ZEROs and the Demon pair chased them down into a cloud where the Japs escaped and the Yanks became separated. Nichols and wingman Lacroix then chased a pair of ZEROs and Lacroix flamed his target before it dropped out of sight. Flight Ldr Irv Voorhees and wingman Slocum both flamed an enemy fighter and turned back for another pass, but the fight abruptly ended. Capt. Martin recalled the Demons as darkness fell.

At home, Lt. Lacroix cracked up on landing his battle damaged ship, but was unhurt. Lts. Dittler and Don Sutliff failed to answer the call. After search flights the next day, both men were posted as missing. Word came three days later from a missionary on the north slope of Sutliff's fate, but Dittler was gone without a trace.

## LT. SUTLIFF IN THE BUSH 21 DAYS

Second Lt. Don Sutliff had gotten the best of one ZERO, and was about to send its pilot to meet his ancestors, when a 20mm round from an enemy wingman badly damaged his Warhawk. After elud-

*RAAF Lockheed Hudson bombers from Pt. Moresby often escorted by the 49ers.*

*RAAF Airspeed Oxford V.I.P. liaison aircraft commandeered by the Allied command likewise escorted by 49ers throughout eastern Papua.*

*Left: 9 FS regrouped at new 14 Mile camp in late December. Capt. Peterson (lt.) converses with pipe smoker Woods while Tice surveys the crowd. Landers relax with the USAAF newspapers while newcomer Dick Bong sits quietly behind him. Right: 14 Mile pilots enliven as the bar opens.*

ing his assailant in the clouds, the lieutenant tried to nurse the crippled P-40 over the mountain range, but he had to bail out of the smoking ship before reaching the crest of the mountains. He dropped into a high swampland just north of the Kokoda Trail. Safely aground, he was aghast to find someone apparently prior to this fateful sortie had taken most of the essentials from the survival pouch attached to his chute pack.

With only a quart bag of water, a mosquito head net and a compass, Sutliff reasoned he was not far from Wairope village and knew he must reach the main trail. The lieutenant set off to the east through the tangle of the jungle swamp and after two arduous days of sparse water rations and green bananas, the exhausted pilot crossed a track that led him to a village of friendly Papuans. After a meal and brief rest, the flyer set off on foot for another six days, but only traversed an estimated eight miles. Once he reached the Mobare River, he took a canoe and finally reached a Dutch missionary camp near Wairope. Racked with a high fever and overexposure, the lieutenant stayed in the care of the mission people for more than a week until an Australian patrol could return him to Pongani for transport to Port Moresby hospital.

As if fate would spite the men at 14 Mile, misfortune befell the Demons again on the 23rd. Sqn Ldr Martin led a twelve plane sweep over Buna at midday, but met no aerial opposition and instead brought them down against coastal ground targets. Light flak perforated Martin's radiator and the engine quickly overheated which forced the Squadron CO down on a small kunai field about five miles due east of Popondetta village. After three days in the jungle,

natives led the flyer to an Australian patrol and Martin returned by air transport from Dobodura to 14 Mile in good health. In Martin's absence, senior Lt. Frank Nichols took the initiative and temporarily assumed command while continuing to fly missions. The Flying Knight transferee, Capt. Red Manning, administered to Operations and the Screamin' Demons never missed a beat.

As for the 8th and 9th Squadrons, on November 22nd, the haggard Eightballs would fly three missions without incident while a Flying Knight would be temporarily lost to the mechanical failure of yet another old model P-40E fighter. After an uneventful morning sweep over Buna, Lt. Ralph Wire tried to return in his faltering ship, but bailed out of his smoking stager short of the Moresby area. The lieutenant came to rest on a high plateau near the top of the Owen Stanley range just east of Myola village. Wire had supplies dropped to him by a passing transport and was eventually able to walk down to the Kokoda Trail two days later. Australians took him to the transport strip at Kokoda village and he flew back to 4 Mile Field after his fifth day of absence.

### ROOKIES OVER LAE: NOVEMBER 26, 1942

The 8th Squadron recouped a brief vendetta on the 26th when a sortie to Lae resulted in victories without loss against the veteran JNAF wing. Darwin veterans Lts. Bruce Harris and Earl Kingsley led newcomers Lt. Warren Blakely and 2Lt. John Porteous in the combined Eightballs and Flying Knights fighter sweep sent against

*Rookie 2Lt. Harry Dillworth in mid-December crack-up of Flt Ldr Melikian's new P-40K. 7 FS used fuselage bands in 1942-43 era to designate leaders, evidenced by the slanted blue stripe on "SWING IT," plus an array of ever popular Vargas girls adopted from a G.I. calendar or Esquire magazine.*

*Booze and bucks bring (lt. to rt.) Frank Nutter, Pete Alger, an unidentified pilot, Jimmie Harris, Stan Johnson and another unknown to the 14 Mile craps table.*

*Able Darwin cadre Flt Ldr Earl Kingsley.*

*8 FS Java veteran Capt. Docksteder, Ops Exec in the early 3 Mile campaign.*

the Lae airdrome that morning. As they orbited west of the airdrome, the heavy clouds obstructed a clear view of the target and Flt Ldr Harris in #66, THE SCARLET RECTUM, decided to take his able rookies down to 8000 feet for a closer look. Eight ZEROS crossed their path just west of the Markham River delta and in a headlong, wild "rat race," the Warhawks circled down and around until they were chasing them at tree top level.

The Yankee pursuers became the pursuees as the combatants tightened up the line of chase. Kinglsey was in the lead and was chased by a ZERO that was followed by Harris, who was likewise chased by a second ZERO which was followed by Blakely. The snakelike formation of five combatants twisted about through the forested valleys for several seconds until at long last, Kingsley's superior speed took him out of the ZERO's gun range.

Flt Ldr Harris continued the chase of the lead ZEKE into a steep walled canyon and when it rose up to avoid the slope, the SCARLET RECTUM unleashed an accurate volley of .50 caliber tracers which set the Mitsubishi ablaze, and thoroughly discouraged the remaining Ku wingman. Harris' pursuer tried to break out

of the rat race, but at such a low altitude, the ZERO's superior maneuverability was negated. Blakely quickly closed the gap in his old stager #40, and at point blank range, he touched off a .50 caliber barrage that shattered the grey fighter. Flaming debris from the two disintegrating targets scattered over the green forested slopes. Second Lt. Porteous, meanwhile, had chandelled up to initiate his own engagement and finally won advantage over an opponent. The rookie "second louie", now joined by Kingsley, peeled off after a lone Mitsubishi. Both Yanks opened fire and followed the smoking ZERO down toward the clouds until it dropped out of sight.

At the same time, Harris had swung back up to find the remaining enemy fighters were attempting to draw the Warhawks into a second low altitude chase. Harris was "annoyed by such stupidity" and swooped down to destroy his second ZERO victim. The remaining enemy pilots chose to break off for good and the victorious Eightball quartet chased them until they crossed the river delta. Harris wisely chose not to chance the deadly AA batteries at Lae drome and turned his flight southward.

After a safe landing at 3 Mile Field and a few rounds of G.I. lemonade with Major Sims, the men sorted out the victory claims in the Eightball tag game above Lae that day. Harris was confirmed with his two kills, rookie Blakely with one kill and another as a probable, while Kingsley and rookie Porteous accepted a "half kill" apiece due to the confusion over who really hit the smoking ZERO that dove into the clouds. After another lemonade, all happily agreed the dogfight had been an extraordinary initiation of the two beaming newcomers.

## LOSS OF BURNETT; NOVEMBER 26, 1942

The garrison at Buna held MacArthur's troop advances in the western and southern assaults to a bloody crawl in the waning days of November. The 49ers continued their exhaustive pace of sweeps and bombing strikes. The 7th Squadron hammered away at the reinforced gun emplacements that flanked the embattled garrison vil-

*Senior 8 FS element leader Harold "Bud" Learned and C.C. Whitehead days before the lieutenant's only victory, November 30, 1942.*

lage, but the Demons paid the horrendous price of three pilots lost in four days. On the 26th, 2Lt. Dean Burnett had only been in camp at 14 Mile three days and drew the #4 position in his first flight. The rookie pilot never made it through the murderous flak corridor over the target and his Warhawk exploded in a ball of fire when it slammed down on the shore north of the enemy held village. The blast scattered the debris into the bay and Burnett's remains were forever lost.

## LOSSES OF JOHNSON AND VOORHEES; NOVEMBER 30, 1942

In the late morning hours of the 30th, a strong ZERO force swept over the shrinking Buna garrison in a broad air attack on the Allied lines, just as the 49ers approached from the south. Mission Ldr Lt. Frank Nichols had sixteen Screamin' Demon P-40s in high cover to a dozen dive bombing Eightballs. When the lower flights signalled they were under attack west of Buna village, the Demons wheeled northward.

At an altitude of 8,000 feet, Green Flt Ldr Carl Aubrey, wingman Irv Voorhees, element leader Don Lee and wingman John Johnson searched among the billowing clouds, but the elements fatally drifted apart. Both Demon pairs were caught from behind by a flight of descending ZEROs. Wingmen Voorhees and Johnson were both shot down south of Buna, and their element leaders would have been next if not for the intervention of Nichols' Red Flight quartet.

Red leader Nichols, wingman Lucius LaCroix, element leader Sheldon Brinson and rookie wingman Arland Stanton were joined by Green survivor Lee and the five-ship flight re-engaged the enemy. After three passes against the twisting ZEROs, Nichols and his four wingmen each claimed a victim apiece.

A third flight of Screamin' Demons arrived late in the fracas and newcomer 2Lt. Howard Nelson claimed victory over a diving, smoking ZERO which he chased down into the clouds. As the enemy dispersed, Nichols led one last orbit of the area, then recalled the mission.

While the 7 FS attended to the business overhead, the Eightball dive-bombers had their mixed success in a very brief exchange at their lower altitude. In a turning fight beneath the overcast, newcomer Flt Ldr Ernie Harris and rookie wingman 2Lt. Bob Moose along with Darwin veteran Bruce Harris and rookie wingman Lt. Bryant Wesley maneuvered to fire at their opponents, but only 2Lt. Moose was successful. Moose separated as he chased his victim down to its crash, then wisely set off alone for Moresby.

Lt. Wesley was caught before the guns of a skilled JNAF veteran and his Warhawk was riddled by cannon and machine-gun fire. After a 20mm round exploded in the P-40's rear fuselage and schrapnel slashed his left leg, Wesley prudently rolled the stricken ship over and dropped from the cockpit. The Eightballs saw Wesley's chute canopy drift down into Big Embi Lake south of Dobodura.

Darwin veteran Lt. Harold "Bud" Learned in the lead of his flight also scored hits on a ZERO interloper, but the target vanished in the haze as the fight ended, just as quickly as it had begun. The Eightballs broke for home in a climbing ascent to clear the mountains to the west, and soon, eleven ships safely settled down on the runway at 3 Mile. CO Sims ordered search flights launched immediately to confirm the location of Wesley's parachute descent.

## WESLEY ON BIG EMBI LAKE

Wesley's wet landing in October off the south coast was nothing like his ordeal in the great swamp of Big Embi Lake after the dogfight on November 30th. His descent had put him down on marshy

*7 FS Lt. Nelson and his P-40K #38 "BLACK BOY" at 14 Mile.*

*Confident Lt. Nichols took a new model-K Warhawk, added the distinctive shark mouth which became the epitome of aggressive leadership in the 7 FS.*

*8 FS senior Flt Ldr Dick Dennis MIA on December 18th.*

*Lt. Bill Levitan scored his last victory on December 26 in Manning's old stager #70 "SCATTERBRAIN" then joined the P-38 flight school.*

ground, and after cutting strips of parachute to bandage the shrapnel wound on his leg, he set off on foot for the Samboga River. He had hoped to trek downstream to Dobodura village, but unfortunately, the lake was actually three bodies of water connected by a slimy bog. The stranded flyer was forced to wade and swim for two days before he eventually stumbled wearily into an army engineers camp south of the Dobodura airfield. The next day, the G.I.s evacuated him to the airstrip where he caught a transport flight for the Pt. Moresby field hospital on December 4th. He left New Guinea for good by month's end.

## A SALVAGE SITE NEAR DOBODURA

Natives brought word to the troops near Dobodura that they had found a crash site not far from the army camp and that they would lead the white men there. In a few days, 8 FS engineer Lt. Dick Illing was able to fly to Dobodura via transport and followed the natives to the site, which soon revealed the fate of one of the Screamin' Demons. A muddy crater on the bank of a stream and a wide array of small debris marked the spot of a cataclysmic impact. Illing searched through the debris for the invaluable rubber cush-

*More 8 FS dive-bombing missions to Papua's north coast as Buna falls.*

ions for the Allison engine mounts, but only a service .45 caliber pistol was found which had been issued to Lt. John Johnson.

As for the other Demon lost on November 30th, Irv Voorhees' wreckage was never found. After mid-December, Squadron Leader Martin found time to write letters to the families of the dead and file more acquisition requests for planes and men.

## ACCIDENTAL DEATH OF W/O RAY PEASE; DECEMBER 11 FATAL ILLNESS OF SGT. CALLOWAY; DECEMBER 14, 1942

It seemed odd that any man who had endured the strife of isolation in the jungle should fall victim to an act of fate in a more civilized climate. Yet, on the very same day they found suicide victim Bradley at Rorona, four HQ men on leave 1500 miles to the south in Australia had their trip end in a bitter tragedy.

Warrant officer Ray Pease, and S/Sgts. Francis Divine, Bill Henwicks and Francis Jansen had spent an enjoyable afternoon touring the sights in the town of Ipswitch, near Brisbane, only to have their jeep overturn. Henwicks fractured his hand and Jansen cracked several ribs, but Divine was critically injured with a skull fracture and most tragically, Pease was killed.

Three days after the traffic accident, radioman Sgt. Wilbur Calloway of the 8th Squadron died from complications of heat prostration at Kila. Hutchinson was appalled at the senseless losses of the three men, and to him, the gains of the Allies that month seemed a meager consolation.

## THE FALL OF BUNA; DECEMBER, 1942

The new 5 AF organization had borne up well in the first two months of operations in New Guinea. One of the more successful USAAF components had been the fighter units of Col. Wurtsmith's Fighter Command that continued to persevere in the three-sorties-a-day pace. The objective of aerial supremacy had now become a reality as the mission count grew with an influx of new men and planes against the diminished enemy air force. Even more impressive was the resultant buildup of fresh Allied troops and supplies that crowded the docks and barracks in northern Australia and southern New Guinea.

As for the climax at Buna, Supreme Allied Commander MacArthur moved his Southwest Pacific headquarters from Brisbane to Port Moresby in early November to bring his monumental presence to bear on his field officers and to personally see to operations. Since the Buna defenders had repelled the Allies during four murderous weeks of siege, MacArthur again sacked both Australian and American field commanders, replacing the lot with Lt. Gen. Eichelberger who would ultimately direct the execution of the enemy garrison imbedded on the north shore.

The Japanese, by the bushido code and strategic necessity, were fitfully committed to deny the north coast of New Guinea to MacArthur. Should the new Allied air force commander, Gen. Kenney, establish airfields at Buna, those bases in turn would threaten Lae and eventually put the SW Pacific Imperial HQ at Rabaul in peril. To recover the strategic losses at Milne Bay and Kokoda, area commander Lt. Gen. Imamura would attempt yet another reinforcement of the Buna stronghold. Lae would likewise be reinforced to retry for Port Moresby after the wet season, but until then, the Allied army closing in on Buna had to be stopped at once.

As Gen. Eichelberger stepped up the pressure against Buna, the Japanese sent their troop ship convoy from Rabaul in the last week of November, but the cratered garrison could not be approached beneath the patrols of Allied fighters and bombers. That convoy withdrew to download at the mouth of the Kumusi River, fifteen miles up the coast. The 5 AF would ruthlessly bring down an avalanche of steel on the delta for four consecutive days.

On December 7th, Imamura tried to intervene with additional air power for the besieged troops on the Papuan coast. A flight of G3M medium bombers (Type 96) under escort of the ZEROs from Rabaul would sortie against the Allied forces. By late morning, their formation reached the Papuan coast north of Cape Ward Hunt, then turned toward the Allied forces closing in on surrounded Buna. The 49ers would meet them, just as they reached their objective.

*49ers wondered why the fast RAAF Beaufighters needed escorts of the P-40s which could barely keep pace.*

## NAKAJIMAS AND WARHAWKS OVER BUNA; DECEMBER 7, 1942

Only airborne twenty minutes, Lt. Frank Nichols' Red Flight had just begun to orbit north of Buna at 14,000 feet in escort to the 8th Squadron dive bombers, when the Dobodura air controller relayed an Australian patrol report of a big enemy formation approaching from Lae. Nichols was instructed to hunt nearer the coast and he led wingmen Lts. Hood, Lacroix and Stanton in a northward right turn toward the sea.

After climbing 3000 feet to better survey the cloud dotted coastline, Red Flight turned about to see the raiders flying a parallel course in two line-abrest waves of nine aircraft each. Nichols continued south with his flight until they were slightly ahead of the twin-tailed bombers. The Demon leader called for the break, jettisoned his belly tank and wheeled head-on into the enemy. The four Warhawks were screened by the scattered cumulus in their turning descent and none of the ZEROs attempted to intercept them as they closed at "a mile a minute" against the lead Vee elements on the enemy's right flank. Owing that the obsolete Nakajima Type 96 was not armed with forward firing weapons, not a single defensive round was fired at the Demon quartet.

At 300 yards, the Demon leader's first volley of tracers ripped into the right engine and wing inlet of the lead ship. As they drew

*8 FS veteran Kingsley's old Darwin stager renamed "KAY THE STRAWBERRY BLOND" by rookie F/O Sammie Pierce and flown well into 1943 until turned over to Nelson Flack.*

*Watkins took "CHARLCIE JEANNE" to Pt. Moresby, but flew Donaldson's refitted P-40 in the 9 FS fight, December 26th.*

*Tent mates Walter Markey (lt.) and Dick Bong during the 39 FS era. Bong flew the P-38 better than he played his clarinet in the Knights O-club band.*

into point blank range, trusted wingman Lacroix kept an eye on the escorts who held their position 1000 feet above their twin-tailed charges. At the last second, Nichols and Lacroix rose up over the burning tan camouflaged raider, then banked hard away to the left.

Element leader Lt. Hood and wingman Stanton struck in the next instant as the formation approached the beach near Gona. Hood's gunfire set aflame the element wingman to the right of Nichol's victim. Both flaming hulks plunged into the surf north of

*Newcomer Bob McDaris joined 9 FS in Papua in late 1942, then served briefly with 7 FS, then joined the HQ combat staff in mid-1943. He later flew attached to 8 FS in 1944, the only officer to fly combat in all four squadrons of the 49ers.*

Buna as the Red Flight team regrouped over the foothills for another pass. However, after the raiders dropped their ordinance between Gona and Buna, they quickly vanished within the haze to the east. They eluded the Demons, only to fly directly into the pursuit path of the Flying Knights.

Indeed, a patrol flight of eight P-40s from the 9th Squadron had vectored north at the warning of the approaching enemy formation. Led by veteran "snake bite" Bob Vaught, they had climbed to 18,000 in their hunt and finally overtook the closely formated raiders in their descent east of Buna. Using his interception technique proven at Darwin, Vaught peeled off into a screaming dive against the trailing Vee elements. He sped down through their inaccurate defensive fire, then snapped upward in a climbing attack on the belly of the G3M raiders. He fired at two bombers, then closed in on the straggler wingman as the .50 caliber explosive rounds flash against the silver underside of the slender fuselage. He was unable to repeat the assault as the now alerted ZEROs chased him away.

Veteran element leader Lt. Bill Levitan and rookie 2Lt. Duncan Myers also used the flight leader's assault technique and they too fired on the bombers before the escorts intervened. Both Flying Knights avoided their pursuers, but Levitan exceeded maximum velocity in his dive for the safety of the clouds and flipped into a violent spin. He was badly shaken in the cockpit of his tumbling Warhawk before he regained control far below. Unable to contact his flight, Levitan cautiously crossed the mountains, then skirted northward beyond the weather front covering the south coast and landed safely at Rorona.

## FIRES AT SEA

The Screamin' Demons victims, destroyed before they had reached their objective, sent columns of oily smoke from the sea just north of Buna. The bombers claimed further off shore by Flying Knights Vaught, Myers and Levitan were also confirmed, and it seemed an appropriate underscore for that first Pearl Harbor Day anniversary. Ultimately, the scheme had been far too little and too late for the hapless Imperial troops at Buna, and their battered reinforcements stranded on the Kumusi River delta.

*Landers' "TEXAS LONGHORN" based at Rorona field, but only flown a few times on patrols and never in combat.*

On the 10th, the Australians overran Gona. On the 14th, Gen. Imamura ordered the evacuation of the Buna village garrison northward up the coast to link up with the Kumusi reinforcements, but the 800 stranded, bloodied survivors there had already reboarded their barges in the night and escaped to land still further north at Mambare Bay that same day. In the truest bushido tradition, the remaining rear guard stood in defiance on the shores between Sananda and Gona in a ghastly fight to the death. Finally, General Eichelberger's troops secured the Buna coastline on January 2, 1943. Nearly 12,000 dead and wounded Imperial men had been lost in the jungles and on the shores of New Guinea in the span of the five months.

Following the successful mission on December 7th, the 49ers did not meet aerial opposition over the battle front for ten straight days, even though they kept up their routine of ground assaults and standing patrols. The USAAF and RAAF again combined forces in another strike to Lae on December 18th to seek out the enemy air force. The infamous Lae wing proved it was still very deadly.

### THE LOSS OF LT. DENNIS; DECEMBER 18, 1942

As the Beaufighters and A-20s roughed up the Lae airdrome, twelve Eightballs flew in high cover over the target area. As the fighter-bombers withdrew, another rain front began to close in over the Markham River delta which masked the approach of the defending ZEROs. They swept out of the mist in one firing pass and none of the Americans could bring their guns to bare. The Eightball elements separated and escaped in flights of ones and twos, except for the mission leader.

Indeed, veteran Dick Dennis never returned to 3 Mile. No one saw his ship go down, nor heard a distress signal. Dennis had most

certainly been killed instantly in the sudden attack, and the loss of the beloved cadre officer was a staggering blow to the entire Eightball outfit.

### THE VETERANS OF RABAUL; DECEMBER 1942

Despite the loss of valuable flight leaders such as Dick Dennis, there were many young men newly arrived from America to take his place. As of that first anniversary of the war, new men and equipment had forever swayed the odds in favor of the Allied cause.

In contrast, the Japanese Navy Air Force suffered crippling losses with dismal reinforcements for the crumbling front of Gen. Imamura's Southeastern Area. The losses at Milne Bay, Buna, and Guadalcanal sapped the Imperial forces far beyond Imamura's command. And much to the chagrin of the Japanese Navy command, their beleaguered wing at Rabaul would have to be relieved by Army air units taken from the fronts in China and Malaya.

Beginning in late December, Japanese Army Air Force fighters and bombers ferried through Indochina and the Philippines, or through the atoll stronghold of Truk, eventually to reside at the growing airfield complex surrounding Rabaul. For the time being, the JAAF command settled in the headquarters garrison of Vunakanau Field.

### NEW ENEMY IDENTIFICATION SYSTEMS

Accordingly, the Allied intelligence community became aware of the many different types of enemy aircraft that soon appeared in recon photos, but combat crew reports listed all radial engine fighters as "ZEROs" and all heavy bombers as "TE" for twin engine.

*9 FS Lightnings temporarily at Rorona, mid-December, 1942.*

Col. Frank McCoy, a Georgia native on Gen. MacArthur's S-2 intelligence staff, cleverly adopted a southern tradition of giving simple, short nicknames for the wide variety of Japanese planes to ease the confusion of the pilots and crews in the Pacific theater. Normally, boys names were given to the fighter types and girls names were used for bomber or reconnaissance types.

The new system renamed the navy ZERO to "ZEKE" and dubbed its clipped wing version, "HAMP." The army single engine cousin, the Ki-43, became the "OSCAR." The more common Navy heavy bomber seen in the Southwest was the rotund cigar-shaped G4M which became "BETTY" in S-2 parlance and the large twin engine army cousin became "SALLY." The JNAF fixed gear single-engine Aichi dive-bomber likewise became the "VAL." By early 1943, though not always consistent, use of the nicknames became a standard practice for Allied flyers.

### OSCARS AT LAE; DECEMBER, 1942

The first JAAF fighter unit to arrive in New Britain was the famous 11th Sentai that had gained great honor in the early campaigns in China, and more recently in Burma and Sumatra. The illustrious unit was considered by the Imperial Staff to be the most capable fighter sentai (group) in service, and was therefore designated as one of the first army groups to take the new generation Nakajima Ki-43, an all metal fighter, into combat.

Although not as heavily armed as the ZERO, the Ki-43 OSCAR was perhaps the most maneuverable fighter aircraft in the world. The formidable 11th Sentai, with their lightning bolt unit marking emblazoned on the tails of their ships, soon joined the ZERO units at Rabaul in the escort of bombers and ship convoys that ventured out against the Allies in the Solomon Islands and New Guinea. By month's end, the Sentai posted a permanent squadron contingent of planes and crews at Lae airdrome.

### CHRISTMAS, 1942

As the first anniversary of the war passed, the 49ers at Port Moresby were again embroiled in the logistical tangle of complying with the endless reassignments of men and materials to different bases. As the 39 FS moved their new Lockheeds into 14 Mile, the Screamin' Demons completed the move of their operations up the road to 17 Mile with Hutchinson's headquarters people. The Eightballs at 3

*Landers lost Irvin's old charger "THE REBEL" in the December 26th interception of the OSCARs over Dobodura.*

Mile continued to revamp the older Warhawks in their livery while inducting more pilots into their ranks.

The dispersal of the Flying Knights to three different locations was brought closer to resolve. Ninth Squadron CO Capt. Jesse Peaselee finally convinced the 5 AF command of the dire, miserable conditions at Rorona Field. On the 24th, the captain consolidated his command at 4 Mile Field with his P-40 pilots while his P-38 crews made ready for the move to the new strip being built at Dobodura. Peaslee recalled his P-38 pilots on attached duty to the 370th Materiels Squadron bases in northern Australia where the last ships were finally being readied for combat, and the Warhawks meanwhile flew missions attached to the 7th Squadron operations at 14 Mile Field. By month's end, the majority of Knights were gathered at Port Moresby for duty as a integral unit.

On a rainy Christmas Day, the USAAF distributed canned hams, fresh eggs, fresh milk, real butter, fruit and coffee to the air crews at the Port Moresby complex while missions continued to be flown to the north coast. The Warhawk pilots had decreased the frequency of dive bombing sorties as more coastal patrols over Buna and escorts to Lae were ordered. There had not been contact with the Japanese air force for two weeks, partially due to the monsoons that restricted missions all along the north coast.

### THE BEST VS. THE BEST; DECEMBER 26, 1942

As the 49ers shuttled men and planes at Moresby, the JAAF 11th Sentai began their active participation in the operations from Malahang strip, northeast of Lae Village. After a number of small reconnaissance flights, the OSCARs flew a sweep in force to the south in the improved weather of mid-morning on December 26th.

Likewise, the second Warhawk patrol lifted off from the fields at Port Moresby between the intermittent rain showers and coasted over the Owen Stanley Mountains toward the Buna area. Senior Lt. "Big John" Landers led a dozen Warhawks with White Flight at 14,000 feet, Blue Flight at 10,000 and Red Flight at 8,000, all meant to orbit over Buna. Just as they arrived, the Dobodura air controller urgently called for fighter cover. "ZEKEs" were strafing the landing area and attacking a flight of RAAF Hudson transports, one of which carried none other than Gen. Blamey, head of the Allied army in New Guinea. Landers ordered "tanks off" and the Flying Knights peeled off for the interception.

The "ZEKEs," of course, were the Lae OSCARs that had caught the Hudsons at low altitude. As the OSCARs separated momentarily in their mad chase after the RAAF bombers, Landers' Red and Blue Flights burst out of the hazy overcast and struck the enemy over Dobodura airfield. The Knights latched onto their targets and a vicious dogfight raged from 5000 feet down to the tree tops.

Blue Flight engaged first as veteran element leader Jim "Duckbutt" Watkins and wingman Art Wenige held together to make two coordinated passes against the OSCARs. Blue Leader Bill Levitan and wingman Bill Sells separated in the first hard turn, but they quickly bested a pair of enemy fighters beneath the hazy overcast. Before the Blue quartet was forced to break off due to low ammo and fuel, Levitan, Sells, Watkins and Wenige each claimed to have destroyed one the assailants. As for Red flight, things turned out differently for Darwin veteran John Landers.

In Red Flight's attack descent through the broken overcast, Landers' elements lost formation and remained dangerously separated throughout the fight. In his first combat engagement, wingman 2Lt. Bob McDaris claimed a "ZEKE" destroyed and another heavily damaged, but failed to relocate his flight leader. "Mac" made a solo retreat for Moresby. Likewise, 2Lt. John "Baggie" Bagdasarian had chased an OSCAR off the tail of Blue Flight's Watkins, but Baggie's old stager could not stand the strain and he set the P-40E with its blown Allison engine down safely at Dobodura.

*2Lt. Planck scored his first kill on the December 27th sortie with 39 FS.*

*2Lt. Hyland scored New Year's Eve 1942 on another 39 FS sortie.*

## LANDERS ALONE

Landers, flying #75 THE REBEL (formerly CO Irvin's old ship), plunged right into the midst of a regrouping flight of six OSCARs, and took them all on at once. Big John's wild aerobatics in the REBEL so startled his opponents that he bested two of them before the odds overcame him. One of the sentai masters finally swung his nimble Ki-43 in behind Landers and the lone Knight could not shake free. The REBEL was perforated by a long, accurate stream of 7mm tracers.

Landers broke down and away for the safety of the foothills to the south, but his pursuer riddled the REBEL again before he could drop behind the crest of the forested terrain. Big John pulled back his canopy, stepped out on the wing and was swept off in the slipstream at 1000 feet of altitude. He was jolted in the straps below the burst of his chute and fell into the dense forest due east of the coastal village of Pongani.

The hefty pilot survived a rough tumble through the limbs of a tall tree and came to rest in a dense thicket that took several hours to negotiate. Once able to find better footing in a stream, after three days, Landers eventually waded to a small village not far from Pongani. The tribal elder there graciously took a personal liking to the six foot, four inch "plenty whitey goodfella." They gave the blond giant food and shelter for the night, and on the next day, a native party escorted Landers down the trail to Pongani village. Big John soon caught the next transport flight for Port Moresby.

## THE OUTCOME FOR THE BEST

Understandably, there were vast discrepancies in either side's claims after the skirmish that cloudy morning over Dobodura. There was even a postscript to the Flying Knights engagement when 5 FC confirmed an enemy fighter shot down just north of Buna by a patrolling RAAF Wirraway, bringing the overall score to eight enemy fighters shot down. Unknown to the Allied pilots, they had confronted the enemy's best, yielding only the temporary loss of Landers and Bagdasarian's forced landing. And the contest would continue unabated the very next day.

## THE FIRST 49ERS P-38 KILL; DECEMBER 27, 1942

The enemy staged another attack on Buna the next day and for the 49th Fighter Group, a new era would dawn with the interception flown against that raid. Two former 17th Provisional Squadron lieutenants, now permanently assigned as Flying Knight Lockheed pilots, would score the 49ers' first P-38 victories while flying with the 39th Squadron. They were 2Lts. Richard Bong and Carl Planck. The Flying Knights, the Lockheed P-38, and Dick Bong in particular, would become entwined in a truly heroic epic.

Likewise, the Rabaul Imperial Staff that day set their own precedent. As the missions to the Solomon Islands momentarily subsided due to seasonal storms in the east, the Rabaul command staff swung the might of its air arm against Papua. In the first combined army-navy sortie in the Southern Area campaign, ZEROs, Val dive-bombers and OSCARs gathers for the united strike on Dobodura. The Imperial strike force crossed over the Solomon Sea, and at

mid-day, they could see their Buna objective beneath the dense cumulus clouds hanging motionlessly against the Owen Stanley range. At a quarter past noon, the VALs rolled into the attack on the new Allied garrison at captured Buna, 14,000 feet below.

The air raid sirens all along the Buna complex screamed at the first sight of the approaching dive bombers and the air controller called in the alarm to the standing patrol of four P-38 Lightnings of the 39 FS that orbited directly above Buna at 25,000 feet. Flt Ldr Capt. Tom Lynch, wingman Dick Bong, element leader 2Lt. Ken Sparks and wingman John Magnus simultaneously jettisoned their belly tanks and peeled off into a heart pounding 450 Mph plunge for the dark green dive-bombers that swept over the bomb bursts in the coastal village.

In mid-descent, the enemy escorts crossed the American's attack path. Capt. Lynch lined up on a radial engine fighter with dark red roundels glistening in the brilliant sunlight and pushed down on the gun button of his control wheel. The escort, likely a ZERO, disintegrated as the P-38s thundered onward for the VALs further below.

The Lightning were quickly followed in their howling descent by a flight of HAMPs and Bong slipped his #15 THUMPER aside to fire at a Mitsubishi that threatened Lynch's P-38. The HAMP spun away and Bong looked back to see three others circling in behind him, so he increased his angle of descent and lost his pursuers, finally pulling THUMPER out at over 400 knots "2 inches above the shortest tree in Buna."

Suddenly, there in THUMPER's flight path was a VAL that had just pulled out of its bombing run. Bong swept into point blank range, and before the rear gunner could bring his weapon to bear, the P-38's concentrated firepower struck the Aichi dive-bomber which detonated into a fireball. Too low to regroup for a second pass, the Flying Knight swept upward and turned off for Pt. Moresby with his first victory claim.

## THE LAST 9 FS WARHAWK ENGAGEMENT AND MISTAKEN ENEMIES

As Lynch's Lightnings entered their attack dive, a mixed flight of 7 FS and 9 FS Warhawks would simultaneously join the fray, plus another flight of 39 FS Lightnings accompanied by Flying Knight 2Lt. Carl Planck. Within the haze at 6000 feet above the Dobodura plains, more than fifty fighter aircraft swirled about as tracers zipped through the air from a dozen different directions.

Confusion and bad judgement raised the pitch of the battle. The zealous Lightning pilots could not distinguish the Warhawks from the OSCARs, or ZEROs, and they shot at any single engine profile that appeared within the mist. The 49ers screamed out their identity over the Allied frequency to the trigger-happy P-38 pilots, but five Warhawks pilots found themselves evading the concentrated gunfire of the Lockheeds. The 49ers Warhawks all broke off for Pt. Moresby before they could effectively engage the opponents. By half past noon, all of the fighters had withdrawn.

## AN UGLY DEBRIEFING AT 14 MILE

On the Flying Knights' flight line at 4 Mile, shaken Lt. Neuman surveyed the .50 caliber bullet holes in the radiator cowling, prop blades and rear canopy of his P-40. Squadron mates Clay Tice, Bill Hanning, and Harry Dillworth had fortunately avoided the volleys fired at them.

Meanwhile up at 17 Mile, raging Ops Exec Red Manning landed his P-40 holed by the Lightnings and immediately commandeered a jeep. Three other men jumped on board as the flight leader sped off for 14 Mile Field, and he was still in his flight gear when he confronted the 39 FS fighter jockeys. In a heated shouting match, the red-headed, red-faced Ops Exec reached for his .45 automatic and his squadron mates had to physically drag him back to his vehicle.

Forty-Niner CO Don Hutchinson was furious when he heard the account of his pilots' ordeal against the Lightning wing. Flying Knight CO Peaselee and Demon CO Martin wanted charges filed, but Group Deputy Maj. Morrissey wisely counselled to let the matter drop. It was an unfortunate incident, but thankfully, no one had been killed.

The final accounting of victories for the day was sorted out for the Lightning pilots. Bong's VAL kill was confirmed, and curiously, his offhand mention of the shots he fired at the HAMP resulted in a second confirmed kill. Carl Planck's claim of a radial-engine fighter shot down five miles up the shoreline from Buna village was confirmed for the third Flying Knights kill of the mission.

Although the P-40s and enemy fighters parried briefly, no 49ers Warhawk driver filed claims over an opponent. As for the 9 FS Warhawk pilots, Hanning and Neuman had fired the last P-40 volleys in combat for the Flying Knights as of that day. By New Years Day of 1943, all of the P-40Es were turned over to the 8 FS at 3 Mile while the senior-most Flying Knights were inducted into P-38 school and the junior pilots were reassigned to the two sister squadrons.

On the last day of 1942, Dick Bong and squadron mate Norm Hyland were part of the 39th Squadron formation that flew a retaliatory fighter sweep of Lae. Both Bong and Hyland found airborne targets and Hyland scored his first career victory. Bong's victim was not confirmed, but was recorded as a probable kill.

## THE FIRST CENTURY MARK

The year ended with the 49ers being the highest scoring fighter outfit of the USAAF in the war to date. As of the December 26th engagement and the seven victories claimed, one of those shot down by Landers was declared the 100th kill for the group. Regardless of the historical discrepancies, the ultimate fact was that two fighter forces from two different army air forces had met for the first time, and though the details of the battle were as hazy as the sky where they fought, Hutchinson's 49ers had outscored the best of the JAAF newcomers and the 5 AF ruled the sky over Buna.

## ON TO SALAMAU

The Allied offensive was fully underway. MacArthur's army prepared to move up the north coast against the next objective of Salamaua village. The tiny isthmus town had an accessible port for sea transports and inland was a landing strip large enough to service transports and fighters. Only slightly more than twenty miles south of Lae, Salamaua could provide MacArthur with a landing facility to set his invasion force against Lae proper, which was tentatively planned for early April, 1943.

The 5th Air Force became increasingly important as the most strategic weapon available to keep up the pressure on the retreating Japanese. In the next two years in the offensive along the northern coast of New Guinea, the focus of MacArthur's strategy would turn to the capture of airfields and harbors. As airfields were taken, or built when necessary, the 5th Fighter Command would send its groups forward to secure the skies over the advancing troops. So it was for LtC. Don Hutchinson's 49ers, the Fighter Command's first team, slated for the move to Dobodura.

# 8

# THE LAE CONVOYS IN
# THE PAPUAN CAMPAIGN, 1943

As the situation worsened in the Solomon Islands and in Papua in late 1942, internal politics in the Japanese Imperial Command forced concessions between the contested branches of their armed services. With one army annihilated at Buna and another trapped at Guadalcanal, the humiliated 8th Area Army commander, Lt. Gen. Imamura, requested assistance from the Imperial Navy. Without adequate numbers of air transports, the Mobile Fleet was his only hope.

An elaborate agreement was reached. Admiral Yamamoto would assume overall command in the South Pacific theater and the JAAF would provide supplemental convoy air cover with the air arm of the Imperial Fleet. In return, Yamamoto would organize his navy units, to become known as the "Tokyo Express" by the American Navy, for the perilous, month long sea borne rescue of their men on Guadalcanal.

As part of the new battle order in the Southeastern Area, the Imperial Navy staff realized its depleted fighter force had to be upgraded as early as October, 1942. Aware that the logistics of the South Pacific battle now surpassed the ability of their existing units, several carrier based kokutais were reorganized for shore assignment and sent to the airfields of New Britain as reinforcements. The reorganization, however, merely renumbered the existing units, while the veteran combat pilots continued to fly the staggering distances from Rabaul to both Guadalcanal and Lae. Losses soared throughout November with few replacements, and by late December, many of the kokutais were reduced to as few as ten ZERO-sens and pilots per chutai (squadron).

The Imperial Staff therefore summoned army air units from distant theaters for Gen. Adachi's New Guinea command to bolster the defense of Lae and to fly convoy protection for reinforcements from Rabaul, but only one army fighter sentai had arrived in Lae as of December. Buna would not survive, nor would the Allies be stopped. American and Australian troops continued to pour into the ever expanding camps of Papua in broad daylight against minimal aerial opposition.

The setbacks of the once victorious JNAF was in part due to the affects of Lt. Gen. George Kenney's 5th Air Force offensive. More USAAF bomber units were brought into the Port Moresby airfield complex, while Col. Wurtsmith's 5th Fighter Command moved forward to the new airdrome at Dobodura, only 175 miles from the great Japanese stronghold at Lae.

The 5th Fighter Command would provide critical air cover over the growing north coast complex centered at Dobodura, as well as give escort to the medium and heavy bombers who continued to reduce Lae airdrome and strike the Solomon Sea supply routes. Dobodura Airfield controllers would direct a myriad of Allied medium bombers, fighters and transports, as Kenney's air force flourished against the enemy's meager airborne intervention in the first month of the new year.

Two principle logistical facilities supplied MacArthur's army in the Papuan offensive. First was the airborne materials handled at Dobodura. Second were the U.S. Navy and merchant supply ships beginning to harbor at the former German gold camp town of Oro Bay, about ten miles southeast of Dobodura. The old inland road from Oro Bay would eventually be rebuilt with a new bridge over the Samboga River, and by the end of January, the two supply bases had begun to amass a huge reserve of war materials.

## THE FIRST LAE RELIEF CONVOY; JANUARY 1943

As MacArthur built up the Oro Bay-Dobodura complex, the Rabaul staff simultaneously attempted to reinforce Lae with the first troops to be recovered from the disastrous Solomon's campaign. Of the 35,000 Imperial ground troops that had suffered on Guadalcanal, only a third of that force would survive the epic sea battles fought between Yamamoto's "Tokyo Express" and the relentless U.S. Navy fleet commanded by Adm. Fletcher.

On January 5th, 6000 of the recovered troops who had reached New Britain were reassigned to Gen. Adachi's army and loaded on board five merchant ships in Rabaul's Simpson Harbor for the 600 mile voyage to the garrison at Lae. Their "Tokyo Express" had barely survived beneath the lethal heavy guns of the U.S. Navy in the Solomons, and now they were to fall prey to the aerial onslaught of Gen. Kenney's 5 AF in the hazy skies of the Huon Gulf.

On the 6th of January, coast watchers on New Britain radioed the sighting of an enemy convoy that passed along the south shore toward the west. Heavy bombers based at Port Moresby, with ten P-38 Lightnings of the 39th Squadron led by Capt. Curran Jones in high cover, flew a search and destroy mission against the convoy at mid-day. The enemy ships were found off the southern New Britain coast near Gasamata and an intense air battle broke out between Curran's P-38s and the Ki-43 fighter escorts. Attached Flying Knight 2Lt. Walter Markey scored a victory over one of nine OSCARS claimed in the engagement. That evening after the 39th Squadron debriefing, Gen. Kenney ordered a maximum effort by all available flight crews for a morning strike against the Lae bound transports.

*Former 39 FS Lightning purportedly adopted by 9 FS Walt Markey in January 1943. Old name and aircraft number on the nose have been covered over with standard O.D. paint.*

*7 FS crews rearm P-40K "SCATTERBRAIN" flown by Ops Exec Capt. George "Red" Manning for another strike to Lae.*

## THE AIR BATTLE ABOVE THE LAE CONVOY; JANUARY 7, 1943

On the evening of the 6th, LtC. Hutchinson and his new Group Ops Exec, Major Wyatt Exum, consulted with their flight leaders. Hutchinson's team would be made up of the Warhawk pilots of the Screamin' Demons from 17 Mile Field and the Eightballs from 3 Mile Field. The Flying Knights, who were still attached to the 39th Fighter Squadron, would provide top cover under Maj. Prentice's command at 14 Mile Field.

The Demon Ops Exec, Capt. George Manning, and new Eightball Ops Exec, Capt. Ellis Wright, devised an elaborate mission plan for 36 Warhawks to strike both the convoy and the Lae harbor area. Twenty Demon and sixteen Eightball P-40s would be ready for the mission the next day.

## THE 7 FS DIVE BOMBERS FOR THE CONVOY

Newly promoted Major Bill Martin, the Demon CO, took charge of the mission high cover that day and chose his senior pilot, Ops Exec Red Manning, to lead the strike on the convoy. Since the Demons' newer P-40Ks were more capable of striking the heavier blow on the convoy, two flights of four P-40Ks, each to be armed with two 300 pound HE bombs, were made ready at 17 Mile for the

*7 FS cadre veteran C.T. Johnson (lt.), Red Flt Ldr Frank Nichols and veteran A.T. House cited at 14 Mile Field immediately after their part in the Lae convoy strike on January 7th.*

first strike. The two flights were designated as Capt. Manning's White Flight and "Nick Nichols 'Nip Nippers'" Red Flight.

Lt. Ray Melikian's Green Flight quartet would fly close escort at 10,000 feet, then Lt. Yancey's Yellow Flight would follow at 11,000 feet and Lt. Vodrey's Black flights would finally take high cover positions at 12,000 feet. Red Manning's principle objective with the P-40K dive bombers was to hit the convoy as they entered the confines of Lae harbor.

After a restless night, and an unnerving stand-down during the morning rains, Capt. Manning answered the phone at the Ops shack on 17 Mile Field just after the noon hour. He was told that the convoy had been followed by an RAAF Catalina flying boat which had sunk the trailing freighter in the morning darkness, and now the Catalina reported the convoy had diverted for Salamaua. Manning scrambled his pilots and the Screamin' Demons were airborne at 1300 hours.

## JANUARY 7TH, FIRST STRIKE; 2 O'CLOCK OFF SALAMAUA

All five Demon flights got off in good order and quickly joined formation over 17 Mile Field, then swung north on a direct heading for the hour long flight to the isthmus of Salamaua. The bomb ladened lower flights slipped past the 12,000 foot peaks of the Owen Stanleys and began their gradual descent down the north slope toward their target. Vodrey's Black Flight and Yancey's Yellow Flight held their higher positions beyond the mountain crests where their pilots soon made out the dark shapes of nine enemy ships in convoy, still 50 miles from the northern shore. Even higher overhead was an escort cap of eight 39 FS Lightnings led by Capt. Lynch, including the successful Flying Knights team of 2Lts. Dick Bong and Carl Planck.

Far below, Mission Leader Manning's two flights of dive-bombers cruised over Salamaua at 9000 feet and circled twice about the area, expecting to find the ships in the bay. The harbor however, was empty, and Manning chose to attack the ships at sea. The Mission Leader ordered the flights to drop their centerline tanks, but much to his annoyance, his own tank stubbornly clung to the belly shackles. Manning knew the handicapped plane would hinder the mission, and reluctantly, he passed the mission lead to the Red Flight Leader. Red Ldr "Nip Nipper" Nichols turned the flight of seven bomb laden P-40s toward the approaching convoy still 40 miles off shore, while Capt. Manning remained behind to drop his pair of 300 pounders on the isthmus south of the harbor.

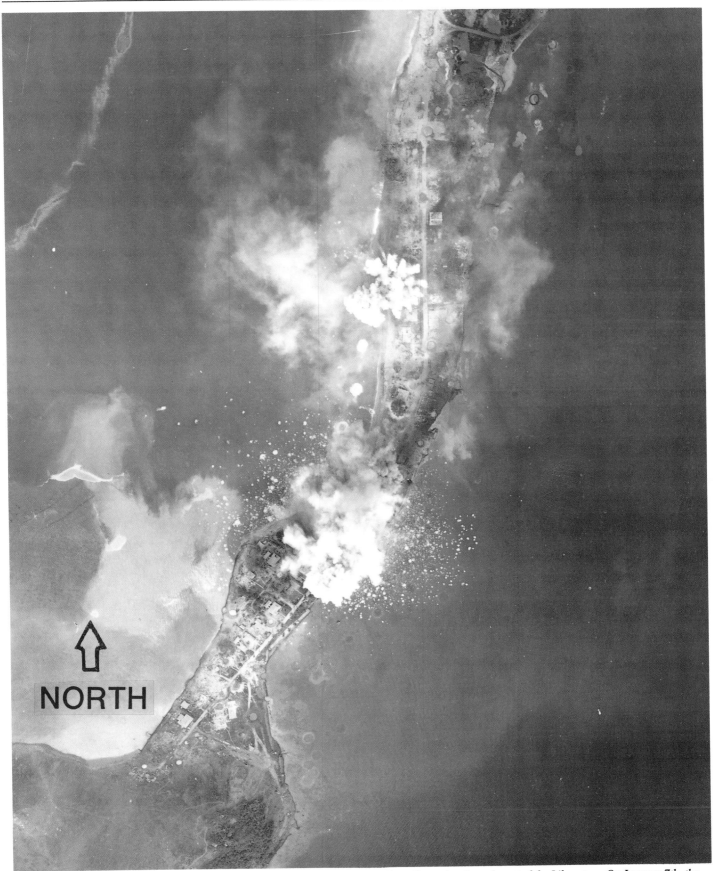

*A mile above the narrow land bridge of Salamaua peninsula with the village and auxiliary airstrip under attack by Liberators. On January 7th, the Screamin' Demons went to this target in search of the Lae convoy before they ventured eastward over the Huon Gulf.*

*Left: 7 FS P-40K #29 "PATSY RUTH" assigned to Lt. Arland Stanton at 14 Mile during the January-February offensive. The aircraft displays two kill flags, one of which was gained by the pilot on February 6th, plus four yellow bomb mission markers. In late February, Red Flight was orders to repaint their red spinners in the 7 FS designator color. PATSY RUTH's spinner is actually a highly polished sky-blue contrasted with the darker blue of her number and name. Nichols' unit was allowed to retain the famous "NICK NICHOLS' NIP NIPPERS" name above the exhaust pipes. Right: Burtnette's aircraft #31 "STEWHEAD IV" which mortally damaged the Myoko Maru on February 7th.*

## YELLOW and BLACK vs OSCARS

Black Flt Ldr Vodrey had momentarily lost visual contact with the dive bombers through the expanding cumulus clouds offshore. Vodrey led 2Lts. Carl Houseworth, Joe King and Birge Neuman (just transferred from the 9 FS) down among the clouds to join Lt. Yancey's Yellow Flight at their lower position. Once there, the two flights turned back toward the harbor in search of the Mission Leader. Black Flight tail-end elements King and Neuman had just completed their circuit of the harbor and were headed back toward the convoy at about 13,000 feet, when the Yankee pair caught site of three planes approaching head-on to their right and a thousand feet above. Both King and Neuman hesitated to call out a warning of the looming fighter trio, thinking they might be Warhawks. As the three strangers passed directly overhead, their lead ship snapped into a lefthand wingover, displaying crimson wing roundels, red spinner and red radial engine cowling. Neuman cried out the warning as three 11th Sentai OSCARs plunged down on his element. In seconds, Black Flight was scattered by the attack.

At the same instant, Yellow Flt. Ldr. Yancey had just looked back and above to verify Vodrey's high cover position, only to see the descent of the OSCARs upon the rear element of Black Flight. Yancey abruptly wheeled about to counter the OSCARs and throttled forward with Yellow wingmen Irv Bagdasarian (another former Knight), and rookie element 2Lts. Sheldon Brinson and John Griffith close behind.

As Warhawks and OSCARs closed in on one another, Yancey's P-40K stalled out in his initial ascent and the lieutenant chose to fall away briefly to pick up speed. Yancey then re-engaged, rolled into firing position, but could not hold an advantage long enough over the wildly maneuvering green and brown enemy plane. Second element leader Lt. Brinson, countered against an OSCAR that had followed Yancey, and after several high speed turns with the Ki-43, Brinson's P-40 stalled and dropped away no longer in the fight.

Yellow Flight had become hopelessly separated. Second Lt. Bagdasarian never did regain altitude and had set off for home after the initial attack. Lt. Yancey turned out of the fight to see his num-

ber 4 man, 2Lt. Griffith, chasing an OSCAR northward toward Lae. The Yellow Leader set off in pursuit too, but the rascal escaped and both Yellow men turned back toward the enemy convoy.

After the fight had dispersed, Yancey flew offshore to orbit the convoy once, then rejoined Griffith and Red Flight's dive bomber pilot, 2Lt. David Allen, for a safe return to 17 Mile Field. During the return flight over the Owen Stanley Mountains, Allen jokingly asked the Yellow Flight Leader why his ship still carried its drop tank. Startled at the onset of the dogfight, Flt Ldr. Yancey had simply forgotten to jettison the contraption.

## GREEN vs. ZEROS

Lt. Melikian's Green Flight had meanwhile escorted Lt. Nichols' two dive bombing flights all the way to their convoy objective, unaware that the top cover flights had engaged the OSCARs high overhead. As the dive bombers peeled off to hit the first ship in the convoy, Lt. Melikian spotted four ZEROs below in descent toward

*Refit 8 FS stager "A DIPLOMAT (To Tokio)", also named "KANSAS CITY KIDDIE" on the port side, flown by newcomer 2Lt. Bob White who scored his first two kills on January 7th. The lighter spinner half is orange-yellow, a bit darker than the standard USAAF insignia shade and purportedly acquired in trade from Navy personnel.*

*Left: 7 FS newcomer Lt. Joe King flew escort to the P-40K dive-bombers sent against the Lae convoy. Right: Newcomer "pineapple man" Lt. Ernie Harris, seen here weeks later on his motor cycle at Dobodura. Unshakable Harris disproved any doubts of his previous Hawaiian tour when he scored three victories over Lae on January 7th.*

the dive bomber team, and dropped his belly tank to engage. As the Green flight quartet rolled down to the right, just as with the other Warhawk escorts, the entire Green Flight team became separated.

Melikian quickly cut off one of the attackers. His wingman, 2Lt. Duncan Myers, a former Flying Knight, fired a long volley at another ZEKE until his left wing guns jammed. Green Flight's element leader, another former Knight, 2Lt. "Mac" McDaris, also fired at a lone ZEKE, but Mac dropped too close to the convoy and was forced to break off his pursuit as accurate AA flak burst near his Warhawk. Rookie wingman 2Lt. Al Smith could not keep up the chase in his sputtering Warhawk, due to water contaminated fuel. Separated from his leader, Smith tried to return over the mountains, but could not regain enough altitude and had to set down at Dobodura.

Flt Ldr Melikian saw an unidentified P-40 followed by an enemy fighter and fired a long range burst at the ZEKE with little effect. Luckily, the pursued Demon pilot shook off his assailant, and the dogfight dissipated. Melikian's flight had kept the enemy escorts from disrupting the Warhawk dive bombers, but not a single P-40 pilot could claim a victory over the ZEKEs or OSCARs that had intervened above the transports.

## RED and WHITE vs THE CONVOY

As the dogfights snarled high overhead, Flt Ldr Lt. Nichols had reached the target and all seven Warhawk pilots would try to bomb the convoy. Nichols' two flights in line formation approached the in-line convoy of five transports, flanked on both sides by two destroyer escorts that sailed in a defensive weave of "S" turns throughout the attack.

Nichols did not hesitate and ordered his Red Flight to attack the lead transport. From 8000 feet, Nichols rolled his shark-mouthed #24, NIP NIPPER, down on the 5500 ton Clyde Maru, its deck crowded with troops. Just to his right on the way down, the Red Leader saw three ZEKEs flash by, but after release of his bombs at

1000 feet, neither enemy fighter nor flak from any of the ships threaten the NIPPER as it sped away at 500 feet above the brilliant blue sea. Nichols' bombs exploded just to the right of the freighter's stern.

The Red Flight leader's wingman, Lt. Allen in #18, GLORIA, was next and he descended on the Clyde, too, but the pair of 300 pounders fell 100 feet wide to the right. Allen pulled GLORIA out only 50 feet above the waves and sped off for five miles before swinging back to observe any damage. All he could see in the distance was AA flak bursts over the convoy, but no Warhawks, so he turned GLORIA back for the long flight to Port Moresby. Allen passed over Buna where he joined Yellow elements Lt. Griffith and Flt Ldr Yancey, whose P-40 still carried its drop tank. They turned once around Buna, then climbed inland over the mountains for 17 Mile field.

Red Flight's third man was Darwin veteran C.T. Johnson in #25, ROSIE, who dropped down on the Brazil Maru which was second in the convoy, but he was suddenly distracted in mid-descent by a ZEKE that passed beneath him at 5000 feet. Johnson tried to fire at the ZEKE and drop ROSIE's bombs all at the same time, but accomplished nothing as the ordnance detonated harmlessly to starboard over 100 yards away. The ZEKE twisted around and followed Johnson down, but the wily Yankee veteran quickly lost the pursuer and returned to strafe the Brazil in a second pass. The AA flak was heavy and accurate, forcing Johnson to withdraw. Short of fuel, he turned ROSIE off for Moresby.

Red Flight's last man was Lt. Stanton who also dropped his bombs off the starboard side of the Brazil without effect. Stanton pulled #29, PATSY RUTH, out at 50 feet and swung to the rear of the convoy to avoid the enemy fighters. The lieutenant was not pursued and he was able to observe the strikes of the three Warhawks in White Flight.

The three remaining White Flight dive bombers were flown by the Darwin veterans, Flt Ldr A.T. House, Lt. Claude Burtnette and newcomer 2Lt. Larry Succop. Lt. House in his #13, POOPEY the 2nd, led the White trio down the right flank of the convoy to bomb the last ship in the chain. At 8000 feet, House passed over the last transport, the Chifuku Maru, and rolled POOPEY over to the right into an ear popping 60 degree plunge toward the 5800 ton vessel. Heavy machine-gun fire rose up from the Chifuku deck and House returned a stream of .50 calibers in response, dropped both bombs and broke off to the left away from the convoy escort destroyers.

## FINALLY, SUCCESS

Burtnette was next in his #31, STEWHEAD the 4th, and also flew through a barrage of heavy but inaccurate tracers. Burtnette targeted the next to the last merchant, the 4100 ton Myoko Maru, and unlike all the other Demon dive bombers in the preceding attempts, he scored a direct hit amidship with one of his 300 pounders, then broke away to follow Flt Ldr House. The bomb smashed into the base of the funnel and exploded in the engine room, sending up a roiling yellow plume with debris streamers rising 500 feet high into the air. The Myoko's engine was heavily damaged by the blast, and she would limp into Lae harbor to offload her troops onto barges later that evening. She would inevitably be beached and abandoned at Lae village.

Lt. Succop also attacked the Myoko Maru, but did not hit the mark. Unlike his White Flight wingmen, Succop broke away in the opposite direction to escape beneath a hail of AA from the destroyers on the left flank. Miraculously, Succop's plane was not hit and he encountered no ZEROS. During his flight to Buna, Succop crossed "Nip Nipper" Johnson's flight path and the two men subsequently crossed over the mountains for 17 Mile Field. Johnson's ship landed with less than five gallons of fuel in his main tank. Red Flight's Stanton, with White Flight Burtnette and House, also returned to 17 Mile to land shortly after 3 O'clock. All the Demons were safe.

## WHERE WERE THE P-38s?

Unknown to the Warhawk band, their high escort of Lightnings from the 39th Squadron had scrambled from 14 Mile at Port Moresby and had crossed the mountains headed directly for the convoy from the onset. Because the dive bombers vectored first to Salamaua, the Lightnings met the convoy escort of JAAF fighters much sooner, 65 miles out over Huon Gulf. The 39 FS claimed six OSCARS destroyed, which resulted in the relatively lighter resistance against the P-40s nearer Salamaua.

In the initial engagement at sea, Lt. Dick Bong claimed one of the escort OSCARs for his third victory. The Lockheed flight quickly returned to Dobodura for refueling to fly a second strike at Lae before dark. As the Eightballs were descending on Lae proper, Bong and the 39th Squadron would meet the OSCARs again, high above the Markham River delta.

## JANUARY 7TH, SECOND STRIKE; 3 O'CLOCK TAKEOFF FROM MORESBY

As the Demons' debriefing was quickly analyzed and compared to U.S. Navy and RAN reports, the Port Moresby command staff confirmed that the enemy convoy had turned north for Lae and the second strike was launched. Eightball CO Major Eck Sims appointed his senior flyer, Ops Exec Ellis Wright, to lead the Eightball assault. Wright's White Flight would go in at 4000 feet followed by Lt. Ernie Harris' Yellow Flight at 6000 to strafe the transports. Lt. Larry Kirsch's Green Flight and Lt. Rufus "Bo" Jordan's Blue Flight would hold at 8000 feet in top cover.

The Eightball skipper led the sixteen ship strike force all the way north for well over an hour, but found his old P-40E model stager could not keep up the pace. Capt. Wright, just minutes from the target area, turned back with his wingman for 3 Mile Field, while element leader Lt. Lowell Lutton and wingman 2 Lt. Bob Moose joined up as the third element to Yellow Flt Ldr. Harris who assumed the mission command.

## THE 8 FS STRAFERS AT MARKHAM BAY

Lt. Harris led his fourteen plane force straight to the mouth of Markham River outlet where the late afternoon shadows of a great cumulus front darkened the Lae coastline. As the Warhawks approached the river delta, the pilots could make out the dark silhouettes of enemy ships offshore from Lae village. Harris mistakenly

identified one of the destroyers as a heavy cruiser, and noted three transports near two smaller burning ships. With the six Warhawk strafers in the combined elements of White and Yellow Flight at 7000 feet, Harris dropped his belly tank and led the plunge toward the ships below. In their descent, all of the Americans were immediately engaged by OSCARs of the 11th Sentai that had just regrouped from their assault against the Allied bombers who had struck the convoy only minutes before.

## YELLOW-WHITE FLIGHT AGAINST THE TRANSPORTS AND OSCARS

The six Warhawk strafers swerved to reach the transports beneath the threatening OSCARs, but the Sentai succeeded in forcing the P-40s apart. Only Harris broke through to strafe one of the troop vessels, and he pulled his #67, CAROLINA BELLE, out of its screaming dive to rocket back up through the thin overcast at 6000 feet to engage the enemy fighters. Harris closed unseen behind an enemy who pursued another P-40 and quickly dispatched the Ki-43 which rolled over and burst into flames. He then attacked a second OSCAR which fell away in a flat spin and disappeared beneath the haze. Harris fired on his third victim to within 100 yards and followed the smoking Ki-43 down through the clouds. Momentarily separated from his target in the haze, Harris' BELLE soon dropped beneath the overcast where he saw three crash sites on the surface of the bay.

Now over the enemy ships, Lt. Harris encountered the HAMPs likely of the 582nd Kokutai, but the three resultant passes he flew against them were unproductive. Low on ammo, fuel and altitude after nearly 30 minutes of dogfights, Harris called his scattered squadron to regroup. He set his CAROLINA BELLE southbound for home and reached 3 Mile Field at 1830 hours.

## DICKEY LOST IN THE BAY

The remaining strafer pilots had struggled to ward off the aggressive attacks of the 11th Sentai, but the maneuverable OSCARs were most dangerous at low attitude and minimal speed. The P-40s and

*"Pineapple man" Warren Blakely flew stager #40 as did many other 8 FS pilots in the January-February operations.*

*Tough "SARAH 2nd" flown by 8 FS cadre Flt Ldr Bo Jordan who retained the trusty stager throughout the January-February mission era.*

Ki-43s twisted about until Yellow element leader Lt. Warren Blakely in #68, bested two opponents above the haze. Blakely dropped into the overcast momentarily, but his rookie wingman, Lt. Eugene Dickey, failed to keep his position and quickly fell prey to a more nimble enemy. Dickey's P-40 was heavily damaged and he set it down in the shallows of the river delta just west of Lae's airstrip. As the other separated strafer pilots sped away, Dickey was last seen wading ashore on the delta's southern beach. All of the strafers set off to the south for Port Moresby on Lt. Harris' signal.

**BLUE AND GREEN vs. THE OSCARS ABOVE**

When the Yellow Flight elements had engaged the OSCARs above the overcast, the high cover Blue Flight simultaneously spotted ten OSCARs looming 2000 feet above their own level and more HAMPs orbiting further below nearer the transports. Flt Ldr Jordan ordered Blue wingmen Lts. Littleton, Day and White to gain altitude quickly in order to counter the OSCARs who wheeled into the glare of the sun. The sky over Markham Bay was littered with belly tanks as Warhawks, OSCARs and HAMPs wheeled about to gain the advantage.

Green Flight, trailing the rest of Eightball strike group, had just broken out of the scattered cumulus at 7000 feet and was approaching the bay when Flt Ldr Lt. Larry Kirsch spotted the rising ZEKEs below and the OSCARs overhead that had just begun to peel off. Lt. Kirsch wanted to cut off the descending Nakajimas, but the enemy passed through the sun's glare and Kirsch lost visual contact. Wingman 2Lt. Cyrus Lynd, element leader Lt. Ken Johns and wingman 2Lt. Bob Howard each singled out an OSCAR at the same level. Only Lt. Johns could hit his target, and a heavily smoking OSCAR dropped toward the bay as the other Green Flight members were forced to dive away and re-engage.

Blue Flight turned hard to the right. Flt Ldr Jordan and wingman 2Lt. "Injun" Joe Littleton held formation for a complete circle with the first pair of OSCARs that had dropped in behind their Warhawks. Jordan's greater speed placed his #62, SARAH the 2nd, behind one of the Ki-43s and he sent it down in flames into the bay before he became separated from Littleton. After "Injun" Joe freed himself from another OSCAR by diving through the overcast, he swooped back up to meet a head-on attack by another Ki-43 which exploded instantly from his .50 caliber counter volley.

Blue element leader Lt. Bill Day and wingman 2Lt. Bob White also held formation, slightly higher than the Blue Flight Leader, and both fired on the same OSCAR that appeared before their guns. The OSCAR fell away in flames. Day and White broke away briefly and cleared their tails, then re-engaged. Each bested another opponent, but they momentarily separated. White flew #54, KANSAS CITY KIDDIE, within range of a plunging Nakajima's 7 mm guns and the sentai pilot put twenty-seven rounds through KIDDIE's rudder, cutting the control cables.

However, the descending OSCAR pilot overran his target and lost sight of White who quickly turned the tables and swung KIDDIE through an aeliron turn in behind his attacker. The lieutenant fired a point blank volley, the Ki-43 exploded, and he broke off down through the haze for home. White rejoined Day south of Salamaua and both reached 3 Mile Field safely.

As Lt. Kirsch's Green Flight wheeled away from the OSCARs to gain safe distance before re-engagement, Kirsch and wingman Lynd ventured within gun range of the destroyer in the bay and heavy flak burst near their Warhawks.

The enemy navy AA separated them, and in his attempt to rejoin his leader, Lynd fell victim to an 11th Sentai OSCAR. The Sentai veteran pounced on the single Warhawk and shot out Lynd's right wing guns before the hapless rookie could escape into the nearby clouds. Lynd regained 10,000 feet of altitude, but he had lost contact with the other P-40s and prudently swung southward out of the fight. Unsure of the damage to his ship, Lynd chose not to chance the mountain crossing. He set his fighter down at Dobodura where ground crews counted twenty-three 7mm bullet holes in the wings, fuselage and tail surfaces.

**BLUE and GREEN vs. THE HAMPS BELOW**

Blue Flt Ldr Bo Jordan, and Green Flight's #4 man, Bob Howard, had become separated from their respective wingmen in the first passes against the high altitude OSCARs and both would encounter the HAMPs below the 6000 foot ceiling. After chasing his first burning victim down toward the bay, Jordan was challenged by a dark green "square-wing-tipped ZERO" that dropped from the hazy cloud cover, forcing Bo to dive SARAH away for a safe distance. In his second ascent to 5000 feet, another HAMP turned headlong into SARAH, and Jordan closed the gap firing away. As they passed one another, both the Yank and the Jap zoomed their fighters upward, then stalled out and dropped away to challenge one another again. After the second and third such pass, the Kokutai flyer snapped out of his fourth ascent and whipped across Jordan's line of flight. The Blue flight leader pulled the trigger as SARAH passed a mere 30 feet off the tail of the dark green machine, which flew through the .50 caliber barrage. The combat ended and Bo set off for 3 Mile Field without further interruption.

Meanwhile, Green Flight's 2Lt. Howard was less fortunate. He had chased his JAAF opponent from 7000 feet down to 4000, and once beneath the haze layer, he became embroiled in a head-on challenge with a cannon armed ZEKE. While concentrating on his target ahead, Howard fell victim to one of the "invisible" HAMP wingman who shot out his hydraulic and electrical lines. The Warhawk's guns were knocked out too, and he peered down at the gaping 20mm hole in his left wingroot. Howard desperately tried to spot his assailant, but could not see the HAMP in the hazy sky, so he turned at full throttle for the clouds over the shoreline. Low on gas and with poorly responding controls, Howard dead reckoned for Rorona Field, and landed there an hour later without flaps or brakes. The holed Curtiss was actually not critically damage, and after hurried repairs, Howard flew down the coast to 3 Mile Field the very next day.

The strikes of January 7th had been an immense success for the Screamin' Demons and Eightballs. The 49ers were collectively rewarded with thirteen aerial victories, all in the 8th Squadron, as well as credit to the Group for sinking the Myoko Maru. Only Eightball Eugene Dickey, known to have reached the mainland, was eventually posted as the only man missing in action during the span of the January Lae operations. Whether victim of the cruel jungle, or executed by the Japanese, evidence of Lt. Dickey's fate was never known.

On the evening of the 7th at 17 Mile Field, General Whitehead had seriously considered the feasibility of a night dive-bomber mission to be flown by the 7th Squadron, but the plan was soon dismissed after an adamant argument from Demon CO Martin and his weary pilots, who were backed up by Col. Wurtsmith. All the fighter units stood down.

## FLYING KNIGHTS OVER THE HUON GULF

Word soon came down from the Lockheed squadron at 14 Mile Field that 39 FS-attached Flying Knights had made contact with the OSCARs east of Lae only minutes before the Eightballs had struck the convoy.

It was their second sortie of the day and Capt. Lynch had taken his two flights eastward at 18,000 feet in search of the transports when they came upon the JAAF escorts who had just refueled at Lae airdrome. Sixteen OSCARs were intercepted by the seven high flying Lightnings which included the element team of Bong and Planck. Both Knights damaged a Ki-43 target in the first pass, and Bong claimed his forth aerial kill in his second pass. When the OSCARs escaped below in the clouds near the Markham River outlet, it was then that they engaged the 8 FS in a great dogfight at the lower altitude.

## NEW ACE DICK BONG; JANUARY 8, 1943

On the very next day, Bong and wingman Normand Hyland flew as wingmen in two afternoon missions. Hyland heavily damaged an OSCAR which plunged toward Lae airdrome during the mid-afternoon fighter sweep. During the second mission while on escort to B-17s and B-24s over Markham Bay, Bong claimed his fifth aerial kill after a head-on pass against an OSCAR, just five miles offshore in the twilight of the day. Bong was the first official Lockheed ace of the 5th Air Force with five confirmed victories in only three encounters with the enemy.

For two days, the 5 FC squadrons returned to hit the Lae complex, but there was limited contact in the marginal weather. On the afternoon of the 9th, Demon Lt. A.T. House engaged a lone OSCAR over Salamaua harbor, and claimed hits, yet the subsequent crash of the Ki-43 which was witnessed by another unit in the area

*A.T. House and his crewchief on the wing of their P-40K "POOPEY II." Gregarious A.T. irritated the more serious types at 14 Mile and Flt Ldr Nichols never accepted the tale of the ramming incident 12 months early at Horn Island. House posted a third kill on March 9, 1943, and it would be 50 years before it was finally confirmed.*

was never correlated to House's combat report. Ironically, A.T. House would survived the war, and his fifth kill would not be confirmed until a half-century later by Air Force authorities.

## THE AFTERMATH OF THE AIR ATTACKS IN EARLY JANUARY, 1943

The Imperial Command's attempt to relieve the Lae garrison had been a measured success. Two transports were lost, but the majority of the onboard troops had survived to disembark at Lae proper during the Allied air raids. Much to MacArthur's displeasure, five thousand enemy infantry reinforcements were now in position to oppose the advance Australian forces nearer Salamaua.

The escort pilots of the JAAF and JNAF were honored by their Imperial commanders for the protection given to the Lae convoy during the operations that had spanned four days, but their losses greatly reduced their effectiveness for the next three weeks. In particular, the superior P-38s had badly mauled the 11th Sentai who posted seven pilots killed, three badly wounded and seventeen Ki-43s lost in combat. Six of the Nakajimas had been lost outright in aerial engagements and the others were written off after heavy landings due to extensive combat damage. Likewise, the surviving OSCAR pilots were not allowed to totally recuperate. The 11th Sentai was withdrawn from Lae back to Rabaul to refit for more convoy escorts to the "Tokyo Express" by month's end.

## THE WAU GARRISON BUILD-UP

Throughout the remainder of January, Gen. MacArthur used the respite to reinforce his Australian troops who had moved further north up the coast nearer Salamaua. The enemy reinforcements that had reached the Lae garrison would next confront the advance Australian forces who had taken a flanking route inland to occupy the old German mining camp village of Wau, with its tiny dirt airstrip, only twenty-five miles southwest of Salamaua.

The 49er Warhawk squadrons flew armed reconnaissance of the coast from Buna to Salamaua, hunting barges, landing areas and coastal village supply dumps. Salamaua was dive bombed and strafed repeatedly. Routine P-40 and P-38 escorts to C-47 transports were also flown to the isolated Aussie garrison at Wau which grew solely by air supply.

## NEW COMMANDERS AND THE NEW HOME AT DOBODURA; JANUARY, 1943

Fifth Air Force crews returning from late day sorties began to stay overnight at Dobodura Field. On January 17th, engineer Lt. Fred Hollier and his 35-man advance team reported at Dobodura to establish permanent 9th Squadron flight services for their P-38s, as well as the air echelon's bivouac facilities near the village of Horanda. Two days later, the first official 9th Squadron Lockheed missions were flown from 17 Mile, while four ships were posted daily to Dobodura's main northeast-southwest runway, referred to by the Flying Knights as Horanda Strip.

## ROTH DOWN AT DOBODURA; JANUARY 18, 1943

One of the first broken aircraft officially tended to by the Flying Knights crews was not one of their big Lockheeds, but a war-weary Warhawk from the Eightballs that nearly killed Darwin veteran Lt. John Roth. The pilot was making a mail run for the USAAF personnel at the advanced base when his old P-40E-1, #65, seized up on the landing leg to the main strip. Roth plowed into the savannah just east of the field where old #65 cartwheeled once, then slammed down on its back. The lieutenant miraculously survived the total destruction of his plane, but a deep head wound from hitting the gunsight required immediate surgery. Luckily, the Eightball medical team headed by Flight Surgeon John Wexler had just set up their dispensary west of the field and Roth was quickly taken there by jeep. He recovered fully at Pt. Moresby and returned to combat after a month's rest.

*Newcomer future ace Bob Hagerstrom and his new Eightball squadron patch. The hand painted figure-8 pierced by a winged lightning bolt was never official and did not appear much after April of 1943.*

Shortly after the Roth accident, Lt. Dick Illing and the 8th Squadron engineering team moved into the jungle camp at the north end of Dobodura's shorter northwest-southeast strip. They would receive the old Eightball Warhawks from 3 Mile in the first week of February at this new strip which they named "Kalamazoo."

LtC. Don Hutchinson had performed his task brilliantly by bringing an entire fighter group organization into the New Guinea offensive while his 9 FS simultaneously converted into a new type of aircraft. The group had posted 124 aerial victories as of late January, and of eleven aces acknowledged by the Fifth Air Force Command, seven of them had been with the 49ers at one time. Though aces Reynolds, Kiser, Wagner, Hennon, Morehead, Landers and Donalson had all returned home by the end of January, their legacy would be carried on by the remaining Darwin veterans now reinforced by the newcomer Warhawk and Lightning pilots, including P-38 ace, Dick Bong. For the 49ers part in the Papuan offensive, they would garner their second Distinguished Unit Citation.

Summarily, Don Hutchinson was promoted to colonel and transferred to the 5 FC as the new Chief of Staff. The 49th Fighter Group was handed down to Hutch's hand picked successor, Maj. Bob Morrissey, who initiated the next phase of the transfer of the 49ers' operation on the north slope of the Owen Stanley Mountains. By month's end, veteran Major Jim Selman would rejoin as Group Deputy, while Demon CO Major Martin moved up to 49er Group operations. The Screamin' Demons' command would be passed on to Capt. Red Manning.

More replacement pilots arrived from duty in Hawaii and from training bases in the States. Most were Warhawk pilots and were appropriately assigned to the 7th and 8th Squadrons. By late January, twenty-four Lightnings had been totally refitted for permanent combat assignment to Capt. Jesse Peaselee's 9 FS and were moved up to 14 Mile Field. In the first week of February, the Knights were able to stage three full flights of Lockheeds in rotation to Horanda strip for patrols and escorts. The twelve ships would normally return to 14 Mile Field in the evening, until the entire air echelon could move to the Horanda camp.

There was an immediate appeal from Major Morrissey to upgrade the equipment of the tattered Eightball outfit, as more P-38s were due to arrive at Townsville. But the distribution of the Lockheeds was already set in the 5 AF command decisions reached by General Kenney and his deputy, Enos Whitehead. The men of the groups who had fought in the earlier defense of Pt. Moresby had been promised a chance to avenge the losses suffered against enemy. Despite FC CO Wurtsmith's interceding on behalf of his old friend, Morrissey was told the matter was closed. The 80 FS, recuperating at Townsville, would be the next unit to get the Lockheeds.

On January 22nd, Capt. Lechleitner and his 49th FCS had advanced to their new control center at Oro Bay and by early February they directed all air traffic in the Oro Bay-Dobodura area now designated as Fight Sector 10. The old U.S. cadre friendships were renewed as 49er personnel travelled the log-covered corduroy road between the harbor and airfield stations.

## ANOTHER COUNTERATTACK IN FEBRUARY, 1943

The Imperial JNAF and JAAF had resorted to small bomber formation night raids against the Allied buildup, but there had been only minimal damage done to the Australian camp at Wau, to Dobodura Field, to the Port Moresby complex, or to Allied shipping at Oro Bay. In the first week of February, the weight of the enemy's combined air efforts was focused once more against the Solomons front to provide cover for the last Imperial troops who pulled back to Rabaul. In two weeks those soldiers would be refitted as the next reinforcements bound for Lae.

To ensure that no major Allied ground operation would advance from Wau down the mountain trail into Salamaua, the Imperial staff directed the first major daylight air strike of their Army air force medium bombers against the Australian camp. The twin-engined Kawasaki Ki-48 Type 99, flown into Rabaul by the veteran 45th Sentai crews from their China campaign, staged into Lae airdrome in the first week of February. The Ki-48s, known by the Yankee code name of LILY, were tasked to pit the dirt runway at Wau and strafe the Australian bivouac area. Once more, the battle ravaged OSCAR veterans would fly close escort over their JNAF bomber crew brethren. The mission would prove to be the most fateful confrontation between the 11th Sentai and 49th Fighter Group of the Papuan campaign.

## FEBRUARY 6, 1943; WAU AIR STRIP

The Wau airstrip was nestled in a steeply walled canyon at an altitude of 3500 feet between heavily forested 9,000 foot mountains. The 4000 foot runway laid north to south, barely long enough to accommodate the heavily laden C-47s that flew continuous supply flights to Gen. Blamey's soldiers encamped near the strip. In a strategic sense, Wau was deemed a "compact target" and great pains were taken to provide adequate air defense of the crowded valley, including a battery of 40mm Bofor guns manned by Aussie crews. All C-47 supply flights were heavily escorted.

On the 6th, newly promoted Capt. Frank Nichols was posted on the flight roster at 17 Mile Field and drew a routine mission for escort of six C-47 Dakotas bound for Wau. Nichols was most surprised when he read the name of the flight leader in the second element of Lt. John Hood's Blue Flight; none other than Group Commander Bob Morrissey. The colonel had just been approved for flight duty after his bout with malaria and was anxious to be, "a group leader by example."

At 0945 hours, Nichols led the eight ship Screamin' Demons team off from 17 Mile Field. They were to rendezvous with the C-47 transports that were flying in from Townsville for the first supply run of the day to Wau Strip. The Dakotas and Warhawks joined up on schedule just above the Owen Stanley peaks at 14,000 feet and set off together through the rising cumulus clouds for the north.

After a half hour's uneventful descent toward Wau, the Americans arrived over the deep green rolling foothills that surrounded the Wau garrison. As was the routine for the escorts, Nichols led the "Nip Nippers" Red Flight elements of Lts. David Allen, Don Sutliff and Arland Stanton in an orbit of the Wau area at 10,000 feet. Two thousand feet overhead, Lt. Hood's Blue Flight elements of Lt. Bob Greene, LtC. Morrissey and 2Lt. Larry Succop trailed a few minutes behind and they momentarily lost site of the C-47s in their final approach to the Wau runway.

Another flight of Dakotas, escorted by 40 FS Airacobras, were also descending into Wau air space. For a brief moment, there was

*Nichols' P-40K "NIP NIPPER" which gave him the last two aerial victories of his 7 FS tour on February 6th.*

confusion in the Demons flights in keeping track of all the USAAF planes in the area.

## ENTER THE JAPANESE

At that precise moment, a maximum effort by twenty-eight 11th Sentai wingmen in escort to nine LILY bombers of the 45th Sentai broke out of the clouds at 9000 feet just west of Wau. As the LILYs descended in their bombing run on the tiny Aussie garrison, Frank Nichols' Red Flight members saw the dark green twin-engined planes and mistook them for RAAF Beaufighters. Suddenly, the 45th Sentai was fired upon by the Wau strip Bofor guns and the Demon pilots saw the flak bursting near the three LILYs in the lead Vee.

*7 FS P-40K #18 "JAYHAWKER" ("GLORIA" on the lt.) assign to Lt. Allen who got a pair of LILYs on February 7th. The pilot left the Demons in May and scored seven more kills with the 475 FG.*

## RED FLIGHT'S ENGAGEMENT

As the LILYs dropped their bombs east of the strip, Nichols saw their red wing roundels and called for the break. With belly tanks plummeting away, Red Flight peeled off from 10,000 feet in hot pursuit of the raiders who sped off toward Salamaua. In seconds, Nichols sharkmouthed #24 closed the gap to the LILYs and he poured a stream of tracers into the wingman on the right flank of the lead trio, then broke hard right and ascended at full throttle to set up for another diving pass. Climbing toward the Wau strip, the Red Leader saw P-39s come under attack by the OSCAR escorts and chose to engage the enemy fighters instead.

Nichols saw one OSCAR turn to counter his attack and he briefly dove #24 out again for more speed and another zooming ascent. Back up to 11,000 feet, Nichols firewalled the Warhawk down on an enemy fighter which followed another Airacobra. Nichols' broadside deflection volley caused the OSCAR to immediately burst into flame. The Ki-43 rolled slowly over and glided gently toward the earth, then abruptly increased its descent into a fiery explosion on a hillside north of the landing field.

Nichols could not tarry as another OSCAR loomed above him and he dove off to the west for more speed to re-engage a third time. He then maneuvered twice with the nimble enemy fighters until one stalled out well within gun range. The captain riddled the OSCAR until it fell away in a flat spin toward the jungle. Threatened again, and now low on ammo and fuel, Nichols pushed the nose of #24 down and sped away at 350 Mph for Port Moresby.

The Red flight leader's wingman, Lt. Allen, had stayed in his position for the attack on the bombers and had closed in to fire at the same LILY formation, damaging the Ki-48 on the left flank. As his flight leader maneuvered off for the OSCARs, Allen was able to elude the Ki-43s and approached the LILYs from beneath for his second attack. Partially hidden by the clouds, Allen closed in on two Ki-48s and fired on both ships before the escort detected his position.

Certain that the two bombers were mortally hit, and with OSCARs turning toward his line of flight, Allen descended at 400 knots back toward Wau to escape through the flak corridor, just 500 feet above the runway. He was intent to re-engage after his zooming ascent, but another chase by a Ki-43 and an escape down the flak corridor a second time found him headed south for good. He reached 17 Mile Field safely.

The second Red Flight elements of Sutliff and Stanton had reached the bombers several seconds after their mission leader's assault and they had mixed success. While in pursuit of the LILYs, Sutliff and tail-end-charlie Stanton, in #29, PATSY RUTH, were attacked by a pair of OSCARs. The sentai veteran who fired on Stanton put ten 7 mm rounds through PATSY RUTH's fuselage before the lieutenant could break free. After four attempts to climb back up to the fight at 10,000 feet, Stanton finally hit an OSCAR in a head-on pass northwest of the strip. A fifth counterattack by another OSCAR forced the lieutenant to break off for the last time. Assured of one kill, Stanton returned alone to 17 Mile Field.

Element leader Don Sutliff, after he found he had not flipped on his gun switch, flew a substantial distance to rearm his guns before re-engaging. With guns recharged and separated from his wingman, Sutliff set off alone to the northeast toward Salamaua, hoping to cut off the escape of the LILY formation. At 12,000 feet,

the Demon pilot saw three enemy fighters in a spread formation, two thousand feet below and cruising toward the coast. Targeting the trailing OSCAR on the left, Sutliff dove in from the rear. His .50 caliber burst flamed the Ki-43, which fell and struck a hillside in a brilliant orange flash not far from the north end of the Wau strip. Sutliff broke down and away for Wau, made a head-on firing pass at another escaping OSCAR along the way, and swept over the field to find the fight was over. He soon regrouped with Capt. Nichols and Blue Flight's Lt. Bob Greene and the trio pushed on for Moresby.

## BLUE FLIGHT'S ENGAGEMENT

Once Lt. John Hood's Blue quartet finally found the airfield beneath the clouds, they saw the flak bursts above the runway, the bomb bursts along the east side of the strip and the big tangle of Warhawks, Airacobras and OSCARs. Hood led his Blue team down against the second wave of LILYs and each of the four Demons were able to hit a bomber before the OSCARs intervened.

After his firing pass on the LILY in the left element position, Morrissey was chased far to the north by the OSCARs before he could escape in the clouds and turn back for Wau. The other Blue Flight elements had been forced apart as well.

Flt Ldr Hood dropped down beneath the LILYs and was about to attack again from the rear, but was forced to withdraw when an enemy fighter bore in from above. Hood plunged down and zoomed back up to 16,000 feet and encountered LtC. Morrissey, and Lt. Succop soon after. Unable to re-contact the combatants, Hood, Succop and Morrissey turned south for the flight home.

Hood's wingman, Lt. Greene, had been the only Blue Flight man to sustain contact with the enemy in a second pass. Greene had made his diving attack on the left flank of the LILY formation without effect. Zooming back up to 11,000 feet, the lieutenant cut off an OSCAR turning with a P-39 and shot it down just northwest of the field. He climbed back to 12,000 feet, but the fight had ended and he joined Red Flight's Sutliff for company on the flight home.

## THE FIRST 9 FS OFFICIAL P-38 VICTORY

As the Demons debriefed at 17 Mile Field at noon, the Lightnings of the 9th Squadron at Dobodura were prepared for the follow-up strike against the Lae airdrome. In a large strike force composed of four Flying Knights accompanying the P-38s and P-39s of the 35th Group, the 5 AF formation encountered another OSCAR formation over Wau at one o'clock.

Second Lt. David Harbour in the Flying Knights flight led by Capt. Sid Woods was able to overtake an OSCAR in a dive begun at 18,000 feet. Harbour's Ki-43 victim spiralled down in flames for the first official confirmed victory by a Lockheed pilot flying under 9th Squadron colors. Several 35 FG claims were made as well.

It is difficult to verify all of the individual victors in the many sorties flown by either army air force on February 6th, but the losses for the proud 11th Sentai had been nothing short of devastating. Their sentai commander and several veteran flight leaders had been lost that day, and their unit was forced to stand down. The JAAF command would be forced to bring in an entirely new fighter organization by mid-February to relieve the stunned OSCAR pilots.

## THE CAPTURE OF GUADALCANAL AND THE PAPUAN BUILD-UP; THE 1st WEEK IN FEBRUARY, 1943

Three days after the small but significant air battle over Wau, the Japanese completed the evacuation of their defeated legions on Guadalcanal. Adm. Yamamoto's rescue efforts would yield only eleven thousand of the original 35,000 men sent to the Solomons front, and those survivors had little time to recuperate. They too were regrouped in Adachi's army at Rabaul, and soon sailed off to meet their fate at the Lae garrison which lay in the shadow of MacArthur's great army in Papua.

After the dogfight above Wau on the 7th, the 49ers entered into a realm of relative calm on the New Guinea front. All three squadrons of the group continued to fly tactical strikes near Lae, while they inducted new pilots into their ranks. The Flying Knights also increased the number of P-38s at the old Demon facilities of 14 Mile Field. Some of the big Lockheed fighters were ferried in by the senior Darwin cadre and subsequent patrols were flown with those veteran pilots in command. More escort missions to the 5 AF heavy and medium bombers took the Flying Knights farther up the New Guinea coast, well beyond Lae and over western New Britain, but no contact was made with either the Lae, or Rabaul Imperial wings during the last weeks of February.

## NEW FLYING KNIGHTS BOSS

Captain Jesse Peaslee's Lockheed squadron had become one of the most important offensive weapons in the 5 AF arsenal, but unfortunately for the captain, he would not preside over their greater accomplishments. The Darwin veteran was an excellent administrator to his fighter band, but Peaslee was not regarded as an exemplary combat pilot by the more aggressive officers in the 5th Fighter Command, particularly by his Group Commander, Bob Morrissey.

Morrissey was a politically driven officer who adamantly believed a combat unit should be "led by example." The colonel often flew his P-40K on sorties with either the 7th or 8th Squadron. His promotion to group commander confirmed his principles of command and Morrissey demanded equally of his squadron leaders.

*New 9 FS CO Sid Woods.*

*8 FS CO inductee Capt. Jim Porter, formerly of the Flying Knights.*

Peaslee, studious and somewhat reserved, fell out of favor with Morrissey early on. When Peaslee reported to Pt. Moresby with a case of jungle fever in late February, the Group CO temporarily replaced him with 9 FS Ops Exec, Sid Woods. Two months later, Peaslee would transfer out of theater to the United States, never to fly fighters again.

Captain Sid Woods was a robust, square-jawed, pipe smoking Darwin veteran and an excellent pilot. As a lieutenant back in December, he had survived the crack-up in his old P-40 at Rorona, but refused transfer to the States and instead, opted for qualification training in the Lockheed school at Townsville. Promoted to captain, he made the transition smoothly from Warhawk to Lightning and displayed an exceptional proficiency as a capable flight leader. Eventually appointed Assistant Squadron CO, he proved to be a fearless combatant, a stern but fair disciplinarian, and the Flying Knights seemed to come alive under his steady demeanor. Woods interim command of the Knights in March was the driving force that made the squadron the scoring champions in the Southwest Pacific.

## EIGHTBALLS FOR DOBODURA

By the end of January, Maj. Eck Sims had completed his tour and the Eightballs celebrated the CO's good fortune in being mustered out with a much deserved trip to the States. Sims would always be remembered for his irregular military manner, but he had proven himself to be one of the most competent flying commanders in Col. Wurtsmith's Fifth Fighter Command. Sims, the oldest flying fighter pilot in New Guinea, had presided over an operation of the oldest Warhawks flown in the 5 AF inventory, and yet, his 8 FS had posted 46 victories to date, and 28 of them had been gained under his leadership.

Capt. Ellis Wright had hoped to follow Sims in the 8th Squadron command slot, but the irascible, arrogant captain was not liked by the Eightball personnel. Wright would grudgingly accept promotion to Wurtsmith's FC staff as assistant Ops Director in mid-March.

Morrissey was fortunate to have had the able senior captain, Jim Porter, available to carry on the work of departing Eightball

*8 FS CO Major Ek Sims (lt. front) left his squadron to able men such as Capt. Ken Johns on his left who would be backed up by proven rookie 2Lts. (lt. to rt.) White, Blakely, Bellow, Howard and Littleton.*

Sqn Ldr Sims. Veteran Porter had been transferred over from the Flying Knights in January expressly to assume the command of Eightballs. By mid-February, Capt. Porter took charge of the Squadron's move over the mountains to their new base at Dobodura Field. The Corps of Engineers had completed the installation of pierced steel matting on the 5000 foot, northwest-southeast "Kalamazoo" leg of Horanda strip, which would enable Capt. Porter to move all of his 8FS Warhawks there for full time operations by the end of March.

However, in the February interim of the staff changes in preparation for the new operations at Dobodura, Morrissey's administrative prowess would be put to the optimum test. As the 49ers gathered their gear at their respective bases for the impending move to the northern side of the Owen Stanley Mountains, the 5th Air Force was about to become embroiled in the largest operation ever to take place in the Papuan theater to date.

# *9*

# THE BATTLE OF THE BISMARCK SEA

The Japanese Imperial Staff at Rabaul had reached the proverbial cross-roads in the Pacific campaign. Buna was lost, the Solomons front was collapsing toward Rabaul, and Lae was vulnerable. But, with another refit division of the rescued troops in bivouac at Rabaul, the Staff chose to put the 6900-man force, accompanied by a 250-man contingent of army air echelon, on board sixteen ships for the next Papuan excursion, code named "81-Go." Again, the plan did not have a consensus of all the commanders. Some counseled for the division to be put ashore further north up the Papuan coast, and to be force marched down the coast to Lae, but Gen. Adachi was adamant.

The January relief convoy had been quite successful, despite the intervention of Allied land based aircraft. The 18th Army commander further reasoned that his air force had inducted more Imperial Army air units into its planned counter-offensive against MacArthur's forces in New Guinea. The 1st Sentai, another veteran OSCAR unit which had flown convoy escort in the January Solomons operations, had advanced to Lae airdrome in late February to reinforce the battered 11th Sentai in preparation for this very operation. By his erroneous assessment of the strengths of the two opposing air forces, Gen. Adachi convinced his skeptical compatriots of the soundness of the perilous 81-Go plan. And there was simply no time left for the Lae garrison.

As of March 1st, the order of battle was set. In the following days, a confrontation would begin off the north coast of Papua which would culminate in the epic Battle of the Bismarck Sea.

Allied reconnaissance had kept watch over the growing fleet of enemy ships and aircraft at Rabaul. On the morning of the first day of March, a report reached Gen. Kenney at Port Moresby of another convoy sighted westbound along the northern coast of New Britain. Determined not to allow the enemy troops to reach Lae as they had done in January, Kenney sent his heavy bombers with several P-38 escorts to stop the convoy, but inclement weather foiled the mission.

Kenney advised Col. Wurtsmith of 5 FC to curtail the current tactical operations and enter into a high state of readiness. The long range bombers continued the search for the enemy ships that sailed through the stormy seas, somewhere northeast of Lae.

## LYND IS LOST; MARCH 1, 1943

On March 1st, the 7th and 8th squadrons flew two missions from their respective Moresby bases. On the strafing missions against Malahang strip, they destroyed two planes on the ground, but met no aerial opposition. On the Eightballs' return flight to 3 Mile Field,

Lt. Cyrus Lynd experienced engine trouble and the shuddering Warhawk failed to clear the mountain crest. Lynd spun into a fatal crash not far from Kokoda village where Aboriginals led an army recovery team four days later to find his body. The young lieutenant had shown bravery in the previous combat missions and also shown great promise as a flight leader, but another old model P-40E Warhawk had killed a good man.

The Eightballs could not mourn Lynd for long as their Ops Exec, Capt. Wright, advised everyone to get as much sleep as possible, for a new offensive against Lae was about to be launched. All pilots and crews were put on full alert to await the signal from Wurtsmith's 5 FC center at 17 Mile Field.

## THE VITIAZ STRAITS

In the following morning twilight beneath a heavy overcast, a B-24 reconnaissance plane found the sixteen ships of the enemy convoy off the western tip of New Britain, 100 miles northeast of Lae. The ships were sighted in the Vitiaz Strait, the wider of two sea lanes between New Britain and Papua's Huon Peninsula. Kenney ordered the 43rd Bomber Group, with the P-38s in high cover, for the next long range strike over the strait. Three B-17 mission sorties would pummel the enemy fleet of eight escort destroyers and eight troop-cargo ships in the Vitiaz Strait throughout the day. Beneath the overcast in the lashing rain, the Flying Fortresses sank two transports and dispersed the convoy formation.

The Lightning escorts could not penetrate the cloud cover and failed to make contact with the main force of convoy escort fighters over Huon Gulf. Only the 39th Squadron found limited action near the New Britain west coast during the morning sortie. The Flying Knights would have to try again the next day.

## DAY ONE - MARCH 3rd; THE AIR STRIKE IN HUON GULF

On the morning of Wednesday, March 3rd, Gen. Kenney unleashed his great Allied air force to strike the enemy vessels and Lae airdrome in the largest Allied air operation to date in the Papuan campaign. From a force of nearly three hundred fighters and bombers, the USAAF and RAAF continuously pressed their assaults through the storm clouds for three days to hammer the airdrome, or to descend upon the six remaining troop ships that attempted to reach safe harbor at Lae.

In mid-morning, thirteen B-17 Fortresses flying at the base of the breaking storm clouds, and fourteen heavily armed B-25 strafer

*Crossing traffic at the intersection of Horanda and Kalamazoo.*

gunships streaking in low over the dark sea, attacked the regrouped convoy sixty miles east of Lae harbor in Huon Gulf. Numerous medium bombers followed at mid-day to drop a withering avalanche of high explosives on the hapless, crippled Imperial ships. High overhead, 39th Sqn Ldr Prentice led fourteen of his Lightnings, including six Flying Knights led by Lt. Ed Ball, in a sweep to engage the great swarm of enemy fighters which failed to halt the butchery of the fleet below. Warhawks and Beaufighters kept a constant net over the Lae airdrome complex. The Japanese reeled beneath the aerial onslaught.

## FLYING KNIGHTS OVER THE GULF

On March 3rd, the majority of fighter engagements above the Lae convoy were accomplished by the long range P-38s, including twelve of Capt. Sid Woods' Flying Knights. After a brief delay in the dispersal area at 14 Mile Field, the Knights launched three flights, but the last quartet, led by Capt. Clay Tice, was forced to reform while airborne. Flight Leader Tice had taken off in his #88, ELSIE, only to find a fuel tank cap had snapped free and was clattering against the wing in the slipstream. He descended back to 14 Mile and had a line crewman refit the cap, then took off in ELSIE again.

Capt. Tice ascended over the peaks in pursuit of his flight, which was now led by Lt. Ed Ball, but the captain had to settle for flying

*An unidentified pilot (lt.) passes the time in the Dobodura mission rotation with Flying Knights Ed Ball, Bill Bleecker and Flt Ldr Floyd Finberg in a card game at 14 Mile Field.*

singular escort to eight of the B-17s bound for the convoy. Tice orbited the Fortresses as they dropped their ordinance on the enemy transports. When the air controllers signalled the next vector, the captain tried to jettison his tanks, but the drop switch failed and he had to turn his malfunctioning P-38 back to Dobodura. In his 350 MPH descent, the left tank broke free. The disgruntled Flight Leader landed at Horanda strip, had the line crewmen free the starboard droptank mechanism, and then had ELSIE refueled. For the third time, Tice set off for the battle.

Upon arrival over the bay at 22,000 feet, the captain saw a burning warship surrounded by six rescue barges and turned ELSIE toward the scene to record the event with her gun camera. In the shallow descent, Tice sighted an OSCAR just ahead and 4000 feet below. He immediately turned ELSIE to the attack. The OSCAR pilot attempted to elude the plunging P-38 and turned hard to the left, but Tice laid out a perfect deflection volley of two hundred rounds of .50 caliber and thirty rounds of high explosive 20mm cannon fire. The OSCAR, camouflaged dark green and banded with a dark stripe across the tail, lit up in its midsection from the blow of the concentrated gun fire, spiralled onto its back and dropped into the overcast that hung one thousand feet above the sea. Tice swung upward to survey the area briefly for other planes, but seeing none, set off for 14 Mile Field.

Meanwhile, Tice's original flight now under Lt. Ball's command had also engaged the enemy. Flt Ldr Ball led wingmen 2Lts. Clay Barnes and Leroy Donnell into the target area at 12,000 feet, with another trio of leader Lt. Bill Haney and wingmen 2Lts. Dick Bong and Bill Gersch directly below at 11,000 feet. The two flights orbited beyond the gun range of the convoy AA batteries, until Bong called out the presence of enemy escorts above the ships and peeled off to his left. The other five Lightning pilots followed Bong's descending P-38 for the enemy planes far out over the gulf.

The 9th Squadron drove down in numerous passes on the mix of OSCARs and ZEKEs until Lts. Ball, Leroy Donnell, Clay Barnes and the redoubtable Bong, each claimed destruction of a Ki-43 and damage to several others. Flt Ldr Haney and wingman Gersch both downed a ZEKE apiece before low fuel and ammo forced them all back to 14 Mile Field. In the skirmish, Haney had been hit in his right rear fuselage and Gersch had received slight damage to his starboard engine which caused it to run rough, but all the Flying Knights were ecstatic with their success; and they were safe.

## AN EIGHTBALL AMBUSH AT MALAHANG

As the surviving JAAF and JNAF fighter pilots descended toward Lae airdrome, the flights headed for Malahang were ambushed from above by the Eightball Warhawks, led by the irascible Capt. Ellis Wright, newly promoted to 5 FC as Assistant Ops Exec.

Wright took his White Flight quintet of Eightball Warhawks beneath the breaking overcast and orbited the shoreline east of Lae at 8000 feet. As the first ZEKEs withdrew from the dogfight with the Lightnings, Wright swept in behind four of them, beyond the shoreline at 400 feet above the waves, and cut off their approach to Malahang. Wright brought his guns to bear on his first two victims who fell into the sea, while wingman 2Lt. Bob White shot down a ZEKE which exploded on impacting the jungle off the south end of the strip. Minutes later, Wright sped up the Bulu River toward

*Capt. Tice's "ELSIE" tipped up due to a broken nose strut when landed by 9 FS 2Lt. O'Neill at Dobodura, some days after the Battle of the Bismarck Sea. ELSIE's outer tail surface displays a vertical white bar designating Tice as a senior flight leader.*

Malahang, closed in unseen behind another ZEKE foursome and blew up the trailing Mitsubishi at point blank range.

The second element leader in White Flight was Lt. Ernie Harris with wingmen 2Lts. Bob Moose and tail-end, Warren Blakely. The leader and wingman Moose made a firing pass at another ZEKE, with the victory later confirmed for Harris. Lt. Blakely shot down yet another before a lone ZEKE chased him from the area.

Red Flight led by Lt. Charles Galatka and flying top cover at 11,000 feet to the 7th Squadron dive bombers, did not encounter any ZEKEs or OSCARs at their greater height. Following the Demon dive bombers attack on Lae's main runway and their strafing of the straggler landing barge on the Markham River delta, Gelatka led the Eightball Red quartet down to riddle the smoking barge until it settled out of sight. The Eightballs withdrew on Capt. Wright's signal to regroup, and they returned together to 3 Mile Field in mid-afternoon.

## BLUE DEMON DIVE BOMBERS

Many new arrivals in the 5 FC who had not yet drawn permanent assignment, were pressed into attached squadron duty for the mammoth offensive against the newest Japanese reinforcement attempt at Lae. One such officer was senior Capt. Bob McHale who led the Demons' Blue Flight dive bomber quartet from Dobodura to the Lae area. Flt Ldr McHale had hoped to hit the convoy at anchor in the harbor, but by the time the dive bombers reached the bay in the early afternoon, the convoy had already been heavily damaged and its survivors dispersed. McHale diverted his bomb ladened P-40Ks up the Markham River delta to hit the main runway.

In a stacked in-line formation, McHale began his bomb attack from 9000 feet toward the north end of the Lae strip, followed closely by wingman Lt. John Benner. Seconds later, the other Blue Flight duet of element leader Lt. House and tag-a-long, Major Jim Martin, followed in a screaming descent toward the broad dirt runway. McHale and Benner released their 500 pounders at 1200 feet before the enemy field AA batteries could accurately target the two speeding Warhawks.

*Darwin 9 FS veteran Lt. Ed Ball made the P-38 team and gained his two aerial victories in the March campaign over Huon Gulf.*

House and Martin were both forced to pull out of their initial descent after the Japanese gunners quickly adjusted their aim. The lieutenant and major leveled off momentarily at 6000 feet as heavy caliber flak burst in front of their P-40s, then rolled their Warhawks over into a near vertical plunge and dropped their bombs near the north end of the strip, proceeded by a strafing run down the east flank of the landing area. Luckily for the Lae wing, the airdrome was vacant.

All four Blue Flight pilots had broken off to the right over the delta beneath scattered, inaccurate flak. Flt Ldr McHale spied the errant lone barge that was to become their first victim. The four Warhawks chased the lugger toward the western shoreline and slaughtered all on board, then strafed the smoldering hulk until it lay motionless in the muddy delta shallows. In his third pass over the smoking barge, Lt. House pulled up over the shoreline just above the trees in time to see eleven enemy fighters approaching from the east, 3000 feet overhead.

McHale and Benner had both expended all their ammunition in strafing the barge, and at House's warning of enemy planes, the Blue Flight Leader and his wingman immediately withdrew at full throttle, low over the bay.

House and Martin had not used up all their ammo and they wheeled north over the mainland to engage the approaching ZEKEs who had begun to separate into paired elements for their attack. After their climbing turn to the left back to 2000 feet over the delta, House's plan to cut off a lone ZEKE was quickly foiled by enemy wingmen approaching from the front and rear of the Blue team. House pushed the throttle forward in his trusty #13, POOPEY 2nd, and set up for a head-on pass against the onrushing ZEKE. As the dark green fighter's tracers fell beneath POOPEY's polished silver spinner, House returned a long burst which slammed into the Mitsubishi's engine. The Yankee pilot rocked POOPEY into a hard climbing left turn above the stricken ZEKE which disintegrated in flames. Martin broke around to his right and dueled briefly with two of the pursuing ZEKEs while House regained control of POOPEY, which had stalled out in the abrupt maneuver. As the element leader re-engaged, one of the ZEKEs erred and pulled out in front of House. The Darwin veteran closed into the rear quarter of his second victim, sending the ZEKE down in flames into the surf near the enemy strip.

Outnumbered and low on ammo, the Yanks dropped down to the water for a 350 MPH escape inland for cloud cover. House and Martin searched within the broken cumulus at 3000 feet for the rest of Demon Blue Flight, but both were low on gas and they climbed out of Markham Valley for home. The rising rain clouds on the north coast forced them to cross the mountains far north of Port Moresby and they landed at Rorona Field. Thankfully, all of the 49er combatants were able to return to their respective bases early the next day.

## LEVITAN IS LOST; MARCH 3, 1943

As for the men at 14 Mile and Dobodura, many Flying Knights were saddened by the loss of a veteran who never fired a shot in the day long fight. Senior Lt. and Java veteran, Bill Levitan, high in combat hours and awaiting transfer orders for the States, had flown by transport to Townville to pick up a refurbished P-38 for ferry

*7 FS veteran A.T. House coming to rest at 17 Mile in trusty P-40K #13 "POOPEY II" which garnered him the fourth confirmed victory on March 3rd. Like so many of the Darwin era pilots, House opted for home in May.*

flight back to 14 Mile Field. He had just crossed the coast of Cape York in company to a B-17, but the Lockheed pilot became separated in a rain squall and never reached New Guinea. The 9 FS Darwin veterans who had learned their combat techniques from the energetic, wiry little man found his loss almost unbearable. Levitan's death made sleep all the more fitful that night.

## DAY TWO - MARCH 4th; BISMARCK SEA BATTLE AND HUNTING NEAR LAE

On the evening of March 3rd, the weary pilots of the 5th Air Force ate sandwiches and drank strong coffee before collapsing in their tents. Many of the heavy bomber crews would sleep for only a few hours before rising to fly night missions in search of enemy survivors, but rain squalls curtailed the majority of the sorties.

The crew chiefs worked late into the night to repair and rearm the Lightnings and Warhawks, while the Operations people conferred over targets and new sorties. Group CO Morrissey stayed up late into the night reviewing the assignments for the next day and Group Ops Exec Reddington counselled with Wurtsmith's staff. The 49ers would be ready at first light on the morning of the 4th.

## BACK TO LAE ON MARCH 4th WITH THE FLYING KNIGHTS

Kenney was resolute in wanting to smash the remnants of Lae airdrome and ordered the fighters back to Lae for the coup de grace.

*Markey's reliable #74, still in service at Dobodura during the March campaign. Early flight line operations rarely included power equipment and refueling was by simple gravity and siphon hand-pumps.*

*9 FS aircraft #81 landing at Horanda after another March patrol.*

Though several enemy planes were strafed on the airstrip, there was no airborne opposition for the Warhawks of the Screamin' Demons or Eightballs in the earlier raids of the day. Later missions were aborted due to heavy rain.

At midday, however, the 9th Squadron made contact beyond the range of the Warhawks farther up the Huon coast. Eight Flying Knights were part of the nineteen-ship high cover that took the medium bomber strafers to Lae. As the Beaufighters and Havocs pounded the airfield, the 39th Squadron tangled momentarily with the Lae wing, claiming four shot down and several damaged. As the Beaufighters withdrew for Port Moresby, the blooded Lightning pilots continued east in a sweep of the Huon shoreline. Just past noon, Lt. Harry Brown called out the position of a dozen patrolling OSCARs forty miles east of Lae and dove to the attack. Brown and wingman 2Lt. John "Jump" O'Neill raced through the Ki-43s in three looping passes, and each pilot claimed one OSCAR destroyed before the enemy escaped into the clouds. All the Lightning pilots returned safely to 14 Mile Field.

### DAY THREE - MARCH 5th; DEMONS AND KNIGHTS AT LAE

The missions were repeated the very next day. Twelve Eightballs and sixteen Demons, in escort to the RAAF Beaufighters, would set off from 17 Mile at daybreak. At half past eight, just as the

*P-40K #32 used by Bob Baker on March 3rd seen in the Demons engineering work area during an engine overhaul.*

Beaus began their strafing runs, the Demons' Green Flight made contact with the 1st Sentai OSCARs in a brief, vicious skirmish over the Markham River valley, northeast of Lae village.

Green Flight's fourth man, Lt. Myers, aborted the mission early on when his gear failed to retract. Green Leader Capt. Melikian continued on, short one man, and set his trio in close formation to the Beaufighters beneath the hazy cloud ceiling at 6000 feet for the cross-island flight to the target. The assault on the Malahang strip was straight-forward. As the Beaus descended for their strafing run from the seaward approach, their flight leader immediately called out, "OSCARs to the east, just off shore." Melikian saw two light tan Ki-43s a thousand feet below and signaled his wingmen to attack. They kicked off their belly tanks and wheeled over into an in-line pursuit of the enemy planes.

Melikian, element leader Lt. Lee and wingman 2Lt. Dave Baker roared inland bound over the Malahang runway at 4000 feet, but the OSCARs looped up through the cloud ceiling. As the Beaus broke off and escaped to the west, Melikian circled his Green Flight 180 degrees to the east, back toward the shoreline, and crossed the Malahang landing pattern. Melikian and Lee each subsequently intercepted an OSCAR and chased them upward in looping maneuvers, but neither 1st Sentai pilot could reach the safety of the clouds in time. Two OSCARs fell in flames toward the hills northeast of Lae.

Lt. Baker's engagement was not as brief. The Yankee lieutenant, flying P-40K #32, also cut off one of the Ki-43s in similar fashion, but the Sentai man beat him in the race for the clouds. Baker sped upward through the haze and broke out above the overcast to see his quarry engaged by a flight of Lightnings. Badly outnumbered and outgunned, the Oscar quickly dropped away in a twisting "split S", beyond the gun range of the P-38s. Baker throttled #32 after him in a 400 MPH plunge down through the haze, but the Sentai man repeated the looping escape and the persistent Demon flyer followed him once more. A second time above the clouds, Baker came within gun range, but the OSCAR rolled over again. Baker again followed the enemy down through the clouds in hot pursuit, and spotted the OSCAR 1000 feet below in a broad opening within the overcast. From his height advantage, the Demon pilot dropped down to slay the OSCAR pilot with a long accurate volley from #32's six .50 caliber guns. Baker closed in from dead astern and flamed the Ki-43, which dove to a fiery explosion against a hillside north of Lae village.

The fight was over for the all the Demons, and Baker momentarily formed up with White Flight, until they saw Melikian and Lee in the distances west of Lae. Baker sped off to rejoined Green Flight for the trip back to Port Moresby. Those three 7 FS victories would be the last aerial victories for the Screamin' Demons in the March air battles.

### FATE AND VAUGHT MEET AGAIN

Only minutes after the Warhawk sorties, the Flying Knights would enter into another dogfight where one of their most beloved flight leaders would fall, not to the enemy, but again to inexplicable fate. Flamboyant "Snake-Bite" Bob Vaught, in ship #94, would lead the eight-ship flight of 9 FS Lightnings as part of the high cover for the mid-morning strike. In limited action, the Lockheed pilots would

*Victorious Baker poses with #32 at 17 Mile. The able flyer eventually joined the 49ers HQ staff and was one of the few men to put in a third combat tour which would take him to the Philippines in 1944.*

*5 FC CO Wurtsmith congratulates Flt Ldr Frank Nichols one last time before the able flyer transferred to the new 475 FG.*

*Senior Flt Ldr Bob "Snakebite" Vaught at 14 Mile Operations, just days before the captain's fateful mission of March 5th.*

engage a scattered enemy fighter formation within the heavy clouds high above the Lae target where they collectively claimed six destroyed and several damaged.

Capt. Vaught was the only Flying Knight who claimed any enemy planes destroyed on that sortie, having flamed two in dead astern firing passes, but he was forced to withdraw when #94's left engine failed. As the Knights departed for Dobodura, the captain's right engine also began to run rough, just as they flew east of Wau village. Unwilling to gamble on the single engine lasting all the way to Horanda, or to chance a bail-out and possible capture, he decided Wau was a viable alternate strip. Besides, old #94 had just provided him with his fourth and fifth kills, and the new ace wanted to save the valuable ship.

Vaught descended into the Wau pattern, certain that the big fighter would halt upon the 4000 foot strip if he landed uphill on the sloping valley floor. He lowered his landing gear and turned into the southern approach above the rows of red-ripe coffee trees that surrounded Wau village and the narrow dirt strip. With a little more air speed than usual owing to the urgency of landing on one engine, Vaught dropped full flaps to aid in slowing the approach, when suddenly, the fighter's coughing right motor shut down short of the runway. Vaught had no time to react as #94 sank without warning from its 100 foot height. The powerless Lockheed slammed into the end of the dirt runway at 120 knots, sending up a great cloud of mud and debris. It slid off the edge of the strip and plowed through the coffee trees, finally coming to rest in a grotesque twisted hulk. The P-38's residual fuel did not ignite and the field crews immediately rushed to the broken plane laying in an ocean of brilliant red coffee beans. The pilot's lifeless body was carefully pulled from the wreckage and taken to the small Aussie dispensary where a medic pronounced him dead.

Vaught's body was wrapped in canvass and put aboard a C-47 for transport back to Port Moresby. As the transport was about to take off, the loadmaster told a crewman to better secure the dead man, but to the crewman's shock, when he tried to lift the purported corpse, the shrouded body let out a deep moan. The C-47 pilot flew at full-throttle for the hospital at Port Moresby. Rugged Bob Vaught had outlived the odds once more. This time, he was going home for good. He recovered from his injuries and transferred to the States, where he later signed on to fly another combat tour in the European theater.

Vaught's squadron mates continued in the Papuan campaign with a rapid pace of victories in the phenomenal Lockheed twin-engined killer. Maj. Jesse Peaselee's pilots would rival the high scoring 39th Squadron P-38 pilots and outscore all other units in their deadly pursuit of the enemy over Papua and the Solomon Sea. While the short range Warhawks returned to their tactical missions, or patrolled over Dobodura and Oro Bay, the 9 FS enjoined in missions of even greater distances to find the enemy during March. Vaught had become their newest ace, but his score would soon be far surpassed by many of the Flying Knights who soldiered on in New Guinea.

## THE DEMISE OF THE LAE REINFORCEMENTS

Kenney's three day campaign against Operation 81-Go had been an immense success. Of the more than 7000 troops in Gen. Imamura's 18th Army contingent, nearly half had been lost, including the entire 18th Army HQ staff. Five Imperial Fleet destroyers which had escaped the 5 AF onslaught were able to pick up 2700 troopers from the Gulf, who were then returned safely to Rabaul. Only 900 men from the convoy would ever reach Lae garrison, while thousands of tons of crucial war supplies had been sent to the bottom of the Solomon Sea.

The survivors at Lae and Rabaul mourned for the Imperial soldiers, airmen and seamen who had been killed, or were missing as a result of the withering attacks of heavy bombardment and ruth-

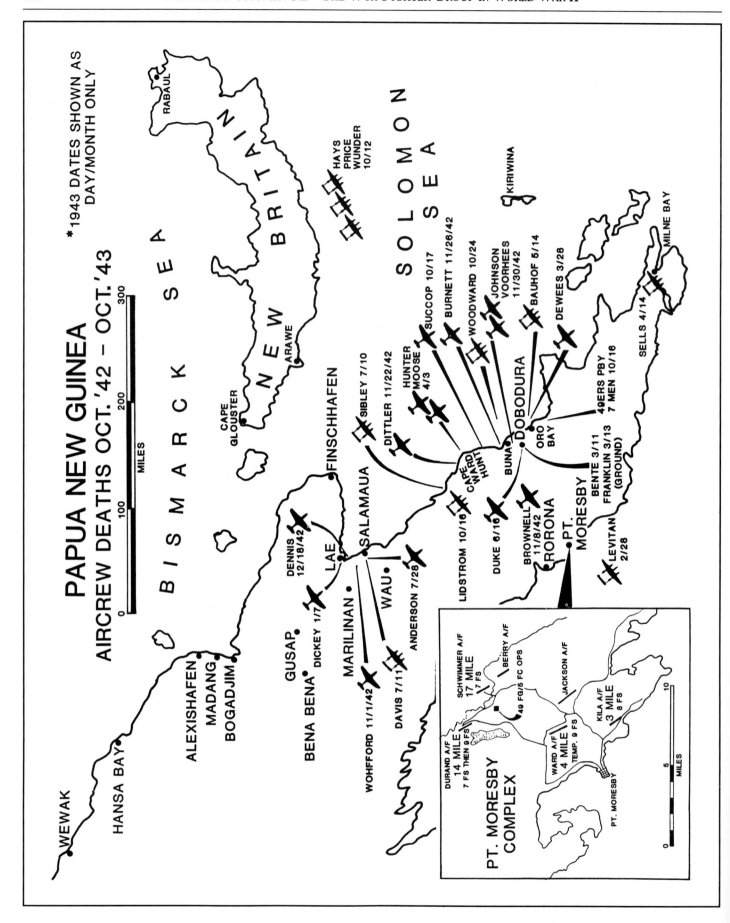

PAPUA NEW GUINEA
AIRCREW DEATHS OCT. '42 – OCT. '43

*1943 DATES SHOWN AS DAY/MONTH ONLY

MILES
0    100    200    300

RABAUL

NEW BRITAIN

BISMARCK SEA

ARAWE

CAPE GLOUSTER

FINSCHHAFEN

SALAMAUA

DENNIS 12/18/42
LAE
DICKEY 1/7

MARILINAN

WAU
ANDERSON 7/28
DAVIS 7/11

GUSAP
BENA BENA
WOHFFORD 11/1/42

ALEXISHAFEN
MADANG
BOGADJIM

HANSA BAY

WEWAK

SIBLEY 7/10

DITTLER 11/22/42

HUNTER MOOSE 4/3

SUCCOP 10/17

BURNETT 11/26/42

WOODWARD 10/24

JOHNSON VOORHEES 11/30/42

BAUHOF 5/14

DEWEES 3/28

SOLOMON SEA

HAYS PRICE WUNDER 10/12

KIRIWINA

MILNE BAY

SELLS 4/14

CAPE D WARD HUNT

BUNA
DOBODURA
ORO BAY

LIDSTROM 10/16

DUKE 6/16

BROWNELL 11/8/42
RORONA
PT. MORESBY

BENTE 3/11
FRANKLIN 3/13 (GROUND)
49ERS PBY 7 MEN 10/16

LEVITAN 2/28

PT. MORESBY COMPLEX

DURAND A/F
14 MILE
7 FS THEN 9 FS

SCHWIMMER A/F
17 MILE
7 FS

BERRY A/F
49 FG/5 FC OPS

JACKSON A/F

WARD A/F
4 MILE
TEMP. 9 FS

KILA A/F
3 MILE
8 FS

PT. MORESBY

MILES
0    5    10

*The Screamin' Demons honor guard assembly at 17 Mile Field before their move to Dobodura in late March.*

less strafing. Fourteen merchant ships and eight war ships had been sunk, and nearly 60 aircraft had been lost in combat or to related causes. Kenney's 5th Air Force had successfully retrieved the dismal achievements of January. As of the first week in March of 1943, the Allies had negated the last real hope of an Imperial offensive to be based at Lae, New Guinea. From that moment on, initiative in the jungle island war was in the hands of the Allies.

MacArthur and Kenney did not tarry in the glow of this victory. The two American generals rallied their respective army and air force to pick up the offensive pace against the New Guinea front and to expand into the New Britain campaign. There would be a brief period of news headlines for the American public, citations for the brave, and then the immediate return to the mission to capture Lae proper.

LtC. Bob Morrissey presided over his high scoring 49th Fighter Group, proud to lead the best in Wurtsmith's 5th Fighter Command. Morrissey had not lost a man in the grueling three days of missions against the great convoy bound for Lae, and had personally received kudos as one of Gen. Kenney's most capable strategists, having played a key role in the operations planning of 5 FC at 17 Mile Field. As testimony to the men of the Screamin' Demons, Eightballs and Flying Knights, the entire Group completed its move to permanent encampment at the new base of Dobodura immediately after the March campaign against Lae, while their P-40 and P-38 missions continued without interruption. As of March, 1943, Dobodura would be known as the home of the 49ers, the most deadly fighter group in the Pacific theater.

# 10

## THE 49ERS OF DOBODURA 1943

For the first time in the New Guinea campaign, General George Kenney had an air base that could hold the majority of his Fifth Air Force fighter groups. The Dobodura complex on the great savannah plain below the northern slopes of the Owen Stanley Range afforded a broad dispersal area for fighters, medium bombers, transports and reconnaissance squadrons.

On the west side of the T-runway landing area was a dense jungle forest, and beyond those tree, another kunai savannah. It was in this forest and prairie that the Fifth Fighter Command dispersed the personnel of the fighters groups, including LtC. Bob Morrissey's Forty Ninth Fighter Group HQ and their three squadrons. For the next seven months, this great complex of men and machines would be the center for Col. Paul Wurtsmith's 5 FC air offensive against the Japanese who were based 175 miles to the northwest at Lae and 400 miles to the northeast at Rabaul, New Britain.

As more aircraft began to fill the dispersal areas of Dobodura's broad landing field, the Japanese immediately launched a counter-offensive against the growing Allied airdrome. Japanese army and navy aircraft would strike the Allied bases of Dobodura and Oro Bay throughout 1943, and both sides would pay dearly with the losses of many good young men.

### ALERT AT DOBODURA; MARCH 8, 1943

The Lockheed P-38s and Operations shack of the Flying Knights was located on the south side of Horanda runway in the forest that grew between the landing field and the Samboga River. At the sound of an alert, they would taxi directly onto the main strip and lift off to the northeast, often in flights of four ships abreast on the 500 foot wide dirt track. It was common practice for flights of transports to land or take off parallel to the P-38s operations.

Just off the north end of the shorter Kalamazoo runway was "Warhawk Row" where the P-40s of Capt. Manning's Demons and Capt. Porter's Eightballs were dispersed among the trees. Their take-offs were usually by pairs of P-40s, southeast bound over the dispersal area of the Flying Knights. This northern dispersal area was also used by the 22nd BG Marauders, as well as a staging area for Moresby-based Airacobras in escort to the C-47 transports.

The alert system was tested from the very moment of its inception. The majority of alert sorties were far beyond the range of Capt. Porter's Eightball Warhawks. Capt. Woods' Lightnings immediately proved their superior range and speed.

### TAYLOR'S INTERCEPTION; MARCH 8, 1943

At 1:00 p.m., sixteen 9 FS Lightnings at Horanda got off in the alert to pursue an enemy formation off Oro Bay. The trio led by Capt. Dick Taylor became separated in the scattered cumulus over the Solomon Sea as they searched for the nine BETTY bombers which had just struck Oro Bay and were now reported heading back toward Gasmata. At their pursuit altitude of 17,000 feet, Taylor's flight overtook the triple V formation of dark green raiders. The Knights passed 4000 feet overhead until Taylor could peel off to his left for a head-on pass against the Mitsubishis' right flank. The captain swept beneath the bombers and fired at point blank range across the breadth of the enemy formation. One bomber temporarily fell from the V, but struggled back into position.

Taylor repeated the tactic twice again, only to be suddenly cut

*Eightball P-40Es on the alert line at Kalamazoo strip.*

*8 FS engineering facilities off the north end of Kalamazoo.*

off in his attack by eight escorting OSCARs which approached from a greater height. The Flying Knights rolled away in full throttle descents to the nearby clouds where Taylor eluded one OSCAR, then wheeled hard about to attack again. In a whistling plunge through 6000 feet, the captain overtook two OSCARs, one which he flamed from dead astern, and then set upon the bombers in a final pass against the BETTY in the far right position. The explosive ammo of Taylor's 20 mm cannon and four .50 caliber machine guns flashed on the engine nacelle and forward fuselage of the rotund twin-engine ship. It shuddered from the blows, fell from its position and plunged straight down for a mile into the sea. Taylor looked about for more OSCARs, but seeing none, he recalled his flight. All sixteen Knights safely returned to Dobodura and Taylor was official awarded with both the OSCAR and BETTY as confirmed kills.

Patrols and alerts continued for the next five days, but neither the Flying Knights nor the Eightballs made contact with the raiders. Then on March 11th, the JNAF at Rabaul sent the kokutais to again strike the Dobodura area. It would result in one of the most dramatic interceptions ever flown by the 49ers from Dobodura.

## THE INTERCEPTION ON MARCH 11, 1943

Shortly before 10:00 a.m., a U.S. Navy patrol ship reported an approaching enemy formation over the Solomon Sea, due east of Oro Bay. The 49th Fighter Controllers at Oro Bay, code named "CATER", immediately signalled the airborne patrol of four P-38s in Green Flight at 15,000 feet over Buna village, to gain altitude and rendezvous with the 8th Squadron over the Allied port. Darwin veteran flight leader, Lt. "Tiny" Tom Fowler, with his wingman

Carl Planck, element leader Lt. Bill Hanning and his wingman, 2Lt. Keith Oveson, executed a climbing turn southward, up through the billowing cumulus clouds that topped out at 18,000 feet.

Simultaneously, the Eightball alarm sounded at Kalamazoo strip and their mission leader, Capt. Larry Kirsch, responded with eight P-40s which took off in a full throttle climb out to sea. As the old model E's struggled up to 10,000 feet, they were informed by CATER that the enemy was headed for Dobodura and Kirsch brought his flights about through a 180 degree climbing turn. At 20 minutes past ten, the Eightball pilots looked down at the bombs bursting upon their landing field, and caught sight of the raider's formation up through the clouds at 19,000 feet. Then the bombers turned out to sea and Kirsch's Warhawks followed, still climbing.

Down below, the alerted standby Red Flight of four Flying Knights, led by CO Sid Woods, took off as the string of enemy bombs erupted behind them upon Horanda strip. Capt. Woods, wingman Lt. Jack Mankin, element leader Dick Bong and his wingman, 2Lt. Theron "Pappy" Price, all escaped the attack. They set off eastward in pursuit of the raiders, but in their ascent, Price reported engine failure and had to turn back. Woods, Mankin and Bong continued the chase.

## GREEN FLIGHT'S ATTACK

Meanwhile, Lt. Fowler's Green Flight had climbed to 26,000 feet, well above the scattered clouds. CATER informed the alerted 49ers that the enemy had now dropped to 15,000 feet, so Green Flight dropped their belly-tanks and gradually descended to pick up speed for the attack. Soon, Flt Ldr Fowler called out on his right, a formation of twenty-four BETTY bombers with an escort of an equal

*8 FS Operations center at Kalamazoo.*

*9 FS motor pool facilities in the dispersal area south of Horanda strip.*

number of ZEROs in trailing position. Green Flight passed over the Kokutai formation to place themselves "up sun" at 23,000 feet against the enemy's right flank. The Flight Leader looked about one last time for enemy fighters at his altitude, then dropped the left wing of his big fighter and plunged for the enemy below. Wingman Planck followed immediately, then Hanning and wingman Oveson followed a few seconds later.

As the Lockheed quartet descended, three kokutai ZEKEs broke into the approaching P-38s which diverted their attack on the bombers. Both ZEROs and Lightnings fired at each other head-on. Fowler struck his target with a sustained burst and immediately broke to the right as Ku wingmen chased him out of the fight. Wingman Planck simultaneously broke left to protect his fight leader from a turning ZERO and raked the dark grey-green fighter from nose to tail at point blank range. Other ZEROs intervened and Planck was then forced to speed away some distance to protect himself, then turned hard about and climbed to reengage. From 25,000 feet, Planck looked down on a P-38 in a shallow dive and trailing smoke. Someone was in trouble, but another threatening pass by the kokutai forced Planck to withdraw before he could cover the falling Flying Knight.

## HEAD-ON WITH HANNING

The crippled P-38 was that of element leader Bill Hanning. He and wingman Oveson had also engaged the ZEKEs, just as Fowler and Planck had done, but Oveson had quickly been forced out of the match and Hanning had to fight on alone. After an initial high speed turn against three ZEROs, Hanning flamed an enemy with a perfect 90 degree deflection shot and turned to descend upon another, but the Ku wingman countered his attack and wheeled toward him, face to face.

They closed in on one another and both fired, but the closure rate was far too great for Hanning to avoid the fateful collision. His P-38 jolted as the right wingtip tore through the ZERO's cockpit. Hanning quickly regained control of his bent bird, then turned northwest and throttled back his shuddering engines which streamed prestone coolant. He looked down at the crushed Mitsubishi which fell away trailing smoke and saw another ZERO wingman turn toward his own smoking Lockheed.

For 20 miles, Hanning kept ahead of the persistent Ku pilot who had now entered into a shallow dive to run down the crippled Lockheed over the coast. The vulnerable Flying Knight had no recourse. He dropped the nose of his ship into a diving turn and braced himself for another headon exchange. Twice more, ZERO and Lightning closed upon each other with guns ablaze, but Hanning's aircraft had suffered too much damage from the previous collision and gunfire. Unable to maneuver out of the ZERO's line of lethal cannon fire, Hanning's canopy collapsed and the Allison engines erupted in flames. The Flying Knight released his straps, stood up and arched his back until the slipstream ripped him out of the shattered cockpit. Hanning pulled the cord of his chute, just as the Lockheed exploded. He blacked out and later awoke in his inflated May West, floating amongst the debris and ashes of his destroyed ship. Luckily, he had come down within sight of Oro Bay and was soon picked up by a RAN tug, "the Pacific", which took him to the harbor's field hospital. He would convalesce there for a week to allow his shrapnel cuts, black eye and strained back a chance to heal.

## RED FLIGHT AND THE EIGHTBALLS

The scrambled flights from Kalamazoo and Horanda could see Green Flight's engagement east of Oro Bay. Capt. Kirsch's Warhawks desperately pushed upward for the battle that spread beyond the shore, but Capt. Woods' superior twin-engine P-38s dropped their belly-tanks and quickly outpaced the old stagers P-40s. The Flying Knights' Red Flight would be the next to strike the kokutai.

Capt. Woods, with Mankin and Bong in close echelon formation to his left, overtook the BETTY formation thirty miles beyond the shoreline. The Yanks sped out in front of their quarry to be in position for a slightly higher frontal assault. The three Flying Knights swung into a sustained firing pass against three Vee elements on the right flank then turned back for a second pass, but all were forced to disperse by a superior number of ZEKEs. Woods dropped the nose of his #86 and dived for the coast at 450 Mph until the pursuing escorts turned away.

Jack Mankin had shaken his pursuers among the clouds and tried to find the bombers again, but they had disappeared in the cumulus. After a few minutes of hunting, he chanced upon the trailing elements of the ku escorts, and maneuvered against two of them until he hit one that stalled out in a climbing turn. As his victim fell away trailing smoke and flames, the other Ku wingmen gained the advantaged. Mankin rolled his big Lockheed over and dived for the coast.

Tail-end Dick Bong had come well within range of the intervening ZEROs and twisted his #80 into a vertical descent in excess of 475 mile per hour. He pulled out just above the waves of the Solomon Sea and sped off ahead of his pursuers for several minutes to get some maneuvering room, when he realized he was headed due east and deeper into enemy air space. He craned his neck to look to the rear and spotted only one plane following some distance back. Deciding it was now probably safe to reverse course, Bong racked #80 into a 180 degree turn and immediately acquired the on-coming ZERO in his gunsight. The ZEKE still carried its centerline tank, assuring the P-38 ace that his opponent was not expecting the head-on pass. He fired a long burst of tracers into the radial-engine fighter, then kicked left rudder and swept past as it erupted in flames. Bong was startled to encounter a second tank-toting Zero which also appeared head-on. The lone lieutenant quickly adjusted with left rudder and fired a short string of tracers which flashed upon its grey fuselage.

Then seven more nose-on silhouettes appeared and Bong laid on right rudder to fire a long 20 degree deflection shot at the closest ZEKE, then reversed with left rudder as the other Ku wingmen wheeled out of the path of the twisting, tracer-spitting, twin-engine monster. The lone Knight quickly looked back at the first two enemy planes now falling in flames and the third one trailing smoke, but he could not get another in his gun sight. Bong pushed the throttle full forward and hunched down behind the armor plate as the ZEROs wheeled in behind his accelerating P-38. After he had only run a short distance, one of them made a pass from the left rear quarter and hit #80 with a short burst. But Bong had the jump in this race and he out distanced the last of the kokutai before his left engine lost its coolant. He would come down safely for a single engine landing at Horanda.

*Although contemporaries mustered out of the mission roster for HQ staff positions, or furloughed home, 8 FS Darwin cadre pilot Clyde Barnett returned from medical leave to resume his flying tour. He took charge of rebuilt Model-E stager #55, named it "WEST PALM BEACH PLAYBOY" and took up the Deputy Ops Exec job at Kalamazoo.*

## EIGHTBALLS HIT THE ENEMY ESCORTS

With belly-tanks drained and dropped off, the eight Warhawks had picked up speed and finally caught the kokutai 50 miles off shore. Capt. Kirsch had seen the Red Flight Lightnings make their unproductive pass at the bombers and he was determined his rookie wingman, 2Lt. Leo Mayo, and the veterans Ops Exec Clyde Barnett and his wingman, Ben Duke, would get their chance. The Warhawks approached the BETTY formation from 21,000 feet and Kirsch rolled to the attack as the P-38s pulled away.

Unfortunately, the nimble ZEROs were able to regroup and cut off Kirsch's flight before the Eightball's reached the BETTYs. The four Americans maneuvered through several turns with the ZEKEs until Lt. Mayo's P-40 took a 20 mm round which entered through the left-rear canopy window and exploded in the cockpit. Shrapnel cut Mayo's left hand and arm, and blew out half of his instruments. That was plenty of combat for the rookie and he rolled straight down for shore.

Only Ops Exec Barnett in #55, PALM BEACH PLAYBOY, caught a ZERO in a left turn. Barnett torched the Mitsubishi's engine, then closed in and hammered the fuselage until the Ku pilot slumped down out of sight. The Ops Exec then tried to re-engage, but the PLAYBOY had lost too much speed and the victorious Darwin veteran wisely dropped away for Kalamazoo.

The second quartet in the Eightball scramble would fare better against the BETTYs. Veteran Lt. Bill Day had led rookies Lt. Bill Lown, 2Lts. Danny Moore and Bob Hagerstrom, up to 22,500 feet and were several seconds behind the descent of mission leader Kirsch. Although Day's foursome had struggled to hold formation at the extreme altitude in their old Warhawks, they were able to use the height and speed advantage to reach the bombers while the first quartet engaged the ZEROs.

Second Lts. Lown and Hagerstrom fell in some distance behind the bombers and fired as they closed in at high speed, but they badly judged the range. Both men were forced to drop out as their old stagers would not put out the power to catch the bombers again,

*Left: An unidentified man poses by CO Sid Woods' aircraft at 14 Mile which displays the captain's BETTY kill made on March 11th. The curious yellow number "05" is likely a designator of a 13 AF unit which turned the P-38 into the Townsville maintenance center which in turn reissued the aircraft to the 9 FS. The wolf-shield is likely a personal design of the previous 13 AF pilot. Right: Rookie and future ace Bob Hagerstrom with the old stager that garnered him his first career kill on April 11th.*

but in their descent, a ZERO crossed Hagerstrom's path. He fired and claimed the hits were fatal.

Day and Moore joined up in a duet pass on the same BETTY wingman in the right V element that had received all the attention in the previous attacks. Both Day and Moore scored hits on the BETTY and swept beneath the formation, then wheeled about for another run, just as the ZEROs dropped to their level. Moore could not gain any advantage and withdrew, but wiley veteran Day in his trusty #43, JERRY 2nd, intervened against an adversary who had momentarily pursued Lown. Day closed inside the ZEKE's turn and saw his .50 caliber explosives light up on the grey fuselage, but five of his six guns jammed during the high G turn. With only one gun working, Day riddled the Mitsubishi's cockpit and engine until JERRY stalled out. The Flight Leader pushed the nose of #43 down and heard the clatter of machine bullets clank on JERRY'S hull. He shoved the throttle forward and JERRY dutifully carried him safely for the cover of the clouds below. The fight was over. All of the Eightballs would returned to Kalamazoo.

## AFTERMATH of the MARCH 11th RAID

Several ground units at Dobodura had sustained casualties in the attack that day. The 49ers returned to their base and found their operations area had borne the brunt of the bombings.

The Warhawks set down on Horanda strip and taxied for the Kalamazoo dispersal area, but were instructed to park their Warhawks on the north side of the main strip near the control tower. The 8th Squadron ordinance team had already roped off the northern dispersal area and had begun to search for unexploded bombs.

During the air battle, the Eightball line crews had attempted to ready another quartet of Warhawks for a follow-up flight, but several men had been caught in the open as the BETTYs paraded over their dispersal area. Sgt. Charles MacDonald and PFC Joyce Zumbrennen scrambled for the air raid trenches, but both men were hit by flying shrapnel. Thankfully, their wounds were minor and easily treated at the scene by 7 FS Flt Surgeon Capt. Wexler.

*8 FS pilots in opposition to I-GO (front lt.-rt.) 2Lts. Carter, Grant, Hagerstrom and Polhamus. Standing (lt.-rt.) are Lt. Ernie Harris, and 2Lts. White, Vodra and Flack.*

*8 FS pilots in the Dobodura battles (front lt.-rt.) 2Lt. Sawyer, F/O Pierce, 2Lts. Wolfe and McCullough. Standing (lt.-rt.) are Flack, Peterson, Lown (MIA-1944), Deputy Ops Exec Barnett and Ops Exec Wright.*

## SGTS. BENTE AND FRANKLIN FALL

Far across the airfield, the Flying Knights were not as lucky. They were caught in the path of an enemy salvo, just as Red Flight P-38s departed. In the dispersal area, Sgt. Fred Bente was in a P-38 cockpit and Sgt. Obert Franklin was standing on the ground nearby to assist in the test of the engines while Cpl. Rob Woodfin watched from a short distance away. The first bombs landed squarely on the Lockheed, killing Bente outright and setting the plane on fire. Woodfin and Sgt Franklin were cut down by the blast, the sergeant being mortally wounded by the shrapnel.

As the other bombs erupted down through the flight line, Cpl. Garland "Texas" Black drove his truck for the trees, but he had to abandon the vehicle when a bomb burst in his path. He got out and crawled underneath the vehicle for protection, only to be pinned to the muddy ground as the whistling shrapnel flattened the tires. He would lay there in the mud for an hour before he could be rescued.

In the meantime, the Demons surgical team found the wounded 9th Squadron men and took them to the HQ field dispensary. Corporal Woodfin's wounds were easily treated, but Flt Surgeon Wexler could do little for mortally wounded Sgt. Franklin. The sergeant's shattered right arm was amputated and his extensive chest wounds were cleaned, but it was to no avail. Franklin died three days later.

The Flying Knights found little consolation in the ensuing confirmation of six enemy kills in the interception that day. Bong was awarded two ZEROs, Fowler, Planck and Mankin a ZERO each and CO Woods a BETTY, but they would be without wounded Hanning for the next two weeks and they had lost their first enlisted men to enemy action.

## A WARHAWK ACE IN NEW GUINEA

The Eightballs had been extremely lucky as all their old stager P-40s and all their men had survived the March 11th raid. After Ops Exec Barnett, and newcomers Moore and Hagerstrom were each officially given credit for their ZERO kills, the Eightballs gave a toast to the new celebrity in their ranks. The popular young flight leader, Lt. Bill Day, had his BETTY and ZERO kill claims confirmed for his fourth and fifth victories, making him the first

*C.C. Ed Gillam (lt.) and new ace Lt. Bill Day a few days after the March 11th sortie.*

Warhawk ace in the New Guinea theater. By tradition in the flying ranks, Day spent a small fortune buying drinks in the Eightball officers club and enlisted club, too.

The Eightballs renewed their patrols over the Dobodura-Oro Bay complex, and the Flying Knights resumed their long range escorts to the Fifth bomber command, yet neither unit would contact the enemy for the next two weeks. Group Commander Morrissey meanwhile pressed the Screamin' Demons to bring up the last of their ground and air echelons to Dobodura, and the colonel informed 8 FS CO Jim Porter to expect the arrival of the Demon Warhawks by the end of March, as both the Demons and Eightball P-40s would operate from Kalamazoo strip.

## THE INTERCEPTION ON MARCH 25, 1943

As Capt. Red Manning's Screamin' Demons were making their way to their new facilities, the Japanese again sent recon missions in preparation for the next interdictions at Oro Bay. Numerous high speed reconnaissance planes had been reported over the coast and the Flying Knights finally caught one of the spy planes above Dobodura.

The five-ship patrol led by newly promoted Capt. Bill Haney, flew over Buna at 20,000 feet when they were vectored by the CATER air controllers to seek out a lone plane in their area. Capt. Haney turned north and spread his quintet far apart to hunt for the intruder they soon spotted a lone BETTY bomber cruising at 24,000 feet, headed due west. Haney was joined by Lt. Ed Ball and they set after the rotund Mitsubishi in the brilliant clear sky. As the BETTY passed over Dobodura, Ball attacked first and killed the rear gunner, then Haney closed in for the coup de grace. Both of the Flying Knights scored hits on the swerving giant as it turned back toward the east, until Haney pulled to within point blank range. The captain raked the bomber on both sides of its fuselage until the Mitsubishi rolled inverted and plunged straight down into the sea.

## INTERCEPTION ON MARCH 28, 1943

The Japanese continued to send small raids against the Allies both day and night, as well as daily reconnaissance flights, but three days of 49er patrols and scrambles failed to intercept any of these lesser intrusions. On the 28th, the fighter force from Dobodura would execute another deadly interceptions resulting in one of the most intense dogfights of the war

In mid morning, a great air armada of JAAF and JNAF planes lifted off from their New Britain air fields to strike an Allied convoy of a dozen ships that had just reached Oro Bay. It was their largest formation thus far in the campaign, and though the kokutai heavy bombers would successfully evade the American interception, LtC. Morrisey's P-40s and P-38s would exact a bloody toll from the ZEKES, and VALs, and OSCARs, caught just beyond the bay.

## BLUE FLYING KNIGHTS

At a quarter past eleven o'clock, a standing "Blue" patrol of five 9 FS Lightnings, led by the Darwin veteran Lt. Clyde Harvey, was vectored from their position east of Dobodura, southward for Oro Bay. CATOR reported a large formation approaching from the east at 16,000 feet and Blue Flight made a climbing turn for "twenty-seven angels." Once at their position five miles above the harbor area, Harvey soon caught sight of the sprawling armada of single engine planes, which he estimated as a force "unable (to be) counted as they were too scattered, and I estimated 50 to 60 ZEROs scattered all over." The Knights could see the Allied convoy ships dispersed about the bay. Smoke rose from two stricken freighters and from the fires that raged on the bombed docks. Four BETTYs were also seen escaping through the billowing clouds, well out of range, but the greater swarm of VAL dive bombers and fighter escorts were directly below, just turning off from their attacks on the harbor.

Flight Ldr Harvey did not hesitate and immediately jettisoned his belly tanks. Only the last man in Blue flight, 2Lt. Keith Oveson, failed to drop his tanks and he would remain in his high position as a spotter for CATOR. Flight Ldr Harvey, 2Lts. Clay "Mother" Peterson, Walter Markey and "Jump" O'Neill, peeled off into a 400 mph plunge for the escaping enemy formation below. The four Blue Flight pilots thundered down through a broad "S" turn and spread apart to choose their individual targets, but the Blue quartet was not alone.

## BLUE and RED EIGHTBALLS

Just as the Flying Knights Blue patrol had responded from its position east of their field, two standing patrols of Eightball Warhawks over Buna village would also answer the 1115 hours call from CATOR.

The Red quartet was led by Mission Leader, Capt. Ken Johns, with wingman 2Lts. Bob Howard, element leader Cecil Dewees and rookie wingman F/O Merle Wolfe. Blue Flight was led by Darwin veteran Lt. Bo Jordan, with wingman 2Lt. Stan Hunter, element leader Lt. Bob Moose and wingman 2Lt. Russ Francis. Capt.

Johns led the P-40s parallel to the coast up to 24,000 feet, where the Eightballs soon looked down on the burning freighters and docks, and the escaping VALs just above the water. At the same moment that the Blue Flight P-38s had entered their attack dive, mission leader Capt. Johns ordered "tanks off" and eight P-40s roared into the fray. Twelve 49ers had struck in unison in their initial assault.

## MORE FLYING KNIGHTS IN GREEN and YELLOW FLIGHTS

The scramble alarm also brought aloft the alert flights from Dobodura. Fifteen minutes before the 49ers' air borne flights had attacked, the Green Flt Ldr, Capt. Bill Haney, with wingmen Lt. Floyd Finberg and newcomer 2Lt. Grover Fanning, took off from Horanda strip, followed closely by the Yellow Flight trio of Ops Exec Harry Lidstrom, wingman 2Lts. Arthur Beauhof, and Martin "Big Pete" Alger. The Green-Yellow force swept upward to 24,000 feet and Capt. Haney soon witnessed the approach of the VAL dive bombers at Oro Bay, and heard over the radio, the rattle of gun-fire and shouts of attacking 49ers who called out the enemy positions. Haney ordered the flights to spread out, then dropped his tanks, and all six P-38s roared down at 400 Mph against the fleeing enemy.

Meanwhile, the initial 9 FS Blue Flight attack was immediately engaged by the JNAF escorts, and Flt Ldr Harvey, Markey, and O'Neill, each flamed a mottled green ZEKE. In the ensuing passes, the dogfight became a blur of Curtiss, Lockheed, Mitsubishi and Nakajima fighters. Warhawks and Lightnings fired upon ZEKEs and OSCARs in the same instant. Flaming wreckage fell and oil slicks spotted the ocean. For over 30 minutes, the 49ers pressed their assaults above the watery graveyard of the Solomon Sea.

Capt. Johns' and Lt. Jordan's respective Red and Blue P-40 flights had initially been engaged at 5000 feet by the close escort OSCARs and ZEROS, but both side had mixed success. Red Flt Ldr Johns and wingman Howard had slashed through the intervening OSCARs and brought their .50 caliber guns to bare upon the

*Resilient Eightball Flt Ldr Capt. Ken Johns.*

*9 FS Darwin cadre veteran Floyd Finberg finally scored in his P-38 on March 28, 1943.*

*9 FS veteran Lt. Howk flew a year of sustained combat but never hit an opponent, even in the P-38.*

VAL dive-bombers. Each man splashed a victim, and together, they heavily damaged four others. Johns and Howard then set off for home, but just off shore, they joined with the P-38s and parried with the bronze-colored OSCARs. Captain Johns fired a wide deflection volley in defense, but missed the sentai opponent. He and Howard finally broke off for a safe landing at Kalamazoo.

## THE LOSS OF 2LT. DEWEES

Red Flight's second element was far less fortunate. Element leader Dewees and wingman Wolfe had separated a short distance from their Red Leader, due to Wolfe's slow ascent in his sputtering old stager. After Dewees and Wolfe had crept up to 22,000 feet, they sped down together to engage at 7000, where Dewees fired at a Vee element of VALs, but struggling Wolfe could not get the enemy in his sights. Wolfe fought to hold formation as Dewees maneuvered for another pass, but the frightened rookie failed to see the circling kokutai opponent who closed in from behind. Wolfe peered out in horror as 20 mm cannon explosions shattered Dewees' canopy. Instantly killed, the lement leader's P-40 snap-rolled into an inverted flat spin.

Cannon tracers now bracketed Wolfe's ship and the terrified rookie dropped away for the coast. He pulled out just above the waves and sped westward beneath the last elements of enemy planes, until he crossed the shoreline just south of Buna. Wolfe climbed to 6000 feet in search of his squadron mates, only to be attacked by a pair of Warhawks who suddenly swept down out of the hazy overcast, and then just as abruptly disappeared. It was more than the terrorized rookie could bare. Merle Wolfe, totally exhausted, finally reached Kalamazoo alone.

Meanwhile, the Eightball Blue Flight elements had also taken hits in the exchange with the kokutai, but the damage was only one bullet hole in Francis' rudder and only two holes in Howard's tail. Blue Flight claimed victories and probables in return. Flt Ldr. Jordan and his wingmen had become widely separated after the first pass, but in the individual encounters that followed, Jordan, Hunter and Francis, each claimed one green ZERO apiece. Moose posted an impressive claim of three brought down. All four men of Blue Flight safely returned to Kalamazoo.

Several minutes after the initial assault by the Knights' Blue Flight patrol, Haney's Green-Yellow sextet came down against the rear action defense flown by the HAMPs. The combined elements of the Lightning squadron proved to be too much to handle for the inferior Mitsubishis. Blue Flight's Walter Markey claimed a square-wingtipped fighter in the first pass, and in the ensuing maneuvers, Flt Ldr Harvey and wingman Jump O'Neill claimed two more. Darwin veteran Finberg dispatched a fourth HAMP, and Ops Exec Lidstrom gunned down the fifth victim.

Number four "Big Pete" Alger was the only Flying Knight hit in the exchange. The tall, quiet wingman had taken his Lightning #90 down to low altitude to assist a P-38 which was pursued by five ZEKEs and Big Pete singled out the trailing Ku wingman as his target. After a long chase, Alger closed in on the ZEKE's rear quarter and torched the Mitsubishi, which rolled over and fell the short distance into the ocean. Alger immediately applied power to #90, and pulled the nose up, only to fly through the cannon fire from a pair of trailing kokutai wingmen. A 20 mm round exploded

on his horizontal stabilizer, and Alger stood his Lightning on its wingtip in a high speed turn to face his opponents. His gunfire dispersed the ZEKEs and Alger quickly regained altitude, flew several headon passes against some other ku opponents, but low fuel soon forced him to withdraw. Alger carefully brought his holed P-38 down safely on Horanda strip at half past noon. The fight had ended with all the Knights accounted for.

During the later raid on March 28th, the last Eightball flight led by Lt. Ernie Harris scrambled from Kalamazoo, but the old E models again failed to reach the contest in time. Flight Ldr Harris did pursue a trio of ZEKEs bound northward for Lae, but could only fire at the stragglers without effect. An intervening enemy flight force him to break off his pursuit. Harris' sortie woefully pointed out the very weakness of the Fifth Fighter Command defense. The old Warhawks simply had to be replaced.

## 5 AF REALIGNS THE NORTH COAST DEFENSE;
## MARCH-APRIL, 1943

Of the small fighter force at Dobodura in early 1943, the area defense relied most heavily on the Warhawks and Lightnings as the Airacobras failed to make contact with enemy during all of March. In particular, Capt. Porter's 8 FS had distinguished themselves time and again by maintaining their operations with the oldest Warhawks in the USAAF extant, yet, their assigned patrol sector which stretched from Cape War Hunt to Salamaua was really beyond their operational means. The Screamin' Demons newer P-40Ks were actually too few in number to cover the airspace from Salamaua to Lae. The coveted Lightnings were fewer in number still. Fifth Fighter Command simply needed more modern fighter aircraft.

## THE HUNTER-MOOSE TRAGEDY;
## APRIL 3, 1943

Additional hardships befell the Eightballs with the mysterious incident that occurred during the morning patrol of April 3rd. Of the eight Warhawks airborne off Cape Ward Hunt, Lt. Bob Moose and 2Lt. Stan Hunter unexplainably collided and both men were lost. Only Hunter's body was recovered by a Navy patrol ship that witnessed the event, and all at Kalamazoo mourned the tragic loss of the capable new men.

Eightball CO Capt. Jim Porter reported only eighteen P-40Es now serviceable, and parts for the Warhawks were down to absolute minimums. Engines, tires and radio equipment were in particular shortage. Pilots rarely flew the same ship in consecutive sorties, and the number of flyers on forty-eight hour rotation was at a new low. Even Dobodura's fuel dump was on critical ration.

When airborne, the war-weary P-40s could barely reach effective altitude in the time it took the stand-by Lightnings to scramble from Horanda strip and reach 20,000 feet. Luckily, Lae had not presented a current threat due in part to the monsoons. Anticipating renewed airborne threats from New Britain, eight Warhawks from Capt. Manning's 7th Squadron were reassigned to relieve the Eightball patrol area. But those Warhawks would never be the equal of a flight of Lightnings.

Captain Sid Woods' 9 FS Lightnings had proven to be the most successful squadron in the campaign with the majority of kills posted by the Knights who out-climbed and out-distanced the Warhawks. But they were at the limit of their operations, too, with only twenty ships being combat ready a majority of the time.

## WAR WINDS OF APRIL, 1943

Likewise, the political shuffle in Fighter Command continued to directly affect the 49ers ranks. The Lightning outfit of the 39 FS "Cobras" at 14 Mile strip in Port Moresby had just completed their reorganization under their new commander, leading 5 AF ace Capt. Tom Lynch. Former CO Major Prentice moved on to form an new all-Lockheed fighter group, scheduled for operations in early May and had been given carte blanche to recruit the necessary crews from the existing units in the Fifth Air Force. Several veteran pilots of the 49ers, sensing the improved chances for survival in a superior plane plus a promise of promotion, opted out of the Warhawk units for the new P-38 group. Experienced line crews were stunned to learn they simply had been shanghaied by the new group commander.

As qualified mission leaders and crewchiefs transferred out of the 49ers, the depleted ranks of the 7th and 8th squadrons soldiered on. Ltc. Morrissey and Group Ops Exec Martin inducted a number of staff officers from Fighter Command to fill in the flight rolls, though only on a temporary basis.

## BARNES AND BONG STRIKE OVER DOBODURA; MARCH 29, 1943

Again on the 29th, the Lockheeds proved their worth on high altitude patrol. A 9 FS four-ship flight north of Buna, led by Darwin veteran Lt. Bob McComsey, with wingman Lt. Leroy Donnell, element leader 2Lts. Clay Barnes and wingman Dick Bong, was vectored southward to search for a lone aircraft, but the ship eluded the Flying Knights in the great cloud formation that rose to 25,000 feet. Flight Ldr McComsey spread apart his elements to broaden their search, and Lt. Barnes soon spotted the sleek DINAH, a twin engine JNAF speedster, which had turned northward toward New Britain. Barnes and Bong closed in after a 20 mile chase at 400 mph down to 18,000 feet and both men fired at the swerving enemy plane. On the fourth firing pass, Bong braved the return fire of the enemy rear gunner and his .50 caliber/20 mm barrage from dead astern set off the DINAH's fuel tanks. It disintegrated into a huge ball of fire and tumbling debris. Bong had scored his ninth kill, and tied with the rival 39 FS commander, Capt. Tom Lynch, for the highest victory count in the Southwest Pacific.

## A QUIET WEEK IN APRIL, 1943

March ended and early April brought a momentary lull in the raids on Papua. As the last of the 49ers' HQ staff moved into the Dobodura camp, the Screamin' Demon, the Eightballs and the Flying Knights celebrated their accomplishments in the New Guinea campaign. The group had added fifty more victories over the enemy air force,

and the Yanks proudly displayed the current total of 182 kills painted on the big sign at the 49ers HQ. Despite their perilous location within the range of a very desperate enemy, the Yanks considered their new home in the great jungle camp to be an improvement over the desert wilderness of dusty Darwin. As a part of a new Allied air force, the 49ers had now gained the full attention of a great enemy force based only 400 miles away, but when not in the slit trenches, Dobodura was considered a very pleasant camp.

While MacArthur's forces continued to swell the camps in Papua, his counterpart at Rabaul, Adm. Yamamoto, had designed a major offensive for his Combined Mobile Fleet to rid the Southern Area of the Allied air force, once and for all. By the Imperial officer's bold plan, the Allies in the Solomons and in Papua would come under the most aggressive air attacks since the war began. For Yamamoto, it would be the fateful engagement of his career. For the 49ers, it would be but another era of combat and victory.

## THE 49ERS AGAINST OPERATION I-GO

Imperial fleet carriers entered the waters of the Philippines Sea and added their Mobile Fleet air wings to the units who queued up on the air strips at Truk lagoon and at Rabaul. By the second week of April, nearly 350 JNAF and JAAF combat aircraft choked the dispersal areas of New Britain. On the 7th, Yamamoto unleashed an aerial armada against the American army and navy air units at Guadalcanal, and the harbors and airfields of Papua. For seven days, Yankee aviators and flyers rose up to meet wave after wave of attacks by the Imperial airmen in Operation I-Go.

## I-GO MISSION TO ORO BAY; APRIL 11TH

There had been many enemy reconnaissance flights following the Barnes-Bong interception of the DINAH on March, 29th. Fifth Air Force Intelligence also reported exceptionally heavy radio communications over the enemy channels and Allied recon flights over New Britain detected many aircraft parked on the airdromes. The 5 FC staff was advised of heavy engagements taking place in the Solomon Islands. A maximum effort to have fighter patrols up above Dobodura during all the daylight hours forced 5 FC CO Paul Wurtsmith to call upon his staff captains and majors to rejoin the fatigued fighter units.

In the 9th Squadron, newly promoted Major Jesse Peaslee had just returned to flying status following his bout of jungle fever. The CO would lead his Flying Knights during a time when the enemy would send its two largest air assaults against Oro Bay, yet each time, the CATER air controllers would curiously deny Major Peaslee a chance to engage.

## WHITE FLYING KNIGHTS ON APRIL 11th

At 1130 hours on April 11th, Major Peaslee was airborne with fourteen wingmen over Dobodura at 24,000 feet, when CATER vectored them due east to the shore line at the alert of a huge enemy formation approaching Oro Bay. Down below, the stand-by units at Horanda and Kalamazoo scrambled into the air and headed upward

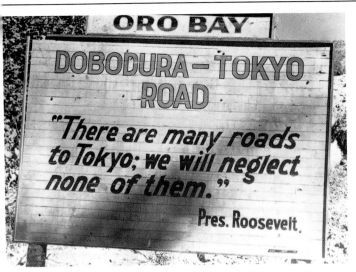

*Oro Bay, one of the two principle targets of the April 11th assault in Yamamoto's I-GO operations.*

to their attack positions. As the 5 FC war planes converged toward the bay, Peaslee was amazed when CATER altered the vector of his White Flight to hold over Cape Sudest at the mouth of the Samboga River. Senior Flt Ldr Lt. Clyde Harvey, likewise appalled by CATER's misdirection, was ordered by the Major to take his quartet down toward the harbor. Hopelessly out of range, Peaslee and his remaining nine wingman held their position and orbited the area while Harvey, Bong, Holze and Price sped south.

In their initial descent, element leader Bong reported engine trouble and dropped out for Dobodura. Flight Ldr Harvey, with Lts. Theron Price and Harold Holze still in close formation, dropped down to 20,000 feet in search of the enemy. Just north of Oro Bay, they spotted a dozen black Ki-43 OSCARs of the 1st Sentai cruising above the thin overcast that blanketed the coastline at 15,000 feet. The three Knights dropped their belly tanks and peeled off to engage.

*9 FS aircraft #82 "DOUBLE TROUBLE" assigned to team pilots Francis Nutter and Frank Wunder. Nutter may have scored his lone career kill in #82 on April 11th. After a July crackup, the aircraft was rebuilt and renumbered #91. It was finally written off after another landing accident in September.*

As Harvey, Price and Holze swept down, "Pappy" Price was forced to break away and turn into an OSCAR that had suddenly threatened their rear quarter. Pappy successfully fired a distracting burst at the sentai attacker who rolled away, then entered into several high speed turns with the other OSCARs that now fought for position. The counter maneuvers split up the White trio and Holze dropped away at 400 Mph with three OSCARs in hot pursuit.

Price and Harvey fought it out at the "2 by 12" odds, but only Price could mortally hit one of the ebony Ki-43s. Suddenly, a 7 mm round splintered Price's canopy splattering him with plexiglass and shrapnel. They could not locate the position of the attacker, and both of the Knights rolled into their escape dives within a hail of 7 mm tracers.

Harvey and Price soon found Holze down at 7000 feet, and the regrouped White Fight trio climbed back up over Oro Bay, but the enemy was gone. They turned back for Horanda strip.

The scrambled four-ship Green Flight from Horanda did not fare any better. Flight leader 2Lt. Bill Gersch and wingman Eddie Howes took off first, followed three minutes later by elements Lt. Leon Howk and 2Lt. Frank Nutter. Neither Gersch nor Howes could find the raiders in the growing cloud formation offshore.

Only Darwin veteran Lt. Howk and wingman 2Lt. Nutter could overtake the last elements of the 1st Sentai that had ventured north of the harbor. As with White Flight, the Green Knights team entered the area at 25,000 feet and were attacked from above by the black OSCARs. Howk was literally swarmed by OSCARs and he shot at several opponents, but could not hold his fire long enough to sustain any damage. Nutter fired and saw debris fall from the escaping Ki-43, but he could not finish the job. The Green duet plunged down toward the coast to safety. Just south of Buna, the pair climbed back up to 12,000 feet, but the OSCARs had withdrawn.

## SCREAMIN' DEMONS FINALLY BACK IN ACTION

Capt. Red Manning's eager 7 FS pilots had wanted to get back into the air action after the month long spell of boring patrols and dive bombing missions nearer Salamaua. With a revised patrol schedule, Manning's Red Flight of eight P-40Ks at 24,000 feet near Oro Bay, answered the 1150 call and climbed seaward for the incoming enemy formation. But the Red Demons would separate as they hunted in the clouds. Several miles out of range, Red Flight could only hear the radio transmissions from the other 5 FC flights.

## WHITE DEMONS SUCCESS

The successful 7 FS attack would be flown from Kalamazoo strip by eight P-40Ks of White Flight which lifted off at 1150 hours. They too became separated in the clouds as they rose up to 24,000 feet, but White element leader 2Lt. Bob Greene with wingmen 2Lts. Joe O'Connor and John Quinliven, would consequently find twelve of the VALs who had just set up at 17,000 above the overcast for their dive bombing attack on the merchant ships outside the harbor.

Greene, O'Connor and Quinliven slipped into the glare of the sun above the right flank of twelve VALs in three Vee elements and rolled into the attack. Greene targeted a straggler dive-bomber that

*Left: 8 FS Darwin veteran Flt Ldr Bo Jordan scored his last career victory in the I-GO opposition. Right: Capt. Larry Kirsch, one of the Eightball's best combat leaders in 1943.*

was several yards from the main group, and just as it extended its dive flaps, Greene poured in a long volley of tracers from dead astern. The Nakajima burst into flame and fell straight down before the rear gunner could return fire.

O'Connor and Quinliven held close formation and covered Lt. Greene until the flight leader dropped safely away. O'Connor then circled about in search of escorts, and lost Quinliven in the maneuver. Quinliven went on to join the Eightballs in the greater dogfight which raged overhead.

O'Connor neither saw any enemy escorts, nor could he relocate his flight, so he chose to set off alone in pursuit of the VALs for a second pass. The kokutai had closed ranks and descended into the overcast, save for one unfortunate straggler. O'Connor bored in on the swerving Nakajima whose valiant rear gunner opened fire with his single 7 mm weapon, but the Screamin' Demon fired two murderous burst that killed the gunner and flamed the VAL's left wing. The burning dive-bomber fell through the overcast, and the Demon Warhawk followed with four more firing passes until the enemy pilot jumped free in his chute. Now at 8000 feet, A/A batteries from the Allied ships sent up a broad, inaccurate barrage and O'Connor broke off to a safer altitude, then turned for home.

## THE EIGHTBALLS STRIKE THE MAIN FORCE

Once again, the trusty old P-40E's of the 8 FS would struggled up to 21,000 feet and execute another successful interception. Three flights made contact, and though badly separated in the dogfight, all of the Eightballs would survive.

Once the P-38s had cleared Horanda strip, twelve Eightballs rose off Kalamazoo and vectored for the interception, just at the noon hour. The Yellow Flight foursome was led by Lt. Ernie Harris, followed by wingman F/O Sammie Pierce, element leader Maj. Bill Martin of 49th HQ, and his wingman, 2Lt. Roger "Bitsy" Grant. Next came the Green Flight veterans Lts. Bruce Harris and his wingman John Roth, followed by 5 FC Ops Deputy Capt. Ellis Wright and rookie 2Lt. Dick Vodra. Last to take off was Red Flight, led by Capt. Kirsch with his rookie wingmen, 2Lts. Jim Hagerstrom, element leader Marlin Smith and Bob Aschenbrenner.

## YELLOW FLIGHT STRIKES

Ernie Harris' Yellow flight managed to stay together in their initial pass against the escorts. Harris and Pierce flamed a ZEKE apiece, then the Yellow elements set after the dive-bombers. Harris and Pierce held a loose formation as the leader splashed a VAL. Then they turned back on the intervening HAMPs where Harris shot down his second fighter victim and Pierce damaged another.

After Yellow elements of Maj. Martin and 2Lt. Grant also hit the escorts in the first pass, Grant lost control of his prop and dropped out momentarily to allow his engine Rpm to slow down. Meanwhile, the major was pursued and hit by a single 7 mm round which encouraged him to dive away for safety. Martin returned to 10,000 feet and watched Harris and Pierce in their final engagement overhead, then he wheeled off alone for Kalamazoo.

Grant recovered control of his wind-milling prop, he latched on to a flight of P-38 Headhunters in pursuit of the VALs, but the lieutenant could not over take them. As the Lockheeds turned back for Dobodura, several ZEROs dropped down between Grant and the P-38s. He carefully applied power to his rough running P-40, and closed the gap after a twenty mile pursuit back to the coast. He made one firing pass on two ZEROs, then sped away alone to safely put his over-heated fighter down at Kalamazoo.

## GREEN FLIGHT AND "BOLTING" ELLIS WRIGHT

Bruce Harris' Green Flight had tried to find the enemy, but the irascible Ops man, Capt. Wright, bolted in the chase to hunt on his own. Bruce Harris could only find a lone OSCAR, which he fired upon, but lost the target in the overcast at 15,000. The errant Wright did find the dogfight and joined Ernie Harris' Yellow element in their assault on the escorts. In the swirl of fighters in the mist at 16,000 feet, Wright claimed mortal hits on three ZEROs.

## RED FLIGHT AT LAST

Capt. Kirsch's Red Flight arrived at the height of the conflict, and all four plunged into the fray. Tail-end Aschenbrenner was cut off by the wheeling ZEROs early on and dropped safely out for home, while the remaining pilots of the dispersed Red team mixed with the other Eightball elements.

Capt. Kirsch roared through the snarl of ZEKEs, OSCARs, Warhawks, and Lightnings, and was forced to dive away into the flight of VAL dive-bombers directly below. Kirsch fired on a VAL beyond effective range, but nearby, the lost White Demon rookie, Quinliven, had entered the fight and had come under attack from another ZEKE. Kirsch intervened and Quinliven dived for safety as the ZERO looped to evade Kirsch's first volley. When the Mitsubishi pilot fatally turned across his path, Kirsch saw the long glistening canopy fill his gunsight and he held down the trigger at point blank range. The cockpit exploded as the ZEKE rolled inverted and plunged straight down into the sea.

Red flight wingman "Hag" Hagerstrom had stayed with his flight leader through the initial pass and had found a target in the second pass, but in the excitement, had forgotten to flip on his gun switch. As he fumbled with his instruments, he nearly collided with the ZEKE. Hag broke off to regain his composure, then joined two P-38s in the chase of another ZEKE. The lieutenant soon pulled inside the turn of the kokutai pilot who had foolishly banked gently to his right. Hag raked the unsuspecting grass-green ZEKE from its tail to the cowling with his explosive .50 caliber ammo. The Mitsubishi's engine belched smoke and flame, then the ZEKE stalled out and dropped through the overcast.

Green Flight element leader Lt. Marlin Smith had likewise shot his way past three escorts in the first encounter, then dropped down to chase the VALs. He hammered a target which dropped down toward sea, but the VAL leveled out and its valiant pilot turned about in a defiant head-on challenge. Smith pulled away a safe distance and was about to re-engage when he looked back to see the stricken Aichi dive-bomber burst into flame and fall into the water.

## RESULTS OF THE ORO BAY RAID ON APRIL 11TH

It was almost an hour from the first attack by the 49ers until Capt. Larry Kirsch rejoined with wingman Hagerstrom for a final survey of the ocean beyond Oro Bay. The sky was filled with great billowing cumulus and the overcast at 16,000 feet stretched all the way to the vacant eastern horizon. Hearing no Allied distress calls, Kirsch and Hag turned inland for home. They set down on Horanda at half past one o'clock.

The raiders had taken a sever beating at the hands of the 49ers. The bomber pilot who had bailed out after Demon O'Conners attack was picked up by a U.S. Navy patrol boat and imprisoned at Oro Bay. The JNAF aviator was the only enemy flyer to actually see how little damage his wingman had inflicted on the harbor. Only one ship was hit by the VALs and it limped into the bay later that night.

Enemy planes had also been reported over Dobodura, but no American made an interception there. Essentially, the first I-Go raid on Oro Bay had been a very meager feat.

## I-GO MISSION TO PORT MORESBY; APRIL 12TH

Admiral Yamamoto's schedule called for the next air attacks to be flown against the harbor and air strips at Port Moresby. Once more in late morning, the alarm at Horanda and Kalamazoo strips was answered by the weary 49ers. Demons, Eightballs and Knights waited for the vector orders for the nearby harbor, but were surprised to find the enemy force would pass Dobodura and press on for Port Moresby.

## EIGHTBALLS ANSWER FIRST

The action on the 12th began at 0730 hours, when the three planes in escort to a flying boat bound for Oro Bay, were warned of a single approaching plane. The Eightball trio at 9500 feet, led by Red Flt Ldr George "Pinky" Davis, with wingmen 2Lt. Merle Wolfe and Joel Thorvalson, turned inland over the fogged-in shoreline toward Dobodura in search of the intruder reported above 29,000 feet.

*8 FS Rookie F/O Art Talmadge (lt.) with veterans Bruce Harris and Bo Jordan in May just days before the senior men left for home.*

In the clear air high above their airdrome, Flt Ldr Davis spotted the lone DINAH and set off due east on a parallel course to intercept. The Red trio jettisoned their belly tanks, and set their Warhawks in a steady climb to overtake the sleek reconnaissance ship. The DINAH crew soon spotted the rising Eightballs and the JNAF pilot crept up to 31,000 feet, certain that the Warhawks would never reach that greater height. The high flying DINAH, with the three P-40s trailing two thousand feet below, cruised out of sight over the mountains as the other Eightballs readied their aircraft on Kalamazoo strip.

As Davis' Red Flight followed the DINAH over the hazy blue mountains, the pilots at Dobodura waited for word from CATER of the enemy bombers that would most certainly follow the reconnaissance overflight. At 0930, the alarm sounded and six more P-40s from Warhawk Row sped off for the great formation of BETTYs and ZEROs escorts that passed high above. Senior Flt Ldr Bo Jordan led 2Lt. Art Wenige and tag-along 5 FC Capt. Ellis Wright as

*9 FS pilot Lt. Ralph Wire (rt.) and his crewchief in the April mission period.*

the make-shift Yellow Flight, but the Fighter Command ace soon dropped out in his sputtering old stager.

Veteran Flt Ldr Bruce Harris followed immediately with 2Lts. Pleasent Barrett, Bob Howard and F/O Art Talmadge of Green Flight which sped off Kalamazoo, over the ominous armada of P-38s warming up on the perimeter of Horanda strip. As the last Warhawks got underway at 0945, Dobodura crews were deafened by the continuous roar of twenty-four Lightnings that rose up from Horanda strip who then thundered upward toward the Owen Stanley Mountains.

## FLYING KNIGHTS TO PORT MORESBY

Within the swarm of Cobras, Headhunters and Flying Knights P-38s, the 9 FS elements of Lts. Ralph Wire, Grover Fanning and Big Pete Alger pressed upward to 27,000 feet and topped the spine of the mountains, just as the enemy position was called out north of the harbor. Flight Ldr Wire had a radio malfunction, and with hand signals, passed the lead to Alger. As the Lightnings poured down the southern slopes, the elements split up to hunt for the raiders. The Knights at 28,000 passed over their old home of 14 Mile Strip, when Pt. Moresby's fighter controller, code named ELSIE, vectored the Lightnings north. Alger soon saw the nine Vees of three BETTYs each in a broad formation at 21,000 feet, followed closely above by equally as many escorts. Alger targeted the left flank of

*Below: Lt. Pete Alger in his #90 leads another alert scramble off from Horanda. Pilots on alert stand-by seldom knew the location of the enemy intruders until their Warhawks or Lightnings were airborne for several minutes. Alger was stunned when his flight was sent all the way to Pt. Moresby on April 12th.*

the great enemy formation as the Lockheeds dropped their tanks, then Big Pete shoved #90's throttle forward, and the battle was on.

Alger led the attack upon the left flank of the BETTYs, who had just toggled off their bombs for the harbor docks. Alger and Fanning fired on the closest dark green bombers in the nearest Vee, then plunged beneath the enemy echelon and swept across the formation to fire on the elements on the right flank. The black and dark green OSCARs of the 1st Sentai immediately dropped down on the American who had mortally hit two of the Mitsubishi giants. Alger broke left, Fanning broke right and Wire, flying cover for his wingmen, pulled head-on into the intervening sentai. A brutal dogfight incurred as the sky over Port Moresby filled with tracers.

Fanning rolled away momentarily to the north, gaining speed and altitude, then re-engaged and fired again at a second bomber from point blank range. The BETTY fell from the formation, quickly to be joined by an OSCAR in singular escort, and the enemy pair drifted due east for home. Fanning quickly eluded the other OSCARs and set a direct pursuit for the wounded bomber which was attempting to reach the safety of the clouds beyond the spine of mountains. Just past the summit, Fanning swept down on the right rear quarter and flamed the Mitsubishi, which fell away on its left wing toward the jungle. The OSCAR looped upward to counter Fanning's pass, but misjudged his opponent's speed and failed to fire at the rocketing Lockheed. With his great speed, Fanning easily slipped from beneath the rolling Ki-43, then wheeled hard about and caught the Nakajima at the top of its second loop. Fanning's fusillade hit the forward fuselage of the Ki-43 which erupted in flame. The mottled green fighter spun out of control toward the forest below.

Lt. Wire had attempted to fend off the dark green OSCARs that rose from beneath the Americans and sent one down trailing heavy, black smoke, but the odds quickly worsened. Unable to recover his flight, Wire rolled down and away from the fight, then

climbed to 32,000 feet in search of another target. The bombers were now disappearing in the clouds to the east, and his pursuit quickly proved pointless. Low on fuel, Wire set off for Horanda strip and landed shortly after Lt. Fanning.

Unfortunately for Big Pete Alger, he would not return to Dobodura that day. His #90 was caught by the diving ZEROs, and one "old Navy hand" refused to let the P-38 get away unscathed. Big Pete plunged in a twisting dive through 16,000 feet while the ZERO's 20 mm cannons knocked out his right engine and 7 mm rounds holed the right tail, right fuselage boom and shattered his canopy windscreen. He finally outran his assailant south of the harbor, but knew the flight for Horanda was out of the question. Alger turned for nearby 7 Mile strip with hydraulics lines leaking, the rudder trim shot out, and the left engine running rough. Old #90 flopped down to a safe landing where ground crews quickly gathered to gaze at the ravaged Lightning which would never fly again.

## PASSING DOBODURA

The mission was far from over for the Japanese crews who had withstood the onslaught of the Lightnings over Port Moresby. As the Lightnings expended fuel and ammo, they withdrew for Horanda strip and left the retreating enemy to the Warhawks that patrolled over the escape routes on the north shore. The impatient Eightballs were ready.

Lt. Jordan's Yellow flight and Bruce Harris' Green Flight had orbited over the airdrome, waiting for the return of the raiders. But weather was closing in on the northern coast which would negate the full force of the Eightball flights. Still, four P-40 pilots were able to make one last pass against the kokutais.

As the Eightballs searched among the clouds over Oro Bay, several enemy planes were sighted in scattered formation up and down the coast. Jordan targeted a trio of BETTYs and led the Eightballs down from 16,000 feet into a rear quarter attack on the glistening green Mitsubishis. Jordan made three passes on the twin engine ships, then swept upward at the sight of a lone ZERO which suddenly set upon the Warhawks. The veteran mission leader quickly dispatched the ZEKE intruder, while Green Flt Ldr Bruce Harris, Howard and Talmadge each butchered a BETTY bomber. In twenty minutes, it was over, and the six men set off for Kalamazoo.

## THE FIRST ARE LAST

Oddly enough, the first men to pursue the raiders were also successful in the end. From the onset of Flt Ldr Davis' initial pursuit of the lone DINAH which preceded the raid, the Red Flight trio had followed the recon plane from Dobodura to Port Moresby and back, finally pulling to within gun range as the DINAH passed over Cape Ward Hunt. After a 300 Mph chase down through scattered overcast thirty miles out to sea, Davis closed to within 300 yards and flamed the DINAH's left engine. His guns jammed, so he recharged and fired until they jammed again. Debris fell from the stricken twin engine speedster, but the P-40 was soon down to only one functioning gun and then none. The DINAH slipped down into the overcast leaving an inky smoke trail. Red Flight immediately turned back for Kalamazoo, where Davis set down with empty gas tanks, but was awarded confirmation of the kill.

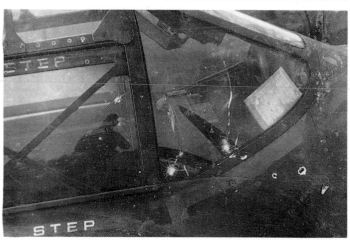

*Above: Big Pete Alger in "his office" which took a real beating over Pt. Moresby. Below: Alger's holed P-38 down at Pt. Moresby. The aircraft took hits in several places, including the right rear boom seen here as well as the horizontal stabilizer and the right supercharger coolant radiator.*

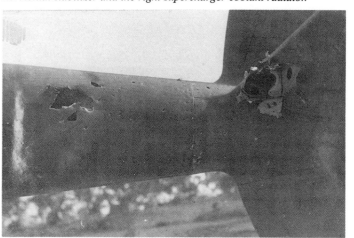

## I-GO MISSION TO MILNE BAY; APRIL 14th

On the 13th, weather shut down operations over the Solomon Sea and the Fifth Fighter Command was given a brief respite from the grueling missions that had sapped the strength of its pilots and crews for nearly a week. On the 14th, another mid-day raid was signalled, but only four 9 FS Lightnings out of the entire Dobodura force would make limited contact with the enemy. For those four Flying Knights, a sortie underscored in blood would mark the end the April campaign.

On the morning of April 14th at Vunakanau airdrome across the harbor from Rabaul, the young Imperial Navy air crews gathered their gear and boarded their BETTY bombers for the next mission. They would dispatch 27 heavy bombers accompanied by a VAL kokutai and heavy fighter escort for the Allied harbor and airfield of Milne Bay on the very eastern tip of New Guinea. By 0830 hours, the great formation had taken off and turned due south out over the Solomon Sea. Clouds had already begun to spiral upward in white cumulus towers. The air crews pulled their formations tightly together, and climbed up to the cloud tops at 21,000 feet. The Imperial airmen then settled in for the ocean crossing to the Papuan target which would take nearly three hours.

Just before noon, the outer islands off the eastern Papuan shoreline appeared through the heavy, scattered clouds. The blue spine of the Owen Stanley Mountains tapered downward to the south-

east, pointing the way to their target. The gunners began to scan the clouds for the swarm of Allied fighters that certainly would appeared at any moment. But only one twin-engine interceptor would strike the BETTYs that day.

## FLYING KNIGHTS TO MILNE BAY

The alarm sounded at Dobodura and several flights were sent up to their stations for the incoming raid. As the Flying Knights sped upward to their 25,000 foot position above the coast, CATER directed eight of the P-38s to hunt for a large formation sighted over Goodenough Island, 130 miles southeast of Oro Bay.

Veteran mission leader Lt. Bill Sells called CATER for clarification of the distant vector, and the air controllers confirmed the sighting. Sells led the Knights in a climbing pursuit, due east for the great cumulus clouds that obscured the far horizon. After several minutes, the flight began to deteriorate. Sells' Red Flight had a wingman declare a power loss and he was ordered back to Horanda. Green Flight fared much worse. Newly designated flight leader, Lt. Dick Bong, quickly lost half his fight when 2Lt. Milliff experienced engine failure and turned back for Horanda. Only minutes later, 2Lt. Nutter lost power and he turned away. Lt. Carl Planck, with a dead generator and loosing power, closed in on Bong's wing and the pair pressed on together.

Mission leader Sells was duly concerned. Flight control repeated the vector and confirmed the size of the enemy formation, but Sells' five remaining Lockheeds were the only P-38s in the vicinity for the interception. Sells reluctantly ordered the elements to keep each other in view, but to separate and expand their hunt.

As the Flying Knights passed over Goodenough Island, Sells could not find the raiders and decided to extend the hunt even further. He led his Blue Flight wingmen, 2Lts. Ralph Hays and Edie Howes down from 25,000 feet to search at a lower level within the scattered clouds. Bong and Planck of Green Flight would hold their position as high cover. The Knights orbited south of the island once, found nothing, then set off for Milne Bay. Blue and Green were now out of sight of one another. Sells and Bong held radio contact as they approached the mainland shore, when both Blue and Green Flights fatefully crossed the paths of the sprawling enemy formations.

## GREEN FOR THE BETTYS

Lieutenants Bong and Planck met the BETTYs at 26,000 feet, just as the kokutai released their bombs on the Milne Bay harbor. The Green Flight duo dropped their belly tanks and climbed one thousand feet above the kokutai, placing themselves in the sun's glare against the left flank of the trailing Vee. As Planck advanced his throttle, his ship dropped suddenly to the right as the starboard supercharger belched smoke and flames. Planck was out of the fight as he struggled to control his crippled Lightning, while Dick Bong alone plunged for the BETTYs.

On board the enemy bombers, the crewmen shaded their eyes in an attempt to keep the pair of speeding P-38s in sight, but the fighters passed before the glaring sun. They shouted to the rear gunners to shift their attention to their left, but it was too late. Dick Bong targeted the wingman on the left flank and poured in a barrage of .50 caliber and 20 mm tracers which exploded in the cockpit. The crew panicked as they fought for balance in the lurching Mitsubishi with its left engine bursting into flame.

As the BETTY slipped down through the overcast, it was overtaken by RAAF Warhawks which made several more firing passes before it slammed into Milne Bay.

Bong's murderous pass against his first victim had ended when six black OSCARs dropped from overhead into firing range. The Flying Knight ace quickly separated with his superior speed, then wheeled about for the next victim. After a short pursuit to the north, Bong quickly overtook the left flank of the escaping kokutai as it passed over the mainland. The lone Knight closed in on the leftmost ship and fired at point blank range from the left rear quarter. The tail gunner fired only a few errant rounds until the left side of the cylindrical fuselage erupted in flames. It abruptly began to descend in a steep angle and Bong maneuvered for another firing pass, but two more ebony OSCARs dropped down behind him. As the burning bomber slipped beneath the overcast, he broke off his attack and evaded the Ki-43s, then radioed for Sells to regroup, but the mission leader had long since gotten into serious trouble.

## BLUE FOR THE VALS

While Bong assaulted his two BETTY victims, Sells' Blue trio had swung over the VALs and the ZERO escorts who were in a stacked formation which ranged from 20,000 through 16,000 feet. Sells ordered tanks off and accelerated across the enemy flights to the "up sun" position against the enemy's left flank. Sells directed Howes for the dive-bombers while he and Hays would try to hold off the ZEROs who were turning to meet the Lockheed intruders. Sells and Hays rolled into a 400 Mph plunge for the ZEKEs, and a split second later, Howes broke for the VALs.

Diminutive "Legs" Howes in ship #71 charged into the nine VALs huddled in three tight Vees of the trailing echelon and opened fire in an attempt to spray the entire group. He nearly rammed one of them as the kokutai elements swerved violently to avoid the howling P-38. Now scattered, Howes wheeled about and targeted a lone VAL, but the ZEROs intervened too soon. Howes rolled away for safety and in his escape, he saw a P-38 surrounded by a dozen green

*Milne Bay's airdrome target in the I-GO assault of April 14th.*

*Left: Pilots catch up on some light reading and napping in the peaceable 9 FS day room. Right: Despite the intensity of the April raids, the camps in the Dobodura forest were virtually untouched. The 7 FS mess tent held up throughout the ordeal.*

striped ZEKEs. Howes regained altitude and re-engaged in an attempt to reach the cornered wingman, but it was hopeless. After numerous turns against the ZEROs, Howes mortally hit a green mottled Mitsubishi, but #71 was too low on fuel, and "Legs" had to make a run for home.

As for Sells and Hays, the task of taking on the escorts had been foolhardy at best. In their initial assault, they immediately became separated when Hays was forced to withdraw due to gun failure. Hays quickly recharged his weapons and returned to the fight where he raked two VALs with gunfire before he was overwhelmed. Hays separated with his superior speed, then came back to follow the escaping raiders toward Goodenough Island, but the young lieutenant was not about to attack again without his flight leader. Alone, Hays set off to the northwest for home.

## SELLS DEAD AT MILNE STRIP

The P-38 caught in the midst of swirling ZEKEs had indeed been that of mission leader Sells. The veteran lieutenant fought until the ZEROS riddled his Lightning literally to pieces. He miraculously avoided being wounded and finally escaped within the clouds, but the return flight north was out of the question. Sells had to attempt an emergency landing at the tiny dirt strip of RAAF's Gurney Field, just on the western shore of Milne Bay.

The Flying Knight mission leader carefully entered into the approach to the east-west strip from the bay side when his holed right engine finally seized up. He quickly adjusted full flaps and left rudder just beyond the shore line, when without warning, an RAAF Warhawk perilously dropped into the Gurney landing pattern in front of the vulnerable Lockheed. Sells desperately swerved out of a certain collision, but his battle damaged Lightning could not hold in the air. It slammed into the forest at the east end of the runway and blew up in a red fire ball. Captain Bill Sells' body was incinerated in the inferno.

## THE AFTERMATH OF OPERATION I-GO; APRIL, 1943

The Japanese Imperial staff at Rabaul declared the I-Go operation completed as of April 14th. Admiral Yamamoto was hailed as the Empire's most famous warrior as his Imperial Combined Mobile Fleet posted claims for nearly 200 Allied aircraft either shot down or destroyed on the ground. The actually Allied losses were far less

than these claims, and the overall effect was an equally exhausting depletion of the Imperial air crews. The Imperial Navy units stood down from missions during the last two weeks of April as battle worn planes were flown back to Truk, New Ireland and Rabaul for overhaul. Army air units transferred to the western airdrome of Wewak in preparation of the next Papuan operations which were scheduled for May.

Immediately following the I-GO operations, Yamamoto dispatched a coded radio message of his plan to personally survey the forward air strips of the Solomon Islands. The Allied intelligence team accurately decoded the message in time, and a flight of Thirteenth AF Lightnings from Guadalcanal were sent on a precision interception of Yamamoto's BETTY transport near Bougainville on the 18th. The admiral was assassinated, along with his entire staff. The final sum of Operation I-Go was the loss of the Empire's most capable field commander.

For most Americans, the death of the infamous admiral who had planned the treacherous raid on Pearl Harbor was a high point of resolve in the national vendetta. But very few Americans would ever understand the scope of the battle for air supremacy over New Guinea that had been waged in April. LtC. Bob Morrissey and the 49ers were genuinely more concerned with the day to day survival of their fighter group at the remote jungle air field in Papua. They had fought the best that the enemy could muster in the growing Pacific war, and still had held their ground at Dobodura.

## NEW ACES AND THE 2ND CENTURY VICTORY MARK

The 49ers Ops Exec, Capt. Ellis Wright, had become their first staff ace with his triple victory on the 11th. In the dogfight over Oro Bay on the 12th, Eightball Flt Ldr Lt. Ernie Harris took the lead as highest scoring Warhawk ace in New Guinea when his score rose to seven, while one of Flying Knight Lt. Grover Fanning's three victories was declared to be the 49th Group's 200th tally. In the New Guinea air war, the undisputed leaders were the men of the LtC. Bob Morrissey's 49th Fighter Group.

The toast of the 5 AF was again the quiet Flying Knight, Dick Bong. The destruction of the BETTY which fell into Milne Bay was confirmed as the lieutenant's tenth victory, establishing him as the first official double ace in the Pacific theater. Other pilots would score as many kills, but none would ever exceed Bong's count. The quiet killer from Wisconsin was on his way to becoming the most famous fighter pilot of the war.

# *11*

# THE 49ERS LAST SOLO DEFENSE OF DOBODURA: MAY 1943

In the first few months of 1943, the Far East Air Force began to receive new troops from the training bases in the America. For the 5th Air Force personnel who had been in combat for over a year, the relief personnel were a most welcome sight. Veterans anxiously scanned the first furlough list posted with the names of the senior-most men who were eligible to return home. On the basis of a point system which awarded credit for time in the combat, the enlisted mens' clubs hosted their first farewell parties for the crews who had acquired their total points. Any man who had put in his time was bid a hearty good-bye, and no one questioned his choice to leave that jungle hell. Any who chose to extend their tour were accused of temporary insanity, all in good spirits, but their decisions were always greatly respected.

In the 49th Fighter Group camp, the veterans were ecstatic with the news of the first 49ers posted for transfer back to the United States. Several of the privates and corporals were summarily promoted, sometimes by two grades in rank. Some were transferred to other units, as determined by the 5 AF Command, while others were given leave for the training centers in northern Australia.

For the lucky fellows who could find passage back to Australia, they reveled in their extended furloughs. They donned regulation uniforms, resumed shaving daily and adapted some trace of military demeanor, but those were reasonable burdens. For the first time since their mobilization in March of 1942, the enlisted 49ers would soon be socializing with the Aussie lassies, and drinking cold beer in the rowdy pubs "down under."

The 49ers had dropped well below its personnel quotas and CO LtC. Bob Morrissey quickly inducted the available new replacement pilots and crews. Many veteran flight leaders were promoted in rank, but all three of the Group's squadrons were still short of combat veterans. By the end of April, the 49ers had virtually become a new organization with a substantial number of novice fighter pilots on its roster.

At times, a newcomer's professional demeanor was sharply juxtaposed to the irregular military nature of General Kenney's jungle air force. The old hands from the 49ers' prided themselves in their independence, and at first, the newcomers felt a distinct distance between themselves and the veterans. Despite the disparity, the initiation of these new men into the 49ers came with the shared misfortune of their great isolation. As the new pilots and crews joined the battle, the 49ers were drawn together once more as another fellow died in the wilderness war.

## LT. PROPS IS LOST; APRIL 28TH

In the 7th Squadron, rookie Lt. Christ Props flew an escort mission to Lae airdrome at mid-day, but on the return to Dobodura, his P-40K mysterious fell from the sky in an inverted spin. Faulty oxygen gear was suspected, but little could be ascertained from the debris that was found near Popondetta. Props' body was interred at Port Moresby's Allied cemetery.

For Morrissey and his squadron commanders, every man was absolutely critical in the defense of Oro Bay and Dobodura. But Col. Wurtsmith's 5 FC was struggling to keep its operations intact with only nine combat fighter squadrons, and only five of those at Dobodura. Just as in the previous months, the Airacobras that flew from Kalamazoo strip were ineffective in high altitude interceptions. The 49ers Warhawks and Lightnings continued to carry the burden of defending their airdrome and the nearby Allied harbor.

The 49ers flew their routine escorts and patrols over the northern shoreline, but failed to intercept the enemy recon flights with good reason. The group was often down to four flights of sixteen operational fighters per squadron. Eight-ship patrols had become a rarity. The old P-40Es of the 8th Squadron now averaged more than three hundred hours of combat per Warhawk, and Capt. Porter's Eightballs were about to be tested again.

## THE AIR RAID OF MAY 14, 1943

In the second week of May, spy flights from Rabaul reported the arrival of another large convoy of Allied merchant ships and barges in Oro Bay. Inclement weather held down any major effort until May 14th. On that day, the Imperial Command dispatched 18 BETTY bombers from the 751st Kokutai based at Kavieng, New Irelands, to hit the Allied harbor. Departing Kavieng at daybreak, the BETTYs flew 130 miles south to Rabaul and rendezvoused with 32 ZERO escorts of the 251st Koukatai. They set off south together and reached the north coast of New Guinea at 1020 hours.

In the clear sky above the Solomon Seas, the raiders were spotted far beyond the northern Papuan coast. Fifth Fighter Command was well prepared at the approach of the 751st Kokutai. Once again, the 49ers would rise up in the alert, but this time, all three squadrons would join in one of their most brutal interceptions of the war.

## FIRST CONTACT WITH THE FLYING KNIGHTS

At 0800 hours, Red Flt Ldr Lt. Floyd Finberg took wingmen Grover Fanning, Big Pete Alger and Clay Petersen up to investigate the first sighting alerted by CATER. After only twenty minutes in the air, Finberg had radio difficulty and passed the lead to his second element, led by Lt. Alger. Big Pete immediately caught sight of the DINAH intruder, and with Petersen close by, the duo closed in at 350 Mph on the fleeing ship. Both Alger and Petersen fired, and the damaged DINAH began to drop for Cape Ward Hunt. Alger methodically swept down on the enemy's left side, flamed the port engine, then slipped to the right and set fire to the starboard engine. The helpless DINAH drifted aimlessly into a slow roll as Alger bore in from dead astern and poured in the final high explosive rounds. The enemy ship's fuel tanks erupted, tearing the DINAH apart. The debris fell into sea off the Cape, marking the watery grave with a pier of oily smoke.

The Red quartet quickly returned to Horanda strip where elements Finberg and Fanning, still fully armed, had their Lightnings refuelled. Finberg's crewchief quickly corrected his malfunctioning radio, just in time for the lieutenant and wingman Fanning to attach themselves to Capt. Bill Haney's Green Flight, which would take off at 0930 hours. Thirteen Lightnings roared off Horanda strip and passed by the great dust cloud that was rising from Warhawk Row on the north end of Kalamazoo.

## EIGHTBALLS UNDERWAY

Sixteen old stagers from Capt. Porter's 8th Squadron faithfully roared off from Kalamazoo at the 1000 hour alarm. There were four flights who circled upward to 20,000 feet and waited for the vector against the enemy. CATER garbled the original plot of the enemy formation and mission leader Capt. Larry Kirsch faced a most difficult decision. If the vector was true, only Kirsch's Green Flight was in the immediate vicinity of the airdrome. The captain gambled and led F/O Art Talmadge, element Leader Bruce Harris and wingman rookie Elferd "Fats" Elofson back to orbit above Dobodura. It was a fateful choice by the fiercely competitive Kirsch, for he had effectively taken his quartet out of what was to be the 8th Squadron's most successful interception of the New Guinea campaign.

Senior Lt. George "Pinky" Davis, leading the Eightball's Red Flight, assumed the mission lead for the southern vector and guided his three Warhawk wingmen off to the coast line just below Oro Bay. Thirty minutes later, as Red Flight swung inland south of the harbor, Flt Ldr Davis saw the looming BETTY bombers just to the east of the harbor. Davis signalled "drop your tanks" and led 2Lts. Tom Farley, Leo Mayo and Dick Vodra down from 20,000 feet for the enemy half a mile below. Only seconds away behind Red Flight were twelve more 49er Warhawks.

## THE DEMONS REACH ORO BAY

The 7th Squadron was led by their redoubtable Deputy CO, Capt. Frank Nichols, who had taken his eight P-40Ks up to 22,000 feet. Capt. Nichols and Yellow Flt Ldr Capt. John Yancey, saw the enemy bombers at the same moment Lt. Davis of 8th Squadron had seen them. With their combined P-40 squadrons now in the sun's glare against the enemy's left flank, Nichols and Yancey signalled "tallyho" and plunged into the head-on, in-line attack behind Lt. Davis' Red Flight Eightballs.

## BLUE EIGHTBALLS ARE NEXT

Blue Flt Ldr Warren Blakely, wingman Merle Wolfe, element leader Bob White and rookie wingman Bob Aschenbrener saw Nichols' flight peel off and follow Eightball mission leader Davis in the plunge for the kokutai. Blakely accelerated forward and swung to the right so as to target the center of the enemy echelon. At his signal, Blakely's Blue Flight rolled into the attack.

The 751st Ku began to jettison their ordinance and turn to the north, just as Flt Ldr Pinky Davis and element leader Mayo chose their targets on the left flank of the raider's formation. The leaders rolled in behind two of the rotund Mitsubishis from the left rear quarter and both men poured in a steady stream of tracers until the stricken BETTYs fell out of position. The Eightballs sped past the other bombers to the enemy's right flank and immediately drew within range of the 251st Ku escorts. Davis' flight engaged and fought down to a thousand feet above the sea until Davis splashed a Hamp, and Mayo claimed victory over a ZEKE. Rookie Dick

*Senior Flt Ldr Lt. George "Pinky" Davis, 8 FS mission leader on the May 14th interception at Oro Bay.*

*8 FS 2Lt. Dick Vodra and the old P-40E-1 #57 "SQUIRLBATE" that got him his two career kills on the May 14th.*

Vodra in his sputtering old #57 SQUIRRELBATE splashed a pair of ZEROS as well.

Capt. Nichols' Demons fared equally as well. Both Nichols' Red Flight and Capt. Yancey's Yellow Flight struck the same elements as Davis' Eightballs had done only seconds before. Nichols' quartet turned in behind the turning formation and would have duplicated the Eightballs' attack, but Nichols' and two wingmen were forced out of the fight by the riled ZEKEs. Only Red element leader Arland Stanton was able to gain an advantage over the ZEKES and he followed the kokutai out to sea where he delivered the coup de grace upon a straggler, just above the waves.

## YELLOW DEMONS' ASSAULT

Yancey's Yellow team would be the most successful Demon flight of the day. From their descent at the rear of the Warhawk column, the Yellow wingmen gained the necessary speed to overrun the kokutai's left flank and turn into the bombers from head-on. Yancey fired on a twin engine Mitsubishi that fell from its left wing position and he turned in time to see it fall in flames toward the ocean. Element leader Larry Succop swerved to the right in his attack and fell in behind the right flank of the BETTYs. Succop closed in on a G4M and killed the tail gunner from dead astern, then shot up the left engine which exploded and covered his Warhawk with oil. With oil streaming down his windshield, the Demon pilot drifted down and carefully set off for Kalamazoo beneath the battle which rolled out to sea.

Then Warren Blakely's Blue Flight Eightballs roared in against the middle Vee elements of the 751st Ku echelons. Blakely, Wolfe, White and Aschenbrenner made numerous passes against the leading bombers and White succeeded in flaming the right engine of one BETTY which fell far below the formation. White, in #54, KANSAS CITY KIDDIE the 2nd, would have followed to finish the job, but four dull green ZEROs wheeled into his path. The other blue elements dropped away, but White kept his KIDDIE in the fight until he hit a ZERO in a head-on exchange. Another ku wingman chased him back toward the coast where Lt. Farley intervened on White's behalf. Farley and White then set off for home together.

## THE FLYING KNIGHTS SEE ALL

As the first Warhawks engaged, the first elements of scrambled P-38s entered the scene at 24,000 feet. Yellow Flt Ldr Lt. Ross Blachly, Lt. Don Byars and 2Lt. Art Bauhof passed south of Oro Bay, just as the long string of attacking Warhawks was twisting down toward the BETTY formation. The enemy bombers paraded over the bay where their bombs sent up geysers near the ships and explosions on the docks.

Blachly continued over the melee as the combatants swung to the north beyond the harbor and back out to sea. The Yellow Flight trio crossed the shore line and soon paralleled the right flank of the enemy Vee formations under assault by the last P-40s. Blachly jettisoned his belly tanks and signalled nearby Green Flight led by Capt. Haney, with wingman Lt. Frank Wunder and foundlings Finberg and Fanning in trail. All seven Lockheeds rolled down into a 400 Mph dive for the fight.

Only Yellow Flt Ldr Blachly, who was well out in front, avoided early contact with the escorts and he alone attacked the bombers. As the other Knights engaged the fighters, Blachly twice came in head-on and fired at a straggler bomber on the Ku's right flank. In his attempt at a third pass, Blachly was finally drawn into the swirling dogfight. The Demons, Eightballs and Knights twisted about for position against the green ZEKEs, but a pair of Ku veterans singled out Bauhof and caught his Lightning in a murderous crossfire. Don Byars tried to aid Bauhof, but Byars was drawn into a fight that led him down to 1000 feet. Byars finally gained the advantage and splashed a HAMP, but he could not recover in time to reach his flaming wingman.

## BAUHOF IS DOWN IN HIS CHUTE

The Knights were overwhelmed as more ZEKEs from the main force overhead fell upon them. As the Demons, Eightballs and Knights broke off combat, some of the escaping 49ers caught a glimpse of Bauhof's Lockheed followed by the two ZEKEs which rendered it into junk. The P-38 nosed over into the sea and a parachute popped open just above the crash site.

## FAR OUT OVER THE OCEAN

In the meantime, Major Peaslee and with five wingmen in Blue Flight, were also trying to sort out the confusion of the original vector. Peaslee had again ventured within range of the fight, but refused to attack beyond his assigned area. His rookie wingman, 2Lt. George Alber, stayed in formation as Peaslee orbited back toward the coast, but Darwin veteran Lt. Jim "Duckbutt" Watkins bolted at the sight of the enemy. Watkins ignored the last CATER plot and with three brave souls in tight formation, Duckbutt pushed headlong after the BETTY formation that turned out over the Solomon Sea.

## BRAVE BLUE KNIGHT OVESON

Watkins, Lt. Keith Oveson, 2Lt. Frank Nutter and Lt. Leroy Donnell pursued the air battle out beyond the shore. Their pursuit line brought them along the left flank of the eastbound kokutais and Watkins wheeled out in front for a head-on pass. But the veteran 251st pilots pulled in between the Knights and the BETTYs, allowing the Blue Flight team only one thundering pass through the bombers. Only Keith Oveson fired on the BETTY which drifted from its left wing position and the lieutenant shot out its port engine before he was forced to contend with the intervening ZEKEs. The four Blue Knights dispersed and maneuvered against the escorts, but once again, only Oveson hit his target. Badly separated, the Blue quartet rolled for the coast in a 450 Mph escape.

## THE LAST of the DEMONS AND EIGHTBALLS

The follow-up flights from Kalamazoo had also pursued the kokutais back toward New Britain. Demon Blue Flt Ldr Lt. Ray Hilliard led

(Text resumes on page 160)

# AIRCRAFT OF THE
# 49TH FIGHTER GROUP

The 49ers displayed a wide variety of tactical insignia as well as the personal markings applied by pilots and crewchiefs. Typically, USAAF serial numbers on the tails of their aircraft were stripped or painted out, but there always exceptions. The practice was apparently one of convenience, not of confidential intelligence logistics, and resultant Air Force records do not track the exact number of planes assigned to the group. An exact count of the hundreds of planes flown by the 49ers cannot be ascertained.

## PROFILE AIRCRAFT

**(1)** Curtiss P-40E s.n. unknown - 7 PS A/C #36 of Flt Ldr Capt. Bill Hennon at Darwin - April, 1942. Taken from the RAAF at Brisbane, it was the first A/C to displayed the namesake "bunyap" screaming demon of the 7th Squadron on the left side of the rudder only. Red centers of the cocardes are painted out. The red spinner was used by a number of Philippines-Java veterans. A single photo reveals #36 was lost in a collision, but no other record details the incident. Hennon survived Java, Darwin and New Guinea, only to disappear off the coast of New York on March 31, 1943, while test flying an early model P-47, the very plane he had requested as a replacement for the Warhawks in Papua.

**(2)** Curtiss P-40K-5 s.n. unknown - 7th FS A/C #13 POOPY II of Lt. A.T. House at 14 Mile Field, Pt. Moresby - October, 1942. The camouflage is standard U.S. olive-drab and tan, roughly equivalent of dark-green and light-earth required for RAF day-fighters circa 1941. House scored three final victories in POOPY II, the last being his April victim which was confirmed 50 years after the fact. When his tour ended in May, 1943, both the ace and POOPY II passed into total obscurity.

**(3)** Curtiss P-40E, s.n. unknown - 8th PS A/C #44 of Java-veteran 2Lt. Jim Morehead at Darwin - April, 1942. One of the original A/C assigned to the squadron, it displays the early black in-flight #209 beneath the newer yellow #44. A thin coat of white paint covered the red centers of all the insignia. Morehead returned to the States and joined a P-47 unit for a tour in the ETO which the ace survived with equal distinction, despite gaining no more aerial kills. Warhawk #44 was destroyed in Lt. Eisenberg's crash-landing after combat on June 13, 1942.

**(4)** Curtiss P-40E-1 s.n. 41-35972 - 8th FS A/C #43 JERRY II of Lt. Bill Day and C.C. Gilliam at 3 Mile Field, Pt. Moresby - November, 1942. Rebuilt JERRY II was used by ace Day to score his last four kills as of April, 1943, so recorded with five small round dots below the pilot's name under the canopy. He stood down from combat in May and JERRY became a hack trainer. After a brief stint as a 5 FC gunnery trainer, athletic Day returned to the States and after the war, gave up flying for professional tennis.

**(5)** Curtiss P-40E s.n. 41-24872 - 9 PS A/C #94 BOB'S ROBIN of Lt. Bob Vaught and C.C. Petraitis at Darwin - May, 1942. The ROBIN was another former RAAF type with the fuselage insignia painted over in olive-drab which foiled a plain star, a marking not unique to early 49ers A/C. Some were flown without fuselage insignia, and eventual applications at Darwin varied greatly in size and position, particularly in the 9th Squadron. BOB'S ROBIN yielded a single kill for the future ace, but unlike pilot BOB who went on Pt. Moresby in September, A/C ROBIN never left Australia.

**(6)** Curtiss P-40E-1 s.n. 41-36090 - 9 FS A/C #83 MAUREE of Lt. Jack Donalson and C.C. Christopherson at Darwin - July, 1942. One of the first replacement A/C, she was the second MAUREE. Her eagle was a noble attempt by Christopherson and then-assistant Bill Pascalis, the co-author, to copy the logo of ace Flt Ldr Reynolds. Terse Donalson asked, indeed, if it was a parrot. Whatever the bird's breed, MAUREE gave ace Donalson his last two victories. When he went State-side, she went to the fight in Papua.

**(7)** Curtiss P-40K-5 s.n. unknown - 7 FS A/C #10 at Dobodura, N.G., circa July, 1943. The Warhawk displays the twin fuselage stripes of the either CO Capt. Bill Martin, or Ray Melikian. Flown by several pilots in its waning service era, A/C #10 displayed the new theater markings of white tail plus the white ailerons and horizontal stabilizers adopted in both the 7th and 8th Squadrons. No E-model or K-model advanced beyond Dobodura.

**(8)** Curtiss P-40N-5 s.n. 42-105820 - 7 FS A/C #19 SUZY of Flt Ldr Capt. Duncan Myers at Gusap, N.G., late 1943. Myers flew the E-model, the K-model and the N-model in combat, and SUZY was the pilot's favorite. She tried to make him an ace, but he lost his fifth victim at the toss of a coin to wingman Jarman. In May, 1944, Myers mustered out for the States and a distinguished military career while SUZY vanished within the A/C pool at Nadzab.

**(9)** Curtiss P-40E-1, s.n. unknown - 8 FS #49 DOTTIE II circa April, 1943. Blacksheep veterans recall one of the most colorful old stagers was DOTTIE II photographed at Dobodura. Often flown by 8 FS Ops Exec Ellis Wright, she is very likely the P-40 that made him an ace with six victories. When Wright moved on in 5 FC, DOTTIE II went back for another overhaul and was never seen again.

**(10)** Curtiss P-40N-5 s.n. 42-104947 - 8 FS A/C #67 The CAROLINA BELLE of CO Ernie Harris and C.C. Carl Wingo-November, 1943. The N-model was the second belle so named after the pilot's mother, and proved to be just as deadly as the old E-model. In November, 1943, the BELLE made Harris and Wingo the first double-ace Warhawk team in the Pacific.

**(11)** Lockheed P-38H-5 s.n. 42-66845 - 9 FS A/C #97 of team pilots Harry Lidstrom and Grover Fanning - September, 1943. Likely a former 39 FS A/C, it continued to serve Lidstrom and Fanning well, yielding some of their ten collective victories. Lidstrom was lost in another plane, ace Fanning briefly flew the Thunderbolt before he mustered out in early 1944 and A/C #97 was last seen in the Nadzab scrap heap.

**(12)** Lockheed P-38F-2, s.n. 43-2208 - 9 FS A/C #95 of Capt. Bill Haney and C.C. Ray Holman at Dobodura. Replete with red flight leader bands and enlarged in-flight numbers on the nose for the Rabaul operations, it was purportedly flown by Haney on both the October 29th and November 2nd missions resulting in several unconfirmed victories for the would-be ace. When the Lightnings were taken from the squadron in December, Haney mustered out for the States.

**(13)** Curtiss P-40N-5, s.n. unknown - 7 FS A/C #24 of Lt. Elliott Dent at Gusap in early 1944. Dent's newest model-N was one of several to reach the 49ers in late 1943, baring the red bordered insignia despite a three month old USAAF directive to have the red overpainted. Dent got two kills in the A/C over Wewak on January 23, then named it ANNE the B'HAM SPECIAL and stayed with her all the way to Biak Island that following July.

**(14)** Curtiss P-40N-5, s.n. unknown - 7 FS A/C #20 KEYSTONE KATHLEEN or EMPTY SADDLE of CO Arland Stanton at Gusap in early 1944. The ace recalled the bawdily decorated N-model was a rebuilt stager, but was the best fighter he ever flew in the theater. KATHLEEN gave him three kills over Wewak on three different missions before she played out for good in April. Stanton got his last kill in a new N-model in May over Biak, then furloughed home from Hollandia in June.

**(15)** Curtiss P-40N-5, s.n. 42-105834 - 8 FS A/C #51 of Lt. Don Meuten at Gusap in early 1944. Other than the ace's name and six kill flags beneath the canopy windscreen, little else distinguished A/C #51 in the February-March assault on Wewak. Plane and pilot were in the first flight to advance to Hollandia on May 5th, only to vanish 48 hours later on a mission abort, just minutes from the airfield.

**(16)** Curtiss P-40N-5, s.n. 42-106363 - 8 FS A/C #45 of Lt. Marion Felts at Gusap, mid-1944. After Felts got two victories in this Warhawk, a heavy landing in May resulted in the repairs yielding the fighter-bomber denude of camouflage at Biak in August. Felts would find his fifth aerial victim over Leyte while his trusted silver Warhawk soldiered on in a tactical reconnaissance unit.

**(17)** Republic P-47D-4RE, s.n. unknown - 9 FS A/C #83 of CO Maj. Gerry Johnson at Gusap - January, 1944. Johnson and Capt. Markey were the only Knights to each score double kills in the Thunderbolt, fully half of the squadron's eight victories gained in the five months of the P-47 era. Johnson then had eleven kills officially confirmed, but his own count always exceeded 5 FC by two; hence, thirteen kill flags on his scoreboard.

**(18)** Lockheed P-38L-5, s.n. unknown - 9 FS A/C #91 of CO Maj. Wally Jordan at Biak in September, 1944. His garishly marked Lightning gave him six aerial victories as he led the Flying Knights into the final Lockheed era. As the Philippines invasion drew near, the tri-color rudder colors were adopted by several other FEAF fighter groups, but rarely by the Screamin' Demons and never by the Blacksheep.

**(19)** Lockheed P-38L-5, s.n. unknown - 7 FS A/C #13 of Capt. Bob DeHaven at Tacloban - October, 1944. The Screamin' Demon ace usually flew this distinctly marked Lightning in the early Leyte operations, but at least one of his last four kills came in another plane. DeHaven considered himself a triple-ace, especially since one of his P-38 kills was lost in a coin toss to an 8 FS pilot. Not long after the ace went stateside, A/C #13 was believed to have been written off after an enemy bombing raid.

**(20)** Lockheed P-38L-5, s.n. 44-25327 - 7 FS A/C #19 of Lt. Fernley Damstrom at Tacloban - December, 1944. Damstrom was the leading 49ers ace in the Philippines campaign with eight kills. Unlike the black scoreboards on most 5 AF P-38s, A/C #19 had a white one. Other Demon P-38s displayed the blue just on the upper tail surface, but after the Leyte campaign, tail-markings in the 7th Squadron ceased.

**(21)** Lockheed P-38J-15, s.n. unknown - 8 FS A/C #46 at Biak - October, 1944. Logistics at Biak forced the Blacksheep to take some of the refit J-model A/C up to the Philippines operations. Even though squadron markings were applied, few of the old stagers lasted long enough to receive personal markings. Ace Nelson Flack purportedly flew A/C #46, one of several Blacksheep A/C to be lost in the late November bombing raids at Tacloban.

**(22)** Lockheed P-38L-5, s.n. unknown - 8 FS A/C #61 at Tacloban -December, 1944. Once they were at Tacloban, the besieged Blacksheep commandeered more P-38s from the other units held in reserve. Despite all unit markings being painted out with silver dope, former 13 AF Lightnings could often be identified by their distinctive anti-glare panels which extended over the gun portals. A/C #61 was such a replacement P-38 purportedly used briefly by ace Nial Castle during the closing stages of the Luzon airwar.

**(23)** Lockheed P-38L-5, s.n. 44-26407 - 9 FS A/C #84 CHARLCIE JEANNE of veteran ace Jim Watkins in 49ers HQ at Linguyan - July, 1945. While waiting for a command assignment, Duckbutt flew several missions with his old squadron in the A/C bearing his old number, which he again named after his wife. True to form, Duckbutt and CHARLCIE JEANNE prevailed in scoring their twelfth kill over Hong Kong in April. In the post-war occupation, Watkins took charge of the Screamin' Demons and a new L-model #1 CHARLCIE JEANNE.

**(24)** Lockheed P-38L-5, s.n. unknown - 49ers HQ A/C #10 ELSIE of Group CO LtC. Clayton Tice Jr. at Linguyan-July, 1945. This is the configuration of the colonel's plane on the fateful mission to Kyushu and the infamous landing at Mittigahara. Each squadron command aircraft likewise had triple-chevrons in their respective squadron colors. Spinner colors were solid red, yellow or red, without contrasting bands. By the end of October, FEAF completely restructured its forces and the 49ers forfeited their Lockheeds forever.

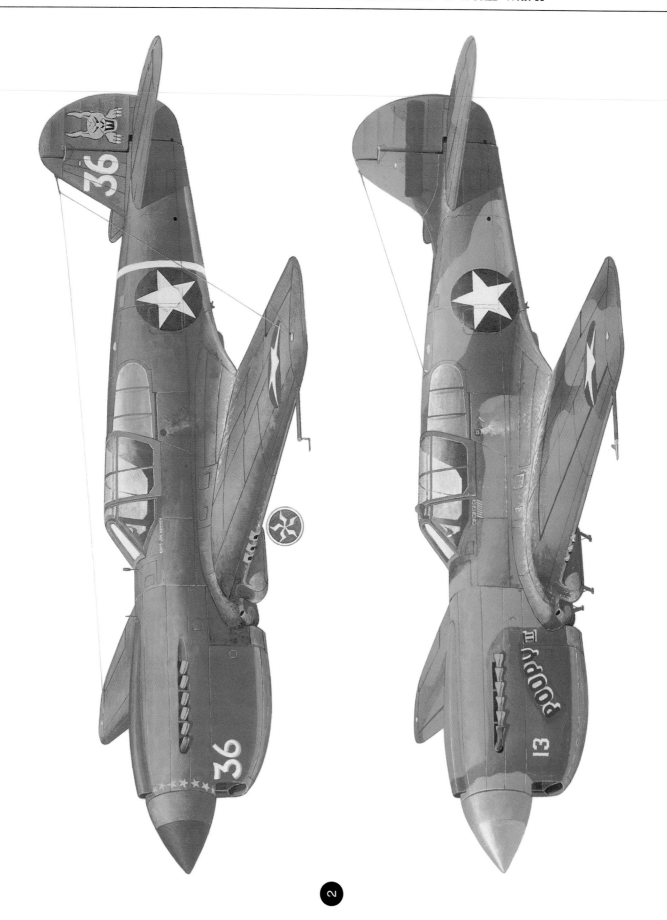

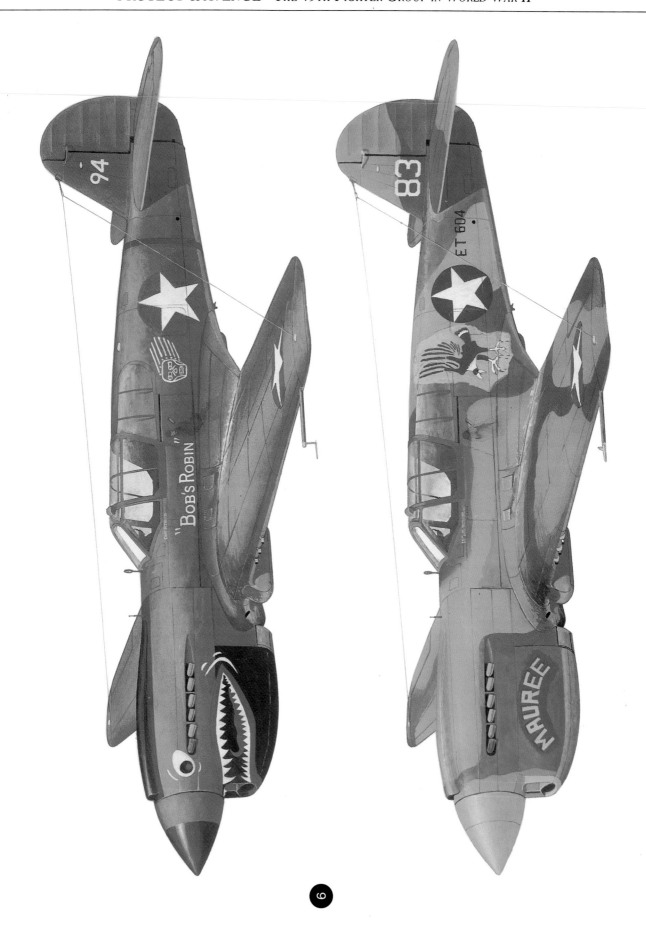

5

6

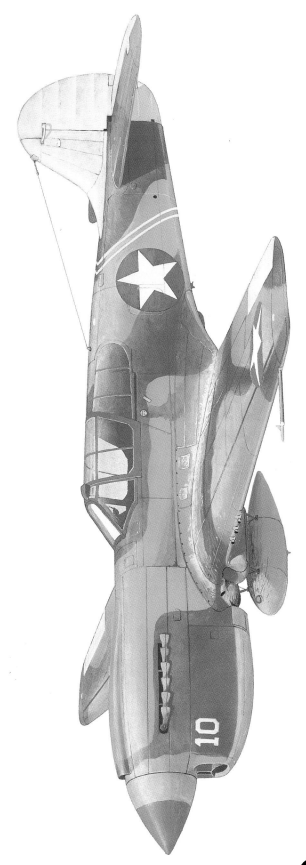

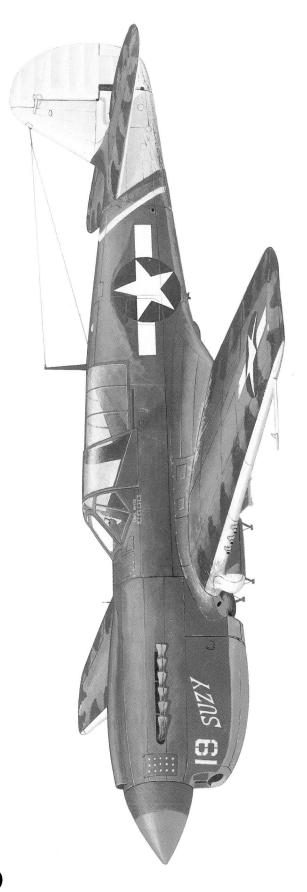

7

8

**9**

**10**

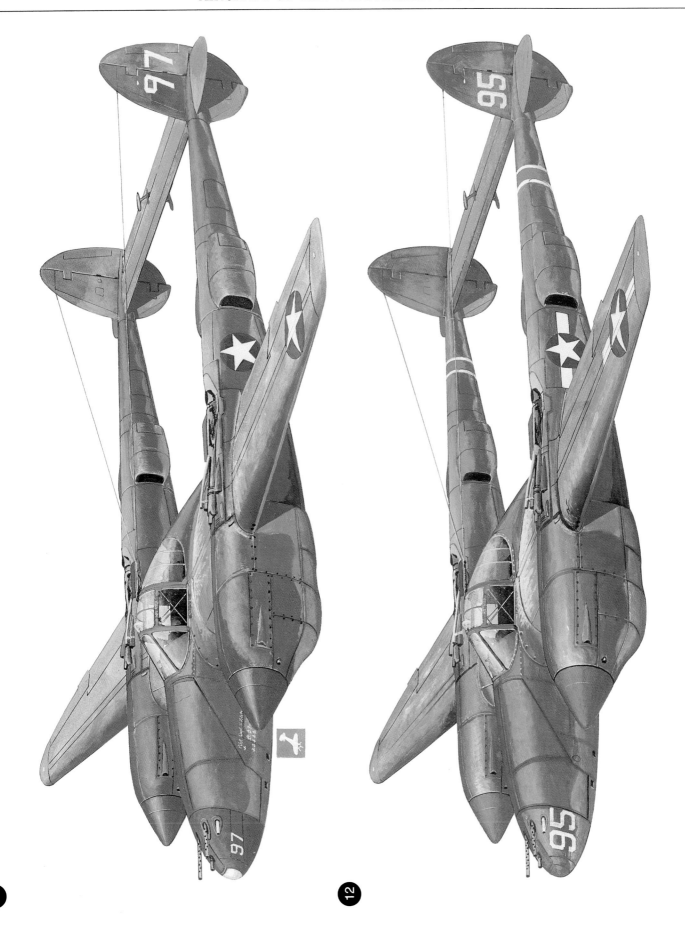

**11**

**12**

13

14

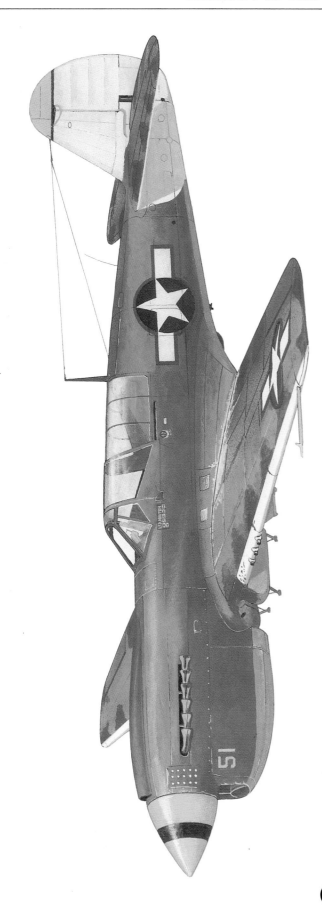

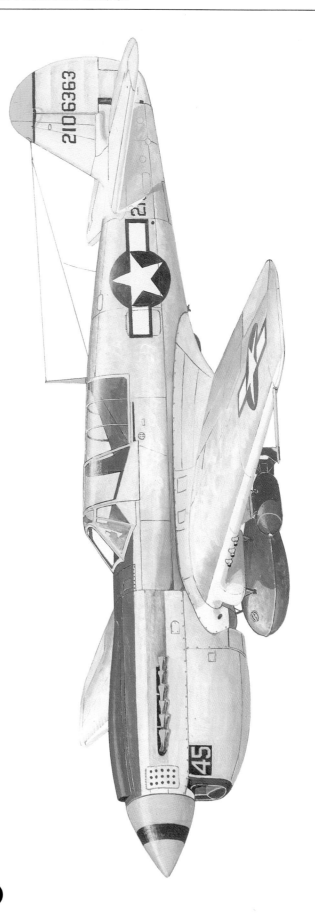

17

18

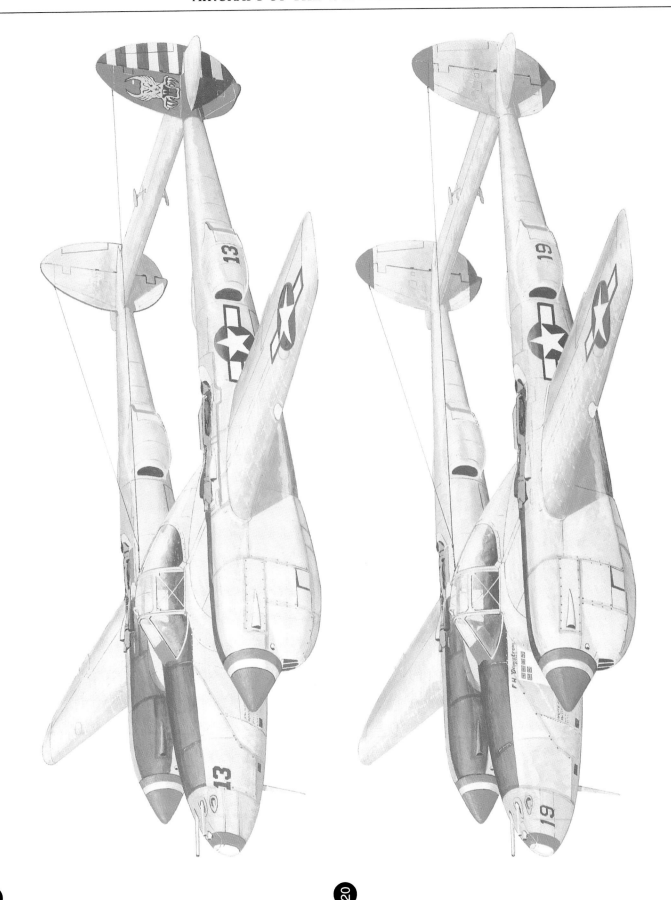

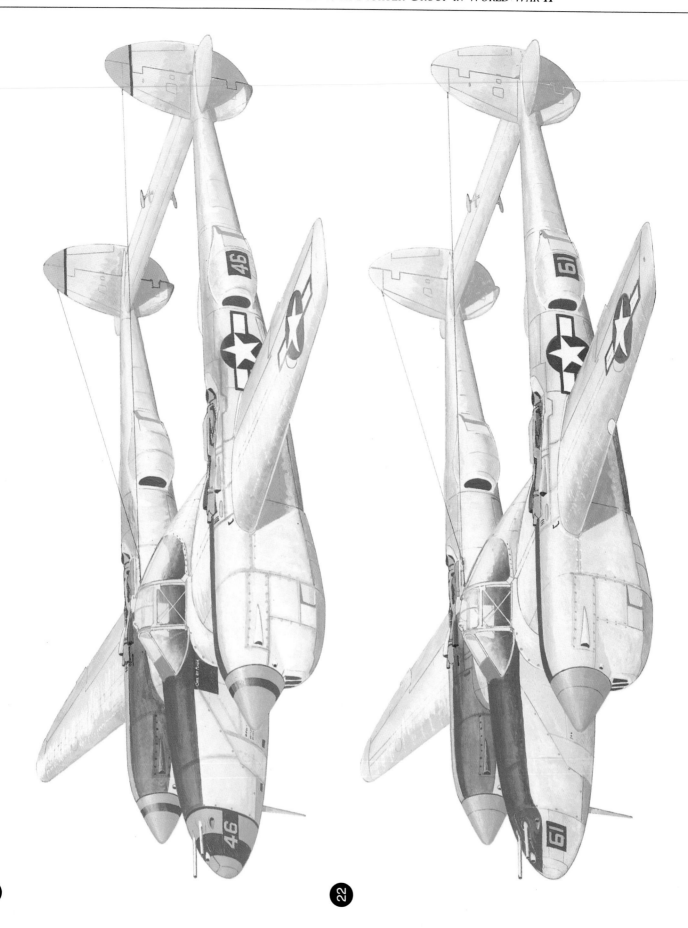

21            22

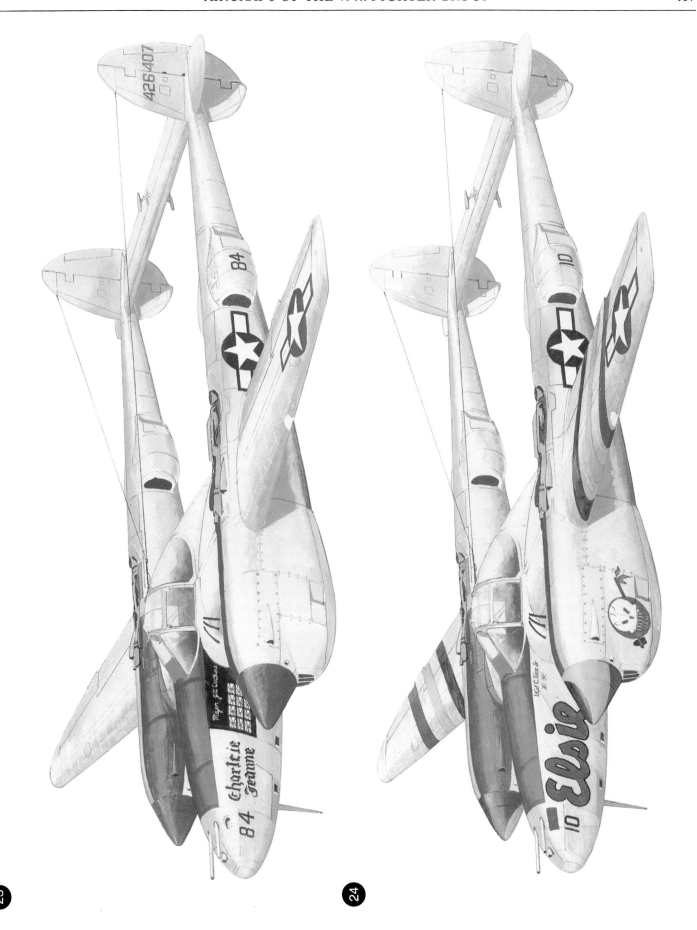

**DeHAVEN'S DILEMMA** - Depicted is the December 10, 1943 engagement described by 7 FS participants Capt. Shel Brinson and wingman Lt. Bob DeHaven. Unknown to the lieutenant at that moment, the TONY in the foreground had become his fifth career victim, but the ace's full attention was soundly captured by the enemy flight leader bearing down in the background. By DeHaven's estimation, only "pure luck" extricated him from the dilemma. The end result was DeHaven's affirmation of a definite combat style. From that fateful December day onward, he only attacked when the advantage was his and his airborne opponent was alone. DeHaven believed his next nine confirmed victims never saw him coming. *(From the John A. Hallberg collection)*

**FLYING KNIGHTS OF NEW BRITAIN** - Depicted is 9th Squadron Commander Capt. Jerry Johnson with wingman 2Lt. Ray Swift on October 23, 1943, on their first successful escort over northern New Britain. Above Rapopo airdrome, the captain scored the seventh confirmed kill of his tour. These long-range missions wore down both the planes and their resilient crewmen, but with rarely more than a dozen P-38s in service at a time, the Knights racked up 22 aerial kills in just four missions to the Japanese stronghold of Rabaul. When the P-38s were finally decommissioned in November, the Flying Knights had accounted for 169 aerial kills to become the undisputed leaders of 5th Fighter Command. *(From the author's collection)*

2Lt. Harry Dilworth, Lt. Sheldon Brinson and Lt. John Griffith twenty miles out to sea before the Blue quartet overtook the raiders. Hilliard had oxygen equipment failure and stayed with wingman Dilworth at 13,000 feet in hopes of catching a straggler, but no enemy plane fell within their range. Blue element leader Brinson and wingman Griffith were able to draw near enough to see Nichols' Red Flight, but neither Brinson nor Griffith could make an effective gun pass on the 751st bombers. Brinson tried, but he was chased away by a wildly maneuvering 251st veteran. He dove away to join up with the other 49ers who circled about the smoldering crash site of Flying Knight Bauhof.

Blue Demon wingman John Griffith pushed his luck further than his cohort had done. In his #21 VERA, he first fired out of range on the left flank of the bomber echelon and then swung off to the left where he overtook a lone ZERO. Griffith flamed the unsuspecting Ku pilot's engine, only to have another ku wingman send several 7 mm rounds through VERA's cowling. The Demon pilot dove VERA away and chose to re-engage, but his prop controls would not respond due to the damage inflicted by the ZEKE. He foolishly attempted to follow his opponent through a loop, only to have the enemy aviator slide in on VERA's right rear quarter and shoot out her hydraulics. Griffith rolled his riddled #21 into an escape dive and limped back for Kalamazoo.

Demon Green Flight, led by Lt. Don Sutliff, was the last 7th Squadron element to overtake the descending raiders, but Sutliff's people were strung out in a loose formation. Only Sutliff and rookie wingman 2Lt. Carl Houseworth reached the left flank of the retreating Japanese formation. They made one pass at the bombers at 17,000 feet, and Houseworth broke off in the opposite direction from his leader. Sutliff dove away for safety to 3000, and though alone, the Green flight leader turned back toward the enemy overhead.

Sutliff then sighted a BETTY straggler and three escorts only 50 feet above the sea. In a full-throttle dive, Sutliff sped between the ZEROs and made a concentrated firing pass on the bomber's right flank. The explosive .50 caliber rounds flashed on the right

*Above: Howard's #59 named "GREMLIN'S RENDEZVOUS" on the right side. Right: Howard's "JAYNE CARMEN" named for the girl back home who would become his wife.*

wingroot as Sutliff flashed by and wheeled hard about for home. The ZEKEs turned to follow but they could not catch the lone Warhawk that sped over the waves toward Dobodura.

## GRAND FINALE by the EIGHTBALLS

At 0940 hours, Flt Ldr ace Lt. Ernie Harris, wingmen 2 Lts. Pleasent Barrett and element leader Bob Howard, and F/O Sammie Pierce, were the last four men to lift off in the alert. The quartet, named White Flight, set off at full throttle and Flt Ldr Harris wisely chose a straight-line coarse due northeast to overtake the raiders. For nearly thirty minutes, the White team pressed their weary old Warhawks up to 22,000 feet, but Barrett's ship lost power and the rookie turned

*Armorers immediately disarmed Demon John Griffith's #21 "VERA" after it skidded to a halt on its broken left landing gear at Kalamazoo, while nearby, Flt Ldr Ernie Harris mounted up in his #67 "CAROLINA BELLE" for the last 8 FS pursuit flight in the May 14th interception.*

back. The remaining White elements kept up the chase. Sixty miles from their base, Harris, Howard and Pierce finally overtook the 751st Kokutai. With the ZERO escorts widely dispersed during the course of the escape, Harris took the trio down the right flank of the ragged formation without opposition. The three Warhawks pulled ahead of the BETTYs, then peeled off to the left for a line-abreast head-on run against the right wing elements.

Flight Ldr Harris in his #67 CAROLINA BELLE, went in first against the second Vee of bombers on the ku's right flank. Howard in his trusty #59 JAYNE CARMEN, attacked the next bomber to the right and Pierce, in his yellow-ruddered #50, swung wider to the right to attack the ship further most in front of the kokutai formation.

Harris' gunfire sent his target down and it crash landed on the ocean. Howard's fire set his target in flames and it began to slowly descend out of the Vee. Pierce's element leader victim also was set afire and it began to loose altitude. The White Flight trio wheeled hard about to the left and sped back for the second pass.

They approached the rear of the disintegrating formation where Harris and Howard both chose victims which had fallen behind the main force. Harris passed over Howard's first target which trailed a long streamer of brilliant red flame, "and it looked like one of those movie newsreel films." Harris drew into point blank range on another cripple and raked the dark green fuselage from tail to nose until his guns were empty. Howard pressed in through the defensive fire from a BETTY's turrets, but JAYNE CARMEN's .50 caliber burst killed the gunners. She nearly rammed the target as Howard bore in for the coup de grace. With their ammo expended, both of the Eightballs rolled away beyond the gun range of the ku survivors who descended into the safety of a distant cloud bank.

Flight Officer Sammie Pierce, the ornery North Carolinian "country boy", had swung off from his wingmen and was prepared to attack another bomber further down the echelon, but he suddenly caught sight of a lone ZERO which had taken a firing position against unsuspecting Howard. Pierce desperately turned and fired a broad deflection shot at nearly 500 yards. He was surprised when his tracers "hit th' ZEKE right in the bung-hole" which forced the Ku pilot to roll his green fighter down for the sea. Pierce's old "yeller-tail" model E had just been completely overhauled and Sammie put its Allison engine to the test. He plunged through six thousand feet at 450 Mph and "outran th' rascal" for the kill. As the ZEKE dropped straight into the water, Pierce pulled the stick into his stomach and #50 rocketed back up to 5000 feet. No other fighters were present, so the lone Eightball wheeled back toward the bombers. Sammie passed near a BETTY with a burning left engine which had fallen far behind and he made a long firing pass with the

*Georgia country-boy Sammie Pierce in his trademark Atlantic triple-A team red baseball cap.*

*F/O Pierce's rebuilt P-40E-1 #50 speedster that gave him two kills and carried him safely out of the May 14th battle. The future 8 FS ace declared the old stager was the best Warhawk he ever flew, including numerous combat hours in the updated N-model.*

last of his .50 caliber ammo. The cripple swerved aside for a shallow cloud bank, and Pierce orbited overhead, but the big Mitsubishi vanished within the haze. He turned back for the mainland.

Pierce passed over the wreckage of Flt Ldr Harris' first victim. The stranded crew had crawled out on the wings of the floating hulk, but he had no means of strafing them. He pressed on, and minutes later, encountered another ZERO which turned nose-on into his line of flight. Sammie could only feint a head-on exchange with his empty guns, so he pointed #50's spinner at the challenger. The mottled grey fighter snapped into a loop and rolled for the Eightball's rear quarter, but Pierce slammed his throttle forward and dropped #50's spinner below the horizon. He "bid the bastard sweet adieu" as the old "yeller-tail" responded with another 450 Mph sprint which took him safely home.

Harris and Howard had meanwhile formed up at 8000 feet and made one last reconnaissance of the area. They passed over two glistening oil slicks and three plumes of smoke which rose from the peaceful cerulean ocean. They swung south and at noon, Flt Ldr Harris and wingman Howard were the last fighters to put down at Horanda strip.

## THE AFTERMATH OF THE MAY 14TH RAID

Prior to the bombing strike, The 151st Kokutai reconnaissance unit at Rabaul had sent a plane to Oro Bay, but that crew had avoided the Allied patrols. The second sortie flown north of Dobodura by the DINAH which was intercepted by 9 FS's Pete Alger, was not followed by a tactical strike. There was only the raid on Oro Bay.

Of the eighteen 751st Ku G4M bombers that reached their objective, six bombers failed to return, including their veteran mission leader, Lt.Com. Nishioka. The other twelve BETTYs all took hits, and upon return to Kavieng, several wounded crewmen would be hospitalized.

In effect, the duplicated claims of eleven BETTYs destroyed by the 49ers came from three separate flights which attacked over a span of 45 minutes. There was confusion and contradiction which appeared in the many mission reports filed by the rookie officers. It would take several days to verify all of the cross references and subsequent testimony. Some of the younger rookie pilots effected substantial revisions in follow-up reports and the vacillation of these witnesses brought a stern reprimand from LtC. Floyd Volk, the intelligence chief of Fighter Command.

Most certainly, the same elements on the kokutai's left flank had been hit numerous times by the long procession of P-40s in the first assault. These same ships were also hit from the front by the first P-38s. It was also probable that the 8th Squadron's firing pass on the center elements while over the harbor, was duplicated in the final head-on attack farther out to sea by White Flight. Likewise, the two gun passes by Lightning pilot Blachly on the right flank may have resulted in damages which made those bomber crews all the more vulnerable to the final butchery inflicted by the final P-40 trio.

There were also the ten ZERO kill claims contrasted by the purported safe return of all the 251st Ku fighters to Rabaul. In turn, the 251st Ku, which had just refitted for duty during the previous month, was made up of seasoned veterans who boasted 13 enemy fighters destroyed and 5 more as probable. The only 49er planes lost were the P-40K of Lt. Griffith and the P-38 of 2Lt. Bauhof. Griffith's VERA reached Horanda with fifteen 7 mm rounds in its fuselage and a 20 mm cannon round which destroyed the left landing gear strut. The gear collapsed on landing and VERA was written off, but Griffith was unhurt.

As for rookie 2Lt. Art Bauhof, his position at sea was reported by several pilots, including Capt. Tice who circled the his position as a marker for the rescue boat. However, when a "water wagon"

*9 FS CO Woods' aircraft with the unique white and red command stripe on the tail. The ship was likely one of the earlier 39 FS aircraft and Woods flew it to full attrition in September, just before his tour ended.*

rescue tug got to the site, they only found a raging school of sharks, causing them to suspect the ill-fated Flying Knight had been wounded, which attracted the predators. Obviously, no trace of Bauhof was ever found.

## NEW EIGHTBALL ACES AND A MISSION RECORD

Despite the erroneous total of the 23 enemy planes accredited to Morrissey's Group, the 49ers had made a stunning interception. In particular, Major Jim Porter's war weary Eightball Warhawks had been awarded the lion's share of seven BETTYs and six ZEROs. After confirmation by 5 AF HQ, 2Lts. Bob Howard and Bob White were awarded their fifth kills as the newest aces in the 5th Air Force. The Eightball outfit would later be honored with a Distinguished Unit Citation for their part in the May 14th interception, the first ever for an individual squadron in World War Two.

On the day after the famous raid, the 49ers returned to their patrols and alerts in anticipation of a follow-up by the enemy, but unlike the greater series of raids in April, there was very little contact. On the 15th, the Japanese sent a heavily escorted search flight of BETTYs to find their missing crews, but only ran up against a sextet of Mitchell bombers, and three 251st ZEKEs were lost in the

*9 FS crewman Sgt. Harlerode posing along side Lt. Johnson's aircraft "SOONER" in late May. The plane was formerly #80 and it's "0" is in the process of being changed to "3," since "83" was the pilot's "lucky" team number from his Oregon high school football days. The captain's black scoreboard would not display a victory flag until late July.*

*8 FS Bob Howard and his scoreboard of a rising-sun flags designating three confirmed ZEKE victims and the more recent pair of BETTY kills on May 14th which made him an ace. Howard would score against the BETTYs again four months later.*

*New 8 FS ace Bob White and his trusty #54 "KANSAS CITY KIDDIE II" at Dobodura. The name is white and the number is yellow. KIDDIE served the pilot until the new N-model Warhawks reached the Eightballs in July. Right: White posing with "KIDDIE's" scoreboard after the May 14th interception.*

brief exchange with the B-25 gunners. No American fighters were involved.

On the morning of the 16th, a small formation made a sudden raid on Dobodura, and again, no 5 AF unit made the interception. The hit-and-run tactics continued for a week, but fortunately, damage at the Allied airdrome was minimal. In the last week of the month, the Japanese Navy was forced to turn their attentions on the new Allied offensives in Alaska and the Solomon Islands. The JNAF raids against the Allied camps in Papuan subsided.

## A NEW ENEMY AIR FORCE; MAY, 1943

In the May doldrums, the Imperial Command designated a new 4th Army Air Force to be headquartered at Rabaul, and its first contingents were flown into the Southeastern Area in mid-month. To counter the Australian troops who now ventured deeper into Markham Valley, the remnants of the 1st and 11th Sentais at Wewak were joined by the Indo-China veterans of the 24th and 59th OSCAR outfits. They would fly escort to the LILY light bombers of 45th Sentai and HELEN heavy bombers of the 61st Sentai. At Rabaul, the 68th and 78th Sentais brought in the new Kawasaki Ki-61. The Kawasaki fighter bore a striking similarity to Italian types seen in North Africa and would be summarily named the TONY. The 68th and 78th TONYs began to escort bombing raids and convoys between Rabaul and Wewak by month's end.

Meanwhile, LtC. Morrissey's fighter group attempted to uphold their patrol duties with fewer and fewer of the war weary P-40Es. While the squadrons waited impatiently for the arrival of promised replacement Warhawks from Townsville, the majority of escort missions against Lae were more often flown by the 7 FS model K's and the 9 FS P-38s.

On the 24th, Eightball ace Ernie Harris returned from a patrol north of Cape Ward where he had fallen into a brief, vicious maneuver against a wily OSCAR veteran, and barely escaped with his skin. Harris had proven himself as the most accomplished fighter pilot in the 8th squadron with his fantastic acrobatics in the old

CAROLINA BELLE, but this mission had finally taken all the old girl could yield. Caught in the gunsight of the sentai veteran, Harris escaped in a desperate "outside loop", feinting a turn in one direction and falling off toward the other. Upon his safe landing back at Kalamazoo, crewchief Carl Wingo watched as the faded old stager wobbled into the dispersal area on its badly splayed landing gear. The rugged Warhawk had sprung its main wing spar, but had held together long enough to bring Harris back. The BELLE was finished as Wingo informed Op Exec Barnett that another old bird was out of the line-up. Only a few days later, a rookie second lieutenant ground looped Flt Ldr Bruce Harris' old #66, the SCARLET RECTUM which had to be written off. The Eightballs were down to a dozen serviceable planes in the first week of June.

## NEW FIGHTERS FOR NEW GROUPS

June marked another great transition in Fighter Command as LtC. George Prentice began his 475 FG "Satan's Angels" operations at Dobodura. The 49ers who had applied for promotion and transfer to the new Lockheed outfit said goodbye to their old comrades and moved their gear into the Angels bivouac area. More of the old cadre had been posted for transfer to the States, and others still were transferred south to man the training facilities in Australia.

As newly promoted Major Red Manning and his Screamin' Demons returned to their tactical missions in support of the Australian troops near Salamaua, Capt. Nichols left for the new Lockheed group, and Ray Melikian took over as the Deputy CO. Senior Lt. Arland Stanton assumed the Ops Exec role and the Demons carried on in the old K models, but neither of the Warhawk squadrons would encounter any airborne action for the next month. There would be only one encounter with the JNAF in June by the long ranging P-38s.

Sid Woods took over formal command of the 9th Squadron with the late May departure of Jesse Peaslee. Senior Capt. Bill Haney took up the assistant CO duties and Capt. Ross Blachly became the squadron Ops Exec. The Flying Knights extended their escort sorties and fighter sweeps beyond Lae and across the Huon Gulf to hunt over the new enemy air strips spotted at Cape Glouster and Gasamata, on western New Britain.

## LT. YEAGER'S DIVERSION; JUNE 2, 1943

On June 2nd, the Knights were part of the escort team that struck 125 miles due north of Lae at the coastal staging air field of Madang. The mission was completed without incident until they approached Horanda where Lt. Paul Yeager reported engine failure within sight if the airdrome. The lieutenant tried to bring the Lockheed in on a single engine, but the starboard mill burst into flame on the final leg and Yeager bailed out south of the field. As the line crews watched from Horanda strip, Yeager's chute took him down safely into the great swamp of Embi Lake where the nylon canopy snarled in a tall gum tree.

Capt. Woods landed and personally organized a rescue effort, including the dispatch of an Aussie infantry team to try for the stranded flyer from the west side of the swamp. The next morning, CO Woods, Ops Exec Blachly, and an Army medic, set off from the east side along a hunting trail and reached Yeager who had hung in the tree all night. The Aussie patrol arrived soon after and Yeager was cut down. All spent the night on dry ground, and on the third day, Yeager was carried out by litter. Dick Bong flew ahead of the rescue group and strafed the crocodiles that laid in their path along the swamp perimeter. After a week of rest in the Dobodura field dispensary, "tree-top" Yeager was pronounced fit to return to flight duty.

*Griffith's battle damaged P-40K #21 "VERA" was dragged into the dispersal field east of Kalamazoo and summarily scrapped out for vital parts.*

## MACARTHUR'S ADVANCE; BENA-BENA STRIP, JUNE 1943

Operations next sent the Flying Knights on a series of their most taxing missions to date. On June 7th, the 9 FS Lightnings became part of the escort team which staged south to Pt. Moresby's 7 Mile Strip, now called Jackson Drome by the RAAF, to await the arrival of C-47 Dakotas from Australia. All planes would fuel at Jackson for the 380 mile flight to the advanced base at Bena-Bena village, 175 miles northwest of Lae. The missions were flown for five days without incident.

*Attacks on staggered BETTY elements in formations of this type understandably resulted in duplicated kill claims by the 49ers on May 14th.*

On the morning of June 12th, Capt. Woods led the next sortie of eleven wingmen down to Jackson Drome, but the mission went awry. The 11th Service Squadron was ill prepared to handle the Yankee fighters, and Woods became furious as the fueling crews struggled with the cumbersome 150 gallon belly tanks. At 0800 hours, the Dakotas got underway, but Woods, element leader Dick Bong and element Jack Mankin were forced to leave wingman Harry Lidstrom who still waited for gasoline. Lt. Jim Watkin's Red Flight took off intact, but Blue Flight element leader Gerry Johnson also stayed behind due to fueling problems. Forty minutes after the Dakotas had gone, ten Flying Knights headed north in the futile hopes of finding the transports in the worsening weather.

Woods took Green Flight up to 11,000 feet as top cover, but Mankin soon turned away for Horanda with a faulty oxygen gear. Woods and element leader Bong continued on above the Red elements of Flt Ldr Watkins, George Albers, John Howard and Frank Wunder who were just ahead at 8000. On Red Flight's right flank was Blue Flight's trio of Flt Ldr Barnes with wingmen 2Lts. John Stowe and Francis Love.

For more than an hour, the nine Flying Knights flew over the cloud covered valleys of central New Guinea, when Lt. Watkins broke radio silence and reported to Sqn Ldr Woods that the Knights had surely passed their objective. Watkins led his Red Flight elements down through the billowing cumulus to 7000 feet as the entire formation circled through one complete turn. Watkins brought his Red quartet back for 10,000 feet and turned west in search of the Allied camp, just as sharp-eyed Dick Bong called out "OSCARs coming down on Blue." To their right and above at 14,000 feet, eight shiny tan Nakajimas nosed into their attack. It was their old nemesis, the 1st Sentai from Wewak, out on a strafing mission to Bena-Bena.

## BLUE FLIGHT ENGAGES

All of the Knights dropped their tanks at that moment. Blue Flight's trio dove a short distance to gain speed, but Francis Nutter could not get rid of his port tank. He swept upward to 10,000 feet and

*Lockheed technician Frank Bertelli who lived with the Flying Knights and ingeniously created a myriad of field modifications that kept their temperamental Lightnings airborne.*

then wheeled right with Flt Ldr Barnes and wingman Stowe to face the descending OSCARs. Barnes was the only man to hit a target and Blue Flight watched as the OSCAR rolled over and slip down through the clouds. Barnes repeated the maneuver and another OSCAR looped in front of his guns. Barnes kept his tracers on the ascending brown fighter until it stalled out and dropped off in a slow vertical spin. It plunged straight for the jungle and Blue flight momentarily dispersed.

## GREEN'S EXCHANGE and BOSS VS. BOSS

Woods and Bong wheeled hard to their right to cut off the eight OSCARs overhead, but Woods, in his #86 with the red diagonal command stripe across the tail, was singled out by the lead Ki-43 similarly marked with broad red wing bands. The sentai commander skillfully gained a dead astern position behind the 9 FS boss. Sid Woods responded with cool logic and rolled away in a 400 Mph sprint into the clouds.

Fearless Dick Bong, in #79, pressed on alone in a head-on assault against five of the twisting OSCARs, but nothing resulted from the first firing pass. Three Ki-43s wheeled in behind him and the ace separated through the clouds, then climbed back for another go. At 12,000 feet, Bong sighted seven single engine planes a mile ahead and targeted the nearest Ki-43. He fired a long burst from 600 yards down to 50 yards without effect, and was chased away a second time. He re-engaged for the third nose-on pass, but one of the OSCARs drifted to his left and Bong fired a perfect shallow deflection into the green-mottled silver plane. Two 20 mm rounds exploded in mid-fuselage on the target which slowly rolled into a sinking spin. Bong quickly tried to fire on another, but the odds played out against him. Enemy rounds rattled on #79 and the Knight wheeled out of the fight.

Red Flight had also turned into the sentai which passed over them and Flt Ldr Watkins could only feint at a speeding OSCAR that whistled by. Wingman Alber got off an errant shot at the attacker, but lost his flight leader in the maneuver. Lt. Howard also failed to drop one of his tanks and ventured only one firing pass before he broke off for Pt. Moresby. Tail-end Francis Wunder also fired a poorly aimed volley at one enemy ship, and swung about to re-engage, but his flight had separated. Wunder joined on Capt. Woods and Bong as the fight ended. Red Flt Ldr Watkins was totally separated and drifted off for Jackson Drome. He landed there at 1100 hours to find wingman Howard and Blue Flight's Barnes and Stowe there, too. At the same time on the north slopes of the Owen Stanleys, Capt. Woods, and Lts. Bong, Alber, Wunder and Nutter reached Horanda strip, all nearly out of gas.

Upon landing, Bong's #79 swerved drunkenly in its roll-out and stopped short of the dispersal area with a flat right tire and the hydraulics lines severed by 7 mm gunfire. It had been a very close call for the Flying Knight ace, but Bong only smiled as he surveyed the riddled right boom, plus the two additional bullet holes in each wing. He seemed genuinely indifferent to the whole event.

The missions to Bena-Bena continued, but the OSCARs were absent for the remainder of the June. Soon, the 80th Squadron Headhunters and 475th Group Satan's Angels joined in the escorts to Bena-Bena which provided some relief for Capt. Woods' pilots. Further relief came as replacement pilots arrived from Australia.

Although there was no aerial combat, the pace of the missions for the Flying Knights was unyielding. For their sister squadrons at Kalamazoo strip, the Demons and Eightballs also had been out of contact with the enemy, but the war still took a ghastly toll at their remote jungle encampment.

## DIVERSIONS IN JUNE, 1943

The squadrons at Dobodura had been under fire throughout May and the relative peace in late June led to a spirited challenge from the Screamin' Demons to take on all comers in a round-robin baseball tournament. Colonel Morrissey initiated the event with a fly-over in the 49ers Piper Cub liaison hack, BETTY BOOP. The teams roared with laughter when the colonel threw out the game ball through the arch of BETTY BOOP's prop. The ball exploded in a cloud of sawdust, and a wad of shredded leather and string plopped on the playing field. Another ball was found and the Demons vanquished all pretenders to reign as the baseball champs of Dobodura.

## THE GREAT MACKAY TRAGEDY; JUNE 17, 1943

The revery of the games vanished when the 49ers spirits were crushed by the tragedy on the 17th. Major George Powell, the much admired Group Exec and former Fighter Controller commander, was returning with five 8th Squadron men on leave in Australia when their B-17 transport crashed at MacKay Air Drome in Queensland. Major Powell, Capt. John Berthold, S/Sgt. Charlie LaRue, Sgt. Carl Cunningham, Pvt. Jerome Abraham and Pvt. Charlie Montgomery were among the forty men lost. Col. Paul Wurtsmith personally bore the grim news to the units at Oro Bay and Dobodura. As if the losses were not enough to break the hearts of the old cadre, on the next day, another 8th Squadron veteran fell.

## THE DEATH OF THE "CHOCTAWAHATCHEE KID"; JUNE 18, 1943

In an attempt to improve the gunnery skills of the replacement pilots who came to Dobodura, 5th Fighter Command instructed its engineers to develop a tow-target program which would utilize the combat experience of the veteran pilots at the front. In April, Sgts. Charlie White and Bob Burton of the 7th Squadron had gone to Townville and fabricated an electrically powered winch system which could be installed in the lower rear fuselage of a P-40. The winch hauled a cable which towed a thirty foot-long, four foot-wide nylon target 150 yards behind the Warhawk. Pilots could fire at the trailing target from wide deflection positions to experience rates of closure on the rectangular fabric which approximated the length of an enemy fighter.

The winch-fitted Warhawk was the old 9th Squadron P-40 E-1, "Scatterbrain," previously flown at Darwin by Demon CO, George Manning. The war-weary plane had been transferred to the 7th Squadron during the Pt. Moresby mobilization and then turned over to the salvage squadron when the Group moved to Dobodura. As a tow-plane, the old stager was brought up to Dobodura and maintained by the 8th Squadron flightline, even though the ship pro-

*8 FS Lt. Ben "the Choctawahatchee Kid" Duke.*

vided gunnery training for all of the 49ers pilots. Tow-pilots were chosen from the flight roster of fighter pilots in the 7th and 8th Squadron rotations.

On June 18th, senior flight leader Lt. Ben Duke of the 8th Squadron drew tow-target duty. The boyish lieutenant was a soft-spoken Southerner, affectionately called the "Choctawhatchee Kid" in reference to his home in the Gulf Coast forests of the Florida panhandle. Although "the Kid" had not scored in combat, he was judged to be an exceptional fighter-pilot and an able gunnery instructor. On the roster to muster out for the States, Duke had flown only a few routine combat patrols until that final fateful flight. "The Kid" rolled out in the tow-plane, but the Allison engine seized just after lift off from Kalamazoo Strip. SCATTERBRAIN snap-rolled and slammed down on its back, killing Duke instantly. His body was buried the following day in the American cemetery at Pt. Moresby.

*Broken aircraft #83 "Scatterbrain" uprighted in the dump at Dobodura after Duke's death on June 18th.*

*Kalamazoo operations in July with the new N-model P-40s of the Eightballs. The hectic schedule often resulted in missions being planned and meals being eaten on the flight line.*

*Eightball missions being mapped out on the hoods of the jeeps at Kalamazoo operations. The first of the new N-model Warhawks gave Porter's squadron new life.*

## TANGLE AT MORESBY; JUNE 29, 1943

The missions wore on routinely as the 49ers sought out the Japanese over central New Guinea without result. Losses occurred, but only to the Demons' chagrin in the self-inflicted setback at Pt. Moresby on the 29th. The Demons staged sixteen P-40K's to 5 Mile Strip as escorts to Milne Bay for C-47 transports supporting the renewed Solomons offensive. At 0700 hours, the Demons landed at the Aussie strip which was crowded with aircraft. The Warhawks rolled safely past the transports, but Lt. John Crowley's ship blew a tire and swerved toward Lt. John Benner's plane. Crowley's wingtip snagged Benner's rudder, then careened off the side of the dirt strip across the path of Lt. Bill Ferris' ship. Crowley and Ferris hooked wingtips and both planes suffered substantial damage. In seconds, the Demons had lost three aircraft, but luckily, Crowley, Benner and Ferris were not injured. It would be several days before the planes were back in service.

## SALAMAUA LANDINGS; JUNE 30, 1943

The Allied offensive finally closed in on the Japanese garrison at the harbor town of Salamaua on the last day of June. An amphibious landing put Australian and American infantry ashore 20 miles south of Salamaua at Nassau Bay beneath an aerial armada of Allied bombers and fighters. All three squadrons of Morrissey's 49ers flew cover over the beachhead, but the Japanese air units did not intervene.

Simultaneously, Gen. MacArthur also took hold of Kiriwina Island, 100 miles northeast of Oro Bay. Army engineers landed there unopposed and immediately began to construct the newest advanced staging field as a precursor to the missions that would soon be sent against the great enemy stronghold of Rabaul. Another 400 miles to the northeast, American forces were assaulting the northern most islands in the Solomons as MacArthur closed the pincers of the two-pronged thrust for Rabaul.

## END OF THE MORRISSEY ERA; JUNE 30, 1943

Lieutenant Colonel Bob Morrissey had become a man of substantial reputation in the 5 AF. At the summons of Deputy CO Gen. Whitehead, the colonel relinquish his fighter group command and joined the general's staff. Morrissey was promoted to full colonel and assumed the role of one of the principal task force planners for the demanding operations that lay ahead.

In the preceding five months, Morrissey's had seen his outfit play a key role in establishing the offensive now being executed against the Japanese. Eight of his pilots and two enlisted crewmen had fallen in combat at Dobodura, but Morrissey's 49ers had held out under the most strident conditions and with the oldest aircraft in the fighter command. The Demons, Eightballs and Flying Knights had raised their victory tally to 231 aerial kills under his command.

Although several new pilots had arrived in the past three months, the 49ers still had not received any new replacement aircraft for nearly eight months. As of June, 1943, the group was still operating the same model E and K Warhawks that they had originally brought up to Dobodura. Their Lightning squadron was often down to only a dozen operational planes that were flown constantly in the grueling long range escorts to the north.

Deputy Group CO James Selman assumed command of the war weary 49ers on July 1st. Promised by 5th Fighter Command that new Warhawks would soon arrive from northern Australia, Selman was forced to lead his Group in the throws of the Salamaua operation, still flying coastal patrols from Oro Bay to Lae with the derelict Warhawks. The new 49er leader was duly concerned for the safety of his Demon and Eightball P-40 pilots.

As for Squeeze Wurtsmith's beleaguer Fighter Command, there was one consolation. Selman had certainly proven his worth in the Darwin campaign of 1942 and Wurtsmith had no hesitation in approving his old friend for the command of the high scoring 49ers. The legacy of the most successful fighter outfit in the South Pacific was still in capable hands.

# 12

# THE MID-YEAR ADVANCES OF 1943

Rough seas had held back the amphibious landings at Salamaua until June 30th, and then the break in the weather was marginal. The assault landed south of the Salamaua isthmus at Nassau Bay and the Australians pushed inland fifteen miles for higher ground at the village of Mubo.

For the first three days of the operations, the 49ers flew their sorties under heavy overcast as the northern coast of Papua was soaked by daily rain squalls. Fighter-bomber missions were flown against coastal targets from Salamaua to Lae, as well as transport escorts to the Mubo staging area. When weather permitted, the 49ers sortied three times a day. Finally, the Warhawk pilots made contact with the Japanese air force on D-day plus four.

## SCREAMIN' DEMONS OVER MUBO; JULY 3, 1943

On July 3rd, the Screamin' Demons were held down until the weather let the C-47 transports fly to the aid of the Australians at Mubo village in the early afternoon. With CO Red Manning in the lead, 13 P-40K's lifted off from Kalamazoo and set themselves over the long parade of Dakotas for the flight to the battle area.

Major Manning had only been airborne a few minutes when his Warhawk began to sputter and loose altitude. He angrily turned his mission lead over to his second element leader, Lt. Arland Stanton, who took up the point position ahead of White Flight to wingmen Lt. Clyde Knisely and 2Lt. Owen "Onnie" Swartz. The big formation continued north through intermittent clusters of puffy clouds, all beneath a heavy scud that capped the sky at 12,000 feet.

Stanton's White Flight held the lead at 8000 feet as the Warhawks swept inland to the north past Salamaua while the Dakotas dropped their supplies to the Mubo camp. Two thousand feet overhead was the top cover Green Flight trio of Flt Ldr Lt. Carl Aubrey and his elements of 2Lt. David Germain and Lt. Sheldon Brinson. On Aubrey's left flank was Yellow Flight led by Lt. Paul Slocum, accompanied by the rookie 2Lts. Elliot Dent, element leader Ed Peck and wingman George McMurry. On the right flank a slight distance off, Lt. Ray Hilliard led wingmen Lt. John Benner and 2Lt. Chet Phillips at 6000 feet.

The Demons' orbited twice around the region west of Salamaua and when the last C-47s signalled their drops, Stanton turned the Warhawks in formation to the right for home. As the Demons drifted past Salamaua Bay, bombs were seen to burst on the shore line and Flt Ldr's Stanton, Aubry and Slocum alerted their elements simultaneously.

*7 FS Lt. Clyde Knisely flew his P-40K #16 "TYPHOON McGOON" on the July 3rd Mubo mission.*

*7 FS senior Flt Ldr Lt. Paul Slocum who initiated the interception over Mubo an July 3rd.*

*New P-40N of 8FS 2Lt Merle Wolfe, aircraft #40 s.n. 2104977, flown to Marilinan Bay.*

## YELLOW FLIGHT GOES IN FIRST

Lt. Slocum's Yellow Flight, with his elements nearest the coastline, caught sight of eight Ki-48 LILYs in line formation 3000 feet below. The bombers were part of the force of twenty 208th Sentai bombers that had flown down from distant Wewak airdrome under protection of sixteen OSCARs of the 24th Sentai. Likewise restricted by the seasonal storms, the LILYs had hoped to strike the main Allied force on the beach, but the landing ships had long since withdrawn. The belated attack would now cost the raiders dearly.

Slocum called for "tanks off" and began a climbing turn to the left for the LILYs that could just be seen through the spotty cloud cover. Then the Yellow quartet dropped into a left turn diving attack on a bomber with a pair of close escorts, but at 5000 feet, the other OSCARs of the veteran 24th Sentai looped up into the Warhawks' flight path.

Flight Ldr Slocum and wingman Dent tightened the turn against the closest pair of OSCARs and both Demons fired as the silver, green-mottled Ki-43s swept beneath them. The Demon pair rolled down on their respective targets as the sentai pilots lost speed and tried to turn off for the clouds, but their escape was foiled. Dent bored in on his victim and hammered it in a 90 degree deflection. The enemy pilot jumped free in his chute as his OSCAR slammed into Salus Lake south of Salamaua. Slocum turned once more with his opponent and caught the OSCAR with a steady volley that sent it down in flames to join Dent's victim.

Yellow Flight's second element of Ed Peck and George McMurry also gained the upper hand in the left-turn assault. Rookie Peck swept through a turn against the OSCARs and failed to get off a shot, while wingman McMurry sped past the escorts and caught up with a straggler LILY just off shore. As Peck broke off and climbed through the clouds to join Hilliard's top cover Red Flight, McMurry persisted in two gun passes against the LILY, flaming the right engine as the bomber crashed in a towering geyser one hundred yards off shore. A smoldering oil slick marked the site of the kill.

## GREEN AND WHITE ENGAGE THE 24TH SENTAI

Seconds after Yellow Flight hit the straggler bomber, the three remaining Demon flights struck the swirling OSCARs. A broad dogfight broke out within the clouds and tracers zipped through the hazy skies as wingmen struggled to hold position. In the course of the fight, many claims followed but only the Americans prevailed.

Green Flight Ldr Aubrey overtook an OSCAR off shore while wingman Germain and White Flight's Swartz ganged up on another. Green Flight's Brinson also fired on an OSCAR which dropped into the Salus Lake, but it may well have been Lt. Slocum's victim. Whatever the case, after only fifteen minutes of combat, the Demons withdrew in some disarray, but would claim five fighters and a bomber shot down. All of the Demons landed safely at Kalamazoo by 1715 hours, and a great celebration broke out. It was the first aerial engagement for CO Manning's outfit since the big interception six weeks ago in May.

## THE FLYING KNIGHTS IN JULY, 1943

The enemy continued to press its sorties against the Allies at Salamaua, and likewise returned to strike the growing Allied camp at Bena-Bena. The Flying Knights had struggled to keep up the pace in the grueling escort schedule with their well worn Lightnings, but luckily, there had been an absence of aerial intervention for nearly a month. Then, in the second week of July, newly promoted Major Sid Woods and his Knights entered into a series of engagements over central New Guinea that would yield several victories and some of the most spectacular encounters with the JAAF veterans from Wewak.

## OVER BENA-BENA; JULY 8, 1943

From their staging base at Pt. Moresby's Jackson Field, once more, Capt. Bill Haney led seven Flying Knights off in the routine morning escort of C-47 transports for Bena-Bena. Above a broken overcast which topped out at 9000 feet, the Knights set up on the right flank of the air convoy while eight 35 FS Cobras protected the left. They were "Bena bound" at 0830 hours.

Only minutes into the mission, Blue Flt Ldr Capt. Larry Smith had to abort with engine magneto failure. Smith took his wingman for cover and turned back as Blue element leader Lt. Fred Sibley assumed the flight lead. The Knights were down to six ships when the Americans reached the drop zone of the C-47s.

Capt. Haney led his five wingmen in a loose formation which was stacked from 19 to 21,000 feet. After a full turn above the Bena-Bena valley, Haney spotted nine twin-engine bombers which he thought to be American. They had approached from due east and now circled above the overcast just above Bena-Bena, when suddenly, four Cobra Lightnings peeled off in hot pursuit of the descending enemy bombers.

The Knights swung north through another turn and scanned the skies for enemy fighters, but the clouds were beginning to close in at their altitude as well. Mission leader Haney had just ordered the Knights to begin a gradual climb for higher position, when six radial engine fighter appeared from the east, directly overhead at 21,000 feet. Haney called out the warning as the 24th Sentai OSCARs dropped against the rear right flank of Lt. Sibley's Blue Flight. As the Knights dove out to gain speed and safety, only the Blue trio would maintain contact with the hit-and-run 24th Sentai.

## BLUE FLIGHT ENGAGES

Blue leader Fred Sibley, and 2Lt. wingmen Ralph Hays and Francis Love were in sight of each other at 17,000 feet when they saw the Ki-43s coming down on their right. Hays had actually watched the OSCARs make a full circle of his flight, some distance off. He heard Capt. Haney's radio alert, just as he calmly dove away to drop his tanks and easily evade the first attack.

Although Blue Flight separated and could not support each others counter attacks, each Blue Knight gained the advantage against their opponents. Francis Love, the trailing wingman in the mission, damaged an OSCAR that had first tried to fire on Sibley. Love turned into the sentai attacker and fired a front-quarter deflection burst of tracers which struck the sleek Nakajima in its rear fuselage. Love's left prop Rpm suddenly increased and he was forced to withdraw before he could fire a second time.

Love's gunfire gave Sibley maneuvering time, and the Blue Leader dove away, then swept back up to re-engage at 15,000 feet. Sibley flew two passes against the escaping sentai and hit one victim from near dead-astern. The OSCAR attempted to loop out of the line of fire, but it stalled out in mid ascent and flat spun down through the overcast into a mountain which loomed dangerously within the haze. Sibley flew other passes and fired at long range as the last of the OSCARs sped off for Wewak.

Wingman Hays also flew numerous passes against his adversaries, almost at will, and like his flight leader, his gunfire sent one of the OSCARs into a flat spin through the cloud deck. Hays re-

*Advanced Australian commando camp at Bena-Bena.*

grouped with Sibley and the victorious pair returned safely to Jackson with their squadron mates.

## THE CRUMBLING FRONT; JULY, 1943

Major Sid Woods' Flying Knights had no time to recoup from the skirmish at Bena-Bena. On July 9th, the 9 FS Lightnings were called back into the patrols over Lae, while still being based at Jackson Drome. New reconnaissance photos indicated new enemy fighters had staged into Lae airdrome and more had been seen at Rabaul. LtC. James Selman 's 49th Fighter Group was thrown back into the thick of Gen. Kenney's final air offensive against the Salamaua-Lae stronghold. Selman's task was to aid in the complete air superiority of the Huon Gulf area in preparation for the planned assault on Lae and Markham Valley, now postponed until after the July-August monsoons.

The Japanese vainly continued to stem the advance of the Allied ground forces in Papua. Their ravaged Army air wing at Wewak was reorganized as the 4th Air Division, and with reinforcements, the new command momentarily revitalized its long range counter-offensive. By the second week in July, yet another OSCAR contingent had staged back into Lae in support of the Imperial Army's besieged 51st Infantry Division at Salamaua. At Wewak, the

*Starboard nose artwork on 9 FS CO Woods' aircraft during the long range escorts to Bena-Bena. The sorties took a heavy toll of the battle weary pilots and planes.*

OSCARs of the 59th Sentai took up permanent residence to escort to the JAAF bombers which sortied against both Salamaua and Bena-Bena.

Likewise, the 68th and 78th Sentais introduced the new Kawasaki inline engine fighter, the Ki-61 TONY, into the Papuan campaign. But the JAAF was still committed to the northern Solomon Islands line of defense as well. Their fighter units continued the hopeless shuttle between the two fronts in the vane attempt to shore up the crumbling Southeastern Area venture. Now more 5th and 13th AF fighters and bombers were encountered than ever before, and the Allied pilots displayed a great ferocity.

As for the average soldier in the great camp of Dobodura, the genuine concern of any man was simple survival. They waited for mail which often answered questions they had sent off from Australia in 1942. There was gambling, but little money. There were movies at the "Zamboogie" open air theater which were constantly interrupted by air raid sirens. There was sleep. The constant heat and intermittent rains held a heavy, wet vapor over the camp, and physical labor would sap the strength of any man.

Only a few of the command staff at Dobodura understood the importance of the greater Allied venture. Selman's 49ers only knew of missions, waiting for the planes, sitting out air raids in the muddy trenches and longing for a pass to the continent "down under." Everyone prayed for the "million dollar ticket " for the States. And there were more burial ceremonies.

## THE LOSS OF SIBLEY; JULY 10, 1943

Only two days after his combat victory over Bena-Bena, Lt. Fred Sibley failed to return from a routine patrol over Lae. A newcomer from the April replacements, Sibley had shown great promise as a flight leader, but he could not overcome fate in his malfunctioning Lightning. He radioed Dobodura of the difficulty and was suspected of having gone down just north of Cape Ward Hunt. His remains were never found.

## RUNNING AFOUL OF FOWLER - F/O DAVIS LOST; JULY 11, 1943

The pressure on the Knights did not let up. The next morning, the 9 FS returned to Salamaua in escort to transports, plus the chance to search for their missing man. As mission leader Woods led his seven wingmen in the routine orbit of the Mubo village drop zone, four OSCARs were sighted circling in from below to strike the C-47s. The Major called for the attack, and all eight Knights dropped down for the enemy, but the Ki-43s turned into the Knights' assault before they could open fire.

Capt. "Tiny" Tom Fowler, whose two wingmen had turned back earlier with engine trouble, had attached himself to the 80th Squadron for the mission. At the warning, Fowler attacked independently from 16,000 feet and entered into the brief turning fight where he first shot at a Ki-43, then turned off to aid his squadron commander pursued by another OSCAR.

Fowler and the sentai pilot turned into each other, but the captain chose to separate in a short dive to regain the advantage. Another OSCAR was seen firing at rookie F/O Archie Davis, and once

*9 FS Darwin cadre veteran Capt. Tommy Fowler, sole Flying Knight to score on July 11th for the last aerial victory of his combat career.*

more, Fowler intervened. As Davis' flaming P-38 dropped into the haze, his killer spotted new the threat overhead and turned toward Tiny Tom, but it was too late. They faced one another for only seconds and the Knight fired first from nearly head-on. He snapped his Lightning aside in an aileron turn to see the drab green Ki-43 plunge straight down trailing smoke into the overcast. The other sentai pilots were in total disarray and they dropped down through the haze, only to be caught by the P-39s of the 36 FS. Three more sentai wingmen would die at the hands of the Airacobra pilots.

Grieved by one man lost on the previous day, and now, a wingman having gone down near Wau, Woods solemnly recalled the flight. Despite the resolve of diminutive Flt Ldr Fowler in the fight that morning, Archie Davis had perished and there was no consolation in the death of his killer.

## LOVE DOWN OFF CAPE WARD HUNT; JULY 13, 1943

Woods seriously thought his Flying Knights were cursed. Like Sibley three days before, fair-haired Lt. Francis Love dropped out of the formation due to engine failure on return from the morning sortie on the 13th. Love coasted south parallel to the shoreline and his P-38 was last seen slipping through the overcast just north of Cape Ward Hunt.

*49ers Group hack Piper Cub "BETTY BOOP," which survived the 43-44 campaigns, all the way to Hollandia.*

Luckily, Love was seen by scout aircraft four days later, walking along the shore twenty miles north of the cape. Sid Woods was determined to see his man back safely at Horanda strip and personally commandeered the Piper Cub hack, BETTY BOOP, for the rescue flight. Woods recovered the blond Flying Knight who was in remarkably high spirits when picked up on the beach. Love was back in the air the next day.

## DEMONS BACK AT LAE; JULY 14, 1943

Major George Manning's Screamin' Demons had joined in the close escort missions for the transports that flew north, but the Demons had missed the actions fought by the Lightning wing. Finally, the Demons got back into scoring on the morning of the 14th. It would result in one of the most dramatic rescues of a downed flyer in the campaign, and would afford newly promoted Capt. Ray Melikian the admiration of the entire 5th Fighter Command.

Mission leader Capt. Melikian took fourteen wingmen on the morning escort to the Mubo drop zone. Leaving Dobodura at 0730, Melikian's force climbed to 21,000 feet over Cape Ward Hunt as the C-47s proceeded to the Mubo camp.

## BLUE AND ORANGE IN PURSUIT

After an hour's time, a signal came from the Australians nearer the coast of enemy bombers striking the beach landing area. Melikian turned south and flew into a clearing in the cloud cover, where 10,000 feet below, he saw two VAL dive-bombers turning out to sea beyond Salamaua. The captain jettisoned his belly tank and spiraled down to the left with his Blue Flight wingman 2Lt. Logan Jarman, element leader Lt. Duncan Myers and wingman 2Lt. Bob DeHaven in a perfect "finger-four" formation attack. Orange Flt Ldr Lt. Don Lee took wingmen 2Lts. Jim Chandler, element leader Del Moore and David Germain down in similar formation at the same moment.

*7 FS Lt. Duncan Myers and his old stager P-40K #19 "FLORIDA GATOR" flown on the July 14th mission.*

*7 FS Darwin cadre veteran Don Lee and his aircraft #34 "PISTOFF" who received the attention of all the airborne 49ers Warhawks on the fateful July 14th mission.*

Blue and Orange dropped through seven thousand feet of altitude in pursuit of the two enemy planes, and at 10,000 feet, Melikian fired a long-range burst at the lead VAL which was about to escape in the haze above the sea. A thin, dark smoke stream emitted from his target, just as it slipped into the cloud. The JNAF wingman banked away to the east while Melikian, Jarman and Myers set after the damaged VAL flight leader beyond the temporary safety of the cloud bank. Alone, DeHaven wheeled down after the east-bound dive-bomber.

Orange Flt Ldr Lee, flying his trusted #34 PISTOFF, also singled out the target heading for Lae. He saw Melikian make the first attack, and then saw the Blue flight trio make their second attack on the north side of the cloud bank. Orange flight finally overtook the dive-bomber whose valiant rear gunner still sent back a lethal string of 7 mm tracers at the swerving Warhawks. Darwin veteran Lee pressed PISTOFF into firing range and sent a fifty caliber barrage into the riddled VAL, but as Lee broke off, his temperature gauge indicated a hot engine. He assumed the Allison had overheated during the prolonged pursuit. Wingman Chandler finished his firing pass and swept over his flight leader to look down on PISTOFF which left a fine trail of white vapor in the sea air. Lee's P-40 had taken a single bullet through the radiator and was loosing its precious glycol coolant.

## LEE DOWN IN HUON GULF

As Jarman and Myers delivered the coup de grace upon the VAL flight leader and DeHaven single handedly dispatched the enemy wingman five miles to the east, all the Demons heard Don Lee's distress signal. The veteran was bailing out.

Lee rode his holed P-40 down to 800 feet above the cerulean Huon Gulf and stepped out on the left wing. He fell away in the slip stream, but PISTOFF suddenly rolled and the lieutenant slammed into the rudder. Although he was stunned, he was able to pull his parachute cord and fall consciously into the gently rolling sea. Wingman Chandler swept overhead to mark the site.

Capt. Melikian was not about to leave the downed flight leader who was still in sight. The mission boss methodically called for the Demons with adequate fuel to set up an orbit over Lee, and to keep the lieutenant in sight until they were relieved. Black Flight, led by Lt. Bob McDaris and Gold led by Lt. Lucius LaCroix, had held their position as high cover. They became critical in the rescue effort as the minutes quickly passed.

Melikian, Myers, DeHaven, and Chandler orbited the site at 4000 feet while Del Moore circled down on the deck. Melikian ordered McDaris to seek help from the Navy patrol craft off nearby Lasanga Island, while LaCroix's people orbited north of Lee's position in a wide pattern to screen any enemy flights from the north, as well as to concentrate on radio communications with other Allied aircraft in the area.

All of the Demons cut their rolled liferafts from their chute packs and dropped them to Lee, but they fell far beyond his reach. Besides, Lee had other problems to deal with. During his descent in his chute, only half of his May West had inflated and he struggled to free himself from his harness while he floated neck deep in the water. Once free, it became painfully clear his left arm was broken just below the shoulder. To further add to his dilemma, his rubber lifeboat would not inflate.

For a moment, the rescue effort appeared to be unraveling. Gold Flt Ld LaCroix passed over a school of sharks only a few yards from the downed flyer, and LaCroix made several strafing passes on the predators until they swam away. Meanwhile over Lasanga Island, McDaris' flight was fired upon by the Navy A/A gun crews. Soon, both LaCroix and McDaris reported their flights were critically low on gas.

Capt. Melikian calmly assured everyone that relief was on the way. True to his word, an escort flight of Eightballs passed overhead and signalled that their old P-40E's would take up the watch over Lee. One of the Eightball flyers finally dropped a raft pack near Lee, and even though it only partially inflated, the sinking

lieutenant finally was able to keep his head well above the calm waves.

A pair of A-20 Havocs soon arrived to relieve the Eightballs who then withdrew. One of the Havocs dropped a large inflated raft to the stranded Demon and Lee climbed aboard the more spacious boat. There was no paddle, so Lee tried to row with his .45 automatic pistol, but that quickly proved pointless. Lee dejectedly floated out to sea and Lasanga Island soon faded from sight. Sharks silently glided by in the clear sea as the afternoon sun beat down on the exhausted Orange Flight Leader.

After an hour afloat, Lee heard the approach of a power boat from the west. Melikian's effort had paid off after all. Lee was hauled aboard the PT boat and was taken to the Navy dispensary at Oro Bay by night fall. Lee eventually was sent State-side to allow his broken arm to fully heal and afford him the opportunity to attend command school. Thanks to Ray Melikian, Don Lee would return to New Guinea the following year, in command for his own squadron.

## NEW GROUPS IN THE BUILD-UP AT DOBODURA; JULY, 1943

Engineers at Dobodura had effected major changes at the jungle air field, including widening Horanda strip and laying Marston mat in the surrounding dispersal areas to handle more planes. The new 348 FG, commanded by flamboyant LtC. Neel Kearby, had arrived in their Republic P-47 Thunderbolts at Pt. Moresby and began to stage into Dobodura. The massive fighters would park on the northeast side of the field, just east of Warhawk Row. Few of the 49ers line crews had ever seen the portly Thunderbolt which was nicknamed the "Jug" because of its rotund, bottle-like shape. The Warhawk and Lightning mechanics walked down the flight line to gaze in wonder at the huge fighters with their entire tail sections painted white, so as not to confused them with the radial engine ZEROs and OSCARs. The markings seemed pointless, since everything about the huge P-47 negated any resemblance to the sleek Mitsubishis and Nakajimas. Even the Flying Knights' crewchiefs who were expert on maintaining the complicated P-38 were amazed at the "Jug's" elaborate turbocharged engine plumbing and awesome firepower of eight .50 caliber guns.

*New P-40N aircraft on the Kalamazoo flight line in July, 1943.*

*P-40N s.n. 42-104981 and designated #65 in the 8th Sqn was assigned to F/O Art Talmadge, homage to the pilot's skill and not just his rank.*

The arrival of the Thunderbolts would offer Selman's depleted band respite in flying both base patrols and support of the Salamaua operations. As part of their orientation, the 348th would assume the standing patrols of the Oro Bay area, allowing the Warhawks to add more tactical punch for the missions over Salamaua and Lae.

### NEW EIGHTBALL BOSS, NEW EIGHTBALL P-40s; MID-JULY, 1943

Veteran Jim Porter had completed his tour as commander of the 8th Squadron and was called up to join Group CO James Selman as the 49ers new Operations executive. For the first time, the Eightballs would choose a replacement commander who was not a Darwin veteran. Senior Capt. Ernie Harris, the "pineapple man" who had come to Dobodura via Hawaii, was respected by the Eightball pilots and crews without question. Easy in temperament and informal in the "Eck Sims tradition", the pipe smoking ace led by example and that was enough for LtC. Selman. Fifth Command readily concurred.

Not only did the Eightballs induct Harris as their new squadron boss, the crew chiefs hailed the arrival of the first new Warhawks for the Kalamazoo flight line since Dobodura had gone operational. As of mid month, brand new Curtiss P-40 model N's had been flown in to replace the oldest of the war-weary E's.

Essentially like the older planes, the N model fuselage was longer by a foot and a half and was the same gross weight as the K model. However, the Allison engine in the new ship provided more horsepower at higher altitude and gave the 49ers a P-40 with a faster climb rate. Lighter weight struts and smaller wheels would cause some additional maintenance with the landing gear, and the vacuum driven instruments would eventually be replaced with salvaged electrical systems from the older planes. But still, a revised cut-down rear fuselage with enlarged canopy area, and a top speed 25 Mph

faster than the best overhauled old stager, gave an Eightball pilot the sense he was in a modern fighting machine.

In the meantime, the last of the old E models would fly with the newer N's until more replacements arrived. As time permitted the Demon and Eightball crews, they would also begin to have their tail sections and wing aeilrons painted white, similar to the Thunderbolts, as an official fighter identification aid. RAAF fighters also began to appear with the white tails which would eventually become the standard marking for all Allied single engine combat planes in the South Pacific.

### MOVING THE EIGHTBALLS UP TO MARILINAN; JULY 20, 1943

No sooner had LtC. Selman brought his group back together in the Dobodura operations against Salamaua, Squeeze Wurtsmith summoned the 49er CO and 8 FS CO Ernie Harris to 5 AF HQ in mid-month and told them of the next element in the Lae invasion scheme. While infantry forces had been securing the areas around Mubo near Salamaua, and Bena-Bena in the north, Army engineers had secretly advanced 80 miles north of Wau into the Watut Valley. At the village of Marilinan, the engineers had scraped out a 5000 foot dirt runway on the west bank of Watut River which flowed north 40 miles into greater Markham.

Dakota transports had made many flights to the new air strip under escort by the 35 FG Airacobras, but Marilinan strip had now been discovered by the enemy. The need of P-40s for base defense there had become a priority and Capt. Harris eagerly jumped at the chance to move closer to the action.

On the evening of July 19th, CO Harris and Ops Exec Clyde Barnett informed all senior flight leaders to take charge of a new Warhawk and pack any essential gear for immediate transfer. The next day, Harris and Barnett with ten wingmen, took off in the morning twilight for an undetermined location, somewhere north far beyond the jungle base that had been their home for the last five months.

Harris' contingent flew to Wau and then continued down the Watut Valley north-northwest along the river until they could see the broad S turn in the stream which marked the location of Marilinan. Harris dropped down over the village and turned south into the landing pattern, finally coming to rest on the south end of the coarse red dirt field.

After dispersing their P-40s in the forested parking area at the southern end of field, the pilots took jeeps a short distance up into the foot hills to a primitive bivouac area where they set up quarters and stored their gear. Their new home was only 80 miles due west of Lae airdrome.

The Eightballs began patrolling over the Markham Valley the very next day. The Warhawks were maintained by the advanced flight crews who served the Airacobras and Dakotas that daily flew in and out of Marilinan. Pilots rotated back to Dobodura on a weekly basis until more flights of the new Warhawks were available. By month's end, the 8th Squadron ground echelons would join their commander at the new jungle camp.

## NEW PLANES FOR THE SCREAMIN' DEMONS

In late July, more P-40N's arrived at Dobodura and Red Manning's 7th Squadron refit with the new ships. They flew area patrols in conjunction with the newcomer 348th Thunderbolts, as well as the continuous escorts to the southern end of the Markham River Valley. Although LtC. Selman's refurbished Warhawk squadrons were now better equipped to engage in combat, the P-40 pilots would not score an aerial victory for more than two months. The brunt of the dogfighting would fall upon Major Woods' Flying Knights.

As the Australian troops closed in on the surrounded Salamaua garrison, Gen. Kenney stepped up the pace of bombardments on the coastal targets. The fighter escorts centered their sorties in and around Lae, as well as flying sweeps to western New Britain. In particular, the Lightning wing fought several intense engagements against the new JAAF units now thrown against MacArthur's forces.

## ESCORT FOR THE MARAUDERS; JULY 23, 1943

Capt. Ross Blachly led eleven wingmen off from Horanda to escort the 22nd Bomb Group B-26 Marauders in the morning strike on Salamaua. Once airborne, Blachly's radio went out and Lt. Harry Lidstrom temporarily took the Yellow Flight lead as they ascended to 15,000 feet. Lt. Gerry Johnson held his Blue Flight off to the left at the same altitude, and Lt. Bleecker's quartet went up to top cover at 22,000.

The target area was spotted with broken clouds and Lidstrom lost sight of the bombers, so he latched on to a transport flight that was also headed north. After leaving the transports west of Salamaua, the Knights patrolled for nearly an hour and a half. At 1000 hours, the lower Yellow and Blue flights caught sight of a huge fighter formation coming down from the north. Blachly first suspected they might be P-40s because of their pointed-spinner profile, but he quickly changed his mind as the red roundels appeared on the wings. At Lt. Lidstrom's signal, all the Knights dropped their tanks to engage the newcomers of the 68th Sentai.

*Left: The instruments of the new Model-N were vacuum driven which Demon and Eightball crewchiefs judged to be far too troublesome. Most were swapped out for salvaged electrical units from the old Model-E and K aircraft. Right: 8 FS Flt Ldr Runey displays the latest fashion of a USAAF fighter pilot.*

## YELLOW-BLUE VS. THE TONY'S

Capt. Blachly, still without a working radio, was uncertain of wingman Lidstrom's intentions and instantly grew impatient with the waiting. The captain shoved the throttle forward and plunged for the enemy fighters racing in head-on at 15,000 feet, just as Gerry Johnson's seven-ship Blue flight targeted the same enemy planes. In seconds, eight Lightning pilots entered into their first dogfight against the new Ki-61 "in-line types" which closely resembled the Italian Macchi 202. The new opponent had been code-named MIKE, an acronym for Michelangelo, but later would be known throughout the Pacific theater by the more familiar Italian acronym of "TONY."

As Yellow Flight held intact in the turn against the enemy, tail-end Wunder switched his turn in the opposite direction and came head-on against one of the heavily camouflaged, long-winged fighters. Wunder fired at point blank range, then rolled aside and looked down at the Ki-61 as it sped straight into the overcast. He was sure that the TONY was mortally hit.

Blue Flt Ldr Johnson likewise made a head-on pass, but his gunfire was ineffective. He re-engaged, and like Wunder only seconds before, claimed a kill after a head-on exchange of gunfire.

## OSCARS, TOO

Blue element leader Charles Ralph held formation for the first pass against the TONYs, but he separated from his flight leader when he saw OSCARs over the coast line. Lt. Bleecker's Green Flight top cover trio also saw the OSCARs and they sped down to the interception as well. At 17,000 feet, the OSCARs were met where Lt. Ralph and Green wingman 2Lt. Wandrey each claimed one of the sleek silver fighters destroyed.

When rookie Wandrey tried to make a second pass on the OSCARs, a pair of TONYs intervened and one of them put a 13 mm round in Wandrey's left wing. Fortunately for the rookie Flying Knight, the explosive round lodged in the spar but did not detonate.

After nearly 20 minutes of continuous maneuvers in the clouds over Salamaua, the combatants separated and withdrew to their respective fields. At Horanda strip, the Knights exuberantly recalled their success versus the new in-line Ki-61s from Wewak. They had been most fortunate in their first encounter with the sleek fighters as Wandrey's plane was the only 49er's ship damaged in the fight. They had no way of knowing that in three days, they would give the TONYs another go-around in a most historic battle.

## LIGHTNINGS AND TONYS AGAIN AT SALAMAUA; JULY 26, 1943

The Flying Knights had fallen into a fever pitch with the renewed aerial engagements. All the senior flight leaders vied for the most favorable missions in the pursuit of the much touted air victories. One fellow in particular had become obstinate in his want for action. It was the Knights' Deputy CO, Capt. Jim "Duckbutt" Watkins.

About to end his extended tour, veteran flight leader Watkins was bound and determined to score at least once more before he

*Crewman Lynch points out the bullet hole in Lt. Wandry's aircraft to C.C. Wilson after the July 23rd meeting with the TONYs at Salamaua.*

was furloughed back to the States. The captain had missed out on every scoring opportunity since his first and only kill in his P-40 over Dobodura, back in December. Now, exactly six month to the day, he was about to exceed beyond his wildest dreams.

On the 26th, senior Capt. Larry Smith was on alert status at Horanda when a mid-day alarm called for an interception at Salamaua. After takeoff, two men aborted with engine trouble and only ten Knights reached the Markham River delta. Not seeing enemy planes, Smith chose to hunt further inland. With wingman 2Lt. Ralph Hays and Jim Harris III, in close proximity, Smith continued due north over the Markham River Valley at 14,000 feet.

Trailing a short distance back on the left flank was the Blue Flight trio led by Capt. Watkins with Lt. Bong and 2Lt. Bob Wood in wing position at 16,000 feet. Some distance off on the right flank was Lt. Gerry Johnson's Green Flight of wingman 2Lt. Stan Johnson and tag-a-long element leader Capt. Blachly with wingman 2Lt. Glade Hill. The accompanying 39 FS Cobras flew their sweep further west while the 80 FS Headhunters ventured eastward.

The Knights probed inland some twenty miles, but found nothing. Mission leader Smith called for a turn back toward the river delta, and as clouds began to close in, Blue Flt Ldr Watkins went into a shallow descent in the attempt to keep Smith in sight. Once back over the delta, the Knights turned north again for their second

*Bell P-39 Airacobra refueled at Marilinan with a gasoline powered portable pump designed and built by the resourceful linecrews of 5 FC.*

*9 FS Maj. Sid Woods and his last aircraft #92 in the final days of his command at Dobodura. Though he scored only one aerial victory in the Pacific, in Europe during 1944, LtC. Woods would become a double ace while commanding two different 8 AF groups equipped with P-51 Mustangs.*

sweep, but in the turn, Smith's Red trio fully separated from the trailing flights. Watkins' Blue Flight momentarily fell into the lead.

Just beyond Lae airdrome in a canyon of dense clouds, the Flying Knights crossed the flight path of ten OSCARs and ten TONYs who were coursing down the Markham Valley. It was the very situation veteran Jim Watkins had been waiting for.

### NEARLY BUNGLED BOUNCE

All ten Knights attempted to drop their tanks in answer to Watkins' signal of "bandits" in front of and behind their position, but Capt. Smith's tanks hung up on the racks. He climbed with Hays and Harris through the nearest clouds, furiously rocking his ship to loosen the pods, but they stayed put. Hays and Harris took the captain out of range to the south, then the two lieutenants wheeled back to the fight.

In the interim, Green Flight suddenly unraveled. Capt. Blachly and wingman Hill had separated from Green Flt Ldr Gerry Johnson. Blachly and Hill were forced to climb out of the fight and join on the wing of the top cover Headhunters some distance off. Green wingman Stan Johnson dropped his tanks and slammed down the throttle, only to blow the right super charger. He stayed with Flt Ldr Johnson through the first pass against the OSCARs, but Stan Johnson could not re-engage. Gerry Johnson was on his own.

Meanwhile, Watkins accessed the logistics of the OSCARs out in front who were turning head-on, while the TONYs were pulling around to Blue Flight's rear quarter. The Blue Leader chose to wheel hard about and face the first pair of mottled-brown in-line fighters coming down on wingman Bob Wood.

### BLUE-GREEN WRECKING CREW

Although rookie Bob Wood tried to keep up with Capt. Watkins and element leader Bong, Wood's right engine blew out and fractured the fuselage. He was out of the fight early on. Unfortunately for the Wewak pilots that day, they still had to contend with the deadly flight leaders who stayed in the contest.

Watkins, flying in A/C #70, hammered the first TONY in the initial head-on pass. The Ki-61 rolled over and the canopy fell away, followed by the sentai pilot in his chute. The captain climbed to re-engage and spotted two more TONYs chasing Gerry Johnson. Watkins cut off the trailing enemy wingman, flaming the inline Kawasaki with an astounding 45 degree shot from the left front quarter. The captain scored his third Ki-61 kill from another head-on encounter and then broke off to regroup. When he took #70 back to 10,000 feet, he was again in the midst of the enemy. Gaining advantage over his fourth Ki-61 victim, Watkins riddled the TONY from the left rear quarter. It did not burn, but it fell out of control into the valley. Watkins concluded the enemy pilot was dead and swept upward out of the fight.

Bong likewise took on the TONYs, but fired without effect in the first pass. As he dove away in #79 to regain speed, Bong encountered his first victim and flamed an OSCAR from head-on. He immediately targeted another Tony and blew away part of its rear fuselage for his second kill claim, then fired on yet another in a left-hand turn from the rear quarter for his third claim. His fourth and last victim resulted from another head-on pass against an OSCAR which disintegrated within #79's concentrated gunfire. Bong fired at several other ships until low fuel and ammo forced him to withdraw.

### JOHNSON SCORES THE HARD WAY

As Watkins shot the TONY off Gerry Johnson's tail, Johnson rolled in behind Watkins and chased an OSCAR off the captain's tail. The OSCAR plunged for the clouds and Johnson rolled his #83 SOONER down after the fleeing Ki-43. From the rear quarter, SOONER delivered a burst of explosive rounds which flash on the Nakajima's slender fuselage. The Green Flight Leader swept upward to regroup as the smoking OSCAR disappeared through the haze below.

Gerry Johnson immediately attempted to rejoin Watkins and Bong, but at 10,000 feet, an inline-type fighter suddenly appeared in SOONER's flight path. The Lightning pilot pressed the firing button on his control wheel, just as the TONY pilot touched off his own guns. Within a hail of enemy tracers, Johnson pumped the controls, rocking SOONER's nose up and down to spray a broader pattern of fire. When the waterhose-like .50 caliber/20 mm stream ripped away the Kawasaki's left wing, the stricken TONY tumbled through the air toward the aghast Knight who wheeled hard over to the right to avoid the collision. SOONER jolted as the shattered Ki-61 tore away the lower tail assembly from the Lightning's port fuselage.

*9 FS crewmen with Capt. Johnson's #83 "SOONER" just days before the July 23rd collision with the TONY.*

*Sgt. Yates inspects the torn tail section of "SOONER" which was scrapped out. Johnson inherited Woods' command and his P-38 which he numbered "lucky" #83 but did not give it a name.*

Johnson quickly regained control of his crippled Lightning and found he could correct the yawing ship with the aelirons. Three 39 FS Cobras soon crossed the Knight's path and they surrounded SOONER for the precarious descent to Horanda Strip.

After Red Flight's Hays and Harris made a belated pass against the last of the OSCARs, all of Capt. Smith's Knights returned singly or attached to other Lightning units. For their latest encounter with the newcomer inline-engine opponents, Watkins four victories belayed any rumor of the purported superiority of "MIKE from Wewak."

Twenty minutes past two o'clock, Gerry Johnson set #83 down at Horanda and rolled to a halt in the Knights dispersal area. The entire line crew gathered around and gazed in admiration as SOONER's crewchief, Gaylord Akin, surveyed his magnificent, rugged Lockheed which had saved the young flight leader and given him two confirmed kills.

## HOT-SHOTS OF DOBODURA

Of eleven victories confirmed for the Lockheed escorts that day, ten were awarded to the Flying Knights. Bong had become the first "triple ace" in the Pacific with the four latest kills bringing his total score to sixteen. Watkins, though his last TONY victim was never officially confirmed, was hailed with four victories by his squadron mates. Crew chief Chambliss added four small Japanese flags on the score board of Watkins' #84 CHARLCIE JEANNE, declaring the captain the newest ace in New Guinea. Chambliss barely had time to clean his paint brush before the captain scored again.

## NEW BRITAIN; JULY 28, 1943

Two days after the big fight over Markham Valley, Major Woods mustered ten Lightnings for an air strike against the western tip of New Britain. In the company of a dozen 39 FS Cobras, Woods' P-38s escorted the B-25s of the 3rd AG "Grim Reapers" who would hit enemy shipping in the bay and strafe the air strip at Cape Glouster. At 0630 hours, Major Woods set off with his wingmen in the clear morning twilight for their New Britain objective, one and half hours due north.

Anticipating heavy resistance over the new enemy complex, the 5 AF mission planners determined Woods' P-38s should stay in visual contact with the 3rd AG at a lower altitude than usual. The Knights took up their close stations over the Grim Reapers, with Red Flight Maj Woods' and wingman Bob Wood in the lead at 4000 feet, followed closely behind by Green Flight's Capt. Bill Haney, wingman 2Lt. Ralph Wandrey, element leader 2Lt. George Alber and rookie wingman F/O H.R. Prince at 6000 feet. Two thousand feet over all in trailing high cover was the deadly duet of Watkins and Bong, accompanied by 2Lt. Normand Hyland.

The Americans reached the target area without opposition and the Grim Reapers were able to hit several vessels off Cape Raoult, just east of the Glouster complex, as well as set fires near the airstrip. Major Woods' close escorts circled the target area as smoke rose high into the hazy sky above the glistening turquoise shore line of the great island. After thirty minutes of watching the Reapers ply their trade, an alert was sounded by the bomber crews of enemy fighters approaching from the east. Wood's men dropped their belly tanks and rose up for the interception.

In a left-turn ascent out over the sea, all three 9 FS flights squarely met the large formation of OSCARs that had sortied from Rabaul. Major Woods and wingman Wood, and Green Flight Haney with wingman Wandrey, all passed directly into firing range against the oncoming enemy at 8000 feet. After four hit-and-run passes in the turning fight, Woods and Wandrey each destroyed a Ki-43 and damaged another, while Capt. Haney downed a third OSCAR.

In Blue Flight, wingman 2Lt. Hyland failed to hold position with the aces and he dropped away with four OSCARs in close pursuit. By the time the lieutenant safely recovered, Watkins and Bong had already done their damage. Watkins first met an OSCAR in a nose-on pass, but missed the mark. The captain then took Bong on his wing for the second pass, and the Flying Knight duet wheeled to each others defense on a pair of sentai wingmen diving in from behind. Watkins' burst exploded his victim and CHARLCIE JEANNE nearly collided with the debris. Bong and Watkins then separated as other OSCARs threatened.

As Bong sped off for the safety of five wingmen some distance off, Watkins plunged down to 4000, only to meet another pair of OSCARs from head-on. Both Ki-43s maneuvered out of CHARLCIE JEANNE's lethal firing line, but as the sentai wingman dropped away, the OSCAR leader looped in front of the captain. Fatally stalled out, the OSCAR seemed to hang in the air by its' prop and shudder as Watkins' barrage of .50 caliber explosive rounds sparkled on its fuselage. The black fighter dropped straight down and shattered in an immense explosion on the water's surface.

Meanwhile, Bong was about to overtake the other Knights when he was caught from behind by a diving attacker. Seven millimeter rounds clattered on #79, and Bong pushed the nose down toward the blue sea. He pulled out at 4000 and turned back to re-engage, when two more OSCARs were seen turning after an element of B-25s speeding southward, down on the deck. Bong entered into a shallow diving turn and fired from 45 degrees of deflection on the trailing Ki-43. The OSCAR turned into the source of the .50 caliber tracers, but it was too late. The black Ki-43 flew through the point blank head-on barrage, then slid aside mortally hit. Trailing heavy smoke, Bong's victim drifted away to the northwest and slashed down in Rein Bay. The ace then wheeled back and rejoined the Grim Reapers for the flight home.

Back at Horanda, Bong counted five bullet holes in the upper surface of his left wing, but crew chief Elwood Barden easily covered them with small riveted patches by the following day. Only Bong's ship had been hit in the mission and everyone had made it home safely. Watkins, pleased to have three more kills immedi-

ately confirmed, ceremoniously bought drinks again for everyone at the 9 FS officers' club. He had no way of knowing his bar tab would get even larger.

## AN INCREDIBLE ENCOUNTER EAST OF LAE; AUGUST 2, 1943

The Allies continued to rain down a horrendous assault on the enemy installations at Salamaua and Lae. The crisis deepened as more and more B-24 heavy bombers struck both of the Imperial headquarters at Rabaul and Wewak around the clock. Allied medium bombers raided further up the coasts of New Britain and shipping on New Guinea's shore was under constant attack. Wewak was continually swept by P-38s which hunted down more and more of their veteran sentai pilots. The new American base at Marilinan, only minutes west of Lae, kept a constant patrol of P-40s and P-39s over the Lae air drome. Invasion of Markham Valley was certainly eminent.

In total desperation, the Imperial commanders approved of a bold plan to turn back the tide of the Allied advance. LtGen. Hatazo Adachi, supreme commander of the Imperial forces in New Guinea,

*"Murderers' row" at Horanda strip. A crewchief signs off Tice's old #88 now back into service, still bearing its unique post gunsight in front of the windshield. The supercharger has an added ram-air intake pipe to better feed air into the turbine, a typical field-mod of 9 FS Lightnings. Aircraft #95 displays a red-white flight leader stripe, possibly assigned to Capt. Haney. Aircraft #85 is assigned to Capt. Smith. Fuel heavy #78 sits low on its gear next to aircraft #84 assigned Capt. Watkins, and the last aircraft #79 was assigned to top ace Dick Bong.*

would go to the Lae stronghold and personally take command of the operations. On August 2nd, weather allowed for a single-engine Ki-51 SONIA scout aircraft to carry the general, under heavy escort of an OSCAR squadron, down the coast to the besieged garrison. The venture would end disastrously.

## DUCKBUTT'S CRESCENDO

At Dobodura, thirty-eight B-25 strafers with an escort of thirty P-38s was sent off just before 11:00 a.m. on a barge hunting sortie to the Huon Gulf coast east of Lae. In close escort at 6000 feet, Capt. Larry Smith led a dozen 9 FS wingmen out over the gulf. After the bombers found targets just east of Markham Bay, the Flying Knights swept out to sea as a shield against enemy planes that might venture out of Cape Glouster.

Smith's Green Flight of wingmen 2Lts. Jim Harris and Charles Ralph were at 6000 feet in the lead. On their left flank was Lt. Gerry Johnson's Red Flight of 2Lts. Stan Johnson and Johnny "Jump" O'Neill. On the right was newcomer Lt. Wally Jordan who led Blue Flight wingmen 2Lts. Grover Fanning and Frank Wunder. Overhead and slightly behind was the Yellow Flight top cover of Capt. Jim "Duckbutt" Watkins, with wingmen 2Lts. George Alber and Francis Nutter. After hunting for only a few minutes, all the flight leaders caught sight of an enemy fighter formation down near the ocean surface and headed straight for the B-25 strafers.

## A CLOSE CALL AS YELLOW FLIGHT OPENED FIRE

When Adachi's escort pilots caught sight of the descending Flying Knights, they peered straight down the muzzles of Yellow flt Ldr. Watkin's blazing guns. All discipline vanished as the enemy wingmen broke ranks and bolted for the escape to the north.

Watkins had brought CHARLCIE JEANNE down at full throttle through a full circle to come head-on against a Ki-43 which ap-

*Future 49ers ace Wally Jordan accredited with his first victory during the last shoot-out*

*Lethal #84 "CHARLCIE JEANNE" rolls out for a sortie.*

peared to suddenly rise up alone from the enemy formation. The captain's first volley blew away the canopy and riddled the fuselage. Yellow wingmen Alber and Nutter thundered through the wildly maneuvering OSCARs and looked down at the captain's falling target. Alber was certain the stricken sentai pilot fell free, but he saw no chute.

Yellow flight swung about to re-engage, but quickly separated. The lieutenants wound up in the wild chase of a lone Ki-43 desperately trying to outrun his pursuers just above the rolling waves. Alber fired first and then broke away as Nutter closed in to finished the job. The OSCAR plunged into the sea and vanished in a boiling white whirlpool.

The Yellow wingmen sped upward to find Watkins, but the captain flew on alone as if he was demonically possessed. Burning a second victim after a brief chase, the captain dropped down on his third target and fired as the sentai pilot tried to out turn the screaming CHARLCIE JEANNE just above the waves. As the turn tightened, the Oscar began to slide down lower until it's right wing struck a wave. The mottled-green Nakajima cartwheeled into the water and instantly disappeared within a great rolling swell.

## BLUE FLIGHTS PART

Blue Flt Ldr Wally Jordan also took a curving attack path down upon the enemy fighters. From the left and head-on, Jordan hammered an all-silver OSCAR which belched out a brilliant yellow fireball from its cowling and dropped straight into the sea. Wingmen Fanning and Wunder quickly followed suite and each knocked down an OSCAR, then separated as Wunder entered into the mad dash after the fleeing sentai elements down on the deck.

Fanning, however, had only dropped one belly tank before he engaged. As the left engine's temperature rose, he drifted off to join with the high cover flight from the 80th Squadron Headhunters for the return to Horanda.

## RED FLIGHT'S JOHNSONs

Flight Leader Gerry Johnson also led Red Flight's first pass seconds after Yellow and Blue set out, but Gerry's gun switch fuse had burned out while firing on the first target. His able wingman, Stan Johnson, wheeled into firing position and riddled the OSCAR until

*Capt. Larry Smith rolls out in #85 which displays his single kill made while mission leader on August 2nd.*

in began to fall apart. Both Johnson's watched the torn OSCAR drop into the gulf.

## GREEN FLIGHT FROM THE REAR

Meanwhile, mission leader Smith had led wingmen Ralph and Harris into a rear quarter assault upon the quarry. As the Green trio circled down through the scattering enemy planes, Smith singled out a ship which had already been hit by one of the previous attacking flights. From dead astern, Smith gunned down the already smoking Oscar and his Green wingmen watched it fall into the sea. Then, as they raced down after the last of the fleeing sentai, Harris swung off to the east in pursuit of a lone OSCAR which seemed headed for Cape Glouster. After several minutes at full throttle, Harris fired at 500 yards until the Ki-43 rolled over and struck the sea in a huge white spray.

## THE END OF THE FIGHT

Mission leader Smith, Yellow-man Nutter, Blue-man Wunder, and Red-man Stan Johnson set off together in pursuit of the last northbound survivor. Despite numerous firing passes at wave top on the swerving, green-mottled Nakajima, not one man could keep the sentai pilot in his gunsight. The Knights turned back as the OSCAR escaped into the haze beyond Finschhafen.

All of the Knights reached Horanda by 5:00 p.m. and no one had been hit. Only Grover Fanning was forced to land with a feathered left engine due to the overheating supercharger. They celebrated once again in the culmination of claiming twenty-eight kills in three missions without loss to themselves.

In the outcome of the August 2nd dogfight in particular, "double-ace" Watkins' eleventh kill placed him ahead of the 8th Squadron's boss, Ernie Harris, as the 49ers second highest aerial killer. As for the duplication in the accounts of Watkins, Alber, Nutter and Wunder each having chased a victim into the waves, 5 FC considered each report as a separate event and a total of eleven kills were posted after the mission debriefing.

At Wewak, the Imperial command was in total shock. Their OSCAR unit had been ravaged, including the death of their Sentai commander, and the supreme general officer's plane had vanished. It would not be until late that evening that a coded radio message told of Adachi's incredible escape in the SONIA, all the way to Rabaul.

So it was that the great venture to save the Lae forces had come to an end. Not only was the Lae garrison bombed night and day throughout the month of August, beginning on the 17th, Kenney sent his B-24 Liberators in a high altitude strike to Wewak, followed by a devastating strafing attack by his B-25 squadrons. After three days of such raids, more than a hundred aircraft the 4th Air Army lay in ruin on the newly constructed airdrome.

For the remainder of the August, encounters with the JAAF were understandably few. Within the relative calm, the 49ers once again reformed their own command staff and tended to the losses of more young pilots.

## ROOKIE ANDERSON DOWN AT DOBODURA;
## 26 JULY, 1943

While the Flying Knights closed out the aerial engagements for July, the Warhawk squadrons remaining at Kalamazoo Strip soldiered on with their sorties over the Salamaua battle. Once more, the Eightball's lost two more men in the war-weary Curtiss fighters.

No sooner had CO Ernie Harris' party left for Marilinan, a new pilot at Dobodura was lost on his first mission with the 8th Squadron. On July 26th, 2Lt. Norman Anderson was orbiting over the Aussie lines just west of Salamaua when he signalled engine trouble. He bailed out of the old model E and his wingman reported Anderson's landing near Dali village.

The search flight that went back to Dali the following day saw Anderson's chute hanging in a tree. An Aussie infantry patrol hunted in the surrounding area, but not another trace of the lieutenant was ever found. Hardly anyone at Dobodura could even remember young Norm Anderson's face.

Unfortunately, another man was badly injured in the rescue attempt. Rookie F/O Stew Chowing had only flown a short distance from Kalamazoo when his old P-40E had the engine overheat. Chowing swung about and descended to Horanda strip, but in the excitement, he forgot to drop his belly tank. The fuel heavy P-40E slammed down on the strip and the fuel tank ruptured, engulfing Chowing's ship in flames. Chowing miraculously escaped but was badly burned. He was treated at the Dobodura field dispensary and eventually transferred out of the unit for more intensive care in Australia.

For all of these events, little was changed in the course of the battle. The Japanese had gambled and their general had almost been killed. Neither Salamaua nor Lae would be saved. Despite a spirited stand in Markham Valley, many thousands more of the Imperial forces had been sacrificed in a hopeless cause. For the glorious honor of the Emperor, their pilots had tried to reclaim air superiority over Papua and the Huon Gulf, but the sky there now belonged to LtC. James Selman's 49th Fighter Group and the 5th Air Force.

# 13

## TAKING MARKHAM VALLEY

The Papuan tribes had lived in comparative harmony with the Dutch and German merchants and miners for many generations, but with the monsoons in mid 1943, more dangerous strangers had ventured deeper into the New Guinea jungle than ever before. The recent Japanese invaders had been equally as brutal as their worst tribal enemy. Papuan warriors had fought many fierce battles, but they had never seen the likes of the weapons the strangers used to fight in the forest, or on the sea. No elder had ever fought in the air.

The clans in the Markham River Valley now sent word of more strangers building their great camps ever deeper in the forests and the Papuan elders counselled their families to wait patiently. Just as the Japanese had gone from the Pongani valley, these white strangers would surely leave their river valley camps. Even the wisest elder had no way of knowing that the great Allied airdromes would grow even larger. They believed the forest was the only permanent thing, but New Guinea had changed forever.

General MacArthur's great land army was now ready to advance into the central river valleys of the great island, and the 5th AF commander, Gen. George Kenney, had indeed put into motion the air borne mobilization for the Lae invasion. Thousands of troops were camped at Pt. Moresby, Dobodura and Milne Bay, and many more were waiting in northern Australia. When the rains subsided in September, the Americans and Australians would be ready for the greatest land based Allied offensive of the Pacific war.

### A NEW 49ERS TEAM

Though LtC. Selman's Screamin' Demons, Eightballs and Flying Knights continued to keep up the pressure on the Lae airdrome in particular, the August weather held down many of their routine patrols. In the rain soaked interim, combat points were tallied and Selman's veteran crews received the most prized citation of all. More names of the senior 49ers were posted for the voyage to the States. By August 9th, many had reached Brisbane and boarded the USAT Lurline for San Francisco.

### THE LAST OF THE DARWIN FLYING KNIGHTS; AUGUST, 1943

After the big dogfight over Lae on August 2nd, Flying Knight CO Maj. Sid Woods was notified that his extended tour was over. Likewise, the majority of senior flight leaders had well exceeded the

*Capt. Balwin (lt.) and 5 FC pilot Latane flank Flying Knights Flt Ldrs Clay " Mother" Peterson (lt.) and Dick Taylor, two of the 49ers best, during citations in late August. All four captains went home by month's end.*

necessary combat points for release. As of the third week of August, the last of the Darwin cadre pilots would stand down from all flying. By the following month they were homeward bound. Group CO Selman had to quickly rectify the resultant gaps in squadron commands.

Upon review of the remaining officers' records in the 9th Squadron roster, the Alaska campaign veteran Lt. Gerry Johnson was found to be senior by date of commission to all the others. Before Woods left, Gerry Johnson was promoted to captain and the handsome young Oregonian assumed the role of Squadron Deputy boss until

*Broad Markham Valley and the landing fields of 5 BC in November 1943.*

*Lae village and its harbor once again under attack, this time from 10,000' by 90 BG Liberators. Wrecked aircraft cover the famous airdrome to the west which was hit continuously prior to the September 4th invasion. In the lower right corner is the long abandoned Myoko Maru beached after the 7 FS attack on January 7th.*

August 27th. When Johnson formally took command, Capt. Wally Jordan then became deputy and senior Flt Ldr Harry Lidstrom was promoted to captain with the new duties of 9 FS Ops Exec.

Captain Lidstrom's task was certainly no less ominous than his predecessors. The departure of the veterans had left his operations roster tactically bankrupt. Rarely with more than a dozen 9 FS Lightnings in service at one time, the Knights had been able to rotate the mission rosters with different elements, yet always with senior captains to lead. As of August, that was no longer the case. Group CO Selman could only offer the new pilots sent down from Fighter Command, plus a few rebuilt Lockheeds to resolve Ops Exec Lidstrom's dilemma.

## ROTATION OF THE DEMONS

As of the last week in July, Major George "Red" Manning had turned over his 7th Squadron Command to his deputy, Capt. Ray Melikian.

Red Manning left for home in early August to be succeeded by the tall, sensitive captain and the contrast in character could not have been more dramatic. Manning was confrontational at best, while Melikian was much more studious. On July 14th, Melikian had displayed his keen, rational manner while leading the mission sortie and simultaneously coordinating the rescue of Lt. Lee.

Unlike the depleted 9th Squadron, Capt. Melikian still had many senior flight leaders in his organization and the Demons were taking on more new P-40N's each day. Even though Lt. Logan Jarman had bailed out south of Salamaua back on July 27th, the lieutenant had been quickly rescued, and the ship had immediately replaced with a new Warhawk. Melikian's 7 FS was sound.

## MUDDY MARILINAN

Eightball CO Capt. Ernie Harris had inherited an absolute mess for his pilots now flying patrol from muddy Marilinan air strip. Harris'

*Left: 7 FS Lt. Ray Hilliard kept P-40K #37 in combat service well into August when Allied single-engine types adopted the theater-wide white empennage markings. Even the last of the Eightball model-E stagers received white tails and ailerons, but neither E nor K-models advanced beyond Dobodura. Right: Only the new N-model Warhawks advanced north to Marilinan in August like this 8 FS P-40N believed to be s.n. 42-105515, not yet receiving the new theater marking.*

"irregulars" were certain they had been sent to the mired camp on the west bank of the roily Watut River as some strange punishment devised by a "depraved bastard general down in sunny Sydney."

The incessant rain poured down on Marilinan in the first week of August for five straight days. The 8 FS bivouac eventually flooded and Harris moved his men to a new camp closer to the air strip. Ops Exec Barnett was hard pressed to get his patrols up off the muddy runway and his soaked Eightball pilots grew restless.

Lanky Flt Ldr Joe Littleton, a wild hearted Cajon from Louisiana, brooded as his flight was grounded again. After fortification from a bottle of whiskey, the Cajon madman brandished a long butcher knife and challenged all comers in the mess tent. As the aircrews scrambled for cover, burly CO Harris intervened and flattened the wild lieutenant with a thundering right hook to the face. The incident seemed to vent everyone's frustration as Littleton was carried away to sleep off the whiskey.

*(Lt.-rt.) Hagerstrom, Drier, Carter, Flack, Sawyer and Talmadge pose in front of Pierce's new N-model #55 "KAY THE STRAWBERRY BLOND" shortly after arrival at Marilinan.*

*8 FS 2Lt. Dick Vodra challenged his flight members to adopt the checker-board rudder marking on his aircraft #57 as a taunt to a particularly aggressive enemy pilot dubbed "WEWAK WILLIE."*

It was equally difficult for the Eightball ground echelon who struggled to mobilize at Dobodura for their move to the new northern camp. The men packed their gear, but it sat in the steaming humidity as the air transports waited for clear weather. The Eightball camp reeked of mildewed khaki and rotted leather. And their aircrews still had to service the old stager Warhawks for the patrols over Lae.

The Warhawks and Lightnings struggled into the air from their respective muddy air fields, and thankfully, the Japanese suffered the same torment. The forces at Wewak and Rabaul could only send lone raiders or reconnaissance planes down toward Oro Bay, and there was rarely any contact.

On August 11th, a Screamin' Demon patrol was vectored north in search of a suspected Japanese photo plane. One Warhawk flight pursued two unidentified planes, but the targets vanished in the clouds east of Lae. Later that afternoon, the 9th Squadron sped north to the Markham River delta for an interception. From 20,000 feet, the Knights spotted a dozen radial engine ships far below, cruising west of Lae. The Lightnings dropped their tanks and entered into a

400 mph assault on the unsuspecting intruders, only to break off at the last instant when someone called out "JUGs, don't fire. They're JUGs." The Flying Knights roared with laughter as the 348th FG Thunderbolts wildly maneuvered out of the path of their howling P-38s.

Back at Dobodura, Capt. Johnson graciously delivered two bottles of bootleg gin to Major Neel Kearby's disgruntled Thunderbolt pilots. Soon, the squadrons toasted their bogus battle, and wished each other had been the real enemy. How the fighter pilots hated "the god-damn Japs, almost as much as the god-damn rain."

## THE BATTLE OF ZAMBOOGIE THEATER

By the fourth week in August, the 8th Squadron ground echelon had moved out of their Dobodura bivouac. Unfortunately, the Eightballs would miss the arrival of the first U.S.O. tours to come to New Guinea. At the rustic Zamboogie Theater, thousands of troops and aircrews crowded up to the stage to see the first white women any of them had seen in months. Show girls, Hollywood stars and Vaudeville entertainers danced and sang as the troops whistled and cheered themselves hoarse. Beautiful Phyllis Brooks, an actress from the entourage that came with famed film star Gary Cooper, gave one of the more memorable performances.

At the chivalrous invitation of the Flying Knights, Miss Brooks had joined in several toasts to her arrival in New Guinea. After the pre-show libations, she returned to the Zamboogie Theater just the as band struck up her musical number. With her inhibitions totally subdued, she entered into an impromptu striptease that ignited the crowd. As the enthusiastic soldiers surged toward the leggy beauty, two husky M.P.'s swept the bewildered actress from out of the grasp of the gregarious fans and spirited her away in a waiting jeep. So ended the Battle of the Zamboogie. The victory was grand and the heroine was safe.

On August 31st, several units in the New Guinea theater were served a wonderful evening meal of turkey with all the trimmings, including real egg custard and chocolate pudding. The younger troops were eager to ask for seconds, but the wily veterans doubted the sincerity of the Army's generosity. "If its Thanksgiving dinner,

*Long, lean Flt Ldr Moore, Ops Exec Barnett and Lt. McCullough gather at the bold black and white checkered rudder, but quickly concluded Vodra "was nuts," even if "WILLIE" was fictitious. Wiser Eightball pilots chose not to make their P-40s even the least bit remarkable.*

*8 FS Bill Runey took on aircraft #43 seen here with its newly painted white rudder as of mid-September and kept the trusty stager in service for six months.*

its from '42. If it ain't Thanksgiving, you ain't gonna like breakfast." As if the shrewd old campaigners had some premonition of the fates at hand, the following morning brought fair weather over eastern New Guinea and a flurry of missions.

Airfields at Milne Bay, Pt. Moresby and Dobodura swarmed with the largest airborne maneuvers ever assembled in the Southwest Pacific campaign. Gen. George Kenney had devised an immense aerial assault by the 300 aircraft available in support of Gen. MacArthur's infantry units who would invade Markham Valley.

The fighter groups at Dobodura were tasked with escorts to the endless parade of transport that flew to all of the Allied camps. Enemy airdromes and coastal installations throughout the Huon Peninsula region were struck daily by Allied bombers and fighters to deny the Japanese any semblance of where MacArthur's invasion force might land.

*9 FS aircraft #73 "KWITCHERKICKEN" of Lt. Price flown in the September 2nd escort to Cape Glouster. His resultant kill flag is visible off the Sgt. Akin's left shoulder.*

## FLYING KNIGHTS BACK TO CAPE GLOUSTER; SEPTEMBER 2, 1943

On September 2nd, Capt. Gerry Johnson led his first successful aerial engagement as the 9 FS commander. As part of the escort team for the 22 BG Marauders and 43 BG Fortresses sent to strike the enemy installations at Cape Glouster, Johnson's Flying Knights would execute one of the most unique interceptions of the campaign. The dogfight that day would occur between twin engine fighters from both contesting air forces.

Their opponent that day would be the new Kawasaki Ki-45 twin radial-engine fighter, code named NICK, but as yet unknown to the combat flyers in the theater. Only slightly smaller in dimensions than a P-38, the Ki-45 was heavily armed even by Allied standards, carrying a 20 mm cannon in its nose, a forward firing 37 mm cannon in the belly and a rear gunner with a hand-held 7 mm defensive weapon. The JAAF hoped the interceptor would at last be the "bomber killer" that could knock down the high flying B-17s and B-24s. The Flying Knights were about to prove the new weapon was certainly no match for their Lightnings.

## BLUE AND YELLOW LIGHTNINGS

Gerry Johnson's team of fourteen wingmen had taken off from Horanda strip at first light and rendezvoused with the bomber force out over the sea. At 0930 hours, the strike team reached New Britain where the Marauders struck some freighters off the Cape at a lower altitude while the Fortresses bombed the Glouster airdrome from 8000 feet, just above the scattered cloud deck.

Johnson set his Knights in a stacked formation from 7000 through 15,000 feet to cover as wide an area as possible. The Mission Leader's Blue Flight of wingmen Lts. Grover Fanning and Theron Price, circled just over the shoreline at 7000. Directly overhead, Yellow Flight led by Big Pete Alger held top cover.

For several minutes, the Lightnings orbited directly over the Fortresses who warned of scattered flak reaching up to 10,000 feet, but it did not threaten the P-38s. As the raid ended and the B-17s turned back out to sea, the bomber crews reported they were under attack by a twin-engine fighter just north of the target area. Of all the elements in the vicinity, only Blue Leader Johnson and his two

wingmen caught sight of one such intruder which closed in on a separated B-17. Johnson erroneously identified it as a "Dinah" and rolled his Lightning into a heart throbbing dive for the attacking newcomer NICK.

At nearly 400 Mph, Johnson overtook the NICK as it twisted to the right and plunged for the clouds. The P-38's accurate volley shattered the NICK's long canopy and debris tumbled from its riddled hull. Johnson pulled up sharply and lost sight of the target as Lt. Price fell into firing position. Price, also at break-neck speed, snapped a quick burst at the twisting Ki-45 which continued down and away to the right. As Price broke away, wingman Fanning followed suite and the NICK shuddered as the third volley slammed into its riddled hull. Trailing smoke, it drifted slowly down toward the shoreline.

## YELLOW FLIGHT'S PASS

Price wheeled hard about to attack again, only to cross directly behind the second NICK hunting for the American bombers. Immediately overhead, Yellow Flt Ldr Pete Alger and wingman Love drew near and would be the only high cover elements to see the same intruder. Price and Johnson hauled their P-38s through a tight turn for the second Ki-45 and Pappy Price fired first which set the port engine on fire. "Pappy" peeled out of the way as Capt. Johnson snapped off a short accurate burst, then quickly broke off as the Yellow wingmen attacked.

From above and behind, Alger fired, then Love made a run at a high degree of deflection, then Alger fired again. Alger broke away, just as Fanning rushed in from dead astern.

## THE NEXT ACE

From above, Love turned toward the battered NICK for the last time, just as Grover Fanning closed in from below for the kill. Concentrating on their target, yet not seeing each other, Love and Fanning simultaneously butchered the twin-engine interceptor until it fell into the bay not far from the airdrome. Love turned away to regroup with Yellow Flight, but Fanning cut his speed and dropped down to survey the burning wreckage floating in the midst of the great oil slick. That steaming pile of junk was his fifth career kill.

## THE LAST 13TH SENTAI HEAVY FIGHTER

As ace Fanning cruised over the smoldering hulk sinking beneath the waves, yet a third NICK came upon the scene and tried to slip in behind the victorious Knight. Fanning caught sight of the new threat still some distance off and he shoved the throttle forward to easily outpaced the approaching Ki-45.

The NICK pilot foolishly followed the ascending Lockheed for a short distance, only to sicken at the sight of the twin fuselage beast which suddenly stood on its wingtip and wheeled about to bring its four .50 caliber guns and 20mm cannon to bare for the dreaded head-on firing pass. The pitiful fellow turned his new fighter hard about and throttled forward for the Glouster airdrome, but it was futile.

Fanning quickly ran down the hapless enemy flyer to open fire at point blank range. The last of his ammo was expended until only one .50 caliber gun fired, but the damage was done. He pulled up over the shattered Kawasaki interceptor as it slammed down on the end of the runway and exploded in a roiling fireball.

Meanwhile, Price and Johnson had dropped down for the final pursuit over the shoreline. The two Knights overtook their first damaged target, thinking it was a fourth interceptor. Price and Johnson fire at it once again, but the green-mottled cripple slipped into the overcast lying against the inland foothills and vanished. Certain it would crash, Johnson confirmed it destroyed by Price.

After one last survey of the target area, Johnson recalled the Lightnings and they regrouped out over the gulf for a safe return to

*An A-20 at Dobodura with wing-mounted smoke canisters which the Screamin' Demons escorted during one of several sortied to Lae landings on September 4th.*

Horanda strip. Ironically in the mission debriefing, the targets hit by Johnson, Love, and Price, regardless of redundancy, were appraised as three individual kills. Price was also awarded a probable, while Fanning had two kills and his ace ranking confirmed. Despite how many enemy fighters had actually been over the target that day, the 49ers would not see another NICK in the air until the Philippines campaign a full year later.

## THE LAE-NADZAB INVASION; SEPTEMBER 4, 1943

On the morning of September 4th, naval bombardment and 5 AF air strikes pulverized the beach just east of Lae proper. As the main force of Aussie and Yankee troops made their amphibious landing and pushed inland for Malahang air field, the second element of Kenney's brilliantly coordinated air assault was put into play.

Aussie commandos had advanced from their base camp at Marilinan and floated down the Watut River into the western plain of the Markham Valley, then turned due east for MacArthur's principle objective; the big air field at Nadzab village. As the commandos attacked from the west, Kenney's C-47 transports delivered 1700 American paratroopers with precise timing, down on the north bank of the Markham River. The Aussie and Yanks overwhelmed the tiny remnant garrison and Nadzab was secured within hours after the first shots were fired.

Above the one hundred Dakotas and their airborne troops, the 5th Fighter Command set an umbrella of fighters in multiple layers to screen out any possible intervention from the enemy. Johnson's Flying Knights were part of the high cover, while Harris' Eightballs orbited over Markham Valley to the west and Melikian's Screamin' Demons patrolled the east flank. The mission ended with total success for Kenney's air force. As but a few enemy plane sventured into the Markham Valley air space that day.

LtGen. Adachi's escape plan for his Salamaua-Lae garrisons had indeed affected a minimal resistance at the Huon beachhead. The retreat was to proceed through the narrow pass at the northern end of the Finistere Mountains which lay on the east flank of the Markham flood plain. Through that pass was the road to Madang and relative safety. And the oncoming seasonal monsoons would provide some respite from the Allied juggernaut. Despite such logistics, Kenney's 5 AF and the U.S. Navy ravaged Adachi's supply routes throughout the Solomon Seas. MacArthur had Adachi on the run and would never let him rest.

*9 FS ace Lt. Grover Fanning.*

## THE PUSH FOR MADANG

The capture of Markham Valley was especially critical to the expansion of Kenney's air force. The broad kunai plain at Nadzab was many times larger the airdrome at Dobodura. With the creation of new bomber groups, the great valley would allow the 5th Bomber Command bases to stage medium and heavy bomber missions against all of the enemy airfields in western New Guinea. Nadzab would eventually become the 5 AF HQ while satellite air strips for the fighter groups would be built near by. As engineers constructed the Nadzab facility, the fighter groups maintained a constant vigil over the area. This task became a priority for the Warhawks of the 49th Fighter Group.

The loss of Nadzab by the Japanese had totally shifted their posture to defense and counter-attack. The Wewak forces would try to knock out the new Allied complex before the entire Huon Peninsula was overrun. Despite the monsoons of the equatorial summer, engagements would increase once again as the two great powers clashed in the Allied offensives of 1943.

## INTERCEPTION OVER MOROBE; SEPTEMBER 6, 1943

The Imperial 4th Air Army at Wewak quickly rallied a major effort to thwart the Allied advance which split north of Lae. Australian infantry pushed east along the coast in pursuit of the Japanese who escaped for Finschhafen. On the 6th, enemy heavy bombers raided the big supply camp inland from the beachhead at Hopoi village. Two 49er squadrons would intercept the bomber formation, but the mission debriefing that followed was clouded by fouled radio communications, duplicated claims and the loss of a young wingman.

## THE EIGHTBALLS ARE BACK

Capt. Ernie Harris' people had braved the monsoons of July and August to advance to their new airstrip before the Nadzab maneuvers, but their only contact had been when the Japanese bombers raided Marilinan between rain squalls. The Eightball Warhawks had not been in an aerial exchange for three and a half months.

At mid-day on the 6th, the 8 FS patrol from Marilinan had just gotten airborne and passed over Lae at 1330 hours when their controller SHADOW alerted the Blue Flight leader, Lt. Bob White, of a large formation coming in from the east. White, with wingman

*8 FS Flt Ldrs White, Jordan, Moore, Littleton and newly appointed 5 FC instructor Bill Day near the end of their combat tours.*

2Lt. Willie Drier, element leader Lt. Elfred "Fats" Elofson and rookie wingman 2Lt. Bob Sherman continued beyond their patrol area in search of the contact. As the four Eightballs passed over the beachhead at 20,000 feet, they found they were the only patrol in the vicinity. White requested that SHADOW vector another unit for the search.

## FLYING KNIGHTS GO NORTH

Meanwhile down south at Horanda strip, Flt Ldr Lt. Ralph Wire had just taken off in the lead of fourteen Flying Knights for their patrol when the southern area controller CHARTER relayed the northern vector. Wire led his men north as the four flights spread apart for the hunt. On the left flank was Capt. Dick Bong's Blue foursome and Mission leader Wire's Red foursome was on the right. Overhead in trailing high cover was Yellow Flt Ldr Lt. "Pappy" Price with a pair of wingmen at 16,000 and to their right was Lt. Walter Markey's Green quartet.

## OVER HOPOI VILLAGE

Over the beachhead at Hopoi village, the Eightballs searched through the billowing clouds, but found nothing. After the hunt continued for forty-five minutes, the trailing rookie wingman glanced out to sea. Down below at 15,000 feet, Bob Sherman saw the enemy for the first time. The young lieutenant hurriedly tried to count all of the enemy planes in the two chevron formations, but they were partially obscured by the clouds. Although there were two Vee chevrons of nine BETTY bombers each, Sherman excitedly reported twice as many. He barely made out a similar number of fighter escorts, but the exact count was pointless. Blue Flight was grossly out numbered and Flt Ldr White repeated the back-up request to SHADOW.

Suddenly, a signal was received over the Allied channel from the enemy. Some Japanese crewman identified his formation as friendly. CHARTER control asked White to confirm the contact, but the Blue quartet had no doubts. The Eightballs sped out to sea in a climbing turn to the right behind the enemy bombers. White, Drier, Elfson and Sherman were going to attack.

Thirty miles off shore, Blue Flight passed through the bright glare of the sun and looked down on the left flank of the BETTY formation heading toward Hopoi. Partially hidden by broken clouds and undetected by the escorts, Flt Ldr White pulled as far ahead as he dared, then rolled his #42 KANSAS CITY KIDDIE the 3rd into a righthand turn for the trailing enemy chevron. All three wingmen followed. The Eightballs thundered down head-on from the left quarter where Flt Ldr White opened fire on the second element aircraft in the second Vee. The BETTY shuddered as White broke down and away to the right. He looked over his shoulder at the falling Mitsubishi.

Wingman Elofson fired at the bombers from head-on, too, but his aim was poor. He dropped and then swept back for a second shot, but the escorts suddenly pulled in behind him. Elofson left the fight. Drier also fired from head-on, and like Elofson, he tried a second run, but escorts cut him off. Willie Drier separated to the left and eluded the escorts in the clouds.

*8 FS ace Bob White wheels out in his last aircraft #42 P-40N "KANSAS CITY KIDDIE III" at Marilinan.*

Tail-end Bob Sherman dropped down on the chevron, but the lieutenant slipped past Elofson and came down on the lead BETTY of the second Vee. From overhead and behind, Sherman fired from out of range and broke off to his right to re-engage. He quickly formed up with Flt Ldr White and the pair sped off for another pass as the enemy paraded over the beachhead toward Malahang air field north of Lae. The enemy dropped their ordinance and turned back out to sea, just as White and Sherman hit them in a climbing head-on attack.

White lined up KANSAS CITY KIDDIE on the greenhouse nose of the approaching bomber and poured in a murderous stream

*8 FS Lt. Willie Drier about the time of his close call with the Flying Knights off Lae on September 6th.*

of tracers which flashed in the enemy cockpit. Sherman pressed in on the same ship through point blank range and raked the rotund fuselage along its full length. The lieutenant's explosive rounds nearly severed the tail section from the brown and green giant which fell seaward trailing heavy smoke and strewing debris into the water.

As White sped beneath the bombers and pulled up, his ascent took the KIDDIE right into the trailing flight of TONY escorts. He wheeled into a turning deflection against a heavily mottled TONY and his converging .50 caliber tracers sawed off the Kawasaki's left wing. The tumbling fighter slammed down into the jungle just north of Malahang as White broke down and away.

White and Sherman rejoined and departed for Marilinan, but separated Willie Drier in his #60 LITTLE MAGGIE, decided to track the escaping enemy and report their position beyond the shore until the next Allied fighter unit arrived. Alone in the glare of the sun on the enemy's right flank, his scheme seemed to be pretty sound until he looked up into the sun for enemy escorts, and instead, saw Ralph Wire's blood thirsty Flying Knights. Instantly, Drier knew he was in the wrong place at the wrong time.

**FIFTEEN FLYING KNIGHTS**

From some distance to the south, Mission Leader Lt. Wire had seen the BETTYs turn back toward New Britain. At the signal, all fifteen Flying Knights jettisoned their belly tanks and throttled forward.

As Wire was in the lead, he and Red element leader Lt. Wilbert Arthur targeted what they thought was a lone TONY in escort over the right flank of the BETTYs. It was actually Willie Drier in LITTLE MAGGIE. Drier stood MAGGIE on her wingtip to display her star insignia and called out over the radio to the descending Lightnings, but the 9 FS was still on the CHARTER frequency. Wire and Arthur's tracers whizzed over MAGGIE and the Eightball pilot called it quits. He took MAGGIE down for the Salamaua beach in a full throttle dive.

Nine of the Knights thundered past the in-line fighter streaking toward the sea and slammed into the right flank of the BETTYs over the shoreline. After two passes against the bomber echelons

*Drier's #60 "LITTLE MAGGIE" which nearly became another Flying Knights victim.*

*9 FS Sgts. Akin (lt.) and Lynd clown beside Lt. Bong's scoreboard on aircraft #79 in the first week of September.*

which held their ranks, both Wire and Arthur claimed heavy damage to one of the lead ships which dropped toward the sea. Yellow Flt Ldr Price claimed another and Blue Flt Ldr Bong also claimed fatal hits on two others before the Lightning were overwhelmed by the OSCAR escorts. There on the Lae shoreline, a sprawling dogfight broke out.

## NOT A GOOD EXCHANGE

Although one bomber had been lost in the interception over the target, the OSCARs held fast in their formation and were ready when Wire's Lightnings struck. In the clash, Wire claimed two "Zeros" and Arthur claimed hits on a third, but the sentai pilots held their ground. At the same altitude as their opponents, they out maneuvered the Knights until all the P-38 were forced to dive away. Several P-38s had been threatened, but none were hit as hard as Blue Flight.

Blue Flt Ldr Bong and his wingman had turned for the attack on the left flank of the BETTYs while his second element wingmen momentarily engaged the OSCARs. With near blind obsession, Bong pressed his #79 in on the enemy lead ship for the third time, only to suddenly realized his right engine had been hit. The captain dropped away to his left and slipped down through the clouds to check the severity of the damage. Bong shut the right engine down and feathered the prop for the long flight home, but the weather to the south had begun to close in. After his emergency signal, only Marilinan was ready to receive the crippled P-38. The ace gently took #79 down into the Watut River Valley.

## DOWN IN WATUT VALLEY

Marilinan was clear and dry despite the low hanging clouds over the surrounding hills. Lt. Bob White, the newest ace in New Guinea, had returned there with all of his wingmen, but the Eightballs crews could not celebrate White's victory just yet. Everyone was on the lookout for the damaged Lightning which was due in at any moment.

Minutes later, the awaited P-38 was seen at the landing field's northern perimeter in it's straight-on approach. In a routine single-engine landing, Dick Bong settled on to the narrow red strip only to have his left engine seize as the landing gear touched down. Without power and the hydraulics gone, #79 slid side ways momentarily and then righted itself in a fast roll-out for the drainage ditch on the left side of the runway. Bong slumped down in the seat for protection just as his stricken P-38 slowed to a crawl at the brink of the gully. The nose wheel sank in the soft dirt at the runway's edge and the left gear quickly followed. The red loam gave way as the big fighter gently slumped over and stuck its left wingtip in the mud. With his right wing and tail pointing into the sky, there sat the leading ace of the Fifth Air Force.

As the rain began to fall on Watut Valley, 8 FS CO Ernie Harris dispatched a message to Dobodura that Bong was safe. But the celebrity ace had been hit again in combat, and this time, he was noticeably shaken. The weather socked Marilinan in and muddied the Eightball air field for two days before the errant Knight could catch a transport for Horanda.

*Aircraft #79 slumped off the end of the Marilinan fighter strip after Bong had his right engine shot out by the BETTY gunners over Lae on September 6th.*

*9 FS warhorse #91 (formerly #82) pranged for the last time at Dobodura in the September campaign.*

## WHERE IS 2LT. JIM FAGAN?

Once he reached his 9 FS quarters, Bong learned that his two bomber kill claims in the fight of September 6th could not be confirmed. But the most telling blow to the young captain came with the news of his rookie wingman who had not yet been accounted for. Apparently 2Lt. Jim Fagan had been shot down over the gulf.

After consulting with CO Johnson and Ops Exec Jordan, Bong asked to fly his future missions as an unattached pilot. He felt great responsibility for Fagan's loss, and said he could not bear to loose another wingman. The idea was disregarded by the senior officers, but war-weary Bong was given two weeks of furlough. The war had begun to take its toll of the youngster from Wisconsin.

## DEMON HARBOR OVER THE BAY; 7 SEPTEMBER, 1943

While Dick Bong languished at muddy Marilinan with his 8th Squadron hosts, the Japanese raided the Hopoi beachhead again on the 7th. Despite the rain squalls, the Screamin' Demons were able to get seventeen planes over the Huon Peninsula and execute their first interception since mid-July. Unfortunately, it would only be a singular feat by errant Lt. David Harbor.

After a late takeoff form Kalamazoo due to oxygen equipment trouble, Lt. Harbor set out on patrol at a lower altitude than normal and pressed into the Lae area through the heavy weather. SHADOW control vectored several interceptions to Harbor's vicinity, but he failed to contact any of them. Eventually reaching the end of his fuel, he turned back for base, only to spot a pair of weather-worn radial engine fighters passing below through a break in the overcast.

Harbor swung down in a firing pass on the trailing OSCAR whose dirty grey camouflage had peeled away to the bare metal on its upper wing surfaces. The sentai pilot tried to evade the P-40 in a turn to the left, but Harbor laid in a perfect rear quarter deflection. The lieutenant watched a Ki-43 slam down on the beach and turned back to re-engage the wingman, but the OSCAR leader escaped to the north beyond Lae. That was the only 49er contact of the day.

Missions continued for a week, but neither Warhawk nor Lightning from LtC. Selman's 49ers could find a victim. The hunt stretched from Finschhafen to Lae, yet the Japanese avoided all of the 49er patrols. There was brief revery as news came of the Italian

surrender in the Mediterranean theater on September 9th, but it quickly became old news. Six days later, U.S. troops invaded Markus island only a thousand miles from the Japanese mainland. Everyone hoped the Axis "Nips" would surrender as the "I-ties" had done. But the Oriental rascals raided Nadzab the next day.

## NADZAB DEFENSE; SEPTEMBER 13, 1943

At mid-day on the 13th, Eightball ace Lt. Bob Howard led the standing patrol from Marilinan. After orbiting the coast at 18,000 feet directly over Lae, Howard's fourteen Warhawks were warned at 11:00 a.m. of enemy bombers approaching the area. As Howard turned the patrol for the hunt to the east, the Eightballs immediately caught sight of the raiders just overhead through the broken cumulus clouds. Twelve BETTYs were counted at 21,000 feet with twice that many "Zero" escorts in a higher trailing formation.

Howard signaled his flights to drop their tanks and turn to an ascending parallel course for the interception, but the P-40s were barely able to keep pace with the Mitsubishi formation which pushed deeper into Markham Valley. After several minutes of frustrating pursuit through the clouds, only Howard's Blue Flight foursome and Lt. Bernie Makowski's Yellow Flight trio could maintain visual contact. The seven Eightballs crept up to 500 feet above the enemy bombers' left flank, but the P-40s were too strung out and too low on fuel to mount a sustained attack. Unwilling to gamble on regrouping while in range of the escorts in higher position, Howard signaled his men to attack individually.

Howard banked slowly to the right, hoping to slide in undetected against the bombers' rear quarter, but the wily veterans of the 24th Sentai had watched the P-40s from the onset. As the Warhawks turned for the BETTYs, the OSCARs pounced upon them. The P-40 pilots fired at the looming targets, but the Ki-43s prevented them from causing any serious damage. Outnumbered and out of position, all of the Eightballs peeled off for home.

## TAIL-END-THORVALDSON'S VOYAGE

The seventh man at the end of the strung-out Eightball flight bore the brunt of the escort intervention. Tail-end Lt. Joel Thorvaldson had just chosen his very first airborne bomber target, only to be cut off by the OSCARs. His "split-S" turn ended beneath the enemy at 10,000 feet where he pulled out to re-engage, only to have the automatic prop control fail. As one of the pursuing OSCARs threatened again, Thorvaldson knew his survival chances in a broken fighter called for desperate tactics. At 300 Mph, the lieutenant stomped down with full left rudder and pushed the stick hard to the left. The engine torque whipped the howling P-40 completely around as the rugged Curtiss fighter shuddered on the brink of a high speed stall. As the OSCAR flashed by, Thorvaldson kicked the rudder to the right and slammed the throttle to the fire wall. He fell in deadastern of the would-be attacker and they twisted downward, still at 300 indicated. Thorvaldson finally hit the swerving dark green Nakajima and smoke poured from its round cowling, but the victim's wingman drew within range. The lone Eightball rolled away and plunged for the clouds within a hail of tracers.

As the streaking P-40 broke out into the clear air above the Markham River valley, the combined damage of enemy rounds and windmilling prop set the nose ablaze. Thorvaldson leveled off in preparation to bail out, but the fire ceased just as quickly as it had begun. The magnificent Warhawk would allow Thorvaldson one last chance.

Knowing he would never reach Marilinan, the pilot chose to belly land on the open river bed and raise the odds of being rescued. He glided the crippled ship down along the great river until he spotted the broad sand beach at the junction of the Markham and the Waffir River tributary. With cool expertise, Thorvaldson fired off the last of his ammo, lowered the flaps and settled down into a gentle slide which ended on the grey sands of the north bank. He turned off the switches, radioed his position over the emergency channel, then stepped out of the trusty Warhawk which had saved his life. Now it was up to CHARTER control at Nadzab, 50 miles to the east. But as night fell, no rescue flight came.

The next day, Thorvaldson waited until noon, but the only planes he saw were far out of range and could not be identified. With a sound combination of Scandinavian and Yankee reasoning, the stranded pilot chose the course any good Viking would take. He took the life raft from his parachute pack, gathered his essential gear and set off down the river for Nadzab. Two days later on the 16th, brave Eightball Viking Joel Thorvaldson drifted into Kaiapit village just west of Nadzab. After a night's rest at the 5 AF HQ, Thorvaldson was shuttled off to Marilinan for the homecoming celebration.

## ANOTHER EIGHTBALL ADVENTURE IN THE WILDS; SEPTEMBER 21, 1943

No sooner than the Eightballs had Thorvaldson back, they would loose another man four days later. After the fight on the 21st, Lt. Roger "Bitsy" Grant would survive one of the most legendary jungle treks ever experienced by a 49er.

Eightball CO Ernie Harris took fifteen wingmen up for the last patrol of the day at 1630 hours. They had cruised over the shoreline for an hour when CHARTER signaled the approach of another enemy raid. At 18,000 feet just east of Lae, Harris' Red Flight tried to catch a speeding DINAH, but they could not overtake the twin-engine ship. As Harris ordered the hunt to resume back toward the east, a trio of OSCARs passed below his flight.

## NEW DOUBLE-ACE

The captain wheeled down after the lead Ki-43 which peeled off for the deep shadows of the nearby clouds, but Harris' new N-model CAROLINA BELLE quickly overtook its prey. The BELLE's explosive rounds burst on the OSCAR's canopy and mid-fuselage. By wingman Polhamus' confirmation of that kill, Ernie Harris became the first "double ace" Warhawk pilot in the Pacific war.

Red element leader Lt. Dan David and his wingman 2Lt. Hal Sawyer also engaged the enemy fighters and both men fired at a silver ship that sudden appeared beneath them. After a rambling dogfight that took them up over the rolling hills of the Cromwell Mountains, both David and Sawyer claimed an enemy fighter de-

*8 FS Joel Thorvalson and his "Viking raft" which carried him through the crocodile country of the upper Markham River. He kept his flare pistol, medicine bag, canteen of fresh water and the mosquito netting, but opted for bare feet so as not gouge a hole in his rubber boat.*

stroyed. The Red Flight pair then pulled back to 11,000 only to find a chevron of nine BETTYs directly ahead. By that time, Harris had also pulled to within range of the Mitsubishi bombers and the Red Flight team made their first attack on them before the escorts could re-engage.

Red element leader David, in his #49 KATHLEEN, turned from his firing pass on the BETTYs, only to have a radial engine fighter pull in behind him. David dove for safety through a split-S and dropped right into the main force of OSCARs which immediately swirled about him. He put KATHLEEN into another turning dive, but three sentai wingmen quickly fell into pursuit of the white-tailed Warhawk that plunged for the valley below.

In full throttle at tree top level, David slid left and right as brilliant red tracers whizzed past his ship. Now down deep in the long shadows of the valley, David knew he had few options left. As one the sentai men closed into gun range, the lieutenant caught site of a narrow pass on the mountain ridge. At 300 Mph, KATHLEEN sliced through the narrow gap with the OSCAR right behind, but the sentai man could not match the maneuver. His Ki-43 was snatched from the sky as its right wing tip snagged one of the gum trees. David looked over his shoulder as the other sentai wingmen

*8 FS Dan David relaxes during a maintenance session at Marilinan.*

broke off above the tumbling, flaming wreckage that seconds before had been their flight leader.

## WHITE FLIGHT CHASES THE BETTYS

Lt. Roger "Bitsy" Grant's White quartet had flown a similar engagement. After a headon pass against the OSCARs, Grant's people set after the bombers that had turned inland for the escape toward Madang. Flight Ldr Grant, with one OSCAR kill to his credit, was joined by his fourth element wingman, 2Lt. John Hanson, as White Flight had become separated in the clouds after the fight with the escorts. The two men could barely make out the dark silhouettes of the twin engine ships to the north, but Grant was determined to put the last of his ammo and fuel to good use.

Likewise, Blue Flt Ldr Lt. Bob Howard avoided the OSCARs and closed in on the fleeing bombers. With the setting sun at his back, the Blue Flt Ldr ace flew into point blank range and expended all of his .50 caliber rounds into three bombers on the left flank of the bomber formation. Soon, the left element wingmen fell out of position with a burning left engine. Howard would claim that victim as the sixth and final kill of his tour.

Finally, White Flight's Grant and Hanson caught the raiders as they neared the crests of the Cromwell Mountain Range. In near

*Radiator tub cowling of David's aircraft #49 "KATHLEEN II" that outran the OSCARs at treetop over Huon Peninsula on October 15th.*

darkness, Grant could barely make out the twin engine planes against the dark jungle slopes, let alone identify their type. Guessing they were "Lilys" which lacked rear defensive armament, Grant pressed in on one of the dark silhouettes, only to be struck by the 20 mm cannons of the BETTY tail gunners. Grant returned fire, but his windscreen clouded over with glycol coolant which streamed from his damaged Allison power plant. Hanson also closed in for two firing passes at the bombers who dropped from sight for the north coast. Confident both targets were destroyed, the rookie pulled up into the last rays of twilight at 12,000 feet, but he had completely separated from his flight leader. Hanson drifted down for the Markham River and was the last to land at Marilinan. Everyone was home accept Bitsy Grant.

## SURVIVAL ON THE BUHEM RIVER

Roger Grant awoke in the pale evening twilight beneath the great forest canopy which covered the southern slope of the Cromwell Mountains. There was a moment of complete confusion as he peered down at the dark jungle floor forty feet below, and then up at his parachute straps which held him motionless in the forest branches. Suspended in the evening mist, dazed Grant could barely recall how he came to this lofty perch. There had been a dogfight. And tracers coursing through the night sky. There was the spine-numbing jolt of his chute snapping open. After a brief survey of the forest from his high perch, Grant mused at being "as far from Los Angeles as a guy can get."

After his senses aroused, he realized he must get to the ground and recover as much of his gear before total darkness set in. He rocked in his chute straps until he could catch hold of the tree trunk, then cut his liferaft and survival pack free and dropped them to the jungle floor. Once down from the branches, Grant inflated the rubber raft and cut a large cover from the chute. Totally exhausted, he fell asleep in his makeshift shelter for the duration of the night.

In the morning, the stranded flyer tried to get his bearings. He fought through the forest for three hours to reach a small clearing only one hundred yards from the point of his descent. Through the opening in the dense forest ceiling, Grant could see the Buhem River which coursed due south for the gulf and Hopoi village, but he had no way of knowing which river he was on, or if any one knew of his location. Lugging the inflated raft, he pressed on through the dense undergrowth hoping to find a foot path, but by late afternoon he was worn out by the burden. He reached a small stream and collapsed in the cool water.

After several minutes, the lieutenant washed his face and wondered of his fate. As his mind swirled with many memories of his home in California, a voice called inside his head to seek help at the top of the mountain. Pages of the Bible appeared to him beneath the surface of the stream and Grant took the mysterious sights and sounds to be his salvation.

## A SPIRIT GUIDE

All that next day, the delirious pilot struggled through the jungle until he crossed over a path near the summit of the hill. He followed the trail in one direction, then pointlessly turned the other way. Bitsy happened upon a great wash-out which plunged two thousand feet to the river. Certain he had found the way home, Grant descended into the gorge, only to be accosted by the apparition of Lt. Harry McCullough, one of the men from his flight.

The apparition asked, "Where are you going?"

"Well, Mac, I'm going down to the river and float home", answered the bewildered Grant. Ghostly McCullough, attired in his dress uniform, advised the distraught flyer not to leave the higher path. The river was dangerous.

Grant cautiously continued down to the water, but found the river was too shallow and rocky for his raft. And to his amazement, far down stream he could make out a Japanese patrol searching the river bank. With his raft draped over his back, the stranded flyer climbed back up the gorge. Mid way up the wash-out, the exhausted pilot collapsed as rain began to fall. On a narrow shelf, he crawled beneath his raft and built a small fire. When darkness fell, McCullough reappeared wearing his flight suit and appeared to be badly wounded. Grant and McCullough talked long into the night, but the lost pilot awoke the next morning to find his ghostly friend had vanished. Grant crawled out of the gorge and set off down the trail. He abandoned his raft in the underbrush and never ventured near the river again.

After several days of eating nuts and drinking rain water, the starved lieutenant wandered into the perimeter of a native village just as the silent darkness fell upon the jungle. Grant waited for several minutes, uncertain if he should call out. Suddenly, the inner voice said, "Go on." At the position of attention on wobbling legs, he marched passed the huts, but no one, not even a village dog, heard him go by. Late that night, he reached a small, tumbling river and had to cross over the swaying foot bridge by the light of the full moon. Neither village on either bank saw the lone American.

Fifteen days passed until Roger Grant walked out of the forest and into the coastal prairie north of Hopoi village. He found a friendly tribal village whose elder told him they had seen him come down in his chute after the big fight, but none of the friendly scouts had been able to find him. The elder seemed greatly amused that Grant had actually walked through the villages of the fierce mountain people who relished the flesh of the "long pig." Grant also told the elder of his meeting with McCullough, the spirit man. The old man only nodded as if he understood.

For more than two weeks, Roger Grant had avoided enemy patrols and forest cannibals. He returned to combat at Marilinan, and even survived the war. But Harry McCullough had transferred to another unit. Bitsy never saw Mac, in the flesh or in his dreams, ever again.

## FINSCHHAFEN INVASION; SEPTEMBER 22, 1943

The day after the September 21st dogfight, General MacArthur sent the Australian 22nd Battalion on a flanking amphibious landing at Finschhafen to cut off the enemy's coastal escape route to Madang. As with the Lae landings, Gen. Kenney placed a great umbrella of 5 AF fighters above the navy assault fleet that drew down on the narrow coastal plain of eastern Huon Peninsula. As the Aussie troops rushed ashore south of the village, six Rabaul-based BETTY bombers with ZERO and OSCAR escorts attempted to strike the Allied fleet at mid-day. Before the enemy force could reach the beach-

*Astray Eightball pilot Roger "Bitsy" Grant celebrating his return to Marilinan with a cigar and champagne.*

head, they fell victim to one of the most brutal interceptions of the campaign. Lightnings from the 432 FS and Warhawks from the 35 FS slaughtered the BETTYs and ZEROs, wiping out an entire bomber chutai. The Satin's Angels were accredited with fifteen aircraft destroyed, surpassing the old Eightball record of thirteen scored back on May 14th.

The 9 FS Flying Knights could only pick off three of the stragglers as the engagement subsided. At 1130 hours in their mid-day patrol, Mission Leader Capt. Ralph Wire and eight Flying Knights overtook a flight of eight OSCARs which were spotted at 6000 feet over the Finschhafen beachhead. Wire and his wingmen plunged down through the swirling rain clouds and ripped the enemy formation apart. As the Ki-43s scattered, Capt. Wire heavily damaged one of the green-mottled planes which fell into the overcast, while Lt. Francis Love damaged yet another. Newly promoted Capt. Pete

*Able 9 FS Flt Ldr Ralph Wire had hit several targets other than his three confirmed kills, but the two probables over Finschhafen on September 22nd were his last victims in New Guinea. The captain would muster out of the 49ers in December and find his last two victims far off in the China theater with the 14 AF.*

*Left: 9 FS M/Sgt. Woodfin (rt.) and two unidentified armorers surround tee-shirted Big Pete Alger after the captain scored his fourth and last victory on September 22nd over Finschhafen. The popular flight leader would fly in the Rabaul operations and then mustered out for home in December. Right: 9 FS Lt. Jimmie Harris scored his second career victory over Finschhafen on September 22nd.*

Alger and wingman Lt. Jimmie Harris each shot down a fighter just off shore before the remaining sentai wingmen escaped beneath the squall line which eventually closed in over the battle site. All of the separated Knights managed to return to Horanda.

With the Australians firmly entrenched on the east coast at Finschhafen, 5 AF CO Kenney stepped up the pressure against the battered JAAF at Wewak and western New Britain. As the 5 FC Lightning wing rotated its squadrons in the sweeps to either stronghold, the Flying Knights continued to miss the greater engagements with the enemy. For five days, the Satins' Angels under their new commander, Major Charles MacDonald, and the old friendly rivals of the 80 FS Headhunters held all the luck in the quest to find the Japanese air force.

### BLEECKER OVER BORAM STRIP; 27 SEPTEMBER, 1943

On the mission of the 27th, Ops Exec Wally Jordan personally requested the chance to lead the morning escort over Wewak's southern most airstrip at Boram village, but the great enemy fighter force was absent once again. Capt. Jordan stacked his Lightnings from 10,000 through 5000 feet to completely cover Boram's air space, but the Knights caught only one plane during their two hours of orbit over the enemy airfield.

At 1100 hours, a lone TONY approached Boram from the west. Red Flt Ldr Dick Bong, just back from leave and hungry for action, was first to spot the dark brown Ki-61 below which cruised at a thousand feet above the forested slopes. Bong peeled away from 5000 with his three wingmen close behind, but the veteran sentai pilot had already seen the threat. The enemy pilot throttled forward and looped upward into the four diving Lockheeds. As the Ki-61

streaked over them, all four Red wingmen fired and missed. The maneuver might have saved the brave sentai man had he not been so grossly outnumbered.

The TONY slowed down in the top of its' loop and passed directly into the firing line of Blue Flt Ldr Lt. Bill Bleecker. The sentai man wheeled hard to the right, but Bleecker chopped his throttle and pulled into point blank range from dead-astern. The Lightning's guns tore pieces from the TONY until it burst into flame and the pilot bailed out. Bleecker and the Knights regrouped above the parachute which drifted down into the sea. That was the only contact for the day and the last September victory for all of the 49ers.

### BONG BACK OFF GASMATA; OCTOBER 2, 1943

The aerial fighting continued to be very sporadic for LtC. Selman's fighter pilots. Even ace Dick Bong had to settle for another singular encounter on October 2nd. The Knights flew escort to a strike on the new airdrome at Gasmata village on the south shore of New Britain, but no enemy fighters intervened. As the escorts withdrew, a lone DINAH Ki-46 passed below the Americans and its crew appeared oblivious to the lone P-38 which dropped down into a dead-astern pursuit. Dick Bong's #79 poured in four deadly bursts and the twin-engine spy plane rolled straight into the sea.

### HAGERSTROM'S CENTURY MARK VICTORY; OCTOBER 5, 1943

Three days after Bong shot down his DINAH off Gasmata, Eightball

*Dick Bong literally "back in the swing" in a Dobodura September baseball game after a two week furlough in Australia ordered by 5 FC CO Wurtsmith.*

Warhawk pilot Bob Hagerstrom shot down another Ki-46 north of Finschhafen. Of the eight Warhawks on late-day patrol, only Hagerstrom could keep the speedster in sight as it tried to escape to the north.

All of the Eightballs dropped their tanks and tried to catch the DINAH in a climbing pursuit, but heavy clouds and the fading twilight made contact difficult. For a full twelve minutes, Flt Ldr Hagerstrom held his throttle in "emergency war power" and followed the Ki-46 up the coast, nearly reaching Madang. Finally up to within 250 yards, Hag let loose with a barrage from dead astern which blew up the Mitsubishi's left engine. An oil cloud enveloped the Warhawk which permeated the cockpit and caused a burning sensation in Hagerstrom's eyes. The DINAH fell away toward the dead engine with the enraged Yankee right behind and firing all the way. The fuselage ignited and Hag fired several more bursts to run off a gun camera record of the 100th aerial victory for the Eightballs. The recon ship struck the water and disintegrated in a fiery explosion that could be seen for miles at sea.

## WANDREY'S BRIEF MISADVENTURE; OCTOBER 8, 1943

The Flying Knights were forced to write off two P-38s in the same week. On the 2nd, 2Lt. Gil Millif bellied in his ship on Horanda's emergency strip due to total hydraulic failure, and six days later, Lt. Ralph Wandrey washed out his ship on a test hop. Neither man was injured, but Wandrey gave everyone at Dobodura a bit of a shock when they saw his plane fall out of the air. After nearly an hour of searching the crash site, the Knights' linecrew failed to find a body because lanky Ralph Wandrey had mysteriously vanished.

Wandrey had been cleared to check out over-hauled #74 in the late afternoon, so he rolled out on to the runway, pushed the throttle forward and settled back for a routine liftoff. As his big Lockheed began to rise, the pilot kept a wary eye on the B-26 Marauder waiting at the east end of the runway for the P-38 to pass. Mid-way down Horanda strip and only twenty feet off the ground, both Allison engines seized up without warning. Ralph Wandrey's #74 had become a nine ton sled full of aviation gas.

The fuel-heavy fighter sank back to the strip, slammed down on its landing gear at 120 Mph and headed straight for the parked Marauder. Wandrey cranked the steering wheel to the right and his left wingtip just missed the glass nose of the B-26. Out of control, old #74 departed the runway and bolted over the drainage ditch which sheared off its landing gear, then caromed off the culvert that ran beneath the service run and vaulted back into the air. The broken P-38 sailed two hundred yards out into the savannah field beyond the dispersal area. The ground controllers sounded the fire alarm as men and vehicles scrambled off for the big dust cloud that rose up beyond the trees at the east end of the drome.

Miraculously, wiry Ralph Wandrey was unhurt and was fully aware of his predicament. Old #74 was already permeated with gas fumes, so he immediately shut off his switches, released his flight gear and threw open the canopy. He jumped off the wing and ran for the safety of the open field, just as the fumes ignited in a huge fire ball. Wandrey stood helplessly and watched his favorite ship go up in flames. He began to brood over the thought of the written reports and explanations to his fellow pilots. The whole incident was down right embarrassing.

Angry with the loss of the P-38 and even more agitated with the scrambled rescue effort, Wandrey set off on foot for home. He trudged through the kunai stubble and sneered with contempt at the fire trucks and jeeps full of crews who sped down the runway toward the roiling pillar of black smoke. Several minutes later, Wandrey walked through the trees and back to the service road to hail a ride from a jeep returning from the crash site. The driver asked him if he had seen the crash. "Hell, yes, I seen it. I was in it", snapped the frustrated pilot.

The driver offered to take Wandrey to the operations tent but the flyer was reticent. "I need a drink. Take me home, corporal", he grumbled and the soldier drove him back to the Flying Knights camp. Wandrey said thanks and stepped into the 9 FS officers club to gaze in amazement upon his squadron mates. Sure that their comrade was dead, the Flying Knights did what any band of pilots would

*Results of Wandrey's test flight in aircraft #74.*

have done. They were all gregariously drinking to Wandrey's memory and had already begun to distribute his estate.

There was his tent mate Dick Bong who was wearing his leather jacket and his good friend Paul Yeager who had acquisitioned his fleece-lined Aussie flight boots. A celebration broke out and soon the mood turned to good-natured banter. One of the men confessed, "We really missed you Ralph, and we didn't want anyone else to get your gear. By the way, Wandrey, where'd you hide your booze?"

From that day forward, each Flying Knight made a map of his liquor stash location and filed the map with boss Gerry Johnson. If a man went down, his booze would be consumed in his honor. It would only be proper fighter pilot etiquette.

## ROUTINE MISSIONS AND NEW HEROES

The 49ers continued to patrol the Huon Peninsula coast line and sea route over the gulf, but they failed to intercept any other reconnaissance flights after Hagerstrom's kill on the October 5th. A small raiding force completely escaped detection on the 10th and bombed Dobodura, but damage was slight. No claims were made by any of the standing patrols.

On the next day, newly promoted Col. Neel Kearby made headline news when he led his 348th FG Thunderbolts on a sweep of Wewak. Kearby personally destroyed seven of the eight JAAF fighters knocked down in a big dogfight over the enemy airdrome. The "ace-in-a-day" feat was precisely the example of leadership that General Kenney expected of his group commanders. At a ceremony some days later, Neel Kearby would become the first 5th Fighter Command pilot to be awarded the Congressional Medal of Honor.

## THE FIRST TRAGIC ATTEMPT AGAINST RABAUL; OCTOBER 12, 1943 HAYS, PRICE AND WUNDER LOST

On the evening of the 11th, Squadron Leader Gerry Johnson called all available Flying Knights pilots to attend the pre-mission brief-

ing. The captain told his crews and pilots that the morning escort would be for strike cover on the enemy headquarters at Rabaul. Hardly a soul could sleep that night with the thought of the great battle that was sure to follow. But Gerry Johnson's people would receive their single greatest defeat within a dark tempest over the ominous Pacific and not by the hand of the Japanese.

Sixteen P-38s were declared ready on the Knights flight line by line chief M/Sgt. Fred Beech and Ops Exec Lidstrom drew up the mission pilots from the senior most men. The Knights staged to Kiriwina Island in the pre-dawn hours and topped off their tanks, then rose up to rendezvous in mid-morning with the Lightning wing to take up their station over the B-24 Liberators which paraded due north for New Britain. Half way across the Solomon Sea however, the weather had already begun to deteriorate.

By the time the bombers reached their objective, only a small band of 432nd and 80th Squadron Lightnings had been able to hold their position and engage the Rabaul defenders. Flying Knight CO Johnson orbited south of Simpson Harbor as high cover for target egress, but the Knights never even saw the bombers. They turned back for Dobodura when the B-24s radioed they were on their way home.

Tragically, the Flying Knights were forced apart in their attempt to penetrate the great white blanket of cumulus that had closed down on the Solomon Sea. All of the Dobodura crews waited anxiously as individual fighters dropped down through the overcast. By nightfall, Capt. Gerry Johnson was deeply perplexed with the absence of senior lieutenants Ralph Hays, Theron "Pappy" Price and Frank Wunder, Jr. No one had heard a distress call, nor was there any sign found of the trio in the search the next day. A few days later, the CO reluctantly turned over the "booze maps" of the three lost pilots to the officers club.

## FAILED JAPANESE REPRISAL; OCTOBER 15, 1943

The Imperial commanders at Rabaul and Wewak knew the end was very near. The Empire could not afford another series of losses as

*9 FS Frank Wunder, one of three Knights lost October 12th on the first Rabaul raid.*

*Hatless 5 FC Capt. Vaughn and 9 FS Sgt. Akin next to the captain's P-38 at Dobodura. Oddly enough, though the photo exists, no USAAF record of the pilot was ever found, and yet he appears to have scored three aerial victories in aircraft #75 with the Flying Knights.*

those that had occurred in the last ten weeks. Their men at Wewak, Rabaul and Cape Glouster were suffering from disease and starvation, let alone the continuous Allied air raids that struck both day and night.

Five months to the day since their last major strike at Oro Bay, the Japanese tried once more to knock out the Allied camps in eastern New Guinea. The JAAF and JNAF again combined air units for operations against all of the Papuan targets, but this time they would be met by an Allied fighter force which had nearly tripled in size. Just as with the past encounter in May, the 5 FC interception on October 15th would result in wholesale slaughter of the air crews from Rabaul.

*7 FS Ops Exec Carl Aubrey posing on P-40N aircraft #1 "THE SAINT" in which he led the Oro Bay interception on October 15th.*

## MORNING ALERT AT DOBODURA; OCTOBER 15, 1943

Shortly after sunrise, 49er CO Selman was notified of heavy air traffic having been detected over northern New Britain. Ops Executives Capt. Carl Aubry of the 7th Squadron and Lt. Harry Lidstrom of the 9th Squadron hurriedly conferred with Group Exec Jim Porter in an attempt to coordinate the Group's Warhawks and Lightnings for an optimum response. All morning missions were canceled. Then, at 0800 hours, the alarm went off and Dobodura's great fighter force roared into life. More than one hundred fighters would rise up to meet the enemy over Oro Bay.

From Kalamazoo strip, Ops Exec Aubrey led seven Screamin' Demons off as the huge dust storm rose from the Lightnings taxing out of their dispersal area. Minutes after the P-40s cleared the airdrome pattern, Sqn Ldr Gerry Johnson led his seven Flying Knights aloft from Horanda strip, followed by sixty Lockheeds of the 475 FG. The Thunderbolts of the 348 FG took off last, but the Jug would not reach the battle area in time. The fight that day would be another Lockheed show.

After a thirty minute ascent to the south, the pilots of 5 FC made contact at several different points with the large enemy formation of JNAF dive-bombers and fighters approaching Oro Bay. Lightnings and Warhawks plunged into the enemy formation from a dozen different directions over a period of thirty minutes. Major MacDonald's Satin's Angels struck first, followed only minutes later by the Screamin' Demons.

## SCREAMIN' DEMONS AT ORO BAY

Capt. Aubrey's Blue Flight foursome was at 15,000 feet when they began their hunt in the clouds over the shoreline. Immediately, the mission leader caught sight of three Vees of VAL dive-bombers heading back out of the sea. Aubrey called for "tanks off" and wingman Lts. John Roberts, element leader Roger Farrell and wingman John Miller plunged after their captain for the dark green planes cruising one thousand feet above the waves. In that first attack, Blue Flt Ldr Aubrey and element leader Farrell each overtook a swerving VAL and after three passes, two riddled dive-bombers fell into the sea. As Aubrey turned about and finished off his second victim, the other Blue Flight elements tried to regroup, but all hell broke loose.

Frantic voices cried out in Aubrey's headset as his Demon wingmen tried to identify themselves to the lone P-38 which had

come down behind them with its guns blazing away. It was too late. Aubrey called for the Demons to regroup, but the radio channel was filled with the voices of shouting Demon pilots. Yellow Flight had been attacked by P-38s as well.

## HARRISON IN TROUBLE WITH SATAN'S ANGEL

Overhead at 20,000, Lt. Duncan Myers' Yellow Flight had dropped their tanks at the same time and targeted four pale grey ZEROS and six darkly camouflaged HAMPS two thousand feet overhead. The four Yellow Demons swung about and climbed into the glare of the sun, but the veteran 253 Kokutai pilots quickly countered the attack. In a brief exchange high above the gathering rain clouds, only Yellow element leader Lt. Bobby Harrison could bring his guns to bear on one of the dark green Mitsubishis.

As the HAMP dove away trailing smoke, Harrison and wingman 2Lt. Ed Peck wheeled about to try and spot the dive-bombers, but the incident turned ugly when an anxious Satan's Angel dropped down head-on against the Demon Warhawks and opened fire. The Yellow element leader's left ammo bay exploded as the P-38 roared past. Luckily, Harrison was identified by the other Angel wingmen. Rookie Peck had wisely plunged away for the safety of the shoreline.

## A NEW FLYING KNIGHT ACE IN THE THICK OF THE BATTLE

At the very same moment, Capt. Gerry Johnson had reached Oro Bay with eight ships and immediately engaged the wave of eighteen VALs which had just begun its attack on the Allied ships in the harbor. Johnson took his Red Flight rookie wingman, 2Lt. Ray Swift, down for the lead element of VALs at 15,000 feet and each Knight burned a victim. Red element leader Grover Fanning and wingman 2Lt. Bob Wood shot their way through the ZERO escorts, and after four passes, ace Fanning and 2Lt. Wood each torched a dark green fighter from dead astern.

The lead Red elements wheeled around and Johnson was about to fire on a second dive-bomber when the kokutai escorts dropped to his level. Mission Leader Johnson chased a ZERO down through

9 FS ace Fanning scored his seventh kill on October 15th and his eighth and ninth two days later. He participated in the Rabaul raids, then finished his tour in the P-47s.

9 FS C.C. Charlie Kurtz next to aircraft #97 with Lt. G. Fanning and nine silhouettes kills (the last kill is off the photo to the left). Above that, the name of team pilot Capt. H. Lidstrom with a single kill mark. Ironically, Fanning scored his last two kills in this aircraft the day after good friend Lidstrom was lost in another plane.

the haze and fired until the green fighter rolled over and splashed down just beyond the harbor. The victory was his fifth, and it made the new ace hungry for more. The Knights' CO wheeled about for the VALs which had dropped down on the surface of the sea to escape beneath the cloud cover. Johnson bored in on his hapless third victim, killed the rear gunner and shot away the bomber's left wing. The Aichi aircraft exploded in a ball of fire and oily black smoke.

## BAD DEEDS OF THE KNIGHTS' BLUE FLIGHT

Blue Flight led by Lt. LeRoy Donnell nearly duplicated Red Flight's feat, save for two glaring error. As Flt Ldr Donnell and wingman 2Lt. John McLean each shot a victim out of the first VAL formation in the initial attack, Blue element leader Lt. Milby Marling and wingman 2Lt. Charles Kamphausen assaulted the ZERO escorts.

Marling fired on what he thought was a trio of enemy escorts trailing the VALs, but they were really the 7th Squadron's Blue Flight elements. Aubrey and Farrell escaped without being hit, but wingmen Roberts and Miller's P-40s were badly damaged from Marling's attack. Miller turned into the P-38's fire and barely escaped as a single .50 caliber round exploded in the nose of his P-40. Roberts could not shake his pursuer as easily. Twice he turned down and away as .50 caliber rounds tore out huge holes in his left aileron, right stabilizer and rear fuselage.

Not only had Marling failed to heed the calls on the tactical channel, his rookie wingman had violated the first commandment of engagement. Without good reason, Kamphausen had left his element leader to fight alone.

Rookie Kamphausen had momentarily fallen back when his left engine cut out. After his flight leader pulled away, the rookie engaged the ZEROs and chased his first combat victim all the way down to its fiery crash in the sea. Flushed by success, Kamphausen joined a pair of Satin's Angels and the trio hunted 100 miles out to sea toward Gasmata where they overtook a pair of ZEROs.

Kamphausen ambushed his second victim of the day with a hard turn to the left down to 500 feet above the deep blue water for a perfect 90 degree deflection shot. As he looked down at the boiling white whirlpool where the ZEKE had splashed down, a JNAF wingman swept up behind him and put three 7 mm rounds through

his starboard radiator. As the two Angels chased the kokutai wingman back toward New Britain, Kamphausen left the area and returned alone to Horanda.

## MORNING LANDING AT DOBODURA

When the scrambled flights limped back into Dobodura, Screamin' Demon Capt. Aubrey and element leader Farrell were livid. They had flown down into the midst of the enemy formation and had confirmed four kills, only to nearly be killed themselves by the damned Lightnings. Demon CO Ray Melikian, steady and resilient, met with Flying Knights CO Johnson for a more detailed debriefing, then returned to inform his mission pilots that both Marling and Kamphausen would be dealt with under the firm hand of Capt. Johnson.

As for Marling and Kamphausen, Johnson gave them a sounding out that could be heard throughout the Dobodura camp. Johnson admired their aggression, but warned the rookie if he ever separated from his flight leader again, it would be the last time he ever flew as a member of the 9th Squadron. Element leader Marling was fined the price of a case of scotch whiskey which he personally had to deliver to the Demons' officers club. The Satin's Angels had won a brief reprieve after they dutifully escorted Yellow element leader Bobby Harrison's crippled Warhawk back to base. For commanders Melikian and Johnson, the matter was thereafter closed, but the P-40 drivers still considered the cursed Lightning wing to be as dangerous as the Japanese.

## A LATE MORNING ENCOUNTER ON OCTOBER 15, 1943

While the morning mishap between the Demons and Knights was being sorted out, another 9 FS flight fought a brief engaged far out over the Solomon Sea. As the main Lightning force had ventured off to the Oro Bay, the reserve flight led by Lt. Johnny "Jump" O'Neill was vectored 300 miles further east to Woodlark Island in search of a downed transport. Flight Ldr O'Neill, wingman Lts. George Alber, Francis Love and Frank Nutter searched for over an hour until they had to set down on Woodlark's rough staging strip to refuel.

*Either 9 FS Lewelling or O'Neill in aircraft #99 "MY BEAUTIFUL LASS" in close formation to a wingman on a Rabaul mission.*

Airborne again by ten o'clock, O'Neill decided to hunt north of the islands on the return flight to Dobodura. At 1500 feet, the four Knights skirted the southern squall line of the storm growing over the sea. Only minutes from Oro Bay, the quartet passed directly beneath two New Britain-bound ZEROS. Jump O'Neill and Alber toggled off their tanks and closed up in attack formation. The two Knights wheeled in unseen through a climbing turn to the enemy's rear quarter and neither kokutai pilot knew what hit them. O'Neill's burst instantly killed the trailing kokutai man and Alber torched the leader when he turned gently to the right to see what had happened to his wingman. The Knights circled over the two steaming oil slicks for several minutes, but no other planes passed by. As the front rolled in from the north, the four P-38s regrouped and entered into a shallow descent for Horanda.

## LATER WITH THE EIGHTBALLS; OCTOBER 15, 1943

While LtC. James Selman's Demons and Knights slugged it out with the enemy off Oro Bay, his Eightballs unit at Marilinan trudged on in their patrol schedule over Lae. The White Flight team had already put in three missions and were about to check in at the bar when the operations people told Flt Ldr Joe Littleton to "saddle up" for one last escort to Finschhafen. The White Flight P-40s were to cover a pair of RAAF Boomerang fighter-bombers which were to be target spotters for the Australian 9th Division artillery north of the village. Littleton wearily protested and said the Aussie fighters could probably take care of themselves. When wingman Bill Runey asked how the Boomerangs fared against ZEROS, one of the Aussie pilots replied, "We don't know, Yank. No one's made it back to tell us." That settled the matter.

By four o'clock, Littleton's tired team had commandeered four refueled P-40s and set off for the forty minute flight to the Finschhafen beachhead. As the Boomerangs slipped down to do their work, Flt Ldr Littleton, wingman 2Lt. Runey, element leader Lt. Bill Elliott and Lt. Jim Carter orbited over the Australian camp. They watched the bright orange fire of the Aussie artillery rounds which burst beneath the dark forest canopy and grew a bit restless as the eastern horizon darkened. They were about to sign off from the patrol when one of the Boomerang pilots called in an intruder. From his altitude a mile above the beachhead, Littleton caught sight of nine silhouettes which suddenly appeared against the blue-grey clouds up ahead. The four Eightballs dropped their tanks and throttled upward one thousand feet until they could turned in be-

hind the Ki-48 LILYs from Wewak who were making the last bomb run of the day. For the hapless 45th Sentai crews on the left flank, the sortie would quickly prove to be their last.

Littleton began the in-line attack against the left Vee trio and raked the right wingman. The other three P-40 pilots each poured in a steady stream of tracers into the same target whose engine began to burn. Tail-end Carter slipped aside to watch the stricken bomber drop down toward the shore.

Littleton wheeled abruptly to the left and the Eightballs spread apart as they came back for the second pass. The next victim was the other sentai wingman and the White flight leader poured five hundred rounds into the LILY whose gunners vainly tried to defend their ship, but the 7 mm tracers soon stopped. After Elliott and Carter fired, wingman Runey saw the LILY was doomed and pushed ahead for the Vee leader.

The sentai gunners of the lead ship initiated young Runey to the thrill of his first exchange of gun fire. The lieutenant closed in on the mottled grey and green bomber which sent out silvery tentacles of smoking tracers and he gasped as they dropped perilously beneath the nose of his Warhawk. He misjudged the closeness of the target in the dim light and once at point-blank range, he fired a short, deadly .50 caliber volley which sparkled all over the center of the bomber. At the final moment, he rolled up to the left and peered down into the enemy cockpit which glowed from the internal fire. The LILY drifted toward the dark rolling hills and erupted into a fireball which lit up the mountainside.

As Littleton maneuvered for his third pass, element leader Elliott called in the warning of OSCARs overhead. The two leaders

*Seasoned 2Lt. Bill Runey accounted for two of the LILYs shot down on October 15th.*

fought for position against a pair of dark grey fighters and Littleton damaged one, but Elliott's guns jammed and he had to exit the fight. As the OSCARs and LILYs withdrew, wingmen Runey and Carter delivered one last bloody pass on the straggler bombers.

Runey had risen up through a thin cloud layer, then turned downward to re-engage the stricken left element LILY hit in the second pass. Once again, he closed through point blank range and briefly exchanged fire with the enemy gunner who withered within the terrible .50 caliber volley. The ship's entire center section between its engines began to burn and the remaining crewmen desperately clawed their way out of the airborne inferno. Three chutes popped open in the LILY's smoky wake.

Lt. Carter had meanwhile relentlessly pursued the very first victim down beneath the hazy overcast. Fifteen miles north of Finschhafen village, Carter overtook the crippled Ki-48 and followed it down through a left hand turn while shooting out both engines. The bomber slammed down just a few yard inland and Carter zoomed back up to catch sight of the OSCARs turning overhead. Not certain of where his own flight might be, the lieutenant wisely sped south in search of Flt Ldr Littleton.

White Flight eventually regrouped off the southern coast and all four men safely returned to land in the deep shadows of Watut Valley. That night, the Eightball crews celebrated the confirmation of White Flight's triple kill in the dusky sky over Huon Peninsula. Runey and Carter had survived their first contact with the enemy and only one 7 mm round had hit Elliott's ship. But that would be the only 8th Squadron victory celebration for the month. The very next day, four more pilots from Marilinan would venture to Finschhafen, but that mission would end in another survival epic.

### A DEBACLE AT FINSCHHAFEN; OCTOBER 16, 1943

The Eightballs once again stood down from a full schedule of sorties over the Huon coast when another late-day summons was made by the embattled Aussies at Finschhafen. Lt. Bob Hagerstrom had just brought his flight down at Marilinan at 1700 hours when Ops Exec Barnett ordered them off to the east again. With four refueled planes, Hagerstrom, 2Lt. Bob Sherman, Lt. Doug Lenore and 2Lt. Sammie Pierce sped off through the golden twilight for the interception 140 miles away. After a full throttle run for the coast, the quartet wheeled over the beachhead at Finschhafen only to be informed that the suspect raider had turned out to be an errant C-47 transport which had come from the north after getting lost in the storm. Now the storm front was over Finschhafen and Hag's men were in serious trouble. They had burned up their fuel in the hot pursuit and could never make it back to Marilinan. They had to attempt a landing on the rain soaked Aussie strip below. Hagerstrom went in first, but his ship cracked up on the muddy runway and blocked the way for the others. Airborne Sherman, Lenore and Pierce were stranded in the tempest.

The Eightball trio was left with only one option for survival so near the enemy lines. They all agreed to press down for the shoreline and bailout as near the Australian camp as possible. The three Warhawk pilots then separated to avoid a mid-air collision and dropped down through the lashing rain. They probed through the black overcast and were blinded as lightning flashed all around them. Only Bob Sherman bailed out and landed on the beach south of the

*8 FS Flt Ldr Doug Lanore (lt.) days before he led the four-ship flight that was lost in the storm at Finschhafen. The dog is Lenore's camp mut "YALLER GAL" whose name he also gave to his P-40N. The others are (lt.-rt.) ace Howard, future crash survivor and ace Flack, Hurst and Hanson.*

village. Lenore and Pierce blindly tumbled from their P-40s and the wind carried them over the coastal hills deep into the dark forest.

### LENORE AND PIERCE IN THE BUSH

Doug Lenore drifted down to a rough tumble through the trees two miles from the shore. After yelling for help and struggling to free himself from his snarled parachute cords, an Aussie commando called out from the undergrowth, "Shut up, Yank. There's Nips about, right?" The Warhawk pilot was hauled down from the branches and handed a Lewis sub-machine gun. Until the following morning when they reached the Aussie command post, Doug Lenore was an inductee in the Australian 22nd Division.

Eight miles inland, Sammie Pierce came down in his chute near the goldcamp village of Sattelburg. Sammie immediately took off his chute and buried it, then escaped into the forest and jumped into a deep stream bed. With his .45 automatic at the ready, he waited until dark, but no Japanese patrol followed. Hoping the steady drizzle would hide his tracks, the lieutenant set off down the narrow stream valley.

On the next day, the rain let up momentarily and Pierce rested until he heard voices of a Japanese patrol coming from the high ground behind him. After the voices faded into silence, he left the stream bed and tried to avoid paths or clearings. For three days he kept to the slow pace through the dense undergrowth and eventually crept down the hill to the shore. Sammie headed south and on the morning of the fifth day, he crossed the perimeter of the Aussie lines.

Sammie peered out from beneath a clump of ferns, only to dive for cover as a burst of machine gun fire tore through the trees overhead. He quietly drew his pistol and braced himself for a close quarter shoot-out when a wonderfully thick Aussie accent broke the grim silence. "Come on out, Yank. It's about time you showed up." The Aussie commandos put the last lost Eightball pilot on a transport bound for Marilinan the next morning.

## NOT LOST, JUST ASTRAY - the 8 FS "BLACKSHEEP"

With the safe recovery of the last six flyers who had gone down in combat, the Marilinan crews began to take great exception to their dubious "eightball" name. After a rousing songfest at the Marilinan officers club, the lyrics of the Yale whiffenpoof tune became a standard with the rebellious 8th Squadron crews who declared themselves "poor little airmen gone astray" and not just unlucky trouble makers.

After Bitsy Grant's return, fellow Californian Dick Vodra had sketched out a cartoon of a black lamb wearing a leather pilot's helmet and sent it off in the mail to a friend who worked for Walt Disney Studios. The Disney illustrator quickly returned a formal rendering of Vodra's "black sheep" complete with flight goggles in the shape of the figure eight. CO Ernie Harris readily accepted the idea and by month's end, his squadron adopted their new mascot and name. Like the Screamin' Demons and the Flying Knights, the Blacksheep name became a permanent Army Air Force fixture.

## LONE KILL AT WEWAK and LIDSTROM LOST; OCTOBER 16, 1943

The grueling mission rotation continued at both 49er operation centers as the Demons, Blacksheep and Flying Knights met the exhaustive pace of alerts and escorts. But Group CO Selman's more aggressive pilots were aggravated by the misfortune of missed scoring opportunities while their friendly rivals continued at the deadly pace set in the first half of the month. The weather marginally improved and the 49ers entered into a brief flourish of action, but the resultant victories would be costly.

Fifth Command sent a large air strike against the Wewak complex on the morning of the 16th. The strike force escorts were made up of 348 FG Thunderbolts and 80 FS Lightnings who were met by a large enemy fighter formation south of the target and several kills were registered by the Jug pilots. After the mission debriefing at Dobodura, Flying Knight Deputy CO Wally Jordan put in a request for a follow-up armed reconnaissance of the area, but when the Knights swept over the Madang air strip that afternoon, only rookie 2Lt. George Haniotis would pick off a lone OSCAR.

As the Knights returned down the coast and swung west-south-west at Finschhafen for the descent flight to Horanda, Ops Exec Harry Lidstrom reported engine failure and fell away for the emergency strip at Lae. When the main flight reached Dobodura, Jordan was informed that Capt. Lidstrom was safe at Lae and would return later that afternoon. After some rudimentary engine maintenance at the northern strip, Lidstrom decided to take the valuable Lockheed down to Dobodura before dark. He set off down the shoreline for home in the evening twilight, but flight controllers at Dobodura soon received a signal from Lidstrom that he was just north of Cape Ward Hunt and had again lost power in the troublesome engine. Then the radio signal was gone. Immediately, a scout plane was sent north as darkness settled over the cape, but no trace of Lidstrom could be found. A few days later, Flt Ldr Grover Fanning had the missing man's name painted above the score board of his Lockheed as a memorial to the beloved Ops man. Everyone hoped that the lost pilot would someday walk out of the jungle, but four months would pass before native tribesmen carried the remains of Harry Lidstrom from the fatal crash site in the hills above the Cape.

*Popular Capt. Harry Lidstrom lost on October 16th trying to reach home in a faltering P-38.*

## SEVEN MEN DEAD AT PONGONI; OCTOBER 16, 1943

No sooner had LtC. Selman learned of the missing Ops Exec in the 9th Squadron, his heart sank with the devastating news that the 49ers' hack PBY transport was overdue at Oro Bay. The 49ers' rescue flight team had just come back at twilight after the search for Lidstrom when the pilot reported they could not reach the harbor in the rain storm.

A year later to the month, local tribesmen reported the location of the shattered flying boat not far from Pongani village. The remains of F/O's Cecil McElhiney and Dick Smith, radio officer 2Lt. Bob Mona, T/Sgt. Hal Macha, S/Sgt. Jack Holt, and Sgts. Charles Dawson and Glenn Walter were recovered for burial. The funeral service finally put to rest the bleakest era of Selman's command.

## ANOTHER RAID ON ORO BAY - LOSS OF LT. LARRY SUCCOP; OCTOBER 17, 1943

On the 17th, the enemy air force at Wewak tried to hit the Allied stronghold in Papua. A mid-morning alert put the Flying Knights and the Screamin's Demons back over the coast and though the 49ers' effort was better coordinated than the snafu of the 15th, the day would end with the bitter loss of a senior Demon flight leader.

The Screamin' Demons answered the 10:00 a.m. alarm with only three P-40's and the mission seemed doomed from the start. Lt. Bob DeHaven left several minutes after Flt Ldr Larry Succop and wingman David Germain took off, but DeHaven failed to catch up. While DeHaven hunted alone, Succop and Germain pressed on at 15,000 feet in an attempt to join the Satin's Angels, but even their new N-model Warhawks could not overtake the rapidly climbing Lightnings.

As the Demon pair sped alone through the clouds just off shore from Buna, they were hit from behind by a flight of ZEROs. Germain barely escaped with his life, but Succop disappeared. Several minutes later, Germain found safety with the Angels, but he was forced to fight for his life a second time when they found the enemy again. When a 7 mm round knocked out his prop control, weary David Germain dropped out for Kalamazoo.

*7 FS Larry Succop in aircraft #26 on patrol over the Markham River valley. The front half of the spinner is blue and "26" is white while only the starboard wing bears the white leading edge of the typical theater marking. Quite unique is the yellow s.n. 2105498 replaced over the white painted tail. Flt Ldr Succop vanished in this aircraft on October 17th during the hunt for enemy raiders off the north coast.*

## THE KNIGHTS OFF BUNA

Meanwhile, a dozen 9th Squadron P-38s in three flights also got off. The sortie was particularly unique in that all of the pilots were lieutenants. Senior Lt. George Alber was mission leader ahead with Blue Flight, but he and one of his elements turned back early with mechanical failures. The flights reorganized en route and ace Green Flt Ldr Grover Fanning assumed the lead. Soon Lt. John Stowe fell out with a runaway left prop and the Knights reorganized again. Fanning continued to take the others eastward.

After reaching the coast at Oro Bay, CHARTER fighter control reported the enemy was inbound from the north and Fanning took his team through a wide left turn up to 25,000 feet. In minutes, they reached Buna and flew head-on into a formation of thirty-plus enemy fighters. Fanning called for the break, but Bob Wood could not shake his left belly tank free. He turned south as the remaining eight Knights entered into a steep plunge for the OSCARs and TONYs two thousand feet below. Despite all the difficulty, Fanning's seven lieutenant wingmen would prove to be more than a match for the enemy.

## FANNING'S GREEN TEAM

The Green team of Fanning, rookie wingman 2Lt. Charlie McElroy, element leader Jimmie Harris and wingman Del Moore went straight into the lead elements of four TONYs and scattered the charcoal colored fighters. After two full turns against the Ki-61s, the high cloudless sky was criss-crossed by tracers and rookie McElroy took a single 13 mm round in his left engine which forced him out of the fight. The three other Green elements fought on and wheeled about in classic close formation to catch the OSCARs in their turns. Fanning was about to fire when a TONY tried to cut off element leader Harris. Fanning whipped about at full throttle and pulled in behind the in-line fighter. Debris showered from the Tony until it disintegrated in an immense explosion. Fanning went back to engage the OSCARs.

Meanwhile, Jimmie Harris held on in the turn against the OSCARs until one of the brownish-green fighters stalled out in a high angle wing-over. His three-second burst blew off the Ki-43's left rear stabilizer and it fell away in a spin. Harris swept in behind another mottled Oscar and raked it from tail to prop. Its rolled over and dropped through the haze with its engine ablaze.

*9 FS Jimmie Harris scored two more kills on October 17th, yet all during the Rabaul missions and four months more months in Thunderbolts, he never found his fifth victim.*

Then wingman Moore heavily damaged a third. The enemy fighters dove for the safety of the clouds far below, only to be cut off by ace Fanning who killed one of the sentai pilots with a deadly accurate burst from head-on. Fanning looped back to regroup and looked down at the two geysers which rose out of the sea where his last victim and Harris' second kill had fallen near one another.

## RED FLIGHT'S PART

Red Flt Ldr Jump O'Neill, followed by his only remaining wingman, Ralph Wandrey, made their attack several seconds after the Green team, but it was equally as deadly. O'Neill and Wandrey made a classic wingman assault on a pair of turning sentai fighters and simultaneously knocked them down with precision front quarter deflection shots. They turned into the sentai again and Wandrey heavily damaged another before they were recalled by mission leader Fanning.

The 9th Squadron lieutenants had accounted for six enemy planes knocked out of the fight in a mere five minutes. Oddly

enough, neither Blue element leader Milby Marling nor rookie wingman 2Lt. Alfred Lewelling had hit an enemy plane in their assault, even though they had made three passes together and the rookie had expended most of his ammo.

## DEMON DEHAVEN'S LONE KILL AND THE 3RD CENTURY MARK

Meanwhile, Lt. Bob DeHaven had descended to 17,000 feet in his lone pursuit over the ocean and saw several P-38s harassing the enemy planes overhead. He was only a half mile away when he saw an OSCAR stall out in its turn and be hit by a lone Lightning.

Indeed, the OSCAR with its stabilizer clipped off by Flying Knight Harris continued to spin down through the haze right into the path of the lone Demon. The Ki-43's pale grey underside filled the P-40's gun sight and DeHaven held down the trigger through point blank range. He wheeled his Warhawk off at the last second, then orbited the smoking OSCAR whose pilot fell free and deployed his chute. The fight was over and DeHaven flew off to formate with a flight of Satin's Angels for the return to Kalamazoo.

In the debriefing following the successful interception, Demon CO Melikian was stunned to learn that Mission Leader Succop could not be accounted for. A search flight was hastily sent off to scan the coast, but nothing was ever found. Melikian reassured the two wingmen that no blame was directed toward them, but both Germain and DeHaven dwelled on the loss of their flight leader for several days.

For all of the September and early October madness, LtC. James Selman's men had once again shown amazing resolve. Though some of their brothers had been lost, the Demons, the Blacksheep and the Knights held out against the airmen from Rabaul and Wewak. Though other USAAF squadrons had scored at a faster pace during the previous six weeks, no other group's victory tally could compare. The 5 AF intelligence team eventually accredited 9 FS CO Gerry Johnson's first kill on the October 15th mission as the Knights' 129th victory and the 49ers' 300th aerial victory overall, but Selman's people were far from finished. In the third week of October, Gen. Kenney assembled his heavy bomber force for the final thrust against Rabaul and the 49ers would be right in the thick of the epoch battle.

# *14*

# THE REDUCTION OF RABAUL: OCTOBER-NOVEMBER 1943

The Japanese command had marshaled some 300 fighters at Rabaul to fend off the rush of U.S. Navy and Marines carrier-based and land-based squadrons during the waning Solomons campaign of late 1943. But the momentum was now with the superior numbers of the growing Allied forces. With the appearance of the phenomenal gull-winged F4U Corsair and more of the dreaded P-38 Lightnings coming at the front of the Allies' aerial assault, there had been a disastrous loss of seasoned air crews on New Britain.

General Kenney's 5 AF had also stepped up the southern assault as more of the ominous B-24 Liberators staged with virtual immunity from their distant bases in Australia and the heavily defended airdromes in Papua. Even the re-equipping of some of the kokutais and sentais at Rabaul and Wewak with more heavily armed twin-engine interceptors had proved ineffective against the growing enemy bomber formations. The 4th Air Army at Wewak had been wrecked by the Liberators and B-25 strafers that past August and were yet to be adequately reinforced. Ravaged by dysentery, scurvy and malaria, the Imperial aircrews struggled to hold out in their battered command centers, but nothing could save either Rabaul or Wewak. Both day and night throughout September and early October, the Imperial headquarters rocked beneath an ever-broadening avalanche of high explosives.

## LIBERATORS AND LIGHTNINGS TO RABAUL; OCTOBER 23, 1943

As for the strategic escort squadron of the 49ers at Horanda Field, there was little time to recuperate in the maximum effort against the Rabaul stronghold. Capt. Gerry Johnson's 9FS was down to sixteen serviceable P-38s, and the operations kept line chief M/Sgt Beech's mechanics busy twenty-four hours a day. On the 23rd, Capt. Johnson drew target egress high cover for the strike force going back to Rabaul. By sunrise, Beech's people got all of their Lightnings airborne.

Capt. Johnson and his pilots staged to Kiriwina Island where one man failed to takeoff for the 11:00 a.m. rendezvous with the bombers off the southern New Britain coast. Another aborted en route, but Johnson had fourteen sound aircraft in high cover on the right flank at 26,000 feet when they reached the target area at noon.

Unlike their first crossing to Rabaul, the 9th Squadron pilots would see the northern coast of New Britain through scattered clouds for the first time. They coasted over the sharp prow of the Cape Gazelle landmark which jutted north-eastward into the brilliant blue

St. George Channel. Fifteen miles to the west lay the volcanic peaks of the c-shaped peninsula which protected the village of Rabaul and Simpson Harbor. Directly down below lay Rapopo airdrome on the northern shore and Tobera airdrome about ten miles inland southwest of the Cape's point. Allied intelligence had long since called out these bases as the home of the regrouped 253rd Kokutai which flew air defense for the eastern and southern approaches to Simpson Harbor.

As the Knights made their first turn over the JNAF airdromes, the tactical channel crackled with the excited voices of the Satin's Angels who had engaged the enemy directly over the harbor. Capt. Johnson turned his flights out over the channel and peered north into the searing blue Pacific sky. He could just make out the bombers as they paraded over the enemy ships in the bay and then made their turn toward the Knights' position. When the Liberators winged beneath the 9 FS elements, Johnson called out ten green single-engine fighters closing in from the north one thousand feet below. Lockheed belly tanks littered the sky as the ace Mission Leader plunged to the attack.

Johnson's Red Flight quartet included his wingman 2Lt. Ray Swift, element leader Capt. Bill Haney, and wingman Lt. Stan Johnson. Young Swift had been told to stay close to the commander if he wanted to see any action and the Captain was true to his ward. Even when flak suddenly burst within the line-abreast Red Flight formation and Haney swung away with Stan Johnson to spoil the Japanese gunners aim, rookie Swift held his place on Capt. Johnson's

*9 FS CO Johnson waiting for the signal at Kiriwina Island in the Rabaul operations.*

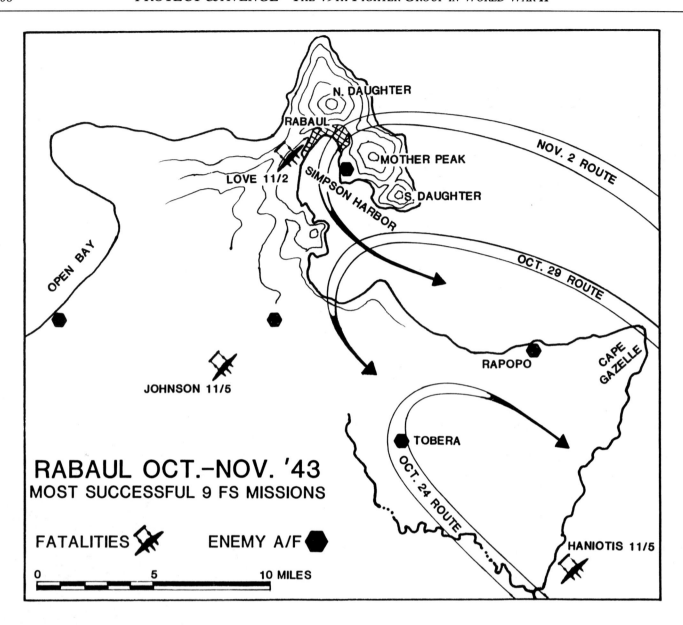

**RABAUL OCT.–NOV. '43**
MOST SUCCESSFUL 9 FS MISSIONS

FATALITIES ✈          ENEMY A/F ⬡

0          5          10 MILES

wing. Seconds later, the CO and Swift immediately latched on to a lone ZERO which had just flown a pass at an echelon of B-24s. Down to 21,000 feet, the CO cut his throttle and fired a dead-astern burst into the Mitsubishi which flamed and rolled straight down. Swift watched the burning fighter fall away until it faded from view against the emerald green forest of Cape Gazelle.

In the mean time, Green element Francis Nutter and Yellow element Francis Love both chased an enemy plane down below 10,000 feet, but neither man could overtake his target. Their strict orders were to cover the escape of the Liberators and Capt. Johnson recalled his elements before anyone else felt the urge to extend the chase any further.

Capt. Johnson's team safely returned to Horanda strip where their crew chiefs immediately swarmed over their Lockheeds. Canvass shelters were erected over the ships and the crews worked long into the night to refit the planes which were required for the maximum effort that would following in just a few hours. Line chief M/Sgt Beech reported two of the P-38s would require engine

changes and two other were marginal, but a dozen of the mission weary ships would be ready at daybreak.

### CLOSER TO TOBERA; OCTOBER 24, 1943

Twelve new pilots in the 9 FS rotation ate a breakfast of fresh bread and eggs and washed it down with strong coffee, then drove down to the Horanda dispersal area. They stepped down from the jeeps and looked north across the runway to the dispersal field which was choked with an awesome arsenal of sixty B-25 strafers of the 345 BG and 3 AG. Unlike the previous escort missions, this would be a massive low level assault against all of the major Rabaul airdromes to knock out the enemy fighters prior to the B-24 strike. This time, the Flying Knights would be right in the thick of the battle on the deck at Rabaul's Tobera airdrome.

Just as the day before, the Knights staged to Kiriwina and waited until mid-morning for word that the bombers were on their way. At

*Another flightline poker game passes the time while the P-38s are off on the seven-hour long mission to Rabaul.*

0830 hours, mission leader Capt. Dick Bong led his eleven wingmen up from Kiriwina to join the sprawling Lightning wing formation over the Solomon Sea. Minutes later the Lockheeds wheeled into position above the strafers and the Knights dropped down in close escort position on the right flank of the 3rd Attack. An hour later, the strike force reached the New Britain coast and passed over Jacquinot Bay when the B-25 mission leader broke radio silence. The final check point for their turn into the target was just minutes ahead.

When the Mitchells reached the mouth of the Warangoi River, they swung to the northwest up into the billowing fair weather clouds that hung on the hill sides of the river valley. Capt. Bong led Red Flight rookie wingman 2Lt. Woodson Woodward, element leader Norman Hyland and wingman Gil Milliff inland at 2000 feet, while Lt. Bill Bleecker's Blue Flight of Lts. John Stowe, Jimmie Harris and Milby Marling followed nearby on the right. Overhead in trail at 6000 came Lt. Jump O'Neill's Green Flight of 2Lt. John McLean, Lt. Ralph Wandrey and Lt. Del Moore. The 3 AG Mitchells suddenly called for the turn to the right into Tobera airdrome's air space and accelerated down through the haze. Bong's men were about to become embroiled in the fight of their lives.

## IT BEGAN WITH RED FLIGHT AND THE LOSS OF 2LT. WOODWARD

As the Mitchells skimmed over the trees toward the enemy airstrip, the 39 FS high cover flights warned the Lightning wing of several contacts with enemy fighters all along the northern shore of Cape Gazelle. Bong's Red Flight elements peered up through the cumulus and soon caught sight of three radial engine fighters speeding in from the north. Bong and rookie wingman Woodward dropped their tanks and throttled upward, followed seconds later by element leader Norm Hyland and wingman Milliff. The Red team rushed toward the ZEROs and Bong fired at all three but missed. The ZEROs turned into the Lightnings and the other Red Flight elements separated without firing a shot. Only Bong and Milliff reformed and sped back to the 3 AG Mitchells while Hyland pressed on for the fight developing north of Tobera. Rookie Woodward had disappeared.

## RED FLIGHT HYLAND AND BLUE FLIGHT BLEECKER

Hyland flew into the vicinity of the Blue Flight elements who had also engaged the enemy at the same moment. The Blue Flight foursome had swept beneath ten ZEROs and rose up to engage, but the Blue Knights also separated in the maneuver. As the three Blue elements escaped to the open seas, Blue Flt Ldr Bleecker and Red element Hyland combined forces and each prevailed in the encounter just north of Tobera airdrome.

After Hyland fatally hit a turning ZERO in a high angle deflection, Bleecker wheeled in behind a kokutai aviator who had dropped into a shallow dive and foolishly tried to out run the Lockheed beast. Bleecker followed for several seconds and butchered the ZERO until it plowed into a hill side. Then Bleecker and Hyland turned due east to join up with the Satin's Angels who had withdrawn to the designated rendezvous point off the coast.

## GREEN FLIGHT'S NEW ACE

Jump O'Neill's Green team at their higher position had also seen the ten ZEROs and the quartet came down in a rear-quarter attack. O'Neill twisted through several passes with the kokutai pilots who swept in and out of the clouds until one enemy aviator slowed down at the top of a wing over. The Green Leader sent out a line of "blue-nose explosives" which sawed off the ZEKE's tail section for his fifth career kill. As the other kokutai wingmen attempted to reach the safety of the clouds, ace O'Neill overran another dark green fighter and killed the kokutai pilot from dead astern.

Green element leader Wandrey and wingman Moore also held on in the wild dogfight that swirled within the clouds above the

*New 9 FS ace Johnnie "Jump" O'Neill scored his 5th and 6th victories in the wild dogfight over Tobera airdrome on October 24th.*

*Veteran Del "Moo" Moore, originally with the Demons but now in the Knights as a Rabaul raider, scored his only confirmed career kill on October 24th. His Lightning (# unknown) carries the victory as a four-leaf clover, as well as tree and tent which he had knocked down in his earlier escapades. Moore stayed with the Knights for over a year through nearly 300 hours of combat.*

## WITHDRAWAL FROM RABAUL; OCTOBER 24, 1943

Mission Leader Bong was hopelessly frustrated by the loss of wingman Woodward and the scattering of the Flying Knights over the Cape. The ace mission leader recalled his flights, but the 9 FS elements had withdrawn from the cloud covered battle site all along the eastern shoreline of Cape Gazelle. As Bong and wingman Milliff circled over the sea in search of their errant squadron mates, the captain spotted three small luggers hugging the safety of the coastline and vented his anger on the hapless Imperial sailors. After the pair made a brutal low level firing run, they left one of the boats burning at the stern and turned south for home.

Bong's fears were confirmed after his landing at Horanda strip. The intelligence people confirmed that 2Lt. Woodward had last been reported east of Buna low over the water in his badly shot-up Lockheed. That night in the Flying Knights bar as the liquor dulled the pain of the day's events, hardly anyone could recall the missing man's face. Woodson "Woody" Woodward had only been on the flight roster a week.

## STILL A WAR UP NORTH - LT. DAVID IS DOWN; OCTOBER 24, 1943

The Warhawk squadrons were still fully engaged in the reduction of the enemy camps on the Huon Peninsula and the men at Marilinan again had to rescue another stray Blacksheep on the 24th. Lt. Dan David had been hit by ground fire while strafing barges south of Madang and had nursed his holed P-40 all the way to the Watut Valley where the engine shut down. Just as squadron mate Thorvaldson had done seven weeks prior, David attempted a belly landing on the Waffir River sandbar, but his plane cart wheeled and slammed down in the heavy brush. Luckily, an L-5 liaison hack reached the flyer who had barely been able to crawl from the wreckage despite a sever back sprain. The injured man was eventually evacuated to the hospital at Oro Bay, and then back to America.

The harrowing crash completed changed Lt. Dan David's personality and he never flew again. After the war, he changed his last

enemy airfield and damaged several ZEROs in the exchange, but neither pilot could confirm a kill as their targets disappeared within the clouds. Finally, a pair of ZEROs challenged Wandrey and Moore head-on and then fatally broke off the maneuver well within range of the Green Knights' guns. The Green element leader beat the lead HAMP on the inside of the turn and his barrage rendered the Mitsubishi into smoldering junk. Moore duplicated the feat against the ZEKE wingman. Both flaming Mitsubishis fell straight down into the jungle.

As Wandrey and Moore tried to rejoin, a TONY suddenly appeared and Wandrey wheeled in behind the Ki-61 to knock pieces out of its forward fuselage. His Lightning passed through a spray of oil as the sentai pilot rolled into a escape dive and vanished within the mist. Unable to focus through his gunsight beyond the fouled windscreen, Wandrey called wingman Moore and withdrew to the coast. The fight was over for the Flying Knights.

*9 FS latecomer to the Lockheed era was 2Lt. Bernie Krankowitz. He flew throughout the Rabaul missions and on into 1944, yet would not record a victory until the Philippines invasion a year later.*

*After Bong missed all of the airborne targets over Tobera, he expended his ammo at the barges off the south coast of New Britain. Still with seventeen kills as of late October, the armorers reloaded aircraft #79 for yet another mission.*

name to Rowan and gained great fame as a television entertainer. Oddly enough, Dan David "Rowan" never talked of the October 1943 incident or his 49ers career throughout the remainder of his life.

## MOBILIZING AGAIN AT MARILINAN; OCTOBER 27, 1943

The war also took a immense change for Lt. David's cohorts at Marilinan. The base had been turned over to the RAAF as a major infantry supply depot for the Australian troops who would push north to link up with the advanced commando units in the Ramu River Valley. The Blacksheep were forced to take off across the flight path of the 35 FG and likewise avoid the approach of C-47s which rose against them from the opposite end of the field. There simply was no longer any room for Harris' men on the traffic clogged strip.

On the 27th, the first flight of Blacksheep Warhawks lifted off for their new home 150 miles further north. Lt. Bill Runey skillfully soared over a pair of Airacobras, then sped beneath a rising C-47, and finally wheeled hard to the right over the river. He skimmed above the forest where the familiar wake of white cockatiels rose beneath his P-40 for the last time. Crowded, muddy Marilinan had been a miserable camp and the only thing Runey and the 8 FS would regret leaving behind was the camp cook who had gained great fame as a consummate baker. Other than the cook, the RAAF was welcome to the wretched airdrome, which they called Tsili-Tsili after their camp just a bit further down the river. Regardless of the name, any base would surely be better than "silly-silly" Marilinan.

Unfortunately for Capt. Harris, Lt. Runey and all of the other Blacksheep, they were sent to the primitive dirt strip roughed out on the valley floor of the Ramu River valley near the village of Gusap. There was no improvement in their lives at all and their Warhawks were immediately thrown against the enemy on the mountain pass road which ended just sixty miles to the north at the Japanese coastal garrison at Bogadjim.

## THE LAST DEMON SWEEP FROM DOBODURA; OCTOBER 27, 1943

With the Blacksheep committed in their move to Gusap and the Flying Knights embroiled in the strategic escort missions to Rabaul, the Screamin' Demons at Dobodura were finally summoned into the fighter cover for the Huon Peninsula's southern shore. Capt. Ray Melikian's 7 FS was also advised to mobilize for the Ramu Valley while temporarily inheriting the Blacksheeps' old patrol area. It had been a particular agonizing lull for the Demons who had been consigned to the mundane patrols over the harbors and airfields down south. The expanded mission area to the northern front was a welcome relief for the more aggressive Demon flyers.

Late in the afternoon of the 27th, Melikian sent a late-day Demon scramble off from Kalamazoo strip. Newly promoted Capt. John Benner led seven wingmen north to rendezvous with the Marilinan P-39s to cover the latest convoy of supply ships approaching the Aussie camp at Finschhafen.

Capt. Benner led Red Flight wingman 2Lt. Allen Osborne, element leader Lt. Bill Ferris and wingman Lt. Bob Croft into the

target area at 10,000 feet and passed directly over Finschafen village at a quarter to six o'clock. Newly promoted Capt. Arland Stanton with Green Flight wingman Lt. David Germain, element leader Lt. Duncan Myers and wingman Lt. Bob DeHaven momentarily hunted ten miles off shore on a parallel course. The Demon flights passed just beyond the beachhead through the deepening shadows of the heavy cumulus and Benner took his Red Flight up another 3000 feet to take advantage of the final rays of sunlight. Capt. Stanton took his men down a thousand feet and began to drift westward toward the shore to reform with mission leader Benner. The Demons had been northbound for a only a few minutes when nine enemy bombers with sixteen escorts drifted into view overhead to the north. The Warhawks and Airacobras dropped their tanks and climbed upward to engage. The Screamin' Demons got there first.

## RED DEMONS ENGAGES THE ENEMY ESCORTS

Benner's Red Flight closed in on the LILY bombers just as they turned to the west. The LILYs began to salvo hundreds of small parachutes upon the high ground and it dawned on the Demons that they were not bombs, but supplies being dropped to the trapped Japanese soldiers at Sattelburg village. Capt. Benner and wingman Osborne rose up through the rambling OSCARs who did not seem to be in any particular formation and both Demons made two passes before they gained advantage over a pair of green-spotted silver Ki-43s which attempted to escape within the haze far below. Flight Ldr Benner's concentrated dead-astern volley obliterated his target which fell in a myriad of flaming pieces. Osborne cut off a P-39 in its attack on an OSCAR and chased the victim down into a shallow valley where the Ki-43 rolled over and slammed down in a brilliant orange explosion. Benner and Osborne re-engaged and the captain flamed a second OSCAR which plunged into the jungle. The bombers had long since turned back to the north and there were only Airacobras in the area. Mission Leader Benner withdrew to reform his group.

Meanwhile during the initial assault, Red element's Ferris and Croft had also made firing passes at the OSCARs, and Ferris heavily damaged one target while Croft was momentarily chased off by another sentai wingman. Ferris would have finished off his flat-spinning victim, but the Red element leader was interrupted by an aggressive TONY which jumped into the midst of the fight. Through several turns, Ferris struggled to hit the twisting dark green Kawasaki with faded orange wing roundels, but the acrobatic enemy pilot continually avoided each .50 caliber volley. It was a wondrous display of flying skill, but the sentai man pushed the odds much too far. He was about to fall victim to an equally skilled opponent from Green Flight.

## GREEN FLIGHT HITS A TRANSPORT

As Stanton's Green team crossed over the beach, they saw the supply drop and fought their way through the escorts in an attempt to reach the Lily transports. After a rambling dogfight that sprawled thirty miles inland, element leader Myers and wingman DeHaven each downed an OSCAR while Germain heavily damaged another.

*Capt. Bong showing the strain in the pursuit of the Rickenbacker record.*

*Jump O'Neill's faithful lady, displaying his final victory tally after the October 29th mission.*

Then Germain joined Flt Ldr Stanton in a head-on attack against a straggler LILY. Germain wheeled about beneath the riddled Ki-48 and fired a second time from the rear right quarter in a climbing pass. Engulfed in flames, the pale green-striped transport slid aside in a shallow left turn and drifted down into a spectacular explosion in the trees. Red Flight regrouped and turned south.

Just as they were reforming, wingman DeHaven in his blooded #13 passed over the deadly dance recital being held by Red Flight's Ferris and the shifty Kawasaki acrobat. After Ferris completed another head-on parry, DeHaven decided he had seen enough and elected to cut in on the sentai interloper. The TONY pilot caught site of DeHaven's approach and tried to escape to the north, but ole #13 had the down-hill edge. The Demon's volley instantly flamed the Ki-61 and its pilot-acrobat took to his chute. The fight was finally over.

Melikian's men continued to fly missions over the entire southern realm of the Huon Peninsula, but as of the first week in November, the Japanese had effectively abandoned the area. As the air war swept further to the northwest into the Ramu River Valley, the Screamin' Demons kept up the monotonous routine of defensive patrols over the southern half of the Markham Valley, but there were no raids against the new 5 AF HQ at Nadzab. More bomber groups moved into the Dobodura and Nabzab airdromes as Ray Melikian and his people soldiered on in the anticipation that their new base would soon be ready somewhere up north.

### ONCE MORE TO RABAUL; OCTOBER 29, 1943

Capt. Gerry Johnson's mission-weary Flying Knights still held up their quota in the aerial onslaught against Rabaul. The Knights had flown every day in the mission rotation without firing a shot since the low level raid on Tobera five days previous. On the 29th, the Knights were switched from their close escort assignments over Cape Gazelle to their first sortie to Rabaul proper. That day would mark their single most successful New Britain mission with six confirmed kills and everyone returning safely to Horanda.

At mid-day, Capt. Bill Haney took his place as Flying Knight mission leader. With only one man failing to takeoff from Kiriwina, the Knights joined the Liberator strike force and proceeded on schedule to northern New Britain. They paraded over Cape Gazelle, then turned to the west-northwest on to the bomb line for the shipping in Simpson Harbor. Haney's three flights were stacked between 20 to 22 thousand feet in the clear sky and easily saw the rising swarm of fighters arching in from the north. In near perfect execution, all but 2Lt. Glade Hill would drop their tanks and plunge into the enemy formation in one thundering pass.

### HANEY'S BLUE FLIGHT

Blue element wingman Hill separated momentarily and rocked his Lockheed to loosen his stuck belly tanks, but Haney did not wait. With element leader Lt. Jump O'Neill and wingman 2Lt. John McLean following close by, Haney peeled off for the enemy as Hill finally jettisoned his tanks, only to find his starboard supercharger did not run at full power. Though Hill was several seconds to the rear, all four Blue elements hit the JNAF fighters at 18,000 feet and made two firing passes in their 400 Mph spiraling descent down to the tree tops. Just above the jungle, ace Jump O'Neill in his howling #99 BEAUTIFUL LASS gunned down ZERO kills number seven and eight for the last two victories of his tour.

### BONG'S RED FLIGHT TRIO

Although Bong's Red team was short one wingman, the trio duplicated Blue Flight's score. After chasing their quarry down to the hill tops west of the harbor, Bong and element leader Norm Hyland each hammered a ZERO in a shallow diving head-on pass. Wingman 2Lt. George Haniotis desperately tried to hold position with Bong, but the ace's third victory in as many missions seemed to renew his wild hunting spirit. Bong roared after the escaping enemy wingmen all the way north to Open Bay and shot down his nineteenth victim who fell in flames into the sea.

## YELLOW FLIGHT'S PART

From their high trailing position at 22,000 feet, Yellow Flight Leader Lt. Charlie Ralph brought down wingman 2Lt. Ray Swift, element leader Lt. George Alber and wingman Lt. John Stowe as the last elements to enter into the dogfight at the lower lever. While elements Ralph and Swift each sent down a smoking mottled fighter into the jungle, Alber and Stowe were momentarily distracted by flak bursts over the harbor's western shore. As the two tail-end-charlies regained composure and flew south to find the rest of the Knights, a lone ZERO suddenly swept out of the haze over the mountains and latched on to the lagging Yellow wingman. John Stowe's P-38 jolted as four 20 mm and twenty 7 mm rounds exploded in his starboard nacelle. Luckily, the Flying Knight was not wounded and could control his plummeting Lockheed down to the relative safety of the clouds along the south coast.

When Stowe safely put down on Kiriwina, his ravaged Lockheed was dragged away for scrap. The Flying Knights were then down to twelve war weary model-F and model-G P-38s. The other planes eventually reached Horanda by nightfall where line chief Fred Beech performed those mechanical miracles in the nightbound dispersal area. That next morning, all twelve Lightnings were waiting for CO Gerry Johnson.

## HELL ROSE UP OVER SIMPSON HARBOR; NOVEMBER 2, 1943

On November 2nd, Gen. Kenney's heavy bombers attempted an early morning raid, but weather set the mission back. A large B-25 strafer force waited at Kiriwina with the P-38 escorts, but they too were held down until weather reconnaissance flights could find a clear route to Rabaul. In mid-morning, Kenney received confirmation of broken clouds over Simpson Harbor which was choked by the Mobile Fleet warships and freighters. Over 200 enemy aircraft had staged into the surrounding airdromes. The mission was hurriedly reinstated.

By late morning, an aerial armada of B-25 strafers and B-24 heavies beneath an umbrella of 80 Lockheed escorts were on their way to the enemy stronghold. Capt. Johnson was at the lead of the twelve Flying Knights in close escort to the 345 BG Mitchells which were slated to hit the docks and ships of the harbor. En route to the southern New Britain coast, Green Flt Ldr Wally Jordan angrily reported mechanical failure and turned his Green Flight over to element leader Lt. Carl Planck. Jordan turned back for Kiriwina alone as the remaining eleven Knights pressed on within the formation in stacked position from 1000 up through 3000 feet on the Mitchells' right flank.

The strike force proceeded north to the outer islands in St. George channel, then swung west toward the northern side of the twin volcanos named Mother and Daughter which stood over the target of the German colonial town and its deep harbor. At 1345 hours, the B-25s and P-38s pressed on into the shadows of the two peaks and swung hard to the left through the shallow pass between them to initiate the second wave of the low level attack. It was if the 5 AF crews has passed through the very portal of hell.

The turbid air over the sprawling harbor was smeared with black flak bursts from the hundreds of anti-aircraft guns which ringed the target plus the firepower of the Imperial Navy warships at anchor. Thick grey smoke rose up from the fires burning on the docks and the fires on two of the merchant ships which had been hit by the first wave of strafers. More heavy grey smoke rose from Lakunai airfield.

The fearless Mitchell crews skimmed through the tree tops and down to strafe the docks within a blizzard of flak bursts and tracers. Johnson's three flights dropped their tanks and swept directly over the village where they saw airborne targets in every direction, but their job was to protect the Mitchell's flank at all costs. And that was precisely the price paid by trailing Blue element Lt. Francis Love.

## BLUE FLIGHT AND THE DEATH OF FRANCIS LOVE

The air over Rabaul was criss-crossed by the most murderous A/A gunfire any Flying Knight had ever braved. Capt. Johnson's Red quartet was over the docks within range of the anchored warships, while Lt. Planck's Green Flight and Lt. Norm Hyland's Blue Flight were to the left over the heavy guns in the hills above the town.

Just as the Americans passed over the town, Blue Flt Ldr Hyland was suddenly met head-on by a mottled ZERO and he pressed the trigger on his control wheel purely by reflex condition. As the Knights' first kill of the mission tumbled into the forest, Hyland looked back to check on his elements, only to see Love's P-38 falling in flames. Whether he had been hit by flak, or shot from the end of the line by enemy fighters, it was impossible to tell.

The Mitchells turned for the escape back to the east and the Knights wheeled after them. There over the massive volcanic cone called Crater Mountain which rose on the west bank of the harbor was an ominous swarm of some fifty ZEROs. The Knights' test had only begun.

The ten remaining Flying Knights pulled the noses of their P-38s into the air and opened up a murderous return fire at the radial-engine fighters which fell upon them from every direction. Blue wingman Del Moore reached 3000 feet, then dropped his guns on a ZERO which shuddered from the .50 caliber blows and rolled straight down into the bay. Blue wingman Doug Barrett clobbered a ZEKE at point blank range just above the water and it cart-wheeled into a geyser of silvery spray. Barrett damaged another as his Blue teammates finally fought their way to safety beyond Cape Gazelle.

*9 FS wingmen Doug Barrett with "pistolero" Francis Love who crashed in flames west of Rabaul village during the great November 2nd raid.*

## GREEN FLIGHT and PLANCK'S COLLISION

Lt. Carl Planck's Green trio pushed through the smoke drifting over the western shoreline and peered ahead at the wall of enemy planes. As they turned with the bombers and rose up to counter the assault, Flt Ldr Planck exchanged gun fire with an onrushing ZERO and the enemy took a fatal hit, then exploded. Planck fired at a second opponent from head-on, and as his rounds struck home, the ZERO plunged straight into his left engine and sheered off the prop, then slid beneath his Lightning and slammed into the left tail assembly. Even without his rudders, Planck managed to drift downward through a full turn to the left and set off to the southeast.

In the same time frame, Green wingmen Al Lewelling and Bob Wood had also fired at the oncoming horde. Lewelling's OSCAR opponent had already bailed out when the lieutenant looked to his right to see his flight leader's collision. Instinctively, Lewelling and Wood swerved violently aside, but neither Green Flight wingman could account for their stricken flight leader after that moment. Eastward bound at high speed, Wood reported enemy gunfire had knocked out his left supercharger. The two surviving Green wingmen closed ranks and pressed on together for Kiriwina.

## RED FLIGHT'S MAD DASH OVER THE HARBOR

The Red Flight team of Squadron Leader Johnson, wingman Lt. Stan Johnson, element leader Capt. Bill Haney and wingman 2Lt. Glade Hill all fired at the first wave of ZEROs which assaulted them north of the village. Mission leader Johnson's first victim fell just west of the town and when the Red quartet turned east, he destroyed his second target while wingman Stan Johnson flamed another which dropped away to crashed near Vunakanau strip. The Red elements climbed for greater advantage and entered into the monumental dogfighter that broke out just east of the anchored enemy ships.

Red element leader Haney entered into the last and most dangerous engagement of his life. He and wingman Hill turned through four firing passes with the enemy, but the exchange was so fierce,

*Capt. Bill Haney hit four enemy fighters in the swarm over Simpson Harbor on November 2nd, but none could be definitely confirmed. Likely an ace and one of the most respected 5 FC pilots, the weary captain gladly opted for home after the 9 FS P-38s stood down and no one questioned his decision.*

neither Flying Knight could confirm the final demise of the captain's four heavily damaged targets. As the Red pair withdrew, Haney swung aside to chase off a ZERO which had pounced upon a smoking Lightning, but the captain was in turn distracted by another enemy plane. Unable to find the stricken P-38 again and out of ammo against the myriad of targets, frustrated veteran Bill Haney safely withdrew from the onslaught.

## THE ODYSSEY OF CARL PLANCK

When the nine surviving Knights debriefed after the great November 2nd raid, they tried to make sense of all the incidents that had passed within that horrid 15 minutes of absolute madness over Simpson Harbor, but the two missing men overwhelmed everyone's recollections. There was no question that Francis Love's ship had exploded in the jungle, but there was the burning plane that Capt. Haney had tried to cover during the withdrawal. Indeed, the stricken P-38 was Planck's battle-rammed machine.

Diminutive Carl Planck had endured cannon rounds and a mid-air crash to nurse his battered aircraft all the way to the east coast of New Britain, well beyond Cape Gazelle. He made a ditching in Wide Bay and gashed his head, but was able to reach the shore before nightfall. He pressed into the jungle interior for cover and collapsed of exhaustion. He did not stir until morning light.

He started into the high country to seek out any friendly native camp, but found no one for at least six days. Living off coconut meat and rain water, he finally found a friendly tribe who nursed back some of his strength. In two weeks, he was escorted in darkness deeper into the interior highlands. His host tribe eventually provided him with medicine stolen from a Japanese camp, and his head wound finally healed over. After several more days, the pilot was taken to another tribe who was in contact with the local Australian coast watchers.

Planck provide the tribesmen with a note bearing his physical description as well as his Clemson College class ring. The Australians immediately responded to his message, particularly to the reference of the downed flyer's premature baldness. He was thrilled to learn the Australians had a safe coastal encampment and he readily joined the coast watchers to better his chances for a submarine escape from New Britain. Although he was forced to wait for two months, Carl Planck and three other survivors were finally spirited out of Wide Bay by a U.S. Navy sub.

The 49ers had long since moved forward to the big airfield complex north of Nadzab, and his old mates were stunned when the ghostly frail lieutenant met them in the Flying Knights bar. Planck was under security restrictions and did not tell any details of his adventure, nor did he linger with the 9 FS men. After his brief, happy reunion, Carl Planck went home to America and never flew again. He never spoke to another 49er for fifty years.

## BONG PASSES THE TWENTY VICTORY MARK; NOVEMBER 5, 1943

Three days after the infamous raid, two refurbished war-weary P-38s were put back in the 9 FS flight line and another eleven Knights were once again bound to Rabaul. Capt. Bong led the mission as

*Near exhaustion and suffering a nagging toothache, leading ace Dick Bong had to settle for twenty-one victories, five shy of the Rickenbacker record. When the Lightnings were struck from the 9 FS roster in mid-November, weary Bong furloughed home.*

high cover for the Liberators, but the smashed Japanese fighter wing could only put up a meager effort. At a quarter past noon, Bong's elements swept high over Vunakanau airdrome where a widely scattered formation of enemy fighters were seen three thousand feet below.

In the initial descent, Blue element leader Francis Nutter fired his last rounds in anger at an enemy aircraft, but he completely missed his mark. Green Flt Ldr Bill Bleecker fared better when one of his two targets rolled into an escape dive leaving a trail of debris. But no one saw it crash.

Ace Dick Bong was the only pilot to have a pair of ZERO victories confirmed. The first was hit from dead astern and blew up before the enemy aviator ever had a chance to maneuver out of the way. Seconds later, the ace caught his 21st victim at 5000 feet above Vunakanau, and it too, disintegrated in a fireball. The fight was over as quickly as it had begun. Bong recalled the Knights and set off for Dobodura.

## HANIOTIS BAILS OUT OFF THE SOUTH COAST; NOVEMBER 5, 1943

The Knights had only flown a short distance from the target area when Lt. George Haniotis radioed his position to the standby res-

cue flights at Kiriwina. Haniotis bailed out several hundred yards off shore and was last seen afloat a few miles east of Arawe.

On the following day, the search flight from Kiriwina hunted all along the south New Britain coast, but Haniotis had disappeared. Two days later, a returning flight of B-25s reported an Allied raft floating off shore at Cape Glouster and heading out into the Vitiaz Strait. It was most likely Haniotis, for two weeks after that last sighting, the deflated raft washed ashore on the New Guinea shore north of Cape Ward Hunt. The serial number verified the raft as the one assigned to the missing Flying Knight, but his body was never found.

## BONG'S LAST DAYS AS A FLYING KNIGHT

The night of November 5th, Gen. Kenney attended the celebration in the Flying Knights' bar and praised the young woodsman from Wisconsin for his extraordinary bravery. Capt. Dick Bong, four times an ace, was the toast of the Pacific campaign as the first man to break the twenty victories mark. The captain was now very close to the standing American record of twenty-six aerial victories set by Eddie Rickenbacker in World War I. Everyone wondered where Bong would find his next six victims to break the tie and Kenney, eager to use Bong's feat as a promotional bargaining chip with the

War Department in Washington, would give the young captain every chance possible.

## STAN JOHNSON LOST OVER NEW BRITAIN; NOVEMBER 7, 1943

Two days after Bong's last "double" over Rabaul, newly promoted Capt. John "Jump" O'Neill led seven tattered 9 FS Lightnings on another high altitude sweep of Rabaul and Simpson Harbor. Once again, O'Neill's flight dropped on a small formation of ZEROs and several were hit, but none were confirmed, not even for accompanying Flt Ldr Bong.

The mission also ended in tragedy when another senior man failed to return. Bong's wingman, Lt. Stan Johnson, was last seen chasing a target inland from the harbor, but he never returned to Dobodura. Bong was devastated and refused to fly another mission with any other wingman.

Four days later, the last six serviceable aircraft in the 9 FS sortied with the Lightning wing to Rabaul. Cocky ace Lt. Ralph Wandrey reassured Bong that on that mission, he would fly the captain's wing and keep pace in his determined hunt for those six tempting victories, regardless of the threat. He had no idea of Bong's resolve.

The mission progressed normally to Simpson Harbor, but the P-38s found no action. Driven to break the Rickenbacker record, Bong decided to hunt a little closer to the source. From high over the Mother and Daughter peaks, Bong took wingman Wandrey on a heart-stopping race straight between the volcanic cones and right down the main street of the European colonial village. Roaring over the trees tops of the dusty boulevard median, Wandrey nervously chuckled as pedestrians scrambled for cover and vehicles careened on to side streets. Wandrey rocked his big fighter up in an aileron turn and glanced down at a man who burst out of his room in his bathrobe to gaze up from his second floor balcony at the audacious American pilots. In tight formation, the aces pulled up into a screaming climb with flak bursting in their wake. Still, no enemy aircraft would answer the challenge and Dick Bong never fired another round in his war-weary Lightning.

After the aces' wild promenade down Rabaul's main street, the 9th Squadron stood down from the mission schedule. The last

*New 9 FS Republic P-47 Thunderbolts on the Horanda flightline in the last week of November, 1943.*

*Capt. Bong with C.C. Elwood Barden and A.C. Art Finkle at the end of the 1943 Lockheed era. Had crewmen been accredited with victories, Barden would have outscored all the 49ers since aces Andy Reynolds, Dick Bong and Gerry Johnson ran up over 40 victories in the sergeant's P-40 and P-38s, respectively.*

of the P-38s that had carried them through countless sorties to a total of 169 aerial kills were too battle-worn to continue. On November 12th, Capt. Gerry Johnson formally announced what every man had expected for some time. The faded Lockheed's were turned over to the maintenance squadron at Dobodura and the majority of senior officers, including Dick Bong, were given the option to return Stateside. As of that day, the remaining Flying Knights would take up duties with the Republic P-47 Thunderbolt.

## END OF AN ERA AT DOBODURA; NOVEMBER, 1943

Dobodura had changed dramatically for LtC. Selman's fighter group. With the loss of the Flying Knights' P-38s, Melikian's 7 FS was the last 49ers unit on flight status at the expanding airdrome, but more bomber units were taking up permanent residence at Horanda strip and air traffic there had become a tangle. The Demons were told to gear up for the move to their new base at Gusap in the Ramu River Valley.

Some of the 49ers actually regretted abandoning the jungle camp that had been home since they had ventured there in the great Buna campaign of 1942. But the enemy soldiers had long escaped to the north or had been killed in the terrible destruction at Salamaua and Lae. The 49ers part in that defeat, and particularly the Flying Knights part in the Rabaul raids, would result in the unit's third Distinguished Unit Citation.

With the fighting now far beyond the range of their P-40s and P-47s, and it was time to move on. While the men at Dobodura broke camp for the November advance, the enemy likewise attempted to fortify their weakening grasp of the northern New Guinea coast. More Imperial soldiers and pilots were marshalled to aid their besieged forces at Wewak, but the Empire was desperately short of supplies and fresh troops. There was no force strong enough to stop MacArthur's juggernaut which had gained ominous momentum beneath General Kenney's 5th Air Force, nor could any man on the island of New Guinea foresee the awesome destruction that would yield forth in the next twelve months.

# 15

# ADVANCE INTO CENTRAL NEW GUINEA

By November of 1943, Central Pacific U.S. Navy forces and the 13th AF in the Solomon Islands had grown sufficiently in strength to effect the final assault on Japan's crumbling command post at Rabaul. Simultaneously, General MacArthur turned the full weight of his Southwest Pacific command for the liberation of central New Guinea.

The scope of the New Guinea front had expanded ever further to the west, and Gen. Kenney again found his 5 AF to be Mac-

Arthur's most potent strategic weapon. In targeting Japan's 4th Air Army headquarters at Wewak, Kenney designated an aerial task force composed of attack bombers, fighters, transports and the necessary ground support which would move beyond the Markham Valley headwaters into the contiguous Ramu River Valley. The new strategic group was named the 308th Bomb Wing Air Task Force and its designated commander was none other than the 49ers' former boss, Colonel Don "Fighter" Hutchinson.

*Blacksheep Lt. Drier' aircraft #52 "SUGAR" slow-timing a new Allison engine over the Ramu Valley in December, likewise displaying new 8 FS marking of yellow/black spinner and tail cap. The Finistere Mtns. lay beneath the usual overcast that veiled the approach of Madang-based raiders just ten minutes flight-time to the east.*

## NEW RESIDENTS ON THE RAMU RIVER; EARLY NOVEMBER 1943

In this interim, Australian Commander Vasey's vanguard 7th Division had pursued the retreating enemy into the Finistere Mountains on the eastern flank of the Ramu Valley. In the highlands called Shaggy Ridge, the Australians stalled in a vicious battle with the entrenched rear guard. Vasey once again called upon the trusted 5 AF airborne artillery, and Hutchinson dutifully responded by calling up Capt. Harris' Blacksheep in the last week of October to the sprawling airdrome nearing completion at Gusap village. The Blacksheep set up camp in the sparse forest five mile east of Gusap and began operations from the dirt strip nearer the village designated as Gusap #3.

Only five air minutes from the highlands battle line, the Warhawks hefted their 500-pounders up to blast the enemy off the northern most five-thousand foot promontory known as the Pimple. By month's end, the 7th Division was able to push the Imperial survivors deeper into the coastal valley for the final bloody assault on Bogadjim.

Task Force CO Hutchinson had also been well appraised of the increased enemy activity at the airdromes of Bogadjim, Madang and Alexishafen, just thirty miles beyond the Finistere range. Other Gusap airstrips would soon be ready and aircover for Ramu Valley would become the 49ers top priority, but until the runway construction was finished, base defense fell squarely on Ernie Harris' Blacksheep.

While the 8th Squadron air echelon fit the tactical campaign against the Finistere high country, the ground echelon attempted to improve their bivouac. Despite intermittent rain showers, the enemy welcomed them each morning with air raids which sent everyone clambering into the rain soaked trenches. Although an early warning radar team and A/A flak units were installed for additional base defense, the Blacksheep crews never felt secure as the enemy usually struck Dumpu before the alarm could sound.

## BARNETT'S REPLY

Blacksheep Ops Exec Clyde "Smiley" Barnett was the last Darwin cadre veteran to hold a flying job in the 5th Fighter Command. Temporarily set back in the Papuan campaign with an ear infection, Capt. Barnett had bid his time as a ground officer and intelligence man, but he hoped his overseas tour would culminate in the cockpit. Now once again in a Blacksheep Warhawk and within range of the enemy, Smiley had a personal vendetta to settle on behalf of the "old timers."

The able Ops Exec had built up an intense, personal contempt for the abysmal base defense setup and the constant interruptions brought on by the Wewak raiders. Within the incredulous muddle of building shelters, pumping water from the bomb shelters and servicing the mud-spattered Warhawks, Barnett's pilots were hard pressed to keep a patrol aloft each day plus flying the dive-bomber missions to the highlands. The Blacksheep rarely had more the twenty P-40s airworthy at a time.

After obtaining reconnaissance photos of the Madang and Bogadjim airfields, Smiley Barnett thought it high time to return the favor to the rascals on the coast. Blacksheep CO Harris readily

concurred and notified Fighter Hutch who jokingly reflected that "Smiley's tenacity was such that lesser men dare not contest." The colonel gave Barnett the green light.

## MORNING MISSION; NOVEMBER 7, 1943

On the 7th, Ops Exec Barnett, wingman F/O Walt Linder, element leader Lt. Jim Carter and wingman Lt. Nelson Flack lifted off just before 7:00 A.M. and climbed due north through the thin haze over the Finistere range. After reaching the coast in merely ten minutes, the Blacksheep quartet swept ten miles out over the sea past Bogadjim to put the sun at their backs and then proceeded to hunt northward at 10,000 feet. They momentarily followed what appeared to be a squadron of B-25s which soon disappeared in the haze far below. Only minutes later, they came abreast of Alexishafen and it was there the Blacksheep caught sight of a broad formation estimated as twenty-five muddy-brown, radial-engine fighters. Barnett, Linder, Carter and Flack did not hesitate an instant. They toggled off their belly tanks and dropped out of the sun against the three rear-most Nakajimas.

It was "damned near perfection" by Barnett's estimation. In the first pass, the flight leader, Linder and Flack closed to within dead-six o'clock, point-blank range of the trailing enemy trio and all three targets erupted in flames before any of the sentai wingmen knew they were under attack. The remaining OSCARs wheeled about in confusion as Barnett, Linder and Carter plunged to the southwest for home.

Nelson Flack, however, bravely took advantage of the circumstances and after three complete turns with the wildly maneuvering sentai, the lone lieutenant killed his second victim with a wide deflection shot. Flack climbed out to 16,000 feet to peer back down on Barnett's victim burning on the beach and three smoking oil slicks in the water. Unable to contact his flight, the lingering lieutenant turned off for home.

Flack touched down at Gusap to an ecstatic welcome. Barnett led the cheering mob that met him as he stepped down from his Warhawk which bore a single bullet hole in the fuselage. It was 0745 hours. The four-victory mission had spanned only fifty minutes of flight time.

Two more flights were sent back to Alexishafen that day, but the Japanese did not return until the last P-40 sweep flown early in the afternoon. The CO himself had strapped on his #57 CAROLINA BELLE and led the final eight ship sortie off at 1300 hours. They proceeded straight to Bogadjim.

*Ops Exec Barnett lifts off in his last aircraft #55 P-40N "MIAMI MISHAP" at Gusap. While promoted Maj. Harris languished on restricted flight duty, Darwin veteran Barnett effectively led the Blacksheep and scored his last career victory on November 7th. Barnett's tour also ended in late November and he left with Harris.*

## AFTERNOON MISSION; NOVEMBER 7

Capt. Harris took Lts. John Hanson, element leader Charlie Petersen and wingman Phil Hurst up in his Red Flight while ace Lt. Bob White headed up the Blue Flight quartet of Lts. Joel Thorvaldson, element leader Fats Elofson and wingman 2Lt. Merle Wolfe. They climbed to 12,000 feet over the coast where the next sighting occurred. Harris pursued the enemy planes north beyond Alexishafen, but they disappeared within the overcast just as the Gusap controller called in a radar contact back over their home base which was coming in from the southwest. The Blacksheep reversed course and headed back inland. While southbound, they made contact directly over Bogadjim village.

## RED FLIGHT STARTS THE FIGHT

A northbound line astern formation of twelve OSCARs pulled into view below at 5000 feet and Harris immediately set after them from head-on. The OSCARs responded by climbing into the Blacksheep attack and Harris executed a split-S with wingman Hanson to cut off the leading Ki-43. When the missions leader's target typically countered with a tight aerial loop, he riddled it as it stalled out in the top of the arc, then half-rolled out of his descent to escape the enemy wingman.

Red element leader Petersen had held on throughout the initial maneuver and kept the other OSCARs in sight. As the enemy wingmen turned to fire, Petersen cut across their flight path and raked a Ki-43 with .50 caliber tracers in a wide defection shot. The "blue nose" explosive rounds flashed on the wingroot and canopy, but before he could see it crash, the lieutenant was forced to evade the other sentei wingmen. Meanwhile, wingman Hurst clobbered another OSCAR in mid-fuselage and Harris saw that victim explode on impact in the forest west of Bogadjim.

## BLUE FLIGHT'S ENGAGEMENT

Lt. Bob White's Blue Flight also had a flawless encounter. Just as ace Harris had done seconds before, the blue leader and wingman Thorvaldson followed one of the sentai men upward where White's deadly accuracy sawed off the OSCAR's left wing for the ninth and last victory of his combat tour. Blue element leader Elofson also fired at White's victim, then both of the lead Blue elements picked out two more targets. That next go around, Joel Thorvaldson was successful after a head-on firing pass. Tail-end Merle Wolfe would confirm Thorvalson's only career kill.

Harris signalled for the two flights to regroup and they all returned to Gusap where Lt. Hanson experienced the only bad luck of the day. Hanson's prop control failed on final approach causing him to over shoot the dirt strip. The Warhawk pancaked in the rough and would be dragged off for salvage, but luckily, Hanson walked away without a scratch. What mattered most to Capt. Harris that day was his pilots had won hands down with six confirmed, two probable and no losses. General Kenney was so pleased with the entire Ramu Valley operation that he sent his personal congratulations to the 308th Bombwing staff. Graciously, Hutchinson responded with high praise for the Blacksheep leader's part in the

*Blacksheep ace Flt Ldr Bob White after his final career victory on November 7th near Bojadjim.*

venture and he summarily promoted Ernie Harris to the rank of major on November 8th.

## SCREAMIN' DEMONS TO GUSAP; NOVEMBER 10, 1943

On November 10th, Lt. Paul Kell led the first echelon of 7 FS personnel into their new bivouac twenty miles southwest of Gusap village and five miles below the junction of the main Ramu stream and smaller Gusap River. Engineering personnel erected a tent facility for Line Chief M/Sgt Robert Witteberg and his crews in the kunai grass next to the rough hewn 5000 foot long dirt runway. It lay east-west and terminated not far from the east bank of the Ramu. The crews were ready to receive their Warhawks by the second day at their strip which was designated Gusap #7.

Within the week, LtC. Selman moved his 49ers Group HQ people into their new bivouac just a few miles southeast of Gusap #7. Operations began in earnest and the Demons assumed daily patrols to orient themselves to the new surroundings.

At the same time, a squadron of 3rd Attack A-20 Havocs began to fly from the longer strip called Gusap #10, just north of the Demons on the north side of the Gusap River. All of these runways were essentially in the open as there was no forest to provide a secure dispersal area. Shallow earthen revetments had been piled up by tractor graders as the only protection against enemy attacks. At Gusap #7, the Demons dispersed their P-40s on the north side of the runway via a dirt track that wound through the earthen stands.

## MORE GREETING FROM WEWAK; NOVEMBER 15, 1943

The Imperial commanders at Wewak had feared for months what now was taking place in the valleys of the interior, just beyond the coastal mountain range. The threat of Vasey's army at Dumpu in early October had certainly been a serious omen, even with their retreating forces holding the high ground. But the arrival of Warhawks and A-20s at Gusap which now swept the coast, plus the presence of even more B-24s and Lightnings in the great airdrome at Nadzab now made the situation critical.

The JAAF answered with a broad aerial assault across the breadth of Col. Hutchinson's tactical command, striking as many

*8 FS Bob Aschenbrener's aircraft #46 "NAUGHTY MARIETTA" flown at Marilinan and Gusap. The aircraft name was from a popular movie musical as well as an homage to the pilot's mother. "MARIETTA" got the first two victories for the future ace on November 15th.*

airfields in the Ramu valley as possible. In particular, the 208th Sentai LILY bombers with heavy escort from the 1st and 248th Sentai OSCARs sortied into the 49ers airspace on November 15th.

After formating at Madang, the raiders flew south just above the haze capping Shaggy Ridge until they were due east of Gusap village. At 14,000 feet just across the plain from their objective, the LILYs wheeled westward on to their bombing run.

## MAKOWSKI'S BLACKSHEEP PATROL

At that same moment, senior Lt. Bernie Makowski was in the lead of an eight-ship Blacksheep patrol which was stacked between 8000 to 12,000 feet. The Warhawks had just turned north over Gusap proper when they spotted the raiders still some distance to the east. Makowski requested confirmation of the suspect formation, but the air controller's response was unclear. Makowski turned his flights eastward to have closer look through the haze and came head to head with the Nakajimas.

Makowski's higher Yellow Flight wingmen were Joel Thorvalson, Don Meuten and Jim Reynolds. Blue Flight at the lower level was led by lanky Lt. Danny Moore with wingmen Bill Runey, Bob Aschenbrener and Willie Drier. When Moore called for the attack, one the OSCARs was so close that Runey thought, "This Jap must think I'm his wingman."

## BLUE FLIGHT FIRES FIRST

Moore, Runey, Ash and Drier dropped their tanks and lifted the Warhawks' noses above the horizon at full throttle. They managed to momentarily loose the OSCARs and in five minutes, the Blue team was at 13,000 wheeling over the LILYs in their brown and green-streaked camouflage. All four of the Blue Flt Warhawks pushed ahead down the Vee's right flank until they well out in front. Moore called for the break and they rolled headlong in perfect formation right back into the face of the enemy.

Flight Ldr Moore and wingman Runey fired on the two LILYs on the formation's right side. Moore's rounds flashed against the dark fuselage of one ship, as did Runey's and Aschenbreners' vol-

leys on another. Drier was about to fire at a bomber, but the OSCARs finally intervened. In a series of tight turns, the Blue Flight pilots exchanged gunfire with the looping Ki-43's until Moore and Runey had both downed a fighter and Ash had dispatched two others.

## RED FLIGHT IS NEXT

Only seconds behind Moore's team came their redoubtable squadron mates of Red Flight. Mission Leader Makowski watched as Moore's people sped down the right side of the enemy formation, so the lieutenant held his Red Flight at bay until Blue Flight attacked. But the OSCARs began to turn toward his Warhawks and Mak could wait no longer. He called for the break and Red Flight thundered down against the LILY elements on the left flank.

Just as Blue flight had done against the right flank, so Mak's Red Flight did against the left. Mak, wingman Meuten and element leader Thorvaldson were able to bring their guns down on the bombers while their number-4 man Reynolds kept an eye on the OSCARs.

Rookie 2Lt. Meuten put on a awesome display of aerial marksmanship. After their initial pass, Meuten returned to the bombers while Mak, Thorvaldson and Reynolds tangled with the escorts. After a chandelle out of the dogfight, Meuten dropped down on a LILY from behind and methodically shot away the canopy, then gutted the cockpit and finished by sawing off a hefty portion of the right engine. The LILY with its dead crew drifted down to belly-in near Gusap where Aussie commandos would eventually take stock of the carnage.

Makowski and Thorvaldson treated the OSCARs with equal contempt. They joined in the duel between Blue Flight and the OSCARs until the Red Flight pilots each sent a Ki-43 down in flames. As the fight dropped lower in the air, the opponents began to withdraw. But the battle was not yet over.

## HARRIS' FINAL FIGHT

With the first alarm, Sqn Ldr Ernie Harris led another eight planes off from Gusap #3 and headed due south, but by the time they reached 15,000 feet, the fight had broken up. He split up his two

*Blacksheep CO Maj. Ernie Harris' P-40N #67 "CAROLINA BELLE" after his eleventh aerial kill on November 15th that was never officially confirmed. Passed over many times due to the number of senior captains in the 49ers, 5 FC typically restricted his combat time as a major. Harris disliked the politics and opted for command training in the U.S. when his tour ended in December.*

flights and took his own Red quartet off toward Madang to hunt for stragglers. En route to the coast, Harris took on errant Blue Flt Ldr Danny Moore and the five Blacksheep pressed on through the thin haze as they chased the raiders north. As they passed over Bogadjim, they caught sight of the escapees, but the bombers were much too far ahead.

The four Red Flight men dropped their tanks, and with Blue Flt Ldr Moore, they accelerated down toward the trailing OSCARs. The Blacksheep separated as they pursued the Nakajimas down closer to the ocean where Maj. Harris overtook his next victim and riddled the mottled fighter from dead astern until it burned. With his greater speed, the ace drew along side and quickly glanced at the sentai pilot who had released his seat straps and was stepping out onto the wing. But other OSCARs had drawn within gun range and Harris turned away before his victim bailed out. It was the last victory of his career, but without a witness, double-ace Harris would never have that eleventh kill officially confirmed.

## LAST MAN HOME

Lean, mean Danny Moore had also caught up to another victim beyond the shoreline and his flaming target was seen falling into the sea by members of his adopted Red Flight. With his Warhawk virtually running on fumes, he turned back down the Ramu Valley after Harris' flight turned away. Moore was the last Blacksheep to set down at Gusap strip.

It had been another successful interception for the Blacksheep and only one plane from Red Flight would crack up on landing back home. Second Lt. Hal Sawyer's ship #56 swerved off the runway in its rollout, but the pilot was unhurt and the P-40 would later be repaired.

Bill Runey's trusty old stager #47 had been the only Warhawk to take a hit against the OSCARs. A 12mm round had entered the left rear fuselage, knocked out the radio, cut the hydraulic lines, then passed on through to sever the right wing control cables and crack the rear gun mount. He landed the tough old bird without incident, but its combat days were over. Runey later took charge of old #43, another trusty mount that would serve him for another six months.

The war had taken a very positive turn for the Allies in the New Guinea theater. The advances into the central river valleys had been at the greater expense of the enemy and Gen. Kenney knew he had the right men in command at the right places. In particular, Col. Hutchinson task force and LtC. Jim Selman' 49er Warhawks seemed to have firm grasp on the airspace over Ramu Valley. And more units would soon take up operations from Dobodura to Gusap to further increase the pressure on the Japanese retreating to Wewak.

## BRINGING UP THE FLYING KNIGHTS P-47'S;
## LATE NOVEMBER, 1943

Despite having his Flying Knights still in training with their new P-47s at Dobodura, LtC. Selman would not have his group separated for long. Aggressive 9 FS CO Gary Johnson had pushed his remaining ex-Lightning pilots, as well as the newly arrived Thunder-

*Capt. Johnson signs off a flight log during the P-47 operational training era at Dobodura in December, 1943.*

bolt pilots, to qualify for attached combat duty with the veteran 348 FG as quickly as possible. The 36 FS of the 35 FG had also taken up operations with the P-47 and Maj. Johnson had already flown with both groups on several occasions.

The only setback during the month for Johnson came as the result of his own aggressive nature. During a fighter sweep to Finschhafen with Col Kearby's 348 FG, Johnson bolted from the formation and bounced a radial engine aircraft cruising just above the trees. After landing at Dobodura, Johnson soon learned his victim had not been the enemy, but an RAAF artillery spotter in a Wirraway. Badly shaken F/O R.M. Stewert survived, and Johnson personally bore a case of bootleg gin to the unfortunate Aussie.

Despite the near tragedy, Johnson was undaunted. In the first week of December, he declared enough Flying Knights had acquired adequate instruction in the big Republic fighter to resume combat. And there was now plenty of room for his Thunderbolts up north at Gusap.

As of the first week in December of 1943, LtC. Jim Selman began to orchestrate one of the most convoluted mobilizations his

*9 FS line chief Sgt. Harley Yates (lt.) surveys the salvaged P-47 purportedly flown by Flying Knights CO Johnson on attached combat duty to the 36 FS in late December. The sergeant recalled the captain had ventured too near a returning B-25 over Markham Valley and the nervous turret-gunner shot out Johnson's hydraulics. No official record of the event was recorded.*

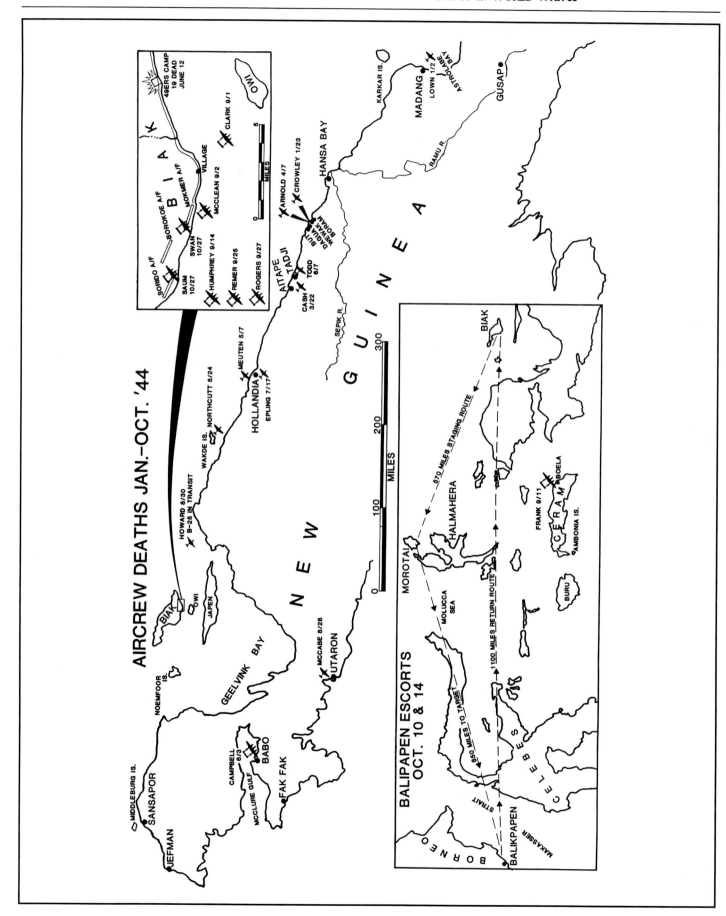

AIRCREW DEATHS JAN.–OCT. '44

BALIPAPEN ESCORTS OCT. 10 & 14

7 FS P-40N #10 carries the Screamin' Demons version of napalm bombs with detonators fitted externally to standard under-wing Curtiss drop-tanks filled with gelatin-gasoline.

Screamin' Demons country at Gusap #7 strip.

49th Fighter Group would ever experience. Their latest mission in the Wewak campaign included the change of command in two of their squadrons, plus the adaptation of a new type aircraft, and the complete transfer of their ground echelon by air to the new Ramu Valley airdrome.

Simultaneously, Selman presided over the many new commendations and advances in rank for his group. There were also senior captains who had reached command grade. Several officers took up duties with the new 49ers headquarters unit at Gusap while others continued to fly attached to whatever squadron might be in need of an experienced flight leader.

Maj. Ray Melikian of the 7 FS had seen to the preparations at Dobodura in October for the Demons' move, but had chosen to muster out for the States by month's end. Captain Arland Stanton assumed command on November 1st, and in his #20 KEYSTONE KATHLEEN, led the first of a dozen Screamin' Demons Warhawks up to Gusap strip #7 on the 16th.

New Screamin' Demons CO Arland Stanton at Gusap, December 1943.

## SCREAMIN' DEMONS LOOSE LT. GERMAIN; NOVEMBER 18, 1943

Other Demon pilots followed with the last of the 7 FS aircraft that had been in the Dobodura repair depot, but tragically, not Lt. David Germain. While on takeoff from Kalamazoo the 18th, his engine seized and the P-40 crashed. He was critically injured and immediately air transported to the hospital at Pt. Moresby where he lingered for two months. David Germain would expire on January 18, 1944.

## NEW BOSS FOR THE BLACKSHEEP

After his final engagement on November 15th, Major Ernie Harris reflected on his 250 missions and the many combat engagements over the past year. He was a candidate for relieving LtC. Selman of the group command, but that would not occur until after the New Year. Eligible to return stateside, the major passed the Blacksheep command over Capt. Bernie Makowski on November 22nd.

Harris' leadership had truly been one of the high points in the annals of the South Pacific war. He had been cited for his bravery many times and was the highest scoring P-40 ace in all the USAAF. Gen. Kenney and 5th FC Squeeze Wurtsmith were hard pressed to find another leader who possessed the calm assuredness that Harris had always displayed.

Harris returned to a stellar career as a test pilot for the USAAF bureau of development. Later as a group commander, he took the first American jet-equipped fighter unit to the European theater in 1945, only to die in a landing accident in Italy three years after the war ended.

## ERRANT CROFT TO THE FLY RIVER; DECEMBER 4, 1943

The shear ruggedness and magnitude of the New Guinea interior required a pilot to be totally familiar with all of the landmarks along the mission routes, but to newcomer Lt. Bob Croft of the 7 FS, a radio receiver knocked out by the Madang flak guns and a solid cloud deck would make his return to Gusap a nightmare. Croft

*8 FS aircraft #47 flown by Lt. Winternitz closes in for a close look at an escorted B-25 in the December campaign.*

coasted past the Ramu Valley until his fuel was consumed and he was forced down 200 miles to the southeast on the broad plain of the Fly River. Luckily, his emergency transmissions at the time of his crash landing had been monitored by the Australians at Marauke on the south coast. He left his P-40 on the kunai field and was picked up by liaison aircraft which took him Pt. Moresby. He eventually caught a transport back to Gusap on December 9th.

## FLYING KNIGHTS' THUNDERBOLTS;
## DECEMBER 10, 1943

Up at Gusap, a second, parallel airstrip had been prepared on the south side of the 3rd Attack's strip #10. This slightly shorter runway covered with pierced steel matting was called #5 and designated for the 9 FS. When word reached Dobodura that #5 was complete, CO Gerry Johnson hand picked wingman 2Lt. Ray Swift, element leader Capt. Walter Markey and wingman Lt. Ralph Wandrey to join him in the first official combat sortie to their new home.

The line crews quickly gave a final pre-flight check to the four chosen aircraft. They particularly fine tuned the Major's #83 with its bold twin command stripes around the portly fuselage and the

score board displaying thirteen Japanese flags under the cockpit. As the highest scoring 49ers ace in residence, cock-sure Gerry Johnson believed in showing the Flying Knights' best, even if it was himself.

The flight was particularly well attended in that the Knights' oldest Darwin veteran would fly along in Ralph Wandrey's Jug – none other than the 9 FS mascot – big white Huckleberry Duck. With the fowl firmly wrapped in a sheet and stuffed under Wandrey's seat, the slender lieutenant settled into the spacious cockpit and chuckled to himself as Huckleberry chattered away beneath his butt. The quacking was drowned out as the pilot revved the 2000 horsepower Pratt & Whitney Double Wasp engine in the pre-flight check. Wandrey peered down the line-up at the commander's plane and the Major signal "thumbs-up." The lieutenant closed his canopy, then noted the time and weather in his log; 0740 hours and clear. The P-47 quartet rolled forward and true to the brute fighter's name, they literally thundered off Horanda strip.

They rose up to 9000 feet for the hour's cross-country flight and set course due north toward the fair-weather clouds drifting over the north end of Markham Valley. The four Thunderbolt drivers had no inkling of the frantic reception awaiting them beyond the hazy horizon.

*9 FS CO Capt. Gerry Johnson's P-47D-5 at Dobodura in December with his thirteen kills acquired in P-38s being stencilled beneath the cockpit.*

## THE GREATER GUSAP RAIDS OF DECEMBER, 1943

The enemy at Wewak once again attempted a maximum effort against the swelling Allied airdrome. The TONY pilots of the rested 68th Sentai had recently returned from Manila and with the sister 78th Sentai, they staged into Madang in the first week of December. Those veteran units were reinforced by the newcomer OSCARs of the 33rd and 63th Sentais who had recently deployed to the Southwestern front. The veteran OSCAR crews of the 24th and 248th also staged into Alexischafen in the following week, providing the 4th Air Army with over eighty fighter aircraft for the next blow to be leveled at Gusap.

On December 10th, the Japanese commenced with the main fighter sweep of TONYs from Madang which took off at daybreak and paraded straight into Ramu Valley. The Ki-61s normally flew in four-ship elements while the greater number of Ki-43s formated at random and usually at a higher altitude. They masked their approach within the veil of broken clouds above the Finistere range and the first wave of mottled TONYs dropped down to strafe the Gusap runways before the alarm was sounded. As the first machinegun rounds and small bombs rained down on the Allied airdrome, the call was heard by the standing patrol of Warhawks cruising over Gusap.

## BAD BEGINNING FOR THE NEW BLACKSHEEP BOSS; DECEMBER 10, 1943

Newly installed 8 FS CO Capt. Makowski had been airborne with an eight-ship patrol for only thirty minutes when the alert was broadcast. The captain turned his Red Flight foursome due south at 9500 feet over Dumpu and headed up the Ramu. White Flt Ldr Lt. Carl Lambert led his people along the same heading on the CO's left.

The Blacksheep were desperately twisting through the broken cloud formations in the hunt when off to the east, Captain Mak caught sight of four dark-brown, inline-engine types at his level which were followed by a larger scattered formation of OSCARs at 14,000 feet. For an instantaneous, uncertain moment, Mak studied the situation. He disliked the odds, so he fatefully decided to turn off and climb to a higher attack position. As his Red Flight slowly entered a climbing right turn, Mak suddenly reversed direction when they entered a cloud and the entire flight completely separated. The interception disrupted into a route.

As Lambert's White Flight entered their climbing turn and lost sight of the captain's leading planes, all hell broke loose. Tail-end F/O Walt Linder heard the sickening thud of 12mm rounds exploding on his Warhawk and he called for the break. Warhawks, belly tanks, OSCARs, TONYs and tracers whirled about in the misty sky.

## LINDER LIMPS FOR HOME

Linder had been clobbered and truly had to fight for his life. As Prestone coolant streamed in a fine white vapor from his Warhawk's ripped cowling, he could not run, but was forced to fight it out alone. He fired on the wheeling sentai pilots, but they had the full advantage of surprise and numbers. The F/O scored only a few hits while the enemy chopped his Warhawk to pieces.

There was only an instant when Linder found the way clear to the south. He nosed his smoking Warhawk downward, but the Ki-61s were equal to the P-40 in a sprint and quickly negating his escape. Another explosive round detonated on the back side of Linder's headrest and shrapnel whistled through the cockpit slashing his left ankle. The battered Allison engine sputtered and fully seized eight miles north of the airfield. Luckily, the F/O was able to belly land on the kunai prairie and he safely stepped out of the shredded P-40 without further injury. Inspection later confirmed more than a hundred rounds of enemy gunfire had hit his plane.

Meanwhile overhead, veteran Red element leader Bill Runey in his reliable old #43 would be the only Blacksheep to reach an altitude advantage over one of the OSCARs. In a head-on pass, Runey raked the Nakajima from wingtip to wingtip and knocked a piece off its right wing. He wanted to turn and finish the job, but the odds against him were much too great. He dove away to the north as more of the OSCAR wingmen swarmed in from above.

Runey landed back at Gusap to find his opponent had put one 12mm round through #43's right wing, but once again, the trusty Warhawk had brought the lieutenant home without a scratch. In spite of the Blacksheeps total disarray in the interception, Runey, Linder and the rest of Makowski's men had been incredibly lucky.

## THE FLYING KNIGHTS HAVE ARRIVED; 0900 HOURS

Maj. Johnson and his three 9 FS wingmen had just entered Gusap airspace and were descending for their landing at 0845 hours when they were alerted by the broadcast on the Gusap air controller "NEPHEW" channel. They eagerly armed their gun switches and pushed back up to 9000 feet among the scattered clouds. After a fifteen minute hunt 20 miles beyond Gusap village, the Thunderbolt quartet turned back and instantly crossed the flight path of eight dirty brown TONYs heading for the coast at 5000 feet. The veteran Flying Knights dropped their tanks and nosed the huge P-47s over into a head-on attack. In seconds, the massive fighters were closing in on their quarry at well over 400 Mph. Mission leader Johnson and element leader Capt. Markey each open fire with their eight .50 caliber guns. The major's target was only damaged, but Markey's victim crumpled within the barrage and the burning Ki-61 dropped straight down to the valley floor.

The speeding Thunderbolts zoom-climbed and wheeled about for the next frontal assault which produced Markey's second kill of the day. That Ki-61 would be the last confirmed victory of the captain's career and it dropped into the hills due south of Bogadjim. Gerry Johnson latched on to a turning Kawasaki and flamed its engine with a fine deflection shot. The Tony pilot tumbled from the cockpit and parachuted into the valley near a commando camp. He was promptly captured by the Aussies and executed on the spot.

As for elements Swift and Wandrey, they had been in perfect position to fire at several targets, but they could only feint at the TONYs and OSCARS due to both of their P-47s having faulty gun switches. Ace Wandrey was all the more disgruntled to find that his frantic passenger, Huckleberry Duck, had wriggled free from its hiding place under the seat. Wandrey was resigned to fly combat in a fighter without guns, plus wrestle with a terrified bird who covered the cockpit floor with molted feathers and excrement. Luckily for the Flying Knights, all were able to land at Gusap #5 unscathed.

*7 FS Ops Exec Capt. Bobby Harrison holds up one finger to signify his confirmed career kill after the December 10th interception in aircraft #23 "MY PET."*

Unluckily for Huckleberry, he later fell victim to one of the camp dogs. Wandrey could not have cared less.

## BLUE SCREAMIN' DEMONS STRUGGLE; 0920 HOURS

As the raiders withdrew to their coastal bases, the Screamin' Demons were simultaneously inland bound from a fighter sweep to Hansa Bay. The mission was led by newly appointed Assistant Ops Exec Lt. Bobby Harrison. His Blue Flight wingman was the new CO, Capt. Arland Stanton and they were accompanied by element leader Capt. Sheldon Brinson and his wingman, Lt. Bob DeHaven. As the clouds closed in during the egress from their objective, the other four-ship flight led by Ops Exec Capt. Carl Aubry separated from view.

At 0920 hours, the Blue quartet had just passed Madang a few miles inland at 12,000 feet when Flt Ldr Harrison called out the mixed flight of TONYs and OSCARs down below headed for Alexischafen. Immediately, Harrison went on the attack with Capt. Stanton in close support. Seconds later, element leader Brinson and wingman DeHaven followed. What ensued would be the fight of Bob DeHaven's life.

Harrison's accurate volley sent down one of the TONYs which crashed near Alexischafen. Capt. Stanton dispatched one of the Ki-43s which slammed down in the missionary churchyard in Madang village. Capt. Brinson was about to fire at a TONY when DeHaven spotted another enemy wingman who in turn had targeted Brinson. DeHaven fired a wide angle deflection to distract the attacker, but was forced to break away when yet another Ki-61 swept into firing range. As Brinson momentarily withdrew, he was surprised to see DeHaven's target, though seemly not damaged, be abandoned by the pilot who dropped into the jungle beneath his chute. Brinson reengaged in the pursuit of two other targets, but was unable to relocate the young ace wingman who had just saved his neck. Indeed, DeHaven could have used some help for he had gotten into an very tight spot.

## DeHAVEN'S DILEMMA

The trailing sentai pilot who fell in behind young DeHaven's #13 was obviously a veteran of some substance. With his first burst of machinegun fire, DeHaven's rudder controls went dead. The Demon pilot racked the P-40 into a mind-numbing aileron roll and started down in a twisting descent, but the TONY pilot coolly held his position at DeHaven's six-o'clock. Each time #13 bottomed out in its rolling maneuver, the sentai ace laid in a devastating volley of 12mm rounds. DeHaven's radio was shot out. The ammo bay in the left wing exploded. A quick glance over his shoulder only confirmed his executioner was closing fast. DeHaven frantically peered down the long nose of his riddled Warhawk and could see the Gusap airfields still minutes away. He didn't think he was going to make it.

DeHaven had run out of altitude and could only skim over the treetops in his last attempt to shake his pursuer. He looked back for what he thought was the last time, and was elated to see the TONY abruptly snap upward into a chandelle to formate with four other sentai wingmen who were passing in the opposite direction for the return to Madang. DeHaven was going to make it back after all, if #13 would just hold together until they reached Gusap #7.

His dilemma was far from over. Once in the landing pattern, DeHaven discovered that not only was his radio dead, but the sentai marksman had shot out his hydraulic lines. Without landing gear, flaps or any communications, he reckoned to fly straight for the east end of #7 and belly in on the side of the strip. Throttling back as far as he dared, the holed Warhawk shuddered at the edge of a stall. DeHaven gingerly swung to and fro with aileron control to bleed off his air speed. His confidence was on the mend, when suddenly there head-on from the west came a C-47 Dakota with its flaps down and landing gear extended. DeHaven advanced the throttle and dropped his left wing, using his engine torque to slip past the transport, but only by a few feet. Back at only a hundred feet above the kunai, he flew over the river and made a broad flat turn to try again from the west.

DeHaven's chest heaved as he fought to keep the shaking #13 airborne. With the Dakota now off the far end of the runway, the lieutenant drifted down on the shoulder of the track and slid to a halt in a cloud of dust. He cleared the switches, then pulled himself out of the broken ship and stood there shaking from head to toe as the scrambling squadron mates drew near. After a stiff belt of G.I. lemonade and a lot of nervous laughter, exhausted Bob DeHaven went to his quarters and slept for twenty-four hour. He was back in the air in forty-eight. (See artwork on page 158 for artist's rendering of this scenario).

## GUSAP RAID OF DECEMBER 12, 1943

Intermittent fighter sweeps were flown by both sides on the 11th, but neither side made any significant contacts in the marginal weather. On the next day, the Japanese mustered an even larger force to hit Gusap. This time, the OSCARs of the 24th and 63rd Sentais would fly cover to their big Nakajima sisters, the Ki-49 heavy bombers which the Allies code named HELEN.

At mid-morning on December 12th, Demon Blue Flt Ldr Sheldon Brinson was back on patrol with Lts. Russ Cash, element

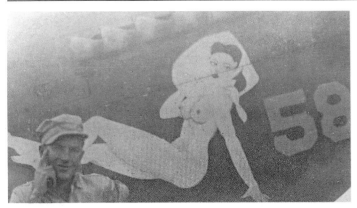

*In the third week of December, Reynolds got his new Warhawk #58 which was renumbered #68 and also named "NORMA."*

leader John Miller and ace DeHaven in the number-four spot with a brand plane. Red Flight was led by Lt. Joe O'Conner with wingmen 2Lts. Fernley Damstrom, element leader Lou Martin and wingman Lt. Lew Smith. At 1000 hours while passing over Gusap at 10,000 feet, the Demons saw a triple-Vee bomber formation and the familiar swarm of OSCARs in escort approaching from the east. O'Conner's Red Flight was closest to the enemy and he led his Warhawks in a climbing pursuit as the intruders turned away from their bomb run at 11,000 feet. As the Red quartet dropped their tanks, O'Conner's engine momentarily lost power and he fell out of formation in a flat spin. Wingman Damstrom lost contact with his flight leader and left for home. Element leader Lou Martin assumed the lead of the struggling Red Flight.

## DEMONS RED FLIGHT ONE-FOR-THREE EXCHANGE

Martin and Smith overtook the HELENs just over the foothills and bored in on the right flank of the formation. Both men targeted the nearest ship furthest to the right and fired until the HELEN's right engine began to burn. The Red pair flashed past, then swung about beneath the bomber formation and set off again against the left flank. However, a sentai tailgunner on board one of the left flank HELENs made the Demons pay dearly. Both Martin and Smith had their radiators holed and were put out of action. Both drifted down for home with overheating engines.

Red Flt Ldr O'Conner had meanwhile regained control of his sputtering P-40 and tried to overtake the bombers again. He could see the ship on the right falling behind with its right engine ablaze and was about to pull within firing range when his Warhawk shook from the blows of 12mm tracers pouring in from behind. An OSCAR had dropped into point blank range and proceeded to render O'Conner's P-40 into scrap. The flight leader miraculously escaped being wounded and was able to reach Gusap #7 for a safe landing, but the Warhawk was summarily dragged off to the junk heap.

## BLUE FLIGHT FAIRS AS POORLY

In the meantime, mission leader Brinson's Blue foursome had gained slightly more altitude than hapless Red Flight. Brinson had witnessed Red Flight's first pass and saw the smoking HELEN drop

from the right side of the formation. The Blue Flt Ldr closed in intent to make his own firing pass after Red Flight's second pass on the left flank, but just as Brinson peered through his gunsight, the deadly Ki-49 tailgunner fired another lethal burst which exploded on his canopy.

The blinding flash knocking Brinson out cold. He awoke from the concussion moments later partially blinded by the smoke and the glass shards in his eyes. There were searing shrapnel lacerations in his left arm and both legs. The captain jettisoned the shattered canopy, but when the smoke cleared, he found his instruments were in order and the Allison was still running strong. Knowing he would never survive a bail-out into the no-man's land of the coastal mountains, wounded Sheldon Brinson turned his P-40 for home.

Meanwhile, DeHaven fought it out single-handedly with the OSCARs all to way up the valley to Alexischafen. He had turned against several opponents, but was now near enough the enemy base to be concerned about groundfire. As he turned back for Gusap, he ventured upon a pair of Ki-43 stragglers and could not pass up the opportunity. He rolled over through a split-S turn to dead-astern on the trailing sentai ship. A P-47 whizzed by on his right, but the Demon ace was not distracted. The OSCAR wheeled right and DeHaven poured in a deflection burst which set fire to the Nakajima's right wingroot. DeHaven and the P-47 orbited over the falling Ki-43 which finally exploded on a hillside just southwest of Alexischafen village.

## FOUR THUNDERBOLTS

The interloping P-47 driver was the resilient Maj. Gerry Johnson. He had gone back to Dobodura to lead another four-ship cross-country excursion to Gusap and had again arrived as the enemy was leaving. Although the hefty fighters had reached Gusap at 8000 feet and used most of their fuel in the climbing pursuit of the higher Japanese formation, element leader Capt. Wally Jordan was able to overtake and damaged an OSCAR. The others were consigned to confirm DeHaven's sixth career kill and the smoking HELEN which fell into the foothills. The bomber kill was eventually awarded to Red Flight element leader Lou Martin.

## THE LAST AERIAL VICTORIES OF 1943

Those last nine victories in December would cost the 49ers five Warhawks and able Capt. Sheldon Brinson. The Demon flight leader had attempted to put his badly damaged P-40 down in a belly landing at Gusap #7, but his blurred vision and shrapnel wounds had reduced his flying skills a bit too far. Brinson overshot the runway and plowed 100 yards into the rough. He was pulled from the steaming wreck and immediately transported to the surgery facility at Port Moresby.

Forty-niners Co Selman and 7 FS CO Stanton later inquired of Brinson's recovery from surgery and the doctors confirmed the captain was one, tough fighter pilot. Even after the removal of one of his lacerated testicles, wry Brinson demanded, "Issue me one of them nurses and I'll test-hop your handy work, Doc." He soon left for America with a good prognosis, but Shelly Brinson would never fly fighters again. The 49ers had lost one of their best.

*7 FS Sheldon Brinson then a lieutenant in his P-40K at Dobodura. A seasoned combat leader at Gusap, the able captain ran out of luck on Dec 12, 1943.*

As the pace slackened briefly, LtC. Selman was finally able to consult with Col. Squeeze Wurtsmith in choosing a successor for the 49ers command. The 5 FC CO indeed had the popular veteran David Campbell of the 35 FG as the next in line for a group leader slot. By Christmas, Maj. Campbell was making the rounds of all the Gusap airstrips to meet the pilots and crews, as well as to fly attached with the Warhawk and Thunderbolt missions.

## QUEUING UP FOR CAPE GLOUSTER; DECEMBER 26, 1943

For the remainder of the month, LtC. Selman's pilots received somewhat of a reprieve. The 4th Air Army at Wewak took another terrific beating by the B-24s on the 22nd. Gen. Kenney sent the devastating raid to insure the JAAF would not come down against the Allied invasion of Cape Glouster, New Britain, planned for the last week in December.

The 49ers P-40s and P-47s flew escort for the bomber raids from Finschhafen to Wewak and even flew their own search and destroy bombing missions, but the Japanese air force was not met in the air. Ace Bob DeHaven had to resort to sinking a freighter with a 500 pound bomb in Astrolabe Bay. Everyone rotated in the mundane patrols over their home valley, but still, there were no airborne encounters.

The mess shacks at Gusap served an abbreviated Christmas dinner of some kind of canned fowl with fresh fruit, and milk for the first time in weeks. Weeks-old mail was hauled into the camps and weary veterans were elated with the news from the families back home. On the day after Christmas, word soon came to Ramu Valley of the great air battle that had taken place over the bloody beachhead at Cape Glouster. Apparently the Japanese had saved everything for the defense of that last escape route outpost from Rabaul, but the 5 AF annihilated the Imperial fighters and dropped the greatest concentration of heavy ordinance on a target in one mission since the war had begun. New Britain was cut off and Wewak was next.

Immediately, the pace of ground support sorties resumed in earnest as Vasey's 7th Division closed in on Bogadjim. Both the

Demons and Blacksheep took to carrying modified detonator-armed drop tanks filled with napalm (gelatin-gasoline). The fearsome fire bombs were dropped on the camps and supply depots from Bogadjim to Hansa Bay. Major Johnson's P-47s with their eight-gun armament became a deadly strafing unit as they marauded over the shipping lanes and docks of the coastal villages. The 49ers intelligence teams and the Ops Execs scoured the daily recon photos for targets and harassed the Japanese at every turn.

## DEMONS OVER SAIDOR; JANUARY 2, 1944

The New Year passed with little fanfare as the mission schedule only seemed to increase. On the day after New Year's, MacArthur again cut the northern escape route to Wewak for the ravaged Imperial 18th Army. Under another 5 AF aerial armada, seven thousand troops of the 32nd Division made an amphibious landing a hundred miles north of Finchhafen at the old coastal mining village of Saidor. Although the 200-man enemy garrison fled into the forest, there would be a brief, spirited aerial intervention from Wewak.

An A-20 flight of the 3 AG was to strafe the beach and small staging airstrip at Saidor shortly after the noon hour. Their close escort was provided by twelve 7 FS P-40s led by Capt. Duncan Myers with flight leaders Capt. Bill Lown (attached from 49ers HQ) and Lt. Bob DeHaven.

The A-20 strike went well and after regrouping, they headed due west to be picked up by the egress escort of P-47s from the 9 FS. As prearranged, the 7 FS with fuel still in their drop tanks, left the bombers and swept northwest up the coast to interdict any Japanese units coming down from Wewak.

## CROSSED PATHS AT ASTROLABE BAY

Wewak headquarters learned of the surprise landing from a early morning reconnaissance flight which found the Allied fleet of 18 destroyers and 30 transports laying off the Huon coast. An attempt was made to send a morning fighter assault, but bad weather delayed the sortie. When the front broke, a meager counter-attack of

*Shown here is Flt Ldr Duncan Myers who led the 7 FS massacre on January 2nd.*

*Ace Bob DeHaven's old stager "orchid" #13 ("RITA" on the rt. side) as of early January 1944, displaying the new 7 FS spinner colors of sky blue and white. C.C. Paul Pogapohl also had installed a venturi intake cup below the windscreen to provide fresh air in the cockpit. Aggressive DeHaven flew this fighter hard until the war-weary bird was turned over to the Gusap maintenance squadron for a complete refitting in late January. It was reissued to the 8 FS in late February, or March.*

thirty-four fighters and nine light bombers was launched as the only response the battered airdrome could muster.

Just as the Wewak group reached the north shoreline off Madang, Capt. Myers approached them head-on out over Astrolabe Bay. Myers called in the Japanese as two flights of TONYs in high cover and OSCARs in close support of three Vees of LILY bombers. The Screamin' Demon leader called the break from his greater altitude above the enemy, dropped his belly tank and plunged straight for the leading escort element of OSCARs.

Myers' aim was true as the foremost OSCAR rolled over in flames and dropped straight into the bay. The Demon leader's wingman Lt. George Allen fired on another OSCAR which also erupted into flames. The sentai broke ranks and wheeled about in frantic aerobatics to fend off the diving Warhawks as the brave bomber crews pressed on toward Saidor.

Lt. DeHaven brough his element down on the TONYs and the ace's lethal deflection shooting sent down the third victim of the interception. The Demons wheeled about to reform for the second pass and saw a smoking P-40 falling toward the gulf. Despite the loss, the engagement had turned in complete favor of the Demons as the sentai elements totally dispersed.

As the dogfight subsided, Capt. Myers swung beneath all of the combatants and next turned on the LILY formation. Maj. Wells, attached from the 312 BG for this mission, had struggled with the fuel transfer while dropping his belly tank, but now he also had reached the battle and had singled out a bomber. Both the captain and the major sent a bomber down in flames.

## LOST CAPT. LOWN

With fuel and ammo gone, Myers called for regroup, but on the descent into Gusap airspace, Capt. Lown did not rejoin, nor did he answer on the emergency channel. Rescue flights were held down by weather on the 3rd, and flights the following day turned up nothing. Bill Lown was listed as missing in action.

The late response to the Allied landing at Saidor had resulted in yet another pointless sacrifice of the indispensible aircraft and airmen from Wewak. More of the Imperial refugees trapped on the north coast would forever be denied the coastal escape route to the west. The enemy's assaults against the Ramu Valley airfields had been of minimal effect., The 49ers and their brethren of the 5 AF had taken the central valleys and could not be stopped.

# 16

# AGAINST WEWAK:
# JANUARY-FEBRUARY 1944

Though the capture of Saidor village in the first week of 1944 was tactically insignificant on the grander scale, the venture yielded one of the most important intelligence prizes of the Pacific war. For some obscure reason, the Saidor garrison staff chose to bury, rather than destroy, a large cache of the master code books for the Imperial Army communications network. Since early in the war, the Imperial Navy and merchant marine codes had been deciphered, but after the new find, MacArthur knew the majority of his opponent's movements. Despite their staggering losses throughout the last sixteen months of the conflict, the Japanese never surmised their logistics had been so thoroughly compromised.

From the newly discovered codes, Gen. Kenney was appraised of the vulnerability of the enemy bases in the Admiralty Islands on the north flank of the Solomon Sea, and quickly realized their capture would further deny Wewak another source of reinforcements. The schedule for the Philippines could be advanced by months. MacArthur readily approved of the Admiralties venture and Kenney called for a cap over the New Guinea coast from Finchhafen to Wewak.

The resultant increase of escorts and sweeps for the 49th Fighter Group was more than acceptable to Col. Selman and CO-designate Campbell who wanted their unit to keep up the scoring pace. The 49ers were assigned their first maximum effort to Wewak proper and the Blacksheep drew the first sortie. Their new Ops Exec Capt. Bob McHale posted the names of the men tagged for the sweep to Dahlman Harbor, just off shore of the enemy headquarters.

*7 FS Lt. Warren, always present in aircraft #12 "LITTLE JEANNE", but not able to knock down any of the remnant defenders of Wewak.*

## BLACKSHEEP TO DALLMAN HARBOR; JANUARY 6, 1944

There were four main airfields that made up the Wewak complex. All of the strips were simple, dirt runways which once had served the coastal plantations and mining stores of the opulent Dutch and German trading empire. The Japanese simply widened the existing tracks to facilitate their heavier military transports and bombers. Accept for some service areas which were provided with thick bamboo matting or split log trestles, the runways were not covered with hardened surfaces as the Allies had done in eastern Papua. The soil of Wewak was constantly rain soaked, and even marginal weather made operations there nearly impossible.

Two-hundred and fifty miles northwest by air from Gusap came the first coastal strip named Borum after the nearby village. Five miles further west came Wewak village on narrow Cape Moem. The 4th Air Army headquarters was housed there in the former governor's mansion on the bluff which overlooked the main airstrip laying parallel to the shoreline of Dallman Harbor.

Ten miles up the jungle covered shoreline beyond Wewak lay Dagua field, and finally another five miles to the west was rustic But village and its earthen runway. The entire complex was shadowed by the rolling foothills of the heavily forested Alexander Mountains.

On January 6th, the 49ers flew their first strike to the Wewak airstrip, but the mission was not nearly as dangerous as most of the pilots had anticipated. Their objective was essentially a fighter sweep in support of the Blacksheep who were tasked with hitting the docks of Dallman Harbor. The Demon P-40s in company of several 475 FG P-38s set up a mission cap over the foothills from Borum to Wewak as the Blacksheep swept in over the harbor from the seaward side. The defensive flak was sporadic and inaccurate. A small tanker was sunk and two barges were set on fire, but there was no aerial opposition.

The 8 FS tried to return to Wewak again on the 8th, but a weather front held them to the secondary target of Uligan Harbor at Alexischafen. Only minimal damage was done to the docks and jetty. They would return to Uligan the following day.

Within that first week of January, the 9 FS had fully intended to re-enter the mission schedule with their ungainly P-47s, but they were momentarily sidelined by an outbreak of dengue fever. Medics completed cleaned the water supply facilities and by January 10th, the 9 FS was back in the rotation. That day, sixteen P-47s joined the escort to Alexischafen, but there was still no airborne contacts in the marginal weather. On January 12th, fifteen P-47s went on a sweep and dropped down to strafe shipping at Karkar

*9 FS Doug Barrett poses with ace Wandry's P-47. With several hours in single engine fighters before his Lockheed tour in 1943, Barrett proved to be an able formation instructor to many of the senior officers during the operational training era in the P-47.*

Island north of Alexischafen. Still the Japanese air power could not be found. In three days however, things changed dramatically.

## JAPANESE RAID ON GUSAP; JANUARY 15, 1944

On the morning of January 15th, Wewak was back in business. As 5 AF crews prepared their planes for the day's flights, the Japanese struck Ramu Valley with another mixed force from the north. Again, there was no air raid warning of the TONY fighters which swept in low over Gusap #5's flight line and strafed the dispersal area. An A-20 on the 3 AG flight line was put out of action by a bomb blast, two 9 FS Thunderbolts were torched and a jeep carrying four Knights was bracketed by a burst of machine gun fire, but the men escaped being hit. The Knights engineering tent was flattened and the Ops tent was riddled, but again, there were no casualties. Only Lt. Charlie McElroy received cracked ribs in a crowded slit trench near Operations.

*Heavy landing by P-38 veteran Wilbert Arthur at Gusap in the demanding Thunderbolt. Arthur persisted in taking on a second aircraft #92 and rose to the proficiency of flight leader in the big fighter.*

## FLYING KNIGHTS BACK AT WEWAK; JANUARY 18, 1944

Maj. Johnson led his Flying Knights on the retaliation raid of January 18th. While the 7 FS and 8 FS flew an uneventful escort to the B-24s, the 9 FS gave high escort over the target to the 22nd BG. Johnson again provided a prime example of "command by doing" as he chalked up his eleventh confirmed kill, which he personally accounted for as his thirteenth, over a lone OSCAR south of Wewak during the strike force withdrawal.

More escorts, armed reconnaissance and valley patrols were flown for five days, but no contact was made with the enemy. Finally on the third week of the month, Gen. Kenney's reconnaissance flights found a major force staging into to Wewak from the far west. He laid another of his ruinous assaults on Wewak.

## A GROUP VISIT TO WEWAK; JANUARY 23, 1944

After several Japanese aircraft were seen waiting at But and Dagua airstrips, Col. Selman was advised to martial all of his 49ers for the next maximum effort. Fifth Command was not going to have a repeat of the unannounced raid of the 15th. On the 22nd, air activity was seen to increase at Wewak proper and Kenney decided it was time to beat the Japanese to the punch. On January 23, a long parade of 5 AF medium and heavy bombers raided all four Wewak strips.

The 49ers Warhawks and Thunderbolts were up from their respective Ramu Valley bases with improved weather at 0940 hours. They rendezvoused with the north-bound bomber force immediately over the Finistere hills and flew a direct route to the target. They reached Borum village at 1100 hours.

## SCREAMIN' DEMONS OFF CAPE MOEM

Capt. Arland Stanton was at the lead of his seventeen Demon P-40s stacked from 21,000 through 24,000 feet over the right flank of the B-24s, and he looked down as the formation passed directly over Borum strip. From his position above the right-most elements of Liberators, the captain peered ahead and accessed the dogfight between the pre-strike sweep of P-38s and OSCARs out over the sea. The Lockheeds appeared to have the advantage as the engaged sentais struggled to reach the approaching B-24s.

After the Liberators salvoed their heavy ordinance on Wewak airdrome, Stanton held his position and followed them five miles through their inland turn until it was certain none of the defenders were in pursuit. It was only then that the first enemy planes began to approach the B-24s. Directing White Flight to stay in high cover, mission leader Stanton signalled his Blue, Green and Red elements to drop their tanks and engage.

## HAHER'S GREEN FLIGHT

From their lowest position at 21,000 feet in the Demon escort group, Green Flt Ldr Lt. John Haher had ventured into the mission despite one of his elements having dropped out early on with engine trouble. With his remaining rookie second lieutenants Jay Rogers and Fred

*7 FS future ace Elliott Dent (rt.) and his crew pose with their P-40N #24 displaying two new kills gained on the big escort mission of January 23rd to Wewak.*

*7 FS aircraft #26 "PARALYSIS VI" which barely reached Gusap with Jack Suggs after the January 23rd dogfight at Wewak. The riddled Warhawk was scrapped out and Suggs took a replacement #26 which would last until September.*

Dick, they were the first Demons to register aerial kills in the mission.

Even though they flew a single firing pass through the OSCARs down to 2500 feet, Rogers damaged one and Dick splashed another in their cover of the Flight Leader who shot down two more. They swooped back up and headed south to reformate above the retreating Liberators. Green Flight's "green wingmen" had passed their combat initiation with flying colors.

## STANTON'S BLUE FLIGHT

Squadron Ldr Stanton took wingman 2Lt. Jack Fenimore, element leader Elliot Dent and his wingman 2Lt. Mic Zuniga down on the approaching dark-green OSCARs from head-on. Only element leader Dent scored. He hit his first target squarely in the nose, then wheeled about and hit his second victim with a wide deflection shot. As Dent's last victim spun downward into the bay, the Blue Flight team saw yet another burning aircraft hit the water some distance to the north. That falling aircraft was probably the sole victim of Red Fight.

*7 FS Flt Ldr Jack Suggs who barely escaped from the dogfight over Wewak on January 23rd, persevered and returned to exact revenge at Wewak on March 12.*

## DEHAVEN'S RED FLIGHT

From their highest position in the escort team, Lt. Bob DeHaven's Red Flight quartet had been the last to pass over the target. In his #13 adorned with a painted orchid on the radiator tub, DeHaven had seen the preceding Demon flights engage and when he passed over Dallman Harbor, he began to drop down through a left turn for an attack on the enemy's rear quarter. It was at that moment that Red Flight was attacked from behind.

DeHaven and his rookie wingman 2Lt. Marion Hawke were registering over 300 Mph when the OSCARs intervened. The Red flight leader and his wingman instantly countered the assault by converting their diving speed into a mind-blurring climb back up to the bombers, but element leader Lt. John Crowley and wingman Lt. Jack Suggs apparently had not seen the threat to the rear. It was a fatal oversight.

As Hawke momentarily greyed out at the top of the wild maneuver, the experienced DeHaven quickly nosed his "orchid" downward again just as the lower Red elements were overwhelmed far below. The ace flight leader, with Hawke just seconds behind him, plunged straight down to the aide of their Red Flight mates, but they were too late.

## CROWLEY DOWN OFF CAPE MOEM; JANUARY 23, 1944

The wingmen of Red Flight had indeed entered into great peril for they were ambushed by the veterans of the 59th Sentai. Suggs' ship was heavily damaged, and when Hawke finally intervened, his left aileron controls were shot out and a 12mm round shattered against his headrest, littering the cockpit with shrapnel. Somehow, they both were able to reach the safety of the clouds hugging the foothills, but ill-fated Crowley had pulled out of his dive much too low. Forced to attempt an escape just above the water, one of the OSCARs quickly drew down on the trapped Demon. Crowley's P-40 rolled over and dove straight into the sea.

Skillful DeHaven, however, swept down through the whirling OSCARs to fall upon Crowley's killer and closed into point blank range. At the last moment, DeHaven rolled up over his eighth ca-

*8 FS Flt Ldr Hagerstrom just days before he took new aircraft #50 up to Wewak on the January 23rd ace-maker mission.*

*New 8 FS aircraft #65 "RAGGED BUT RIGHT" assigned to wingman John Bodak which served him well in the Hagerstrom rampage on January 23rd.*

reer victim whose cockpit had become a raging inferno. It was very likely the burning plane seen by the Blue Flight Demons some distance to the south.

## HAGERSTROM IN THE HORNET'S NEST; JANUARY 23, 1944

Blacksheep CO Capt. Bernie Makowski brought his fourteen Warhawks over Wewak thirty minutes later above the second wave of Liberators. Just as the Demons had done moments before, the 8 FS P-40s would engage the sentais over Cape Moem, and a new Blacksheep ace would prevail.

*An unidentified 7 FS crewman sits on DeHaven's new P-40N #13, s.n. 42-105405 which was likely the aircraft used to gain the ace's eighth victory scored in the wild January 23rd fight over Wewak. The victim may well have been 59th Sentai leader Col. Nango who was reported missing in the vicinity of the Screamin' Demons engagement.*

Blue Flight was a remnant duet whose other two elements had dropped out en route to the target. Blue Flt Ldr Jim "HAG" Hagerstrom decided to stay with the mission since he was flying a brand-new P-40N-5 #50, as was wingman 2/ Lt. John Bodak in his new mount #65 named RAGGED BUT RIGHT. Not having scored in three months plus an intermittent bout with malaria had put Hagerstrom in a surly mood and he was spoiling for a fight. The JAAF was about to accommodate him.

At their right flank position at 18,000 feet, the Blacksheep Warhawks crossed the flight path of an estimated thirty enemy fighters that approached from their right. Just as the mission leader called out their position, Hagerstrom saw a P-38 from the 475 FG high cover team diving downward with several OSCARs in trail. Hag called the break to Bodak, dropped his tank and peeled off across his wingman's line of flight. Startled Bodak took a deep breath and followed the ever accelerating Hagerstrom down into the fray.

It was the most exciting combat maneuvering Bodak had ever seen, and every effort was spent to keep his whirling element leader in sight. Hagerstrom closed at a tremendous rate on the nearest OSCAR and fired a short burst into the its wing root. He wheeled aside to avoid the explosion, and still with Bodak in close formation, pressed onward with their diving speed to reengage. At a range of 500 feet, both Blacksheep opened up and shot their way through the enemy formation and two more OSCARs fell in flames.

It got "very crowded" and Hagerstrom rolled out above the dogfight which placed Bodak in the lead. Again, they set off back into the mob. Bodak leaned hard into a curving firing pass on an OSCAR until flames spewed from its belly. Again and again, Hag and Bodak scissored back and forth in textbook support of each other.

As the pair broke out of the melee at 3000 feet, another P-38 passed at high speed in the opposite direction to the P-40s' path. A TONY was in distant pursuit of the P-38 and the Kawasaki changed its course into Hagerstrom as they closed upon each other. The Blacksheep leader suddenly stood his #50 on its wingtip and nearly blacked out in the high-G turn, but #50 leveled out at "6 o'clock" behind the Ki-61. Hag's six .50's tore the TONY to shreds and it rolled straight over into sea from 1500 feet.

*8 FS aircraft #69 "THE BASTARD" assigned to Carl Lambert who scored his only kill in the January 23rd dogfight. The womanizing wolf motif was truly a play on words, more accurately describing the crewchief's reputation and not that of the pilot. Indeed, very much like Walt Disney's cartoon character "Lambert, the sheepish lion," demure Blacksheep 2Lt. Lambert was only a terror in the air.*

## BRIEFLY WITH WHITE FLIGHT

White Flight element leader Lt. Lou Graton with wingmen 2Lts. George Smerchek and Carl Lambert also joined the big dogfight. All three were likewise accredited with their first career victories, but the story for this day was Hagerstrom with 4 confirmed and wingman Bodak with 2 kills. Hag and "Johnny Zero" Bodak were certain they had hit others, but the violence of the fight made further claims impossible to confirm.

## STANDING DOWN AT GUSAP AND DOOMED LT. MARION HAWKE

Considering the plight of the Demons Red Flight, the escort to Wewak had ended quite successfully for LtC. Jim Selman's 49ers. The surviving P-40 pilots returned to Gusap despite their damages, where as the Flying Knights in their P-47s had missed the whole show.

At Gusap #7, the two Red Flight junior elements bravely landed in their holed Warhawks. Suggs was able to get his gear down and safely land, but the P-40 would require the replacement of its shredded left aileron and rudder, plus substantial patchwork over the numerous bullet holes. Hawke's riddled P-40 lost power in the landing pattern and was bellied in short of the strip to later be hauled off for scrap. But neither Suggs, Hawke nor any other 49er had been wounded. Missing John Crowley had been the only casualty of the entire mission.

Unfortunately, Lt. Marion Hawke was a marked man. The lieutenant was given two weeks leave and returned to Northern Australia. At Iron Range on February 15th, he was on the flight line when a training plane swerved wildly off the runway and its wing struck him in the head. Marion Hawke died instantly of a crushed skull.

## ANOTHER CHANGE FOR THE 49ERS; JANUARY 25, 1944

On the 25th, Jim Selman was promoted in rank and sent up to join the 5 FC operations staff at Nadzab. Having led the original 9th Pursuit Squadron cadre from Florida into combat in Australia, plus his role in the planning for the New Guinea offensive, able Jim Selman had built a reputation as an idea man who could make his schemes come to fruition. During his Group command tenure, he had maintained the highest scoring record in the entire USAAF which had help secure the air over New Guinea. Selman officially handed the 49ers over to newly promoted LtC. David Campbell who was likewise determined to uphold the Selman legacy.

*Group CO select Campbell saddles up for a 9 FS sortie.*

## A NEW FLYING KNIGHT CO

On January 28th, Maj. Gerry Johnson was furloughed to command school in the States and he turned his Flying Knights over to the Deputy CO Capt. Wally Jordan. Jordan, an outstanding fighter pilot and tactician, had first been a candidate for the Group Ops Exec slot, but both Johnson and LtC. Campbell wanted the cool head of Jordan to keep the rookie Thunderbolt pilots "in family hands." Dapper and even tempered Jordan was seen by the high command as an "ice man" who led by example, just as Johnson had done.

Word came to the pilots in Ramu Valley that Capt. Dick Bong had returned to fly combat. But the leading ace did not join up with his old outfit in their P-47s. Fifth Fighter Command had given him, and his good friend LtC. Tom Lynch, a special operations job at Nadzab where they would remain in their P-38s and fly attached to the unit of their choice. The pair of all silver Lockheed fighters became a common site in escort formations over the north coast. Although Gen. Kenney cautioned restraint in their hunt for enemy targets, everyone was rooting for the USAAF aces to overtake U.S. Marines aviator Greg Boyington who had tied the Rickenbacker record of twenty-six back in January over Rabaul. But Boyington was lost in action, and surely Bong could break the record over Wewak.

*Survivor Carl Planck (second from lt.) reunited with his old 9 FS friends at Gusap. The flyer's return was a shock to everyone who believed Planck had died in the collision at Rabaul on November 2, 1943.*

*7 FS Farrel off on the February 3rd sweep to Wewak which resulted in his third and last kill.*

The greatest surprise, of course, was the startling appearance of veteran Flying Knight Carl Planck and the story of his incredible adventure after being lost over Rabaul. The lieutenant visited briefly with his comrades, but could relate very little of his ordeal as he was under strict orders to protect the secrecy of the other survivors still in the New Britain highlands. In a very emotional ceremony, the frail fellow personally removed his memorial cup from the Flying Knights Shelf of Honor in the pilot's bar and painted out his name from the Honor Roll on the big score board. Carl Planck was the only 49er who ever do so.

## BLACKSHEEP INDUCT A NEW BOSS

Capt. Bernie Makowski opted for a new position with the Fighter Command staff and handed over the 8 FS at Gusap to senior man Bob McHale who was summarily promoted to major. The new major took senior Capt. Carl Petersen for his Ops Exec as the 8 FS pilots and crews soldiered on.

All of the 49ers returned to the mission grind of fighter sweeps and armed reconnaissance of the coast, but the Japanese had once again dispersed their shattered air force to the west. For two weeks,

the 49ers hunted as far west as the satellite airfield of But, however, targets had become quite sparse.

## A LONE KILL OVER DAGUA; FEBRUARY 3, 1944

While escorting B-25s to hit Dagua airfield on the 3rd, the Screamin' Demons lead flight caught three OSCARs which had just taken off from Dagua when the strike force arrived. Only element leader Lt. Roger Farrell could overtake one of the fleeing Kawasakis before they reached the safety of the cloud bank hovering far off shore. After Ferrel's target splashed down, he joined his squadron in strafing targets all the way back to Muschu Island just off Cape Moem. The mission concluded without further incident.

## A NUISANCE NEAR MUSCHU ISLAND; FEBRUARY 6, 1944

Three days later during an early morning escort to the A-20s of the 3 AG to strafe Muschu Island, a meager attempt to intercept was made by a small mixed flight of OSCARs and TONYs. Capt. Stanton was at 8000 feet above the target when the first enemy plane swept

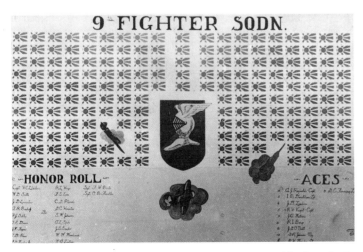

*Planck was the only 49er to ever retrieve his squadron goblet from the 9 FS O-club bar. He next went to the Knights victory board and with a shaking hand painted out his name from the Honor Roll, third from the top of the middle row, then bid farewell to the Flying Knights for good.*

*CO Stanton's aircraft #20, the bawdy "EMPTY SADDLE," was a reliable old stager and his favorite fighter aircraft.*

*7 FS CO Stanton poses with his aircraft #20 "KEYSTONE KATHLEEN" at Gusap after his ace-maker mission on February 6th at Wewak.*

into the area. He dropped down on the all-silver Ki-43 and made several firing passes until it fell into the sea. The pilot dropped in his chute into the water next to the burning oil slick, easily confirming the captain as the newest ace in 5 FC. It was also the last victory Stanton's bunch would see that month.

Meanwhile, the close support escort flown by the three Blacksheep lieutenants of Blue Flight had just strafed a pair of barges when the flights above called in the intruders. Flt Ldr Ellie "Fats" Elofson, Marion Felts and Don Meuten were a mere 400 feet over the water where they wheeled about and quickly would down three interceptors.

Meuten dropped one OSCAR for his third career kill, while Elofson shot down another Ki-43 for his very first victory. A TONY was flamed by Felts and the fight ended. Back at the Blacksheep bar, the three victorious pilots related that the fight had been very intense, but much too brief. They wanted more.

## THE FIGHT OF FEBRUARY 14, 1944

Maj. McHale's men got their wish three days later back over Muschu Island, along with four Demons in company. At 0945 on the 14th, the Warhawks lifted off their dusty runways and picked up the A-20s over the hills just to the east. After the hour and a half cross-country to the coast, Blacksheep mission leader Lt. Fats Elofson spotted the first aerial targets over Wewak proper.

*(Lt-rt.) 7 FS pilots Farrel, Harrison, Dillworth and O'Conner in residence at Gusap. Flt Ldr Farrel was the only man in this foursome to score in 1944. His second career kill came on February 3rd, the sole victim on the escort mission to Dagua.*

Elofson took his Blue Flight elements down on a pair of black-cowled ZEROs patrolling over Dallman Harbor at 4000 feet. Element leader Don Meuten got to the trailing ZERO first, and again with lethal marksmanship, sent the dirty grey-green plane down with the first burst of .50 caliber tracers. The other ZERO escaped to the west and Blue Flight reformed over of the A-20s now descending for their island objective.

As the P-40s crossed over Cape Moem, the Blacksheep descended to 2000 feet. As they headed out to sea, several elements called in more enemy fighters at the same height and closing in on the rear of the A-20 squadrons. All four Blacksheep flights turned to intercept the approaching OSCARs and TONYs. Simultaneously, the trailing high cover flight of Demons led by Lt. Farrel at 8000 feet descended in a perfect ambush.

## DEMON FARREL'S FLIGHT

Demon leader Farrel led wingmen 2Lt. Fenton Epling, element leader Lt. Bob Croft and 2Lt. Jim Keck down on the foremost OSCARs. As the sentai maneuvered to engaged the turning Blacksheep, Farrel's foursome struck from the rear and four OSCARs fell in flames. The Demons zoom-climbed back to their high cover as the greater dogfight erupted below.

*7 FS wingman Lt. Bob Croft with his P-40N #18 "IKEY" scored his sole victory along with Flt Ldr Farrel who scored his third career kill over Wewak on February 14th.*

## MAD SCRAMBLE BLACKSHEEP BLUE AND RED FLIGHTS

The loss of four sentai wingmen without having fired a shot completely dispersed the onrushing OSCARs and a wild turning fight broke out as the Blacksheep engaged. Blue leader Elofson with wingman Felts, Red Ldr Lt. Bob Aschenbrener with wingman Lts. Tom Holstein and element leader Dave Winternitz, all fired on the nearest OSCAR. After a series of hard turns to the left, the Ki-43 finally was set on fire after Winternitz's second volley and the flaming hulk plunged into the sea.

Blue and Red flights had completely separated during the chase which put the Red Flight rookie fourth element Lt. Ed Glascock at the mercy of a diving TONY. Glascock wheeled about for the head-on pass and fired, but the TONY's 12mm rounds had already found their mark. Glascock's P-40 shook as the Ki-61 shot out his radio, his hydraulics, and blew out several large holes in his left wing which also severed the control cables. The TONY abruptly vanished into the mist toward the west.

*Blacksheep astray
Nelson Flack.*

## BLUE AND YELLOW AGAIN

Blue Flt Ldr Elofson and wingman Felts had turned away as the others joined the mad scramble for the first OSCAR. Elofson instead targeted the TONY which had just shot up Glascock and had summarily come under attack by Yellow Flt Ldr Nelson Flack and his wingman Lt. Jim Reynolds.

Indeed, the incensed Kawasaki pilot who had riddled Glascock from head-on had now taken on Flt Ldr Flack in the same vain. As the other P-40s fired from different deflections, Flack bored in nose-to-nose with his .50 calibers ablaze. He pulled up over the speeding Ki-61, just as it nosed over and plunged into the Pacific.

Mission leader Elofson called for the Blacksheep to regroup, yet they were scattered all over the area. Glascock and Flt Ldr Flack both limped back over the foothills alone. Luckily, the wingman would reach home, but not the flight leader.

## FLACK'S LONG WALK HOME

Nelson Decoursay Flack Jr. had set course toward the southeast and just cleared the Alexander Mountain range when his Allison engine overheated and began to smoke. As the P-40 lost power and began to drift downward, Flack radioed his position, but was not at all sure of his accuracy. He was descending into the swamps of the Ramu River over 60 miles from Gusap where few white men had ever ventured.

The terrain of the swamp was much more rugged than was first judged by Flack. He attempted to slide in on the deep kunai of a small clearing, but the abrupt halt threw him into the gunsight and he split open his forehead. After crawling out of the P-40 and bandaging his head wound, the shaken pilot reasoned to burn his plane so as not to let it fall into enemy hands. The net result was a column of smoke which marked his location for friend and foe. Retreating pilots flying back to Gusap mapped his location and a rescue was quickly set in motion.

At Gusap, Blacksheep CO McHale was advised that since his man Flack had gone down in such a hostile place, an experienced guide should go in first and assess the terrain. Australian commando Sgt. Hector Henstridge agreed to paradrop into the site and help the stranded American prepare a landing strip, if possible. On the second day, Henstridge drifted down into the crash site, but Flack was gone. The Yank had set out on foot alone. Later that day, Aussie pilot Sgt. Eugene Saltirnik attempted to land his L-5 Stinson on the treacherous site, but the L-5 cracked up. The stranded Aussies were weighing their dwindling options when Nelson Flack suddenly approached through the ten-foot tall kunai. He had unknowingly walked in a mile wide circle back to his crash site.

The Yank was in poor condition. His cloths were in shreds. His flesh was red from the sun and the welts of a hundred insect bites. Henstridge attended to Flack's cuts and bruises, gave him new trousers and then the threesome ate a hot meal. Flack readily improved after a full day of rest and was able to join in on the construction of a rough hewn runway which became known as Flack Field.

After six days, the next man to attempt a landing at the remote site was Sgt. Jim Nichols of the 25th Liaison Squadron. His L-5 tipped up on the kunai stubble, shattered its wooden prop and bent the gear struts. Nichols was not injured and he joined the team in pushing the plane into the growing scrap heap. Another man would try the next day.

Indeed, Sgt. Tom Stallone was able to safely land the following morning, but the field was much to dangerous to attempt a takeoff with two men on board. After long deliberation, Stallone regretfully left the four behind and barely lifted off from Flack Field in his Stinson. The next day, commando Henstridge led Flack, Saltirnik and Nichols off to the nearest Aussie outpost, 60 miles away.

## IN THE HANDS OF COMMANDO HENSTRIDGE

For the next twenty-one days, Hector Henstridge directed their path through the swamps while food supplies were airdropped along the way. After reaching the forest where the airdrops ended, the commando rationed the last of the food until they were forced to live off the land. Raw fish, lizards and birds plus a variety of fruits, nuts and roots brought on dysentery until frail Jim Nichols withered to a mere one hundred pounds and tall Eugene Saltirnik became a stumbling, silent wrath. Henstridge temporarily lost vision in one of his eyes from an insect bite and all of their shoes rotted away. When they were finally retrieved by an Australian patrol, the four men could barely walk, but they all eventually recovered. After a week in the care of his Aussie mates at their jungle camp, Nelson Flack was eventually transported back to Australia where he completely recuperated, thanks to the rugged commando Henstridge. The Blacksheep pilot returned to flight duty at Gusap by the end of April.

*Rugged Commando Sgt. Henstridge (lt.), Lt. Flack, RAAF F/Sgts. Nichols and Saltirnik, all bearded and gaunt after three weeks in the bush, but alive.*

*8 FS aircraft #64 "NORMA" which got veteran Jim Reynolds his sole career victory on February 15th.*

## THE FINAL FIGHT; FEBRUARY 15, 1944

While their squadron mate Nelson Flack was entering into his ordeal in the swamps, CO Bob McHale took his Blacksheep back to Wewak to even the score for his missing flyer. At 1030 hour on the 15th over Cape Moem, they had it out once against with the tenacious defenders.

Maj. McHale led the four flights into the target stacked from 12,000 up through 15,000 feet where they came upon the morning harbor patrol of an estimated fifteen OSCARs and TONYs. The major did not hesitate and signalled the attack to all of his elements. As the Warhawks drew into firing range, the enemy turned toward them to counter-attack. Another swirling dogfight erupted over the sea.

## WHITE FLIGHT STARTS OFF

White Flt Ldr Lt. Bob Aschenbrener, wingman Lt. Ed Glascock, element leader Lt. Dick Polhamus and wingman Lt. Jim Reynolds were the lowest in altitude of the Blacksheep and reached the OSCARs first, just beyond the cape. Leader "Ash" fired at a Ki-43, then broke off to sweep down nearer the water to fire on the TONYs. A Ki-61 engaged him in two head-on passes until the White Flight

*8 FS veteran Reynold's old #58 renumbered #44 "DOROTHY MAY" reassigned to 2Lt. Porteous in the Gusap-Hollandia era.*

leader bettered the Kawasaki in a tight turn and killed the pilot with a dead-astern volley. The TONY rolled, dipped its wing into the waves and disintegrated within a towering spray of water.

Meanwhile, Aschenbrener's first OSCAR target dropped down to escape above the ocean, only to fall into the gunsights of the trailing White Flight elements. Glascock, Polhamus and Reynolds fired in turn on the fleeing Ki-43 which dropped so low, it glanced off the harbor surface within a shower of spray kicked up by the White Flight volleys. Reynolds was sure he had mortally hit the OSCAR.

## BLUE FLIGHT STRIKES

But the soaked OSCAR rose from the water's surface, only to be hammered again when Blue element leader Lt. Hal Sawyer swept in and delivered the coup de grace. The riddled Ki-43 struck the surface for the last time which sheared off the cowling and right wing.

Blue Flight leader McHale also joined in the chase of the TONYs while his flight assaulted the OSCARs. The major overtook one of them not far from the south shore of Muschu Island. As the Ki-61 circled low over the water, McHale cut inside his turn and blew away the canopy. The TONY nosed straight in.

## YELLOW FLIGHT WRECKING CREW

As Yellow and Red Flights plunged to the attack, they passed directly over Dallman Harbor which was obscured by the smoke rising from the smug pots on the cape. Flak bursts appeared in the vicinity of Hagerstrom's Red elements, but they were of no consequence. The Yellow quartet led by Lt. Averette Lee swept off momentarily to the east and then dropped into the fray.

Both Yellow and Red flights entered into the incredible tangle of OSCARs, TONYs and Warhawks. After numerous firing passes at several opponents, Yellow Flt Ldr Lee withdrew with claims of one Ki-43 killed, another damaged and a TONY which was probably destroyed after two accurate volleys. Trailing Yellow Flight element Lt. John Porteous likewise had two other OSCARs confirmed as destroyed. Red Flight had at least gotten in the last of the firing passes on the OSCARs caught down on the harbor surface, but none of the Red elements could claim any fatal hits.

All of the Blacksheep returned to Gusap in good order and though there was duplication in credits given out for the kills that day, no man had been hurt. Maj. McHale's vendetta for missing Nelson Flack had momentarily been fulfilled.

## MONTH OF THE ENEMY'S ABSENCE

After the costly exchanges with 5 FC during February, the JAAF essentially abandoned operations at Wewak to repair 250 miles further west up the coast at their airdrome complex of Hollandia. Inclement weather and the 800 mile round trip to Hollandia made it virtually impossible for LtC. Campbell's short range Warhawks and Thunderbolts to find any airborne action. Even the latest sweeps to the staging air strips at Tadji a hundred miles west of Wewak was a logistical hardship for the 49ers machines.

*8 FS pilot tent mates Runey, Reynolds, ground echelon officer Plicta and pilot Lee very near the end of their combat tour at Gusap, April, 1944.*

*(Lt.-rt.) Seated veteran pilots Bleecker, Arthur, Markey, Fanning, and Hyland wait with latecomer Jimmie Haislip at the Knights operations shack for another monotonous Gusap patrol. All of the veterans would muster out as of May, 1944, while Haislip would soldier on until September.*

The Flying Knights bid their time with the restricted operations in the portly Thunderbolts, but the senior ex-Lightning pilots considered the big fighter to be an engineering nightmare with wings. Their ships were predominantly production model D-4 types which topped out at six and half tons when fully loaded, and even after burning off fuel, the Jugs could not effectively maneuver in the heavy wet air over the jungle. The exhaust from the aft-mounted supercharger blew out directly on to the tailwheel which swelled and eventually shredded into ribbons on the Marston mat. The main gear tires also blew out much too often in the oppressive 100 degree heat of Ramu Valley. A disgruntled P-47 driver summed up the beast's greatest shortcoming by saying, "If the Army engineers built a runway all the way around the world, Republic would build an airplane that needed every foot of it to take off."

In the meantime, the hefty Thunderbolts were consigned to high altitude escort where they could employ their great weight and horsepower to advantage. Nothing in the theater, not even the regal Lightnings, could outrun one of the Republic monsters in a full power dive. The 348 FG CO Neel Kearby had proven the fact by racking up twenty kills to date in his P-47. Now the debate had drawn down to the final test; Would Kearby in his Thunderbolt, or either Bong or Lynch in their Lightnings break the Boyington/Rickenbacker 26-victory mark?

## THE DOGFIGHTS OF MARCH AT WEWAK

After two weeks of meager hunting, the pilots in Ramu Valley jokingly speculated that the Japanese had abandoned the jungle island all together. Their spirits lightened as the ever popular USO shows ventured into the headquarters at Nadzab and even the Hollywood movie idol, John Wayne, toured the advanced bases at Gusap. More mail arrived and fresh meat, eggs and beer was scrounged from the supply bases in eastern New Guinea and distant Australia. All was on the up-swing when the intelligence reports began to sound a familiar warning. Enemy planes were staging back at Wewak, and CO Campbell hoped his high-scoring outfit could make good use of their esprit de corps.

Regardless of the marauding bombers in Gen. Kenney's juggernaut, the Imperial merchant fleet was able to reach Wewak with a sizable reinforcement of men and materials. In the palm orchards of Brandi Plantation which lay just west of Borum village, and upon the slopes of the foothills west of Wewak, thousands of Imperial troops and tens of thousands of tons of equipment lay in wait to repulse the Allied invasion.

## STANTON PICKS OFF A SINGLE NEAR WEWAK; MARCH 8th

However, on a routine armed reconnaissance of the Wewak complex on the 8th, the Screamin' Demons led by the Squadron CO only found a lone OSCAR flying over the foothills just south of Wewak village. The sentai man never knew what hit him as Capt. Stanton closed in at 350 Mph from above. The Ki-43 went straight down in flames.

When more aircraft did reach the enemy airdrome, the 5 AF heavies struck again. Beginning on the 11th, the Wewak coastline rocked under an avalanche of high explosives for four straight days. One thousand pounders dropped by the B-24s pitted the four airfields with immense craters and newcomers were forced to circle over their once safe headquarters airdrome where the Allied fighters now hunted in swarms.

On the 11th, LtC. Campbell was disappointed after leading the early morning escort and thereby missing the dogfight over Wewak at noon where the Thunderbolts of the newly refitted 35 FG, along with the veteran 348 FG, scored a dozen kills. On the 12th, the two Warhawk squadrons of the 49ers flew close escort to the A-20s which bombed the bivouacs of Brandi plantation. Campbell flew top cover in his P-47 with the Flying Knights, only to be at the right place, but at the wrong altitude. All of the victories fell to the P-40s at the lower altitude, and the colonel wondered if he would ever see another airborne target while in command.

## STANTON'S DEMONS AT WEAWK; MARCH 12, 1944

The first contact on the 12th was made by Capt. Stanton who took fourteen Demons into the target in a spread formation from 8000 to 12,000 feet on the A-20s right flank. As the Havocs swept through the mist near Borum village, they were set upon the small interceptor force of OSCARs and the Demons immediately engaged. In a single pass, Capt. Stanton and Lts. Bill Ferris, Jim O'Neill, Lem Pollack and Jack Suggs each downed a Ki-43. Three of the stricken OSCARS fell in flames into the Borum camps and the other two plunged into the bay. The survivors quickly broke off and headed west.

## McHALE'S BLACKSHEEP

On the A-20's left flank came Capt. McHale's sixteen Blacksheep who flew straight over the retreating OSCARs just ravaged by the 7 FS. Caught in their descending escape, the hapless sentai elements had only placed themselves at the disadvantage of fighting again at that lower altitude.

In a violent turning fight, McHale gained his second career victory, then damaged another. Wingman 2Lt. Burt Hall got his lone career kill and Lt. Marion Felt gained his second career kill. Element leader Lt. Averette Lee knocked down an OSCAR in the first pass, as did wingman Lt. Bob Sweeney.

But the performance of the day once again was turned in by the deadly marksman, Lt. Don Meuten. The Blacksheep lieutenant wheeled in behind an old 11th Sentai Ki-43 still bearing the lightning unit marking on its tail. It rolled over and fell away in flames. His second victory came over an all silver Ki-43 which exploded and fell in pieces into the bay. The third kill was over an OSCAR whose canopy was shot off from a phenomenal 90 degree deflection. It exploded on impact on the harbors surface. The 8 FS had a new ace and Meuten had made it all look so easy.

*7 FS Lem Pollack sitting on the damaged wing of his Warhawk after the exchange on March 12th which yielded his only career kill.*

## THE NEXT DAY WITH THE DEMONS AND KNIGHTS; MARCH 13, 1944

LtC. Campbell chose to join the Warhawks who seemed to have all the luck in their lower realm. The 49ers CO mounted up in his P-40 and with staff Capt. Bob McDaris as his wingman, they joined the 7 FS in their mid-morning escort. It proved to be a timely choice.

Had the colonel stayed with his P-47 squadron, he might have scored with them as well. Newly promoted Capt. Ralph Wandry had sixteen Thunderbolts at 16,000 feet over Wewak at 1100 hours when the OSCARs appeared overhead. Wandrey ordered "tanks off" and rose to the attack. As the P-47s drew within range, the OSCARs dropped for the safety of the clouds below, but the mission leader's big Republic sprinter easily overtook one of the trailing sentai men. He fired a long burst into the Ki-43 until it rolled over and plunged into the sea. It was his sixth and finally victory of his career.

*Left: 7 FS aircraft #3 "BUCKET O' BOLTS" normally flown by Jim O'Neill who scored his first confirmed kill on March 12th at Wewak. Right: 8 FS Marion Felts playfully slumped against his P-40N at Gusap after a heavy landing in May. The aircraft displays his first two kills, the last which came on March 14th at Wewak. The aircraft stripped of camouflage would be back in service at Biak.*

*8 FS veteran Averette Lee was long overdue to furlough home in March, 1944, but stayed on as a Flt Ldr until the 49ers moved up to Hollandia. Lee is seated on White's old #42 which he flew on the March 12th mission to score his last air victory.*

As the chase leveled out far below, the Knights tried to picked off the other stragglers in several head-on passes, but Lts. John Crowder, Bernie Krankowitz, and 2Lt. Fred Helterline only scored ineffective hits. In exchange, Krankowitz took two 12mm bullets through his fuselage and 2Lt. Bill Huisman had his hydraulic lines cut by a single explosive round. Luckily, they were all able to re-joined on ace Wandrey's command and safely returned to Gusap without further incident.

Meanwhile, the Demons reached the coast and Campbell caught site of three OSCARs skimming over the hills in their escape from the assault of the P-47s. In seconds, the colonel, Capt. McDaris and wingman Lt. Joel Paris closed in and dropped all three targets. Finally, the colonel had personally added to the 49ers score.

## ANOTHER KNIGHTS' MISSION; MARCH 14th

On the 14th, the B-24s pounded Borum field and Brandi plantation again with Capt. Wally Jordan's 9th Squadron in escort. Just as Capt. Wandrey's flights had done on the day before, CO Jordan and his Red Flight wingmen fell upon the OSCARs who plunged away at the approach of the deadly, high flying P-47s. And like Wandrey, the CO drew down on one of the fleeing Nakajimas and sent in down in flames into the sea. Lts. Eddie Howes and Will Treadway each overtook a hapless sentai victim as well. This time, no Flying Knight aircraft was hit in the exchange.

## AND THE LAST; MARCH 15, 1944

Capt. Wandrey was in the lead again on the 15th, but unlike the past mission when he attacked thirty enemy planes, on that day there were only three. In their thundering dive for the enemy trio, several of the 9 FS elements fired and 2Lt. Huisman evened the score for the damage he received two days prior. After a head-on pass that nearly ended in a collision with a Ki-43, Willis Huisman wheeled in behind a fleeing TONY and fired until it fell into the Pacific. It was the last kill made by a Flying Knight in a P-47.

Simultaneously, Demon ace Bob DeHaven scored the last 7 FS kill in the Wewak campaign. In another classic, blind-side firing pass, the lieutenant shot down his ninth career victim just south of the enemy harbor.

*Aircraft P-40M #99, essentially a lengthened export version of the model-K, was purportedly the only model-M assigned to the 49ers and subsequently used by CO Campbell in the Wewak operations to score his fourth and last career kill on March 13th at Wewak. It was his only victory with the 49ers.*

*Left: Ace Ralph Wandry was one of only six Flying Knights to get a confirmed kill in the P-47 which the lieutenant considered a worthless weapon. After his sixth and last victory on March 13th, Wandry made the transition back into the P-38 in May, then furloughed home in September. Right: 9 FS crewmen inspect the gaping bullet hole at the base of the radio mast on Krankowitz's P-47 on March 13th.*

*Left: Senior Flt Ldr Treadway in his Thunderbolt pilot gear at Gusap. He scored hits on his first career victim over Wewak on March 14th, but the OSCAR was never officially confirmed. The significance of the roman numeral on the nose of his aircraft is unknown. Right: Latecomer P-38 pilot Jacobs posing with 9 FS CO Jordan's aircraft #91.*

*Left: 9 FS Flt Ldr Jimmie Haislip with his crew and their P-47 #80 "JO." Right: Unidentified crewmen next to 7 FS ace DeHaven's "RITA" used for the ace's ninth victory on March 15th. The wheel covers display a blue-white yin and yang design.*

*Purportedly Huisman's P-47 #85 with a bullet hole in the fuselage just behind the canopy and its hydraulics knocked out in the March 13th fight.*

*9 FS CO Jordan in his dual striped command ship with Flt Ldr Haislip in formation.*

## ON TO TADJI AND THE LOSS OF CAPT. CASH; MARCH 22, 1944

The pace never let up. Meant to bomb the enemy camp at Tadji, the Warhawks could reach the 300 mile objective with a full belly tank and two 300 pound bombs, but little else. On the grueling mission of March 22nd, the Screamin' Demons encountered light but accurate flak. Capt. Russel Cash, the Group Operations executive, was last seen turning inland from the target, but he never reached Gusap. On hearing of the Ops Exec loss, LtC. Campbell was badly shaken. The colonel and captain had become fast friends.

## ANOTHER CENTURY MARK AND A MOMENTARY VICTORY; MARCH 25, 1944

On the 25th, supreme Imperial commander Gen. Adachi ordered the 4th Air Army headquarters staff to withdraw to Hollandia and abandon shattered Wewak for once and for all. The remaining troops dispersed into the Alexander Mountains. Many would die of starvation and disease, or fall victim to the aboriginal headhunters of the interior. The victory at Wewak was ultimately gained by the combined air power of the 5th Air Force and the U.S.Navy carriers. So complete was the destruction of Wewak, like the other garrisons to the east, it would be passed over for invasion. Gen. MacArthur quickly advanced his New Guinea strategic schedule ahead by four months as of April and set his sights on Hollandia.

*LtC. Neel Kearby CO 348 FG, KIA March 5, 1944.*

*Tommy Lynch as a captain at 14 Mile Field in late 1943, KIA March 9, 1944.*

*On April 12th, Bong finally exceeded the World War I victory tally and set the new record at twenty-seven. By the time the first 49ers reached Hollandia in late April, Bong was on his way home for the second time.*

In the wake of the battle for the north shore lay a brutal legacy for all of the pilots who had fought and gained the high praise of their comrades and commanders. Many had reached the touted rank of ace, while others had stayed in combat too long. Gen. Kenney had counseled his high scoring veterans to not be foolhardy in their race for the Rickenbacker record, but none the less, two of his adventurous young leaders were lost. Neel Kearby had been killed in a dogfight over Wewak on March 5th. Four days later, Tom Lynch was killed when he fell to enemy flak at Tadji. Dick Bong, now with 25 confirmed kills, was the last man capable of reaching the elusive victory record.

Operations in April became more routine for the pilots of Ramu Valley. Only the P-38 wing at Nadzab was able to keep up the chase of the JAAF at far off Hollandia. On April 12th, Bong scored two more victories over Hollandia to set the new American record at 27. The event was fleeting, however, as the record was matched in May by Thunderbolt pilot Bob Johnson of the 56 FG in England.

As for the disgruntled 9 FS saddled with their ungainly P-47s, they were still in the lead with a tally of 177 confirmed kills, even though they had not seen the enemy for nearly a month. For the 49ers overall score, Blacksheep Don Meuten's kill on February 6th was confirmed as the 400th aerial victory for the group.

## ONE BRAVE SENTAI MAN; APRIL 11, 1944

By April, the bombing missions to Wewak had become a milk run for the veterans of 5 BC and new bomber crews were often initiated to combat by hitting the once great enemy complex from low altitude where light, inaccurate flak would be sent up by the airdrome refugees. On April 11th during such a mission for the 312 BG in their new A-20s, the escort pilots in the Blacksheep formation were amazed to find an airborne target over forsaken Wewak. There over the abandoned airdrome at 10,000 feet came a lone Tony.

Mission leader Lt. Bob Aschenbrener called in the target and initiated a climbing attack, when the sentai pilot did a most peculiar thing. Rather than turn off and escape at his superior altitude, the enemy flyer plunged down toward the shoreline and headed west. Five hot-blooded Blacksheep killers sped off after the tragic fellow who suddenly wheeled around to fight it out. Aschenbrener fired over 700 rounds into the Ki-61 and the others hit him as well, until mercifully, Lt. Ed Glascock put an end to the farce. Back at Gusap, the Blacksheep drank to Glascock's health and quietly wondered, "Was that last guy over Wewak just sayin' sayonara, or was he just another crazy Jap?"

# 17
# HOLLANDIA, 1944

The acceleration of Gen. MacArthur's plan for the Philippines invasion had left the war-weary 49ers out of the advanced force for the first time in the war. With two squadrons still in the short-range P-40 and the other squadron about to reequip with the P-38, LtC. David Campbell's high scoring fighter group was consigned to wait in the sweltering heat of the New Guinea jungle while the air battle raged over the new JAAF headquarters at Hollandia. In that great contest, the 80 FS Headhunters went on a killing rampaged and surpassed Maj. Wally Jordan's Flying Knights as the top scoring squadron in the Pacific. It was almost more than the Knights could bear.

During that period, the P-40's of Arland Stanton's 7 FS and Bob McHale's 8 FS upheld their tactical role. When the 49ers were not strafing targets along the coast or flying up to Tadji to escort the returning Liberators and Mitchells back to Nadzab, the pilots found their names posted to the new training schedules. The Screamin' Demons, Blacksheep and Flying Knights ventured off to the neighboring air strips and checked out in the P-40s and P-47s respectively. Others were sent down to Nadzab or Dobodura where many a 49er flew the P-38 for the first time. The Lightnings were old stager F and G models in the Nadzab and Dobodura maintenance squadrons which were held in service specifically for familiarization flights. But the old Lockheeds could be treacherous.

## ANOTHER TRAINING FLIGHT DEATH;
## LT. BOB HARPER, APRIL 12, 1944

On a training sortie from Nadzab, the Knights' Lt. Bob Harper was killed after his older model ship crashed near its base. Two other 9

*Tumultuous Humbolt Bay at Hollandia in May, 1944. The 49ers ground echelons who downloaded there actually bivouacked just a few yards beyond the stocked piled materials and munitions.*

*Veteran Flying Knight Jimmie Harris and his crewchief during an overhaul of their Thunderbolt #71 just days before the pilot mustered out for home in April. His P-47 was turned in at the Nadzab complex, only to be lost with a 312 BG pilot on a training flight in late April. The wreckage was found thirty-five years later in the mountains by British explorers.*

FS men experienced landing accidents, but if LtC. Campbell was to fulfill his promise to get them all back in the P-38s, they would simply have to take their chances in the rebuilt Lightnings.

## LEAVING RAMU VALLEY; APRIL, 1944

As of the first week in the month, Screamin' Demon CO Stanton had received word from 5 FC CO Wurtsmith to mobilize once again, and there was very little prodding needed to encourage the 7 FS crews to leave dreary Gusap. The ground echelons readily took down their tent city and crated up their gear once more. By mid-month, the enlisted men from HQ and the 7 FS waited for the C-47s to take them out of the remote valley for once and for all.

*9 FS Lewelling and aircraft #99 in late March at Gusap in the twilight of the P-47 era. The aircraft bears the veteran P-38 pilot's Rabaul kill of November 2nd, 1943.*

Major McHale had also been advised to make ready for the 8th Squadron's next advance. Trucks transported their gear up to the 49ers Gusap headquarters for the pending move and operations began to lag as a skeleton line crew kept up the 8 FS mission schedule. All of the Warhawks were soon relegated to the target egress escorts.

## POINTLESS LOSS OF LT. DALE ARNOLD; APRIL 7, 1944

No sooner had Campbell recovered from the loss of Group Exec Cash, another 7 FS man fell from their ranks. On the routine mission of April 7th, Lt. Dale Arnold had descended along the shoreline of Cape Moem to investigate a possible target hidden in the plantation groves when his P-40 struck the water. Flight members watched as the fighter rose off the harbor surface, but the plane stalled out and dropped into the sea for good. The last sign of Dale Arnold was the bubbling whirlpool where his P-40 sank into the deep blue harbor waters.

## BLACK SUNDAY; APRIL 16, 1944

Nine days after Arnold's singular loss, an incident occurred in the New Guinea war that would result in the highest operational loss for the 5 AF on a single day. And it was once again at the whim of New Guinea's unpredictable weather.

Most of the flights from the Ramu airstrips were down on that afternoon of April 12th due to a spreading storm which had risen high over the coast. By mid-day, the coastal entrance to greater Markham Valley was completely socked in. Aircraft returning from that day's mission desperately tried to reach Nadzab, but soon, hundreds of planes were signalling any field for help. Warplanes of every description dropped through the wind-whipped rain into Ramu Valley and made for Gusap.

At Gusap #10, the line crews were alerted to the approach of a Liberator which was down to its last few gallons of gas. Badly damaged in combat, the huge aircraft finally drifted down for the runway, but the heavy landing was more than the B-24 could take. As it slid to a halt, it twisted into a gruesome tangle of aluminum, wires and shredded control surfaces. All was doused in oil and gas. Blacksheep ground personnel immediately joined in the rescue of the trapped Liberator crewmen. Lt. Emila Plichta, T/Sgt. Bruno Topik and Sgts. Irwin Blount, Bernie Tate and Mike Slavik struggled down into the wreckage and withdrew two men, but they were the only survivors.

There were thirty-one other such incidents of aircraft losses throughout central New Guinea. Thirty two crewmen in all would die. Luckily for everyone at Gusap, the line crews kept the residual fuel from exploding and killing even more.

## REBIRTH OF THE LIGHTNING SQUADRON; APRIL 17, 1944

True to his word, on April 17th LtC. Campbell posted the names of the Flying Knights to fly the first combat mission in a P-38 since November of 1943. Seven reserve Lightnings had been completely

*5 AF CO Enis Whitehead (lt.), 5 FC pilot Bong and 5 FC CO Wurtsmith at Nadzab and the publicity session for the ace's new American victory record as of late April, 1944.*

refitted and were approved for duty at Gusap #10. Campbell flew lead in the only J model, a silver machine formerly flown by the 80 FS, while Squadron CO Jordan and five senior flight leaders took charge of the old F and G stagers. The sortie was just a routine escort to Tadji, but Capt. Wandrey aptly remarked, "They're tired old tubs, but they're not those damned P-47s."

By the end of the April, the older ships were replaced by more of the refurbished, uncamouflaged J models which were handed down from the Headhunters and Satin's Angels who in turn received newer Lockheeds. The P-38J was essentially the same as the old model G, but was easily distinguishable by the deeper beard radiators under the prop spinners. The supercharger cooling radiators on the rear fuselages were also enlarged.

## DEMON/BLACKSHEEP INGENUITY

As the Knights refitted in their hand-me-down P-38s, the Warhawk squadron engineers and mechanics tried to convert their short-range fighters into a more strategic weapon. To reach distant Hollandia, the P-40 simply had to go beyond its normal 400 mile combat radius.

The line crews worked around the clock at Gusap to fit each 7th and 8th Squadron P-40s with a temporary fuel line plumbed to each underwing bomb shackle. A free swinging 75 gallon fuel tank was then bolted on to each wing shackle in addition to the one hung beneath the fuselage. Since the two wing tanks could not be dropped, their fuel was to be consumed first. One of the Demon pilots tested the setup and remained airborne over Ramu Valley for seven hours that was roughly calculated as a range of 1200 miles. A round-trip sortie to Hollandia would have been a cinch, but the field modified Curtiss was too late for the April campaign, and was never approved for combat.

## CAPT. GEORGE ALLEN DEAD; APRIL 20, 1944

The Screamin' Demons were cursed. On the 20th, senior Capt. George Allen, only days from completing his tour, was in the lead of a training flight when the captain's P-40 mysterious plunged from the sky. Allen apparently attempted to bail out and his chute failed, or he was possibly thrown clear from the spinning Warhawk just before impact. Whatever the case, his body was recovered a short distance from the crash site and was buried at Nadzab in the American cemetery. LtC. Campbell sternly reiterated to all of his men to stay sharp and not consider any flight as merely routine.

## TADJI AND HOLLANDIA FALL; 22 AND 24 APRIL, 1944

Campbell's 49ers ground echelons eventually boarded air transports at Gusap and flew off to the Allied staging harbor at Finschhafen. In the interim, the air echelons awaited transports to the north, but due to another change in Gen. MacArthur's scheme, their destination had become somewhat of a logistical quandary.

Far to the west, the invasion of Tadji on the 22nd and Hollandia on the 24th had been a unqualified success. On the 23rd, newly

*9 FS newcomer Jim Poston and "DOPEY-BESSIE J. IV" in the last days at Gusap.*

*9 FS Thunderbolt pilot Dick Kirkland about to take his first solo flight with Sgt. Charlie Kurtz in the jump seat of an old stager P-38 at Nadzab. The lieutenant had a probable kill in the P-47 on March 14th, and would have one of the first confirmed kills in the second Lightning era on May 19th over Manokwari Island.*

promoted Gen. Paul Wurtsmith and air task force coordinator Col. Bob Morrissey had flown their P-38s up to rustic Tadji where they judged the primitive sandy strip unsuitable even for the rugged Warhawks, let alone the heavier bombers. MacArthur's amphibious offensive had gotten too far ahead of the tactical air force and the fighter pilot commanders opted to move their operations all the way to Hollandia.

The end result of the altered logistics stranded the 49ers ground echelon at muddy Finschhafen with no tents and no guarantee of portage to a better facility. Some of the men borrowed Navy tarpaulins and bivouacked on the beach. At the same time, the Group's air echelon lingered in Ramu Valley purportedly waiting to muster out for Tadji. LtC. David Campbell sat in Gusap in command of a unit whose ground personnel was scattered throughout the rear lines while his pilots were about to advance to the front.

## P-40'S TO HOLLANDIA; MAY 4, 1944

The 49ers operational dilemma was finally put to rest when the Screamin' Demons' air echelon was picked up by the Dakota transports and taken directly to Hollandia on May 3rd. On the 5th, the Blacksheep echelon team flew off for the new base and the Flying Knights team followed on the 6th.

On the morning of May 4th, the Screamin' Demons with CO Stanton in the lead, rose up from Gusap in their triple-tank toting fighters and lumbered off to the north. Two days later, CO McHale took his Blacksheep north in the same fashion. The Flying Knights followed on the 10th in the rebuilt P-38s and with their passage, all of the 49ers aircraft successfully made the 450 miles cross-country to Hollandia. Group CO Campbell was greatly relieved for the moment.

## DUSTY AIRSTRIPS OF MUDDY HOLLANDIA

A 49ers veteran recalled many years after his brief stay at Hollandia, "It was the only place a guy could stand in mud up to his knees while the wind blew dust in his face." Indeed, Hollandia had turned out to be some what of a hollow prize. Like Tadji and Aitape, the loamy soil was unsuitable to repair the bomb-cratered Hollandia complex. With enough Marston steel matting, the Warhawks and Lightnings could make due, but Gen. Kenney's bombers would still had to operate from distant Nadzab for the time being.

Meanwhile, thousands of Allied troops disembarked at crowded Humbolt Bay which served the old mining outpost village of Hollandia proper. Inland to the southwest through a shallow pass in the coastal Cyclops Mountains was the broad valley which held long narrow Sentani Lake. On the north shore of the lake were the three landing fields which had been hastily constructed by the enemy's 4th Air Army.

There was only one narrow dirt road which climbed through the pass and it quickly proved to be inadequate for the parade of trucks which attempted to clear the choked beachhead of men and supplies. After a truck crew overcame the muddy, crowded ascent for the first three miles, they would descend inland another seven miles until they reached Cyclops airfield and adjacent Sentani strip, and then the final three miles to Hollandia field.

There was total devastation everywhere. The aerial assault in April had been equal to the great raids brought down on Rabaul, Cape Glouster and Wewak, but at Hollandia, the fields were closer together in the narrow valley which seemed to magnify the destruction. Crushed, burned out aircraft, vehicles and buildings littered the valley floor and there was more wreckage on the slopes of the hills above the airdrome. Over four-hundred enemy aircraft had been lost in the maelstrom, the greater percentage of them being caught on the ground.

*Refit 8 FS aircraft #44 renamed "GEORGIA'S JILTED" at Hollandia shortly after the May advance. The Blacksheep pilot is unidentified.*

*7 FS John Miller in aircraft #16 with the distinctive blue diamond pattern on the rudder about to make one last Gusap patrol.*

*P-38s of 5 FC pilots Col. Morrissey and Gen. Wurtsmith on their inspection flight to Tadji on April 23rd. The Lightning on the left is Bong's old aircraft "MARGE" commandeered by Morrissey and still retaining the red wingtips and spinners, but minus the 27-victory scoreboard. Wurtsmith's personal aircraft s.n. 2104004 with the command tri-colors of blue, yellow and red on the spinners and tail tips was one of several aircraft maintained by the Nadzab aircrews for 5 FC officers.*

The Army engineers spent the better part of their labors pushing aside the tangled debris from the airstrips for the arrival of the first 5 AF fighters for base defense. It was at wreckage strewn Sentani runway that Major Arland Stanton's 7 FS P-40s landed, followed by Major Bob McHale's Warhawks at Cyclops field. When Major Wally Jordan's Lightnings arrived on Hollandia main field, LtC. David Campbell proudly informed Fighter Command that all of the 49ers were ready for duty. Indeed, the Warhawks were in action within forty-eight hours.

## LT. ANTHONY SPEARS DEAD AT FINSCHHAFEN; MAY 5, 1944

After settling in at Hollandia, a communique reached LtC. Campbell that one of his pilots flying attached to the 58th Materials Squadron at Finschhafen had been killed. Lt. Anthony Spear had been ferrying a P-40 to Finschhafen and had failed the landing at the rain soaked strip. The lieutenant died instantly in the crash.

LtC. Campbell notified Blacksheep CO McHale who woefully saw to the appropriate letter writing to Spear's family while likewise preparing for the next sortie. But none of the Blacksheep could possibly be prepared for the heart rending loss which would occur two days later.

## FIRST ESCORT TO BIAK; MAY 7, 1944

The JAAF command had withdrawn from New Guinea entirely, and once again had abandoned its irreplaceable ground crews to the invaders. From the new headquarters at Manado in the Celebes Islands, the JAAF attempted to stall MacArthur's advance with their depleted air force that numbered barely more than a hundred serviceable planes. The major staging field between the Celebes and Hollandia was at the island of Biak which lay across the entrance to spacious Geelvink Bay on the New Guinea north shore. Biak Island with its hard white coral runways was deemed ideal for 5th Bomber Command operations and it became MacArthur's next objective in his drive for the Philippines.

On May 7th, the 49ers put eleven Blacksheep and sixteen Demon Warhawks over the B-24s which raided Biak at 1100 hours. The Japanese interceptors there, though small in number, were some of the most aggressive pilots the 49ers would ever encounter.

## ELOFSON'S 8 FS ENGAGEMENT; 1150 HOURS

Despite only having twelve P-40's operational and one of those not making the 300 mile ocean crossing, Capt. Fats Elofson had his three flights stacked between 12 to 15,000 feet over the strike force when they reached the target. Elofson was in Red Flight with Lts. Bob Sweeney and Marion Felts on the high left flank in front of the

*One of the first 49ers aircraft to reach Cyclops airfield at Hollandia was Bob DeHaven's old stager "RITA" still displaying the ace's seven kill flags beneath the port-side windshield. Refit and issued to the Blacksheep, the old charger toted three drop tanks and flew from Gusap non-stop to Hollandia on May 5th.*

formation. To their right was Lt. Nelson Flack's White Flight team of Lts. Bill Runey, Howard Wayne and John Davis. To the rear came the Green Flight trio that remained in trailing high cover and would not engage in the impending fight.

The B-24s had completed their bombing run and had just turned due southeast to escape when Elofson saw two enemy planes closing in on the Liberators from the right. He was about to call for the break for the two ZEROs when the Screamin' Demons from the opposite side of the strike force formation called out more fighters in the area. Elofson scanned the sky overhead one last time and then looked back to see the ZEKE pair turn for the B-24s. The captain could wait no longer and turned for the dark green enemy planes just as a aerial phosphorous bomb showered its white tentacles behind the Liberators formation.

All of the Blacksheep in Red and White Flights wheeled into the pursuit behind the mission leader and chased after the Mitsubishis. In spite of gunfire from all seven Warhawks, the leading kokutai aviator pressed in on the bombers and fired at one of the Liberators. He might have escaped if he had then broken off his attack, but Elofson caught the fearless aviator as he rose up for

another pass. Flames erupted from the black cowling and the aviator tumbled free to deploy his parachute. White Flight wingman Davis swept in and executed the enemy pilot before his reached the sea. Meanwhile, Red wingman Felts overtook the other ZERO for one trailing gunnery pass, then half-rolled out and came back down for the head-on coup de grace.

## STANTON'S DUPLICATE ENGAGEMENT

The Screamin' Demons had indeed seen the same two ZEROs at the same time as the Blacksheep. The 7 FS CO himself had taken his four wingman down for the chase and Major Stanton fired at the same ZERO fired upon by the Blacksheep mission leader. Likewise, Stanton's trailing wingman Lt. Fenton Epling also shot at the enemy pilot who had bailed out of the stricken ZEKE.

However, while the Blacksheep withdrew, Stanton called down his other three Demon flights after he spotted a large group of OSCARs which next drew into view. In seconds, Blue Flight leader Capt. Ed Peck and Green Flight element leader Lt. Joel Paris both

*7 FS Jack Langenburg's #25 "PAT'S CHATTER" resting at dusty Cyclops in early May.*

*Left: Jim Reynold's old stager #68 "NORMA" made the Hollandia advance only to blow her left tire when she touched down. The left strut sheared off in the drainage ditch paralleling the strip, but the tough old girl was set upright and put back on duty within a week. Right: Blacksheep aircraft #59 takes off from Cyclops on a mission to distant Biak in the second week of May.*

*7 FS Ops Exec Hap Chandler brought aircraft #1 "BETS" up to Hollandia.*

*Typical of many Screamin' Demons P-40Ns, Chandler's aircraft #1 also displayed the girl of "DAWN PATROL" painted by talented Dunne.*

dispatched a Ki-43 apiece. Blue wingman Lt. John Roberts made three firing passes at a swerving OSCAR until the riddled ship stalled out in an inverted flat spin. Only seconds from an assured kill, Robert's left aileron was struck by a 12mm round which forced him to break down and away before the victory could be confirmed. Paris quickly re-engaged and fatally hit his second OSCAR of the sortie while Green wingman Lt. Fred Dick destroyed yet another.

As the Demons sped back to attack altitude, Lt. Dick caught site of his second target that day. Below at 11,000 feet was the newest addition in the Japanese arsenal, the more powerful cousin of the Ki-43. Code named the TOJO, the new Nakajima Ki-44 had a bigger power plant and distinctly smaller wings, but it was much faster than the OSCAR as this fellow was proving by outpacing six P-40s in hot pursuit.

Lt. Dick saw the opening growing between the TOJO and the nearest Warhawk. At a attack speed of 450 Mph, the lieutenant dropped into line directly behind the stubby-winged sprinter and raked its fuselage from prop to rudder. After the tail section separated and the sentai pilot dropped free in his chute, Dick kicked his speeding P-40 into a hard rudder turn and fired at the descending pilot, but his shot went wide. He pulled his rocketing P-40 skyward to recovered at 6000 feet, only to find himself all alone two miles south of Biak. Minutes later after heading east, he found squadron mate Epling and they set off together for Hollandia. All of the Blacksheep, including Roberts with his torn left aileron, safely reached home.

## DeHAVEN'S TENTH

The whole fight had only lasted about ten minutes and the trailing elements of Lt. Bob DeHaven's Green Flight had never been in position to attack the sparse number of airborne targets off Biak. Resigned to confirm the other 49ers victories, DeHaven's Demon quartet was the last to withdraw behind the bombers when mission leader Elofson called off the fight. When they reached the New Guinea coast, the ace Green Flight leader saw a single OSCAR far below tracking the retreat of the B-24s.

It was almost too easy. DeHaven and wingman Lt. Ray Rogers slowly dropped out of formation and plunged unseen behind the lone Ki-43. DeHaven closed to within fifty feet of the pathetic sentai pilot and killed him with a three second burst of fire. The OSCAR rolled and dropped inverted straight into the sea for the ace's tenth aerial victory.

## MISSING DON MEUTEN; MAY 7, 1944

It would have been a perfect mission for the victorious Warhawk pilots except for the mysterious loss of leading resident Blacksheep ace Don Meuten. Originally in the lead of Green Flight, he dropped out only minutes after takeoff due to a loss of power. Within sight of Tanahmera Bay, just fifteen air miles west of Sentani strip, he signalled that he was sure the sputtering P-40 could clear the Cyclops foothills, only to radio minutes later he was bailing out.

Don Meuten vanished. For three days, search flights scoured the Tanahmera coastline but not a single trace was found. The men at Sentani airstrip were mortified. The missing ace had been an inspiration to everyone.

## VOYAGE OF THE USAT DAVID BERRY; MAY 10, 1944

In the meantime back at Finschhafen on May 10th, the stranded 49ers ground units finally embarked on the USAT David Berry and two smaller LST craft for the voyage to catch up with their flight team at Hollandia. The Berry and the LSTs were also packed with additional equipment for other units which made life on board the crowded ships chaotic at best. The only consolation was the relatively short crossing to Humbolt Bay which lasted four days.

When the three ships arrived at Hollandia late in the afternoon of the 14th, the 8 FS personnel were amazed to find an immense military camp completely covering the harbor beach. Infantry were bivouacked everywhere along with other USAAF crews who could not find portage inland. Three miles south of Hollandia village, the Blacksheep were down loaded at the village of Pie, just inland from one the principle ammo dumps. On the afternoon of the 15th, a Japanese air raid swept overhead and a stick of bombs fell on the ordinance stockpiled on the beach. There was a tremendous explosion which echoed all the way inland to the airdrome and the fireball was seen far out to sea. The fires would rage all through the night and well into the following day.

## DEATH OF CPL. WILLIAMS ON PIE BEACH; MAY 16, 1944

Unfortunately, the personnel of the newly arrived 49ers ground echelon were not spared. On the night of the 15th, Blacksheep crewman Cpl. Woodrow Williams was mortally wounded when the burning ammo erupted in a secondary explosion which showered the 8th Squadron bivouac with shrapnel. Later that night as the troops fought to put out the blaze, many more of them were hit by yet another blast, but none very seriously. Williams died the next day in the field hospital and LtC. Campbell furiously demanded the Army motor pool get trucks to his besieged 49ers and get them off the bloody beach.

## ROUGH TREATMENT AT BIAK; MAY 15, 1944

At the time the Japanese were raiding Hollandia, the 5 AF was likewise back over Biak. In escort to a pair of 71st Reconnaissance Squadron B-25 Mitchells, the Screamin' Demons would enter into their second dogfight with the Biak defenders, but this time, four Demons would barely escape with their lives.

7 FS pilots (1) Jarrell, (2) Keck, (3) O'Neill, (4) Atkinson, (5) Langenburg and (6) Paris at Hollandia in late May. Langenburg has a grip on the Demons only prisoner of war, a starved Japanese airman who was left behind in retreat. MPs had no facilities for the many refugees who were caught trying to steal food from the Allied camp and the Demons had to keep the miserable fellow in their care as a house boy for several days.

At half past eleven, Demon Capt. Owen "Onie" Swartz had his four flights stacked from 15 to 20,000 feet over the Mitchells when they reached their island objective. Biak was predominantly covered with heavy cumulus clouds, so the eight P-40s of Swartz's Red Flight and Lt. Menger's White Flight dropped down beneath the cloud cover to stay in contact with the B-25s who soon disappeared under the overcast. After several turns southeast of the obscured target, Swartz called for the Demons to withdraw. Unknowingly, the captain flew east for home as his top cover briefly engaged in a vicious exchange with a mixed flight of OSCAR and ZERO veterans.

## GREEN FLIGHT ENGAGES THE ZEROS

Blue Flt Ldr Lt. John Haher and Green Flt Ldr Lt. Lew Smith remained in high cover as ordered, but had none the less descended to 11,000 feet to keep the other eight Warhawks and the two Mitchells in view. Smith's four Green elements were on the left flank when they caught site of eight OSCARs and four ZEROs approaching head-on 2000 feet overhead. The four ZEROs to Smith's left immediately began to let down and turned toward his Green elements.

Green Flt Ldr Smith knew the situation was not good and instantly countered by turning into the diving ZEKEs. In seconds, the two opposing flights were nose to nose and both groups opened fire. Smith was right on target as his blue-nosed rounds sparkled on the center fuselage of a ZERO which snap rolled and its pilot bailed out.

Flight Ldr Smith and wingman Lt. Nic Zuniga wheeled to the left to re-engage. Again from head-on, Smith blew the left wing off a ZERO whose debris slammed into Zuniga's Warhawk leaving a five-foot long gash in the leading edge of the P-40's right wing. As Zuniga momentarily fell away in a spin, the OSCARs struck in a

*7 FS Lt. Zappia and his aircraft #14 "BROOKLYN'S BAD BOY" at Hollandia in late May, always in the fight but never an aerial killer.*

a heart-pounding 500 Mph escape within a hail of tracers while Gregzyn twisted down through the swirling OSCARs in his last attempt to fight back.

Finally too low on fuel to continue, tail-end Gregzyn found an opening and plunged out of the fight at 450 Mph. He found no other Warhawks, so he continued downward for the distant New Guinea coast and soon overtook three retreating Mitchells and their lone escort, Green element Jack Fenimore. Two OSCARs also were sighted there in pursuit of the four planes, but the Green flight escort was out of ammo. Gregzyn tagged on to the Ki-43 which had just opened fire on swerving Fenimore. The OSCAR's right wing exploded in flame and it rolled down into the deep cerulean Pacific. Gregzyn wheeled about for the other Nakajima, but the fellow obviously did not choose to play out the reversed odds. The fight had finally ended.

## DESPERATE DESCENT TO CYCLOPS

The flight home was no easy matter for the ravaged Demons. They were scattered all along the coast, and Larry McInnis, in particular, was in a bad way. Though an enemy round had shattered on the armor plate of his seat and the worst of the shrapnel had been absorbed by the oxygen equipment and his parachute pack, McInnis was now loosing blood from his torn right arm and there were hemorrhaging wounds in both of his legs. He held the control stick as best he could with his knees and reached back with his left hand to pull his medical kit from his chute. He cut the kit free with his knife, then pulled out a bandage with his teeth and somehow managed to apply a tourniquet to his right arm. He jammed another bandage against the bloody wound in his right leg and held it there with his throbbing right hand until the bleeding stopped. Miraculously, two hours later, Larry McInnis reached Cyclops and set his riddled P-40 down in a successful belly landing.

Nic Zuniga also chose to not lower the landing gear of his shattered right wing. He brought his broken P-40 down to a lurching dusty halt, but he was in good shape otherwise. Lew Smith landed and was quickly hustled off to the flight surgeon who treated his minor wound. He was pronounced fit to return to duty.

perfectly timed attack upon the separated Green wingmen. A pair of Ki-43s struck Smith who was wounded by a round which detonated in his cockpit and cut his right arm. As Smith rolled away for the safety of the clouds, he caught sight of Zuniga blasting another ZERO out of the sky which had dropped in front of his torn P-40. Luckily, both Smith and Zuniga got away.

The Green element lieutenants Jack Fenimore and Larry McInnis had managed to stay in the proximity of the lead Green elements, but neither man had fired with effect in the first pass. As element leader Fenimore and McInnis entered into the second pass, they also engaged the OSCARs and Fenimore sent one of them down in a shallow glide trailing smoke. As they watched the sentai man take to his chute, the Green elements were both hit by another pair of OSCARs.

Fenimore was able to outrun his assailant, but trailing element McInnis was not as fortunate. He had been able to score hits on one of the turning OSCARs, but as he turned for another firing run, McInnis came face to face with another OSCAR which opened fire. A thunderclap resounded in the cockpit. Hit hard, the stricken Demon pilot rolled his ship over and plunged away for the clouds. He tried to jettison his canopy and bail out, but after sliding back the mangled frame with his good left hand, wounded McInnis glanced at his instruments. Everything was working, so he decided to try for home.

### BLUE FLIGHT IS HIT

Blue Flight had been a short distance from Green Flight when the ZEROs first struck. Blue Leader Haher had turned for the Mitsubishis in a flanking counter-attack, but was cut off in his approach by the wily OSCAR pilots. Both Haher and his rookie wingman 2Lt. Doug Hart became so widely separated that both men had to dive out of the fight completely.

In the interim, Blue Flight elements Lts. Fred Dick and Warren Gregzyn both held formation long enough to turn into each others respective attacker. Both OSCARs were fatally hit. When they circled to reform for their second pass, Dick and Gregzyn were finally forced apart by the aggressive sentai. Dick plunged away in

*7 FS Jim Jarrell and his P-40N at Cyclops field at the end of the Biak missions. Jarrell and "SPOOKY" would survive the P-40 era to score his four aerial victories in the P-38 era of the Philippines campaign.*

*Above: 8 FS "RACOON SPECIAL" at Hollandia in June, 1944. Right: 8 FS engineering chief Lt. Bazan (lt.) kneels next to an unidentified crewman. Standing (lt.-rt.) are Sgts. Goyer, Watson and Topik, the principle members of the "RACOON SPECIAL" reconstruction team.*

As if to underscore the peril of the day, one of the elements from the Demon flights who had missed the action was injured in his landing. Second Lt. Jim Keck ground looped after touching down and survived with a minor cut on his head. At the debriefing, senior lieutenant John Haher summed up the harrowing mission saying glumly, "The nips were very eager and damned sharp. We were damn lucky."

## WARHAWK LEGACIES and the RACCOON SPECIAL

So ended the battle for Biak on the behalf of LtC. David Campbell's P-40 squadrons. Although other missions were flown over the coastal targets and islands of Geelvink Bay, the 49ers Warhawk pilots never saw another enemy aircraft come within firing range again. Warren Gregzyn's aerial victory at the close of the dogfight on May 15th was officially confirmed as the Screamin' Demons' 112 victory. And Marion Felt's victory on May 7th for the Blacksheep made them the most dangerous Warhawk outfit in the Pacific with an aerial kill record of 152.

The Blacksheep also accomplished something the USAAF engineers had not been able to do since the war began. The squadron engineering officer, Lt. Ed Bazan, commandeered the skillful line crew of S/Sgt Goyer, T/Sgt Topik, Sgt. Hal Watson and Cpls. Thompson and Wiliet to rebuild an enemy fighter. In the trees not far from Cyclops runway, Bazan selected a 59th Sentai Ki-43 OSCAR model II in relatively sound condition. After the team scrounged through other numerous wrecks in the area, they refit their OSCAR with new control surfaces, a rebuilt engine and reconstructed landing gear. Armorer M/Sgt Charlie Mickey even

replumped the 12mm guns. All of the shrapnel holes were spot riveted and Sgt. Topik was particularly impressed by the fine craftsmanship of the metalwork in the OSCAR's fuselage. Everyone was stunned to find the corporate logo of America's Kaiser Aluminum printed on some of the metal panels.

Dubbed the "Raccoon Special" after the Blacksheep call sign, the Ki-43 was stripped down to bare metal and the rudder was painted in pre-war red, white and blue bars. Over-sized national insignia were added to dissuade any overzealous Allied pilot from blasting it out of the air. With the official sanction of 5 AF CO Kenney himself, Maj. Bob McHale took the gleaming Ki-43 up over Hollandia with a pair of 8 FS P-40s in escort and put on a aerobatic demonstration, even though somewhat restricted. Kenney was rightly impressed and personally congratulated the Blacksheep wizards for their initiative. Unfortunately, the prized OSCAR was soon commandeered for further evaluation. S/Sgt John Westbrook etched a small aluminum plate with the names of the Blacksheep men who had rebuilt the OSCAR and riveted the devise to the fuselage beneath the cockpit. To the Blacksheep, the "Raccoon Special" would always be an 8 FS machine.

## COMMAND CHANGES FOR THE WARHAWK SQUADRONS

At the same time, Blacksheep CO Bob McHale left the 8 FS to join the 49ers HQ staff. He handed the reigns over to senior man Charles Petersen who was summarily promoted to the rank of major.

The Screamin' Demons' ace CO had also completed his tour. Maj. Arland Stanton, one of the most decorated pilots in Fighter Command, opted out for the States and command school. He would never tour the Pacific again. Senior Capt. Ed Peck who had only fired once at an enemy aircraft, was next in line for the command slot over double-ace Bob DeHaven, but Peck was considered one of the best tacticians in the group. Boyish DeHaven readily understood and enthusiastically took the 7 FS Ops Exec job.

By that time, Major Wally Jordan had finally acquired a mixed livery of twenty-four P-38 J models and newer L models for the 9 FS. In the last week of May, the Flying Knights were once again inducted into the strategic long range war. Although Jordan was advised by Squeeze Wurtsmith to not take foolish chances, the CO of the Flying Knights and eager 49ers CO Campbell were now pledged to regain the scoring lead and put the rival Headhunters back in second place where they belonged.

With Biak now scheduled for invasion, more sweeps were directed further west to the vestige staging bases of the enemy. At the jungle outpost of Manokwari on the western shore of Geelvink Bay, enemy fighters were seen dispersed in the trees and B-24s were sent there to deny them any opportunity to intervene during the Allied landings at nearby Biak.

## THE 9 FS LIGHTNING WAR RENEWED; MAY 19, 1944

On the morning of the 19th, the Knights had eleven Lightnings over Hollandia to rendezvous with the Liberators for the 475 mile

*9 FS CO Wally Jordan in the second Flying Knights P-38 tour as of June, 1944.*

*New Demons CO Ed Peck and his aircraft #27 "RHODE ISLAND RED", or more to the point, "ROSIE CHEEKS" just days before the move to Biak. Though the captain had scored only a single aerial victory as of the Biak campaign, he was considered to be one of the best squadron leaders to rise up in the 5 AF.*

trip to Manokwari. At half past noon, Maj. Jordan led his Red Flight element Lts. Dick Kirkland, Charles Kamphausen and Willis Treadway west of the objective at 15,000 feet to defend the Liberators' right flank when four stubby winged TOJOs drew into view from the southeast. One of them was in high-cover and the other three were nearer together at 9000 feet. Some distance off and out of sight from Red Flight were four other Ki-44s, but they were seen well in advance by the elements in the Knights' White and Blue Flights.

## JORDAN'S RED FLIGHT ATTACK

Mission leader Jordan pushed his throttle forward and rose up toward the single top-cover TOJO to foil any threat from above, then peeled off and rolled in on a firing pass at the other three enemy planes. Jordan first hit the element leader, then bored in on one the sentai wingman. Red wingman Kirkland followed up on the sentai leader and both of the TOJOs quickly fell in flames. Jordan's victim dropped free in his chute.

## WHITE AND BLUE FLIGHT STRIKE

Indeed, from their top-cover position at 20,000 feet, Capt. Del Moore at the head of White Flight had seen the other four TOJOs approaching from the northwest. The captain with wingman 2Lt. Ed Cooper, element leader Lt. Bill Maddox and wingman 2Lt. Nile Lambert skillfully came down in attack formation on the four Ki-44s and each man fired in succession. Moore knocked the canopy off of his target, but the TOJO left the flight apparently still able to fly. Element leader Maddox made a rear quarter pass, then chandelled back up for a second head-on pass which left his target falling toward the jungle trailing smoke.

Blue Flt Ldr Lt. Charles McElroy with wingmen Lts. Bill Baxter and Huard Norton came down last on the turning TOJOs and all three fired until Baxter overtook a straggler in a 400 Mph chase. At 400 yards, Baxter opened fired again and closed in until the TOJO's stubby left wing broke off. The fight was over and Jordan called everyone to join up for the flight home.

After confirmation by the S-2 division, Jordan's kill was recorded in the Group's roster while the two victories of Baxter and Kirkland were added to the 9 FS scoreboard. The Knights' drank a toast to the picture perfect interception that had brought them their first Lockheed kill since way last November. They were back in the hunt.

## TAKING BIAK; LATE MAY, 1944

Fifth Fighter Command at Hollandia turned its attention back to Biak as a precursor to the amphibious landing. On the 24th, senior Capt. Ralph Wandrey led a hair-raising dive bombing mission with the P-38s against the shore batteries on Biak's southern shore. To avoid the trajectory of the enemy guns, the Flying Knights flew so low in their strafing runs that they would literally look up at the Imperial gun crews. The sorties were concluded without a Lightning being lost.

## NORTHCUTT LOST AT WAKDE ISLAND; MAY 24, 1944

The Blacksheep had been equally fortunate in the tactical assaults over the invasion objective, but one of their men was lost while in

*9 FS pilots in the final mission briefing at the operations center at Hollandia. Maj. Jordan is second from the right in his familiar white flight cap.*

*Crews top off the wing tanks of the refit P-38J's issued to the 9 FS from the fighter pool at Nadzab. Most of the old 8 FG and 475 FG Lightnings continued in service with 49ers until their attrition in the Philippines campaign.*

retreat. On the 24th, newcomer Lt. Bill Northcutt had flown the mission against Biak and experienced engine failure on the way home. He made a safe emergency landing at newly captured Wakde Island on the coast 150 miles short of Hollandia, but in his attempt to takeoff after rudimentary repairs, the P-40 fell inverted into the sea just off the end of the runway. No trace of Northcutt was ever found.

Three days later, Allied infantry waded ashore on bomb-cratered Biak's southeastern beach. Initial retaliation was light, but that night, Japanese defenders hidden in caves further on shore began to lob mortars down on the Allied beachhead. For the next two months, a grueling campaign was fought out in the jungle foothills while Gen. George Kenney's air force advanced into the captured airdrome.

*8 FS C.C. Pop Walker, one of the last of the Darwin cadre who reached Biak and finally muster out in September, 1944.*

*9 FS Kirkland's P-38J-15 "MISS JERRY" s.n. 43-28525 used in the May 19th Manokwari mission.*

*Another spirited basketball game on the flightline while the P-38s venture far off to western New Guinea. Long routes to the targets and long waits at the bases were tiring for pilots and crews alike.*

*9 FS mess crew led by their brawny bearded mess sergeant in the Gusap-Biak era. In spite of a foreboding appearance, the powerful fellow was rather shy and was an accomplished baker.*

## MOVING UP AGAIN; JUNE OF 1944

Newly promoted Major Ed Peck's first duty as Demon CO was to get his ground echelon mobilized at Hollandia once again with the rest of the 49ers for the move up to Biak. On June 2nd, the 49ers were back at crowded Humbolt Bay where they piled on board two LSTs for the three-day crossing to Biak. A remnant air echelon remained at Cyclops field to service the last of the Hollandia sorties. The following morning, the LSTs ladened with 49ers pulled out into the Pacific and steered west along the New Guinea coast just as a sprawling formation of twenty Lightnings rose up from the airdrome. At the lead was the 49ers LtC. David Campbell, going off to hunt for the enemy once again.

## A SINGLE LOSS ON JUNE 3, 1944

Despite the far reaching offensive to eliminate the remnant JAAF, MacArthur's new Allied camp at Biak was still victim to nightly raids. Finally, 5 AF reconnaissance found one of the major sources of the problem far off on the west coast of New Guinea. Five hundred miles due west of Hollandia on the twisting shore line of McCluer Gulf, the Japanese had built a large staging base at remote Babo village. A large force of fighters were poised there for the next strike against Biak and Gen. Kenney directed Gen. Wurtsmith to send his Lightning wing there to eradicate the threat for once and for all.

*9 FS Babo raiders of June 3rd. Standing lt.-rt.; Cooper, Lewelling, Davis, Oglesby, Krankowitz, Treadway, CO McComsey, Williams, Fisher, Curton, Datzenko, Hamburger, Nelson and McElroy. Kneeling lt.-rt.; Poston, Lewis, Hufford, Estes, Swift and Helterline.*

*9 FS veteran Lt. Eddie "Legs" Howes and his trusty aircraft #71 which got him his second career kill at Babo.*

*Helterline poses by the victory flag on his P-38 at Biak several days after the famous Babo raid.*

Squeeze Wurtsmith gave the June 3rd mission to Maj. Wally Jordan's Flying Knights. Group CO Campbell, however, pulled rank in planning the mission and opened the roster to the senior pilots at Hollandia. Major Bob McHale from HQ and the returned veteran Capt. Don Lee, now in command of the 67 FS from the 13 AF, readily signed on. Since the 9 FS only had twenty serviceable P-38s on the line, Campbell again pulled rank and bumped Jordan. The Group CO was determined to lead what would likely be the last big fight over New Guinea.

Setting off at 0830, the Lightnings climbed to 15,000 feet and took a direct route over the interior where one man turned back from Capt. Eddie Howes' Green Flight. Campbell pushed on over Geelvink Bay. All nineteen pilots successfully reached the western shoreline and peered down through the broken cumulus suspended 8000 down to 1000 feet. Directly ahead was the narrow southern isthmus of Vogelcop Peninsula, its broad headlands sprawling off to the north. Beyond the twenty-five mile wide land bridge was McCluer Gulf whose southern shoreline marked the way another fifty miles to the mission objective.

They passed over the isthmus and flight leaders broke radio silence. Weapons were test fired and gun sights were checked one last time. Campbell began to descend for a better look at the obscured target. It was half past eleven.

### THE LAST GREAT DOGFIGHT OVER NEW GUINEA

Mission leader Campbell headed up Yellow Flight with Maj. McHale on his wing, and element leader Lt. Al Lewelling and wingman Lt. Huard Norton in trail. Campbell's quartet dropped down to the top of the clouds and cruised over the jig-saw shoreline where they crossed the flight path of four east-bound OSCARs twisting through the clouds. At that same instant, Squadron Ldr Lee with his White Flight rookie wingman 2Lt. Bob Hamburger, element leader Lt. Jim Poston and tail-end 2Lt. Ed Cooper were flanked to the left at the same altitude as the mission leader when they caught sight of eight enemy fighters headed west.

Just behind Yellow and White Flights came the Green Flight trio of Capt. Howes with wingmen 2Lts. Warren Curton and Fred Helterline who likewise spotted the flight of eight enemy planes headed west. On Capt. Howes left flank, and somewhat lower, came Lt. "Wewak Willie" Williams in the lead of wingmen Lts. Don Fisher, Charlie McElroy and 2Lt. Alex Datzenko of Red Flight.

A short distance in trail to the leading four flights came the Blue Flight high-cover at 11,000 feet. Blue Flt Ldr Lt. Jacob Chandler was accompanied by 2Lt. Nile Lambert, element leader Lt. Leslie Nelson and rookie 2Lt. Carl Estes. Chandler was just entering a turn to the right when he saw LtC. Campbell's flight slip from view within the haze.

### A VERY BRIEF MAULING

As the four OSCARs first seen by Campbell passed beneath his Lightning horde, Campbell signalled the entire P-38 group to wheel to the right in a continuous descent. As the four east-bound targets disappeared within the clouds below, the other eight OSCARs heading west came directly on to the firing line of the turning Lightnings. While Campbell's Yellow team continued their pursuit of the four-ship flight, all the other Knights dropped their tanks and slammed head-on into the unsuspecting eight-ship sentai patrol.

### RED and WHITE

Willie Williams' Red Flight probably got off the first shots over Babo. Red Flt Ldr Williams, despite having to carry his empty left belly tank throughout the fight, fired at one target while registering 400 Mph and had to rolled out to bleed off some of his speed. He immediately re-engaged and fired on another Ki-43 which had pulled out in front of the sentai formation. It fell straight down in flames toward the landing field. Red element leader McElroy overtook his leader's original target, and after a brief chase, sent it down in flames into the gulf. Wingman Datzenko also hit an OSCAR in the first

*Red Flt Ldr Willie "Wewak" Williams who possibly fired at the first OSCAR target over Babo.*

pass and it fell not far from the flight leader's victim. Seconds later, Williams whipped his Lockheed beast around and roared back into the air above the drome where he dispatched his second victim.

Only seconds after Red Flight struck, Sqd Ldr Don Lee and his White team opened fire. After making their first gunnery pass, Lee bent his big Lockheed through a screaming high speed left turn and rocketed right over the swarm of OSCARs taking off from Babo airdrome. He fired at three different targets and heavily damaged two before he was forced to withdraw. Meanwhile, element leader Poston overtook one of flight leader's earlier targets and closed in to dispatch the Ki-43 right over the airdrome. Young 2Lt. Hamburger, in his very first dogfight, hit another from head-on as Red Flight withdrew.

## GREEN FLIGHT TRIO

Green Flt Ldr Capt. Howes took wingmen Curton and Helterline down to 1000 feet over the shoreline and followed their quarry off to the west side of the airdrome. The captain and Curton each clobbered OSCARs, both of which crashed in flames. Curton's victim fell two miles from the airfield just off shore while Howes' stricken OSCAR eventually splashed down three miles further out in the gulf. The two Green Flight victors then fired at their second targets and Helterline closed in on the one damaged by Curton for the coup de grace. Helterline's kill dropped into the jungle west of the airdrome.

## BLUE FLIGHT'S ONLY KILL

Lt. Chandler's Blue Flight arrived several seconds later and missed the more vulnerable targets, but they continued on and passed over the east end of the airdrome. A cross-fire of machinegun tracers bracketed the Blue elements as they passed over the runway, forcing them to separate. Lt. Nelson's right fuselage boom was stitched from its radiator tub to the tail, but his P-38 never faltered. Despite the dispersal of his flight, Nelson remained over the target and became the only Blue element to find a victim, far out over the gulf.

Previous to the flak damage, Nelson had a brief delay due to hung-up drop tanks at the onset, but everything was in working order as he turned out over the gulf. Eventually, the lone Knight

caught up to a single OSCAR which attempted to loop up into the overcast. Nelson's big P-38 followed up to the point of stalling out and he fired a short but lethal burst which killed his sentai opponent. Nelson then rolled aside as the stricken Nakajima plunged into the sea for the final kill of the bloody skirmish.

## WON AND LOST BY YELLOW FLIGHT

When Campbell and his Yellow elements broke out beneath the overcast in pursuit of the four original contacts, they flew right into the midst of a dozen OSCARs ascending from Babo's dusty strip. The Yellow Flight quartet wheeled headlong into the rising sentai and all four P-38 pilots opened fire. They thundered straight over the airdrome and Maj. McHale quickly glanced down at the two flaming wrecks marking the handy work of Williams and Datzenko, but the crowded airspace over Babo was far too dangerous a place to linger. Small caliber flak began to burst directly over the east end of the red dirt runway.

Hungry for his fifth career kill, Campbell set off after a single Ki-43 speeding to the east on the tree tops while McHale quickly targeted a rising Ki-43 still carrying its twin belly tanks. The major opened fire at 300 yards, and the OSCAR burst into flame, then rolled out of sight. McHale was forced to momentarily withdraw. Element leader Lewelling also knocked down a Ki-43 which

*7 FS aircraft #28 "O'RILEY'S DAUGHTER" normally flown by Fenimore, but not in the last Demons Warhawk dogfight on May 15th. The old stager is seen at Biak during an artistic face lift in July.*

slammed down not far from the other two burning hulks. Norton hammered yet a third which drifted downward trailing heavy smoke.

McHale, Lewelling and Norton quickly regrouped and descended for the second firing pass. This time, there was no question as to the fate of the major's next tank-toting OSCAR target. His third career victim rolled over and slammed down in the trees along the beach. Lewelling and Norton both hit targets, but the fight became much too frantic to confirm either kill. Now low on fuel, the flight leaders signalled their elements to regroup at the predetermined rendezvous point over Osmoetoe Island on the eastern end of the gulf.

## AFTERMATH OF THE BABO RAID

Seventeen Lockheed drivers eventually gathered over Osmoetoe and of the two missing pilots, only one was to be accounted for later. Separated Leslie Nelson made a solo return flight and was the last man to put his P-38 down at Hollandia field. After swinging his riddled Lightning into it revetment, the torn starboard boom gave way and the tail section crashed to the ground. Nelson had held out against the narrowest of odds.

The Knights inspected the broken P-38 and asked the lucky returnee if the mission leader had been with him, but Nelson said he had not seen Campbell since the beginning of the great dogfight. So it had been with everyone else. Group CO David Campbell had vanished and there was no way to organize an aerial search to distant McCluer Gulf.

Only two of the returning P-38 pilots had been hit in the fierce exchange which had only lasted fifteen minutes. Newcomer Don Fisher had momentarily struggled with hung-up belly tanks and in his vulnerable state, an OSCAR hit him with a short burst of 12mm gunfire. The rookie's radio was knocked out and his left wing and prop spinner were holed, but Fisher was not injured. Fred Helterline had a single round knock out his electrical system, but his ship brought him home without any difficulty.

Rookie 2Lt. Cooper had the most grey hairs added to his young head. Both of his Allison engines seized for an instant when he throttled forward to join the fight. After a gut-wrenching freefall towards enemy territory, the lieutenant was able to get both of the mills restarted. Shaken Ed Cooper withdrew from the target area without having fired a shot.

*7 FS aircraft #22 "GRADE A" shortly after its arrival at Biak. Despite the memorable artwork, the assigned pilot is long forgotten.*

## A NEW 49ERS SKIPPER; JUNE 5, 1944

Squeeze Wurtsmith was stunned at the news of David Campbell's loss. The young colonel had been carefully schooled as the first of a new generation of group commanders to lead the 5 FC into the Philippines campaign. Good combat veterans like eager Neel Kearby, Tom Lynch and David Campbell would be difficult to replace. For the time being, senior 49ers HQ staff officer LtC. Furlo Wagner agreed to stand in until another officer was groomed for the permanent 49ers command slot. LtC. George Walker, just arrived from command school in the U.S., was assigned as Wagner's assistant and likely successor.

## HORRID BIAK ISLAND; JUNE of 1944

LtC. Wagner immediately contacted Group Adjutant Maj. Alpheus White who was in charge of the 49ers ground echelon at Biak. White signalled that the situation there was far more critical than Hollandia had ever had been. Once again, the 49ers personnel had down loaded from the LST transports into a bustling armed camp, but this time, they were under enemy fire around the clock.

Biak was roughly triangular in shape and about seventy miles long from east to west. Its hilly jungle-choked interior grew right down to the white sands of the narrow beach. The Japanese had scraped three runways out of the rugged forest on the southeastern shore just west of Mokmer village which was their only real strategic foothold on the entire island. MacArthur's amphibious forces came ashore at Bosnek village ten miles east of Mokmer and quickly secured the coast road connecting the two hamlet as the Imperial garrison retreated to their fortified caves. Army engineers immediately set to repairing the bombed out airdrome. Only hours after the landing, C-47 transports were landing at Mokmer strip beneath enemy sniper fire and mortar barrages.

Maj. White was told to set up his 49ers operations on a flat stretch of the roadway beneath the prominent coastal ridgeline two miles west of the beachhead. By the end of the first week in June, 800 49ers had arrived and the camp swelled out on both sides of the crushed coral roadway.

Biak instantly proved to be a miserable place. The clear, fair weather brought on temperatures well in excess of 100 degrees and the humidity was stifling. The seaward side of their camp was swampy and generated a cloud of blood-sucking black flies and mosquitoes. Next to aviation gas, and hot food, insect repellant and atabrine anti-malarial tablets seemingly became the most critical survival staples for the besieged USAAF troops.

Tents and flooring materials had always been a crucial throughout the South Pacific theater, but it was never more serious than on that coral hot spot. It was impossible to dig either air raid slit trenches or foxholes in the packed brittle coral, and without latrines, even the disposal of waste from the Biak garrison became a logistical nightmare.

## TODD LOST BACK AT TADJI; JUNE 7, 1944

Not long after the USAAF had brought Tadji airstrip up to operational standards, the 49ers were instructed to send a man down to

*The packed coral runway known as Mokmer airdrome and the eventual bivouac and aircraft dispersal area of the 49ers to the right. Immediately beyond the dispersal taxiways are the forested bluffs where hidden Japanese fired mortar rounds into the Allied camps. The small open area in the center of the picture just below the point of the coastal inlet is Borokoe airfield while Sorido strip is obscured in the trees on the land point to the left.*

the strip for the purpose of identifying a crash site. Lt. Joseph Todd from the HQ staff requisitioned a Warhawk and flew to Tadji on the 6th where he verified the remains of Capt. Cash who had been lost on the mission of March 22nd.

Sadly however, Lt. Todd took off the following morning to return to Hollandia, only to have the engine seized as he P-40 rose from the runway. The powerless Warhawk slammed into the trees on the west end of runway and the lieutenant died instantly. His body was recovered and transported back to Hollandia for burial.

Meanwhile, missions by the 49ers P-40 and P-38 squadrons continued to sweep the extant of northern Geelvink Bay and the myriad of small islands there, but the Japanese rarely raided the new Allied base in day light. A small force was intercepted near Manokwari on the 8th by the Satan's Angels and then the Japanese held off for the next four day.

## DARKEST HOURS FOR THE 49ERS; JUNE 12, 1944

On the morning of Sunday, June 11th, a few of the off-duty 49ers were attending the church services in the little chapel tent of Capt. Willis Stafford, the Group chaplain. He spoke prophetically that no man there should ever question fate, and that even though the 49ers had seen many comrades fall, that no man should fear for himself alone.

Indeed, LtC. Wagner's fighter group had been extremely fortunate in having been at the front for nearly two and half years with so relatively few combat losses. Now luck was about to play out for the veteran group, when later that night as they fitfully tried to sleep in their hammocks strung within the steamy tropical forest, the war would sorely confirm Chaplain Stafford's sermon.

At 1:30 A.M., the night sky was aglow with a huge full moon which shed a brilliant blue-white light on the coral roadway which

crossed through the 49ers camp. A lone plane was heard approaching from the west and the air raid sirens echoed from distant Mokmer airdrome. Few of the veterans were disturbed by such late-night intruders, for they rarely flew beyond the airdrome where the search lights and the flak guns would ward them away.

That night, however, the lone intruder would pass over the airdrome and fly directly down the coast for the Allied beachhead. Whether the enemy bomber crew intended to hit the new camps, or if their bombardier mistook the white roadway for a runway in the brilliant moonlight, the 49ers would reap the fateful consequences. Six heavy bombs fell into the center of the 49ers camp. Unable to penetrate into the packed coral, the ordinance detonated on the surface where its shrapnel worked to maximum effect on the dull USAAF troops. The first two bombs exploded just west of the main 7 FS bivouac showering them with steel. Four men sleeping between two abandoned gun pits were killed outright. Then another explosion rocked the motor pool and a fourth went up near headquarters where the screams of men rose out of the smoke and fire. Across the road, a searing fifth blast leveled the adjutant's quarters and then the sixth erupted on the east side of camp near an artillery company's bivouac.

There was absolute chaos as tent mates struggled to treat each others wounds while the medics searched through the wreckage for their fallen comrades. Some died in the arms of their friends while others lay mortally wounded only to be found dead in the morning light. Nineteen 49ers perished and thirty more were severely injured. Countless others were hit by shrapnel and debris. Captain Stafford's legs were shattered. Nine of the dead were pulled from the ravaged headquarters area, including the bodies of Maj. White and his entire adjutant staff. Within those momentous explosions which spanned over a period of only fifteen seconds, the 49ers ground echelon had been put out of action.

# 18

# A WAR OF GREATER DISTANCE

## REBUILDING THE GROUND TEAM

The losses in the early morning hours of June 12th momentarily set back the 49ers mobilization. Although many of the air echelon and line crews eventually crossed the sea to Mokmer airdrome on the 15th, missions would still be flown from Hollandia until the ground echelon was reinforced. In that interim, the P-40 line crews immediately set up shop at Mokmer once again under the command of the 308 Air Task Force.

For two weeks, P-40s and P-38s were shuttled from the rear line airdromes to refit the units preparing to move up to Biak. The 49ers provided pilots for those ferry sorties, but another tragedy befell the Demons when Lt. Charles Shoaff made a fiery crash landing at Wakde Island. Shoaff was hospitalized at Hollandia's facilities with second degree burns and would eventually recover, but the lieutenant would never fly again.

## CRUSHED JNAF IN THE MARIANNAS; JUNE 19-20, 1944

The June doldrums in New Guinea were momentarily enlightened by the news of the stupendous defeat of the Imperial Mobile Fleet airwing far to the northeast in the Mariana Islands. In the American assault on Saipan Island, the JNAF attempted to occupy the Marianas airfields in a counter offensive which was totally crushed by the U.S. Navy task force. Although details of the Imperial losses of five-hundred aircraft and most of their crews would not be known to the average airmen in the South Pacific for several weeks, the net result was another advance in the Joint Chiefs of Staff calendar schedule for the Philippines invasion.

## WARHAWKS FOR BIAK; JUNE 22 AND 23, 1944

By June 20th, the 49ers were reassigned to a new camp site just two miles east of Mokmer field. Two days later, Capt. Ed Peck led twenty-four Screamin' Demon Warhawks up to their new field. The 7 FS swept over the throng of cheering troops who had come down to see them land and several of the P-40 show-offs buzzed the strip. Much to Lt. Bill Minto and Nic Zuniga's embarrassment, both failed to safely touch down. Neither man was injured despite the temporary loss of both P-40's and the C-47 hit during Zuniga's roll-out. All three aircraft were sidelined for minor repairs.

Mortified Nic Zuniga pranged another ship during the alert scramble the very morning. After Zuniga's crack-up on takeoff, two of the other 7 FS planes returned from the uneventful sortie with equipment failure. Capt. Peck's outfit had just taken five fighters off the line in one twenty-four hour period.

Luckily for 308 Wing CO Hutchinson, the fighter force was immediately bolstered by the arrival of Maj. Charles Petersen's Blacksheep later that afternoon when twenty-four Warhawks set down in good order upon the freshly crushed coral airstrip. All of the pilots likened Mokmer strip to the concrete runways they had trained on back in the States, but the line crews felt quite the con-

*Looking southward across the 49ers dispersal area of Mokmer airdrome.*

*9 FS quarters built upon the rugged coral. Air raid trenches had to be constructed with sandbags since the coral was virtually impossible to cut with a pick or shovel.*

*Despite the tropical vista, equatorial Biak was hot and infested with ravenous black flies, making it the worst of all the 49ers camps.*

trary as all of the Allison engines in the Warhawks and Lightnings would eventually require complete overhauls due to the wear and tear of the fine, wind-blown coral dust. Nothing good about Biak seemed to last.

### FLYING KNIGHTS TO MOKMER; JUNE 25, 1944

Finally on the 25th, Maj. Jordan was able to transfer his Lightnings up to the new airdrome. After bedding down the twenty-four P-38s for the evening, the Japanese struck that night with another small force, but none of the 49ers aircraft were hit. One bomb came down near the 7 FS quarters east of the field where Lts. Epling, Dick, Jarrell, Paris and Rogers were hit by shrapnel. None were seriously hurt, although they were relieved from flight duty to steady their nerves.

### NOEMFOOR ISLAND; JUNE 26, 1944

One hundred miles due west of Biak was the smaller island of Noemfoor which had a small landing field and shallow harbor at

Karimi village. Both the 7th and 8th Squadrons immediately bombed up their Warhawks and began a series of tactical sweeps on the enemy camp there, but the Japanese had already abandoned Karimi. An American infantry regiment landed there uncontested on July 2nd. Gen. Kenney immediately placed an RAAF P-40 squadron there and the 49ers returned to the tactical missions over western Biak.

Only one 49ers Warhawk was damaged during the Noemfoor raids. On June 28th, Blacksheep Lt. Marion Felts in ship #45 was forced down on Sorido airstrip four miles west of Mokmer field. The P-40 was not critically damaged and repairs were soon made by the 58th Maintenance Squadron. The plane was later reinstated to the 8 FS whose line crews were pleasantly surprised to find their old Warhawk stripped down to bare metal. More silver P-40s were turned out at Mokmer and Sorido as the month wore on, simply because the maintenance of the camouflage paint was pointless. At least eight gleaming Warhawks were flown at one time by the 49ers P-40 squadrons and the 5 FC HQ flight.

Independence Day of 1944 was celebrated at Mokmer airfield with baseball tournaments and the consumption of a cache of Japanese beer found in a shed near in Mokmer village. That night, tiny

*7 FS Dent's #24 "ANNE THE B'HAM SPECIAL" at Biak in August.*

*Two of the stripped Warhawks reissued to the 49ers at Mokmer drome. 7 FS John Miller's old #16 is seen beneath the radiator tub of 8 Fs Felt's old stager #45.*

*Standing lt.-rt.; 7 FS CO Peck, O'Neill, Chandler and Ferrel with Dent (lt.) and Suggs kneeling in front shortly after they arrived at Biak in late July. Only Peck, O'Neill and Dent would stay for the Philippines campaign.*

Owi Island two miles to the south fired off their ack-ack batteries in a terrific fireworks display as the searchlights swept over peaceful Geelvink Bay. The Japanese never appeared.

## FURTHER WEST TO FACFAC; JULY 8, 1944

The Flying Knights had grown restless once again as the war dragged on while they waited in the alert assignment at Mokmer. On the 8th, the reinstated P-38 pilots jumped at the chance to fly another long range sweep back to the west coast. The target was the small satellite base at Facfac village another 75 miles due west of Babo at the very western end of McCluer Gulf.

When the 49ers reached Facfac, they found no airborne competition, so Sqn Ldr Jordan sent down two flights to strafe the airdrome. Lt. Howard Olglesby swept back over the beach and raked the docks with machine gun and cannon fire, only to be blown back up into the air when one of the abandoned warehouses erupted in a huge fireball. The flying debris knocked a hole in Olglesby's right radiator causing him to shut down the right mill and make the 425 mile return flight on one engine. The lieutenant and his mission mates reached Mokmer without further incident.

*New Guinea Demons veteran Jack Suggs and his last P-40N #26 "ALABAM' WEST ANNISTON RAMBLER" at Mokmer airfield near the end of his tour.*

## LONE-EAGLE LINDBERG

Mokmer continued to absorb more air units and the 7 FS camp was forced to move another mile to the north as the flight dispersal area grew nearer their camp. The 345 BG Mitchells at one time had blown down the Demons' operations shack. The 475 FG Lockheeds also took up residence there, along with their distinguished quest, legendary Charles Lindberg. The "lone eagle", as Lindberg was known in the flying community, had been sent to the South Pacific theater by the War Department as an technical advisor to teach long range fuel management to American pilots and crews. Lindberg spent several days with the Lightning wing at Biak, but only flew operational sorties under the personal escort of ace Group Ldr Charles MacDonald and his Satan's Angels.

*Military advisor and aviator legend Charles Lindbergh in his flight gear at Biak.*

## BEYOND NEW GUINEA TO CERAM; JULY 14, 1944

The Flying Knights immediately applied the famed aviator's cruise control techniques on the twelve-hundred mile roundtrip sweep to the Molucca Islands on July 14th. The specific objective was another 150 miles beyond Facfac, but Lindberg's method of increasing the Allison's Rpm while thinning out the fuel flow to a trickle gave the Lockheed pilots even greater range and ample loiter time over the target.

Eighteen Flying Knights flew in escort to the B-24s and B-25s which were sent to destroy the Boela petroleum complex on the greater southern Moluccan island of Ceram. No airborne opposition appeared and after the bombers withdrew, newly promoted Capt. Willie Williams found his thrifty Knights had more than enough fuel remaining to finish off some prime ground targets. Barges in the harbor, trucks on the beach roads and personnel trying to fight the refinery fires were caught in the withering fusillade of the summary strafing passes which left Boela a flaming shambles.

## ANOTHER COMMAND EXCHANGE IN LATE JULY

With the 49ers back in the full swing of operations from Biak, 5 FC CO Wurtsmith called Maj. Wagner back into his HQ slot and the group command was placed in LtC. George Walker's hands. Walker began to sortie with all of the squadrons in his group, and though not as forceful a leader as his predecessors, he quickly proved to be very adaptive. He was a good administrator and perceptive enough

*7 FS Bob Croft's final P-40N #18 "MY ANXIOUS MAMA" in its final days of August at Mokmer drome.*

*7 FS Lt. Minto poses by his #8 "POP'S BLUE RIBBON" which was taken over by newcomer Bob Decker at Biak and flown until the Demons received the Lightnings.*

to know he was only an average fighter pilot. Fully aware that his leadership training in the States was only "text book" correct, the young colonel relied on his senior staff and flight leaders to wield authority in the operations.

As Walker took charge, the Screamin' Demons CO Ed Peck had to step down from his command with a case of malaria. After consulting with 7 FS flight surgeon Webster, the new group CO was assured that Peck would easily recover with proper rest. In the meantime, able Deputy CO Capt. Bobby Harrison was placed in charge of the Demons squadron.

## ANOTHER OLD STAGER TAKES EPLING DOWN; JULY 17, 1944

LtC. Walker and Capt. Harrison immediately had to attend to the first death under their combined commands the very day they were sworn in. One of the 7 FS pilots wounded in the June 25th air raid had been killed while on leave back at Hollandia.

Rambunctious Lt. Fenton Epling had just been reinstated to flight duty on July 17th. He eagerly took charge of the refurbished

old Demon stager #10, the MILK WAGON EXPRESS, and lifted off from Cyclops field. After a few low altitude barrel rolls to prove the work of the depot mechanics, the lieutenant wheeled down to buzz the strip. Imprudent Epling misjudged the nearness of another parked aircraft and struck the plane as he rocketed by. He attempted to bring his bent Warhawk back down on Cyclops, but the ISLAND DREAM stalled out in its approach and slammed down inverted off the end of the runway. Fenton Epling died instantly. They buried him in the field cemetery late the next day.

## BEYOND CERAM; JULY 28, 1944

The Allied command was determined to cut off all of the remnant air units in the Molucca Islands from joining in the retreat to the Philippines. On the 27th, the treacherous 80 FS Headhunters struck again and butchered the airborne defenders at Galela airfield on the northern Moluccan island of Halmahera. The Flying Knights pressed Fighter Command operations for the next hot target. On the very next day, Maj. Jordan's people got their wish.

*New 49ers CO LtC. George Walker at Biak, July, 1944.*

*7 FS Harrison (lt.), Epling and Zappia with the war-weary P-40N #10 "MILK WAGON EPRESS" which killed Epling in the July 28th crash at Hollandia.*

*7 FS senior Flt Ldr Farrell and his last P-40N #15 "ISLAND DREAM" in the end of their Screamin' Demons career at Biak.*

*9 FS Lightning pilot McElroy got his second career kill on the second mission to Ambonia on August 4th.*

When enemy planes were spotted on the airdrome on Ambonia Island, just off the western tip of Ceram, the new 49ers CO assigned himself to the Flying Knights elements for the twelve-hundred mile round-trip escort. Gen. Wurtsmith advised Maj. Jordan to keep LtC. Walker and the B-24s under equally dedicated care.

Fortunately for chaperon Jordan and his tag-along Group CO, the mission was a cake-walk. After the long crossing to Ambonia, the Lightnings orbited at 10,000 feet above the airdrome where fighters and bombers were seen on the ground, but only two VAL dive-bombers were found airborne. Seven Knights dropped down to catch the hapless pair and everyone fired until one of the Aichis plunged into the Ceram Sea. Credit was given to senior Lt. Jimmie "Slip" Haislip. Wingman Wade Lewis hit the other Val with a heavy volley knocking off several large pieces, but it vanished in the mist before it could be confirmed as a kill.

### BACK TO AMBONIA; AUGUST 4, 1944

For the next two weeks, the Lightnings continued to hunt in a 650-mile radius west of Biak, and Jordan's squadron continued to miss

the diminishing Japanese air force. They flew escort to the dive bombing Warhawks and swept all of the known southern enemy dromes, but they would only find a solitary victim back at Ambonia on August 4th.

From their position at 17,000 feet directly over the island in escort to the raiding B-24s, Blue Flt Ldr Lt. "Mac" McElroy and wingman Arthur Hufford spotted two dark green radial engine planes at their level against the white cumulus clouds. The OSCARs first turned into the Blue elements, then the higher Ki-43 turned toward the Liberators. Before either Knight could fire, the OSCAR nearest the B-24s dropped an aerial phosphorous bomb which burst harmlessly behind their ranks. McElroy quickly cut off the approach of the lead OSCAR who had already come dangerously close to his rookie wingman, and after a brief chase, the Blue leader caught the Ki-43 with a devastating volley to its mid-fuselage. The OSCAR attempted a chandelle loop, only to stall out at the top where it exploded in a huge fireball. Mac and Hufford rejoined for the long trip home.

*9 FS wingman Lewis only could claim a probable VAL kill on July 28th over Ambonia.*

*Veteran P-47 pilot Jimmie Haislip finally got a kill in his P-38 on July 28th over Ambonia.*

*An unidentified Blacksheep armorer with his loaded P-40N fighter-bomber at Mokmer field in the last of the Biak tactical strikes.*

*8 FS Lt. Hall's #43 "TEXAS BABY" in the best "Vargas girl" tradition at Biak in August.*

## TACTICAL WARHAWKS AND 2LT. MARTON LOST; AUGUST 13, 1944

While the P-38s continued the long range hunt, the P-40 squadrons honed their dive-bomber skills to an even finer art form and any target within 400 miles of Biak became fair game for the Warhawk heavy-hitters. For closer objectives, they carried a three-hundred pounder on each wing, plus the five-hundred pounder on the belly rack. Enemy movement in the Geelvink Bay area during daylight virtually ceased.

On August 8th, an infantry battalion went ashore at the northwestern most point of Vogelcop Peninsula at Sansapor village and two days later, engineers landed just off shore at tiny Middleburg Island to build a 5000-foot strip there. The Warhawks temporarily moved to Middleburg for the mop-up of Sansapor and the only operational setback was the fatality of Demon newcomer 2Lt. Charles Marton in a crash west of Biak on the 13th. Marton's body was never recovered.

Meanwhile back on Biak, the geniuses of the 8 FS were at it again. Studious Lt. Ed Bazan had further modified the long-range setup for the P-40 to a much higher efficiency by adapting a 200 gallon Thunderbolt belly tank, known as a "fat boy" for its elliptical cross section, rather than the standard tear-drop Curtiss type. Using Lindberg's method of lean-fuel mixture and high Rpm, Ops Exec Capt. Sawyer took off on the main tanks and climbed to 10,000, then switched over to the fat-boy and kept his Warhawk airborne at 200 Mph for four and half hours. The captain landed back at Mokmer with the remainder of his fuselage tanks still in reserve for an addition three hours of flight, had he so chosen. If the Blacksheep had to fly to a base in the pending Philippines invasion, engineer Bazan and Ops-man Sawyer had given CO Maj. Charlie Petersen the Warhawk that could get there.

The Warhawk pilots continued to soldier on and the 8 FS soon moved up to crowded Middleburg Island with the Demons. After the north shore of Vogelcop Peninsula was secured, the Warhawks returned to Mokmer for the final mop-up of the stranded Japanese

*The unit markings on the last of the P-40Ns were far from standard as this immaculate, stripped Warhawk indicates. The black serial number was first applied to the lower rear fuselage only to be overpainted by the white empennage theater marking. It was then painted on the tail surface. The aircraft retains its yellow and black Blacksheep unit colors on the spinner and tailtip, but displays #34 which normally was a 7 FS designator. It is quite likely the Demons and Blacksheep shared any number of refit P-40 aircraft in September as the old fighter-bombers wore out one by one.*

troops on Supiori Island just west of Biak. In the last week of August, the P-40s brought total devastation to the trapped garrison at Korido village. American infantry took the village "standing up" and found hundreds of dead Imperial marines rotting in the sun.

## OLD TEAM FOR HOME, NEW MAN McCABE LOST; AUGUST 28, 1944

Blacksheep CO Charlie Petersen had the promising news of a practical long-range Warhawk overshadowed by the major's better fortune of a furlough back to the States. Many other senior officers and enlisted old timers from the Darwin-New Guinea era were likewise released. Senior Capt. Willie Drier remained for an extended tour and took up the 8 FS command on August 27th.

On the very next day, however, fate would again foul the change in command when newcomer 2Lt. Leighton McCabe failed to return from the day's mission. Blacksheep Ops Exec Hal Sawyer had taken fifteen wingmen on a tactical sortie to Utarom airstrip on the southwest New Guinea shoreline seventy miles due south of Babo. As the P-40s descended through the intermittent cloud cover to find their target, flak burst over the abandoned muddy airfield and Lt. McCabe signalled he was hit. It was the last word anyone heard. Four Blacksheep swept over Utarom the next day only to confirm that the young pilot had vanished.

## ANOTHER LOST SHEEP - 2LT. WAYNE - AUGUST 28, 1944

Even more pathetic was the fact that the very next day, newcomer 2Lt. Howard Wayne would be lost while hitching a ride for the front on a B-25 from Nadzab. The Mitchell transport disappeared en route to Biak and the Blacksheep were notified of the missing young lieutenant ten weeks after the fact. Ironically, Howard Wayne merely passed into history as a name on a USAAF missing crew report.

## FIRST BLACKSHEEP P-38s - LT. CLARK LOST; SEPTEMBER 1, 1944

On September 1, virtually without warning, Capt. Drier was informed that all of his Warhawks were to be turned in to the maintenance pool at Biak by mid-month. All senior flight officers qualified in the Lockheed P-38 were to draw such an aircraft for permanent mission assignments. All junior pilots who were not on the Warhawk mission roster were to report for P-38 transition at Mokmer Field. In the interim, all of the airfields in western New Guinea would continue to be hit by the bomb-slinging P-40s, and aircraft returning with mechanical failure were to be unceremoniously written off, even if they were able to be repaired.

The Lockheed transition was understandably initiated in tragedy. Several accidents occurred in the rebuilt J model Lightnings, including the loss of two planes and the death of one pilot on the very first day. While ferrying a P-38 from Owi Island to Mokmer field, 2Lt. Walter Clark crashed in the sea. Both plane and pilot disappeared beneath the waves. Later that day, veteran combat pilot Lt. Lou Graton came down short in the rough at Mokmer and

piled up his P-38 in a spectacular crash. Graton miraculously lived, but he would be hospitalized with a severe back sprain for weeks. Despite these events, Capt. Drier's resilient crews kept the old Lockheeds airworthy and by the 15th, the Blacksheep flight leaders were taking four-ship patrols out over Geelvink Bay.

## FIRST FIGHTERS BACK TO MINDANAO; AUGUST 31, 1944

On August 29th, the Knights first staged to Middleburg Island and two days later they joined with the Satin's Angels in the first escort by American fighters into Philippines airspace since the great retreat of 1942. Maj. Jordan took fifteen 9 FS P-38s over Buayan airdrome on southern Mindanao in the 1100-mile round trip, but the enemy air force was not there.

## LT. McLEAN LOST OFF BIAK; SEPTEMBER 2, 1944

On September 2nd, the Knights flew back to Mindanao, but the Japanese only responded with inaccurate flak. When the force got home to Biak, the bombers stacked up in the landing pattern while the Lightnings orbited over the water. Lt. John McLean was seen making a low pass just off shore when his Lightning suddenly dipped its wing and slammed down into the sea. Like the 8 FS pilot just two days before, Flying Knight John McLean and his P-38 sank without a trace.

All three squadrons entered into Gen. Kenney's final phase of missions to close the door on the New Guinea theater. From the 5th through the 11th, the war-weary P-40s and P-38s were sent on a myriad of dive-bombing sorties throughout the Molucca Islands. On the 5th, the Demons hefted a five-hundred pounder each to Samate airdrome on Salawati Island just off the western most cape of Vogelcop Peninsula where their eight bombs pointlessly fell on the abandoned airfield. The Demons would stage back through Middleburg and then moved on to Mokmer Field. It would be that way with each of the monotonous sorties.

*7 FS Joel Paris setting off from Mokmer strip in his #7 "SANDY" whose name appeared just beneath the old stager's cockpit.*

*Allied crewmen surround the first two P-40s of the RAAF who advanced to Noemfoor Island instead of the Demons and Blacksheep who were in the throws of changing over to the P-38s.*

## TIED FOR THE SCORING LEAD; SEPTEMBER 6, 1944

On the 6th, four of the Flying Knights flew a rescue escort to the PBY sent to pick up a downed bomber crew at Tifore Island, one hundred miles out in the middle of the Molucca Sea beyond greater Halmahera Island. The PBY found nothing and the mission turned back, when 9000 feet over the west coast of Halmahera near little Lembeh Island, a lone ZERO suddenly appeared to the southeast at the Knights level. Flight Ldr Lt. Ray Swift turned to his right into the path of Mitsubishi which swept in front of the Americans, then climbed up through a chandelle and dropped a pair of aerial bombs at them. The glistening white phosphorous spirals completely missed and Swift's foursome wheeled after the attacker until number-4 man Lt. Bill Baxter ran him down. From dead-astern at 500 feet above the water, Baxter fired and the ZERO dropped down into a broad spray for the Knights 194th aerial kill.

Back at Mokmer, the intelligence team confirmed the victory after debriefing and a few days later, 5 FC published the tally results. It was a dead-even tie between the Flying Knights of the 9 FS and the Headhunters of the 80 FS. The Knights quickly readied their planes for another shot at the Boela oil fields and the possibility of finding more stragglers at that airdrome.

## 2LT. FRANK DOWN ON CERAM ISLAND; SEPTEMBER 11, 1944

In good weather on the 11th, the 9 FS sortied back to Boela, but the airfield was empty so they strafed the garrison buildings and the docks once again. The garrison survivors sent up light defensive flak directly over the pitted dirt runway and newcomer 2Lt. Henry Frank flew right through the barrage. He turned his smoking P-38 to the east, but both engines quit a quarter mile from Boela. His

wingmen circled over his crash site on the shore and Frank was last seen running for the cover of the forest. Successive search flights over the next few days, however, could not find any sign of the lieutenant. He most likely had been captured and summarily executed.

## END OF THE WARHAWK ERA

On the 10th, temporary CO Bobby Harrison led the last 12-ship P-40 mission for the Screamin' Demons in one final assault on cratered Samate airdrome. The next day, Willie Drier's nine Blacksheep did the same. The command captains notified 5 FC CO Wurtsmith that as of the morning of September 11th, all Curtiss P-40 Warhawks were grounded and turned over to the materials squadron at Mokmer Field.

Meanwhile, over in the veteran Lightning squadron, Maj. Wally Jordan transferred into the 49ers Group staff and senior Capt. Willie Williams temporarily stood in as the 9 FS commander. The unit turned over a number of the old J model P-38s to the 7th and 8th Squadrons to aide them in their transition phase, but more accidents occurred as the old had-me-down Lockheeds fell out of the sky.

## PILOTS HUMPHREY, REMER AND ROGERS LOST IN TRAINING

The re-equipping of the 7th and 8th Squadrons was the most abysmal era in LtC. George Walker's group command tenure. There was an onslaught of aborted flights, equipment failures, takeoff and landing snafus, and the inevitable loss of lives. On September 14th, 7 FS rookie 2Lt. Doug Humphrey vanished during an over water

*Returned veteran Gerry Johnson's stripped hack P-40N used at Hollandia in September of 1944. The major's thirteen victory flags can just be seen beneath the white name block under the windshield.*

erans would be available to the 49ers when that critical time arrived.

## BRAND NEW LOCKHEEDS AND OLD VETERANS ARRIVE

While the Demons and Blacksheep struggled with the high-time P-38s at Biak, Capt. Williams began to send his Flying Knights back to Nadzab to ferry up the new P-38 L-1 and L-5 models for induction at Mokmer. And with the new planes came some old hands. Maj. Robert "Crocodile" McComsey, the Darwin 9th Pursuit cadre veteran, arrived to assume command of the Flying Knights as Williams resumed as Deputy CO.

Leading 9 FS ace Maj. Gerry Johnson had also rejoined the 5 FC back at Hollandia and was appointed as the 49ers Group Ops Exec to help LtC. Walker through the more trying times to come. Johnson was even more cock-sure than when he had left back in April. He took charge of a stripped P-40 for his personal hack as well as a new Lockheed and both ships displayed his thirteen victory flags painted beneath the canopy windscreens. The ace challenged all comers to mock dogfights out over Sentani Lake and regularly embarrassed many a P-38 novice while flying his silver Warhawk. Johnson had obviously honed his extraordinary pilot skills to an even finer edge.

None were more impressed, however, or perhaps more intimidated, by the return of leading ace Dick Bong. The major had returned to the Pacific for his third combat tour and was named the 5 FC Senior Gunnery Instructor. Although not expected to fly in combat, Bong introduced himself to George Walker and asked if he might fly attached to the 49ers for a time. The colonel readily ac-

training sortie. On the 25th, the 8 FS lost rookie 2Lt. Dick Remer under similar circumstances. Two days later, 7 FS newcomer 2Lt. Jay Rogers was missing at the end of the day. His aircraft was reported at two different airfields, but neither case was true. Like Humphrey and Remer, Jay Rogers and his war-weary P-38 had vanished somewhere over northern Geelvink Bay.

By the end of the month, LtC. Walker found his group had lost nearly all of the senior flight leaders. Veterans who had gone to the command schools in the States were now returning to 5 FC, but the majority of the officers were assigned directly to the command HQ or at the group staff level. If the Philippines operations were truly immanent, Walker would have qualified squadron leaders and operations executives, but virtually none had combat experience. The 49ers CO pleaded with Wurtsmith to release his staff officers to man Walker's Philippines operations until his junior pilots had gained the necessary experience. Wurtsmith promised the staff vet-

*8 FS New Guinea veteran Ralph Easterling made such a successful Lockheed transition at Nadzab that 5 FC made him squadron CO of the training unit there, even when the young fellow was but a lieutenant. The Nadzab maintenance squadron even enhanced the young CO's P-38J with bold red stripes on the fuselage booms to signify his rank.*

*Gunnery instructor Dick Bong's aircraft #42 at Biak in October before any victory flags were added. Even though many different crewmen serviced this aircraft at Mokmer and later in the Philippines campaign, as with all the P-38s, few ever knew the pilot who flew the plane.*

cepted the ace into the fold and immediately commandeered for him a brand-new P-38 L-1 from Capt. Drier's 8th Squadron. Unlike flashy Ops Exec Johnson, quiet Dick Bong kept Blacksheep ship number 42 with its black and yellow spinners, just as it was.

## A RISING LIGHTNING STORM

In the first week of October, Walker's 49ers were installed in the strategic fighter wing of the 310 Bombwing Air Task Force under the command of veteran Col. Bob Morrissey. The colonel immediately set in motion the next missions which would be the preemptive sorties for the Philippines operation proper. With a P-38 force of nearly one-hundred strong in three fighter groups, ATF CO Morrissey could meet any challenge that Squeeze Wurtsmith and Gen. Kenney might devise.

With the Flying Knights having tied for the squadron victory lead, the 49ers overall tally was then officially recorded as 478 aerial kills. The returned veterans were exhilarated by the idea that their group might fulfill the pledge made so long ago in Australia. At Darwin in 1942, then 49ers CO Paul Wurtsmith had predicted his 49ers would someday reach the century mark in kills and dedicated a magnum of champagne to celebrate the event. But as the 49ers

score climbed, each successive commander declined the honor and postponed the celebration for the succeeding century tally. When George Walker learned of the tradition, he promised Squeeze Wurtsmith he would make good use of the veterans and they would all open that bottle of champagne on the porch of Hirohito's palace.

## PRECURSORY RAIDS TO BALIKPAPEN

In late September of 1944, the Imperial Command consolidated its staff at Manila, Luzon and marshalled a quarter of a million troops throughout the islands to repel the coming Allied invasion. Hope of reinforcement by refugees from the Dutch East Indies had all but vanished as the Americans had continually denied the Imperial Fleet any path through the Molucca Island to withdraw their stranded troops.

Kenney's Far East Air Force was now tasked to deny the Japanese Imperial Fleet, which was still an ominous force despite its set backs in the Central Pacific campaign, any reinforcement from isolated Borneo. On the east coast of the equatorial island was the great petroleum refinery at Balikpapen which had been the objective of many small raids by the long-range B-17s and B-24s since the war began. Now with a force of 400 heavy bombers based at Nadzab and Biak, including the newly inducted elements of the 13 AF, Gen. Kenney had the tools to finally eliminate Balikpapen from the Philippines picture.

## FIRST RAID; OCTOBER 10, 1944

Despite the experience gained in the tactical missions flown by the new 7th and 8th Squadron Lightning pilots, Group Ops Exec Johnson advised Walker to chose the senior pilots of the 9 FS and the 49ers HQ for the demanding Balikpapen mission. Majors Wally Jordan and Dick Bong were therefore chosen as flight leaders for the first mission as much for spiritual support as well as their combat skill. On the 9th, Walker took fifteen P-38s up to the staging base on Morotai, the northern most island in the Moluccas. They arrived at the crowded field and carefully taxied through the closely parked armada of P-47s from the 35 FG.

Early the next morning, the 49ers and Thunderbolts rose up from the Morotai runway at 0700 hours and set off to the south west at 10,000 feet for the 850-mile flight to the Borneo coast. The

*By mid-October, Gerry Johnson had commandeered his new P-38L-5, numbered it "83," added his thirteen kills to the black scoreboard and joined in the Group operations at Biak.*

wingman in Jordan's 3-man flight had equipment failure and turned back before they reached the slender arching peninsula of north Celebes Island. Maj. Jordan took element leader Capt. Williams as his wingman for the remainder of the mission.

All fourteen Knights pressed beyond the Celebes over the Makassar Strait where Walker signalled his flights to start climbing and be on the lookout for the Liberators who had flown a straight-line route from Biak. On the dot at 1100 hours, the P-38s and P-47s intercepted the long formation of B-24s just off the Borneo coast.

The mission check point on the coast line was the river delta ten miles north of the Balikpapen harbor and refinery. When the formation reached the mouth of the river, Jordan drifted inland at 15,000 feet to cover Manggar airdrome which was the known source of defending fighters for the oil fields complex. The Americans immediately sighted six dark green radial-engine aircraft cruising between 3000 to 7000 feet.

LtC. Walker was in the lead with his Blue Flight of Lt. Warren Curton, element leader Maj. Dick Bong and HQ staff officer Capt. Bob Baker. While the pilots watched the single engine interceptors, sharp-eyed Bong spotted a lone twin-engine aircraft passing below the Lightnings at 5000 feet. With trusted friend Baker in close support, Bong signalled his intent to Blue leader Walker and snapped aside in an abrupt wingover. Seconds later, ace Bong overtook the twin-engine IRVING for his twenty-ninth victory. The JNAF pilot drifted away in his chute as the black interceptor exploded and fell in pieces just off shore.

Bong and Baker quickly reformed on Walker who was energized by the gunnery instructor's exemplary marksmanship. The Group Leader signalled White Flight to stay in high cover and for all of the other elements to pick their targets and attack. Ten silver Lightnings dropped upon the OSCARs which had now turned to intercept.

## BLUE FLIGHT FIRES FIRST

Like any anxious combat rookie, George Walker tried to hit every fighter that remotely passed in front of his gun, but he only damaged one fleeting target. Wingman Curton ably protected Walker's every move and tried to keep the colonel in firing position, but the sentai pilots soon proved to be too aggressive. An agile OSCAR drew Curton into a hard turn and the lieutenant momentarily fell away in a high-speed stall. He quickly recovered with the mission leader for one more pass, and in that pursuit, Walker broke up a pair

of OSCARs whose trailing wingman suddenly countered from head-on. Curton caught the Ki-43 with a devastating volley and flamed its engine.

Blue element leader Bong and wingman Baker also joined in the fray with the OSCAR sentai and Bong once again demonstrated his improved gunnery skill. His new method was simple. Just as he had instructed the younger pilots to do, the ace "put the gun muzzles in the Jap's cockpit." OSCAR victim number thirty disintegrated in a ball of fire.

## RED FLIGHT DUO AND A NEW ACE

Maj. Jordan had also caught sight of another lone IRVING hunting at 12,000 feet behind the Liberators when the mission leader signalled the attack. Jordan wheeled through a split-S turn against the sun and the JNAF aviator never saw what hit him. The IRVING burst into flames and dropped straight down into the sea.

Jordan and wingman Williams reformed, and with Walker's Blue Flight, the Red duo next laid into the OSCARs. After several hard maneuvers against the sentai, Williams confirmed Wally Jordan's OSCAR victim which rolled over and plunged into the strait, making him the newest ace in 5 FC. But the OSCARs had finally won an advantage and ace Jordan with his wingman departed down and away to the northeast.

## GREEN FLIGHT ENDS IT ALL

Lt. Eddie Howes had been slightly behind the lead flights and his Green Flight foursome separated in their long turning descent for the battle. Howes eventually overtook a ZERO which he approached from beneath at dead-astern. The Green leader popped up at the last moment within point-blank range and killed the aviator with the first volley. The Mitsubishi snap-rolled and fell into the ocean, just as Howes and wingman Fred Helterline saw a pair of OSCARs wheel overhead. One of the Nakajimas tossed its aerial bombs at the rear flank of the retreating Liberators, but the two weapons exploded well to the rear. Helterline took a pursuit curve after the trailing OSCAR, but the sentai man peeled off and lost the diving Lightning over the hazy shoreline. Howes and Helterline rose up and looked back at the refinery which was sending up a smoke column five miles high. Everyone else was gone and the Green team wheeled off to the northeast.

*Capt. William's aircraft #81 with its dual red command stripes rolling out from the Mokmer dispersal area.*

*The Balikpapen mob. Standing lt.-rt.; 5 FC officer Baker, 49ers Co Walker, Hamburger, gunnery instructor Bong, Howes, Haislip, Wood, Curton, Hufford and Estes. Sitting lt.-rt.; Oglesby, 9 FS CO Jordan, McElroy, Williams and Davis.*

## SECOND RAID; OCTOBER 14, 1944

After four days rest due to marginal weather over the mission route, the next Balikpapen mission was unleashed. To deal with an expected increase in enemy fighters over the target, the 35 FG P-47s would leave fifteen minutes ahead of the main force in a pre-strike fighter sweep. LtC. Walker would follow with his seventeen Lightnings in close escort to the bombers.

The White Flight team was made up of Ops Exec Gerry Johnson in the lead with 9 FS wingman Lt. Hal Oglesby. One of the other element dropped out in route leaving White Flight short one man, but the trailing man possessed enough ego to manage the entire mission by himself. He was obnoxious ace Maj. Tommy McGuire, commander of the 431 FS. Maj. McGuire had taken up the gauntlet to better demure Dick Bong's score and during the leading ace's summer absence, "Terrible Tommy" went on a killing rampage. McGuire had since passed up Gerry Johnson's score, and now with twenty-one confirmed, beating Dick Bong's record became his obsession.

The mission proceeded without a snag and Walker's P-38s reached the Borneo coast, once again in perfect position to the arrival of the Liberators. When the B-24s turned on to their bombing run, the Lightning pilots were spread from 19,000 through 15,000 feet and they looked down at the swirling dogfight raging between the Thunderbolts and the Manggar airdrome defenders. Several burning planes were seen tumbling out of the air battle.

## RAMBLING RED FLIGHT

Johnson, Oglesby and McGuire were high at the front of the strike force and neither of the egotistical aces cared to wait. Mission Leader Walker and his Green Flight were forced to remain in high cover as the two White Flight majors bolted out of formation for the fight.

With Oglesby close behind, Johnson and McGuire thundered down upon the loosely formated OSCARs and both of the majors knocked a Ki-43 out of the air. Oglesby quickly realized he was in the fight for himself, and thus caught up in the hunting fever, the separated White trio descended in a mad dash through the swerving ZEROs, OSCARs and TOJOs. Johnson destroyed one of the TOJOs, McGuire gunned down an old stager HAMP and Oglesby flamed a ZERO.

They attacked again. Oglesby hammered an OSCAR which spiralled down and slammed into Makassar Strait. McGuire raced inland and picked off a TOJO over the shoreline which eventually fell burning into the strait as well. In twelve furious minutes, White Flight had account for more kills than had been tallied by the 9 FS in the previous mission.

*9 FS CO Wally Jordan shortly after his sixth and last career kill added to his command ship at Biak.*

## BLUE WILLIE WILLIAMS

Capt. Willie Williams Blue Flight also came down in the first pass against the OSCARs. All of the element fired, but only the senior captain found the mark. After his first target exploded and fell in pieces toward the water, he fired at another which trailed heavy smoke and descended until it disappeared in a cloud far below. Low on fuel and ammo, Williams recalled his men and they withdrew.

## NOT OVER YET

Newly acclaimed ace Wally Jordan added to the mission score that day as well. At the head of the Red Flight foursome, Jordan and wingman Lt. Ed Cooper made a pass where both men fired and the major scored a kill over a Ki-43 for his sixth and last career victory. Jordan separated in the melee to heavily damage another target as Cooper joined with White Flight McGuire and Oglesby for the firing run against the TOJOs. Cooper's aim was true this time as one of the stubby-winged Nakajimas disintegrated and fell apart before his companions eyes. Cooper stayed with McGuire who had run out of ammo, so they turned out of the fight for home.

As for the other two Red Flight elements, leader Lt. Bob Wood had not been able to jettison one of his tanks as the fight broke out. Wood joined the high cover, so tail-end Leslie Nelson tagged on to Oglesby briefly in the pass against the ZEROs. Nelson fell into a deadly groove as three Mitsubishi pilots went to meet their ances-

tors due to the lieutenant's brutal marksmanship. When Nelson's gun were empty, he swept up to 12,000 feet and looked back at the towering dark cloud rising from Balikpapen which foiled at least a dozen brilliant white phosphorous blossoms. To the victorious P-38 warrior, it was a beautiful sight to behold.

At a quarter past two, the last Lightnings touched down on Morotai. The next morning, the pilots ferried their fighters back to Mokmer to a tumultuous celebration at the Fighter Command HQ. Flight leaders and victorious pilots were cited for bravery on the spot.

After the two longest escort missions of the Pacific campaign, every Lightning pilot was accounted for. The next day, the Balikpapen mission tallies for Squeeze Wurtsmith's fighter pilots were published. The P-47s and P-38s had been accredited with eighteen kills on the 10th and a resounding thirty-eight kills on the 14th. The 9th Squadron lieutenants, Capt. Williams and the 49ers HQ pilots had accounted for thirteen out of the overall total of fifty-six destroyed. The Flying Knights had taken the squadron lead for good and would never be challenged again.

The Balikpapen raiders were lined up in front of the Lightnings at Biak and war corespondents photographed them for the newspapers back home. Bong was an now an ace six times over. It was not only victory, it was blatant hero worship propaganda of the highest caliber. Generals MacArthur and Kenney were making use of every hero they could create. And they would need them all for the next big show.

*Killers of the second Balikpapen mission on October 14th; (lt.-rt.) Oglesby with two kills, Cooper with one, Williams with one, Jordan with one "and a half," Johnson with two and top scoring Nelson with three.*

# 19

# THE PHILIPPINES AIR WAR

As of the second week in October, 1944, the combined forces of Gen. MacArthur's Southwest Pacific command and Admiral Chester Nimitz's Central Pacific fleets came together for the invasion of the Philippines Islands. MacArthur was instructed by the Chiefs of Staff to make Leyte Island his base of operations in the first phase of liberating the 115 thousand square miles of the archipelago from Imperial Commander Yamishita and his quarter of a million troops. Leyte alone was estimated to have a garrison force of thirty-five thousand and there were at least twenty airfields within range of the objective.

The invasion operations began in earnest on October 10th along a broad front when Adm. William Halsey's 3rd Fleet attacked the airdromes and harbors of Luzon, while 600 miles to the south, subordinate Rear-Adm. Thomas Kinkaid's 7th Fleet struck in the southern Philippines in direct support of the Leyte scheme. After the combined aerial bombardments from Kinkaid's fast escort carriers and Gen. Kenney's 5 AF heavies, the main assault fleet entered Leyte Gulf from the southeast on the night of the 19th. Kinkaid's

*Looking due north over Cataisin Peninsula and the famous Tacloban Airfield as of December, 1944, home of the murderous 49ers Lightning Fighter Group.*

naval guns and carrier bombers hammered the entire eastern coastline of Leyte and on the morning of the October 20th, the first wave of the eventual 150,000 invasion troops landed against minimal opposition on the beaches north of Dulag village. As experienced in the past, the enemy garrison there had already retreated to higher ground. The Americans did not meet heavy resistance until they had pushed ten miles inland to the town of Burauen.

Twenty miles north of Dulag was the small coastal inlet of San Pedro Bay at the mouth of the narrow strait separating Leyte on the west and Samar Island on the east. The little bay provided safe harbor for Leyte's provincial capitol of Tacloban. Immediately to the east was the two-mile long narrow peninsula of Cataisan Point which jutted north into the little harbor and it was there that the Japanese had dragged out a primitive runway. A U.S. Army engineering battalion supported by an infantry division immediately overran the abandoned capitol and secured the intact enemy command post known as the Price House which became Gen. MacArthur's new headquarters. On the afternoon of the 20th, the general sent out his famous radio message to the world of his fulfilled promise to return to the Philippines and of the reinstatement of President Osmeno.

## TACLOBAN AIRSTRIP AND THE BATTLE OF LEYTE GULF

The Leyte Air Task Force Commander was Col. David Hutchinson, nicknamed "Photo Hutch" in deference to the 49ers old boss Don "Fighter Hutch" Hutchinson, the new Chief of Staff to FEAF. Photo Hutch was a keen planner who instantly took to improving the Cataisan sand spit runway for the defensive fighter team needed over MacArthur's new headquarters. There was room for three more landing fields on the flat plain between Dulag and Burauen, but those airstrips required far more time to bring up to flight operations. Until the infantry secured the Dulag-Barauen area, the tiny Cataisan promontory would be Gen. Kenney's first base in the Philippines.

While the Supreme Commander and his staff returned temporarily to Adm. Kinkaid's flagship, the USS *Nashville*, the ATF commander requisitioned a convoy of trucks and every available man to retrieve the raw coral found several miles down the mainland beach. After five days and nights of continuous labor on the peninsular runway which had simply become known as Tacloban Airfield, Hutchinson's work force completed a 3000 foot-long section of a reinforced foundation of mixed coral and sand. Two-thirds of that had also been overlaid with Marston mat which was bare minimum length for a P-38 to takeoff or land. Six miles to the south, the 49th Fighter Air Control Squadron set up there air control station at Palo village. Tacloban Airfield was ready, but there were more delays.

The Japanese had kept watch over the growing Allied camp with armed aerial surveillance and a spy network of soldiers who remained in the area masquerading as Philippine workers. Although the resultant air raids were never overwhelming, the Cataisan workforce often had to withdraw to the slit trenches dug among the ever growing stockpiles of supplies and equipment. MacArthur's newly occupied Price House HQ and the surrounding garrison were also bombed. The weather also worsened with the intermittent rains which preceded the first monsoon of the season. On the night of the 25th, however, a far more ominous threat drew dangerously near MacArthur's invasion force. Unbeknown to the weary troops ashore, the still potent Imperial Mobile Fleet had suddenly appeared only 75 miles to the south in the narrow Surigao Straits.

## A NAVY SHOW

The desperate situation at Tacloban had really begun five days earlier, 1500 miles to the west at the Imperial port of Singapore. Adm. Kurita's fleet which had survived the first battle of the Philippines Sea in June had completely refitted in Malaya and set sail again under the operation codename SHO-1 to confront the impending Allied invasion. As a ruse on the northern flank, a diversionary force displaying four carriers with only a small airwing advanced from Japan proper into the northern Philippine Sea to circle above Luzon. After the enemy carriers were sighted by submarines off Formosa, Adm. Halsey presumed they were the true threat and turned his entire 3rd Fleet northward to intercept the shadow force.

When Kurita learned on the 20th of the Leyte objective, the cunning admiral took advantage of the American Navy which blundered in splitting its superior force. In three days, Kurita's dreadnoughts reached the outer islands of the western Philippines where he divided them into two elements of a pincer-like attack force. Kurita steamed due east for the San Bernardino Straits north

*The Philippines invasion fleet bearing the advanced 49ers team pulls in to the Leyte Gulf.*

*9 FS aircraft #75 assigned to Jim Poston had artwork begun at Biak which was never finished in time for the invasion. Indeed, the aircraft was lost shortly after the Leyte battle began.*

of Samar Island while his subordinate, Adm. Nishimura, turned south through the Sibuyan Sea for the Surigao Straits which led directly into Leyte Gulf and the American invaders.

With Halsey's carriers still 700 miles to the north, Kinkaid's smaller fast escort carriers bearing only 800 aircraft, and his comparatively smaller ships of the line, were the last obstacle standing before Kurita on the north flank and Nishimura on the south. Kinkaid put forth an airborne gambit on the 24th, but Kurita steamed down the east coast of Samar by nightfall virtual unscathed. Following a brutal night engagement with Nishimura's force in the Surigao Straits proper, the two pincers of the Imperial Mobile Fleet steamed into the southern and northern Leyte Gulf waters in the morning twilight to come upon the vast array of impotent Liberty ships resting at anchor.

If there had been an American supreme commander over the entire Pacific theater, the situation that day might never have occurred. But Gen. MacArthur was the whimsical victim of the politics which muddled the field logistics. While Central Pacific Commander Nimitz fitfully attempted to warn Halsey of the crisis at Leyte, MacArthur was desperately counting on Kinkaid's diminutive carrier airwing to work a miracle within a mired network of U.S. Army and Navy communiques. At that very moment, enemy cruisers were entering Leyte Gulf and were about to turn it into a shooting gallery which would bring the Philippines invasion to an abrupt halt.

A miracle is precisely what unfolded. On October 25th, Kinkaid's fearless aviators and his destroyer escorts displayed their best. Expecting JAAF aircover, but receiving far too little, Nishimura's southern threat was decimated by the American destroyers which parried in hit and run flanking assaults in the morning darkness. At morning light, the 7th Fleet airwing of Wildcats, Hellcats and Avengers swarmed over the giant war ships and so demoralized Kurita that he believed he had engaged the greater American carrier fleet. Only minutes from their planned rendezvous, Kurita signalled the venture was over and ordered Nishimura to withdraw.

The Imperial Command plan inevitably failed entirely. Hours after Kurita's retreat back through San Bernardino, the greatest sea battle of the Pacific war ended in a devastating crescendo as the American's wiped out the pretenders of SHO-1. Halsey would find the enemy fleet northeast of Luzon and sink all of the carriers. Nishimura's southern group would be harassed so fearfully that only one lone destroyer would somehow survive. Kurita, the last hope of the Imperial Mobile Fleet, slipped away into the western seas and evaded Halsey's final pursuit, but it effected nothing in the final account. The Japanese navy would never be a threat again.

## HOUSE CLEANING AT TACLOBAN

In that tenuous moment in Leyte Gulf, the Japanese introduced a desperate new tactic against the harbored ships. Although Imperial pilots had purposely rammed their opponents in the past, pilots sworn to serve the Emperor in the role of the divine wind called the "kamikaze" came down in suicidal attacks on the USS carriers Princeton, Santee, Suwanee and St. Lo, as well as several Liberty ships. The St. Lo was sunk and the Princeton was beached while their planes diverted to Tacloban, despite the fact the strip was still under construction. In the aftermath of the sea battle, Gen. Kenney counselled with Photo Hutch and after serious appraisal, the 5 AF CO ordered the engineers to sweep the airstrip of all excess construction gear including more than fifty of the stranded Navy aircraft. That night, the crews packed the remaining 500 feet of sand and coral and Wurtsmith radioed the 49ers back at Biak.

## WAITING AT HOLLANDIA AND BIAK

After the operations against Balikpapen, the Flying Knights stood down to fully refit their planes and formally induct their returned veteran Maj. Bob McCompsey as their new commander. Capt. Willie Drier and his Blacksheep bid their time at Biak as the last of his junior officers flew their test hops in the rebuilt P-38 J models. In the 7 FS, Capt. Peck was still grounded from combat, even though his malaria was in remission. For the moment, the impending 7 FS mission to Tacloban would be led by Demon Ops Exec Capt. Bob DeHaven.

The air crews also waited restlessly at Biak for portage to the Philippines. Far back at Hollandia, the ground echelon personnel had manned the troop ships as early as the 16th, only to wait in

*Along with Walker's 49ers, Kenney brought up the P-61 Black Widow night fighters of the 421 NFS as the other half of the Tacloban airborne defense. Few kills were ever attained by the huge fighters, however, and the Navy Hellcats proved to be far more effective.*

anchorage aboard the crowded vessels. In spite of being designated as the 5 FC first team for the Philippines mobilization, as of the October 20th invasion landing, 49ers CO LtC. George Walker sat in the Ops tent at Mokmer Field with no idea of what was happening up north.

## FAR TO THE NORTH WITH THE ADVANCED ECHELONS

Finally, the signal to disembark was sent to Hollandia on October 19th. They steamed out of Humbolt Bay and picked up their convoy escorts coursing down from the Admiralty Islands. Likewise, the aircrew echelons crowded aboard their LST at Biak and joined the Hollandia ships en route. Both ships laden with the 49ers reached crowded Leyte Gulf on the night of the 24th and down loaded early the next morning in the midst of the air battle.

The 49ers had been well informed as to their part in the invasion. The USAAF distributed a packet to each enlisted man which expressed the Supreme Commander's goal of liberating the Philippine nation, plus instructional material on the customs and language of the Leyte population. Thus prepared, the LST's steamed straight into San Pedro Bay and the 49ers fully understood their priority was to get Photo Hutch's airfield operational.

As the shipboard gunners pounded away at the planes overhead, the LSTs lurched into the shallows of Cataisin Point's seaward shore just south of the airfield, but the waters there were too deep. Ground officer Lt. Joe McHenry was even compelled to jump overboard and rescue a military policeman who nearly drowned in the attempt to swim ashore and find the engineers to aide in the off loading. Engineers and Philippine laborers at long last arrived to hastily construct a make-shift dock of sandbags and planking. As the men downloaded, an LST a short distance down the beach was set afire by enemy planes. The Navy AA guns maintained a deafening volley and infantry gun fire sounded from deep within the forest. Errant rounds and shrapnel whizzed through the air from every direction.

The 49ers were immediately inducted into Hutchinson's desperate labor force and moved directly to the bull's-eye of the airstrip target. Cataisan Peninsula was only two miles long from north to south and barely a half mile across at the widest point. The 49ers aircrews could only reach the airfield by boat or the single narrow road from the south and once there, were at the mercy of every incensed dive-bomber pilot in the Philippines. An aircraft dispersal area had been graded out on the peninsula's west bank, but there was virtually no space left for either anti-aircraft gun pits or elaborate air raid shelters. The most novice Imperial pilot could hit the bustling airdrome with the least amount of accuracy. Tacloban was by far the most dangerous camp the 49ers had ever inherited.

## TACLOBAN; NOON - OCTOBER 27, 1944

After the waterborne echelons had been signalled to advance, Walker's fighters staged up to Morotai on the 22nd. But the situation up at Tacloban forced them to hold at Morotai for another four days. Finally, the summons came from Wurtsmith and at 0900 hours on October 27th, LtC. Walker's fighters lifted off from Morotai Field for the 700 mile one-way trip. With a B-25 in the lead, thirty-four P-38s crossed the open sea and passed over the east coast of Mindanao at mid-morning, then pressed on to arrive at Tacloban at noon. Group Ldr Walker, wingman Col. Bob Morrissey, element leader Dick Bong and wingman Gerry Johnson cruised straight in over the bay which harbored more ships than any of them had ever seen in one place before. The lead elements then wheeled to the left into the southbound approach to Tacloban where Walker deferred to veteran Morrissey what he thought would be the honor of the

first landing by a USAAF fighter-pilot in the Philippines since the dark days of 1942. The colonel landed, only to find that 35 FS Lt. Bill Gardner had been forced down just hours before when his P-38 was hit by friendly AA fire during a morning fighter sweep over the invasion fleet.

The other thirty elements followed and taxied to a halt in the dispersal area where the ground crews sent up a cheer and rushed to greet the pilots. Gen. Kenney immediately greeted his favorite young pilot, Dick Bong, and joked with the ace about his non-combat role as Gunnery Training Officer. Bong shyly said he probably would not enter into operations right away, then delighted the gathering when he grinned and asked, "Could I just join up with the first patrol to get to know the place."

The greeting party broke up and Kenney took Walker, Morrissey and Ops Exec Gerry Johnson back to MacArthur's HQ while shy Dick Bong stayed at the airstrip. As the senior officers were greeted by the Supreme Commander, eight 49ers roared over Price House, marking the first operational sortie of the 308 BW in the Philippines. Flights of eight continuously rotated over the west bank of crowded Leyte Gulf while another eight stood in readiness to answer any alert.

## FLYING KNIGHTS INITIATION; OCTOBER 27, 1944

After the meeting at Price House, Col. Morrissey and Maj. Johnson hurried back to the airfield and found Bong. Kenney had personally given them carte blanche to join the next patrol. After checking in at the Ops tent, the staff trio signed on with the next 9 FS patrol and were airborne at 1600 hours. Morrissey had been denied the privilege of being the first USAAF man to land at Tacloban, and he was even more determined to be the first USAAF man to score a kill in the new Philippines campaign.

The staff officer pilots were designated Green Flight and flew as an attached escort to the other eight Flying Knights who each toted a one-thousand pounder to hit the enemy fortifications just south of the Dulag village. As the bomb ladened P-38s went about

*Below: 9 FS CO McComsey's command ship #77 with triple command stripe in red on the fuselage booms. Left: McComsey's scoreboard displays the lone kill made two years earlier in Australia and two bomb silhouettes marking more recent combat missions. Unfortunately, both the major and his plane would soon be written off.*

*Bernie Krankowitz scored the first 49ers Philippines aerial kill in aircraft #72 on October 27th and summarily lost the Lightning in one of the many air raids sent in retaliation two days later. Within six weeks, the 49ers would write off sixty similarly damaged P-38s at embattled Tacloban.*

their business, Morrissey and his ace wingmen swung inland to hunt for enemy planes. Had he stayed in the vicinity of Dulag, he might well have gotten the first Philippines aerial victory in 5 FC.

## FIRST BLOOD AT TACLOBAN

After hitting the coastal target near Dulag, mission leader Lt. Bob Wood recalled his Yellow Flight wingman Art Hufford, element leader Bernie Krankowitz and John Hanisch, then signalled Blue Flt Ldr Lt. Hal Olgesby and his three elements to regroup over the water. As the eight Knights rose up through the overcast, Wood reported engine trouble and turned for home, leaving Yellow element leader Krankowitz in charge. Krankowitz then turned north to follow Woods, only to separate from Blue Flight in the clouds, so he signalled Blue to return on their own.

After Krankowitz' reassembled his Yellow trio the closing rain clouds to 8000 feet, they were about to enter the approach pattern to Tacloban when the flight leader caught sight of the first airborne targets over their new hunting grounds. Three VAL dive-bombers in Vee formation passed the Lightnings at their level going in the opposite direction along a shallow valley just south of Tacloban town.

Krankowitz immediately wheeled about to a rear-quarter attack. As he pulled into gun range on the lead VAL, the rear gunner opened fire. Krankowitz responded with a .50 caliber barrage that killed the gunner instantly. Wingman Hufford simultaneously opened fire on the right element target and both of the flaming VALs plunged into the forest.

Yellow Flight separated as they broke away from the initial attack, but Krankowitz was able to catch the trailing VAL element and riddled it before it disappeared within the overcast. Hufford swept back out over the gulf and found a fourth VAL which he attacked, but his gun-button jammed and all of his weapons fired wildly until the ammo was gone. His smoking victim also escaped in the haze.

## TWENTY MINUTES LATER

Although he was a full twenty minutes too late, anxious Col. Morrissey and wingman Majors Bong and Johnson thought they had found the first Leyte victims twenty miles northwest of Yellow Flight's point of engagement. Bong saw the pair of OSCARs first and closed in head-on, but was too fast. As Morrissey and Bong simultaneously opened fire, Morrissey's Ki-43 fell straight down in flames while Bong overran his target. Johnson, following a bit behind the others, wheeled down on Bong's intended victim from dead-astern and quickly dispatched the Ki-43 with one deadly, five second burst.

Bong quickly set upon another OSCAR pair that appeared, and that time, he closed into point-blank range to set the leading Ki-43 ablaze. The sentai wingman set off for the north and Bong wheeled into a trailing pursuit which quickly separated him from his Green wingmen.

Morrissey and Johnson reformed and hunted back toward their base. Once over the gulf shoreline, the two Green elements passed over a lone VAL raider and both men peeled off for the hapless JNAF crew. Johnson got to the Mitsubishi first and set it afire, then Morrissey swept in and killed the rear gunner. Out of ammo and low on fuel, they triumphantly landed at Tacloban, only to learn that the Flying Knights were buying drinks for victorious Bernie Krankowitz as the winner of the race for the first Philippines kill.

In the interim 300 Mph chase through the rain squalls to Leyte's northern most shore, Bong could only hit his swerving OSCAR target with a few short bursts until the fellow escaped within the billowing dark clouds over Biliran Island. The ace turned back and reached Tacloban to inform his wingmen he would return to the fertile hunting grounds up north the first thing in the morning.

## FIRST 49ERS STRIKE TO ORMOC; OCTOBER 28, 1944

Unfortunately on the following day, weather over the northern half of Leyte made the approach to Biliran too tenuous, even for the eager trio of Morrissey, Bong and Johnson. During the heavy rains, the enemy took advantage of the subdued American air power and brought a convoy of reinforcements into the broad harbor which served the west coast Leyte garrison at Ormoc village.

Gen. Kenney was appraised of the reinforcements, but his weathered-in Lightnings at Tacloban were useless. Kinkaid's Navy carriers to the south sent a small sortie to hit the Ormoc docks in the marginal weather, but the Imperial troops downloaded with minimal interruption. Kenney was forced to counter against the heavily armed camp in the clearer weather later that afternoon. At 1430 hours, weather recon flights reported improved conditions to the north and west. Twelve Demons reached Ormoc Bay and dropped their heavy ordinance on tiny Masisingi Island south of the garrison proper, then turned back to patrol over the mainland interior.

## FIRST DEMON VICTORY IN THE PHILIPPINES

The weather continued to improve and by late afternoon, both opposing air forces were back in operations. Tacloban Field alerted the stand-by flights at 1600 hours and newly promoted Capt. John Haher took off to join the standing patrol. As his flight broke out above the overcast at 15,000 feet, the captain immediately signalled an airborne enemy contact ten miles south of the Tacloban airfield.

Capt. Haher's flight consisted only of two other wingmen, but they readily set after the six OSCARs which approached them 2000 feet overhead. Haher, with wingmen 2Lts. George Spruill and George Rogers, throttled forward and rose up behind the intruders to 27,000 feet without being seen. The Demon leader in his brand-new model L-1 #16 was about to fire from dead astern when the enemy leader and wingman both rocked their wings. Haher momentarily thought the waving planes might have indeed been U.S. Navy types, but the leading four aircraft rose up in a climbing turn and the sight of their red wing roundels abruptly put the Demon captain back on the offensive.

Bearing down on the trailing OSCAR, Haher opened fire and the Ki-43 twisted away in a split-S descent. While Spruill and Rogers fired at the next pair of OSCARs in line, Haher nosed #16 over and plunged after his original target. In seconds, the captain laid in a heavy volley which set the Nakajima's center fuselage on fire. As his victim plunged into the jungle, rookies Spruill and Rogers became targets themselves when the OSCARs out-turned them both. Rogers was able to escape alone in a 500 Mph descent, but Spruill had to be saved with an intervening firing pass laid in by the veteran captain.

Haher continued to chase Spruill's attacker in a twisting descent down to 15,000 feet, and fired several burst without telling effect. The captain's gun suddenly went silent as the G-forces seized the flow of ammo just as the he reached the western shore line. With his rookie wingmen long since separated, Haher was sure he had pushed his luck too far. Out of no where, Lockheed #42 bearing yellow and black spinners swept in for a firing pass and despatched the escaping Ki-43. It was Dick Bong.

## YELLOW KNIGHTS SCRAMBLE

Bong had patiently waited at Tacloban the entire day. With trusted wingmen Morrissey and Johnson, plus Group CO Walker, the four men were the first Flying Knights elements to get airborne in the late-day alert. Designated Yellow Flight, the four staff pilots rose up to set after the very same OSCARs pursued by the scrambling Demons trio. Bong had held off during Haher's initial attack and was in perfect position to take over when the captain's guns went dry. After the wild pursuit to Ormoc Bay, the Yellow quartet momentarily separated and completely lost Johnson, but the other three soon reformed and continued the hunt.

Certain that his recent victim had ventured from a strip on Biliran Island, Flt Ldr Bong wheeled north with Morrissey and Walker all the way to Leyte's northern most point. When the Yellow trio passed Biliran at 11,000 feet, they peered ahead through the broken clouds to the northwest at the peaks of Masbate Island. Only twenty-five miles away over the inland Visayan Sea and still with ample fuel, the wingmen heartily bid the ace Flight Leader to press on to the big island. Just as the Yellow team reached the southern most tip of Masbate, a lone OSCAR was spotted cruising above in a reciprocal direction. Bong entered into a pursuit chandelle and fired at the Ki-43 which carried a single underwing bomb. The Nakajima immediately countered with an escape dive and the simultaneous release of the ordinance, but the bomb struck the rear fuselage which tore away the whole tail assembly. Bong's second kill of the mission fell into the blue waters of the Visayan.

The good hunting inspired the Yellow Flight trio to press on even further up the eastern side of Masbate. They immediately passed over a south-bound flight of seventeen OSCARs estimated at 7000 feet and the Yellow trio turned about to parallel the enemy's course. Bong radioed for additional Allied fighters to rendezvous north of Leyte to effect better odds for an interception, but no one answered. Bong next instructed Col. Morrissey to climb higher and speed ahead to hopefully improve their broadcast while he and Walker continued to shadow the sentai.

Morrissey had just passed from view when the two higher most OSCARs began to rise up from the formation. Bong and Walker, grossly outnumbered, targeted the offending pair of Ki-43s and peeled off to the attack. Slashing through the OSCARs head-on at 400 Mph, Bong hit both of the aggressors with heavy volleys as LtC. Walker safely dove away. When Bong recovered with the 49ers CO, the ace was forced to shut down his over heating left engine. They safely landed at Tacloban and stepped down from the Lockheeds to recount the dangerous long range mission. The ace had garnered kills number thirty-two and thirty-three, plus two other targets as damaged which made the single bullet hole in his left radiator seem rather insignificant.

## ANOTHER LATE-DAY KILL FOR THE 9 FS

While LtC. Walker sortied north, his Red Flight Knights flew another dive-bombing strike to Ormoc. After Red Flt Ldr Lt. Ray Swift's team dropped their ordinance, the foursome entered into another routine patrol of the Leyte interior. When they ventured over the east coast, they saw the bursts of the Navy anti-aircraft batteries and latched on to a lone OSCAR speeding away to the west. Swift fired and hit the Ki-43 which momentarily disappeared beneath the broken overcast. Taking a dead-reckoning heading, Swift continued west and spotted the OSCAR again as it crossed the Ormoc Bay shoreline. The Flying Knight finally overtook the speedster sixty miles beyond Ormoc over the west coast of Cebu Island and sent the Nakajima down in flames.

## KILL #500; OCTOBER 29, 1944

The next morning, Leyte was again covered with rain squalls. Only seven Screamin' Demons were able to take off at 0600 and the two wingmen in Capt. Bob DeHaven's Pinky Red Flight separated in the ascent through the overcast. After a full orbit over the field, DeHaven ventured alone to the northwest. Well after an hour of searching the vast storm front, DeHaven latched on to a flight of Navy Hellcats and shadowed their hunt all the way to the northern tip of Leyte. Off the eastern shore of Biliran Island, the aviators pounced on a flight of OSCARs and while one Ki-43 fell into the sea, another escaped straight into the clutches of the Demon ace.

DeHaven had fired his P-38's concentrated armament at stationary ground targets on previous missions, but had not really given any thought as to what the "four fifties and a twenty" would do to an enemy plane. After running down his wildly fleeing prey 5000 feet over Biliran's shore, he pressed the gun-button on his steering column and his mouth fell open in absolute awe as the "water hose" stream of tracers chopped the OSCAR to shreds. Debris clattered on his Lockheed and DeHaven chandelled out of the smoking wake to watch his eleventh victim tumble into the shallow water.

Meanwhile, the other Demons four-ship Red Flight led by Capt. Elliot Dent stayed intact and broke out of the clouds together at 10,000 feet. After their turn over the base, the air controller vectored Dent's Red team to "16 Angels" on a heading due west. Once over Ormoc Bay, wingman Lt. Searight reported his oxygen gear had failed, so Dent took the quartet down 3000 feet just as they passed over Cebu Island. Up ahead and cruising slowly to the east was a lone OSCAR which immediately fell victim to the firing passes of all four Demons. After being hit by the first three volleys, the fatal blow was delivered by the number-4 man, Lt. Milden Mathre. The lieutenant chopped his throttles and pulled along side to see the sentai opponent wilt into the cockpit which had become a raging furnace. Milden pulled away as the blazing OSCAR finally nosed down and plunged into the deep blue channel.

When all the Screamin' Demons got back safely to Tacloban, victorious Ops Exec DeHaven immediately dispatched Lt. C.O. Archer to fly up to Biliran and confirm the OSCAR wreckage lying on the beach. When Red Flt Ldr Dent's team debriefed from their sweep to Cebu, the Demons phoned the Flying Knights to learn of their score for the day, but a strafing attack had kept the 9 FS on the ground. Although unofficial, the Demons concluded that their own squadron accounting was correct. Ace DeHaven's OSCAR confirmed by Archer and Mathre's OSCAR confirmed by his Red Flight wingmen were the 49ers victories number 499 and 500 respectively.

## FIRST CASUALTY - S/SGT. HODGEPATH; OCTOBER 29, 1944

It would have been a great day to celebrate the five-hundredth kill in LtC. Walker's HQ, but the CO had to attend the ugly business on the Tacloban flight line. Barely an hour after the 7 FS aircraft had gotten airborne in the minimal weather, the Flying Knights would indeed be hit by enemy strafers. The 9 FS linecrews were caught in the open with no chance to reach the slit trenches when a pair of OSCARs slipped under the overcast and shot up the dispersal area. Of the three men hit, S/Sgt Jack Hodgepath would die of his wounds

*A publicity shot of the luminaries in the October air battle. Lt.-rt.; 49ers CO Walker, 5 FC advisor Morrissey, 49ers Ops Exec Johnson, Demon 2Lt. Mathre who scored the 500th Group kill, Jordan temporarily back in command of 9 FS, leading ace Bong, 475 FG rival ace McGuire and Demon ace DeHaven who scored the 499th Group kill.*

at the primitive dispensary the next day. Of the twelve Flying Knights' P-38s on the line for the day's mission, four were damaged and three others were knocked off the roster completely. Replacement aircraft were immediately summoned from Morotai.

## BLACKSHEEP FOR TACLOBAN - SAUM, BILBREY AND SWAM ACCIDENTS; OCTOBER 27-30, 1944

On the early morning hours of the 30th, Tacloban shut down completely as the first monsoon of the season roared across Leyte. The newly arrived Blacksheep echelon joined the other line crews in the fifty-Mph gale to tie down all of the aircraft on the airfield, but torrential rain turned the sandy soil into deep mud and neither man nor machine could maneuver on the peninsula. The storm essentially did in a single day what the enemy could not do in a week. Tents and shacks were torn apart and four-foot waves swept over flat Cataisan Peninsula swamping quarters, vehicles and stockpiles. By mid-morning of the 31st, the weather subsided long enough for 8 FS CO Capt. Willie Drier to finally reach the storm wrecked airfield with sixteen Blacksheep Lockheeds. It had not been an easy crossing for Drier's depleted squadron.

It began on the 27th when the squadron pilots staged to Morotai. Lt. George Saum lost power after lifting off from Mokmer and while on one engine, he was signalled to follow a C-47 which also experienced mechanical failure. As Saum passed over Sorido airstrip eight miles west of Mokmer, his Lightning stalled out and plunged to a fiery crash in the Sorido motor pool. Eight ground personnel were badly injured and the Blacksheep pilot was killed.

Minutes later back at Mokmer, the dead man's wingman, Lt. Joseph Bilbrey, blew both main gear tires on takeoff. The P-38 swerved off the runway and crashed in a drainage ditch. The injured pilot was retrieved from the wreck just before the belly tanks erupted in a ball of fire. Bilbrey was taken to the field hospital where he would eventually recover, but he would never fly again.

As if bad luck came in threes, staff officer Maj. Glen Swam was next in line for his takeoff which ended in the same fiery fate as his hapless squadron mates. Swam's P-38 had just begun to pull up its gear when it stalled out in the ascent and slammed down on the west end of the strip. The big fighter was engulfed in a huge fire ball which killed the major instantly.

The last Blacksheep elements who were delayed by the botched takeoffs at Mokmer waited one more night and took off at first light on the 28th. Lt. Dick McNamara was able to reach Morotai, but on touching down, his left gear collapsed and the Lightning plowed off the runway. McNamara barely got clear before his broken P-38 detonated into a broiling inferno. So it was that CO Capt. Drier was down to only twenty operational Lockheeds as he sat at Morotai and waited for the storm to leave distant Leyte.

Despite being so few in number, Capt. Drier's Blacksheep were a welcome relief to the 49ers commander. LtC. Walker's Group had been hit hard again on the field the day the Blacksheep arrived. Two pilots would be lost, including the Flying Knights' new commander, Maj. Bob McComsey.

Darwin veteran McComsey had only been at Tacloban three days and was working up to operations with his squadron when the Japanese dive-bombers caught the Knights in the open dispersal area. A flight of low flying VALs swept down from the north and dropped their bombs amidst the parked Lightnings where the major had just pulled up in his jeep. The blast knocked him out of his vehicle and he was quickly taken to the field hospital. Staff officer Maj. Wally Jordan again took charge of the squadron with the news that critically wounded Bob McComsey would be going home for good.

## LT. BOB SEARIGHT LOST TO BASE A/A; OCTOBER 31, 1944

While the Flying Knights struggled with the desperate situation on the airfield, the airborne Screamin' Demons lost Lt. Bob Searight who ventured into the landing pattern with engine trouble during the attack. The anxious anti-aircraft crews failed to identify the low flying P-38 and they surely killed Searight with their first volley. The stricken Demon aimlessly drifted out over the gulf until the big fighter rolled over and plunged out of sight in the deep blue water.

Newcomer Demon 2Lt. Francis Hill was the last man inbound to the strip just seconds behind fallen Searight and was only 75 feet over the water when he passed beneath four Aichi dive-bombers. He immediately retracted his landing gear and pulled the nose of his Lightning up to fire at the trailing VAL, but the deadly flak which had just shot down Searight had begun to track his plane.

Hill broke off to the west and headed inland a short distance to avoid the flak batteries, then turned due south and set after the raiders again. Just four miles southwest of Cataisan Peninsula, the Demon lieutenant overtook a VAL skimming over the jungle. The enemy pilot pressed his dive-bomber so low to the tree tops that it sheared off the telephone line running along the Tacloban-Dulag road. In two firing passes, Hill sent the hapless VAL crew down to a fiery death in the jungle.

At the same time, Flying Knight Lt. Charlie McElroy's four-ship patrol had descended into their final approach from the east and they caught sight of three more VALs just north of the airfield.

In a low altitude chase inland in two different directions, wingman Lt. Noah Williams and newcomer 2Lt. Ernie Ambort each sent down a dive-bomber in flames while separated McElroy claimed another VAL shot down south of the airfield. Only the two kills by Williams and Ambort would later be confirmed.

After one last orbit of the airdrome, the Knights landed at Tacloban which was bathed in the amber light of a brilliant Philippines sunset. It was hard to believe such a beautiful place could be so dangerous, but it was only the beginning. LtC. George Walker's fighter group had only confronted but a handful of the enemy airmen.

## THE LEYTE AIR BATTLE BEGINS IN EARNEST; NOVEMBER 1, 1944

The Leyte operations had totally surprised the Imperial commanders at Manila, and with the passing of the late October monsoon, the enemy was finally able to marshalled a stronger counter-offensive. Drawing troops from as far away as China and Indonesia, the reinforcements joined the northern Philippines divisions in their quest to reach the western Leyte garrison. More JAAF and JNAF units moved into the northern airfields to provide escort over the convoys steaming to the battle site as well as to join in the assault on the new Allied airfields.

Despite the fierce weather and brutal fighting in the foothills of the central highlands, ATF CO Hutchinson's work on the Barauen-Dulag airdrome complex was nearly completed with the passing of the great storm. On October 31st, the 8 FG brought their P-38s into the new Bayug Airfield just east of Barauen village and the 475 FG moved to the new airstrip on the coast at Dulag. As more Allied infantry poured into the Dulag beachhead, a proportionate increase in enemy air activity appeared overhead. In the ensuing air battle, 5 FC CO Squeeze Wurtsmith would see his reinforced Lightning wing execute the Imperial airmen in droves.

The first substantive airborne contest began at 0940 hours on November 1st when the Flying Knights beat the Demons in the race to the first vector north of Tacloban. Flight leader Lt. Howard Oglesby and wingman 2Lt. Cheatham Gupton dropped down on a flight of two VALs escorted by a single OSCAR where the leader dispatched the Ki-43 and the wingman knocked down both of the dive-bombers, despite a duplicate claim by Demon Ops Exec DeHaven who fired last on the falling Aichi which exploded in mid-air.

After landing at Tacloban, the typically gregarious DeHaven was somewhat annoyed by the disputed claim being awarded to rookie Flying Knight Gupton. With a huff, DeHaven attached himself to the very next flight and set off for the vector over Dulag. With total disregard for the airspace assigned to the Satan's Angels, DeHaven thundered into the interception and shot down a ZERO directly over the Dulag strip for his uncontested twelfth confirmed kill. The 49ers Ops Exec Gerry Johnson met the Demon ace after the sortie on the flight line and ordered him not to fly again that day.

More contacts were posted throughout the morning. The largest encounter would occur between the 8 FG and a large enemy force over Negros Island to the west where the newcomer Lightning unit would claim a dozen victories. At mid-day, several kills

*9 FS Flt Ldr Oglesby in the dogfight just south of Tacloban which yielded an unconfirmed but certain kill on November 2nd.*

*Looking northward up the west coast of Leyte to contested Ormoc Bay, several weeks after the great battle for the enemy garrison had subsided. Navy ships poured tons of equipment into Leyte by the end of the year for the planned assaults against the inner islands, but the devastating losses of the Imperial Philippines forces left the way clear to Manila far sooner than MacArthur had anticipated.*

were racked up by the Navy patrols. It would be late afternoon when the newcomer Blacksheep finally added their first Philippines kill to the overall tally.

## FIRST BLACKSHEEP VICTORY OVER ORMOC; NOVEMBER 1, 1944

Newly appointed Blacksheep Ops Exec Capt. Nelson Flack had taken up the last patrol of the day when the air controller vectored them across the mainland to Ormoc Bay. The Blacksheep were joined by the Demon foursome led by Capt. Elliot Dent. The eight 49ers Lightnings arrived in a spread formation at 10,000 feet over the broad bay at 1700 hours. After a brief hunt west of the enemy camp, Flack's people made the first contact just off the large land promontory southwest of Ormoc known as Duligan Point.

The Blacksheep captain sighted a lone OSCAR and led the attack down to 3000 feet, only to encounter a larger mixed formation of ZEROs and OSCARs who had been veiled by the scattered clouds. After a short zoom-climb to reposition themselves for a better coordinated firing pass, element leader Lt. John "Johny Zero" Bodak caught an OSCAR with a lethal head-on barrage and it crashed in the narrows just west of tiny Gumalae Island.

The rest of Flack's regrouped elements set into the enemy again. In the second pass, Flack and wingman 2Lt. Nial Castle downed a ZERO apiece and Castle's victim was able to bail out before the Mitsubishi struck the water. Then Castle sent down another ZEKE on the third go-around while Bodak's rookie wingman 2Lt. Walter Meyer downed the second OSCAR of the fight. As the fight dropped down near the enemy ships at anchor, flak bursts erupted in the vicinity of the Lightnings and Flack wisely called for the Blacksheep to withdraw.

## THE DEMONS NEW WET ACE

Demon Flt Ldr Dent had entered into a diving attack on the same OSCAR at the onset, but the Demons handled their resultant dogfight a bit differently than their Blacksheep brethren. It resulted in the gain, and subsequent loss of their newest ace.

As Capt. Dent pursued the OSCAR into the vicinity of the ZEKEs down below, his other three elements momentary lost sight of him in the scattered clouds. Once face to face with the kokutai, Dent decided to fight it out, rather than gamble on trying to outrun his opponents. For a furious ten minutes, the captain wheeled through the enemy formation in a lop-sided fight which dropped down to the wave tops. Although hit several times, he in turn accounted for two ZEROs which crashed in the water and a third which had slammed down in the mangrove swamp of Duligan Point. The dogfight ended when Dent was forced to make a low pass over the enemy ships where his P-38 fell within range of the anti-aircraft batteries. The newest Demon ace bailed out of his smoking hulk and landed in the midst of the merchant vessels which had shot him out of the sky. While in descent, a small caliber round whizzed by him, but he landed safely in the water.

Meanwhile overhead, wingman Lt. Fernly Damstrom struggled to hold position to Demon element leader Capt. Haher despite a faulty right super-charger. Haher covered Damstrom while able 2Lt.

*8 FS Flt Ldr John "Johnnie-Zero" Bodak and his aircraft #65 "RAGGED BUT RIGHT" which got him the first Blacksheep aerial kill in the Philippines on November 1st.*

Hal Harris in his FRAN #6 in turn took on a flight of OSCARs. With the utmost confidence, Harris single handedly beat up the sentai by downing a Ki-43 and damaging another. The Demons then retreated inland to the east and wondered if there was any hope for their captain last seen drifting down in his chute toward the bay.

## DENT IN THE HANDS OF THE VOLUNTEER GUARDS

From the outset of the war, the Philippines citizens had established a fierce resistance against the oriental invaders. Despite a brutal campaign against all vestiges of the old Republic, the stalwart Filipinos established a secret regional militia known as the Volunteer Guards (V.G.), and a highly organized guerilla army, both of which fought a sustained internal war throughout the occupation. When the Americans landed on Leyte, a network of heavily armed rescue teams was already in place to join in the liberation of their homeland. On November 1st, Capt. Elliot Dent would be the first USAAF fighter pilot to be rescued by the Filipinos resistance community. Unlike the abhorrent odds that awaited a downed flier in the past campaigns, the chances of survival in the Philippines were improved a hundred-fold. Had the V.G. battalions of western Leyte not been in existence, the captain would not have lasted beyond a day.

After dropping into the sea a mile off Duligan Point amid the Japanese convoy, wounded Dent found his liferaft was useless. Only half of his May West vest inflated, so, he took hold of a coconut cluster floating nearby. Ironically, the Imperial sailors aboard the destroyer which passed within a hundred feet either mistook Dent's head for another coconut, or they simply were concentrating on finding the flyer's raft. A SONIA plane skimmed over his location, but flew off without notice of him. Finally, in the evening twilight, Filipinos from Taligen village paddled out to him and spirited him to shore. The captain was immediately taken further up the coast a short distance to the Matang village Volunteer Guards battalion station. He would stay in hiding at Matang for eight days.

On the 10th, the Matang V.G. with the aide of several different guerilla companies escorted their American charge northward, and by mid day, they arrived at Port Bello where they stayed briefly at the home of a Dr. Rosete. After acquiring horses there, they continued on until they next reached the V.G. battalion headquarters at Cabaliwan village fifteen miles due west of Ormoc. Dent learned othe airmen had travelled the same route, but he was the only flyer on the course at the time. Dent only stayed the night.

The next day, horseman Dent and the Guards went further up the coast to Sabang. The horses were left there due to the need of Dent's party to continue on foot down the circuitous jungle pathway that skirted around the outpost garrison at Palompon. After another day's walk, the weary party reached their final destination of Tuburan. After a hearty celebration with plenty of food and a potent liquor called tebu, Dent, was led down to the shore at two A.M. on the morning of the 15th to rendezvous with a Navy PT boat rescue team. At noon, he was enthusiastically welcomed back at Tacloban by his squadron mates who had been told some days before of his rescue by the Filipinos. Better still was the news that Elliot Dent, known "the ghost of Ormoc Bay" by his fellow Demons, had his furlough orders waiting for him when he arrived. He never flew another Leyte mission.

## BACK TO ORMOC - 1st ENCOUNTER - NOVEMBER 2, 1944

November 2nd began at first light for the 49ers who were tasked with sweeping the air of enemy fighters prior to the first dive-bomber sorties sent against the newly arrived merchant ships. The Flying Knights and Blacksheep rose up from Tacloban at 0810 hours and reached their assigned patrol areas north and east of Ormoc village respectively. Its was extremely difficult to hold formation in the scattered cumulus which dotted the mountainous interior where both the Knights and Blacksheep continually exchanged position with squadron mates from different elements. At 0830, their earphones began to crackle with the vectors of enemy planes seen to the north. Minutes later, the Flying Knights two-ship flight cruising just east of Ormoc frantically would signal for help as they came under attack.

## HUISMAN AND HANISCH IN TROUBLE

While climbing through the billowing clouds in search of their lead elements, Lt. Bill Huisman and wingman 2Lt. Melvin Hanisch were set upon by seven ZEROs at 6000 feet. Hanisch called out the attackers, but Huisman never acknowledged the wingman's signal until the last critical second. In the break away, the flight leader's Lockheed was hit in the first diving pass by the dark-green Mitsubishis. The besieged Knights were forced apart and had to fight it out alone, but neither man could avoid the inevitable. As their squadron mates desperately raced to their distress calls, Huisman shot down two of his opponents before his P-38 was heavily damaged. Somehow, Huisman managed to escape in his holed ship and limp all the way back to Tacloban.

Wingman Hanisch never made it beyond the western foothills. A kokutai veteran wheeled into dead-astern and shot out his right supercharger, then set fire to his left engine. Hanisch tried to run in

*9 FS wingmen Huisman (lt.) and Hannisch just hours before their fateful sortie of November 2nd to Ormoc. It would be Huisman's last.*

his disabled P-38 within the hail of tracers at tree-top level for another fifteen miles inland, but the right engine final seized up and he was forced to crash landed in a small clearing. His opponent swept down and took a final shot at him in his crumpled fighter, but the volley completely missed. As the ZERO droned away to the west, the dazed lieutenant crawled through the side window of his shattered canopy and swooned as the blood poured out of the deep slash in his forehead inflicted in the rough landing. He held his fist over the wound to quell the bleeding, then drew his pistol and shot out his radio equipment so as not to let it fall into the enemy's hands. The lieutenant then stepped down from the wreck and immediately set off to the east.

## HANISCH IN SAFE HAVEN SOUTH OF ORMOC

Like the Demon flyer lost west of Ormoc the day before, Flying Knight Melvin Hanisch was quickly found by Philippine villagers who led him away to the safety of a local V.G. camp. After the tribesmen cleaned his head wound, the flyer was led five miles south to a guerilla stronghold where the commanding Philippine lieutenant proudly took personal charge of the American. An English speaking doctor was summoned who stitched up Hanisch's laceration, and then the group set off for an eight mile trek to another village to the south. Hanisch first attended a Catholic mass there for a fallen Navy aviator and then was taken by boat further down the coast at twilight to the Philippine lieutenant's home, thirty miles south of Ormoc.

After Hanisch stayed three days as an honored quest, the guerilla leader reluctantly turned the Flying Knight over to an advanced recon patrol of 7th Division infantry at Baybay village on November 6th. Hanisch caught a ride in a heavily armed jeep for a jolting thirty-five mile crossing of the rugged interior, all the way to Dulag.

Later that same day, he hitched a backseat ride in the next northbound Piper Cub and reached Tacloban before sundown.

## FLIGHT LDRS MADDOX AND POSTON TOO LATE

Prior to that 0830 hours encounter on the 2nd, Mission leader Lt. Bill Maddox's White Flight had actually gotten off from Tacloban last. With 2Lts. Ernie Ambort and Alex Datzenko in tight formation, Maddox led them in the mad dash to the west and they even dropped their long-range tanks for greater speed in the attempt to answer the Huisman-Hanisch call for help. In the meantime, Red Flight Leader Lt. Jim Poston had actually seen the Mitsubishi attackers jettison their belly tanks and assault the hapless pair of trapped Knights. Both White and Red Flights simply got to the fight too late to help either Huisman or Hanisch.

As the White and Red elements entered the area of the skirmish, yet another flight of ZEROs appeared and an even larger dogfight erupted. Both Flt Ldrs Maddox and Poston destroyed two ZEKEs each before Poston had his right engine radiator shot out. As Flt Ldr Poston withdrew, Red element leader Ambort covered the flight leader's escape and shot down a trailing TOJO out of a JAAF flight that joined the contest. The Red leader's wingman 2Lt. Paul Nahnibida, just transferred from the 8 FS, likewise picked off an OSCAR.

## BLACKSHEEP ARRIVE

Blacksheep CO Capt. Willie Drier was airborne in the standing patrol closer to Tacloban when he heard the Flying Knights signal for help. When the air controllers released Drier's flights from their base protection assignment, twelve Blacksheep dropped their auxiliary tanks and wheeled due west. Eight of them would reached the Ormoc battle sight at the same time the JAAF arrived.

Like the Knights in their initial ascent, the Blacksheep re-assembled their elements en route. Capt. Drier with wingmen Lt. Bob Campbell and 2Lt. Wright Boyd were soon joined by Ops Exec Capt. Nelson Flack and his adopted element 2Lts. Bill Bechdolt and Ralph Easterling, and FO Hal Bechtold. Enroute they also took on Lt. E.V. May who was the only White Fight element to find the fight.

*Poston's P-38 down in the shallows off Tacloban's runway after the failed attempt to reach embattled Huisman and Hanisch on November 2nd.*

*8 FS Co Willie Drier's aircraft #60 "MY GAL BECKY II" so named on the starboard side by crewchief Goldberg.*

The eight Blacksheep slammed head-on into the fray. Flight Officer Bechtold was the first Blacksheep to close into firing range and he sent down one of the trailing ZEROS as his only victory of the war. The others engaged the swirling formation of OSCARs where Boyd and Campbell each shot down one of the dirty tan Nakajimas. Ops Exec Flack and 2Lt. Bechdolt each destroyed an OSCAR, then tag-along 2Lt. May shot down yet another. Co Drier underscored the interception by downing the last OSCAR for the very first victory of his long combat career.

The fight subsided and Flack's team withdrew, but Red elements Drier, Campbell and Boyd still had enough fuel left over to orbit Ormoc for several more minutes. Thirty minutes later, the Red Flight trio found themselves in perfect position to bounce a flight of patrolling ZEROS and when the smoke cleared, both Campbell and Boyd had again destroyed one each while able squadron boss Drier personally accounted for two more Mitsubishis.

## HUISMAN'S FATAL LANDING; NOVEMBER 2, 1944

Ironically, Hanisch's wingman flight leader who had managed to withdraw in his crippled P-38 would not escape death a second time on the fateful November day. Element leader Lt. Bill Huisman indeed reached Tacloban in his battle-damaged Lockheed only to collide over the end of the runway with a Lightning of the 35th Squadron. The 9 FS crews scrambled to the twisted wrecks where ambulance driver Sgt. Rudolph Ventriglia and medic Howard Darby pulled the 35th Squadron pilot free while T/Sgt. Howard Harlecorde and Sgt. Al Robinson lifted mortally wounded Huisman from his smoldering P-38. The Flying Knight was quickly taken to a hospital ship just off shore, but he did not survive the night. Bill Huisman was buried at sea the next morning.

## 2nd ENCOUNTER - NOVEMBER 2nd

At 0930 hours, fifteen Screamin' Demons in four flights lifted off Tacloban as the first dive-bomber strike force of the day. The mission was headed up by Red Flt Ldr Capt. John Haher who flew directly to the north side of Ormoc village at 12,000 feet where he immediately reported enemy fighters patrolling overhead at 15,000 feet. He also spotted a large freighter anchored near the Ormoc docks.

Determined to hit the ship down loading in the bay, Haher took his two wingmen through a turning descent in order to pick up as much speed as possible. The captain ordered his other three flights to hold in high cover to see if the ZEROS would jump his diving

Red team, but as the dive-bombers dropped beneath the broken overcast, the remaining Demons momentarily lost radio contact with the mission commander.

White Flt Ldr Lt. Fred Dick finally hailed Haher and when he learned that the captain had not yet dropped his two one-thousand pounders, Dick reckoned the remaining P-38s could not hold their high cover any longer while still toting their own heavy ordinance. Lt. Dick ordered the three higher flights to close ranks and they all paraded over the enemy held village where they salvoed their bombs from 12,000 feet.

Haher and his two wingmen eventually hit the "Fox Uncle" merchant ship and it was last seen burning with a heavy list to port. The captain recalled his Demons over Leyte's mountainous interior and then turned back to hunt for the ZEROS but the kokutai had already withdrawn. The Demon flights separated to hunt along the entire west coast and Fred Dick's White team climbed to 22,000 feet where they soon spotted an airborne target south of the bay. Even though the four dark silhouettes were three thousand feet below, the White elements instantly recognized the portly plan-form of the new Mitsubishi JACK, a sturdier cousin of the ZEKE. Dick peeled off with his wingman in close pursuit.

Unfortunately, the diving Demons overshot their mark with their greater speed and element leader Lt. Bob Decker was the only man to score hits on one of the Mitsubishis. As the White team pulled up through a screaming zoom climb, Decker kept his target in sight and quickly separated from his wingmen. Suddenly, six JACKs dropped on to his tail and Decker nosed down to the north and escaped at well over 400 Mph. Low on fuel, Decker chose to press on for Tacloban, only to see a lone JACK down below which had separated from its kokutai and was likewise cruising north. The Demon plunged down to dead-astern and fired a long volley which tracked along the fuselage and shattered the JACK's cockpit. Unbeknown to Decker, wingman Warren Gregczn had witnessed the entire event from high above and confirmed the flaming hulk crashing on the slope of Catangangan Mountain.

## 3rd ENCOUNTER - NOVEMBER 2nd

At 1030 hours, Ops Exec Capt. Flack had re-assembled his Blacksheep pilots at Tacloban, but was only able to muster seven serviceable planes for the next mission. Intent to even the score for the two Flying Knights lost in the first encounter that day, the captain led his two flights off for Ormoc again, only to have his elements split up once more enroute in the cursed weather. Twenty

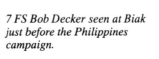

*7 FS Bob Decker seen at Biak just before the Philippines campaign.*

minutes into the mission, only five Blacksheep would rendezvoused twenty miles north of Ormoc.

Capt. Flack had taken Lt. E.V. May as his wingman and they were eventually joined by 8 FS Deputy CO Capt. Phil Kriechbaum with his wingmen Lts. Marion Felts and Tom Holstein. As the five pilots pushed through the towering cumulus at 16,000 feet, they could just make out ships in the harbor up ahead. At that very moment, a single OSCAR came into firing range of Kriechbaum, Felts and Holstein. The three-some descended upon the Nakajima just as four black-cowled ZEROS drifted into view and crossed their path two thousand feet below. Flack and May immediately changed course for the four Mitsubishis, and by that poor choice, entered into a contest with their strength divided. It would cost them dearly.

## AMBUSHED AT ORMOC

Deputy CO Kriechbaum had come to the 8 FS in August of 1943 at Marilinan and was one of their most admired senior officers. A serious, studious type and well seasoned in combat, the captain had been one of those rare individuals to survive over 200 missions without ever having had an enemy aircraft pass in front of his guns. But in his pursuit of the lone Ki-43 which was a certain easy kill, the captain fell for one of the oldest ploys in the fighter pilot game. Kriechbaum was ambushed by a large flight of OSCARs waiting below.

Even veteran Nelson Flack would be drawn into the fray with the veteran OSCAR sentai veiled by the hanging clouds. After several turns against the ZEROs which yielded E.V. May's single career victory, both Flack and May were waylaid by the Ki-43s. Flack registered his fifth career kill over one of the attacking Nakajimas, but his wingman could not hold formation. Before Flack could turn back to his aide, "Evie" May was caught at low altitude by a pair of OSCAR marksmen. Trailing heavy smoke, the lieutenant dropped out of the fight into the clouds and headed home.

May road his burning Lightning all the way to the east coast where the fire spread to the cockpit and forced him bail out. After a jolting tumble down through the trees, the scorched flyer cut himself free of the branches and dropped to the ground within sight of the coast road. He was soon found by 19th Inf. Reg. Lt. Richardson and his four scouts who treated his burns with sulfa powder. Evie May was delivered to the evacuation hospital at Palo village later that very day.

## BACK IN THE FIGHT WITH FELTS

At the time May had been hit, Marion Felts was simultaneously assaulted just a short distance to the west. Felts instantly returned the favor and dispatched one of the Nakajima attackers for his fifth career kill, but the odds were far too great for an extended match. He called Kriechbaum for help while using every escape maneuver he could muster out of his riddled P-38, but the right engine erupted in flames and it quickly spread over the inner wing to the cockpit. Felts radioed his position and tried to open his jammed canopy, but was only able to open the top hatch. He crawled out of his seat straps and stood up to be ripped out of the seat at nearly 400 knots.

Felts was extremely lucky despite having fallen so near the enemy camp. With a badly sprained back, a cracked arm and a sprained knee, he was limping into the jungle within a hail of infantry rifle fire when a Filipino horseman suddenly appeared and carried him to the safety of the highlands. Days later at Cacaliwan, he would join Flying Knight Bob Hamburger. Marion Felts reached home after thirteen days of "absence due to mitigating circumstances."

## KRIECHBAUM KILLED; NOVEMBER 2, 1944

As for Capt. Kriechbaum, he had acknowledged Felts' called for help and broke off his pursuit of the first Ki-43, but the lieutenant had already bailed out by the time the captain reached the scene. As Felts drifted down into the jungle ten miles north of the village, Kriechbaum tried to rejoin with Holstein to fight their way out of the dilemma, but three OSCARs wheeled about and descended upon the captain who was only 3000 feet above the jungle. His P-38 became engulfed in flames and dropped off on its left wing to explode in a huge fireball five miles northeast of Ormoc village.

Holstein had meanwhile pressed after the decoy Ki-43 and raced straight over the anchored enemy ships and garrison town within a barrage of intense anti-aircraft fire. As his OSCAR victim slammed down just northwest of the village, Holstein swept past Felts hanging in his chute. The surviving airborne Blacksheep covered Felts until he was safely on the ground, then climbed up in search of the stricken captain, but Kriechbaum was already dead. Holstein immediately drew the full attention of seven snarling Ki-43s and they entered into a wild rat race at 350 Mph that was inevitably won by Holstein's Lightning which carried him down and away at 400 knots. He was the last Blacksheep to land back at Tacloban.

## FLYING KNIGHTS RETURN THE FAVOR

To reciprocate the effort of the Blacksheep, Flt Ldr Lt. Hal Oglesby scrambled off Tacloban with three wingmen, but the Knights were much too late. As the Knights entered the airspace north of the fight, seven OSCARs tried to catch Oglesby's team with a similar ploy, but the wily 9 FS flight leader disrupted the whole scheme when he caught one of the diving OSCARs in the initial head-on firing pass. Oglesby's return volley gutted the Nakajima cockpit and the other sentai men immediately withdrew to the safety of the clouds up north as their wingman fell in flames.

## 4th AND FINAL ENCOUNTER - NOVEMBER 2nd

Gen. Kenney was far from through with the reinforcements at Ormoc. Missions by all of the 5 AF units continues throughout the day and the Demons were back in the air for another sortie at 1330 hours. Of the fourteen Demon ships airborne, the six planes of Blue and Green flights at 12,000 feet carried a pair of five-hundred pounders intended for the docks of Ormoc. Mission Ldr Bob DeHaven with his three wingmen and the four men in White Flight would provide high cover at 15,000.

*Above: Bob DeHaven's aircraft #13 sits high on its gear at the end of another day's flying at Tacloban. The pace of fighting was so great in the first two weeks that aircraft from the 8 FG and 475 FG were commandeered by Walker's 49ers to hold up operations at Tacloban. Although the Demon ace does not have his victories painted on #13, someone at Biak found time to adorn the tail of this P-38 with the old Bunyap Screamin' Demon of the Darwin days, just barely visible on the left tail. Right: A close-up of DeHaven's tail markings which were similar to the treatment on 7 FS CO Peck's aircraft #1. (See also the color profile of Dehaven's plane on page 155.)*

At 1400 hours, the high cover flights passed over the bay to detract the enemy anti-aircraft batteries. Seconds later, the dive-bombers made a successful run on a "Fox Uncle" merchant vessel which took a single direct hit. As DeHaven's force regrouped over the coast line, the leader caught sight of a lone radial engine fighter headed west several thousand feet below. With his three wingmen in trail, DeHaven set after the dark-green ship which was readily identified as another one of the new JACK types.

The chase ended over the islands which lay on the west perimeter of Ormoc Bay. The Jack pilot offered virtually no attempt to avoid DeHaven's fire as the Mitsubishi drifted slightly to the left before it erupted in a fireball. The Demon ace plowed through the swirling debris, then wheeled about to watch the remnant fuselage of his thirteenth career kill tumble down on Poro Island.

In the meantime, Green Flt Ldr Lt. Fernly Damstrom and Blue element leader 2Lt. Doug Hart had set after a pair of OSCARs cruising due south out of the target area. Like the mission leader's kill only minutes before, both Damstrom and Hart closed in to point-blank range and neither victim attempted to escape. DeHaven arrived and approvingly peered down at the two burning oil slicks on the coastal shallows, then recalled his strike force and they all landed shortly after four o'clock back at Tacloban.

Group CO Walker was duly concerned that his force has been so badly reduced by both weather and combat. Seven of his P-38s and some of his most seasoned flight leaders had been lost in the previous day's combat alone, not including the other Lightnings

that had been scrapped during the continuous bombing raids that struck in the past forty-eight hours. It became necessary to shuttle his remaining aircraft off to Dulag and Baruaen during off duty dispersals while the Tacloban crews turned their attention to the growing scrap heap on Cataisan Peninsula.

## FLYING KNIGHTS ON THE ORMOC-VALENCIA ROAD; NOVEMBER 3, 1944

As a new weather front began to move in, the 49ers pressed on in their tactical missions the very next morning. At 0830, the 9 FS had reached Ormoc garrison again and discovered a large truck convoy pushing inland north of the harbor town on the Ormoc-Valencia road. Trapped on the narrow route by swamps on both flanks, the enemy tanks, trucks and horse-drawn carts were butchered as the murderous P-38s made one firing pass after another until their ammunition was gone.

## HAMBURGER FOUND - BATES LOST

The decimation of the enemy convoy suddenly turned for the worst. The odds against making a third strafing run played out for Lt. Bob Hamburger when he was hit by a barrage of return groundfire. He drifted down in his chute among the rice paddies to the west and safely escaped into the forest. Hamburger, of coarse, was found by another trustworthy V.G. battalion, and later would join Blacksheep Marion Felts on the west coast at Cabaliwan.

Seconds later as the mission force was being recalled, a flight of OSCARs struck at low altitude. Too low on fuel and ammo to offer a sustained counter-attack, there was a moment of panic as the Flying Knights desperately separated to the east. Newcomer 2Lt. Bob Bates radioed his P-38 was on fire, and elements were sure they saw his Lockheed descend to the north. Bob Bates was never heard from again.

## NOVEMBER 4th - NO RESPITE

Missions continued in the marginal weather of the 4th, and the 49ers had two airborne contacts with the enemy, but only one would be successful.

*9 FS Bob Hamburger was shot down and rescued by the Filipinos on November 3rd.*

An early morning armed reconnaissance of the Visayan Islands had been scheduled in the hopes that the P-38s could find the next merchant convoy trying to reach Ormoc, but the Japanese struck Tacloban before dawn and holed the main runway again. The mission was scrubbed until the Marston mat could be repaired, and besides, the weather had again closed in over the area. Demon Ops Exec DeHaven and Blacksheep Lt. Walter Leaf were still in their flight gear at 0730 at the flight line when the air raid siren screamed its warning.

Four OSCARs suddenly dropped through the grey scud right over the airdrome. DeHaven and Leaf ran to the nearest planes on the flight line and in seconds, they rolled out on the Marston mat. They glanced over at the Blacksheep flight line where four ships were rolling forward. Tracers streamed overhead and the field ack-ack thumped in the gunpits back in the trees. DeHaven shoved the throttles forward and sped down the strip veering aside to miss the torn steel matting twisting up out of a smoldering bomb crater. As the captain lifted off the end of the runway, another bomb detonated in the surf beneath his P-38. Leaf followed seconds later, but DeHaven had already vanished into the overcast. The captain burst out alone into the brilliant morning sky and leveled out at 15,000 feet, then turned south with the first vector of VALs attacking Dulag. Walter Leaf never would catch the speeding Ops Exec. Both would hunt alone.

DeHaven reached Dulag air space in a mere ten minutes, but the controller already had a contact confirmation from the 8 FS "Raccoon" flight. DeHaven searched all around to see if the VALs had come with escorts, and sure enough, the sharp-eyed ace spotted three dark silhouettes fifteen miles off to the northwest. He wheeled upward into the sun, gained another three-thousand feet and soon drew near enough to identify them as ZEROs. Just minutes from the north coast, the two lead ZEROs dropped below the cloud deck while the trailing one made a lazy turn to the west. DeHaven quickly dropped in behind the unsuspecting kokutai man and hit him with his first volley. An explosion flashed in mid-fuselage, the ZERO snap rolled and the pilot dropped free in his chute. The ace orbited around the descending enemy pilot until he hit the ground near the mountain village of Jaro.

## LEAF LOST IN TACLOBAN APPROACH; NOVEMBER 4, 1944

DeHaven hunted for nearly an hour more, but no other vector was broadcast. When he landed back at Tacloban, the Demon Ops Exec found he was the only 49er to make good in the interception. Young Blacksheep Leaf had apparently found another flight of enemy fighters, but had not own up to the task. He had limped back to the airfield in his damaged Lightning and was in final approach when another aircraft forced him out of the pattern. Walter Leaf's P-38 fell into San Pedro Bay during the attempt to go around. Both plane and pilot vanished.

By late morning, the weather worsened and a small quiet crowd gathered to celebrate the ace's latest victory. Group Ops Exec Gerry Johnson soon arrived at the Screamin' Demons club bar and announced that DeHaven's victim had just been captured by an infantry patrol near Jaro. He also informed DeHaven that his flying days at Tacloban were over as of that very moment. Fifth Fighter Command had dismissed the fourteen-victory ace from duty ten day prior. The orders had only caught up with Bob DeHaven at Tacloban that morning.

## STORMS OVER TACLOBAN AND MANILA - NOVEMBER 5-7, 1944

On the afternoon of the 4th, the monsoon struck in full force and completely shut down operations. The next day, the heavy rain and fog only lifted long enough in the morning to permit two-plane flights a brief patrol before the weather closed in again at mid-day. Blacksheep Lt. George Smerchek lost his P-38 when it slid on the wet steel mat in a heavy landing and collided with a fuel truck. Smerchek was not injured, but his plane was hauled off to the junk heap.

On the 6th down at Bayug Airstrip, Demon 2Lt. Maynard Oehlbeck was seated in his P-38 on alert standby when a 110 TRS Warhawk botched its landing and slid into his Lightning. The lieutenant was taken to the Palo village dispensary where the flight surgeons attended to his broken leg. Both the Warhawk and Lightning were scrapped.

Meanwhile back at Tacloban, the Japanese bravely pushed through the cloud deck and dropped their bombs on the 7 FS flight line, wiping out three Lockheeds and seriously wounding three men. Staff Sgts. Frank Swartz and James Wilson, and 2Lt. W.K. Korth who suffered a broken leg were all evacuated to the mainland field hospital. Even Flt Surgeon George Webster received a minor wound in the raid which he himself easily bandaged.

Six-hundred miles to the north, however, the Japanese felt the greater wrath of another man-made tempest. Even though Gen. Kenney's 5 AF had claimed over 300 enemy aircraft destroyed in the first two weeks of operations, there was still the persistent flow of enemy planes coming down from the north. At MacArthur's insistence, Adm. Nimitz directed Adm. Halsey's northern carrier air force to bring its full weight down on the great airdrome of Clark Field outside Manila. Reminiscent of the devastating raids at Wewak, Hollandia and the Marianas, Halsey's carrier aircrews caught the bulk of the remaining Imperial Army and Navy planes in the Philippines on the ground. An estimated five-hundred planes were destroyed at Clark Field in two maximum efforts flown on November 5th and 6th.

The weather front lifted on the 7th and LtC. Walker's 49ers were back to their full mission schedule. The effect of Halsey's carrier raids were readily apparent for the Japanese only sent raiding flights of two or three planes at a time against MacArthur's headquarters. The Flying Knights first morning patrol scored the only kills of the day just west of Dulag where Lt. Ed Cooper shot down an OSCAR and damaged another, and wingman 2Lt. Jim Hovik downed a second.

The morning strike flown by the Screamin' Demons to Ormoc did suffer a setback on the part of rookie 2Lt. Hubert Manes. After a late takeoff due to snarled runway traffic, Manes decided to venture off in search of his flight which had continued on to Ormoc. Enroute to the west coast, Manes was bounced by an OSCAR which shot out his right engine. The lieutenant was able to elude the Ki-43 and nearly reached home before the damaged Allison burst into flame. He bailed out west of Tacloban and was immediately found

9 FS cohorts Cooper, Moore and Howes. Cooper scored a probable plus his last career victory on November 11th in defense of Tacloban..

by the guerrillas. Hubert Manes was back in the 7 FS camp that night.

Trading base patrols with the other Lightning units, plus flying dive-bombing sorties to Ormoc drained the 49ers of both their spiritual and material reserves. Crews and pilots were exhausted with the constant cleaning of debris from the airdrome and the ongoing repair of combat damage to the surviving Lockheeds. The Operations people rarely had a reliable count of P-38s available and missions were often formulated in the dispersal area of the airfield. Despite all three squadrons having there serviceable aircraft drastically reduced in number, the 49ers were put back on the tactical offensive once again with the word of another enemy convoy approaching Ormoc on the 8th.

## WURTSMITH JOINS THE 49ERS FOR THE LAST TIME

To help bolster the spirit of Walker's weary men, Gen. Paul Wurtsmith informed the 49ers CO that he would like to join in the flight operations at Tacloban. In the second week of November, Squeeze Wurtsmith "unofficially" placed his personal P-38 mount in the 7 FS flight line, and after a very informal ceremony to mark his reunion with his old group, Wurtsmith brought up the subject of his century-mark campaign. Walker checked the score sheets and was genuinely surprised to find the 49ers had already passed the 500 mark. The general and colonel gladly agreed to wait for number 600.

Gen. Wurtsmith's P-38 at Tacloban for his last sorties with the 49ers in the second week of November.

The Screamin' Demons were also pleased to see their popular commander back in camp. Capt. Ed Peck had fully recovered from his malaria and was cleared for flight duty by Flt Surgeon Webster. The captain skeptically accepted the responsibility of Wurtsmith's temporary assignment and placed the general's name on the Demons pilot roster. When the 5 FC CO or any other staff officer came up in rotation, the resultant flight team would be code-named the "Pinky Special." Peck selected 2Lt. Hal Harris, considered by Ops Exec DeHaven as their best all-around wingman, to be Wurtsmith's permanent shadow in the air. The captain warned young Harris, "If the general doesn't come back, you don't either."

Shortly after Wurtsmith and Peck had rejoined the men at Tacloban, the line crews were uplifted by the arrival of fifteen replacement Lightnings. Although some of them were rebuilt J models, they were a welcome sight, particularly for the Blacksheep who were down to only eight serviceable planes. The replacements ships were equally divided among the three battered squadrons.

5 FC Gunnery Instructor Major Dick Bong.

## 2LT. KANOFF DOWN AT SEA; NOVEMBER 9, 1944

George Walker's fighter group was also running short of pilots and the fact was painfully underscored that same day. The Flying Knights put eight fighter-bombers over Ormoc to strike the convoy which had just arrived in the morning twilight, only to have newcomer 2Lt. Don Kanoff be fatally hit by the shipboard AA batteries. His flaming P-38 fell in pieces into the sea among the enemy ships.

Only a few new men and planes continued to trickle in to the Tacloban complex as the mission count wore on. Other units were likewise slaying the Japanese in staggering numbers, yet the 5 AF had also lost many of its own young airmen. The infantry in the highlands just west of Barauen were still fighting for every inch of territory against a vicious resistance reinforced by the garrison at Ormoc. MacArthur was looking for a bright spot on his stormy battle ground and in the two days that followed, LtC. Walker's 49ers gave him the very spark he was looking for.

## BONG'S LAST SORTIE WITH THE 9 FS; NOVEMBER 10, 1944

On November 10th, acting Flying Knights CO Maj. Jordan was again approached by his old friend, Dick Bong, who asked to fly freelance on the morning mission. Jordan agreed and bumped the scheduled flight leader to head up the sortie himself. At 0730 hours, Jordan led wingman 2Lts. Ismael Corley, element leader Tom Hamilton and wingman Jim Hovik off to escort a flight of 110 TRS P-40s on an armed reconnaissance of the enemy harbor. Dick Bong joined up as the trailing fifth man.

Capt. Ed Peck's Demons were also tagged for escort duty on the same mission and the CO likewise took lead of his own flight. Col. Morrissey soon arrived at the flight line and asked to fly attached, so Ops Exec DeHaven gave the colonel the element lead position. Second Lt. George Rogers would be the captain's wingman and 2Lt. Al Mechino would shadow Morrissey.

The 110 TRS reached Ormoc with their ominous escort of nine 49ers cruising above the cloud tops at 15,000 feet. As the P-40s descended on their objective and disappeared from view, five

Bong's aircraft #42 updated as of November 11th with 36 aerial victories which resulted in Kenney's recommendation for the Congressional Medal of Honor.

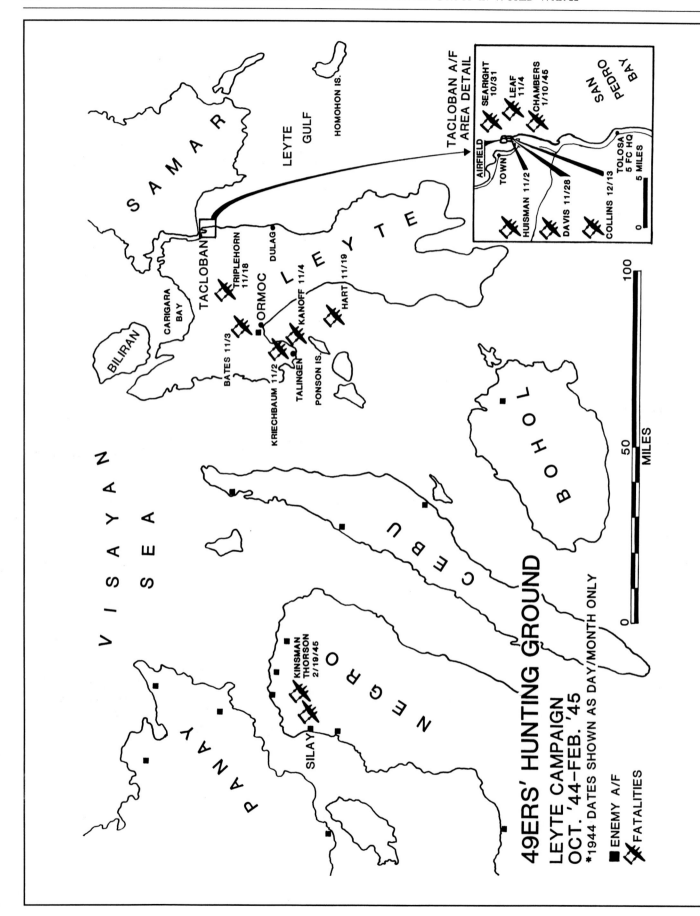

OSCARs ventured into the airspace between the Lightnings and Warhawks.

Bong signalled his intent to hit the trailing Ki-43. All five 9 FS elements dropped their tanks and dove down in mutual support, and in spite of Bong's first target getting away, the ace maneuvered back up through the clouds and quickly sighted another. That second OSCAR burst into flames from Bong's short deadly burst and rookie Corley latched on to another fleeing OSCAR which also fell in flames. Both Ki-43s fell into the clearing north of the village. Seven-thousand feet over the enemy garrison town, Bong made a full circle above the scene of his thirty-fourth victory and counted the enemy vessels anchored below, then peeled off for home with his successful 9 FS flight.

The Demons had also joined in the descent for the OSCARs over the bay, but none of them could reach a firing position. After the foursome regrouped south of the harbor, Col. Morrissey assumed the lead in pursuit of the OSCARs seen escaping west. The Demon team reached the northern cape of Cebu Island and after an orbit over the coastal point, Morrissey spotted one of the escapee Nakajimas.

All four Lightning pilots flew head-on passes against the lone Ki-43 pilot who courageously fought it out for ten arduous minutes. Finally, 2Lt. Rogers hit the fellow with a rear-quarter deflection which slowed the Ki-43 down long enough for Capt. Peck to deliver a coup de grace. The sentai driver took to his chute and Peck tried to snag the billowing white canopy as he overran his sole victim of his combat career. Morrissey fired a wild burst as the enemy pilot swung downward, but he missed. The parachute eventually melted into the mist over Cebu and Peck called for the Demons to withdraw.

The day ended on a high note for LtC. Walker. All of the 49ers were accounted for after their missions.

## BONG'S FINAL 49ERS SORTIE WITH THE SCREAMIN' DEMONS; NOVEMBER 11, 1944

The following day went equally as well. Walker had Bong and Morrissey back in his camp and the Group leader joined them for the next 7 FS mission being led by Capt. John Haher. The captain soon found his leadership preempted when Group Ops Exec Maj. Gerry Johnson assumed command of the sortie. Demon Lt. Bill Minto was tagged as the fifth man and the quintet was airborne at noon to escort a C-47 eastward for an airdrop at Homonhon Island.

The 100-mile round trip over the C-47 took a mere thirty-minutes and once the Lightnings were back over Tacloban, Maj. Johnson led his luminary "Pinky Special" off for a sweep of Ormoc Bay. At 1230 hours, the quintet cruised over the smoldering hulks of the latest enemy convoy which had been hammered by Kinkaid's aircraft carriers. A short distance ahead was a flight of Navy TBF bombers and just behind them was a trailing flight of ZEROs. Johnson instantly peeled away to the attack.

The ZEKEs saw the approaching P-38s and turned into them to initiate an aggressive counter-attack, but the hapless kokutai pilots were up against the two deadliest marksmen in the 5th Air Force. When the fight was over, Johnson had chalked up his eighteenth and nineteenth victories, still two more than the official record, but no one would ever question the major's skill. Dick Bong matched the feat with his thirty-fifth and thirty-sixth victories.

## DEMONS FINALE

Capt. Peck's pilots were far from finished after Haher's team landed at one o'clock. Thirty minutes later, Lt. Fred Dick took off with wingman 2Lt. Hal Harris, element leader Lt. Fernley Damstrom and number-four man 2Lt. Ken Markham for the next Demons patrol and were immediately vectored back toward Ormoc, they arrived over the target at 10,500 feet, where Flt Ldr Dick saw two TOJOs above his elements. He rose to the attack, but the speedy stub-winged fighters escaped to the west. Dick chose to regain altitude and sweep even further west to cut off the escape route to Cebu. Out over Ponson Island, his hunch paid off. Three more TOJOs were seen cruising over the island shoreline at 7000 feet. The sentai leader never saw what hit him.

Fred Dick dropped on the foremost Ki-44 and killed the enemy pilot with the first burst of .50 caliber tracers. The TOJO exploded as the Demon flight leader broke off in a zoom-climb to reposition for another pass, only to look down on the second enemy wingman who had just been killed by Damstrom. Wingman Harris had knocked down yet a third Nakajima and the last sentai Ki-44 was seen diving away to the west.

All four Demons dropped down after the escaping Nakajima and Harris executed the swerving target for his second confirmed victory of the mission. The portly dark brown fighter dipped its wing in the sea and cartwheeled into a shattering explosion. Harris then declared his ammo was nearly expended and Flt Ldr Dick signalled to regroup. They all landed safely back home at half past four.

Hence, the great November 11th battle came to a close. Only one single loss occurred for the group when Demon 2Lt. Huie Manes, returning from a late day patrol, reached Tacloban with a shot up Lightning and had to bail out west of the air field. Manes was quickly recovered and the Screamin' Demons soldiered on.

# 20

# THE LEYTE LEGEND

LtC. George Walkers' 49ers Fighter Group made the headlines around the world. Gen. MacArthur's headquarters staff released the bulletin to the press.

November 12, 1944 - Supreme Command HQ, Tacloban, Leyte:

Today (November 3) the 49th Fighter Group of the Far East Air Force has shot down more than 500 enemy planes since the beginning of the march back to the Philippines. The 49th Fighter Group in the air battles of the Southwest Pacific has set a record for the destruction of enemy aircraft which I believe is unsurpassed by any group in the war. Before coming to the Philippines as our first land based unit, they were crowding the 500 mark and are now shooting for 600. They are unsurpassed in the air.

Gen. Douglas MacArthur

On November 12, 1944, Gen. George Kenney recommended 5 AF Gunnery Instructor Maj. Richard Ira Bong for the Congressional Medal of Honor in attaining his thirty-sixth aerial victory over Leyte.

*Screamin' Demons NCO-club at Tacloban which ran out of beer twice in November as the pilots paid their dues to the crewchiefs for their Leyte killing spree.*

The pilot's aircraft #42, formerly of the 8 FS, had the last two Japanese victory flags painted on the sprawling fuselage scoreboard and Bong was again photographed ad nauseam as the toast of the Philippines campaign. After the publicity affair, Bong quietly asked to be allowed to the return to the mission schedule, but Kenney and 5 FC CO Wurtsmith first required that the ace stand down for at least two weeks of rest. After the break, they agreed to let Bong try for victory number forty, and then retire from combat for good. In the meantime, Dick Bong returned in his trusted #42 to the 49ers aircraft pool and never flew it in combat again. The ship was sorely needed by the war-weary 49ers who were consuming the Lightnings at an alarming rate.

Indeed, the very day after Bong's celebrity party, the Blacksheep wrote off another fighter. Second Lt. Nial Castle's ship blew a main gear tire on takeoff and stalled out as it passed out over the bay. The aircrews watching from the runway held their breath as the big silver plane pancaked on the water and quickly began to sink. Just as the twin tails slipped beneath the waves, Castle popped to the surface and waved to the approaching rescue motor launch that he was all right. Another lost Blacksheep had beaten the odds again.

## SHOOT-OUT OVER TACLOBAN; NOVEMBER 14, 1944

The Blacksheep were tested again the very next morning as two more of their pilots narrowly escaped their demise while on base patrol. Three 8 FS men patrolling between Tacloban and Dulag were jumped by two aggressive ZERO aviators who dropped down from the north. After 2Lt. Irwin Dames' left engine was shot out in the first firing pass, he immediately feathered the burning engine and withdrew the short distance to the safety of the base anti-aircraft batteries. Flight Ldr Lt. George Smerchek and wingman 2Lt. Wally Hickok remained aloft to engaged the intruders, but one of the skilled ZERO drivers next outmaneuvered Hickok and shot out his hydraulics. Smerchek and Hickok withdrew to Tacloban's flak corridor, too. All three Blacksheep landed safely, but the two damaged planes would inevitably be turned over to the salvage crews.

Minutes later, another Blacksheep flight was challenged by one of the same marauders, but Flt Ldr 2Lt. George Reed and wingman 2Lt. Bob Goodwin ended the escapade. Reed fired and hit the ZERO which slipped aside to avoid the second volley, only to pass directly in front of Goodwin's guns. The Blacksheep wingman's barrage torched the Mitsubishi directly over the west perimeter of Tacloban field and the aircrews cheered as it slammed down in the jungle five miles away.

Rainy weather and routine sorties wore on until the 14th when the Flying Knights had a another tense moment in the Tacloban dispersal area. Squadron Ldr Jordan and Capt. Ray Swift were walking out to the aircraft when three unannounced OSCARs swept over the flight line and sent both officers sprawling in the dirt. A bomb exploded nearby and Swift was nearly written off the flight roster by a large piece of shrapnel that imbedded in his chute pack.

The 15th fared no better for the ill-fated Knights. Within the heavy stormfront, the Japanese brought another reinforcement convoy into Ormoc Bay. The early afternoon 9 FS mission to the enemy port ran afoul of a strong storm cell which made the return crossing to Tacloban impossible. Flt Ldr Lt. McElroy first tried to lead his four-ship flight around the towering thunderhead to the south for Bayug Airfield, but he circled back to the north. In the turn the Knights separated and McElroy pressed northward only to run out of gas over the north coast. The flight leader safely bellied in on the beach near Barugo and was quickly rescued by the Filipinos. He return to Tacloban the next day.

Meanwhile, Datzenko, Hanisch and Hovik continued south sixty miles to the southern most point beyond Cabalian Bay, then turned about with empty tanks and looked for a likely spot to crash land. Survival-veteran Hanisch went in first and safely slid to a halt in a rice paddy at Hinunangan village. Greeted by friendly Filipinos, Hanisch signalled for Datzenko and Hovik to follow. The other two also safely bellied in and all three men spent the night at the crash site. The next day, they were escorted by a Filipino infantry platoon a short distance to the north where the Knights boarded a LCM landing craft for the return voyage, only to be picked up after twenty minutes at sea by a PBY flying boat. They flew straight back to Tacloban.

## KNIGHTS BREAK THE WEEK-LONG DRY SPELL; NOVEMBER 16, 1944

On the 16th, the Flying Knights broke the spell of bad luck. The last four-ship sortie of the day led by Lt. Warren Curton was just about to set down after an hour and half of patrolling the east coast when the air controller warned them of contacts approaching Dulag from the west. From his altitude of 9000 feet, Flt Ldr Curton looked directly into the sun and saw ten silhouettes headed his way. He turned into them, but held his fire until he was sure they were the enemy. Out of the sun's glare, five OSCARs sped close by the flight leader and Curton tightened his turn down against the trailing element as the Nakajimas nosed downward to strike Bayug Airfield. Flight Ldr Curton's chosen victim had obviously seen the Lightnings from the onset for the sentai pilot broke away in a frantic split-S maneuver, but the P-38 soon ran down the Nakajima after a brief chase through the broken overcast. At point-blank range, Curton fired and the Ki-43 disintegration in a ball of fire.

Wingman 2Lt. Jack Lewis flew in perfect position and skillfully cut in behind an OSCAR wingman who tried to target Curton. Lewis set the Ki-43 on fire and its smoking wake trailed straight down into the overcast. The lieutenant then used his great speed to follow the other sentai raiders dropping down toward Bayug Airfield and it was there that he overtook another sentai man who had just turned west. Closing to dead-astern, Lewis sent his second Ki-43 kill down to a fiery crash just west of the airdrome.

The second flight of five remaining OSCARs attempted to follow their sentai mates and cut off the lead P-38s, but element leader Lt. Cheatum Gupton and wingman 2Lt. Warren Fowler rudely foiled their scheme. Both of the trailing Knights caught the OSCARs as they bottomed out of their pursuit dives well behind the lead Lightnings. Only a thousand feet above the jungle, Gupton shot down his first victim just west of the Bayug runway, and then Fowler followed suit. Gupton immediately scored again as his second victim fell five miles further west. Fowler latched on to his second target and after a long chase inland, he shot the Nakajima down just a few miles inland from Ormoc Bay.

Flight Ldr Curton had meanwhile been so caught up in the feeding frenzy, he pressed on after the OSCARs even though his guns had jammed. The Knight boldly closed to within fifty feet on the tail of an OSCAR and harassed the poor sentai man all the way to Ormoc before the threat of anti-aircraft fire diverted the meaningless pursuit. Curton rose up to join his three wingmen over the interior highlands and they all returned safely to Tacloban to confirm their seven victories. Not a single enemy round had marked a 9 FS machine in the fight.

Enemy air activity markedly increased even more as the weather broke on the 17th. Even though a VAL fell on the peninsula to the anti-aircraft guns, the other dive-bombers avoided the airborne 49ers patrols and hit the strip again. Early the next morning, another airstrike set fire to the supply dump on the Cataisan beach. Fires were fought throughout the day, and fortunately, no 49ers were injured. Operations temporarily moved their flights to Bayug.

## TRIPLEHORN KILLED DEFENDING THE AIRFIELD; NOVEMBER 18, 1944

Capt. Willie Drier's depleted flights continued to meet the desperate patrol schedule despite the losses. On the 0700 morning patrol of the 18th, senior Lt. Ed Glascock ventured off on a two-ship patrol with rookie 2Lt. Gerald Triplehorn who had only been in camp

*Victorious Blacksheep Ed Glascock who lost a wingman on November 18th, seen later as a captain at Linguyan.*

three days. The Blacksheep pair were immediately vectored south toward Dulag and after a fifteen minute search above the heavy overcast, Glascock caught sight of a lone ZERO just west of Bayug Airfield. In a single pass, the veteran flight leader accounted for the first Blacksheep kill in more than two weeks. Glascock and Triplehorn resumed their patrol.

Thirty minutes later, they were vectored north of Tacloban to contact an enemy flight reported south bound. Glascock led the rookie up to 15,000 feet and wheeled north where they soon crossed the path of four brand-new Nakajima type IV JAAF fighters designated as the Ki-84 and code-named FRANK. A heavily armed, higher powered version of the Ki-44, the FRANK would eventually become the most respected fighter in the enemy inventory. The fight over Leyte that morning would painfully prove the point.

Glascock immediately engaged the Ki-84s and quickly realized he would have to use every one of his veteran skills to survive. He eventually prevailed over one of the speeding adversaries, but young Triplehorn was completely outclassed. Ripped by the 20mm cannon fire of the sentai marksman, the lieutenant tried to turn back for Tacloban, but his ship soon plunged into the mountains. Glascock broke off the engagement and returned alone.

George Walker's group had precious little time to mourn for the fallen Blacksheep pilot. Despite intermittent rain showers, the cursed Japanese pressed down against Tacloban time after time to keep the fires raging on Cataisan Peninsula.

That night when movement over the water was safer, T/Sgt. Orval Wallace, S/Sgt. Reb Colborn and PFC Bernie Peterson of the 9 FS were evacuated to the Navy hospital ship in the harbor due to serious wounds received in the day's raids. Far in the distance, a burning Liberty ship glowed on the horizon. The Cataisan camp watched until the fires blinked out as the hulk silently sank in the dark sea.

## LT. HART LOST IN THE STORM - NOVEMBER 19, 1944

Fighter pilot lore declared, "We live in fame and go down in flames", and nothing was more appalling to the men at Tacloban than to loose a good man to circumstances other than a good fight. Sadly, no one could answer for the missing Demon pilot Lt. Doug Hart. The proven 7 FS wingman failed to return on the 19th after a routine patrol in the damned weather. No trace of Hart was ever found and it was presumed he crashed at sea.

Later in the day, Flying Knight Lt. Leslie Nelson barely missed the opportunity to officially join the rank of aces. The able 9 FS marksman of four confirmed kills had led his foursome to Ormoc at 1400 hours where a single ZERO was seen passing overhead. Nelson rose up and was about to punch the gun button when the kokutai man nosed his Mitsubishi over into an escape dive. For twenty minutes, Nelson pursued the swerving ZEKE at a speed well over 400 Mph across Ormoc Bay all the way to the eastern shore of Cebu Island. Although the ZERO had been hit several times, the enemy pilot finally shook free from Nelson just above the waves and broke across element leader Lt. Tom Hamilton's flight path. Not willing to pass up the shot, Hamilton sent the fellow down with a single burst.

Just a few miles to the north, the other 9 FS elements spotted a second ZERO, and Nelson immediately joined the chase. He took

over the lead and flew down through a lethal point-blank firing pass which blew away the Mitsubishi's canopy and ignited the left wingroot. But Nelson had expended all of his ammo. The flight leader pulled along side the slumped kokutai pilot who somehow managed to keep his riddled plane in the air. With their fuel likewise depleted, the Lightnings pulled off and Nelson looked back at the smoking ZEKE which drifted slowing out of sight to the west just a few feet above the hazy sea. Leslie Nelson would never have the chance to score again during the remainder of his tour, and he would always remember that last ZERO that probably never made it home.

## NO END IN SIGHT IN THE ORMOC STRUGGLE

The Japanese stubbornly refused to abandon their Leyte garrison and on the 21st, yet another convoy was reported entering the area. Another was also expected to arrive on the 24th. MacArthur once more asked Kinkaid and Kenney to again send forth another maximum airborne assault to stop the enemy troops before they reached shore.

## BLACKSHEEP VETERANS REJOIN AT TACLOBAN; MID-NOVEMBER 1944

Luckily for besieged Capt. Drier, his understaffed squadron was reinforced in the second week of the month with two old New Guinea veterans to bolster up the younger men. Capt. Bob Aschenbrener and Lt. Sammie Pierce arrived from their tour of Stateside command school at war-torn Tacloban and quickly proved to be invaluable assistants in Drier's command. Aschenbrener was installed as the new Ops Exec and Pierce as the Ops deputy. Flack became the new deputy CO as replacement to lost Kriechbaum.

It seemed the veterans effected an instantaneous improvement in the Blacksheep morale. Bob Aschenbrener "was one of the most talented boys to strap a fighter on his butt" according to flamboyant Pierce, and the captain proved as much by qualifying for combat

*Blacksheep ace Ops Exec Bob Aschenbrener at Tacloban. The 8 FS personnel boasted that their squadron logo designed by a Walt Disney Studios artist was the only USAAF insignia to display a unit designator. The pilot goggles on their winking Blacksheep is a figure "8."*

*C.C. Seymore "Goldie" Goldberg and his aircraft #60 that garnered 8 FS CO Drier his six Leyte campaign scores.*

*8 FS Co Drier and #60 "LITTLE MAGGIE" shortly after his triple-victory ace-maker sortie of November 24th with Ops Exec Aschenbrener.*

after a mere twelve hours of Lightning transition flights. He joined the Sheep for their major effort sent against the enemy stronghold on the 24th.

## WILLIE AND ASCH - TWO NEW BLACKSHEEP ACES; NOVEMBER 24, 1944

Willie Drier and "Asch" Aschenbrener teamed up as wingmen, and with two other Blacksheep, ventured off on the first morning patrol north of Ormoc. Only having been aloft for half an hour, the controllers vectored Drier's flight at 20,000 feet on a hunt forty miles west of Tacloban. Passing over the Carigara shoreline, Asch called in the first sighting. Leaving the two trailing elements in top cover position, the two veterans plunged on the TONY formation below and treated everyone in the area to a stunning gunnery demonstration.

The newcomer Ops Exec swept in behind a separated TONY cruising at 8000 feet and his first volley tore away the Kawasaki's tail structure and right wing. The Blacksheep pair zoom-climbed to regroup, but on the way up, Drier called out five LILY bombers escorted by an estimated dozen radial-engine types overhead at 18,000. Drier and Asch immediately wheeled about and overtook four ZEROs in formation coursing parallel to the bay shoreline. Drier's gunfire hit one Zero which arched over in flames and crashed ten miles inland. Aschenbrener's second victim dropped straight down into the surf.

The Blacksheep gunmen then turned their murderous intentions back on another four-ship TONY flight and Drier flamed one for his second victim of the day. Asch made his next sentai victim take to his chute after setting the Ki-61 on fire, then astounded his CO by picking off his fourth and final kill with only one working .50 caliber weapon. Drier then closed in and finished off the last Kawasaki for his sixth and final career kill. It was a clean sweep of the entire enemy flight.

## DEMONS SEE ALL

The event over the Carigara coastline had actually begun a few minutes prior to the Blacksheep interception. Demon Flt Ldr Lt. Jim O'Neil had been on patrol with wingmen 2Lts. Hubert "Huie" Manes, Jim Franks and Oliver "Ollie" Atchison just west of Tacloban when they were alerted. O'Neil immediately found a lone ZERO in the area and dove down from 10,000 feet to kill its pilot in a single pass.

The Demon flight only partially regrouped as rookie Atchison separated while climbing back up through the overcast. Still in radio contact, the rookie continued on alone and all four of the team members took the next heading due west to the scene of the greater fight. O'Neil's Demon foursome slammed headlong into the dogfight and effectively kept the Japanese off balance which provided the two Blacksheep captains with superior support.

In the battle over the north coast, O'Neil overtook one of the turning Ki-61s for his second victory of the mission while element leader Franks knocked down one of the ZEROS. Even novice Ollie Atchison damaged a ZEKE when he expended his entire load of ammo in the fracas. As O'Neil fired on another TONY which escaped in the clouds, he passed over the phenomenal gunnery display put on by the Blacksheep pilots and readily confirmed the entire event. In a mere ten minutes, the 7 FS and 8 FS combined for ten enemy fighters destroyed and not a single enemy bullet was taken in return.

## A BRIEF DIVERSION FOR A NEWCOMER FLYING KNIGHT

At the same time returnee Aschenbrener was beating up the enemy over Carigara, newcomer Capt. John Petrovic of the Flying Knights likewise decided to join in his first scramble from Tacloban. Taking up the number four slot to element leader F.O. Hank Hammett, the two found themselves alone after breaking out above the overcast. The Flight Officer and his novice captain wingman continued on their way and eventually were vectored to a DINAH heading southwest away from Tacloban. The Knights dropped their tanks and entered into a thirty minute climbing pursuit of the twin-engine speedster, finally catching the recce 25,000 feet over the north cape of Cebu Island. The captain was readily impressed as Hammett expertly shot out the DINAH's left engine and then drifted to the right and shot out the other motor. The JNAF spy plane dropped away in a flat spin strewing debris in every direction until the burning right wing eventually broke away. The hulk then tumbled wildly down into the clouds.

## O'NEIL'S BUNCH COMES BACK

The only Demon member to miss out on the scoring that morning was element leader 2Lt. Huie Manes. Later that afternoon, Lt. Jim O'Neil's very same flight team was back in the air for their second patrol and the Japanese seemingly obliged Manes with a second chance. As O'Neil's flight passed directly over their home field, the air controller called in a single contact approaching from the northeast. The four Demons rose up to 13,000 feet and were in perfect position for a firing pass when the lone intruder drew within range. In the turning descent on the target, tail-end Atchison fired first with a poorly aimed deflection burst and then the two speeding lead elements overshot the mark. After a full turn, Manes fell directly behind the ZERO and blew the rascal out of the air with a short volley. The Mitsubishi plunged straight down into San Pedro Bay in full view of the airdrome. The foursome regrouped and finished their patrol without further incident, then landed to the cheers from the Tacloban flight line.

## DECKER MEETS GLEN

Improved weather held into the evening of the 24th which would yield another spectacular tropical sunset. The command at Tacloban took no chances and kept a standing patrol of P-38s up as long as the overcast remained broken. By 1820 hours, the jungle shadows deepened in the amber twilight and 9000 feet overhead, Flt Ldr Lt. Bob Decker with wingmen 2Lts. Hal Harris and Nic Zuniga headed home from the last Screamin' Demons patrol. As the trio approached the landing pattern, the air controller signaled a pair of intruders two-thousand feet lower than Decker's flight and coming in from the north. The Demons could not find the enemy at first in the poor light, and after a turn to the right, the flight leader finally caught a glimpse of two planes down through in the billowing mist.

In his descent to firing range, one of the intruders dropped out of sight, but Decker drew near enough to identify the trailing wingman as the small two-man Kugisho E14Y1 floatplane codenamed GLEN. Decker's first burst at 200 yards struck the amphibian's engine and his second burst from closer in set the right side of the fuselage ablaze. The flames quickly spread to the right wing and the GLEN began to slowly spin down into the clouds. Bob Decker's second career victory over the odd little recon plane would be the only sighting of the type by the 49ers.

## GREAT OMENS AND DESPERATE MEASURES; NOVEMBER 24 - DECEMBER 7, 1944

The latest air assault against Ormoc was an omen of the end drawing near in the Leyte campaign. With the fairer weather, the Imperial command accurately surmised another amphibious landing was immanent at Ormoc within a week's time. They desperately tried to reinforce their battered Leyte garrison again on the 23rd.

Gen. Kenney again was appraised of the renewed threat and another air strike was immediately sent against Ormoc. In the great air battle of 24th, the majority of the Imperial reinforcements were caught on the open seas beneath the broken weather front. For three days running, Kinkaid's carrier airwing and Kenney's tactical air groups slaughtered thousands of enemy infantry trapped aboard the transports. Burning merchant ships and war vessels littered the harbor shoreline underscoring the garrison's impending fall.

The 49ers flew continuously throughout the remainder of the Leyte campaign and would not loose a man at Tacloban to enemy raiders, nor to the flak guns of the enemy garrison. LtC. Walker's pilots were able to maintain their scoring pace while the Japanese air units suffered an irreplaceable losses of planes and crews. On the 26th, two different sorties would yield victories again for the Screamin' Demons and Flying Knights.

## 49ERS STILL RULE TACLOBAN

The 7 FS scored first at mid day. Newly promoted Lt. Cecil Archer's Red Flight caught a pair of ZEROs trying to sneak in beneath the overcast and strike Tacloban. Flight Ldr Archer and wingman 2Lt. Olie Atchison swept down into a picture perfect dead-astern attack and both of the Demons dispatched their respective targets in a single firing pass.

Precisely one hour later, Lt. Cheatum Gupton's Flying Knights patrol was vectored ten miles northwest of the base where they found three OSCARs heading east. One of them foolishly tried to outrun Gupton and the Flight Leader caught the Ki-43 with a fine deflection shot at one-hundred and fifty yards. As the target exploded, the two wiser sentai wingmen turned away and disappeared in the clouds.

## POOR HUNTING OVER ORMOC - NOVEMBER 28th and 29th

The enemy was pointedly absent over Tacloban for the next several days. The 49ers had to return to Ormoc to find more targets, but only one was caught by Blacksheep Ops Exec Aschenbrener on the 28th. While on a mid afternoon weather reconnaissance to the north coast and subsequent search for the next expected convoy, Asch chanced upon three in-line types cruising through the mist of the cloud deck at 5000 feet. They quickly dropped into the safety of the clouds and Asch hunted another ten minutes over the area until one of the TONYs reappeared. Before the Kawasaki could disappear again, the Blacksheep ace rushed down behind the target and hit it from dead astern at 300 yards. The TONY burst into flames, rolled over and dropped inverted into the clouds. Although there would be other sightings, Aschenbrener's eighth career kill was the only 49ers contact made that day.

## DAVIS DIES IN BONG'S OLD PLANE; NOVEMBER 28, 1944

While Aschenbrener was scoring that day's only Blacksheep victory over Ormoc, the 8 FS line crews witnessed a fiery crash back at Tacloban which sent a momentary shock through the entire 5 AF community. Aircraft #42, formerly flown by Dick Bong, had stalled out on takeoff and was totally destroyed in the resulting inferno. Witnesses immediately assumed the crash victim was Bong and Gen. Kenney's staff even called to confirm the rumor. Somewhat to everyone's embarrassment, Group Ops Exec Gerry Johnson angrily declared the dead man was his good friend, Ops Deputy Maj. John Davis. The major had signed on to the mission roster just minutes before the crash and he had routinely taken the first available ship on the line which happened to be the top ace's old stager. Bong was stunned when word of his friend's death reached him at 5 FC HQ down in Tolosa village.

The next day, the Flying Knights had to settle for only two confirmed kills. Vectored to Ormoc at day break, Flt Ldr Lt. Wade Lewis of White Flight was the first of the eight airborne Flying Knights to reach the target area. From his lead position at 15,000 feet, Lewis scanned the air over the enemy garrison, but found nothing, so he took his flight in the search further north. As they wheeled away from Ormoc, two ZEROs attempted a half-hearted rear quarter assault from out of the hazy overcast. Lewis' team aggressively turned into the attack which totally foiled the Mitsubishis interception. Lewis ran down one of them, closed to within 100 yards and blew it out of the air. Element leader Lt. Warren Gupton then cut off the enemy wingman who tried to out turn Lewis and hit the ZEKE's black cowling with a devastating head-on volley. The kokutai pilot departed his smoking ship as it rolled over and plunged straight into the ocean.

As Lewis and Curton climbed back up to clearer air, they were ambushed by a flight of nine TONYs. With their throttles shoved to the stops, the victorious Knights turned into the diving Ki-61s and again foiled their scheme. After several high speed passes from head-on, Lewis and Curton each hit a target with deflection volleys which inflicted heavy damage to both Kawasakis. The Knight then safely withdrew.

The Japanese air groups momentarily stood down to refit for the last major effort to Ormoc, only to loose another spy plane on the last day of the month. Blacksheep Flt Ldr Tom Holstein caught the DINAH east of Ormoc village and dispatched it in a single pass. No other contacts appeared until five days later when the Japanese launched the final rescue attempt for their trapped Leyte garrison.

## CROSSED PURPOSES AT ORMOC; DECEMBER 5-7, 1944

On the morning of December 5th, the 7th Fleet assault ships passed out of the great fog bank covering the Surigao Straits and turned north into the open sea for the assault on Ormoc Bay. Throughout the morning, the close aircover of USAAF and Navy aircraft cruised back and forth over the convoy as it spread out into the Camote Sea.

At 1100 hours, senior Flying Knights Lt. Charlie "Mac" McElroy with his Blue Flight wingmen FO Hank Hammett and 2Lt. Ernie Ambort arrived directly over the vanguard destroyers on the convoy's left flank in relief of Lt. Warren Curton's White Flight. Only minutes after White Flight withdrew, the three Blue Knights saw a bomb detonate just off the bow of one of the war ships, and seconds later, Mac saw the VAL attacker speeding off to the west just above the waves. Retreating White Flt Ldr Gupton heard Blue Flight's signal to engage. Disregarding his diminished fuel, Gupton ordered White Flight to turn about and join the interception back over the fleet, but they only arrived in time to confirm McElroy's aerial kill.

## BLUE FLIGHT OVER THE CONVOY - MID DAY - DECEMBER 5th

The three Blue wingmen peeled off after the lone escaping VAL and as they dropped their belly tanks in a curving pursuit dive to their left, Flt Ldr McElroy caught sight of a rambling formation of seven VALs coursing down out of the clouds over the Leyte shoreline. The P-38 drivers immediately turned into the path of the descending dive-bombers and opened fire.

With his guns ablaze, McElroy broke hard to his right and plowed head-on through the Aichi swarm. One of the two targets he hit began to glide downward trailing a thin dark-gray smoke trail and Mac followed the VAL until it crashed at sea some distance off to the south. As the flight leader rose back up to re-engage, he found he was all alone.

Wingmen F/O Hammett and 2Lt. Ambort, on the other hand, had held formation, but separated from their flight leader when they picked out their own targets. In seconds, both of the Blue elements accounted for victories. Ambort's target exploded and he wheeled over to rejoin Hammett who had just overtaken another VAL closing in on a destroyer in the convoy's left flank. After Hammett's volley torched the Aichi, there was a tense moment as its doomed aviator attempted to end his life in the glorious death plunge of a kamikaze. After a frantic chase of the suicidal attacker above the waves, the Knights broke away just as the flaming VAL fell into the wake of the turning destroyer's bow.

Hammett and Ambort rose back up to hunt southward for their separated flight leader, only to cross the flight path of two OSCARs west bound over the shore. The Blue pair wheeled about under the unsuspecting sentai pilots and pulled up behind them at point-blank range. Both of the sentai men were killed before either could jettison his underwing bomb. Ambort's victim arched over into the surf while Hammett's victim slammed down in a brilliant explosion in the forest just beyond the beach. Minutes later, the victorious wingmen found McElroy and the regrouped Blue Flight completed its mission without further incident.

## NEARER TO ORMOC BAY - LATE AFTERNOON - DECEMBER 5th

At 1600 hours, Lt. Warren Curton's White Flight was back over the convoy at 4000 feet for its second escort of the day. During their patrol on the north flank of the convoy, the fog over the coast had spread farther out over the ocean and visibility was quite restricted. When White Flight was alerted to approaching aircraft, Flt Ldr Curton could not see a thing. After a full orbit down to 1000 feet, the flight leader finally caught a glimpse of a squared-wingtip HAMP speeding westward directly over the warships which were sending up a heavy A/A baggage. Curton signaled for the attack and pitched his P-38 downward.

But the lone intruder escaped in the haze before the Knights and a lone Satan's Angel could draw within firing range. As Curton's White quartet momentarily strung out in their continued search, tail-end element 2Lt. Troy Smith was suddenly attacked from behind by another lone ZERO. The lieutenant broke away as the White flight leader turned back toward the Mitsubishi which likewise broke off. The kokutai pilot tried to beat Curton to the cloud bank over Duligan Point, but the Lightning pilot applied full throttle and easily caught up with the offender before he reached the shore. The ZERO desperately wheeled upward to the left into the sun, but Curton stared right into the glare and opened fire. The Lockheed's explosive rounds sparkled all over the fuselage and the stricken ZEKE dropped off in a wingover.

Like his kokutai comrade in the morning interception, Curton's victim assumed the kamikaze role. The doomed aviator targeted a pair of PT boats in the bay, and for a very anxious instant, the flight leader though his victim was going to hit one of the swerving Navy vessels. Curton fired a long volley into the dying ZERO in hopes that it would explode before it reached the boats, but in the end, the flaming Mitsubishi missed them by more than fifty yards. With a sigh of relief, Curton rose back up to finish his escort sortie. Although another enemy fighter would be chased by White Flight, Warren Curton's victory was the last 5 FC kill over the bay that day.

## ORMOC: D-DAY MINUS ONE; DECEMBER 6th

On the 6th, MacArthur's amphibious force held off fifty miles south of Ormoc Bay making its final preparations for the landing scheduled for the following morning. Kinkaid's destroyers paraded up and down the coast lobbing volleys all along the western shoreline to deny the Japanese any semblance of the actually beachhead while Kenney's tactical dive-bombers hammered shore installations at the enemy headquarters further north.

The 49ers were up on patrol again with the day's first light where the first Screamin' Demon sortie yielded the first kill of the day. The redoubtable Capt. John Haher with wingmen 2Lt. Bill Thompson, element leader Lt. Jim Jarrell and wingman 2Lt. Olie Atchison were at 6000 feet above a support convoy in the eastern waters of Surigao Strait off Dinagat Island. They received the radio message of a single plane approaching from the north and Haher could just make out a DINAH five miles away, estimated at 12,000 feet. All four Demons dropped their tanks and advanced their throttles up for the expected routine high altitude pursuit of the twin-engine speedster, but that morning, the JNAF crew intended to have a close look at the American vessels. As Haher's flight turned in behind the DINAH, it suddenly nosed down and headed straight for the convoy ships.

Haher pressed after the spy plane at 400 Mph and after a full minute of pursuit down to a thousand feet above the sea, he had

only closed to maximum firing range. He fired all the way down to point-blank, but despite numerous hits, the victim remained airborne. The captain fired off his last tracers at the sturdy Mitsubishi, then wheeled aside to let elements Jarrell and Atchison have their shots. After Atchison fired and overran the rugged target, Jarrell finally hit the left engine which began to emit smoke. Before Thompson could fire, the wounded DINAH slowly dropped off on its right wing until the wingtip snagged a wave and it tumbled into a spectacular explosion.

The kill off Dinagat would be the only 49ers victory of the day. Later that morning, the Satan's Angels from Dulag would have the greater success over the fleet at Ormoc. The 49ers next big interception would occur the day of the landings.

## D-DAY AT ORMOC; DECEMBER 7, 1944

On the third anniversary of the infamous raid on Pearl Harbor, Gen. Douglas MacArthur sent his troops ashore twenty miles south of the Ormoc garrison. The landing force quickly linked up with the infantry units pushing in from the east to effectively cut the enemy forces in two in the Leyte highlands. The depleted Imperial air force held in reserve to repel the landing was final committed to the battle in its greatest effort of the Leyte campaign, but the resultant blood bath over the beachhead was a total disaster for the JAAF and JNAF. The 49ers were in the thick of the blood-letting from sunrise to sunset.

## D-DAY INTERCEPT #1

At 0730 hours, Flt Ldr Lt. McElroy, wingman 2Lt. Hovik, element leader F/O Hank Hammett and wingman 2Lt. Rentchler were vectored to the first 49ers interception. In marginal weather, McElroy's team searched all the way to the northern tip of Leyte, but only confirmed the presence of the next Japanese reinforcement convoy of seven troop ships and four destroyer escorts. The airborne contacts were made by two other units.

The Flying Knights continued to shadow the enemy vessels for nearly an hour when McElroy signaled his wingmen that four OSCARs had arrived overhead. As the quartet rose up for the interception, Hovik lost power in one of his engines and dropped out of the flight for home. Flight Ldr Mac, Hammett and Rentchler pressed on and finally were closing in at 17,000 feet when the OSCARs counter-attacked. McElroy fired a head-on shot which sent his target falling into the overcast trailing heavy smoke, but the Knights totally separated in the maneuvers and no one confirmed the kill.

After that brief encounter, Rentchler failed to rejoin with McElroy and Hammett, but the flight leader still had plenty of fuel and ammo. The remnant pair hunted all the way across the sea to northern Cebu, but the OSCARs had vanished. McElroy would have to wait until his next sortie to score again.

## D-DAY INTERCEPT #2

Much like the Knights' first patrol, the first Screamin' Demons patrol met with similar frustration. Demon Flt Ldr Lt. Fernly

*A late model heavily armed Nakajima Ki-45 "NICK" like the type intercepted by Demon ace Damstrom on the morning of December 7th.*

*The Nakajima Ki-49 "HELEN" type in the formation butchered by Col. Bob Morrissey's Pinky Black Special Flight on December 7th.*

Damstrom with wingmen 2Lts. Ralph Watson and Bill Fernandez had answered the vector at 0830 and reached the west coast, but lost contact with the enemy in the haze, so they turned back toward Ormoc village. Approaching the besieged village at 11,000 feet, Damstrom saw flak bursts over the American ships which tracked a lone Ki-45 NICK five-thousand feet below and headed straight for his Blue flight. The Demon leader jettisoned his auxiliary tanks and nosed down through a turn into the Kawasaki's rear quarter where he opened fire. Although the target tried to escape in the clouds, the Lightning's explosive rounds set the Ki-45 on fire and it fell inverted into the overcast.

Damstrom called his Blue Flight to regroup, but Watson soon had to withdraw due to a painful eardrum which partially ruptured during his ascent back to altitude. Damstrom and Fernandez resumed their two-ship Blue patrol and eventually joined another four-ship flight of Demons which drifted into view overhead. With the new foursome in high cover, the two Blue Demons hunted just west of the big peninsula beyond the battle front. After an hour passed and their fuel was nearly gone, Damstrom and Fernandez received another vector.

The two Blue wingmen dropped down to hunt at 6000 feet and caught sight of two OSCARs falling in flames just off shore. They wheeled about to their left and immediately saw six NICKs headed east about two-thousand feet below. Confident in having so many other Lightnings in the vicinity, Damstrom decided to attack the twin-engine Kawasakis. The Blue pair dropped into dead astern of the Vee formation which scattered at their approach and Damstrom quickly settled in behind the fleeing left flank wingman. From the

right rear quarter, the Blue leader gutted the cockpit and shot out the right engine of the Ki-45 with two lethal burst. His second kill of the sortie fell just north of Poro Island.

## D-DAY INTERCEPT #3

The two falling OSCARs seen by the Demons in their engagement west of Duligan Point were the victims of another 7 FS flight, but ironically, only one Demon pilot was a member of that illustrious quartet known as the "Pinky Black Special."

*Above and below: Group aircraft #47 of CO Walker with tri-color spinner of red front, sky-blue center band and yellow to the rear. As with Bong's aircraft #42, the 49ers command aircraft were serviced by any available crew, despite the Lightnings have numbers in the 8 FS realm.*

*49ers CO George Walker knocked down one of four HELEN bombers west of Ormoc village on Dec. 7th.*

Knowing the Japanese would throw everything they had at the Ormoc landing that day, staff officer Col. Bob Morrissey had attached himself to the 7 FS as a flight leader in hopes of reaching ace status in the imminent air battle. Group Ops Exec Maj. Gerry Johnson liked the idea as well and joined his friend in the venture. Group CO LtC. George Walker, still not having scored an aerial kill, sensed that the arrival of the two staff executives might result in his own success. So it was that 2Lt. Hal Harris, the designated on-call "Pinky Special" wingman, would fly cover for the three highest ranking Tacloban pilots in the air that day.

The Pinky Black Special took off at 0830 hours with Morrissey in the lead and they reached the Duligan peninsula in good order at 12,000 feet. With some frustration, Morrissey hunted for an hour and half, until finally at ten o'clock, Black Flight was in the vicinity of a productive vector. Morrissey had just toggled off his tanks to join in the pursuit of the very flight of NICKs which would fall victim to Blue Flight. In their descent down through the clouds, the Pinky Black team stumbled upon an even closer flight of an three OSCAR in high escort to six HELEN bombers cruising down the coastline.

The colonel whipped his descending P-38 around against the three Nakajima fighters and fired off a poorly aimed burst which only sent the agile OSCARs into their routine evasive loops. As element leader Walker turned toward them, wingman Harris flew wide to cover him, but the CO overran the targets due to his excess speed.

Impatient tail-end Ops Exec Johnson had seen enough. With absolute finesse, the major swept in behind the OSCAR which slid out of the sentai formation and dispatched it with one deadly deflection burst. The ace pushed the throttle forward as the two remaining OSCARs rose up through another loop, and in view of the entire interceptor force converging over Duligan peninsula, he hit both of the ascending OSCARs in a spectacular climbing firing pass. All three victims fell within a few yards of one another upon the cerulean sea. "Count 'em. One, two, three", Johnson exclaimed over the radio. Several Lightning pilots would later confirmed the twentieth, twenty-first and twenty-second kills for the Ops Exec.

Morrissey called his Black Flight to rejoin and immediately set after the HELENs. The colonel finally reached the silver twin-engine raiders as they neared Duligan Point and he opened fire on the Ki-49 element flying furthest to the right. In seconds, the big Nakajima had both of its engines shot out and it dropped straight into the sea for Morrissey's third and last career victory. Seconds later, LtC. Walker dropped into firing position dead astern of the next element on the right of the sentai formation. The bomber crew gunners never fired a shot in defense as the Group Leader's volley gutted the rear fuselage and torched the right engine. George Walker finally had achieved an aerial kill. Trusted wingman Harris was next and the third HELEN soon fell away in flames. It ended when ace Johnson caught the straggler Ki-49 directly over Duligan Point for his fourth kill of the sortie. The enemy aircraft, victory number twenty-three, dropped into sea just offshore from Tilagen village. Johnson looked about for the other two bombers, but they had long since escaped into the clouds to the north.

## D-DAY INTERCEPT #4

There was virtually no letup as the air battle heated up again at half past eleven. The rambling fight was a combined effort between the two-ship Blacksheep flight of Lt. Bob Campbell and wingman 2Lt. Francis Hill, the Demon foursome led by Lt. Joel Paris and two Satan's Angels.

At the onset, the Blacksheep pair took on six OSCARs which they found cruising over Duligan Point at 12,000 feet. Flight Ldr Campbell rose up behind the sentai swarm and cut out a straggler which led him on a wild chase to its demise fifteen miles due west of the point. Meanwhile, wingman Hill chased another OSCAR which dropped down to sea level and passed in front of the guns of Paris' Demon bunch.

Indeed, the Demons readily took on the OSCARs in the furious dogfight which eventually descended to the deck. All four Demon elements fired several times without effect until element leader Lt. Milden Mathre spotted a lone Ki-43 turning below. Five other Lightning pilots with the same lethal intent descended in firing passes on the hapless Nakajima driver, but Mathre was credited as firing the fatal volley. The victorious Demon broke off to rejoin his flight as the OSCAR splashed down due south of Duligan Point.

About that time, Blacksheep Campbell returned to the scene as the last of the OSCARs vanished in the haze, but another target suddenly appeared. A lone Ki-21 SALLY bomber crossed Campbell's path at 10,000 feet and he quickly turned in behind the unaware intruder. After his first volley struck home, the SALLY pilot wheeled away and Campbell momentarily lost his victim in a hard right turn through the overcast. As he broke into the clear, he spotted the Ki-21 below, and with ten successive firing passes throughout the ensuing chase to distant Cebu Island, Campbell rendered the bomber into a piece of flying junk. It finally dropped into a flat spin from 8000 feet and plummeted down to a crash landing on the northeast coast of Cebu. With his ammo gone, the victorious Demon orbited once over the dusty wreck, and could not help but admire the capable opponent who had somehow kept his torn airplane airborne for so long.

Back over Ormoc, the fight ended with the final kill of the sortie scored by element leader Mathre. After the OSCARs had withdrawn, Flt Ldr Paris tried to overtake a lone NICK which appeared at the same as Campbell's SALLY. Unfortunately for Paris, the NICK's rear gunner hit his Lightning with three 7mm rounds which knocked out the right engine. Paris relinquished the task to able Mathre who was the last man in the immediate vicinity with .50 caliber ammo left over. After Mathre's one pass, the twin-engine Kawasaki splashed down in the misty sea and four minutes later, sank out of sight. The Demons then withdrew and escorted Paris back to a safe landing at Tacloban.

## D-DAY INTERCEPT #5

The frantic pace kept up throughout the afternoon. The deadly Flying Knights team of Lt. McElroy and 2Lt. Ambort went back over the bay at 1400 hours where they engaged in another horrendous dogfight. The contest finally produced an confirmed OSCAR kill for the flight leader and the confirmed fifth career kill of a ZERO for the newest 9 FS ace, Ernie Ambort.

Demon Flt Ldr Fernly Damstrom had also returned to Ormoc Bay and joined the same interception. Within the swirling mass of OSCARs, ZEROs and Lightnings, the boyish Demon marksman maintained his composure and clobbered a turning Mitsubishi in mid-fuselage. Damstrom's fifth career kill was seen by wingman Huie Manes to explode on impact on Ponson Island's east shore.

The fight over Ponson came to a close shortly before five P.M. with the lethal firing passes flown by the Satan's Angels. Their ace commander Col. Charlie MacDonald accounted for his twentieth career kill while freelancer Bong accounted for his thirty-seventh. In the interim, the 49ers withdrew to Tacloban to refuel and rearm.

## D-DAY INTERCEPT #6

Twenty minutes past five, 9 FS Thunderbolt veteran Capt. Willis Treadway, wingman Lt. Cheatham Gupton and 2Lt. Troy Smith were off on a dive bombing mission to Ormoc when the flight controller ordered the trio to salvo their ordinance and execute the next interception. As they passed directly over the embattled garrison, they dropped their five-hundred pounders from 9000 feet and quickly rose up to the vector at "12 Angels." As they passed directly over the landing fleet, Treadway spotted eight ZEROs three-thousand feet below in loose formation. He led his elements into the glare of the sun over the enemy's right flank and the quarry was apparently fixed on the ships in the bay, for the Knights drew into dead-astern without being seen. Treadway and Smith both fired on the two trailing kokutai wingmen. Both targets burst into flame in mid-fuselage and disintegrated in matching fireballs.

Gupton tried to overtake the ZEROs further up ahead, but the kokutai was on a divine mission for their emperor and they entered into near vertical kamikaze death plunges. The fleeting targets were quickly lost in the clouds below and Gupton watched in sickened frustration as another Allied ship exploded from the impact of one of the suicide planes.

*8 FS Walt Meyer on December 7th shot down a kamikaze only to see it reach its target.*

As the overcast became even more dense, the next Blacksheep patrol also struggled to maintain contact with the latest intruders in the dwindling sunlight. Ops Exec Nelson Flack had brought wingman Lt. Walter Meyer and 2Lt. Hal Strom into the area at 1430 hours, but they did not contact any of the targets for a full hour. The Blacksheep trio finally joined in the Knights interception of the kamikazes, and after Strom damaged a DINAH which escaped in the clouds, wingman Meyer was able to mortally hit a ZERO kamikaze for his second and last career kill. Sadly, the dedicated kokutai aviator still reached a small freighter and the huge explosion enveloped the vessel. Meyer orbited once above the stricken boat which stopped dead in the water, then burst into flames at the stern. The hulk soon became an inferno, but there was nothing more distraught Walt Meyer could do. He turned away for home.

## D-DAY INTERCEPT #7

Ten minutes after the Blacksheep set off for home, another wave of JNAF fighters swept over Ormoc. The Satan's Angels along with Maj. Bong were waiting and the ensuing air battle rolled out to sea all the way to Cebu Island. It was a complete route, for in forty-five minutes, eleven more enemy fighters fell into ocean, including the thirtieth victory for 431 FS CO Tommy McGuire and the thirty-eighth victory for the 5 FC Gunnery Instructor.

With the word of the big fight reaching the men waiting at Tacloban, anxious 9 FS Flt Ldr McElroy was determined to attain his fifth victory that day before the sun went down. At 1630 hours, he bolted off the runway for the third time. After hunting for an hour and half, Mac was about to begrudgingly take his foursome home when the air controller called. McElroy wheeled hard about and climbed to the interception of the single contact reported directly over the bay.

The event could not have been more frustrating to the driven flight leader. There at 7000 feet was a lone LILY which should have been an easy kill, but the persistent bomber pilot led the Knights on a weary chase, all the way to the south cape of Cebu. McElroy

*8 FS Meyer's aircraft #63 "HONEY CHILE" with the typical yellow nose and black bands which foil the yellow number. The yellow aircraft number also appeared on a black square foil on the outer face of both rear radiator tubs. This particular sun bathing Vargas girl was one of the more popular in the 5 AF and is foiled here by a blue background. "HONEY CHILE" displays Meyer's only two victories scored on November 1st and December 7th respectively.*

expended all of his ammo turning the drab Ki-48 into a riddled hulk with its left landing gear dangling just above the waves, but it would not fall. The flight leader pulled aside as wingman Lt. Noah Williams closed in and shot out the LILY's engines as well as setting its remaining fuel on fire. It suddenly exploded and fell in pieces not far from Cebu's southern shore. After their return to base, McElroy acquiesced with a shrug and confirmed the kill for Williams.

### D-DAY FINALE; INTERCEPT #8

While the Knights returned home, the Screamin' Demons took off for their last patrol at 1630. Mission leader Lt. Joel Paris with wingmen 2Lts. Perry White and Milden Mathre were joined by Capt. John Haher and wingman 2Lt. Ken Markham for a patrol over the north flank of the invasion fleet laying in anchor and they reached their station at 15,000 feet in good order. Forty-five minutes into the mission, Paris ordered tanks off and led the quintet down through the Navy flak corridor in pursuit of six OSCARs, but the fleet anti-aircraft fire forced the Demons to break off their attack.

Back up at "14 angels" for another fifteen minutes, keen-eyed Flt Ldr Haher caught sight of a lone NICK speeding east toward the fleet ten-thousand feet below. The captain rolled his big fighter over and dropped into a dead astern pursuit at 350 Mph. The Kawasaki crew spotted the diving Demon Lightnings and the sentai pilot bent his nimble ship around in a hard right turn for the race back to the safe haven of Cebu. Haher easily overtook the swerving target and made a firing pass which killed the rear gunner and tore open the left engine. Showered with debris, Haher wheeled his spattered P-38 aside with wingman Markham, then radioed the trailing mission leader that his windshield was too clouded by oil spray to finish the job. In seconds, Lt. Paris dropped into point-blank range and shot out the right engine, but just as with the captain, he pulled away in a cloud of debris with a blackened windshield. But the NICK was done for and it shattered to pieces upon the sea fifteen miles short of Cebu.

Both Haher and Paris with their restricted vision chose to leave the mission in the able hands of element leader 2Lt. Mathre. The lieutenant and the other two wingmen returned to finish their patrol over the harbor at 4000 feet where element Ken Markham spotted the second NICK target. The Kawasaki was southwest bound along the leading edge of sprawling cloud front which had closed in five-hundred feet over the sea to the west. Mathre could not spot the dark grey enemy plane against the dark seascape, so he passed the lead to Markham. Plunging down to 1000 feet to nearly dead astern, Mathre ultimately saw the Kawasaki whose crew had apparently had not yet seen the three Lightnings. Closing too fast, Mathre fired a short inaccurate burst and had to pulled away to avoid a collision. Markham's volley was right on the dot. His explosive rounds sparkled down the fuselage, gutted the cockpit and then blew up the right engine. Rookie wingman Perry White never fired a round as he watched the NICK disintegrate and tumbled straight down into the dark sea.

The Demon trio made one final orbit of the harbor and turned off for Tacloban to land at six o'clock. The big P-61 Black Widow night fighters had begun to prowl over the area and the base search light beams swung to and fro through the overcast. But the enemy never came that night, nor would they come to Leyte for the next three days in any great numbers. MacArthur's great offensive for the final capture of Leyte was permanently cast. The Baruaen highlands were secured the day after the Ormoc landings and Ormoc village was overrun on the 9th. An estimated garrison of 15,000 Imperial soldiers and sailors retreated into the wild mountains to the north. The Volunteer Guards and guerilla regiments would hunt them down and execute them, long after the fighting would end.

### PANAY FIGHTER SWEEP; DECEMBER 11, 1944

On the 10th, the Thunderbolts of the 348 FG accounted for another ten enemy planes in a lopsided dogfight southwest of the invasion group. There were still no contacts on the north flank of the island, and therefore on the following day, 5 FC decided it was time to turn the tables. Rather than wait for the enemy over Ormoc, it was time for the Lightning wing to go out and find them at their bases. Deputy CO Bob Aschenbrener was tagged to add his Blacksheep flight to the Satan's Angels for a fighter sweep of the islands to the west.

Beyond Cebu were the two larger islands of Negros and Panay. Triangular Panay, furthermost to the west, had airstrips on its northern coast at the villages of Cadiz and Pilar. On the north shore of Negros lay the airstrips at Fabrica and Silay. Navy and USAAF reconnaissance confirmed a sizable number of several different typed of war planes at all four airfields. At 0600 hours on December 11th, the Lightnings lifted off to sweep the entire complex.

Capt. Aschenbrener had wingmen 2Lts. Hal Strom, George Reed and Demon-transferee 2Lt. Francis Hill at 24,000 feet in the lead of Lightning force. As they crossed the Visayan Sea, the captain kept close watch of a large enemy convoy lurking beneath the cloud deck to the north and rightly figured an airborne escort would be close by. When they reached the waters northeast of Panay at 0900 hours, there in a broad formation stacked from 28,000 through 10,000 feet came an estimated force of thirty ZEROs, OSCARs and TOJOs. At that instant, one of the most fierce dogfights of the campaign would erupt.

The Blacksheep and Satan's Angels simultaneously attacked the superior force. Drop tanks fell everywhere and tracers coursed in every direction as the opponents wheeled into each others assaults. But after twenty bloody minutes, the Japanese lost seven of their fighters to the veteran Lightning wing.

In the first pass, Aschenbrener clobbered a TOJO which lost its hydraulics and dropped its left landing gear. Wingman Strom followed up on the next TOJO wingman in line and knocked pieces from its underside. Next, element leader Reed destroyed a ZERO which tried to dive out of the battle while the Red leader heavily damaged yet another.

Finally, tail-end Hill heavily damaged another ZERO which passed before his guns. The Blacksheep pressed on in the wild chase down through the cloud deck at 12,000 feet, but the Flight Leader was the only man to find a target skimming over the waves. It turned out to be his original TOJO victim with the dangling landing strut and Asch delivered a coup de grace which sheared off the Nakajima's right wing.

The Satan's Angels were more successful in the final pursuit and did the greater damage further to the southeast. Aschenbrener's people were too low on fuel to continue and they returned to

Tacloban to land at half past ten. The captain's flight, however, was far from finished for the day.

## DEMONS TO THE NORTH, TWICE

While the Blacksheep re-equipped, the Screamin' Demons directly overhead were about to enter into a very prolonged engagement that would result in two trips to Leyte's northern cape. Flight Ldr Keck had already returned due to engine failure, but element leader Lou Denkovic continued on with fellow 2Lts. Bill Thompson and rookie Jim McCrary III to their station at 15,000 feet atop the cloud cover. The second lieutenants had just turned north, when at 1030 hours, McCrary spotted the first enemy airplanes seen in his infant combat career. There were three above his level, four directly ahead and two some distance below. All were ZEROs.

The Demon trio advanced their throttles and began to climb as the ZEROs changed course for the north. The lower kokutai pair momentarily rocked their wings, then dropped into the overcast. The middle foursome soon withdrew and Denkovic decided, then and there, to tackled the remaining three. As the chase neared the north cape, Denkovic pulled to within firing range and entered a shallow left turn against the ZEKE wingman to the left. Thompson targeted the leader.

Trailing McCrary immediately warned that one of the lower ZEROs had re-engaged and was closing in through the cloud tops, back toward the Demon leader. Denkovic immediately wheeled harder to the left to counter the renewed threat while Thompson pressed on against the higher kokutai leader. Thompson fired and damaged the lead ZEKE, then broke off to regain his cover for Denkovic, but he was too late.

Denkovic continued his counter-attack on the returned Mitsubishi and raked it with a barrage from nose to tail. But as wingman Thompson separated in his pursuit of the higher kokutai leader, the higher trailing ZEKE number-three suddenly wheeled about and fired a 20mm burst which knocked out Denkovic's right engine before either of the Demon wingmen could recover. Denkovic broke away for the southeast trailing smoke as Thompson and McCrary regrouped to covered the flight leader's escape. Denkovic dove away at a high enough speed to soon put out the fire in his holed engine.

## DENKOVIC'S DILEMMA

After the Demon leader assured his wingmen he could reach home on the sound left engine, they asked permission to return north to even the score and Denkovic relented. As they peeled away for the second venture, the leader continued in his southerly descent, only to experience more difficulty.

En route, the sound port engine overheated and Denkovic shut it down for a dead-stick glide a short distance until it cooled off. He succeeded in restarting the left mill before he reached Tacloban, only to find his landing gear would not lower all the way. His last hope was to ditch his damaged P-38 in the shallows off the end of the runway, and that too, proved to be yet another test.

Denkovic tried to belly in upon the water, but the battered Lightning dropped off on its dead port engine, dragged its right wingtip

in the waves and cartwheeled to a jolting halt. The twisted wreck settled to the bottom, but did not completely submerge. Shaken Denkovic, his legs pinned under the collapsed instrument dash, nearly drowned as the rescue party frantically tried to reach him in their boats. A crewman tried several times to dive beneath the surface and free him, but the rescuer had no leverage point to lift the collapsed dash. The rising tide soon inundated the cockpit and the exhausted flyer had to be held upright to keep his face above the lapping waves. When Demon Flight Surgeon Don Bux finally arrived, he seriously considered amputating the poor lieutenants legs, but gladly abandoned the desperate idea after a man brought forth a six-foot long heavy steel bar. By standing on the canopy frame, the crewman was able to slide the bar through a jagged hole beneath the windscreen and leverage the dash off the pilots knees. Tough Lou Denkovic would live to fly again.

## BACK TO THOMPSON AND McCRARY

In the meantime, rookie McCrary followed the incensed Thompson all the way back to the northern tip of Leyte where they quickly settled the vendetta. They overtook two more ZEROs over the west bank and both closed into firing range before either of their victims could dive into the clouds. McCrary sawed the right wing off of his target and Thompson knocked several large chunks out of his victim before it escaped within range of the anti-aircraft batteries aboard the Imperial merchant convoy laying off Biliran Island. Both of the Demons immediately withdrew and with their fuel nearly spent, they landed back home just before noon.

In the interim, the Blacksheep on standby had attempted to get a pair of P-38s airborne to aide in the Demons venture, but one of their young rookies suffered the same fate of the Demon flight leader. Newcomer 2Lt. Art Terry had become separated from his flight leader in the area of the fight up north and had his P-38 badly damaged. Despite the fact, the game lieutenant fought his dying mount all the way back to Tacloban and gave the line crews a exhilarating moment when his Lockheed cracked up on landing. Everyone was greatly relieved when the youngster stood up in the cockpit of his smoldering wreck, none the worse for the harrowing interception gone awry.

## ASCHENBRENER ENDS THE DAY

After the first morning sweep to Cebu, Blacksheep Capt. Aschenbrener's same foursome flew a second, mid-day sweep off the west coast, but they found nothing. When they landed in mid-afternoon, the captain was instructed to get some hot food while the Lockheeds were refueled for yet another sortie at 1600 hours. The third sortie was to be an escort for a Navy Catalina PBY search flight of the waters off northern Cebu. Two of the pilots from the previous sorties stood down with mechanical failures, so Aschenbrener and wingman 2Lt. Strom took on standby Lt. Bechdolt and 2Lt. Hill.

The revamped Blacksheep team was over their Catalina charge on schedule, but they never got any farther than Ormoc Bay. Just as they crossed the shoreline, five ZEROs crossed their path, and two of them set after the PBY. Aschenbrener cut off the lead attacker

*Grandchild of the rugged Douglas C-47, this new bare metal four-engine C-54 "Cargomaster" ventured into Tacloban in the midst of the November battle. It dropped off freight, then evacuated wounded back to New Guinea.*

and was able to hit him with two volleys which forced the Mitsubishi so low that it skipped off the surface of the bay. However, the captain's guns had become too hot and the next burst blew out the riflings which threw his volley of tracers wildly off the mark. He slipped aside and let his wingmen finish off the rising Mitsubishi which was finally dispatched by number-four man Hill. The lieutenant's burst tore open the ZERO's right wing fuel cell and the gasoline erupted in a brilliant orange fireball. Hill's victim slammed down in a shattering explosion on the shoreline of Duligan Point.

After a brief pursuit of the remaining four intruders which escaped in the haze to the north, Lt. Bechdolt reported a power failure in his starboard Allison. Aschenbrener, with his defective guns, lost contact with the Catalina whose crew had apparently decided to continue on alone. The Blacksheep foursome with its two broken ships was finished. Capt. Asch, Hill and Strom surrounded Bechdolt with his good port engine and escorted him back to Tacloban. They were all safely on the ground at half past five.

## NEW DEMON ACE SHADOWS THE CONVOY; DECEMBER 12, 1944

The sighting of the enemy convoy cruising in the Visayan Sea on the 11th spurred a number of armed surveillances throughout the following day. The mid-afternoon Screamin' Demons reconnaissance proved particularly auspicious as they would find three JNAF heavy bombers, precisely one year to the day from their last such encounter.

At 1400 hours, Senior Lt. Jim O'Neil was mission leader of the Demon Flight sent to shadow the enemy convoy and had just passed over the west coast of Leyte at 10.000 feet when Lt. Joel Paris' White Flight called in a single twin-engine plane far below. The White quartet immediately plunged in unison for the lone BETTY and were first to the target. Paris with his wingman took a

flanking attack position on the left and White element leader Lt. Bill Bauer took up the assault from the right. Before Bauer could push his gun button, Paris opened fire, knocking out the left engine and shattering the long flat canopy. The dark-green portly ship pancaked down in the pale blue water not far from shore. Paris and wingman George Rogers swept back through two strafing passes, setting the floating wreck ablaze. No enemy crewman was seen to escape from the raging inferno which underscored the fifth confirmed kill of the newest ace, Joel Paris.

Mission leader O'Neil recalled his flights and they continued on to circumnavigate the extant of the southern Visayan sea for the next two hours. After patrolling off the north coast of Panay and seeing the U.S. Navy dive-bombers set fire to three enemy vessels, the Demons circled back to the sight of the first interception and found two more BETTY targets. From 13,000 feet, Lt. Warren Greczyn's Blue Flight were the first men to spot the bombers skimming over the water off little Campopo Bay.

Flight Ldr Greczyn and wingman Capt. Dick Suehr, a former 35 FG veteran, swept down on the Mitsubishis and the lieutenant promptly set fire to the right wing of the lead ship. It crashed in flames in the coral shallows, but did not break up. Greczyn and Suehr left nothing to chance. Both men first strafed the wreck, then executed two of the four Imperial aviators who tried to make a run for the trees beyond the beach. On their third firing pass, they heavily machine gunned the treeline where the last two survivors had taken cover.

Meanwhile, White element leader Lt. Bob Decker had done precisely the same for the kokutai crewmen in the other BETTY. After shooting out the left engine, his target splashed down in the shallows and the lieutenant withdrew to find the Blue leader. When Decker passed over the bloody scene on Campopo beach, he wheeled about to returned and strafe his wrecked victim, only to find the ditched Mitsubishi was completely enveloped in flames. He could not image how any crewman could have gotten out in time.

*Gen. Douglas MacArthur bestowing the Congressional Medal of Honor to Maj. Dick Bong.*

## DEATH FOR COLLINS, HONOR FOR BONG; DECEMBER 12, 1944

The 49ers were well embroiled in the hectic operations over the enemy convoy, when without warning, Kenney's heavy bombers suddenly pushed into the Tacloban airfield. Even though LtC. Walker

was not directly appraised, he accurately reckoned his group would soon mobilize again. For the moment, however, the grueling mission schedule seemed to only worsen as the battle began to spread further to the north.

The Flying Knights had not seen an enemy plane for the past several sorties, but neither had any of their men been in recent peril. New planes had arrived during the mission frenzy and new pilots, too, but the older veterans knew the good luck could not last. Mid-afternoon on the 12th, fate struck down a 9 FS man when 2Lt. Jim Collins' P-38 blew a tire on takeoff and swerved into a newly arrived B-24 parked near the runway. A huge fire engulfed both planes and Collins was thrown clear in the explosion. His was badly burned and there was little the flight surgeons could do. Jim Collins died in the field hospital late that day.

While the young Knight lingered in the final minutes of his life, the 49ers staff was directed to a ceremony for a former Flying Knight on the Tacloban flight line. Within an arch of parked P-38s encircling Gen. MacArthur, Gen. Kenney and a horde of war correspondents, Maj. Dick Bong was presented with the Congressional Medal of Honor. Everyone turned their attention to the glory of the moment in hopes of forgetting that miserable stretch of sand which had been the scene of so much bitterness and suffering.

After many congratulations and a tour of the squadron bars, Bong and his fellow survivors all turned in for the night. They hoped their fitful sleep in the tropical heat would have them ready for the next morning. A stupefying number of sorties were already posted at the operations tent.

## MINDORO; DECEMBER, 1944

The December 7th landings at Ormoc and subsequent annihilation of the Imperial Army and Navy left a strategic void in the central Philippines. Allied intelligence confirmed that heavy air raids and guerilla actions on southern Mindoro had left the island garrisons there virtually undefended. MacArthur boldly advanced his offensive beyond Leyte, 375 miles to the north.

To relieve the taxed 308 BW at Tacloban, which included the bloodied 49ers and the 475 FG, Gen. Kenney called up his 5 AF units waiting in New Guinea. The new tactical force set in the order of battle was designated as the 310th BW under the command of C.J.T. Murtha. For the brief interim, the Tacloban strategic groups would principly stand in reserve until the airfields near San Jose were secured for their later arrival, tentatively for the third week of December.

To aid Murtha's 310 BW staff in assuming the leadership role at Mindoro, Kenney appointed proven Col. Bob Morrissey of 5 FC as special liaison and the scheme certainly fit into the veteran's own design. Career-minded Morrissey reasoned that his successful leadership on Mindoro would mean certain promotion. The idea of being the first fighter pilot since Wurtsmith to be promoted to the rank of general was certainly an incentive. After his successful combat mission on December 7th, the colonel stood down from flying and attended full time to the planning of the Mindoro air defense.

The 8 FG was designated as the first team to advance to Mindoro with its newer model Lightnings. The 58 FG with its P-47s would move up to provide tactical support for the invasion troops. The Navy would bring up its escort carrier air wing to add to the air cover, including a number of Hellcat night fighters to provide extended protection after dusk. As of December 13th, the Mindoro invasion force was steaming north through the Mindanao Sea beneath a sprawling net of Army and Navy fighters.

## USS *NASHVILLE* OFF CEBU; DECEMBER 13, 1944

On board the battle-hardened flagship, USS *Nashville*, Morrissey, 310 BW CO Murtha and the West Visayan area task force commander, Col. Bruce Hill, continued to plan the air operations for the Mindoro campaign, never knowing the fearful reckoning awaiting them at sea. Only minutes by air from the surviving kamikaze units at Fabrica air drome on nearby Negros Island, neither the airborne escorts nor Navy gunners could circumvent the tragedy about to take place in the narrow straits off Siquijor Island.

In the heat of the afternoon on the 13th, the three USAAF officers retired to their respective quarters and Morrissey turned his attentions back to his book, "The Case of the Lucky Legs." It was just past 1500 hours when another general quarters was sounded and the anti-aircraft batteries began banging away on the main deck. The colonel rose from his bunk to ask a sailor scurrying down the causeway if he should move to another area. At that very instant, an Imperial aviator brought his bomb ladened plane down through the task force gauntlet and slammed into the *Nashville*'s deck, collapsing the ceiling of Morrissey's room.

Fire and smoke poured down the causeway and men cried out for help. Navy medics soon broke through to the fallen USAAF pilot and bore him to the dispensary, but it was to little avail. His shattered right leg was nearly severed below the knee. The Nashville medics saved the colonel's life, and eventually, a surgeon in Seattle would even reconstruct his mangled leg. But Bob Morrissey's military career had ended.

Other fleet ships were hit in the December 13th kamikaze attack. Seventy-five members of the 58 FG were killed outright when their troop carrier was hit by a suicide plane. Later on board the smoldering *Nashville*, the bodies of colonels Murtha and Hill were found. In mere seconds, Gen. Kenney had lost a future Fighter Command leader, a task force commander, a wing commander, and nearly an entire fighter group ground echelon.

## MINDORO D-DAY MINUS ONE: DECEMBER 14, 1944

Fighter sweeps against Cebu, Negros and Panay Islands were subsequently flown by the Tacloban based groups throughout the duration of the landing force's voyage into the waters of Mindoro. But the 49ers did not score during those sorties. In the hunt over Negros Island on December 14th, all of the victories fell to the Thunderbolts and Lightning of other units, or to Halsey's carrier-based raiders further north.

## FIRST MISSION TO MINDORO; D-DAY, DECEMBER 15, 1944

On the next day at 0900 hours, newly appointed Demon Ops Exec Capt. John Haher took seven wingmen up at 0750 hours as part of the fighter sweep targeted against the Los Negros airdrome just outside San Jose, the provincial capitol on the southern most shore of Mindoro Island. After an hour's flight time, the Lightnings were

*The liberated provincial capitol of Cebu Island and the inland hills where thousands of Japanese hid until long after the war ended. Beyond the hills of the narrow island lies greater Negros Island which still had remnant fighter units operating from its remote airstrips in January, 1945. One of the airfields of northern Negros was likely the base of the kamikaze that struck the USS Nashville on December 13th.*

over the invasion fleet, and immediately, the Satan's Angels made contact with the enemy air force over Seminara Island ten miles south of the Mindoro mainland.

The 7th Squadron, meanwhile, approached the battle sight a few miles off on the west flank. Capt. Haher's Red Flight was still at 9000 feet and Lt. Damstrom's trailing White Flight quartet was in high cover at 15,000. Haher intended to reach Mindoro proper and sweep San Jose airdrome, but his Demons would never reach the shoreline. At 0915, the Red Flight elements spotted a flight of seven ZEROs above and to their left.

The eight Demon pilots jettisoned their tanks and Red Flight accelerated through a climbing left turn. White Flight circled to the right behind the enemy fighters which likewise dropped their belly tanks, but the kokutai displayed very tentative combat skills early on. Caught in the pincer maneuvers of the two Demon flights, the ZEROs fell away in split-S dives and abruptly lost four of their men to the Lightnings which followed them all the way down to the sea deck.

In his first firing pass, marksman White Flt Ldr Damstrom dropped a ZEKE in the straits between Semirara Island and Mindoro's southern cape. Seconds later, White element 2Lt. Olie Atchison dispatched another a few miles to the west. Red Flight element number-4, 2Lt. Milden Mathre, knocked down his target just a few miles south of the invasion beachhead on the southwestern shore. Minutes later, Red element leader Lt. Jim Jarrell sent a ZERO down in the shallows southeast of Semirara Island which ended the fight. Capt. Haher quickly recalled the Demons to regroup at 16,000 feet and found the Japanese had completely withdrawn. The entire episode had lasted less than ten minutes.

The Demons continued to patrol over the east flank of the convoy for another half hour until White Flight answered a U.S. Navy vector to the east at 1015 hours. After a descent due south to 10,000 feet, eagle-eyed Damstrom finally caught sight of his second victim of the day. A lone, war weary HAMP was seen coursing due north for the Allied ships, just above the waves. After a long arcing

turn into the HAMP's rear quarter, Damstrom pulled unseen into point-blank range and fired two long bursts into the ruddy, olive-brown Mitsubishi. Burning at the wingroots, the old stager rolled over and exposed its underwing bombs, then dropped straight down and was obliterated when its' ordinance detonated on impact with the sea, ten miles off Panay's northern most cape.

When the 49ers landed back at Tacloban at noon, the news of the Demons successful engagements was overshadowed by the exploits of the resident Gunnery Instructor. Dick Bong had knocked down an OSCAR during an earlier morning flight. That made his victory count thirty-nine.

## EIGHT TIMES AN ACE - BONG; DECEMBER 17, 1944

Escort missions were intermixed with dive-bombing sorties for two days, but the 49ers failed to make contact in the many vectors over the cloud covered Mindoro beachhead. Late in the afternoon of the 17th, word spread throughout the Allied commands that Maj. Bong had beaten the odds at last and racked up his fortieth kill south of San Jose. MacArthur wired his congratulations to the major and Kenney personally greeted him at the Tacloban flight line. Then, by the 5 AF commander's direct order, Bong was relieved from flight duty and subsequently sent back to the States for good.

## FLYING KNIGHTS SOLDIER ON; DECEMBER 18, 1944

As the leading American ace of all time rested at Leyte, his old squadron was back up over Mindoro for the fifth straight day. In the late day patrol of the beachhead, Ops Exec Capt. Willie Will-

*8 FS Wright Boyd scored his only victory on his first Leyte mission, then flew through the subsequent Philippines mayhem without hitting another airborne opponent. His old stager aircraft #54 is seen after the move to Mindoro.*

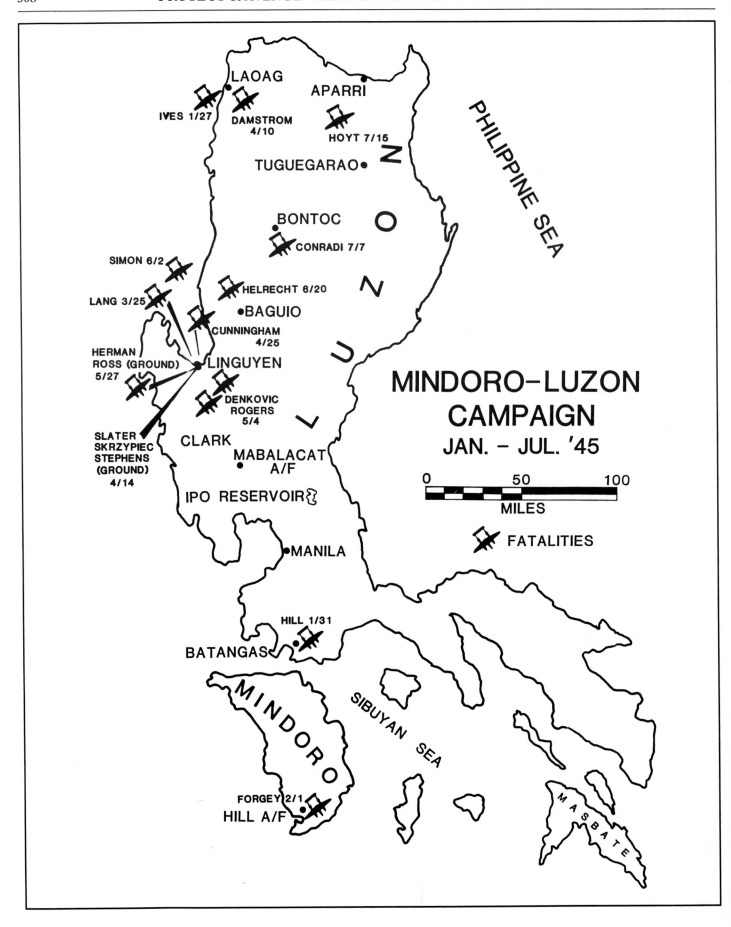

LAOAG

APARRI

IVES 1/27

DAMSTROM
4/10

HOYT 7/15

PHILIPPINE SEA

TUGUEGARAO

BONTOC

L U Z O N

CONRADI 7/7

SIMON 6/2

HELRECHT 6/20

LANG 3/25

BAGUIO

CUNNINGHAM
4/25

HERMAN
ROSS (GROUND)
5/27

LINGUYEN

MINDORO–LUZON
CAMPAIGN
JAN. – JUL. '45

DENKOVIC
ROGERS
5/4

SLATER
SKRZYPIEC
STEPHENS
(GROUND)
4/14

CLARK

MABALACAT
A/F

0     50     100

MILES

IPO RESERVOIR

FATALITIES

MANILA

HILL 1/31

BATANGAS

M I N D O R O

SIBUYAN SEA

M A S B A T E

FORGEY 2/1

HILL A/F

iams had eleven of his Flying Knights ready in a spread formation between 5000 to 7500 feet, but only one contact showed itself.

Capt. Williams took a heading due south and immediately caught sight of a DINAH speeding away toward Panay. In the brief pursuit, the veteran dropped below the Nakajima's flight path and drew to within 200 yards, then rose up to let go with a deadly volley. The right engine of the DINAH belched flames and the ship began to skid aside, but the captain hung on and after checking for his wingman's position, resumed the execution. He completely shot out the smoking right engine, then torched the left engine. The target became engulfed in flames and "Wewak Willie" Williams watched the fourth and final victim of his career crash in the sea, ten miles south of the beachhead.

## MOMENTARY SUCCESS AT MINDORO

Despite the loss of two LST craft during the Mindoro landings, the venture was a huge success. Against minimal resistance by the retreating enemy garrison, a wartime record of tonnage in equipment and men for a single day was downloaded on the flat coastal plain. The new airstrip, named in honor of the fallen task force commander, Col. Hill, immediately began operations to receive the USAAF defensive squadrons, and none too soon.

There was a brief logistical setback when Adm. Halsey's northern carrier task force was lashed by a monsoon in the Philippines Sea on the December 18th. The battered ships had no alternative but to withdraw to distant Ulithi for repairs. Without the Navy to strike the Luzon air dromes, Mindoro came under increasingly severe aerial assaults. Luzon based JAAF and JNAF units were able to sortie at least one hundred times against the Mindoro beachhead on D-Day alone, and as of the 19th, well over a hundred more air raids struck the landing area.

Col. J.A. Wilson, the new commander of the 310 BW, called up the 8 FG Lightnings and 418 Night Fighter Squadron P-61 Black Widows to Hill Field on December 20th. By day's end, the fighters were operating from the 5700 foot sand and gravel runway which held up well, despite intermittent rains which muddied the area. Elmore Strip, a short distance to the north, would be completed by December 23rd to relieve the congestion at Hill.

*8 FS C.C. Sgt. Urrey (lt.) Lt. Bechtold and an unknown crewman after the move to Linguyan. This team would inevitably be together in Japan in the post-war occupation.*

## PARIS' SILVER STAR; DECEMBER 21, 1944

In the interim, Col. George Walker's 49ers would continu to fly cover for the fleet at anchor, as well as provide patrols over the routes through the southern islands. On December 21st, a 7th Squadron VIP escort mission to Mindoro turned into the most memorable for ace Lt. Joel Paris. The entire affair took place directly over the landing forces of the established beachhead.

The mission began for Flt Ldr Paris and his wingmen, 2Lts. Milden Mathre and Jim Jarrell, with a 0930 take off from Tacloban. The three Demons formated at 8000 feet over a U.S. Navy PBY Catalina flying boat bearing USAAF officers who were called up to Mindoro for a staff conference. The flight north went smoothly until the four aircraft reached the waters off the beachhead at noon. Just as the Catalina reached the perimeter of the anchorage, Flt Ldr Paris was notified that Navy radar had detected enemy aircraft in the immediate area. Seconds later, flak bursts dotted the airspace over San Jose Air Drome. Paris ordered the Catalina to land at sea and simultaneously sent wingman Jarrell up to 13,000 feet for high cover.

No sooner had the PBY safely splashed down and Jarrell leveled out at "13 Angels", a single ZERO was seen between Jarrell's and Paris' respective altitudes. Apparently hit by the anti-aircraft barrage from San Jose, the Mitsubishi was trailing a fine trail of smoke as it sped off to the north. Jarrell immediately descended on the crippled ZERO and fired. Paris in his "GEORGIA BELLE" watched the wingman's firing pass and confirmed the kill, then quickly glanced over his shoulder to "check 6 o'clock" for any other intruders. Paris' alertness could not have been more opportune.

Indeed, a second ZERO had slipped out of the billowing clouds behind Paris and opened fire, just as the Demon flight leader looked back. He pulled the BELLE hard about into his attacker just as an explosive 13mm round struck the cross bar in his canopy frame directly above his head. There was a blinding flash and deafening bang which left a six inch wide hole in BELLE's canopy. The slip stream was so great that it sucked the pilot's leather helmet and goggles off his head. The goggles disappeared, but the radio wires retained the helmet. Paris pulled it back over his ringing ears and nosed his ship downward out of danger.

After leveling out at 8000, Paris jettisoned his tanks and called for his wingmen. Jarrell, still in high cover, instantly responded and warned of two more ZEROs closing in behind the flight leader and wingman Mathre. Paris and Mathre throttle forward and rose up through a right turn, only to have the lieutenant separate when they were fired upon a second time. Jarrell arrived in time to cut off one of the attackers, and after a brief chase, he closed in and blew away the canopy of his second victim of the mission. The burning ZERO dropped straight down into the bay.

Paris ascended alone and finally gained an advantage behind one of the aggressive ZEROs. Directly over the Catalina which had begun to taxi over the water to the safety of the Navy gunboats, the Demon ace set the Mitsubishi ablaze and the aviator dropped away in his chute. The ZERO slammed down on little Manadi Island, just off shore from the beachhead. While the lifeless enemy aviator hung in mid-air, Mathre tried to finish him off, but missed. The fellow landed in the bay where he was picked up by the Navy. Soon, another patrol flight arrived in relief and Paris' trio regrouped for the flight home. In the debriefing at Tacloban, the flight members

*PARIS' SILVER STAR – An artist's view of Flt Ldr Paris pulling up as his seventh career victim took to his chute. Paris was nearly deaf after flying back to Leyte with the wind pouring in through the foot-wide hole blown out of in his canopy. At lower left is the V.I.P. Catalina taxiing to the safety of the Mindoro invasion fleet. (Gen. Joel Paris collection)*

related that the Japanese pilots were very capable and that the ZEROs held pace in the fight. Somewhat bemused, Paris reflected, "The Japs flew pretty well, but they couldn't shoot worth a damn."

Parenthetically, when Paris radioed the authorities regarding the fate of captured aviator, he was informed the prisoner had been shot while trying to escape during an air raid. Squadron boss Ed Peck and Group leader Walker were so impressed by the whole debriefing that they immediately filed citations for the resilient flight leader. At the end of his Philippines tour, Joel Paris received the Silver Star for his safe delivery of the VIPs at Mindoro.

### ANOTHER DEMON ACE SCORES AGAIN: DECEMBER 21, 1944

In the U.S. Navy's absence due to the monsoon northeast of Luzon, the USAAF desperately tried to negate the nearest threats in the

north. Aerial reconnaissance found enemy planes at Lipa airdrome on south central Luzon and the 308 BW at Tacloban was assigned to the task. The mission plan was to have a flight of Demon Lightnings glide-bomb with their single one-thousand pounders, then fly high cover for the 35 FG P-47s which would dive-bomb the target and finish off the job with a strafing assault. The fighter-bomber force lifted off at 1415 hours and cruised off on a two-hour long, straight line course for Lipa.

Flight Leader Lt. Fernley Damstrom and his three wingmen arrived over the Lipa coordinates at 16,000 feet in company to the four Thunderbolts below, but the target was completed blanketed by a scud of cumulus. Damstrom's contemptuously surmised the P-47 mission leader, "did not want to use the cloud deck to any advantage", for the Thunderbolts diverted south for the secondary objective on Masbate Island. However, the alternate was nearly as obscured as Luzon and the P-47 pilots broke radio silence. There was lengthy discussion about their fuel consumption and the mis-

they found each plane was down to only a few gallons of gasoline. But the long range mission had been worth it all. Damstrom had achieved his eighth confirmed kill.

## BLACKSHEEP ON THE OTHER SIDE OF THE BATTLE; DECEMBER 21, 1944

Capt. Willie Drier's 8 FS had their engagements on the 21st as well. Seven Blacksheep left Tacloban at 1500 hours and flew north to take up their patrol station at 4000 feet above the anchored Mindoro invasion fleet. Several attempts were made to reach the vectors of attackers skimming low over the waves, but the glare from the setting sun on the sea was blinding and made identification nearly impossible.

Finally at 1730 hours, Flt Ldr Bob Aschenbrener saw an attainable target. A ZERO had just eluded a flight of Navy Hellcats and had risen slightly above the Blacksheep formation. Aschenbrener and wingman 2Lt. Francis Hill rose up to a dead astern firing run and closed in on the unsuspecting aviator. At 100 yards, the Blacksheep ace hit his victim with a single volley which tore away the Mitsubishi's canopy and gutted the engine. The burning ZERO rolled over and plunged straight into the sea where Hill confirmed Bob Aschenbrener's tenth and last career kill.

## BLACKSHEEP BACK TO MINDORO; 22 DECEMBER, 1944

On December 22, Aschenbrener and company ventured back to Hill Air Field for a sortie which he wrote up as "a cross-country flight." Shortly after nine o'clock that morning, the successful team of Aschenbrener and Hill was at 10,000 feet over Seminara Island in their final approach to Hill strip when they were diverted to a vector in their flight path. Aschenbrener immediately accelerated down after a lone TONY cruising at 4000 feet over the eastern shore of the island, but his closing speed was far too great to get off an accurate shot. Hill was in perfect position and caught the Ki-61 as it slid out of the flight leader's firing line. The lieutenant's volley shattered the Kawasaki's cockpit and set the in-line engine on fire. As the stricken Ki-61 plunged into the shallows just off shore, the ace captain readily returned the favor and confirmed the kill, just as Hill had done for him the day before.

What the Blacksheep did not know was that they had just missed one of the greatest air battles in the Mindoro operations. Only minutes before, directly over Hill Airfield, the Thunderbolts of the 35 FG and a flight of Headhunters P-38s had intercepted a large raiding force and claimed nine destroyed. An hour later, Gen. Kenney would retaliate with a sweep of 348 FG Thunderbolts to Clark Field, the expansive, former American airdrome fifty miles north of Manila which was the source of the raids. It resulted in nine more Imperial fighters being claimed.

## THE REDUCTION OF MANILA AND CLARK FIELD; DECEMBER 23-26, 1944

With the combined strength of the 308 BW at Tacloban and the 310 BW at Hill, Gen. George Kenney brought the might of the 5 AF

*8 FS aircraft #41 flown by Bechtold and his two final victory flags.*

sion leader concluded all elements, including Damstrom's foursome, should pattern bomb the target from their present altitudes. Eight heavy bombs were toggled off from over 12,000 feet. Damstrom's ordinance hung up on the rack and he had to rock his Lockheed to shake it free. It fell miles from the target, far out in the Visayan Sea.

The fuel-tapped Thunderbolts immediately set off for Tacloban with Damstrom's flight still four thousand feet overhead and with plenty of gas in their main tanks. Just as the flights reached northern Leyte, a vector to a radar contact far to the east was received. One of the Demons chose not to gamble on his low fuel reserve, but rookie 2Lt. Bill Thompson and able Lt. Hal Harris held position as ace Damstrom wheeled off across Samar Island. They hunted for twenty minutes above the darkening cloudscape, and in spite of missing several contacts, Damstrom drained off every last drop of gas until he found his next victim.

Damstrom's gamble paid off. At the Demons' level of 18,000 feet, two OSCARs approached running due south, parallel to the Samar coastline. The Demons dropped their empty belly tanks as they turned up-sun, but the Nakajima pilots saw them and snap rolled into split-S escape dives in separate directions. Damstrom and Harris followed the lead Ki-43, while Thompson broke away after the other.

Thompson chased his target down to the sea deck and hit it with a short volley, but the Ki-43 reached the safety of the clouds and disappeared. At the same time, Damstrom and Harris both got off several snap shots which hit their wildly maneuvering target. Down to 1000 feet, the game ended abruptly as Damstrom swept in close and blew away several pieces from the Nakajima's rear fuselage. The stricken Ki-43 made one last hard left bank, then drifted out to sea, burst into flame and rolled inverted into a watery grave.

When the Demon trio finally re-assembled and flew back for touchdown at Tacloban, they had to slip through the sweeping search lights and flak bursts of the base defense. Safely in the revetments,

*7 FS aircraft #24 "FRENCHY II" flown by Joe McHenry who scored his only victory on the Christmas Day fighter sweep to Mabalacat Airfield.*

down on the Imperial headquarters complex over four consecutive days. Manila was only 160 miles from Hill Field which allowed every fighter type in the 310 BW to easily reach targets there. Even the war-weary P-40 Warhawks of the reconnaissance squadrons would join the tactical assault on the Philippines' national capitol. The greater task was for the Tacloban fighter pilots who would have to fly eight-hundred miles round trip to well defended Clark airdrome, the principle staging air depot of the Luzon defense.

The first escort to Manila by the 49ers was by all three squadrons on December 23rd. Only one interception by the enemy was attempted in the vicinity of the Flying Knights who took the B-24s to the Grace Park airdrome directly north of the capitol. Both Maj. Wally Jordan and Capt. Eddie Howes of the 49ers HQ staff flew attached to the 9 FS that day and both men fired at enemy fighters which ventured meager feints at the awesome American formation.

Neither the major nor the captain claimed a victory. The Imperial command was stunned by the magnitude of the American force and the Mindoro landings. They had anticipated a landing on southern Luzon, perhaps after the new year, but the new Allied air field on Mindoro was far beyond their most pessimistic expectations. On the evening of the 23rd, they again reinforced the Clark Field air units, only to have them fall victim the next morning to the 348 FG who claimed another thirty-three defenders destroyed.

## THE LAST GREAT DOGFIGHT IN THE PHILIPPINES; CHRISTMAS, 1944

Following the slaughter on the morning of December 24th, later that afternoon, the Imperial command pulled the last of its reserves from the northern most Luzon airfields into the Clark airdrome complex. On the next day, Christmas of 1944, the Lightning groups of the 308 BW struck Clark Field again. Across the twenty-five mile wide valley that cradled the expansive airdrome, a brutal dogfight would erupt and sustain for nearly an hour. It was the last great encounter between the opposing air forces in the Philippines war.

## THE 49ERS OVER CLARK FIELD

Despite having only ten serviceable P-38s from the Flying Knights, senior officer Capt. Willie Williams was summarily designated as the 49ers mission leader against Mabalacat. At 0800 hours, Williams took off from Tacloban and set course for Masbate Island which was their rendezvous point with the Liberators.

Ace Lt. Joel Paris was the senior flight leader designated to head up the Screamin' Demons. Paris and his twelve wingmen took off from Tacloban ten minutes after the Knights, and likewise, set off for Masbate.

*Looking down the 8 FG flight line of new P-38 L's at Hill Field, Mindoro. The fight over southern Mindoro was brief, but bloody. The 8th Group, particularly the proud 80th squadron Headhunters, took a gruesome toll of the Japanese in the third week of December.*

Capt. Willie Drier had intended to lead his Blacksheep squadron, but no sooner than having gotten airborne, his aircraft lost an engine. He signalled Tacloban where Capt. Aschenbrener, waiting in reserve, grabbed his flight gear and commandeered a P-38. Asch roared off and caught up with his fourteen wingmen to assume the 8 FS mission lead.

The Blacksheep had actually been designated as the last to take off from Tacloban in the Christmas Day mission for a very specific reason. The intelligence team anticipated the Japanese would launch every fighter available and be most vulnerable after the raid when they attempted to land and refuel. The Blacksheep and several elements of the Satan's Angels would wait in high cover east of the target area. When the last of the Liberators turned away, the P-38s in reserve would ambush the enemy in the landing pattern.

Therefore, with the Flying Knights in the lead at 13,000 feet and the Screamin' Demons to the left and slightly higher, the Blacksheep fell into formation at 14,000 a fare distance to the rear. Right on time at 0900 hours, the 49ers swept over the sprawling formation of big silver bombers that paraded over Masbate and took up their position on the Liberator's left flank. Across the formation on the east side and some distance ahead flew forty-two silver Lockheeds of Col. Charlie MacDonald's 475 FG, bringing the total count of P-38s to eighty.

The crossing to Luzon went without a snag, and the Americans flew directly down the spine of mountains on the southern mainland, straight to the target. At 1030, the lead B-24 turned due west over the broad plain of central Luzon and set up on the bomb-line for Clark Field. There were high, thin cirrus clouds and brilliant sunshine. Visibility over the mainland was exceptionally clear and afforded a view of the entire Clark Field complex.

Immediately, the bomber crews began to call out the approach of a multitude of single-engine fighters arching in from every direction and at several different altitudes. Far ahead, the rising enemy fighters appeared as dark specks foiled by the turquoise sky.

The air battle began in earnest directly over Clark Field at 1035 with the 431th Squadron. In the first exchange with the Satan's Angels, fourteen victories would be claimed alone. Ten minutes later, the 49ers would sweep over Mabalacat air strip on the eastern fringe of the Clark complex.

## TEN FURIOUS MINUTES FOR THE 49ERS

Of the 49ers who flew over Mabalacat that day, it is impossible to determine who garnered the first kill. At their point of first contact at 13,000 feet, elements of the 7th and 9th Squadrons fired simultaneously at the swarm of airborne targets.

Mission leader Capt. Williams, furthest in front of the group, led a climbing turn with his Red Flight wingmen against a flight of TOJOs which struck from the Flying Knights' left. Initially, the Red elements fired at two fleeting Ki-44s which dropped phosphorous bombs over the Liberators' left flank without effect, but the captain immediately broke off and recalled the Red team to return to their escort station. However, White Flt Ldr Lew Lewelling, 2Lt. Troy Smith, element leader Lt. Noah Wiliams, and 2Lt. Dan Holladay entered into a sustained engagement where, in the final account, veteran Lewelling had a pair of TOJOs verified as destroyed, Holladay had another TOJO accredited to him, and

wingman Smith received credit for a probable victory. Williams had been forced to withdraw when his left engine was shot out.

In the same time frame, Demon mission leader Paris took his elements up to the right in a counter-attack against a flight of ZEROs diving down on the bomber formation. In a rambling fight from 11,000 feet down to the deck, the chase extended ten miles north of the target area. Paris, leading his Red Fight foursome, eventually posted his seventh career victory over a kokutai pilot who bailed out of his flaming Mitsubishi. Red Flight wingmen Lts. Dewey Renick and Joe McHenry each shot down a ZERO, as did Lt. Jim Franks who in turn had his left supercharger shot out. Meanwhile, White Flt Ldr Lt. Bill Minto, element 2Lt. Bob Klemmedson and veteran Lt. Bob Decker each claimed a ZERO destroyed. Veteran Flt Ldr Lt. Jim Jarrell led his Blue Flight quartet into the fray and hammered two targets with accurate volleys, but only element leader Lt. Al Meschino and rookie 2Lt. Bill Thompson would have their individual ZERO kills confirmed.

## THE BLACKSHEEP REAR GUARD

Despite Flying Knight Noah Williams and Screamin' Demon Jim Franks both loosing an engine in combat, both men were able to make it all the way back to Tacloban. The only loss of a 49er over the target would come in the egress action with the Blacksheep. The 8th Squadron was the last to engage the enemy and the last to withdraw.

As planned, Aschenbrener's Blacksheep and several of the 431st and 432nd Squadron elements swept inland as the B-24s turned for home. The Blacksheep captain, leading his Blue Flight quartet, thundered down through a spiral descent just above the village of Bamban which lay between the Mabalacat and Clark landing areas. As anticipated, the Imperial fighters had withdrawn from that airspace, so Aschenbrener and wingman 2Lt. Art Terry pressed ever downward directly over the landing field. There on the northern perimeter of the airdrome, Asch spotted a lone ZERO.

At 400 Mph and five-hundred feet above the dusty field, the Blacksheep ace closed in, but the ZERO aviator saw him coming and maneuvered out of the firing line. Aschenbrener swung wide, then turned inside the ZERO's turned and fired a short deflection volley. Damaged, the smoking Mitsubishi turned away again. On the second go around, the chase led right over the northern perimeter of Mabalacat and the airdrome gunners sent up a cloud of machine gun fire. Aschenbrener was hit by shrapnel which cut his legs, and gashed his forehead. With his left engine knocked out, the captain turned away to the southeast trailing smoke and glycol coolant.

Wingman Terry pressed on through the barrage and hit the ZERO with a burst of gun fire. Blue element leader 2Lt. Jim Atkinson, only seconds behind Terry, swept in and dispatched the Mitsubishi which crashed on the airfield. The Blue flight elements then set about strafing the gun emplacements and parked aircraft on the airdrome, setting a DINAH and two OSCARs ablaze. When they rose up from their work, F/O Hal Bechtold picked off a lone OSCAR over the south perimeter of the field, and five minutes later, 2Lt. Bob Goodwin shot down an OSCAR which attempted the final interception of the day, ten miles south of Mabalacat. Goodwin's victim was the 49ers' fourteenth of the mission and the Lightning wing's forty-second kill overall. The Christmas battle was over.

## BOB ASCHENBRENER'S JOURNEY TO LINGUYAN

Capt. Bob Aschenbrener, Operations Executive of the 8 FS, had come down in a jolting crash landing against a rice paddy jetty, ten miles southeast of the big airdrome. The jetty was more like concrete than packed earth and the recoil against his shoulder harness had severely sprained his back. Unknown to him at the time, two vertebrae in his lower back were chipped and the spinal discs were badly bruised. He was certain two ribs were cracked. The pain was excruciating and he could barely rise from the cockpit, let alone walk.

An electrical fire suddenly broke out in the gun bay and Asch crawled painfully to safety as several rounds of ammo went off before the fire burned out. Lying in the mud, it suddenly occurred to him several minutes after the fact, just as it must be with all downed pilots he reasoned, he was not going to get back to Tacloban that day.

He remembered from the mission briefing that the only hope of rescue from Luzon was on the east-central coast by submarine. His muddled planning for the worrisome trek abruptly dissipate as a small band of Huk tribesmen cautiously drew near. When he struggled to stand, the men shouted for him not to shoot, but that was pointless. The fallen pilot had left his service pistol in his tent, 400 miles away in Leyte.

The Filipinos and the American quickly gained mutual trust in each other. Obviously sensing the flyer was not able to walk, a caribou was brought to the crash site and Aschenbrener was lifted on to its back for a jostled ride to the group's tiny village. He was given a meal of one raw egg and it was clear, the Huk villagers were very poor.

They next explained in broken English that the Japanese were much too near and that they would have to take Aschenbrener to a safer camp. Once back upon the caribou, the captain was delivered, ironically, to a hidden camp of the Huk Bala Hop guerrillas lying at the foot of forested Mt. Arayat, due east of the very airdrome that he had just raided. He was given a meal of barely palatable fermented, spiced fish, brown rice and guava tea. The Filipinos then inflated his life raft from his chute pack for his bed and he slept there for six days. He was so tired, he later could not remember even haven risen to use a latrine.

After his week of rest, Aschenbrener learned that his new hosts were equally as ill equipped as the people who first rescued him. Their spokesman, Doming Aquino, explained that there was a rift between his people and the government backed Volunteer Guards who were in contact with the Americans. When the captain was stronger, they would take him to the Guards camp.

In the interim, the stranded flyer ventured daily down to a beautiful stream not far from the encampment and laid out on a rock outcrop, directly beneath the landing pattern to Clark Field. Every make and model of enemy plane passed so close by that he could easily see the faces of the aircrews.

A few days later, the USAAF pilot was joined by a Navy Hellcat pilot, an Avenger bomber pilot and his gunner. The Aquino family explained that the Americans were to travel north as more Japanese patrols were drawing nearer each day. The guerrillas escorted the flyers to a small railroad and Aschenbrener, still in pain, was put aboard a small handcart along with a small sack of supplies. The captain gave Mrs. Aquino his tiger-eye ring as a token of thanks for

her hospitality and Mr. Aquino responded by giving the captain a Japanese pistol. The Americans then set off across central Luzon.

The Huk guerrillas told the flyers they were to be taken north to the Linguyan coast, sixty miles distant. For two weeks, they advanced from one small camp to another, and eventually rode caribous out of the valley to the safer path through the highlands. There was a tenuous moment when their itinerant Huk guides confronted their adversary, the Volunteer Guards, but the V.G. readily assumed responsibility for the Americans. Aschenbrener returned the Japanese pistol to the Huk leader who in turn gave him a pristine sheathed samurai sword. They all bid one farewell forever.

The dangerous journey continued with the V.G. and more incidents ensued, the most dangerous of which was the crossing of the heavily traveled central highway, but all went well. Finally, Aschenbrener and company reached the safety of a grassy campground, high in the hills and only a short distance from the north coast. During their stay there, the travellers heard the big Navy guns sounding the landings at Linguyan. They would have to wait until the Japanese were off the main roads and the trail to the coast was clear. During this interim, another party passed through the camp in escort to Lt. alex Vraciu the Navy fighter ace with nineteen victories. After a brief visit, the two parties bid each other good luck as Vraciu's group set off once more. Aschenbrener and his people followed the next day. Once at Linguyan, he was flown back to Hill Field.

On the twenty-seventh day since that fateful Christmas mission, Bob Aschenbrener reached his squadron at Mindoro. He would fly one last tour with the 49ers as the 7th Squadron commander and survive the war, greatly in part to the kindness shown by the Filipinos of central Luzon. He schemed for days after his return on how to aide the primitive Huk tribe, but he never saw them again. He would always be indebted to the impoverished tribe who gave him everything, especially his life.

## BACK TO CLARK FIELD; DECEMBER 26, 1944

In the debriefing back at Tacloban after the Clark Field Christmas raid, several Blacksheep reported they were certain Aschenbrener had survived his crash landing, having seen his intact fighter lying in the rice paddy. After a hearty round of drinks to the captain's rescue, the group got back to the business at hand.

The Lightning squadrons posted the rotation of pilots for the follow-up mission back to Luzon, but the strike of the 26th was far less productive than the Christmas Day raid. The mission progressed on the very same schedule as the previous raid, but in marginal weather. The Lightning wing arrived at 1030 hours over the target which was partially obscured by broken clouds rising up to 16,000 feet, and the battered survivors at Clark Field rose up again against the huge bomber force in another one-sided killing affair.

The 49ers were once again accompanied by the Satan's Angels led by their newly appointed Ops Exec, super ace Tommy McGuire. More intent than ever to surpass furloughed Dick Bong's victory score, McGuire initiated the wild shooting spree which broke out directly over the Clark airdrome. But it was the three veteran Blacksheep, Flight Leader Lt. Tom Holstein, wingman 2Lt. Nial Castle and Deputy Ops Exec Lt. Sammy Pierce, who would account for ten of the fourteen total victory claims made in only fifteen minutes.

*8 FS Lt. Ricks ventured to Clark Field in the December offensive, but never found an airborne target. He continued on for the duration and eventually reached Japan in the occupation.*

*8 FS Lt. Robinson hunted over Luzon, Formosa and the China coast, but never saw an enemy plane in the air. He was one of the fortunate to be in Japan in the end.*

## BLOODY BLACKSHEEP BLUE FLIGHT; DECEMBER 26, 1944

Blue Flt Ldr Holstein was the first man to see the wave of seven interceptors which suddenly broke out oft he clouds three miles south of the target and directly ahead. The lieutenant signalled mission leader Drier, but the CO never answered the call. Although Capt. Flack of Red Flight would respond and attack, he would only make one firing pass. Only Holstein's Blue Flight executed a sustained counter-attacked.

Holstein's rookie wingman, 2Lt. Dave Wicks, momentarily fell back with hung-up droptanks and never regained his position. Blue element leader Castle moved up, followed a short distance back by number-4 man Pierce in his old K-model #66 who had tagged on to Blue Flight after their original number-4 dropped out earlier in the mission. Hence, the trio of killers were set for battle.

## DEPUTY SAMMIE'S "TURKEY-SHOOT"

The ZEROs were in a formation of two Vee's of three and a single trailing element, but they suddenly separated when they pulled into the gun range of their opponents. Two elements attempted to cut off leader Holstein. Pierce, trailing slightly above, immediately dove and turned head on against the threatening kokutai pair. He opened fire first and the lead Mitsubishi belched a sheet of blue flame from its cowling. The canopy collapsed, then the ZERO rolled and disintegrated, strewing debris all over the sky. Sammie wheeled over to the right as the fragments clattered on the underside of his Lockheed. A short distance away, he saw Flt Ldr Holstein overtake another ZERO and shoot it out of the sky.

Sammy Pierce did not focus on the falling planes, but immediately rolled his ship over and plunged after a flight of four TOJOs which appeared some distance below. Using his diving speed to full advantage, he targeted the Ki-44 in the third element position. The Nakajimas scattered, but Sammie was not distracted and hit his target with a shallow deflection which knocked pieces from the rear fuselage. The damaged Ki-44 rolled over in an attempt to enter a split-S escape, only to expose the full span of its underside to Pierce's line of fire. His next volley gutted the TOJO which continued straight down, its nose section engulfed in flames.

Assured of his second kill, the Ops Deputy pulled the P-38 into a screaming climb to rejoin his unit, only to see a five-ship flight of ZEROs diving for the Liberator formation. He pushed on after them and arrived above the kokutai, just in time to see ace McGuire shoot down two interceptors, one of which collided with a the tail of a B-24. In seconds, Blacksheep Nial Castle destroyed yet another.

Pierce closed in on the surviving pair of ZEROs and fired on the trailing wingman. It exploded and fell in flames for his third kill. He abruptly turned on the leader to hit it with a brief volley, and was about to finish off the smoking ZEKE when three more kokutai wingmen turned in behind him. Pierce easily separated with his greater diving speed and turned to re-engage, just in time to see Castle slip behind the threatening trio and sent one of them down for his second victoty in the fight.

Pierce returned to the fight for the third and last time to spot a single Mitsubishi far below, hopelessly trying to outrun a twisting snake-like formation of eight raging Satan's Angels, led by none other than ace McGuire. The major had already knocked down his fourth victim in the encounter and was just about to touch off his guns for a certain fifth kill when Pierce dropped from his high perch and overtook the fleeing ZERO. Just as the enemy plane reached the clouds, Sammie laid in a volley which torched the center fuselage, right in front of McGuire's guns.

McGuire was furious. He screamed into the microphone for the man who had just shot down the ZERO to identify himself. Pierce, in his unmistakable Carolinian drawl answered, "This ere's Raccoon Blue numba-fo'ah, Majah."

"Pierce, you little bastard. Is that you ?", was McGuire's coarse reply, followed by a poignant silence, then a chuckle and a closing, "Nice shot."

So ended the December 26th battle over Clark Field, which Pierce would forever recall as "a swell turkey-shoot." The Lightnings broke off to the south and most of the escorts headed for Tacloban, but Pierce opted for Mindoro when the temperature of his port Allison began to rise. With Nial Castle and ace McGuire in close escort, Pierce finally landed and taxied into the Hill dispersal revetments where the nose gear of his battled-scarred #66 collapsed. There were scorch marks on the leading edges of the wings, as well as debris stuck in the left radiator which had caused the mill to overheat. Two holes had been gouged in the lower mid-fuselage, and yet, the trusty Lockheed had proven its worth. Sammie Pierce, the Blacksheep veteran of more than 250 combat missions, had made it back in the battle-torn P-38 with four confirmed kills. With a career total of seven victories, he was then the newest Blacksheep ace.

Later that afternoon at the Hill Air Field O-club, Pierce joined McGuire, now with a total of thirty-eight victories, and they drank heartily to the day's success. No one had any way of knowing those were the last victories to be celebrated by either ace.

## MOVING UP TO MINDORO; DECEMBER 26-30, 1944

Kenney, meanwhile, had already set his 308 BW ground units in motion. The 49ers ground echelons feverishly kept their aircraft in service while they simultaneously geared-up for the Mindoro advance. On the night of the 25th, the men at Tacloban ate a Christmas dinner of canned turkey and fruit cocktail, then gathered up their duffel bags and crowded down to the San Pedro Bay docks. After numerous delays, they were finally put aboard two LSTs by 1300 hours on the 26th and were underway by nightfall. The 7th and 8th Squadrons were on board Ship #556, while the 9th Squadron and the HQ personnel settled down on board Ship #734.

No one was sad to leave muddy, mosquito infested Tacloban. The miserable Leyte airfield fared equally as bad in comparison to any New Guinea camp. Food had never been abundant nor good, and many times, there was a shortage of potable water. It seemed everyone had come down with jungle rot, or malaria, or mild dysentery. The mail was much later than ever before. A shortage of bivouac supplies never allowed the men to even remotely modernize the camp.

But the camp at Mindoro promised nothing new. There had been rumors circulating about the serious situation at Hill Airfield for several days and it only made matters worse when the LST officers asked the 49ers personnel to help man the ship's AA batteries. The Navy only had enough life vests for two-thirds of the company. Lieutenants Leslie Nelson, Don Fisher and Wade Lewis of the 9 FS, all temporarily relieved from flight duty, were commandeered by the Navy to join the aerial spotters on the upper deck while Flying Knight S/Sgt. Othoe Steagall and Blacksheep S/Sgt. Bruing Poplansky, respectively chose senior sergeants and corporals from their sections to man the Navy guns.

On the 27th when the reinforcement convoy turned north into the waters northwest of Panay, the anxiety within the ground echelon ranks grew appreciably. The Navy and USAAF officers claimed there would be adequate air cover for the approach to Mindoro, but after numerous sightings of enemy aircraft throughout the day and more general quarters alarms throughout the night, the 49ers were pointedly skeptical. They saw more PT patrol boats at sea than friendly fighters in the air.

At 0230 hours beneath a full moon on the 28th, general quarters sounded again and everyone huddled in the shadows on deck, but the enemy missed the 49ers ships. At 0500, another alarm sounded and gunfire some distance off could be heard above the rush of the LST's wake. At 1030 hours, the 49ers entered the western perimeter of Mangarin Bay, only ten miles from their destination and right in the midst of the most intense air raid any veteran had ever witnessed, including the Leyte landings. Three kamikaze planes struck the convoy, including the Liberty ship carrying ordinance meant for the 310 BW at Hill Field. When the cargo exploded, the 49ers personnel on the deck were knocked off their feet by the concussion and Lt. Nelson was seriously wounded. A second Liberty vessel was struck and heavily damaged a moment later, and then an LCI craft carrying infantry received a direct hit. All on board the flaming hulk were lost. By late morning, a flight of U.S. Navy F4U Corsairs cruised in over the bay and then the P-38 flights took up their station. There were many more alerts throughout the afternoon, but fighter patrols and shipboard gunners kept the enemy planes at bay. Meanwhile, the 49ers convoy laid off the beachhead and circled throughout the night until morning light when they advanced nearer the shore.

But within the marginal weather of the 29th, the Japanese slipped through the struggling Mindoro air defense in mid-morning. A kamikaze pilot even reached LST #734 bearing the 9th Squadron and HQ personnel. Fortunately, the death plane's course was thrown off by an awesome barrage of anti-aircraft fire from the surrounding destroyer gunboats. The broken kamikaze glanced off the prow of the LST and affected only minor damage. The 49ers were taken back into open waters to try again the next day.

Finally at noon on December 30, Ships #556 and #734 plowed ashore on the Mindoro beachhead despite the ongoing raids and downloaded the exhausted USAAF personnel. Trucks arrived and transported the 49ers inland to the camp at Hill Airfield which actually had received very little damage in the raids. It was obvious the Japanese had principally targeted the ships at sea. And much to everyone's satisfaction, the airdrome was on a high, dry field. Compared to muddy Tacloban far off on rain-soaked Leyte, Hill Airfield was after all, a comfortable place to stay.

## NEW YEAR AND ROUTINE MISSIONS; JANUARY, 1945

As 49ers CO LtC. Walker surveyed his new facilities at Hill, his air echelons far back on Leyte made final preparations for their move to Mindoro. In the meantime, mission escorts to Manila and Mindoro continued at a ragged pace as the older P-38s in the 49ers operations were beginning to show the inevitable wear and tear. Capt. Willie Drier's 8th Squadron Lockheed's were particularly well worn, but Walker informed the captain new aircraft were slated expressly for the Blacksheep. That also meant that Drier's outfit was first on the roster to move up to permanent residence at Hill Airfield at the moment the replacement aircraft arrived.

There was a command staff adjustment to take affect as well. Since the loss of Col. Morrissey in the Nashville incident on December 13th, Gerry Johnson was promoted to lieutenant colonel and began to take up the fallen colonel's duties as the 5 FC coordinator. Major Wally Jordan took over the group's Ops Exec slot and Capt. Willie Williams again took command of the Flying Knights.

## NEW YEARS DAY AT CLARK FIELD; JANUARY 1, 1945

While the last of the 49ers gear was crated up at Tacloban Field, the pilots were off once more for a raid on the Clark Field complex on Luzon. The weather was marginal at best enroute to the target and the high cover Lightning wing was scattered all over at 16,000 feet when it reached the overcast objective.

## LAST DEMON KILLS AT CLARK FIELD AND THEIR NEW ACE

Demon CO Capt. Ed Peck had dropped out in the early going and senior flight leader Lt. Joel Paris took the eleven 7th Squadron P-38s the rest of the way. At 1050 hours on the northern flank of the Liberator formation, a phosphorous aerial bomb detonated over the bombers, followed by the sighting of the first flight of five ZEROs which rose up in defense at Clark field. The five interceptors were swarmed upon by the Lightnings from several different units, but Paris was able to damaged one of the Mitsubishis in a long turning firing pass before it slipped away within the clouds. The Demons reassembled and continued the hunt.

Five minutes later, a second enemy flight estimated at fifteen ZEROs strong, drew near at 16,000 feet. Paris again led the attack and easily overtook one of the Mitsubishis from behind as the kokutai aimlessly scattered. In a long, slow turn, the ace fired from a 90 degree deflection and his eighth career victim burst into flames. Red Flight element leader 2Lt. Milden Mathre executed a similar attack on the enemy flight which resulted in his fifth and final career kill.

## LAST BLACKSHEEP KILLS AT CLARK FIELD AND THEIR NEW ACE

As the fight with the Demons ended high overhead, far across the American formation on the left flank was Capt. Drier's twelve Blacksheep who struggled to maintained their close cover position to the bombers. It was likewise just as difficult to keep their own wingmen in view. When the Liberators salvoed off their bomb load and turned for home, the Blacksheep White Flight quartet ran afoul of the cloud front and rose up for clearer air. One man separated and joined another flight, but Flt Ldr 2Lt. Irwin Dames, element leader 2Lt. Francis Hill and rookie wingman 2Lt. Eldon "Ellie" Brezier stayed together up to 16,000 feet. From the new vantage point, four OSCARs were seen south of Clark and Flt Ldr Dames called for the attack.

Diving down to 10,000 feet, Dames closed in on the trailing fourth element OSCAR and sent him on fire. As the victim tumbled down into the green fields below, the other OSCARs vanished in the overcast. The Blacksheep trio regrouped and headed off to re-join the bombers when 2Lt. Hill called out two more ZERO interceptors down through the clouds and headed their way. Hill rolled his P-38 over, dropped down behind the trailing element from high

*Joel Paris scored his eighth kill on New Year's Day, 1945, on the sweep of Clark Field.*

above and dead-astern. Hill fired and the enemy pilot immediately bailed out, confirming the lieutenant's fourth and last career kill.

Minutes later, the Americans were well on their way south when Blacksheep 2Lt. Nial Castle and wingman 2Lt. Wally Hickok at 8000 feet passed over a twin-engine NICK headed back for Clark Field. Using the clouds as cover, Castle wheeled about into the lower rear quarter against the mottled heavy fighter and pulled to within a hundred yards, then rose up and shot out the Nakajima's right engine. The stricken plane dropped off on its flaming wing and was last seen tumbling in a fiery cartwheel across the Luzon landscape. Just as Demon ace Mathre had done only minutes before, so it was that Nial Castle scored his fifth and final career victory to become the newest Blacksheep ace.

## SUEHR LOST ON THE WAY HOME; JANUARY 1, 1945

The weather only worsened as the Americans pushed out of the target area. The Demons intended to egress down the east coast of Luzon for Tacloban, but several of the elements were forced apart as the clouds closed in over the southern route. Some drifted west and opted for Mindoro.

Veteran Capt. Dick Suehr was leading White Flight whose two trailing wingmen had already separated from view during the fight. With rookie wingman 2Lt. Ralph Watson still in close formation at 13,000 feet, the captain was one of the last to leave the target, and chose the southern route for Tacloban. The White Flight pair became even further detached from the main force, and after 35 minutes, Seurh and Watson were completely enveloped in a clouded sky.

Suehr led Watson due east to make sure they were over broad Lamon Bay, then descended to zero altitude to find a safer southern route under the front. It was standard procedure, but the method failed for the veteran. The cloud ceiling was right down on the sea, and when Suehr tried to turn back, his left wingtip dragged through the waves. The big P-38 cartwheeled and sank out sight in the blink of an eye.

Watson orbited four times around the whirlpool marking the tragedy, but saw nothing. He noted the site as five miles off tiny Coringo Island, then opted for another tack. The rookie began a series a climbing left and right turns across a 150 degree heading.

*7 FS Milden Mathre (rt.) with his crewchief and their aircraft #21 "GOATNOSE" which bore a caricature of the new ace next to his five victory flags.*

After thirty minutes of flying on instruments, Ralph Watson broke into clear sky at 14,000 feet over San Miguel Bay, 100 miles southeast of Lamon Bay. At half past one, the weary flyer put his long range Lockheed down on Tacloban strip and told the story of veteran Dick Suehr, certainly lost to capricious fate.

## BLACKSHEEP FOR MINDORO; FIRST WEEK OF JANUARY, 1945

Missions continued despite the fitful weather. The Demons and Knights escorted the B-24s across the whole of central Luzon, even as far as Linguyan Bay, the prominent twenty-mile wide gulf on the east coast which was the next objective for Gen. MacArthur, but no enemy planes appeared.

On January 3rd, Capt. Drier's 8th Squadron had refit with the new issue of L-model Lightnings and saddled up for the last time at Tacloban. By late afternoon, all of the Blacksheep aircraft had been ferried into Hill Airfield. Drier's unit was reassigned to the strategic operations in Col. Wilson's 310 BW and continued flying missions without pause.

## DEMONS AND KNIGHTS MOVE IN AT HILL A/F

By the end of the first week in January, the Flying Knights and Screamin' Demons moved to San Jose airdrome complex as well. The Demons manned Elsmore Strip while the Knights moved into Murtha. The Tacloban Lightnings would likewise escort every type of aircraft to Mindoro, swelling the dispersal areas with a myriad fighters, medium bombers and transports.

## F/O CHAMBERS LOST; JANUARY 10, 1945

The circumstances for Capt. Williams war-weary Flying Knights only seemed to darken when a replacement pilot died at Hill Field on the 10th. On take off for the afternoon base patrol, F/O Walt Chambers, only with the Knights for two weeks, lost an engine and crashed off the end of the runway. As of that day, the 9th Squadron was down to twenty-three pilots and only sixteen P-38s.

The 5 AF community was truly stunned with the confirmation of Satan's Angels ace, Tommy McGuire, having been killed three days prior to Chambers. And to add to the bewilderment, the ace's fateful event had taken place far to the south on war-torn Negros Island, long since bypassed in the advance to Luzon. On January 12th, the Thirteenth AF lost its leading ace, Maj. Bob Westbrook. The twenty-two victory flyer was killed by groundfire at Kendari Island in the Celebes, even farther removed from the front.

McGuire was posthumously awarded the Congressional Medal of Honor and his memory soon became legendary, even within the ranks of veterans who had once barely tolerated the man's truly irascible demeanor. For the old hands in the 49ers who had seen too many good young men fall, they could only shake their heads and wondered at the senselessness of it all.

# 22

# THE FINAL PHILIPPINES CAMPAIGN

LtC. Walker's 49ers set up camp at Hill Airfield in the first week of January, 1945, and readily found the place to be a vast improvement over the past eight weeks of survival on Leyte. Despite intermittent rains, the new air field drained rather quickly and dried just as rapidly in the hot sun. If there had been shortages at Tacloban, their was a deluge of supplies at Hill. Lt. Jesse Pienezza, the Group Supply officer, found himself the recipient of bivouac gear including pre-assembled flooring palettes, electrical generators for individual tent lights, and complete facilities for the mess kitchens and laundries. There were even baseball gloves, bats, baseballs and basketballs. The Group eventually recovered its mobile camera shop, the old converted ammo trailer they had fit out at Tacloban. Demons 2Lt. Plichta, Sgts. Scheckel and Wycant, and Cpl. Ehrman would take over film processing for the entire group.

The only thing to have made Hill ideal would have been for the 49ers to receive a full compliment of new airplanes and pilots. Capt. Williams' Flying Knights were often down to only a dozen serviceable P-38s, and two dozen pilots on his flight roster. The P-38s in the 7th Squadron were equally combat worn. Only Capt. Drier's re-equipped Blacksheep were able to meet the demanding mission schedule early on, and hence, the 8th CO was able to transfer four of his flyers over to the Knights to bolster their ranks.

Col. Wilson's 310 BW strategic mission was certainly critical. The campaign for the capture of Luzon was well underway as Gen. MacArthur had his amphibious landing at Linguyan, the veritable

"back-door" to Manila, slated for January 9th. The 5 AF air transports barely arrived in time with 600 barrels of gasoline for Wilson's aircraft in the first week of the new year. On January 5th, a Linguyan bound service convoy to Kinkaid's 7th Fleet downloaded ten-thousand barrels of av-gas at the San Jose docks, literally pumping life into Wilson's gasping air units. By the second week of January, the 310 BW was back in full stride as it stepped up the interdiction on the Luzon rail lines and highways linking Linguyan and Manila.

Gen. Yamashita's Philippines forces had logistical nightmares beyond resolve. The Imperial high command, now realizing the gravity of the campaign, refused large scale reinforcements from beyond the Philippines. There was a diverse force of 90,000 infantry, 25,000 airmen and 20,000 Navy personnel on Luzon alone, yet there was no hope of bringing their combined strength to bear against MacArthur. Trapped in the two strangled garrisons at Linguyan and Manila, the Luzon force was likewise denied safe passage between the cities by marauding U.S. Navy and USAAF aircraft. By the time of the Linguyan landing, most of the Luzon garrisons had been abandoned with their men dispersed into the interior highlands.

## CHAMBERS KILLED IN HILL A/F LANDING; JANUARY 10, 1945

The 49ers support of the Luzon invasion got off on a bitter note. As part of the air cover for the voyage of the invasion fleet through the Sibuyan Sea, the Screamin' Demons provided flights throughout the day, but the afternoon mission went awry. Flight Officer Walt Chambers, a veteran who had survived the battle of Leyte, died when his P-38 fell inverted to the ground after engine failure on takeoff.

## ENEMY AIR FORCE GHOST

The enemy air force remaining on Luzon in the first week of the new year was a mere skeleton of an estimated seventy serviceable fighters and bombers. Imperial Philippines Commander Yamashita was thereafter instructed to commit those ravaged air units to kamikaze attacks on Allied shipping rather than squander them against the superior numbers of the airborne opponents. To that end, the Japanese pilots evaded the ever present American air patrols and continued to stage into the Clark Field facilities from the remote satellite fields in the north. Their divine mission was to waylay the American fleet, and not the Far East Air Force.

*The control tower at Hill Airfield, Mindoro. By the time the 49ers arrived, Hill was a thriving, well supplied USAAF community.*

*The terraced interior of Luzon, P.I., where the retreating enemy dug in for the final fight. Fighter-bomber missions to the Luzon targets were never referred to as a "milk-run," not even by the most senior pilots.*

*The mines of Baquio, Luzon, which became the fortified bastions for the Imperial soldiers who chose to fight to the death.*

As a result, the kamikazes raised considerable havoc with Kinkaid's 7th Fleet in the first stages of the Linguyan operations. To halt the dreaded airborne suicide attacks, the largest coordinated airborne operation of the Pacific war to date was convened as Kinkaid and Halsey combined their carrier forces with all available 5 AF groups. The Americans blanketed Luzon on January 7th and summarily crushed the remnant enemy air force. Thereafter, the Philippines air war came in snatches at remote locations.

On the 11th, the collapse of the JAAF was underscored by a fearful ten minute encounter where two P-51 reconnaissance pilots of 82nd TRS shot down a BETTY and nine TONY escorts over the Cagayan Valley. Wingman Lt. Paul Liscomb destroyed three fighters, while the element leader, Sqn CO Capt. Bill Shomo, destroyed the other six and the lone bomber. It was the single highest mission score by a 5th Fighter Command pilot in the war, and understandably, Shomo received the Medal of Honor for the feat.

Although the kamikaze threat from distant Okinawa and Formosa was still of substantial concern, the frequency of the attacks was pointedly reduced. Day after day, airborne contacts became a rarity.

## LAST SCREAMIN' DEMONS PHILIPPINES KILL; JANUARY 16, 1945

The escort missions over the foul weather continued for two weeks and they became so routine, the Lightning wing resorted to shooting up coastal targets and anything that moved on the mountain roads. During a routine VIP escort to Linguyan on the afternoon of the 16th, a Demon pilot would score the squadrons last victory in the Philippines campaign. Like so many other airmen, he would ultimately be tested not by his adversary, but by the cursed weather.

The Demons escort flight comprised four P-38s over a Navy PBY Catalina. The "Cat" cruised below the Demons near the sea while the Lightnings settled in at 8000 feet overhead. No sooner had they reached Linguyan, the Navy aircrew called off the sortie due to the deteriorating weather. The Demons signed off and turned back for Mindoro. They climbed up to 16,000 feet, and were just west of Manila Bay when the flight leader decided to look for a

clearer flight path at a lower altitude. The two lead aircraft dropped through the clouds, but soon radioed for the trailing pair to hold their position above the overcast.

The higher elements were veteran 2Lts. Al Meschino and Huie Manes, both of whom were well accustomed to flying in the Philippines environment. They circled for thirty minutes, then agreed to press on for Mindoro, confident that they would find a break in the cloud deck further south. They reached Balayan Bay on the north side of to the straits separating Luzon and Mindoro, and peered down through the cumulus to confirm their position before the seaward crossing. Just then, they caught sight of a lone, south-bound intruder estimated at five miles distance. Meschino and Manes did not hesitate and rolled to the attack.

Meschino got to the target first and found it to be a rust-colored JAKE seaplane, a pontoon equipped reconnaissance type. The lieutenant pulled out in front of the floatplane which was coasting along, 200 feet above the sea, and the enemy aviator seemed oblivious as the P-38 turned into him from head-on. Just as Meschino opened fire, the JAKE slid off in a flat turn, but the maneuver was not enough to avoid the point-blank volley. Dead at the stick, the enemy aviator crashed, but the JAKE did not burn. Meschino and Manes circled the site until the floatplane broke up and slipped beneath the waves.

Although the interception had lasted only seconds, when Meschino looked about to regain his bearing, the weather had already closed in and completely obscured the coastline. The two Demons rose back up to 12,000 feet, but the situation up there was just as bad. They took a heading due south and pressed on for another hour and half, but could not find an opening in the solid white blanket below.

Finally, darkness and spent fuel forced them into the gloomy overcast until they broke out over the west coast of Negros Island, 160 miles beyond their Mindoro destination. Manes, who had already had the dubious privilege of bailing out of a combat damaged P-38 back in the November, did not wish to experience that sensation again. He bellied his ship down in the shallows while Meschino opted for his parachute. Fortuitously, both men found each other on the beach, and they were later rescued by the Negros tribesmen. After two weeks, a Navy PBY was dispatched to pick up errant

Huie Manes and the last Demon pilot to score a kill in the Philippines, Al Meschino. They caught up with their squadron at Hill Airfield on January 31st.

## THE 49ERS LAST PHILIPPINES KILL; JANUARY 19, 1945

In the third week of January, the 49ers with their 310 BW cohorts were raiding the far reaches of Luzon. On the 19th, a morning strike against the satellite air strip at Guagua village only yielded a barrage of light anti-aircraft fire form the stranded airdrome gunners. Flying Knight 2Lt. Hal Strom had two fair sized holes put in his right wing, but he safely returned to Hill Field.

However, during the mid-day fighter sweep to the northwestern cape, the Flying Knights finally found an airborne target. Red Flight had pressed down to minimum altitude to hunt along the low hanging rain clouds just off shore. When they reached Banqui Bay, they saw a lone twin-engine Kugisho P1Y, code named FRANCES, skimming over the ocean's surface. One of the newer generation of bombers issued to the Imperial Navy, it was not heavily armed, but relied on speed for its defense. The FRANCES broke for the protection of the squall line, but eager newcomer 2Lts. Troy Smith and John Forgey quickly disproved the Kugisho concept of fast bombers having no defensive armament. They easily overtook the dark green machine and Forgey fired, then Smith. Finally, Forgey delivered the coup de grace and the FRANCES tumbled into the gulf, marking the last Flying Knights victory, as well as the final 49ers aerial kill, in the Philippines theater.

## TESTING THE PATH TO CHINA; JANUARY 19, 1945

The 49ers continued to induct new pilots and ground personnel into the Mindoro camps in preparation for the move to Luzon. By the fourth week of January, all three of the squadrons were re-equipped with late model P-38s, bring their serviceability to four full flights per unit. Commensurate with the increased fighter strength, Gen. Kenney expanded the scope of operations beyond the Philippines. The 86th Fighter Wing organization moved up from Biak to deal specifically with the enemy north and west of the Luzon operations.

To intervene against the forces in China, 5 FC coordinator LtC. Johnson devised a bold sweep of the enemy airfields on the south coast at Hong Kong. The colonel held his mission briefing on the night of the 18th and the 49ers operations officers were stunned when the flight charts of the South China Sea were displayed. The flight line led straight to Hong Kong and the route was dotted with the location of rescue submarines and PBY positions.

On the morning of the 19th, Johnson lifted off from Hill Airfield in the lead of the 49ers, each squadron having put up a maximum effort of sixteen aircraft each. But fifteen minutes into the mission, pre-strike reconnaissance reported the sea route was weathered in. The entire 49ers formation diverted back to the Luzon coast to hit their secondary targets. Thereafter, the China venture was postponed until the landings on Luzon were completed. In the interim, Halsey's 3rd Fleet again struck Formosa and the China coastal targets through the 21st.

## PUSH FOR MANILA

With Halsey's fleet in the South China Sea and the noticeable pause in enemy air raids from the north, MacArthur struck out to take Manila. Gen. Kruger's 6th Army began to push south out in two columns from Linguyan as early as the 17th. Enemy resistance immediately stiffened as the American infantry closed in on the Clark Field area, and once more, the 49ers were called back over the western coastal highlands and the interior valley highway in close support. For three day running, Col. Walker's people maintained a mission schedule which would yield three sorties per day in each squadron, despite the intermittent rains. The Demons, Blacksheep and Knights, in company to the deadly P-47 dive-bombers, were so efficient at cutting highways, dropping bridges and annihilating rolling stock that Gen. Kruger declared there was not a single piece of enemy equipment worth commandeering. The general requested that the Hill pilots only hit moving trains and to leave his infantry, "a bridge or two on the road to Manila."

On January 19th, MacArthur put a second landing ashore at San Antonio on the west coast, sixty miles north of Manila Bay. The flanking divisions immediately pushed inland over the pass through the coastal hills to link up with Kruger's main force. Yamashita's western forces were cut in half, and for two weeks, they Americans drove the enemy survivors deeper into the caves of the west coast range, or into the headlong retreat into the coastal forests of the east coast. By the first week in February, Kruger's left flank column would advanced across the interior, cutting off the route to the Cagayan Valley in the north.

## PATH TO FORMOSA; JANUARY 21-23, 1945

Surveillance of the Formosa airdromes as of mid January provided an estimate of six-hundred mixed types of aircraft, predominantly on the fields on the west side of the island. The 49ers became an integral part of destroying the Formosa air arm as Col. Johnson formulated another elaborate Fighter Command epic. On January 21st, the 86 FW executed a 1400-mile round trip sweep to Choso airdrome, one of the major landing field in southern Formosa, but the 49ers and 8th Groups did not find airborne targets. Neither did they make contact on the 22nd at Takao airdrome, nor on the repeat mission there the next day. Despite the logistical hardships, the dual task of escorts to Formosa and the tactical missions against Luzon became the routine for the Linguyan Lightning groups for the duration of the Philippines campaign.

Thus, while part of the Lightning force rotated in the hunt over distant Formosa, the bulk of the tactical air arm swung back over the Luzon objective. After five continuous days of close aerial support, on the January 26th, Gen. Kruger's army overran the vast airdrome of Clark Field. The army commander informed Gen. Kenney that no one could appreciate the total devastation there until seen first hand. There were wrecked aircraft everywhere and every building had been gutted.

## 2LT. IVES LOST STRAFING LAOAG A/D; JANUARY 27, 1945

The weary pace of tactical missions took the 7 FS directly up the western coastline from Linguyan, 150 miles north to the battered airdrome at Laoag village. Once a principle satellite field on the route from Formosa to Clark Field for the Leyte campaign, abandoned Laoag was manned by the stranded JAAF aircrews who could still deliver an effective, light caliber barrage during an air attack. On the raid of January 27th, several buildings were set on fire which was a meager exchange for the loss of 2Lt. Epke Ives. His smoking P-38 crashed at sea, two-hundred yards off the enemy strip. Subsequent search flights did not find any sign of him. Like so many flyer down at sea, Epke Ives vanished.

## 8 FS VETERAN HILL KILLED AT NASUGBU; JANUARY 31, 1945

On January 31st, the third amphibious landing in the Luzon invasion went ashore on the broad peninsula south of Manila Bay at the village of Nasugbu, cutting off the escape route to the south. The 49ers joined in the air cover directly over the troops who quickly advanced inland and encountered heavy resistance just east of the town.

LtC. Walker's Lightnings made their first sortie at dawn's light, each P-38 hefting a pair of "half-tonners" the 130 miles to the beachhead. After a pilot dropped his ton of ordinance which readily flattened the village, the 49ers continued on directly over the infantry and strafed the highway leading away from the beachhead.

Blacksheep Flt Ldr Lt. Tom Holstein and wingman Lt. Francis Hill had come down through their third firing pass against an enemy platoon caught on the road way, and there was only token return fire from the frightened troops. Whether Hill was hit by an errant round, or made an error in judging the rugged terrain, Holstein was stunned to see his good friend's P-38 suddenly plunge without warning into the forest. A huge explosion rose above the trees, marking the fatal crash site of veteran Francis Hill. Capt. Drier and the entire 49ers staff were deeply saddened by the loss of such a well loved, capable young man.

Back at Hill Field, the Flying Knights nearly lost one of their men when his P-38 stalled out after engine failure during takeoff. Luckily, 2Lt. Paul Nahnibidah's Lightning was fitted for patrol and not armed with bombs. He escaped from the burning wreckage with minor burns and contusions.

## BACK UNDER ONE COMMAND AT HILL Airfield; FEBRUARY 1, 1945

As of February 1st, Gen. Kenney transferred his 308 BW tactical organization from Tacloban to Hill Airfield. Logically, the strategic 310 BW team moved up to the new facilities being constructed at the advanced Linguyan air strips. LtC. George Walker's 49ers were reinstated in the 308th wing organization, yet for a brief period, would still operating in the strategic 86th Fighter Wing at Hill.

Despite the politics at the command level, the Demons, Blacksheep and Knights pressed on in the round-robin of mission rotations. As the enemy retreated deeper into the enclaves of Philippines, a 49ers pilot rarely ever knew whether he would be strafing the enemy troops on Luzon or sweeping the airdromes on the west coast of Formosa.

## THE JAPANESE LUZON RETREAT; FEBRUARY, 1945

On the 14th, a fourth amphibious landing assaulted Manila Bay and the island fortress of Corrigador lying at entrance to the gulf. The pursuit of the remnant Imperial army soon ground to a crawl as the refugees barricaded themselves in numerous defensive pockets.

There would eventually be four principle defensive strongholds halting the American advances across Luzon. The largest force was the group which escaped to the northeast into the broad central flood plain of the Cagayan valley. Those troops dug in among the old mining camps on the valley's western slopes. A second rear-guard position was based in the Balete Pass and the Villa Verde Trail highlands which crossed over the hills fifty miles due east of Linguyan. Both the pass and the trail were staunchly defended to prevent Kruger's forces from overrunning the refugees fleeing into the Cagayan interior.

Further south, the third pocket was the Manila defenders who had withdrawn to the forested hills surrounding the big lake of south-central Luzon, Laguna De Bay. The escapees were particularly well entrenched in the hills near Ipo Dam, twenty miles north of the embattled capitol city. A fourth remote group had retreated further south, deep into the rugged coastal hills due east of the lake.

Despite the numerous captured roads and railways, the rainy season did not readily facilitate Gen. Kruger's ground offensive against Yamashita's fragmented command. Due to their restricted mobility and the high casualty predictions of an extended highlands campaign, MacArthur opted for Kenney's air force as the most reliable tactical weapon to keep his infantry losses to an absolute minimum.

## ISOLATING FORMOSA

The American Chiefs of Staff had originally planned to take Formosa following the capitulation of Luzon. The 240 mile-long island laying only 800 miles southwest of the Japanese home islands was a logical base for future B-29 operations, but the late war advances in the central Pacific and the Philippines greatly advanced the final plan to invade Japan proper, projected for October of 1945.

The JCS had first to consider the resolution of the Japanese summer offensive of 1944 in southern China. Despite the Allied setback there, the front stabilized by the end of the year while the Empire mainland subsequently came under ever increasing attacks of the B-29s in October, operating from the new bases in the Marianna Islands. The JCS concluded an air campaign by the China-based 14 AF, plus the presence of Halsey's carriers and the FEAF in the northern Philippines would neutralize the remnant China forces and prevent their organized retreat to Formosa. Nimitz' capture of Iwo Jima on February 19th, only eight-hundred miles from the Empire's mainland, forever negated the invasion of Formosa.

*Throughout the Pacific, many a downed flyer was rescued by the brave liaison pilots in the rugged L-5 Stinson. Like this A/C flown in the western New Guinea campaign, several Stinsons were available at Hill and Linguyan.*

## FRANTIC FEBRUARY FOR THE 49ERS

The targets on Formosa, called Japan's "natural aircraft carrier", would be the twenty-four principle airdromes, eighteen of which were located on the western coastal plain, plus the twenty-odd satellite landing fields. There were targets of strategic importance as well, particularly the sugar refineries which produced alcohol-based synthetic fuel.

In the expanded operations in February of 1945, the 49ers believed Formosa was their own personal hunting ground. Yet, in ten weeks of harassing the heavily defended airdromes, only a single aerial kill by a 49er would be claimed. Despite the taxing execution of strategic missions to Formosa intermixed with the tactical air war against Luzon, the sorties accumulated with of minimum of losses for LtC. Walker's fighter group.

## 2LT. WHITE DOWN IN CAGAYAN VALLEY; FEBRUARY 1, 1945

The Demons were back over Cagayan Valley on the 1st, hitting the satellite airdrome at Tuguegarao. The flights again braved the wild volleys of machine gun fire from the JAAF refugees, and again, another Demon pilot fell out of the air. Second Lt. Perry White drifted beyond the airdrome to the south with a smoking left engine and bellied in near a stand of trees. The lieutenant was last seen in full stride, headed for the forest.

Fleet-footed White was found within minutes by local Volunteer Guards, and for a week, he remained in their care. He was eventually delivered to the American infantry who in turn took him back to Linguyan. Nineteen days after his crash landing at Tuguegarao, he was the glad passenger aboard an Army L-5 liaison plane, bound for Hill Field.

Ironically, the day after White had gone down, CO Ed Peck was desperately trying to confirm word of the lieutenant's survival, only to be stunned by the surprise appearance of missing veteran Capt. Dick Seurh, who walked unannounced into the Operations shack at Hill Field. Returned after thirty-three days of absence, Seurh

told how he had miraculously survived his New Year's Day crash at sea, his rescue, and subsequent escape route with the V.C. eastward to Samar, then at last to Tacloban. Seurh reassured Peck that White would be rescued by the trusted Volunteer Guards of Cagayan Valley.

## FORGEY LOST DURING THE FALL OF MANILA; FEBRUARY 1, 1945

The battle raged on and the 49ers descended upon the Manila defenders for three straight days. Fate overtook the Flying Knights again with the sad loss during the intense operations on February 1st. Newcomer 2Lt. John Forgey, the fellow who had shot down the last 49ers kill over Luzon just ten days before, failed his landing at Hill Field. He radioed his ship had been hit by ground fire over the highway north of Manila, but declared he would be able to make the return flight. Tragically, his damaged aircraft stalled out in the approach pattern at Hill, taking the lieutenant down in a mangled crash. John Forgey's body was recovered and interred at the American cemetery at San Jose. Two days after Forgey died, American infantry were fighting in the streets of Manila.

## DEFENDING THE WEST FLANK; FEBRUARY 13-18, 1945

The Lightnings were immediately turned about to defend the west flank of the Luzon campaign when intelligence reports warned of a Imperial surface convoy seen steaming east of Singapore. From February 13th through the 18th, the 49ers roamed throughout the western Philippines islands, but the ships were never found. Even the 9th Squadron sweep on the 18th over 750 miles to Jesselton airdrome on the west coast of Borneo did not yield a single target, but neither were there any 49er losses.

## INADVERTENT FIRST LANDING ON LUZON; FEBRUARY 16, 1945

The only 49ers mishap during the long range searches to the west did not occur at sea, but rather, over Luzon in the final push into Manila proper. On a ground support mission at San Mateo village, just a few miles north of the capitol, Blacksheep Lt. Bob Sweeney was forced down in an emergency landing, right in the midst of the infantry advance.

Sweeney had ventured too low over the enemy positions and groundfire struck his windshield, showering him with plexiglass shards and momentarily stunning him. Uncertain of the overall damages to his P-38, Sweeney chose to land at the emergency strip established in the northern suburb of Quezon City. An Army mobile air controller who was set up in a jeep on the main highway, brought Sweeney down for a safe landing on a recently secured, broad boulevard, inadvertently making the lieutenant the first 49er to land on Luzon. After receiving first aide from an infantry medic, the lieutenant satisfied himself that the damage to his Lightning was minimal, and took off for an uneventful return to Hill Field.

*Healed Blacksheep Bob Aschenbrener rejoined the 49ers at Mindoro and assumed temporary command of the 7 FS. He would join the 49ers HQ staff later at Linguyan.*

## LT. FAIRBANKS LOST IN THE LUZON STRAITS; FEBRUARY 17, 1945

The Screamin' Demons lost another man to the weather over the Luzon Straits on the 17th. Lt. Leo Fairbanks had made the flight half way home from Formosa when his Lightning lost power. He descended near Itbayat Island, one of the small, northern most rocky isles in the midst of the hazy Luzon Straits.

While the main force pushed on for Hill Field, Ops Exec Lt. Jim Atkinson and wingman Lt. Henderson remained over the area to record an accurate location of Fairbanks' bailout, but they quickly lost contact as weather conditions worsened over the straits. The two searchers fortunately diverted safely to the new airstrip at Linguyan. The next day, Atkinson and Henderson returned to the straits, but a sweep of Itbayat and the immediately area yielded nothing. Leo Fairbanks had vanished forever. The only good news from Linguyan for veteran CO Ed Peck was that Lt. White, missing since February 1st, was safe and would be home the next day.

*The 49ers sign which survived Dobodura, Gusap, Hollandia, Biak and Tacloban. Its last station was Linguyan.*

## SHIFT IN COMMAND AND MOBILIZING FOR LINGUYAN

As of the third week in February, the 49ers again made changes in the squadron commands. Resilient Ed Peck, the man who had served the longest in command of the Screamin' Demons, was promoted to the rank of major and assigned as the Group Ops Executive. Capt. Bob Aschenbrener was fully recovered from his back injury and relinquished his 8th Squadron duties to command of the Screamin' Demons.

The Flying Knights CO Willie Williams was relieved from combat duty and posted for a long deserved furlough back to the States. Newly arrived ETO combat veteran, Capt. John Petrovich, took up the 9th Squadron command, and immediately had to attend to the distasteful review of a pair of deaths.

## THORSON AND KINSMAN DEAD AT SILAY A/D; FEBRUARY 19, 1945

The wide ranging Flying Knights were off again on the 19th with a four-ship sweep over the rear lines. There was an intelligence report of enemy aircraft seen hidden in the trees at Silay airdrome back on Negros Island, the very site of ace McGuire's demise Lt. Noah Williams' flight was sent to eradicate the threat. Always a dangerous target, the bypassed airdrome proved fatal for two of the rookie wingmen.

Flight Ldr Williams with rookie 2Lts. John Kinsman, element leader Wendell Tiffany and Hal Thorson arrived in good order over Silay, but found the airfield was definitely vacant. When they preceded two abreast to strafe the hanger area and the tree line, they were answered with a single barrage of light caliber groundfire. Trailing element Thorson was killed instantly and his P-38 slammed down in flames along side the red earthen runway.

Flight Ldr Williams sped back over the field and peered down at the Thorson's burning wreck when wingman Kinsman signalled he had also been hit and his Lockheed was loosing power. The Knights trio headed for the beach, but Kinsman's riddled ship gave out. The lieutenant hopelessly bailed out at minimum altitude, much too low for his chute to fully deploy. John Kinsman's body was later found by the Negros tribesmen, not far from the burned out wreckage of his plane.

## DEMONS BACK TO CEBU; FEBRUARY 22, 1945

Three days after the Knights' disastrous mission over the rear lines, it was the Demons turn, but they fared much better. The 7th Squadron flew support to the infantry mopping up the last of the enemy camps on northern Cebu, when 2Lt. Eldon Breazier's P-38 was hit by the rifle fire of the trapped Imperial soldiers. Fortunately for the lieutenant, he was able to land on the capture airfield at Tuberan village. Flight leader Lt. Jim Frank followed the damaged Lockheed down, landed and surveyed the damage, then returned to Hill Field with a list of parts for the stranded flyer's P-38. A cargo flight took a ground crew back to Cebu who repaired the P-38 and Breazier was able to fly back to Hill on the 28th.

*Brigadier General Paul Wurtsmith in his new roll as commander of the 13 AF. He would receive his second star before the war ended. Like so many flying officers, he was killed after the hostilities in a peacetime flying accident.*

*Brigadier General Freddie Smith returned from his year of attached duty at the Pentagon and relieved Wurtsmith as leader of 5 FC.*

## 49ERS TO LINGUYAN; FEBRUARY 25-28, 1945

Errant Eldon Breazier arrived back at Hill Field in time to join his Demons squadron mates in the mobilization for Linguyan. The ground echelons of the Blacksheep had already been airlifted north on the 25th, followed soon thereafter by their pilots and the P-38s. The Demons followed on the 26th and the Flying Knights followed the day after. Once the 49ers were at the huge Linguyan airfield complex, LtC. Johnson immediately briefed them for another maximum effort back to Formosa. The Group flew its first Linguyan-based sortie on February 28th.

## PREPARING FOR THE GREATEST INVASION OF ALL; MARCH, 1945

In the first week of March at Gen. MacArthur's new HQ at Linguyan, a realignment of the SW Pacific forces took affect. Paul Wurtsmith relinquished his Fifth Fighter Command to B.Gen. Frederick "Freddie" Smith, the former chief of staff to Kenney who had just returned from his extended "on-loan" tour with the Chief of Staff in the States. Smith was well liked by all of the old hands now seated in the various staff positions of the 5 AF. His inheritance of the Fighter Command had long been anticipated.

As for Paul Wurtsmith, he was awarded his second star, and effective March 1st, Major General Wurtsmith took command of the 13 AF. Likewise, 49ers veteran and organization wizard, Don "Fighter Hutch" Hutchinson, became the only other 49ers officer in the war years to receive congressional approval for the rank of general. Gen. Hutchinson was Kenney's personal choice for his new Chief of Staff for the Far East Air Force.

The induction of the 49ers ground and air echelons into the Linguyan facilities was an awkward transition for the jungle war veterans. The whole sense of the Luzon super-base was that of authority and power. The 49ers had never seen such a concentration of men and supplies, even the veterans of the Nadzab-Gusap era.

Linguyan was literally a super-base compared to the rag-tag coral gravel airstrips of the past. The runways were longer than any previous airstrips and there was actual concrete poured in the re-vetment parking areas. The bivouac area was a well supplied military camp with fully fitted quarters, even for the enlisted. For three-hundred dollars in the right hands, a fellow could secure residence in one of the nicer locations adjacent to the long, white sand beach.

In very short time, the new 49ers residents would be required to draw regulation uniforms from the base supply and would even be subject to routine inspections of their quarters. Many of officers and NCOs of the various field services were professional soldiers since before the war. For the first time, the Demons, Blacksheep and Flying Knights were in the presence of an army that was equipped to win the war, not just hold newly gained ground.

## TACTICAL AGAINST FORMOSA; MARCH 2-6, 1945

Although the 49ers had only been in Linguyan a week, the missions seemed to take on a more urgent sense. There was not a break in the mission schedule, but only a concerted effort to end the enemy resistance in the hills to the east. There was now enough heavy ordinance to arm all of the 49ers elements going on tactical strikes.

The P-38s soon began carrying one-thousand pounders to distant Formosa, particularly concentrating on the airdrome at Koshun on the southern cape and railroad yards at Bozan, twenty miles up the west coast. The missions were immensely successful as 5 FC contributed to the mass destruction of the rail system, and particularly the enemy air fields where a myriad of war planes were caught on the ground. Post-strike reconnaissance estimated that the late-January count of 600 enemy aircraft had nearly been cut in half as of mid-March.

The series of 49ers missions were marred only by the lost of two aircraft which crashed after returning to Linguyan on March 5th. Demons 2Lts. Jim White and Bill Minto were both hit by groundfire at Bozan, and both limped all the way back to Linguyan in an attempt to belly in on the crash strip. White succeeded, but Bill Minto suffered a jolting crack-up, resulting in a multitude of bruises and a slight fracture of his right leg. Both Lockheeds were written off, but immediately replaced from the well stocked service squadron pool.

*The 49ers bivouac at Linguyan in 1945. As the European war wore down through April, materials and food supplies poured into the Philippines camp like never before.*

## AIR BATTLE OVER HAINAN; MARCH 6, 1945

After the many weeks of fighter sweeps over Luzon and Formosa without any airborne sightings, the 49ers finally found the Japanese air force far to the west over the South China Sea on the great island of Hainan. The predominantly oblong island, one-hundred and fifty miles in its widest expanse from east to west, was occupied by a sizable enemy garrison which included the well defended airdrome at Samah on the south shore. To eradicate the JNAF threat to Allied shipping in the South China Sea, a massive formation of B-25 Mitchell strafers was sent to Samah on March 6th. The Demons were tapped for the escort to the target proper while the Blacksheep were assigned to cover the strafers' withdrawal.

At 0845, the Demons left Linguyan in close support to the three groups of B-25 gunships. Forty-five minutes later, the Blacksheep followed. At 1300 hours, the main strike force team drew down on the cloud dotted Hainan coastline and wheeled inland west of the airfield target. Even though the Lightnings were directly over the low flying Mitchells, the haze restricted visual contact with the leading strafers which were nearly five miles ahead.

## IT BEGAN WITH THE DEMONS OF RED FLIGHT

The escorts were led by veteran Capt. Fred Dick with his three Red Flight wingmen at 4000 feet of altitude, at the front of the formation. As the bombers skimmed ever lower in the mad dash across the west perimeter of the airdrome, Dick called out two dark green ZEROs closing in against the hazy sky at a slightly lower altitude. Dick ordered "tanks off", and nosed downward for the kill.

Just five miles northwest of the enemy runway, Capt. Dick scored the first kill of the mission from head-on. The lead ZERO element broke to its right, but was clobbered by Dick's first burst of fire. Red Flight wingman 2Lt. Sisson saw the stricken ZERO roll inverted and its pilot fall free to deploy his chute. Seconds later, Red element leader Lt. Bill Bauer and wingman 2Lt. Dewey Renick, Jr., opened fire on the trailing ZERO which had broken off in the opposite direction. Bauer drifted wide in the high speed turn to the right, but Renick matched the ZERO's turn until they were nose to nose again. Renick laid in a volley which gutted the Mitsubishi's engine and that aviator, too, dropped away in his parachute.

Capt. Dick, meanwhile, sustained the engagement for another go-around and in his third head-on pass, hit his second victim of

*P-38L s.n. 44-23375 A/C #14 in the markings of the Screamin' Demons in the Linguyan era. It sits high on its gear due to empty fuel cells. All such A/C in the Philippines operations were flown by any number of pilots, and few pilots remember a specific crewchief.*

*(Lt.-rt.) Capts. Fred Dick, Jim Keck and Dick Gachan at Linguyan not long after the March 6th Hainan escort mission when Dick became the last Screamin' Demon ace of the war.*

the mission. The ZERO disintegrated in a huge fireball, a fitting way of heralding the fifth and final victory of the captain's career. Fred Dick, the newest Demon ace, broke away to retake his position over the departing Mitchells.

When Dick drew closer to the retreating first wave, he thought he had found a JNAF twin-engine, single tailed heavy fighter in pursuit, but closer investigation found it was a Mitchell straggler with half of one of its' twin-tail surfaces shot away. The captain would later debrief to the staff at Linguyan that Samah was much too tough a target for one Lightning squadron alone to adequately cover.

## DEMONS OF GREEN FLIGHT WERE NEXT

In trail to Blue Flight and six-thousand feet higher was the three-some of Green Flight, led by newcomer Capt. Dwight Henderson. His wingman was Capt. Dick Ganchan, attached from Fighter Command, who in turn was covered by veteran wingman Lt. Bill Fernandez. They were only a minute's flight time from the scene of the first two kills and were on their way down when Henderson caught sight of two more ZEROs closing in from the east at 8000 feet. The lead dark-green interceptor had just entered into a right

*7 FS Flt Ldr Paris went all the way to Hainan Island on March 6th to get his ninth career kill.*

turn as Henderson closed in to within one-hundred yards and punched his gun button. The Mitsubishi's canopy exploded and long streamers of brilliant red flame poured from the fighter which then nosed straight down to explode on the side of a hill, just north of the enemy airfield.

Green Flight regrouped and pushed on pass the airdrome where rolling smoke clouds began to rise into the overcast. As the Green trio broke out over the shore line, they saw numerous barges anchored near the shore and then passed within range of the enemy destroyers lying in deeper water. Anti-aircraft fire rose from the ships in a variety of calibers, and it was far too accurate for Henderson, Ganchan or Fernandez to think about a second pass over the airdrome.

## IT ENDED WITH THE DEMONS OF BLUE FLIGHT

Meanwhile, Capt. Joel Paris had stayed at 8000 feet with his Blue Flight rookie wingman 2Lt. Ralph Oxford, veteran 2Lts. George Spruill and tail-end Al Meschino. When the signal of the first engagement reached them, they were in the proximity of the third wave of strafers, still ten miles from the airdrome which had been well set ablaze by the preceding Mitchells.

Oxford and Spruill both momentarily fell behind with hung-up belly tanks. Spruill rocked his big fighter, but the tanks hung tight, so he gave up on the procedure and throttled forward, anyway. Oxford shook his plane violently one last time to free his clinging drop tanks, and once they fell free, he was finally able to follow the veterans. Only seconds behind in the swirling haze, Oxford unfortunately received a rather unnerving introduction to combat maneuvering from a lone ZERO which suddenly dropped in directly behind him.

All three veterans wheeled hard about to answer Oxford's distress call, and as the rookie broke away, Paris pushed his GEORGIA BELLE beneath Oxford's line of flight to pass directly under the attacker. The maneuver gave the BELLE ample speed to enter into a powerful zoom-climb, bringing the Blue Flt Ldr ace into point-blank range beneath the ZERO. Paris opened fire and blew away the engine cowling of the enemy fighter which would fall on the north side of the airdrome, marking his ninth and final career kill.

The most unfortunate fellow in Blue Flight turned out to be veteran Meschino. He got caught in a wild turning fight against three other ZEROs, and though he shot one of them down, one of the others shot out his left supercharger in return. Meschino was skilled enough to regain control of his damaged Lockheed and exited the area. Over the shoreline, he flew one full circle around a last attacker and finally broke off to find Red Flight for the trip home.

## LAST SCREAMIN' DEMONS VICTORY
## OF THE WAR - #178

Simultaneously, Blue element leader Spruill completed his counter-turn to the left and pulled his guns across the path of another ZERO wingman who entered the scene from above. As the interloper drew within range, Spruill, still carrying his belly tanks, snap-rolled to the left in a high-angle wingover, placing him above his target. He instantly came down in a perpendicular deflection against the unsuspecting victim and fired.

The first burst of .50 caliber explosive rounds sparkled all about the ZERO's long canopy and black cowling. It's prop wind-milled, then quit completely. Spruill watched as the ZERO nosed over and plunged toward the shoreline, not showing any outward sign of damage. But the kokutai man was obviously dead at the stick, for the stricken aircraft went straight in and exploded, just off the end of the Samah runway. There on the beach lay the burning wreckage of George Spruill's one and only career kill. It would eventually be confirmed as aerial victory number 178, the last enemy plane to be shot down by the Screamin' Demons in the war.

When the American bombers signalled that their last elements had cleared the beachfront, Capt. Dick signalled the Lightnings to withdraw to their designated rendezvous point. It was 1330 hours, and they still had 750 miles of ocean to navigate. None the less, Lt. Hal Harris' White Flight not only failed to find the hazy target, they subsequently missed the regrouping to the east and had to fly back home, completely separated from the others. White Flight landed with fuel in their tanks and all of their ammo still in the gunbays. In contrast, Blue Flight's Spruill had his radio go dead en route to the rendezvous and had to settle on a lone crossing. He arrived over Linguyan with empty guns and dry fuel tanks, which negated the chance of a fire as his P-38 safely belly landed on the perimeter of the field.

## AND IT ENDED WITH THE BLACKSHEEP RED FLIGHT

The March 6th fight actually ended for the 49ers far out to sea, long after the strike force had departed. Just as LtC. Gerry Johnson had originally planned, the Blacksheep egress cover flight was orbiting twenty miles east of the target when a Navy PBM rescue plane signalled it was going to venture nearer the target in response to the distress call of a battle-damaged Mitchell. The scud over the target had by then rolled out to sea which made both radio and visual contact nearly impossible, yet, Flt Ldr 2Lt. Irwin Dames and wingman 2Lt. Jack Page set off to the west, intent to provide close support for the rescue attempt.

When Dames and Page approached Samah at 1345 hours, they studied the deathly still column of brownish-grey smoke which had risen out of the coastal overcast, only to be suddenly averted by a great splash which erupted from the sea some distance ahead. They thought it was possibly the crash of the damaged B-25, however, closer investigation of the ocean surface from 1500 feet revealed nothing. Nor was the PBM any longer in radio contact. After weighing their options, the Blacksheep pilots agreed to stay in the area as long as their fuel would last.

They rose back up to 5000 feet, and five minutes later, they crossed the flight path of a lone ZERO coursing for Hainan. After a brief chase, Page finally dropped in behind the interceptor and shot it down. As the smoking plane drifted downward, the pilot jumped free in his parachute, and apparently, landed in good order. He dropped into the water a short distance away from his fighter which struck the sea in a tremendous explosion and cloud of spray. Dames and Page patrolled for twenty minutes more, then turned for Linguyan and landed there at a quartet past five.

*8 FS mission briefing for another strike to central Luzon. Note the variety of flight gear and suits of these Blacksheep pilots. Many of the replacement flyers were highly skilled aviators with high flight hours in cadet training, making the 49ers one of the most skillful fighter units despite so few veterans in their ranks.*

## LUZON FIRES; MARCH, 1945

While the strategic missions played out to the north and west, the tactical missions of the 49ers over Luzon took on an even greater fury with a broad adaptation of napalm strikes against the entrenched enemy. The horrible fire bombs were simply a 150-gallon Lockheed drop tank that the ordinance people fit with a standard bomb tailfin, and an impact detonator to ignite the 140 gallons of the jellied-gasoline within. It was necessary to leave a bit of air-space to allow for some condensation in the hot sun.

Napalm had long been used as a tactical weapon in the Philippine theater, but as of the first week in March, the fighter-bomber sorties were regularly attended by P-38 and P-47 elements armed with the home-made weapons. The targets north and east of the newly captured capitol were saturated with napalm, sortie after sortie, setting fires which raged into the night. American infantry in the coastal hills mopped up the chard forest fortifications which wreaked of the pungent, petroleum fumes.

*Veteran 49er Gerry Johnson temporarily assumed the command of the Group at Linguyan in March 1945 until another lieutenant colonel was in residence.*

*Still carrying two tallies more than officially confirmed, Johnson put his 23 kill flags on "BARBARA" named for his Oregon sweetheart who became his wife on his 1944 furlough. The 23rd victory came over Hong Kong on April 1st, the same mission where Walt Koby shot down the last Flying Knight victory of the war.*

## ANOTHER COMMAND CHANGE

In the second week of March, the 49ers once again realigned their command. LtC. George Walker had presided over the most prolific rate of aerial victories in the 49ers combat history which accounted for 162 confirmed kills in the Philippines operations, and which would yield an unprecedented fourth Distinguished Unit Citation. Now it was time to move on in the growing FEAF which was proportionately enlarging its command staff. The annihilation of the enemy air force and the influx of more qualified combat pilots now in residence at Linguyan precluded any chances of the colonel scoring again in aerial combat. As a senior officer with keen political sense and a stellar combat record, George Walker wisely opted for a promotion to the 308th Bomb Wing staff.

On March 10th, Walker handed over his victorious group to the veteran LtC. Gerry Johnson. Likewise at that time, Johnson had his elaborate fighter sweeps for the China coast reinstated at 5 FC operations. In the lead of the 49ers as their commander for the first time, Johnson took his Lightnings on a extended sweep of the China coast over a two-hundred mile-long area, just east of Hong Kong, but they found nothing.

## THE LAST BLACKSHEEP KILL; MARCH 15, 1945

The 49ers continued to hunt along the China coast from Hong Kong to the shores of the Formosa Straits for five more days, when on the 15th, the Blacksheep finally found a pair of enemy fighters in the air. There would only be one firing pass made by the Lightnings and only one of the enemy planes would fall.

Capt. Willie Drier, the seasoned commander of the 8th Squadron, was in the lead of four other Blacksheep in escort to a U.S. Navy PB4Y flyingboat sent on a rescue mission to the western shoreline of the Formosa Straits. The P-38s were at 10,000 feet, thirty-five miles south of the rendezvous point at tiny Namoa Island, when one of Drier's trailing elements called in a single enemy plane which suddenly appeared out of the billowing clouds behind the Blacksheep flight.

Capt. Drier quickly glanced to the rear and caught sight of the lone Ki-44 TOJO, two-thousand feet below and headed for the mainland. With rookie wingman 2Lt. Jim Ward in attack position, the captain ordered the other three elements to hold in high cover, then peeled off into a split-S dive after the dark-green Nakajima. As Drier and Ward descended through a full turn, another trailing sentai wingman broke into the clear, directly in Drier's path.

Drier snapped off a shot at the lead TOJO which knocked pieces from its rear fuselage. When the sentai leader violently rolled aside, Drier quickly adjusted his aim and fired on the trailing Ki-44. The second victim immediately broke down and away, only to fly straight through Ward's descent path and the rookie opened fire from dead astern. Drier was about to re-engage, but realized Ward's burst was on the mark. The TOJO wingman momentarily pulled out of his dive, then rolled again for the last time, and plunged into the sea. Ward seriously considered pressing straight ahead and picking off the lead target as well, but at the last instant, his exuberance was overcome by the recollection of the adamant veterans who counselled, "always rejoin with your wingman after your attack."

The lieutenant pulled his P-38 "RHAPSODY IN BLUE" up into a zoom climb and immediately found Drier, but when he looked down, Ward realized the other Nakajima had long since vanished in the clouds below. The entire incident over the straits lasted a mere three minutes. After that day, the Blacksheep never engaged

*8 FS A/C #50 "RHAPSODY IN BLUE" flown by Jim Ward who shot down the last Blacksheep victim of the war over the China coast on March 15, 1945.*

*Ward's A/C at Atsugi, Japan, after the war. It was maintained by C.C. Sgt. Sterenet who stayed with the plane and pilot all the way through the Philippines to the post-war occupation.*

another enemy airplane in combat. Rookie Jim Ward had his one and only career victory confirmed by the captain, bringing the Blacksheep final official tally to 207 aerial victories.

### BRAVE LYNCH AND RALPH AT LINGUYAN; MARCH 17, 1945

On the return flight from a search and rescue sortie on the 17th, the aircrews at Linguyan again had a hand in the rescue of a pilot in distress. Rookie Flying Knight 2Lt. Henry Hook splashed down in the surf just off the end of the Linguyan runway in sight of the 9th Squadron crewmen. When the lieutenant popped to the surface, he climbed into his inflated liferaft, but the heavy sea capsized his rubber boat and the rolling waves dragged him under.

T/Sgt Jim Lynch and Cpl. John Ralph had kept an eye on the struggling pilot from the outset. When the lieutenant went under, the two enlisted men ran down the beach, peeled off their trousers, shirts and shoes, and plunged headlong into the tumbling surf. Minutes later, the sergeant and corporal dragged the drenched pilot to the safety of the beach. Brave airmen Jim Lynch and John Ralph were each duly awarded the Soldier's Medal for their fearless rescue of Lt. Hook.

### MORE MISSIONS AND MORE FREE TIME; THIRD WEEK OF MARCH, 1945

As of mid-March, the frequency of sorties for the squadron commanders were just as demanding as ever, and yet, for the first time since the lull in the New Guinea campaign of mid-1944, more leisure time was afforded to the 49ers to take extended leave. There was actually greater efficiency within the Linguyan field operations which afforded officers and enlisted alike time to recuperate in the secured areas of Manila, or to visit girl friends in Australia, or even catch a transport flight to distant Hawaii.

In the second half of the March offensive, the American infantry closed in ever more on the remote hold-outs in the mountains just east of the Linguyan. All three of the 49ers squadrons returned to the aerial assault which concentrated on the Balete Pass and the

Villa Verde Trail area where the enemy had stubbornly chosen to honor their Emperor in a fight to the death. For two weeks, each 49ers P-38 would heft a ton of ordinance, often three sorties per day, up to the highlands. Every man who braved the murderous small arms groundfire there stoically resigned himself to the fact that not everyone would survive the odds.

### LANG DISAPPEARS; MARCH 25, 1945

The next 49ers man to pay the ultimate price on Luzon was Blacksheep 2Lt. John Lang. He had only joined the 8th Squadron in January, but had readily become a favorite with the pilots and crews. On the 25th, he bombed the Villa Verde highway and pulled off the target with a smoking left engine. He nursed the crippled P-38 to within fifteen miles of Linguyan before he had to abandon the burning hulk. He was last seen descending in his chute into the forest, but inexplicably, the lieutenant vanished. Whether the victim of Filipino headhunters or executed by a wayward band of Japanese infantry, no evidence of John Lang's fate was ever found.

### RENICK LOST AT ITOGON; MARCH 27, 1945

Two days after the Blacksheep loss, another Screamin' Demon was killed. Newcomer 2Lt. Dewey Renick had gone on the strike sortie 45 miles north of the Villa Verde road to the enemy fortifications built in the old mining camp at Itogon. The lieutenant made a howling pass, low over the roofs of the red brick buildings of the enemy held village. Apparently killed instantly by the lethal groundfire, his Lightning continued straight past the target and plowed into the hillside. His body was recovered by Filipinos weeks after the fighting there had ended.

Exemplary of that series of missions, the Flying Knights alone dropped 22,000 pounds of high explosives, just on the enemy refugees at Bagiuo village. By the first week in April, small bands of Imperial troops tried to reach Cagayan Valley on foot along the central main roadway, Highway 5, and Kenney's dive-bombers slaughtered them. Everyplace that appeared to be safe haven, or anything that could be used by the evacuees was strafed and napalmed to oblivion.

### OKINAWA; APRIL 1,1945

On April Fool's Day, 1945, the Linguyan camp was electrified by the hourly reports of American troops landing on Okinawa, the largest of the Bonin Islands which was the southern most archipelago of the Imperial homelands. Nimitz' Central Pacific forces had launched the greatest amphibious operation of the war against the enemy garrison and airfields there as a final foothold on the path to the main homeland island of Kyushu, only 350 miles to the north.

Due in part to the intense air attacks on the airdromes of Formosa in March, the Japanese reasoned that MacArthur would surely land his forces there, somewhere on the southern coast. Accordingly, the Imperial command marshalled their air units on the northern airfields of Formosa, and on Okinawa. Their intent was to confront the American fleet in what was surely to be, by their esti-

*One of the Linguyan based B-17 air-sea rescue patrol planes often escorted by the 49ers in the Okinawa offensive. Although the nose turret is replaced with search radar, all of the other defensive guns were retained.*

mation, the decisive sea battle of the war in the northern waters of the Philippines Sea. If the kamikazes could inflict serious losses in the invasion fleet and stall the Formosa venture, the presumption was that the Americans would be coerced into negotiations for a cease fire, and that peace might follow.

The astonishing assault on Okinawa shattered any hopes for the Formosa scenario. In total bewilderment, the Imperial command sacrificed hundreds of novice airmen in wave after wave of kamikaze attacks against the sprawling task force laying off the island objective. Even though the damage was substantial to Nimitz' advanced task force at the beachhead, the inexhaustible reserves were far beyond the scope of the Empire's desperate, pitiful defense. Within a week, literally by the annihilate of entire air units at a time, the U.S. Navy fleet wing overwhelmed the last major counteroffensive of the enemy air force.

LtC. Gerry Johnson's high scoring killers and their FEAF cohorts at Linguyan were relegated to the strategic support of Nimitz' west flank. The 49ers continued to fly interdictions against the west coast of Formosa plus escorts to the many anti-shipping strikes by the medium bombers in the Formosa Straits. There were also numerous escorts to the Navy and USAAF rescue flights.

*Returned veteran Jim "Duckbutt" Watkins and his victory scoreboard after the April 1st fighter sweep which brought him his last career kill.*

## LAST FLYING KNIGHTS AERIAL VICTORY; APRIL 1, 1945

One of the 49ers missions of April 1st along the southern China coast paid off again, and was particularly satisfying since one of LtC. Johnson's old friends from the Dobodura days was there to share the success. Major Jim "Duckbutt" Watkins, the senior-most veteran to recently rejoin the 49ers, had taken up the Group Deputy CO job. Just as in the days when they had been the terrors of the skies over eastern New Guinea, Johnson and Watkins signed on as wingmen to one another for the day's 9th Squadron sortie. And just as in the old days, they would demonstrate to the younger Flying Knights that they still possessed the skills that made them multi-victory aces.

LtC. Johnson flew lead in the sixteen-ship escort to B-24s sent against the airdromes of Hong Kong, one of several such long range airfield suppression strikes in the Okinawa operations. The two veteran aces and the young lieutenants reached the target at 1300 hours to see the bombers lay in an accurate pattern of 500-pounders on the docks and JNAF airdrome, but none of the brilliant explosions started any fires. The Lightnings orbited over the island city at 14,000 feet for forty minutes, when Johnson finally caught sight of two interceptors, estimated ten miles away to the northwest. Watkins had seen them, too, and both of the aces peeled away for the kill before anyone else.

In mere seconds, the ace wingmen attack team closed in on the pair of interceptors, both Nakajima TOJOs, which tried to turn away. It was far too late for that, as both the colonel and the major fired simultaneously. Their respective victims spun straight down, as Watkins later reported sardonically, "right into Mother Earth's bosom."

The other P-38 elements finally arrived on the scene and were searching for the senior officers when two OSCARs swept under the Flying Knights formation. The lieutenants broke ranks in the

*Entertainer Joe E. Brown who performed for the 5 AF at Gusap, visited Linguyan in May and renewed his friendship with the 49ers CO. Johnson shared his quarters with the famous entertainer during his brief stay on Luzon.*

wild pursuit of the new targets, and Lt. Noah Williams eventually gained an acceptable deflection on the lead OSCAR. Williams damaged the Ki-43 with his first volley, and it broke away, only to passed straight out in front of 2Lt. Walt Koby. The young Knight closed in for three, well aimed bursts down to one-hundred yards in range. Koby pulled out at 2000 feet as the OSCAR continued down and slammed into a hillside. The other Ki-43 vanished and the fight was over.

The Flying Knights were signalled to regroup and everyone was accounted for. The mission would have been "a fighter pilot's text book entry" had they not lost a plane en route for home. Fifty miles north of Linguyan, 2Lt. Cliff Peterson had to abandon his sputtering Lockheed. Fortunately, he came down in his chute at Luna village, right on the beach. He returned in good health two days via an L-5 liaison plane. Thus ended the events surrounding the final squadron kill for the proud Flying Knights. LtC. Johnson personally confirmed 2Lt. Koby's one and only career kill, burning away on the hillside north of Hong Kong. It was also victory #254, the last kill of the highest scoring fighter squadron in the Pacific theater.

## DEADLY MISHAPS AT LINGUYAN AIR FIELD; APRIL 6 and 14th, 1945

The most dangerous situations during the Okinawa era of operations actually took place on the ground, right at the 49ers home field. On April 6th, the 49ers dispersal area was momentarily closed down after a bizarre accident involving a P-47 which lost its underwing ordnance on the main runway. The 500-pounder fell on the packed coral and detonated, destroying the Thunderbolt, killing the pilot and showering the dispersal grounds with shrapnel. Flying Knights crewchief S/Sgt Al Valenta was standing atop a Lightning when a single steel chard struck him in the head and knocked him off his feet. After being hauled to the ground, the attending medics declared the tough mechanic was all right. It was only an omen of a more deadly incident which happened eight days later.

On the 14th, Demon Sgt. Rhese Slater and his armament work detail had gone to the ordinance depot to draw out the 1000-pounders for the next 7th Squadron mission. When the team reached the

*7 FS officers in late March at Linguyan. In front (lt.-rt.) are Lt. Spruill who scored the unit's last kill of the war, ace Ops Exec Damstrom and Capt. Ganchan. The two men sitting to the left are Capts. Keck (lt.) and Henderson. Standing in back (lt.-rt.) are Com. Officer Gallagher, veteran Flt Ldr Denkovic, 2Lt. Garrett and N.G. veteran Jarrel. Fernley Damstrom was lost at Laoag, Luzon, on April 10th and Lou Denkovic died in the collision along with George Rogers over the airdrome on May 4th.*

depot, driver Cpl. Gordon Steerock parked and waited at the wheel while Cpl. Ed Bellis stepped out momentarily on the running board. Slater, with Cpls. Ed Bellis, Ed Stephans and Stan Skrzypiec, got out to unhook the trailer, a standard procedure for picking up their issue of bombs at the narrow gateway to the crowded bomb dump.

As the three men stepped to the rear of the vehicles, Cpl. Stephans chanced upon a loose piece of ordinance lying there in the dirt. For some obscure reason, the young ordinance man picked

*8 FS A/C #48 s.n. 44-27120 fitted with the five-point missile rack referred to as the "Christmas tree." The 20mm ammo was routinely omitted when the 60-pound rockets were carried. This A/C only carries a single drop-tank.*

up the eighteen inch-long warhead and held it out for S/Sgt Slater's inspection. Bellis heard Slater tell Stephans that it was probably a dud 5-inch Navy round, and for the corporal to put in down and get back to work.

The last thing Bellis could recall was that foolish Stephans simply dropped the 5-inch round to the ground. There was a deafening thunderclap. Bellis was blown off the running board and driver Steerock was hit in the leg by a piece of shrapnel. Dazed Ed Bellis, only scratched and bruised, got to his feet and looked in horror upon the still bodies of Slater, Skrzypiec and Stephans, all of whom died instantly in the blast.

## DEMONS OPS MAN LOST AT LAOAG; APRIL 10, 1945

Demons CO Aschenbrener was mortified. Only four days prior to the loss of his three armament crewmen, he had likewise lost his newly appointed Ops Exec, Capt. Fernley Damstrom, far to the north at captured Laoag airdrome. Damstrom too, fell in an equally meaningless death.

Popular ace Damstrom and a wingman F/O Sylvan Sisson had flown up to the Laoag strip certainly for sound enough reasons. The sortie would allow them to assess the potential of the field as an advanced staging base, and better still, place them on the flight path of a particularly annoying, airborne intruder that had single handedly harassed the entire Linguyan camp every night for the past week. The trespasser, however, never appeared during the Demon pilots stay at Laoag.

After a couple of nights as guest of the infantry, Damstrom gave up on the interception scheme and took off at daybreak on the 10th, but one of his engines seized up on liftoff. The fuel heavy Lockheed snap rolled and slammed down on the beach. It did not burn, but there was no solace in that. Damstrom died instantly of a broken neck.

There was an ironic twist at the end of the tragic story. An official memo from 5 AF operations was delivered to the Demons several days later. It was the very radio message that Damstrom had filed the night before his fateful morning takeoff. Just as if he had called from the grave, dead Fernley Damstrom's message declared Laoag airstrip was unfit for P-38 operations.

## BREAKING THROUGH THE YAMASHITA LINE; APRIL, 1945

The 49ers once again returned to the tactical operations against the vestiges of the enemy army on Luzon. The American infantry had reached the north coast by mid-April and began to push east rapidly against Gen. Yamashita's troops in scattered retreat for Aparri village at the mouth of the Cagayan River.

Likewise, the 49ers enjoined the concentrated air strikes in the central highlands, roughly on a line from Balete Pass, up through the Villa Verde road crossing and into the hills at Bagiuo, referred to in briefings as "the Yamashita Line. Close air support allowed the 6th Army to break out through the contested highlands and pushed into the southern end of the Cagayan Valley.

By the end of April, ground targets were ever more reduced to fortified enclaves hidden in the gulches and caves of steep, forested slopes. Merely indicated on the mission briefing maps by a circle drawn on an indistinguishable hillside, the sorties required pin-point accuracy to eliminate such hardened targets, and a new weapon was introduced as a likely tool for the job.

Eight late model-L Lightnings had been picked up by the more fortunate Blacksheep pilots gone on leave to Hawaii, and were ferried all the way back to Linguyan via the Pacific route through Wake and Guam Islands. These particular P-38s were fitted with a detachable, underwing racks, each of which could mount five 60-pound high velocity rockets. The Vee-shaped racks hung down nearly twenty-four inches from the underwing surface and were likened to an upside-down "Christmas tree." The 20mm cannon ammo was not carried when the six-hundred-plus pounds of racks and rockets were fitted.

The rockets were only used on a few operational sorties in late April, and May, and proved to be very lethal. The weapons were aimed through the standard Lockheed gunsight and were most effective at a range of up to 500 yards. Many times, the 49ers found the rockets could be fired straight into a cave entrance or through the side of a fortified bunker that otherwise could not be hit with dive-bombing techniques. However, the Ops people considered napalm to be tactically more effective against hidden emplacements, while the awesome firepower of the projectiles might be better suited for high profile targets such as enemy shipping, particularly should the Lightnings be raiding the home ports in Japan's inland sea later that year.

## A NEW ERA FOR ALL AMERICANS

On April 13th, Americans around the world fell into mourning over the death of President Franklin Roosevelt. The loss of the nation's resilient Commander in Chief, a man who overcame his own physical hardships to become the very symbol of the American war effort, seemed all the more sorrowful knowing he would not see the final victory. Vice-President Harry Truman assumed the office as the country carried on in sober resolution to bring the war to a quick conclusion.

## ANOTHER K.I.A.- 2Lt. WAYNE CUNNINGHAM; APRIL 25, 1945

The Luzon slaughter continued throughout April. All of the mountain villages defended by the Japanese were hammered flat by the fighter-bombers and the only vehicles ever seen in daylight were the ones already burned out along the road to Aparri. LtC. Johnson's pilots had become extremely proficient in their routines, and had not lost an aircraft nor a pilot to enemy actions since the Demons lost their last man at the end of March. In was shear luck that a month would nearly pass before the next 49er fell victim over a target.

The unlucky man was newcomer 2Lt. Wayne Cunningham, a pleasant young officer who had only been with the Flying Knights since February. He had joined in on the deadly gambit to practically every target on the big island and finally played out the odds over the Cabuyao village on the west bank of the broad Luguna De Bay. The Knights were in support of the mop-up of the stronghold

*A Sikorsky R-4 helicopter in service on Saipan, Marianna Islands, identical to the type that searched for fallen pilot Cunningham off Linguyan on April 25th.*

when a single round knocked out Cunningham's left engine. He nursed the smoking P-38 all the way back to the Linguyan landing pattern, but the engine erupted in flame and the plane sank in the air. The left wing dragged in the sea, the P-38 cartwheeled and Cunningham vanished in the roiling whirlpool beneath a cloud of steam and smoke.

From the dispersal area, there arose the strangest contraption any of the line crews had ever seen. It was a Sikorsky R-4 helicopter, a rotor-bladed hovercraft with a long boxy, canvass fuselage and drooping, spindly landing gear which gave it an insect-like appearance. The swinging blades popped in the air as it slowly crossed the field, slipped over the beach and drifted out over the bay, just a few feet above the water to the crash site. It just hung there, suspended as if it were a bizarre angel come down to find the fallen flyer. The mechanical angel eventually turned away, not finding any sign of Wayne Cunningham.

Two days later, the Knights had another close call when 2Lt. Walt Koby was shot out of the sky over the raging ground battle at Santiago village in Cagayan Valley. Koby bailed out and landed in the midst of the faithful guerrillas who immediately took him to safe ground, and within a week, handed him over to the infantry. Koby would be gone only eleven days total.

## "RAVIN'" GEORGE LAVEN

Major George Laven was one of the senior officers who had served a tour in the 11 AF as had Gerry Johnson, fighting the Japanese far across the Pacific in the remote Alaskan winter campaign of 1942. Laven arrived for the Linguyan buildup in early March, and was summarily appointed to LtC. Johnson's 49ers as the new Group Executive Officer.

Laven immediately set everyone on edge. He was brash and argumentative, but Johnson tolerated his abrasiveness, particularly when he was in the cockpit. Laven was certainly brave, and at times reckless, but he was a consummate Lightning pilot. He took up the task of personally trying to wipe out the Formosa railroad system single handedly, and by mid-April, bragged of having destroyed more than a dozen locomotives. Still, other senior pilots questioned the veracity of his accounts which were often one-man juggernauts.

While flying in the Alaskan front, Laven had stirred up a substantial controversy there by claiming three enemy aircraft shot down in addition to the one kill which had been officially accredited to him. Like so many cock-sure pilots of his rank, he displayed four victory flags on his P-38 and presumed himself to be in good company with acclaimed ace Duckbutt Watkins, and the leading 49ers ace of all, Group CO Johnson. All of the resident aces at Linguyan declared scores for themselves higher than the tallies confirmed by 5 FC, but none were quite as virulent over the subject as Laven. His tirades eventually gained him the epithet of "Ravin' Laven", and reached such a bitter point on the Blacksheep flight line where his P-38 "ITSY-BITSY II" was serviced that crewchiefs refused to contend with the major's constant demands.

The 8th Squadron Ops Exec Capt. Pierce, much subdued from his own rebellious days back at Dobodura, understood the situation and wisely chose a crewman who could stand toe-to-toe with the irate major and confront him on the same mental plain. The crewchief selected was shrewd T/Sgt. D.C. Todd, one of Linguyan's most notorious operators. The sergeant was a boot-legger, a cock-fight bookie and a suspected fence in the black market business proliferating on Luzon. He would have been court-martialled months earlier accept for the fact that, as Pierce would later muse, "Todd was too damn good at his work."

*The gaudy #44 "ITSY BITSY" flown by flamboyant George Laven.*

## THE LAST 49ERS KILL; APRIL 26, 1945

Therefore, the elements were all in place for the event which followed over southern Formosa on April 26th. The weather that morning was barely marginal, but the aggressive HQ Exec was off again at 1000 hours on another freelance sortie with a single wingman. George "Ravin'" Laven and fellow Maj. Wilson of the 475 FG each carried a full load of ammo in the gun bays, a drop tank and a half-ton bomb to strike the chemical plant at Shinen. When the two staff officers reached the cloudy Formosa coast, they slipped under the overcast at Bozan and continued north for fifty miles at 3000 feet, just beneath the line of rain squalls. They pushed even lower under a 300 foot ceiling to finally reach Shinen at noon, and both men glide-bombed the plant.

Laven was about to initiate a strafing pass on the collapsed buildings at Shinen when he spotted the smoke of a locomotive, three miles to the west. Leaving Wilson to mop up the smoldering chemical plant, Laven turned away and quickly came down on the small locomotive at the lead of a dozen flat cars. He blew up the steam-engine in the first pass, then ventured off at tree-top level in hunt of more rail targets. He strafed a second engine fifteen miles north of the primary target and then turned back for home, when over the coast at 1245 hours, Laven saw what he had dreamed of for the past two years. Up ahead in the mist over Kato village was an enemy fighter, tracking what he thought was an American PBY floatplane.

Laven soon drew into gun range from dead-astern and was thrilled to find both aircraft were Japanese. One was a VAL, which rose up into the overcast and vanished as he approached, but the other was a four-engine JNAF amphibious EMILY bomber which held its course parallel to the shoreline. Laven pushed ITSY-BITSY down below the big floatplane's flight path and closed in, then pulled up within point-blank range and fired. The huge amphibian shook from the blows and immediately crashed in flames on the beach at Kato, scattering flaming debris over the village and setting fire to some of the rustic buildings.

Laven quickly circled the kill site, then wheeled ten miles back to the north to orbit Choso airdrome in hopes of ambushing the VAL, but it never reappeared. After ten minutes, the major drifted south, expended the last of his ammo at the Koshun village sugar mill, then hit the coast and crossed over the sea for home. He landed at half-past two.

The controversy began as soon as ornery crewchief Todd read the major's combat report, then sarcastically painted a PBY-kill silhouette on ITSY-BITSY's scoreboard. Laven was furious and Ops Exec Pierce intervened before it came to blows between the major and the sergeant. But it did not end there.

Long after hostilities had ceased, an Air Force inspection team surveyed the wreckage at Kato village, but found so much debris in the area, it was not readily apparent that it was Laven's EMILY. Though the major's kill over Kato was eventually confirmed, the Air Force continued to offer a caveat for only two of his three disputed Alaskan claims as "official kills scored, but unconfirmed." George Laven, despite nearly a half century of continuous disputes over the facts of his many exploits, stubbornly held his ground in the proclamation that he had reached ace status by scoring the last aerial victory for the 49ers in World War Two.

*Maj. Laven and his scoreboard after the controversial kill claim made on the April 26th recon of Formosa.*

## SEARLE LOST AT SEA; MAY 13, 1945

Maj. Laven attached himself to every mission sent to Formosa for the remainder of the 49ers stay at Linguyan. He was determined to find another airborne victim, and haunted every promising briefing for the most likely prospects. On the 13th, Laven attached himself to the Screamin' Demons sortie to Kagi, one of the airdromes at the extreme range of the Lockheeds. It was the best chance the major had against the dwindling enemy air force, but the opportunity only raised more questions about his aggressive methods when his wingman failed to return.

Once again, the weather over the west coast of Formosa was abominable. Determined Laven, with rookie Lt. Francis Searle on his wing, pressed on despite the rain and reached the target, but did not find any planes on the ground, let alone airborne in the diminishing weather. Laven and Searle turned back and hunted the rail lines for targets, strafing targets of opportunity along the way. When they reached the coastline, they were some distance apart, and Searle suddenly realized one of his engines had lost its coolant. It began to smoke.

The major circled back to support Searle as best he could, but the overheating mill was strictly in the lieutenant's hands. Ten miles off shore, he had completely shut down the troublesome engine. When they passed over tiny Ryukyu Island, Searle appeared to have gotten the plane under control, but the ship suddenly snap-rolled and two brilliant explosions flashed from its underside. In the blink of an eye, the inverted Lightning plunged into the cold Formosa Straits, just south of desolate Ryukyu. Laven could only circle the swirling crash site and report all traces of Francis Searle had vanished.

# 23

# EXECUTIONERS OF LUZON

s of the last week in April, Gen. Kruger's forces had completely encircled the Imperial troops in the hill country twenty miles north of the Philippines capitol city. An enclave of 4700 defiant combat troops dug in for the final defense of their heavily fortified camp at Ipo Dam, an earthen structure at the head waters of the Ipo and Angat Rivers. The reservoir there was one of Manila's principle fresh water sources and MacArthur was fully aware the Japanese could easily bring hardship on the newly captured capitol by contaminating the water, or blowing up the earthen dam. The capture of the reservoir became a top priority.

## IPO; MAY 3-16, 1945

Therefore, on May 3rd, the Linguyan fighter-bombers rose up in the single greatest maximum effort in the Philippines campaign to eliminate the southern highland obstacle once and for all. The operation coordinated over 270 Lightnings, Thunderbolts and Mustangs armed with napalm and high explosives in saturation strikes which reached from Ipo village through the foothills for forty-five miles to the southeast at Santa Maria village. The fires raged for four consecutive days as the FEAF fighters strafed and bombed everything that moved.

## DENKOVIC AND ROGERS LOST; MAY 4, 1945

The Linguyan camp was ecstatic with the news that Nazi dictator Adolf Hitler was confirmed dead by the Russians who had captured Berlin. And with their own resent success against the enemy hold-outs on Luzon, their spirits were as high as ever before. All seemed right, but that changed abruptly with the tragedy that occurred directly over the airfield on May 4th.

A flight of Screamin' Demons had returned from their mission, but congested air traffic forced them to withdraw momentarily. While reforming to land, the Demons began to issue challenges to one another, and understandably, a mock dogfight broke out. Soon, a dozen P-38s were swept up in a "rat-race" tag game around the airdrome. A large crowd gathered to watch the wildly maneuvering Lightnings sweeping from 3000 feet back down to make high speed runs on the deck, straight down the runway. It all came to a startling end with the collision of senior Lts. Lou Denkovic and George Rogers over the west end of the field. Their planes met on converting courses and disintegrated in a fiery explosion. Neither man had time to deploy his chute as both planes broke up and fell in shambles.

The losses of the two men blurred into everyone's memory, when three days later, the camp broke into a spontaneous, wild celebration with news that the war in Europe was over.

*8 FS Lightning rolling out at Linguyan in the fighter-bomber napalm missions to the Luzon highlands.*

*Capt. Ganchan (rt.) and C.C. Voss with their A/C #3 "SOUTHERN MISS" in the Okinawa mobilization.*

## 49ERS FIRE-BOMBING HELL ITSELF

The massed napalm attack at Ipo had been so successful, Gen. Smith of 5 FC repeated the effort on the 16th with a force more than twice the size as the first. LtC. Johnson personally headed up the 49ers and took forty-eight of his pilots north of Ipo as the last Lightning unit in the morning strike of near 680 fighters.

The 49ers orbited over the foothills as the preceding units attacked, and then at 1015 hours, Johnson turned due south with seven 9th Squadron wingmen in line abreast formation. Five other flights of Demons, Blacksheep and Flying Knights, each with eight elements wingtip to wingtip, wheeled into an ascending formation behind the colonel, separated at 300 yard intervals.

At a mere 800 feet above the rolling hills, the flyers peered at the hellish spectacle, four miles up ahead. They paraded straight for the shimmering heat waves and smoke boiling up from the five-mile-square target area. Each man knew he was entering Hades itself as the Lightnings were buffeted by the rising thermals. They passed over the release point and jettisoned the belly tank bombs, each man in unison with the wingmen in his flight. Flight by flight, they fed the awesome inferno.

For the next two days, a similar fate fell upon the refugee troops in the highlands near Santa Maria. The central strongholds were so racked by continuous bombardments, plus the depletion of their ranks due to starvation and disease, the Allies were able to secure the entire shoreline of Luguna De Bay with a modicum of light casualties. Structurally sound Ipo Dam was also captured, virtual without opposition.

Intelligence and operations personnel of 5 FC took first hand assessments of the tactical assaults made by their respective groups. Tours of the target areas near Manila and Linguyan displayed horrible carnage beyond belief. Hundreds of charred corpses were seen in each burned out stronghold, including 2100 of the Ipo defenders

*Wingmen elements add their napalm to the fires raging in the enemy camps at Ipo dam.*

*Philippines veteran Jim Costley and his A/C WINNIE" waiting at Linguyan in July.*

*Philippines combat pilot Ken Clark of the Flying Knights with his A/C #98 "GYPSY" at Linguyan.*

who had likely fallen in the air attacks alone. The wholesale death was not just a symbolic victory, but the settlement of an American vendetta against an adversary pledged to fight until the death. It quite simply was a mass execution.

## CHASING THE GENERAL

The fire-bombing 5 FC turned there proven attack methods one last time against the Imperial Philippines commander's north-central line of defense and burned out the Luzon interior from the 18th through the remainder of the month. Although the May rains quelled the total effectiveness of the napalm, the air raids so pinned down the Cagayan enclaves that Clark Field was put back in operations by the engineers. Kenney had originally planned to have the fields ready for the new 20 AF HQ and its B-29s, but the capture of Okinawa had preempted that scheme. By the third week in May, the 308 BW tactical units moved into spacious Clark and Nichols airfields. By the first week of June, Yamashita's forces were denied further safe haven at Apparri. His strongest army units, still intact in the hills flanking Cagayan Valley, were completely surrounded.

## HERMAN AND ROSS DEAD AT LINGUYAN FIELD; MAY 27, 1945

The operational mishaps at Linguyan field proved once again as deadly as the enemy. On May 27th, 2Lt. Joel Herman of the 7th Squadron had to manually pump down his gear before he could attempt a landing. The gear collapsed in his rollout and the P-38 plowed into two other parked planes. Both pilot Herman, and PFC Bernie Ross who was working on the flight line, were killed out right.

The ensuing fire caused the ammo in the wrecked aircraft to explode, knocking line crewman PFC John Rhodes off his feet. Lt. Joe McHenry, Sgt. Oswoldo Difore and PFC Tim Neasmann were near the scene and rushed to help the fallen private. Difore and Neasmann managed to extract wounded Rhodes safely from the flaming debris, while McHenry boarded a nearby Lightning in danger of catching on fire. The lieutenant started up an engine and taxied it to safe ground.

Minutes later, an airborne Blacksheep pilot reported he was out of fuel, but even more critical was his armed cluster bomb, still hung up on the bomb rack. He diverted to nearby Mangaldon Field where a armament team was waiting. Thanks to the skills of the ordinance people, the ship and pilot were saved, but there was nothing anyone could do for wingman 2Lt. Ken Miners who arrived overhead to report his engines were hot. Traffic was so snarled by that time that Linguyan ordered Miners to abandon his smoking plane off shore. Minutes later, Miners drifted down in his chute and was quickly picked up by a crash boat rescue team.

## FORMOSA ENCORE AND CAPT. ARTHUR DOWN; MAY 31, 1945

Despite the Navy's contentions that the kamikazes would shift their operations to southern Japan, reconnaissance flights in late May discovered many planes were still staging into northern Formosa to strike the Okinawa convoys. Nimitz again insisted that Kenney's 5 AF heavy bombers repeat their reduction of the Formosa airdromes, and Kenney complied with a new maximum effort. The 49ers supported the effort with more of their tactical strikes on the southern airdromes and railroads.

On May 31st, the Lightnings went to the airdrome at Tainan, Formosa. Deputy CO Maj. Watkins was in the lead of twelve Flying Knights, including newly returned Capt. Wilbur Arthur, an old 9th Squadron hand who had been on States-side furlough following the P-47 era in New Guinea. The captain had only been reinstated to the mission roster a short time, and it proved to be a fatefully short second tour.

The mission seemed to progress well enough as the Knights found two aircraft and several vehicles at Tainan which they rendered to junk. When they had expended all of their ammo and Watkins signalled to regroup, Capt. Arthur reported that his ship had been much too heavily damaged by flak. Arthur, flying in aircraft #70 borrowed from Flying Knights CO Petrovich, had already lost an engine. Watkins and the others covered the smoking Lightning in its rapid descent toward the southeast and it soon began to trail flames. Seven miles south of the target, Arthur's chute unfurled and the elements watched as he landed in rugged terrain. The downed flyer hobbled a few steps, then fell to his knees and was last seen crawling for cover.

*Prisoner of war Wilbert Arthur during his P-47 tour in early 1944. He was the only 49er to survive captivity.*

## WILBERT ARTHUR - CAPTIVE

Capt. Wilbert Arthur was the only 49er ever to have fallen in the vicinity of an enemy camp and survive captivity. Even with his untreated broken ankle, the captain endured the harsh working conditions in a labor camp on northern Formosa, and later survived the evacuation to the prison camp at Atsugi airdrome on the Imperial homeland island of Honshu. He would ultimately have the bittersweet satisfaction of seeing his outfit again, and much sooner than anyone expected.

## ATKINSON DEAD; MAY 31, 1945

While the Knights sorted out the debriefing over their man down on Formosa, the Blacksheep also lost a man there, but his fate was sealed. Senior Lt. Jim Atkinson had joined in the strafing attack on a convoy of vehicle along the coast road when his P-38 was hit. The Blacksheep wingmen could only report that the flight leader was low over the burning trucks when he suddenly dropped his wing and cartwheeled in a spectacular, flaming crash. After the war, neither Jim Atkinson's body, nor the crash site, could ever be identified among the many burned out ruins along the bloodied roadway.

## THE GREATEST BUILDUP OF THE WAR; JUNE, 1945

On June 1st, the senior most enlisted men of the past two years in frontline service received the best news of their young lives. They were going home. In days, transport aircraft were packed with USAAF personnel from every unit on Linguyan scrambling for any connection to the States. There was an even greater number of new men arriving with every flight.

For every man that left Linguyan or Clark Field, LtC. Gerry Johnson estimated another five would quickly take their place. As for Johnson, he had been told a senior lieutenant colonel was due at any moment to relieve him of the 49ers command. And the 308 BW staff was already packing for their transfer to Okinawa as the biggest invasion in history was so very close at hand.

## OKINAWA BATTLE ORDER FOR THE 49ERS

In the June buildup at Linuyan, two of the 49ers units inducted new commanders. Bob Aschenbrener relinquished the 7th Squadron to Capt. Clay Isaacson, an able veteran from the European theater. Asch was promoted to the rank of major and moved on with several other personnel to the 308 BW staff.

Blacksheep CO Willie Drier hung up his flight gear and joined friend Aschenbrener on staff. The 8th Squadron went to another ETO veteran, Capt. Mark Vinzant. Both Demon CO Isaacson and Blacksheep CO Vinzant began to work up in their respective mission rosters right away. Isaacson unceremoniously had to belly in after his first abortive venture on the 2nd. But Isaacson was unruffled and immediately commandeered another ship to sigh on for the next flight.

Meanwhile, the 49ers HQ staff welcomed returning veteran Capt. Eddie "Legs" Howes, the diminutive Flying Knights veteran who was assigned as special liaison to Fighter Command. Ace Bob Dehaven had likewise returned to the Demons' staff. By the first week of June, the 49ers were manned with seasoned veterans at ever key position. When the call came down from Okinawa for the 49ers to take their position in the order of battle for the final invasion, the group would be ready as never before.

*ETO veteran Maj. Petrovich took command of the Flying Knights in May, 1945, and subsequently lent A/C #70 to Capt. Arthur for his fateful sortie.*

*Maj. Willie Drier completed his extended tour at Linguyan after more than 300 hours of flight time in combat. No other 49ers pilot came close to matching the ace's stellar command record.*

*After cracking up his first aircraft, 7 FS CO Isaacson quickly commandeered another Lockheed and named it #1 "ALMOST AS DRAGGIN II."*

## MORE NEWCOMERS AND MORE MEN LOST; JUNE, 1945

June began with mixed success for the 49ers. On the 1st, Demon 2Lt. Calvin Madison went down on Luzon's west coast not far from the base. He bailed out and literally landed at the feet of his Filipino rescuers. Madison made it all seem easy, for on the very next day, a man was lost who literally failed to find Luzon.

## SIMON MISSING OVER THE OCEAN; JUNE 2, 1945

Sadly enough the next day, newcomer Lt. Lew Simon had a delayed takeoff, and rather than abort for another mission, he foolishly decided to continue on alone in search of his Flying Knights formation. Simon was a flyer of no less than two-thousand hours in a variety of planes, but fate took total disregard of his skills. When the weather quickly closed in from the north, the lieutenant became hopelessly disoriented and failed to find any other flights, let alone the west coast of Luzon. He transmitted a series of garbled radio messages until darkness set in, and then, Lew Simon simply disappeared.

A week later, two more Flying Knights got equally as lost as their missing squadron mate. Rookie 2Lt. Art Easterbrook accompanied experienced 2Lt. Walt Koby south to Tacloban by air transport in order to ferry two new P-38s back to Linguyan. They left Tacloban in the late afternoon of June 9th, and they too were confronted by a growing weather front en route. Neither man could find an opening and both planes were lost. Easterbrook executed a textbook water landing in the shallows off southern Sibuyan Island, which put him in the hands of the Filipinos in less than an hour.

Koby made one final attempt to reach Luzon. It was a noble effort, but he ran out of gas in pressing further north beyond Sibuyan and wound up bailing out for the second time in his Philippines career.

This time, however, Koby was stunned as he collided with the rudder when his abandoned ship snap rolled. Luckily, he had already grasped his parachute cord and the slip stream pulled his arm hard enough to deploy his chute. Once he regained his senses on splashing down in the inland sea, he was consigned to float in his liferaft for five dreary days. He became so distraught, he seriously contemplated suicide, but a patrolling PBY Catalina arrived in the nick of time. Walt Koby had beaten the deadly odds again.

## LT. KEN MARKHAM DEAD ON FORMOSA; JUNE 18, 1945

The next man to die was another victim of the heavily defended airdrome at Kagi, Formosa. Tacloban veteran, Lt. Ken Markham was the sole loss in the forty-two ship strafing attack of the 18th. His P-38 was snatched out of its low gunnery pass by a power line. Half of a wing was torn away, it snap-rolled twice and slammed down on the airdrome in a fireball, killing Markham instantly.

## NEWCOMER HELFRECHT LOST EN ROUTE; JUNE 20, 1945

Demons CO Isaacson had no sooner placed the man lost on the 18th on the missing roster than another rookie vanished. Victim of the unforgiving weather on June 20th, 2Lt. Bob Helfrecht was last seen descending into the overcast in search of Linguyan. Like so

*Flying Knight veteran Eddie Howes (rt.), Flt Surgeon Bux and an unidentified crewman stand next to #71 "EMBRACEABLE YOU," waiting at Linguyan for a battle that would never be fought.*

*Newcomer Marvin Graham joined the Blacksheep and flew throughout the final Luzon campaign, then moved to Okinawa and the eventual occupation of Japan. His A/C #42 "LITTLE SUNNY BEA" carried him all the way through his tour.*

*Some of the Screamin' Demons of Linguyan, early June. Sitting in front (lt.-rt.): Klemeson, Flt Surgeon Webster, Ops Exec Atchison, CO Isaacson, Spruill, McHenry, Thompson, P. White and Com. Officer Gallagher. Kneeling second row: Manion, Weinberger, Sievers, Hoyt (KIA), Boone, Jones, Gorse, Spindler, Kopecky, J. White (KIA in 8 FS), Costley, Lierly, Thurston and Sisson. Standing (lt.-rt.) DeHaven, Stahl, Wecker, McCrary, Marsh, Jarrell, Mathis, Madison, Cook, Cooper, Bain, Carlisle, Bandy and Powell.*

many of the other young men new to the camp, Bob Helfrecht simply became a blur in everyone's mind when his name was added to the missing crew reports.

Fortunately, a week passed before there was another operational loss, and it would only cost one old stager P-38. Rookie 2Lt. Roy Farrington had both engines seize up on a routine strafing mission near Bagaban village and bailed out of the powerless Lockheed to landed within 500 yards of the American infantry. He would be absent for only two days.

June passed and the 49ers registered a total mission count of more than 1500 sorties in the four week period. Targets on Luzon literally became operational training sorties for the newcomers, as well as the proving grounds for new weapons and delivery techniques. Eventually, the 49ers no longer bombed Cagayan Valley with heavy ordinance, but with surrender leaflets.

## CONRADI LOST IN CAGAYAN VALLEY; JULY 7, 1945

Independence Day of 1945 was celebrated in great array at the Linguyan camp. Baseball games and basketball tournaments were fought out in every section and the food consisted of more fresh portions than any man had seen since before the war. It was a bitter contrast to another newcomer falling victim in the final assault against the pathetic vestiges of the beaten enemy in far off Cagayan Valley.

Rookie Flying Knight 2Lt. Gerald Conradi was not even hit by enemy groundfire. His P-38 struck a tree beyond his target and it instantly slammed to the ground in an swirling fireball. Conradi never had a chance.

*Veteran 49ers Clay Tice with his command A/C #10, not long after his arrival at Linguyan in July, 1945.*

*DeHaven's A/C with the elf riding the cannon armed #13-orchid is reminiscent of his P-40 days. The A/C was flown on several fighter sweeps to the China coast and Formosa, but the Demon ace never saw an airborne target during his brief second tour.*

*7 FS P-38L #6 assigned to newcomer Jim Bandy in the Linguyan buildup of June, 1945. At that time, the Demons began to paint their spinners solid sky-blue and the Blacksheep likewise adopted solid yellow.*

## LAST 49ER TO DIE ON LUZON; JULY 15, 1945

It seemed so strange that on the day LtC. Gerry Johnson turned over the 49th Fighter Group command to veteran Flying Knight LtC. Clay Tice, the group would likewise register its last fatality of the Philippines campaign.

On a milk-run strafing mission in the central Cagayan Valley, Screamin' Demon 2Lt. Harlen Hoyt's P-38 mysteriously fell out of the sky and crashed. No one was certain whether he had been hit by random groundfire, or if he simply blacked out. His plane rolled completely over, enter a flat spin and dropped to the valley floor. The big fighter erupted in a fireball, marking the fatal crash of Harlen Hoyt, the thirty-fifth 49er to die in the Philippines war.

## TICE'S FIGHTER GROUP

Lieutenant Col. Clayton Tice, Jr., like so many seasoned veterans, had returned to the Pacific as a command grade officer with a pur-

pose. He would fairly wield authority in every aspect of his command, and yet, he was more confident and focussed than any of his old group mates could remember. FEAF COS Don Hutchinson was delighted to see that the stern young officer he had met so long ago in Darwin was now definitely of command stature, "as Clay had obviously learned how to smile."

The colonel was equally anxious to get back into the fight and had his P-38 at Linguyan boldly painted in red, yellow and blue stripes which wrapped completely around the wings. When 5 FC CO Freddie Smith asked Tice if the garish chevrons were altogether wise, the colonel coolly responded, "That's why the colors are there. Let'em come, general. The best fighter group in the world is right behind me."

By the last week in July, LtC. Tice had received his dispersal orders for the 49ers ground echelon to move south to the materials supply docks at Manila and for the air echelon to prepare for air transportation from Linguyan. More camp supplies, more tools, and more gear than ever before was to be crated and bagged for the new offensive. Every man was required to update his vaccinations and

*Duckbutt Watkins had his new A/C #1 "CHARLCIE JEANNE" decorated for the invasion which never came.*

*When the Group occupied Atsugi Field after the war, Watkins took command of the 7 FS and his Lockheed was appropriately enhanced with the Bunyap.*

*49ers staff command at Linguyan in late July, 1945. Clockwise from lower lt. are Demon Ops Exec DeHaven, Group Exec Laven, 5 AF liaison Johnson, 49ers CO Tice, pipe smoker Deputy CO Watkins and Deputy Group Exec Jordan. With such qualified combat leaders, Tice was certain the 49ers would reached one-thousand aerial victories over Japan.*

the medics worked around the clock. Everyone was on edge and the Philippines veterans were particularly anxious. The move to Mindoro had been dangerous, but every man felt the move to Okinawa would be the most perilous move of all.

## THE CHINA VENTURE; JULY-AUGUST, 1945

In the interim of the Okinawa mobilization, the 49ers operations people were given a most unusual task. The 86th Wing determined that it would take any surplus fighter aircraft remotely within its domain. A contingent of senior pilots was summarily sent by air transport 1300 miles to western China to commandeer the Lightnings at Kunming.

Indeed, new P-38s delivered in India had reached Kunmimg in good order, but they required additional long range fittings for the ferry flights overseas. The two weeks required for the adjustments left the stranded 49ers in the midst of the rebellion being fought out by the armies of the local war lords. The pilots wore their firearms with at all times.

When the new P-38s were finally ready, the ferry pilots gladly bid their warring host adieu, then stuffed the baggage compartments and rear cockpits with a cache of souvenirs. Unfortunately, when the first Demons flight got under way on the morning of August 1st, Lt. Dudley Fagerstrom's left engine quit as he passed over the lake next to the base. As he turned about to land, the right engine failed, too, and Fagerstrom plowed into the shallow water next to the runway. He survived the crash, but required thirty stitches to close the gash in his head.

## LT. WHITE LOST IN THE CHINA SEA; AUGUST 3, 1945

Two days after Fagerstrom's fouled takeoff, Blacksheep CO Vinzant led his four ferry pilots off for Linguyan. The five pilots were certainly equal to the 1300 mile flight, but the weather over the South China Sea was once again uncooperative. Well out over the ocean, the five-ship flight was forced to fly beneath a squall line where Lt. Jim White misjudged his altitude in the haze and struck the water. His Lightning instantly disappeared beneath the waves and nothing more was seen. The China ferry flights were immediately canceled and three Demon pilots were still there when the war ended.

## WAITING AT LINGUYAN; AUGUST 2-5, 1945

The air echelon was prepared to leave Linguyan as of August 2nd, but the crews and pilots were forced to hold for forty-eight hours as a typhoon raged across the northern Philippine Sea. Tice anxiously awaited word of the fate of his advanced echelons who had sailed off on the 4th, but the fleet easily held out against the comparatively mild storm.

The colonel and his staff pilots grew restless as the days wore on. They had convinced themselves the 49ers were about to enter a battle zone which could surely yield an unprecedented "grand slam" group score of one-thousand aerial victories. Each day, the colonel stood on the Linguyan flight line and fitfully watched while the FEAF transports took other units off to the north.

## HIROSHIMA; AUGUST 6, 1945

On August 6th, everything changed. The first nuclear fission weapon in the history of the world was dropped on Hiroshima, an industrial center on the northern shore of Japan's Inland Sea. The city vanished in the terrifying, blinding flash of one atomic bomb and everything changed, forever.

The news quickly spread throughout the military community, and few really understood the ramifications. Missions were suddenly called back in mid-flight and the operations of all combat units were advised to stand by. Rumors and speculations were spread wildly on the flight lines, in the ready rooms, in the bars and in the barracks. Russia announced it declaration of war against the surrounded island empire. Everyone hoped that peace was at hand.

## NAGASAKI; AUGUST 9, 1945

Three days after the destruction of Hiroshima, a city on the west coast of Kyushu was incinerated in another nuclear blast. Nagasaki and its people vanished, as did Japan's last hope for an honorable negotiated peace.

Clay Tice was a bit bewildered, not knowing exactly what his mission would be with half of his people still at sea and the rest still waiting for air transit to the new base. Orders from FEAF changed by the minute, but there very little to accomplish until his fighter group was reassembled on Okinawa.

On August 14th, President Truman broadcast the long awaited message to his fighting forces in the Pacific. Japan had uncondi-

*Motubo Airfield receiving transport aircraft during the 49ers stay.*

tionally surrendered and hostilities were over. The first LST bearing the 49ers landed at Okinawa the next day and the 49ers air echelon advanced on the 16th.

## A BRIEF STAY AT MOTUBA; AUGUST, 1945

Word of the surrender had reached the 49ers waterborne echelons and everyone was thrilled to land in a peaceful harbor on the morning of the 15th. At noon the next day, LtC. Tice arrived with eighty-five Lightnings after the 850-mile crossing and all safely landed at Motuba Airfield midway up Okinawa's west coast. The strip was the reliable crushed coral surface and the dispersal area was large enough to be shared with a Liberator unit.

Within hours, the newly arrived air echelon began to operate in measured armed reconnaissance, particularly of southern Kyushu. Taking up the cause for the very last time, the pilots routinely would sortie with a full ammo bay, a one-thousand pound bomb and a 300-gallon belly tank. Their principle surveillance was of the airfield and inland sea routes of the southern most homelands, but there were no hostile incidents. newcomer F/O George Coogan was killed in a landing accident on August 31st, the only 49er to perish in the Okinawa operations.

Flights throughout the month even reached as far north as the southern coastal waters of Korea. The most sober sweeps included the reconnaissance of ashen Hiroshima and Nagasaki. The 49ers could not help but wonder at the absolute, sheer devastation seen there.

On August 21st, Japanese emissaries were summoned to MacArthur's HQ at Linguyan to receive the general's terms of surrender. When the Imperial couriers returned to Japan, their two all white BETTY transports with the dark green crosses refueled at Okinawa. The respective Demons, Blacksheep and Knights squadron leaders with three wingmen each were part of the island escort team to take them as far north as southern Kyushu.

## TO THE VICTORS; AUGUST 16, 1945

Of all the successful adventures that befell the 49ers in three and a half years of combat flying, none seemed more appropriate for the victorious group than that memorable flight of August 16, 1945. Group Leader Clay Tice personally led seven Screamin' Demons in armed surveillance of Kyushu and the south shore of greater Honshu Island. The route was plotted as a six and three-quarter hour, 1300 mile round trip. With strict instructions to conserve fuel and to maintain their wing positions, the flight set off at eight o'clock that clear summer morning.

They passed over Nagasaki at 1030 hours, then coursed clockwise over the entrance of the Inland Sea for an hour more until they reached the west coast of Shikoku Island. It was at that point 650 miles into the circuit when F/O Douglas Hall broke radio silence. The youngster reported he had experienced fuel transfer difficulty and had used a disproportionate amount of fuel. His radio transmissions to Tice's ship were not clear and instructions had to be passed through his flight leader, Capt. Kopecky.

Tice directed the flight members to reduce their RPM settings and turn south, but after they were half way down Kyushu's east coast, it was apparent that Hall did not have enough fuel left to reach Okinawa. As the P-38s passed near Nittagahara airfield, Tice made a fateful decision. Unwilling to have young Hall chance a water ditching with a faulty radio, the colonel turned the mission over to Capt. Kopecky, then radioed JUKEBOX air rescue to have one of their B-17 tankers rendezvous with him at Nittagahara. Hall and Tice then jettisoned their bombs into the sea and drifted downward. They were going to land.

Tice led the way and circled the airdrome. Indeed, Nittagahara was rather pastoral and seemed void of any signs of battle. The colonel dropped to a routine landing, then signalled to the uneasy rookie that the way was clear. They both rolled to a halt on the concrete rampart some distance from the hangers. Hall was made all the more nervous when Tice confidently stepped down from his multi-colored Lightning and marched over to inspect what appeared

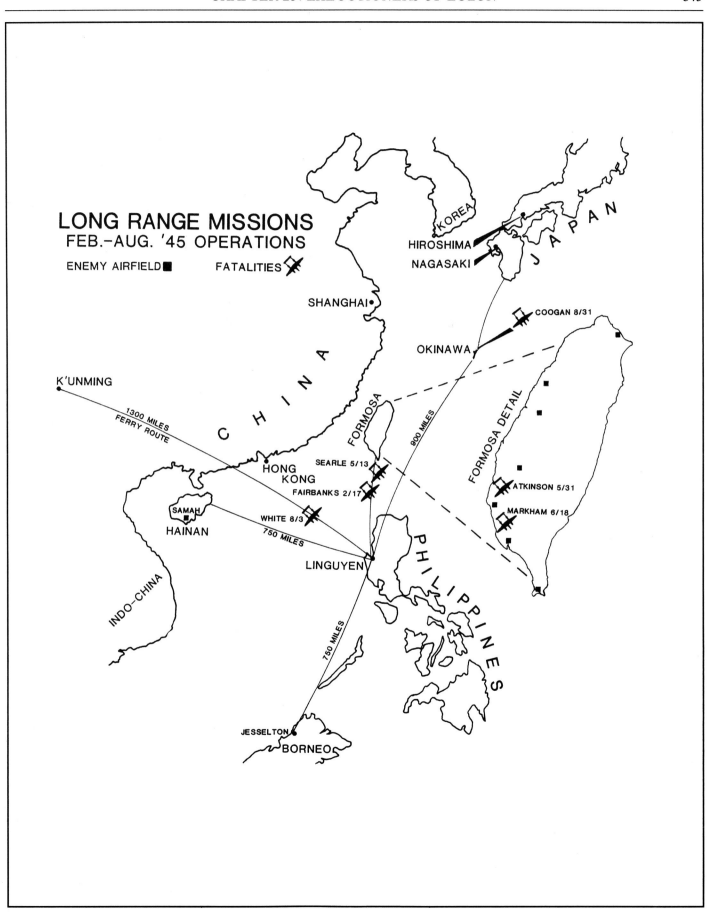

**LONG RANGE MISSIONS**
FEB.–AUG. '45 OPERATIONS

ENEMY AIRFIELD ■          FATALITIES ✕

KOREA

HIROSHIMA
NAGASAKI

JAPAN

SHANGHAI •

COOGAN 8/31

OKINAWA

K'UNMING •

C H I N A

1300 MILES
FERRY ROUTE

FORMOSA

900 MILES

FORMOSA DETAIL

SEARLE 5/13

HONG
KONG

FAIRBANKS 2/17

ATKINSON 5/31

SAMAH •
HAINAN

WHITE 8/3

750 MILES

MARKHAM 6/18

INDO-CHINA

LINGUYEN

P H I L I P P I N E S

750 MILES

JESSELTON •
BORNEO

to be a very serviceable TONY sitting a short distance away. An old man with a snow-white beard slowly wheeled past on a bicycle and curiously gazed upon the two Americans, but said nothing.

In time, there came a man in a uniform which bore no rank who was in the lead of a small platoon of boys. They held up white handkerchiefs, then bowed and drew near the two pilots. After hopelessly struggling with introductions, Tice motioned with his hands that his airplane needed fuel, and the sign language obviously was understood, for the boys ran off and returned with soldiers driving a fuel truck.

The soldiers were extremely accommodating to the tall American colonel who took solemn charge of the event. He refused to shake their extended hands but did accept their siphon hand pumps. He suspected their gasoline might not be high enough in octane for the Allison engines and chose to wait for the tanker. The Japanese waited quietly as Tice paced patiently back and forth near the Lightnings.

Once the B-17 arrived, Tice gave the pumps to the tanker crewmen, which apparently pleased the humble Japanese. Once the crews had topped off the Lightnings, Tice and Hall withdrew from Nittagahara without further ceremony. Both men landed at Motuba and were swarmed by the aircrews, but the colonel dismissed the whole affair as being strictly routine.

It was far from routine for the Supreme Allied Commander. General Douglas MacArthur was furious and sent word through channels that the two pilots who landed in Japan were to be apprehended and held for court-martial. The cohorts of Tice in 5 FC purposefully jumbled the communiques until the matter disappeared within the maze of greater priorities.

FEAF CO General George Kenney purportedly only laughed on hearing of Tice's misadventure. He suspected that the whole affair had been a set-up by the 49ers operators from the beginning. What mattered to Doug Hall was that Clay Tice had made a choice which surely saved his life. And veteran Clay Tice had certainly displayed great gallantry, standing in Japan as a living tribute to every man in the 49th Fighter Group whose motto was "Protect and Avenge."

*CO Tice's "ELSIE" at the time of his landing in Japan, the first ever for the victorious FEAF.*

# EPILOGUE
# POST WORLD WAR II

In the official surrender ceremonies on September 2nd aboard the USS *Missouri*, the 49ers were in the spectacular flyby of the massed Allied air force, and by month's end, they became part of the occupation force. They moved to the Atsugi Airfield southwest of Tokyo, with a brief diversion of the ground echelons to Chofu airdrome. When the Group finally gathered at Atsugi in early October, all of their P-38s were ultimately re-assigned to the 8th Squadron under the command of Major Hap Chandler, a former Screamin' Demons veteran from the New Guinea era. The resultant abbreviated flying operations terminated by month's end as the unit released the majority of its personnel to the long awaited furlough home, and finally, their reentry into civilian life.

Despite the drastic reduction of the American Armed Services after the war, the 49ers "paper air group" remained on duty in Japan for several years. The Group was sustained as a new Fighter Wing in the creation of the United States Air Force in 1947 and was one of the first jet equipped units available in the Orient at the outbreak of the Korean War in 1950. The 49ers flew three years of tactical fighter-bomber missions in the Lockheed F-80 and Republic F-84.

With the permanent cease-fire in Korea in 1953, the Group stood down and would later transfer its operations to the North Atlantic Treat Organization (NATO) in Europe in 1957. In the tense decade of air defense in the front lines of the Cold War era, their principle aircraft were the North American F-86, the F-100, and the Republic F-105. The unit received two Outstanding Unit Citations in NATO service while stationed at Spandalem AFB, West Germany.

In 1968, the well travelled 49th Fighter Wing took up the new missile fighter, the McDonnell F-4, and the concurrent re-assignment to the Tactical Air Command (TAC) in the United States. Thus ended more than a quarter-century of continuous overseas duty. The Wing settled into its permanent residence at the desert air field complex at Holloman Air Force Base in southern New Mexico, and remained the "first team" in the deployment missions of TAC. More unit citations were garnered upon the Wing, particularly for the numerous mobilization exercises throughout the 1960s and 1970s to both the Orient and NATO.

The Holloman operations continued apace with the new generation of fighters born in the next decade, highlighted by their adaptation of the superb McDonnell-Douglas F-15 in 1978. After yet another fifteen years of continuous wing-strength service, an abrupt shift in world politics and the subsequent reductions of military threats brought an end to need for the elaborate TAC community. As of 1993, the re-constituted force would be known as the Air Combat Command with many of the fighter squadrons being disband by the close of the 20th Century.

Just when it seemed the 49ers would pass into history, a cadre of World War II veterans in of 49th Fighter Group Association petitioned the USAF to retain the numbered squadron designators and names of the Screamin' Demons, the Blacksheep and the Flying Knights. Even though their ranks are diminished, they adapted to the new age of stealth flight technology in the revolutionary warbird from Lockheed, the F-117 fighter bomber. As of this writing, the legacy of the first team still resides with the 49ers.

*The P-38 Lightnings of the 49th Fighter Group in the occupation forces at Atsugi Airfield, Honshu, Japan.*

# APPENDIXES

## *Appendix 1*

# World War II Aerial Victories

This historical treatise was never meant to confirm or deny any of the long contested aerial victories awarded to the pilots of the 5 FC FEAF. Japanese archives compared to English language archives simply add more contradiction to the elusive resolution of "how many were lost ?' or `who killed who ?"

By example, there is a curious, common descriptive phrase in JAAF and JNAF records which roughly translate into aircraft that "destroyed themselves" without reference to combat damage being the likely cause. Their missions are described in "Tokyo time" hours and occasionally are offset on the calendar by plus or minus twenty-four hours. There are likewise implications that within the bushido code, the loss of an honored commander may well have overshadowed the loss of pilots of lower military and social rank. Numerous Allied aerial victories confirmed by more than one witness simply do not correlate to Japanese records.

In fair comparison, many 49ers aircraft losses are evident in the photos and dated diaries of 5 AF veterans which are not recorded in either Missing Aircraft and Crew Reports (MACRs) or in the Group's official archives. The 49ers pointedly avoided the listing of aircraft serial numbers and rarely listed the one or two-digit aircraft designator numbers. It was in part due to the difficulty of recording the staggering attrition of the older planes in the New Guinea order of battle, and the even greater fierceness of the Philippines era. From late October through early December of 1944, the group lost over sixty P-38s and many of those were aircraft commandeered from other groups. No record was found to detail either those acquisitions or those losses.

There is also substantial evidence of a continuous revisionist method used by USAAF intelligence in confirming not only the scores of the ace's, but all combat reports during the war years.

One could argue that ace Dick Bong either had only thirty-three confirmed kills, or ironically, forty-one victories, which is of course, one more than the official declaration. Confirmation by 5 FC intelligence, it seems, was motivated as much by politics or the presence of war correspondents, while accounting at the squadron level more often came down to a man's word. Final confirmation often came weeks, months, or as reported here, years long after the air battle had faded into many a flyer's memory.

There is also the argument as to what types of victories were used in tallying the final scores. The fighter groups in Europe awarded their pilots aerial kills plus those grounded targets hit in the dangerous strafing attacks against the heavily defended airdromes of the Third Reich. Similar strafing assaults on the jungle airstrips of New Guinea and the Philippines were not accounted for in 5 FC, and indeed, many Pacific veterans proudly declare a "ground kill" was an unworthy claim for an "aerial duellist."

Therefore, this text concludes with a simple comparison of victories for the top scoring USAAF groups in service in all theaters. The all time leader in aerial victories is the 354 FG flying the P-51 Mustang with the 9 AF in England, currently reported as 701, and they are the only group to reach the seven-hundred mark. Next comes the 56 FG flying the P-47 Thunderbolt in the 8 AF, also in the ETO, achieving 674 aerial kills. The only other unit to pass the six-hundred mark is the 357 FG, ranking fourth overall.

The third highest scoring fighter team in the history of American military aerial combat is the 49th Fighter Group, claiming 668 aerial victories accumulated by the pilots in the 7th, 8th, 9th squadrons and staff pilots of 49th HQ. Although other units may have scored momentarily at a faster pace, no other organization in the Pacific theater ever came close to reaching the 49ers record, not even the U.S. Navy carrier fighter units.

# THE ACES

Becoming an ace was no mean feat, but neither was it the absolute confirmation of a fighter pilot's skills. Bob DeHaven, sternly confident that his score was higher than the official 5 FC tally of fourteen, rather humbly related that the best fighter pilot was the man who "made it back alive and brought his wingman with him."

## 7 FS Screamin' Demons Aces

Robert DeHaven ............................................................. 14
Joel Paris ..................................................................... 9
Arland Stanton .............................................................. 8
Fernley Damstrom .......................................................... 7
William Hennon ............................................................. 7
(5 victories with the 17 PPS)
Elliott Dent .................................................................. 6
Fred Dick ..................................................................... 5
A.T. House .................................................................... 5
Milden Mathre ............................................................... 5

## 8 FS Blacksheep Aces

Robert Aschenbrener ....................................................... 10
Ernest Harris ................................................................ 10
Robert White ................................................................. 9
George Kiser .................................................................. 9
(5 victories in 17 PS and 17 PPS)
Sammie Pierce ................................................................ 7
James Morehead .............................................................. 7
(2 victories with the 17 PPS)
Willie Drier ................................................................... 6
James Hagerstrom ............................................................ 6
Robert Howard ............................................................... 6
Don Meuten ................................................................... 6
Nial Castle ................................................................... 5
William Day .................................................................. 5
Marion Felts .................................................................. 5
Nelson Flack .................................................................. 5

## 9 FS Flying Knights Aces

Gerald Johnson ............................................................... 22
(11 victories with 49 HQ)

Richard Bong .................................................................. 21
(19 victories later with 5 FC)

James Watkins ................................................................ 12
(1 victory with 49 HQ)

Andrew Reynolds ........................................................... 9.33
(3.33 victories with 20 & 17 PPS)

Grover Fanning ............................................................... 9
John O'Neill .................................................................. 8
Wallace Jordan .............................................................. 6
(4 victories with 49 HQ)

John Landers .................................................................. 6
Ralph Wandrey ............................................................... 6
Ernest Ambort ................................................................ 5
Warren Curten ............................................................... 5
Jack Donaldson .............................................................. 5
(3 victories with 21 PS)

Cheatam Gupton .............................................................. 5
Robert Vaught ................................................................ 5

## 49th Headquarters

Ellis Wright ................................................................... 6

Other pilots went on to fly with other units, sometimes in other theaters, where they either added to their Pacific scores or became aces with the new unit.

Steven Andrews, 7 PS to ETO ............................................... 7
Frank Nichols, 7 FS to 475 FG .............................................. 5
John Hood, 7 FS to 475 FG ................................................... 5
Harry Brown, 8 FS to 475 FG ................................................ 5
Lowell Lutton, 8 FS to 475 FG .............................................. 5
John Landers, 9 FS to ETO ................................................... 10
Sidney Woods, 9 FS to ETO .................................................. 10
Art Wenige, 9 FS to 475 FG ................................................. 5
Joseph Kruzel, 9 FS to ETO .................................................. 5
Ralph Wire, 9 FS to CBI ...................................................... 5
Jack Mankin, 9 FS to 475 FG ................................................ 5
George Preddy, 9 FS to ETO .................................................. 26

## VICTORIES BY SQUADRON and A/C TYPE

7th Squadron - 180 kills / 18 probable / 24 damaged
P-40 victories ................................................................ 114
P-38 victories ................................................................ 66

8th Squadron -207 kills / 23 probable / 17 damaged
P-40 victories ................................................................ 152
P-38 victories ................................................................ 55

9th Squadron -254 kills / 63 probable / 20 damaged
P-40 victories ................................................................ 39
P-38 1943 era victories ...................................................... 130
P-47 victories ................................................................ 8
P-38 1944-45 era victories .................................................. 77

49th FG - 27 kills / 1 probable
P-40 victories ................................................................ 8
P-38 victories ................................................................ 19

Group Total Kills ........................................................... 668

Despite all the claims and counter-claims, in the end, it was all given over to fate.

## RICHARD IRA BONG

Dick Bong left the Philippines, and entered the USAAF test pilot program in California. After his many combat escapade and countless brushes with death, like so many battle veterans, he died in an airplane crash far from the war. As the 49ers waited for their final move to Okinawa, word reached the Philippines veterans that Bong's new Lockheed P-80 prototype jet fighter had crashed on takeoff on August 6th, the day before the first atomic bomb was dropped on Hiroshima.

## GERALD RICHARD JOHNSON

Technically, Johnson was the highest ranking 49er, if one accounts for all of his aerial kills being gained while permanently assigned to the 49ers. Johnson is accredited with twenty-two overall in comparison to Bong who gained twenty-one while assigned to the Flying Knights during 1943. The comparison is, after all, quite prosaic. Like his high scoring counterpart, Johnson perished in a flying accident after the hostilities. Promoted to full colonel and awaiting his likely congressional appointment to the rank of general, Gerry Johnson would never leave Japan, or see his son. While flying a B-25 over the Inland Sea just south of Tokyo on October 7, 1945, he was caught by a sudden typhoon which swept over the area. After three of his four passengers safely bailed out over land, Johnson tried to ditch the Mitchell near a small island, but he and the man who chose to stay on board as co-pilot died when the heavy seas and sank out of sight. Neither of the bodies were recovered. In his memory, the JAAF air station at Irumagawa was renamed Johnson Air Force Base.

### ROBERT MARSHALL DEHAVEN
Handsome ace Bob DeHaven returned to California after the war and led a rather idealistic life. After his military career, and somewhat of a celebrity's life in Hollywood, he developed a business relationship with aviation genius and industrial mogul, Howard Hughes. In time, DeHaven became one the world's foremost authorities in aviation weaponry. He became a world traveler and a connoisseur de haut cuisine, yet he always returned to his Hollywood home.

### ELWOOD E. BARDEN
Any good pilot will readily admit his combat prowess was only measured by the skill of his crewchief, the fellow who truly kept the airplane in the air. Such being the case, Flying Knights Staff Sergeant Elwood Barden could rightly be awarded the leading victory score of forty-four enemy aircraft shot down by "his airplanes." He was crewchief to ace Andy Reynolds at Darwin, and to aces Bong and Johnson at Dobodura. Barden's most touching memory was his return to the States and his last gracious reunion with Major Bong in California just days before the ace's death. After a successful career as a civilian aviation mechanic, El Barden retired quietly to his home in Alabama, and would always consider himself most fortunate in having three such able 49ers pilots placed in his charge.

### CARL G. PLANCK, JR.
Carl Planck bid farewell to the fighter pilot's life at Gusap in early 1944, and though he remained at some distance from his old comrades, he never completely abandoned his fascination with flight. Staying in the administrative branch of the new U.S. Air Force, he rose to the rank of colonel by the 1960s and became one of the most respected leaders in the Apollo astronauts program. He retired with honors in the late 1970s after a distinguished career, yet few of his "spacemen" cohorts were aware of his combat record.

### WILBERT ARTHUR
When the 49ers moved to their post-war occupation assignment at Atsugi airfield southwest of Tokyo, one of their duties was to muster a large number of prisoners of war out of the Japanese camps. One man who hobbled forth on crutches was their fallen comrade, Capt. Wilbert Arthur, who had been shot down over Formosa in April of 1945. As with so many lost flyers, everyone had virtually given up missing Capt. Arthur for dead. By default, Arthur had actually been the first 49er to reach the Japanese mainland ahead of flamboyant Clay Tice. The quiet survivor soon boarded a flight to the east and left the 49ers for good. He was never heard from again.

### JAMES PHILO "HAG" HAGERSTROM
In the late 1940s, Blacksheep ace Jim Hagerstrom's stellar transition to jets earned him command of the 67th Fighter-Bomber Squadron flying F-86 Sabre Jets in Korea in 1953. The colonel not only became the sole ace in the 18th Fighter Bomber Wing, he would be the only 49er to become an ace after World War II. With eight MiGs added to his combat portfolio, Hag left the service and gave up flying for the law, becoming a highly successful "ace" investor in South Pacific and Caribbean business ventures.

# *Appendix 2*
# Operations and Combat Fatalities

**U.S.A.**
February 14, 1941 - Pvt. William C. Riley; Illness - Selfridge Field, Michigan

September 20, 1941 - 2Lt. Carlyle C. Loverud; P-35 crash near Jackson, Georgia

December 18, 1941 - 2Lt. Howard D. Cory; P-40 crash near St. Louis, Missouri

**AUSTRALIA**
March 14, 1942 - 7 PS 2Lt. Frank S. Steirtz; P-40 crash, Daly Waters, N.T.

March 17, 1942 - 9 PS 2Lt. Albert L. Spehr; P-40 crash, Bankstown RAAF Field, N.S.W.

March 28, 1942 - 8 PS 2Lt. John J. Musial, 2Lt. Neal T. Takala; Both P-40 crashes near Eden, N.S.W.

April 4, 1942 - 9 PS2 Lt. John L. Livingstone; KIA, 34 Mile Strip, Darwin, N.T.

April 21, 1942 - 49 FCS; All in Lockheed C-40 crash at Mt. Bundy, N.T., Cpl. William Bedford, Cpl. Antony A. Gattamelata, Pvt. Robert W. George, Pvt. Nick Hinich, Pvt. Ray E. Love, Pvt. John J. Faris, Pvt. Walter M. Feret, Pvt. Richard D. Schmidt, Pvt. Buford D. Willard, Pvt Wyatt H. Wiley

April 27, 1942 - 8 PS 2Lt. Owen R. Fish, Capt. Allison W. Strauss; both KIA, Darwin, N.T.

April 29, 1942 - 49th HQ 2Lt. Robert D. Jasper; A/C ground accident, Batchelor Field, N.T.

May 28, 1942 - 8 FS Pvt. David F. Bible; Gun crew accident Adelaide River Field, N.T.

June 6, 1942 - 8 FS 2Lt. Edward M. Miller; P-40 crash at Livingstone Field, N.T.

June 9, 1942 - 7 FS 2Lt. William H. Payne; P-40 crash at Brocks Creek, N.T.

June 16, 1942 - 8 FS 2Lt. Chester T. Namola; MIA Darwin, N.T.

June 23, 1942 - 8 FS 2Lt. Arthur E. Fielder; P-40 crash at Livingstone Field, N.T.

July 12, 1942 - 9 FS 2Lt. John S. Sauber; P-40 aerial collision near Livingstone Field, N.T.

September 11, 1942 - 49er HQ 2Lt. Robert G. Hazard; P-40 crash off east coast of Cape York, Q.T.

June 17, 1943 - 49 FG; B-17 transport lost at Mackay, Q.T., Pvt. Jerome Abraham, Capt. John O. Berthold, Sgt. Carl A. Cunningham, Pvt. Charles D. Montgomery Maj. George N. Powell

February 15, 1944 - 7 FS Lt. Marion J. Hawke; Ground accident at Iron Range Field, Q.T.

**PAPUA - NEW GUINEA - NEW BRITAIN**
November 1, 1942 - 8 FS 2Lt. Glenn L. Wohfford; MIA Lae

November 8, 1942 - 8 FS 2Lt. Nelson B. Brownell; KIA Kokoda Pass

November 22, 1942 - 7 FS Lt. Donald C. Dittler; MIA Buna

November 26, 1942 - 7 FS 2Lt. Dean F. Burnett; KIA Buna

November 30, 1942 - 7 FS 2Lt. John C. Johnson; KIA, 2Lt. Irving W. Voorhees; MIA, Both near Dobodura

December 18, 1942 - 8 FS Lt. Richard H. Dennis; MIA Lae

January 7, 1943 - 8 FS 2Lt. Eugene D. Dickey; MIA Lae

February 28, 1943 - 9 FS Lt. William A. Levitan; P-38 lost off Papua south coast

March 1, 1943 - 8 FS 2Lt. Cyrus J. Lynd; KIA Kokoda Trail

March 11, 1943 - 9 FS Sgt. Frederick H. Bente; KIA Dobodura

March 13, 1943 - Sgt. Orbert Franklin; KIA, wounded March 11 at Dobodura

April 3, 1943 - 8 FS Lt. Robert A. Moose, 2Lt. Stanley J. Hunter; KIA aerial collision off Cape Ward Hunt

April 14, 1943 - Lt. William D. Sells; KIA, Milne Bay

April 28, 1943 - 2Lt. Christian J. Props; KIA Popondetta

May 14, 1943 - 2Lt. Arthur R. Bauhoff; MIA Oro Bay

June 18, 1943 - Lt. Benjamin F. Duke; P-40 crash at Dobodura

July 10, 1943 - 2Lt. Frederick J. Sibley; MIA Cape Ward Hunt

July 11, 1943 - F/O Archie C. Davis; MIA near Wau

September 6, 1943 - 2Lt. James W. Fagan; MIA near Lae

October 12, 1943 - 9 FS Lt. Ralph L. Hayes, Lt. Theron D. Price, Lt. Frank G. Wunder Jr.; MIA Solomon Sea

October 16, 1943 - 9 FS Lt. Harry C. Lidstrom; KIA Cape Ward Hunt - 49 FG Sgt. Charles E. Dawson Jr., S/Sgt. Jack W. Holt, F/O Cecil R. McElhiney, T/Sgt. Harold W. Macha, Lt. Robert E. Mona, F/O Richard W. Smith, Sgt. Glenn A. Walter; KIA in PBY near Pongoni

October 17, 1943 - 7 FS Lt. Lawrence N. Succop; MIA Cape Ward Hunt

October 23, 1943 - 9 FS 2Lt. Woodson W. Woodson; MIA Solomon Sea

November 2, 1943 - 9 FS 2Lt. Francis S. Love; KIA Rabaul

November 5, 1943 - 9 FS Lt. George C. Haniotis; MIA Solomon Sea

November 7, 1943 - 9 FS 2Lt. Stanley W. Johnson; MIA Rabaul

January 2, 1944 - 7 FS Capt. William D. Lown; MIA Astrolabe Bay

January 18, 1944 - 7 FS Lt. David P. Germain; Crash landed Dec. 18 at Dobodura

January 23, 1944 - 7 FS Lt. John F. Crowley; KIA Wewak

March 22, 1944 - 7 FS Capt. Russell D. Cash; KIA Tadji

April 7, 1944 - 8 FS Lt. Dale F. Arnold; KIA Wewak

April 12, 1944 - 9 FS 2Lt. Robert N. Harper; P-38 crash Nadzap

April 20, 1944 - 7 FS CApt. George C. Allen; P-40 crash Gusap

May 5, 1944 - 8 FS Lt. Anthony Spears; P-40 crash Finschhafen

May 7, 1944 - 8 FS Lt. Donald W. Meuten; MIA Tannamerah Bay

May 16, 1944 - 8 FS Cpl. Woodrow C. Williams; KIA Humbolt Bay

May 24, 1944 - 8 FS 2Lt. William E. Northcutt; P-40 crash Wakde Is.

June 3, 1944 - 49 FG LtC. David A. Campbell; MIA Babo

June 7, 1944 - 49 HQ Lt. Joseph W. Todd; P-40 crash Tadji

June 12, 1944 - KIA Biak Island air raid - 49 HQ; Pvt. Arthur Berg, Cpl. Wallace N. Brown, S/Sgt. Albert L. Edgeman, Pvt. Jules Fiegenbaum, Lt. Arnold L. Hayworth, 2Lt. Quinten K. Rizor, Capt. William F. Smoots, S/Sgt. James E. Stroud, Maj. Alpheus B. White; 7 FS; T/Sgt. William C. Gibson, S/Sgt. Aubrey C. Holland, Cpl. Clarence H. Rinnan, Cpl. John A. Tommy, Cpl. Myer H. Wilks; 8 FS; Pvt. William S. Gray, Sgt. Matthew J. Vaessen; 9 FS; S/Sgt. Oscar P. Johnson, Pvt. Morton Pinelas, Sgt. Roger L. Stoor

July 17, 1944 - 7 FS Lt. Fenton G. Epling; P-40 crash Hollandia

August 13, 1944 - 7 FS 2Lt. Charles D. Marton; P-40 crash off Biak Is.

August 28, 1944 - 8 FS 2Lt. Leighton R. McCabe; MIA Utarom

August 30, 1944 - 8 FS 2Lt. Howard B. Wayne; B-25 transport lost east of Biak

September 1, 1944 - 8 FS 2Lt. Walter A. Clark - P-38 crash off Biak Is.

September 2, 1944 - 9 FS Lt. John C. McLean; P-38 crash off Biak Is.

September 11, 1944 - 9 FS 2Lt. Henry J. Frank; MIA Ceram Is.

September 14, 1944 - 7 FS 2Lt. Roland D. Humphrey; P-38 crash off Biak Is.

September 25, 1944 - 8 FS 2Lt. Richard H. Remer; P-38 crash off Biak Is.

September 27, 1944 - 7 FS 2Lt. Jay C. Rogers; P-38 crash off Biak Is.

October 27, 1944 - 8 FS Lt. George B. Saum; P-38 crash, Sorido Strip, Biak Is., Capt. Glen G. Swan; P-38 crash, Mokmer Strip, Biak Is.

**PHILIPPINES ISLANDS, FORMOSA and LATE WAR**
October 29, 1944 - 9 FS S/Sgt. Jack B. Hedgepath; KIA Tacloban airraid

October 31, 1944 - 7 FS 2Lt. Robert W. Searight; KIA crash off Tacloban

November 2, 1944 - 9 FS Lt. William S. Huisman; KIA crash at Tacloban - 8 FS Capt. Philip E. Kriechbaum; KIA Ormoc

November 3, 1944 - 9 FS 2Lt. Richard M. Bates; KIA Ormoc

November 4, 1944 - 8 FS 2Lt. Walter O. Leaf; KIA crash off Tacloban

November 9, 1944 - 9 FS 2Lt. Donald J. Kanoff; KIA Ormoc Bay

November 18, 1944 - 8 FS 2Lt. Gerald W. Triplehorn; KIA Leyte interior

November 19, 1944 - 7 FS Lt. Douglas G. Hart; MIA Ormoc Bay

November 28, 1944 - 49 FG Capt. John C. Davis; P-38 crash at Tacloban

December 13, 1944 - 9 FS 2Lt. James R. Collins; P-38 crash at Tacloban

January 10, 1945 - 7 FS F/O Walter B. Chambers; P-38 crash off Mindoro

January 27, 1945 - 7 FS 2Lt. Epke T. Ives; MIA Laoag, Luzon

January 31, 1945 - 8 FS Lt. Francis J. Hill; KIA Nusuglu, Luzon

February 2, 1945 - 9 FS 2Lt. John I. Forgey; P-38 crash Mindoro

February 17, 1945 - 7 FS 2Lt. Leonard C. Fairbanks - MIA Philippines Sea

February 19, 1945 - 9 FS 2Lt. John F. Kinsman, 2Lt. Harold H. Thorson; Both KIA Negros Is.

March 25, 1945 - 8 FS 2Lt. John R. Lang; MIA off Linguyan

March 27, 1945 - 7 FS 2Lt. Dewey C. Renick; KIA Itagon, Luzon

April 11, 1945 - 7 FS Capt. Fernley H.Damstrom; P-38 crash Laoag, Luzon

April 14, 1945 - 7 FS Sgt. Rhea K. Slater, Cpl. Stanley Skrzypiec, Cpl. Edwin L. Stephens; KIA Linguyan

April 25, 1945 - 9 FS Wayne E. Cunningham; KIA Linguyan

May 4, 1945 - 7 FS Lt. Louis J. Denkovic, Lt. George M. Rogers; KIA Linguyan

May 13, 1945 - 7 FS 2Lt. Francis A. Searle; MIA Philippines Sea

May 27, 1945 - 7 FS 2Lt. Joel G. Herman, Pvt. Bernard J. Ross; KIA Linguyan

May 31, 1945 - 8 FS Lt. James R. Atkinson; KIA Formosa

June 2, 1945 - 9 FS Lewis S. Simon; MIA Philippines Sea

June 18, 1945 - 7 FS 2Lt. Kenneth H. Markham; KIA Formosa

June 20, 1945 - 7 FS 2Lt. Robert E. Helfrecht; MIA Philippines Sea

July 7, 1945 - 9 FS 2Lt. Gerald A. Conradi; KIA Bontoc, Luzon

July 15, 1945 - 7 FS 2Lt. Harlen H. Hoyt; KIA central Luzon

August 3, 1945 - 8 FS Lt. James E. White; MIA S. China Sea

# *Acknowledgements*

**7 FS 49ers HQ & 49th Fighter Control**
Oliver Atchison, David Allen, Jack Holt, Curtis Biggerstaff, Jimmie Barlett, Earnest Knight, Nathanial "Nate" Blanton, Donald Krohe, Russell Brady, George Laven, Sheldon Brinson, Robert McDaris, John Bush, Wilson "Chip" Chapman, Frank Slade, James Costley, Frank Stetson, Spencer Cram, William Wyant, Robert Croft, Family of Fernley Damstrom, Robert Decker, Robert DeHaven, Elliott Dent, Fred Dick, Harry Dillworth, Samuel Goodrich, William Dodson, Ralph Holcolm, William Ferris, Virgil "Chief" Holcolm, Charley Ford, Horace Levy, Elford "Fats" Elofson, Clay Swan, James Fennimore, Jules Teck, William "Franco" Fernandez, James Gallegher, James Gordon, Douglas Hall, Harold "Hal" Harris, James Hill, Mr. Hoffstater, Family of James Jerrel, Alvin "Jack" Jones, Joseph "Kappy" Kaplowitz, Ivan Kunert, Family of Lucius Lacroix, James Langenberg, Don Lee, Paul Manget, Charles Manion, George Manning, Alphonse Mechino, John Miller, Family of Robert Morrissey, Duncan Myers, Frank Nichols, Joel Paris, Edward Peck, Lemuel Pollack, John Plosila, William Redington, Salvatore "Sal" Santora, Donald Schwall, Paul Slocum, Arland Stanton, Edward Steere, Vincent Straus, Jack Suggs, Samuel Tweed, Nicholas Vitaco, Gwyne White.

**8th SQUADRON**
Melvin Allen, Robert "Asch" Aschenbrener, Clyde "Smiley" Barnett, William Bean, Ferman Bishop, Warren Blakely, John Bodak, Roy Bopp, Wright Boyd, Frank Brooks, Wasco Bungo, Nial Castle, William Day, Wesley Downer, Ralph Easterling, Elford "Fats" Elofson, Family of Nelson Flack, Ed Glascock, Seymore Goldberg, Marvin Graham, Louis Graton, Rodger "Bitsy" Grant, Ken Hanson, Bruce Harris, Family of Earnest Harris, James Hagerstrom, Jerome "Jerry" Holtwick, Family of Robert Howard, L.F. Howerton, Thomas Horne, Dale Hughes, Phillip Hurst, Richard Illing, Earl

Kingsley, Joe Littleton, James Morehead, Family of Bernard Pappas, Sammie Pierce, Dan Regan, Clete Reymann, James Reynolds, William Runey, John Roth, Mike Sabetti, Donald Schwall, Robert Skinner, George Smerchek, Marlin Smith, Tony Svogoda, Ralph Tuscano, Robert Tydemann, Robert Van Auken, James Ward, Guy Watson, Richard "Bud" Werner, Carl Wingo, Harvey Wishart, Ezra Young, Edward Zimmer.

**9th SQUADRON**
Martin "Pete" Alger, Elwood Barden, Douglas Barrett, Garland "Tex" Black, Family of Richard Bong, Paul Brown, Donald Bux, Earl Campbell, Ken Clark, Family of Warren Curton, I.B. "Jack" Donalson, Family of Cheatham Gupton, Jimmie Haislip, Henry Hammett, James Harris III, Clyde Harvey, Fred Hollier, Ray Holman, E.B. Eddie Howes, Albert Jacobs, Dick Johnson, Family of Gerald Johnson, Wallace Jordan, Charles Kurtz, John Landers, Alfred "Lew" Lewelling, David Lind, Howard Olgesby, Clinton Palmer, Jesse Peaslee, Carl Planck, Stephan "Polly" Poleschuk, James Pou, Family of George Preddy, Fred Quick, James Selman, George "Spider" Smith, Richard Taylor, Clayton Tice, Louis Vratil, Ralph Wandry, Norman Wilford, Robert Wood, Samuel Tweed, Harley Yates, Paul Ziegler.

**EDITORS and RESEARCHER CONTRIBUTORS**
Bob Alford - Australia Richard Gardner - Battery Press, U.S.A. L.J. Hickey - International Research & Pub., U.S.A. William Hess - U.S.A. Bruce Hoy - Australia Lex MacCaulay - Australia Ernest McDowell - U.S.A. James Landsdale - U.S.A. Lindsay Peet - R.A.A.F. Assn., Australia John Stanaway -U.S.A. Duane Reed - United States Air Force Academy Library, Bob Rocker - Cactus Air Force Project, U.S.A. Ken Rust - U.S.A. Ray Wagner and George Welsh - San Diego Aerospace Museum Ian Witney - Aviation Engineering, Australia American Fighter Aces Museum Foundation - U.S.A.

# *Bibliography*

*Atlas for the Second World War, Asia and the Pacific*, T.E. Griess ed., 1985.

Steve Birdsall - *Flying Buccaneers* - Doubleday, 1977

Richard M. Bueschel - *Nakajima Ki-43 Hayabusa I-III in the Japanese Army Air Force* Arco, 1970
— *Kawasaki Ki-61/Ki-100 Hien in the Japanese Army Air Force* Arco, 1971

Hata and Izawa (Don C. Gorham translater) - *Japanese Naval Aces and Fighter Units in World War II* - U.S. Naval Institute Press, 1989

Dr. Rene J. Francillon - *Imperial Japanese Navy Bombers of World War II* - Hylton Lacy, 1969
—*American Fighters of World War II*, Volume 1 - Hylton Lacy, 1971

Roger A. Freeman - *Republic Thunderbolt* - Ducimus Books Ltd., 1978

B.H. Lidell Hart - *History of the Second World War* - G.P. Putnam's Sons, 1970

Maj. Gene Gurney - *The War In The Air* - Bonanza Books, 1977

Lawerence J. Hickey - *Warpath Across the Pacific* - International Research and Pub., 1984

George C. Kenney - *General Kenney Reports* - Duell, 1949

Robert C. Mikesh - *Zero Fighter* - Crown Pub., 1981
—*Japanese Aircraft: Code Names and Designations* - Schiffer Pub., 1993

R.Natkiel/R.L.Sommer/S.L.Mayer - *Atlas of World War II* - Bison, 1985

Frank J. Olynyk - *USSAF Credits For The Destruction Of Enemy Aircraft in World War II* - author, 1985

Alan Powell - *The Shadow's Edge* - Melbourne University Press, 1988

Chistopher F. Shores - *Curtiss P-40D-N Warhawk* - Arco, 1969

John Stanaway - *Cobra In The Clouds* - Historical Aviation Album, 1982
— *Possum, Clover And Hades* - Schiffer Pub., 1993

John Vader - *New Guinea: The Tide Is Stemmed* - Ballantine, 1971

F.C. Van Oosten - *The Battle Of The Java Sea* - Ian Allen Ltd., 1976

John Winston - *War In The Pacific: Pearl Harbor To Tokyo* - Mayflower Books Inc., 1978
— *Pictorial History of the Second World War*; Volume I-X - Wm.H. Wise and Co., Inc., 1948

U.S. National Archives: *Army Air Forces In The War Against Japan 1941-1942* - USAAF, 1945

*The Battle Of The Bismarck Sea and Development of Masthead Attacks* - USSAF, 1945

*Materials, Bases and Logistics: SW Pacific Area* - FEAF - USAAF, 1946

Historical Study 85 / *USAF Credit for the Destruction of Enemy Aircraft in World War II* - 1978

and Record Group 18 / Microfilm M1065 - Modern Military Branch

# INDEX